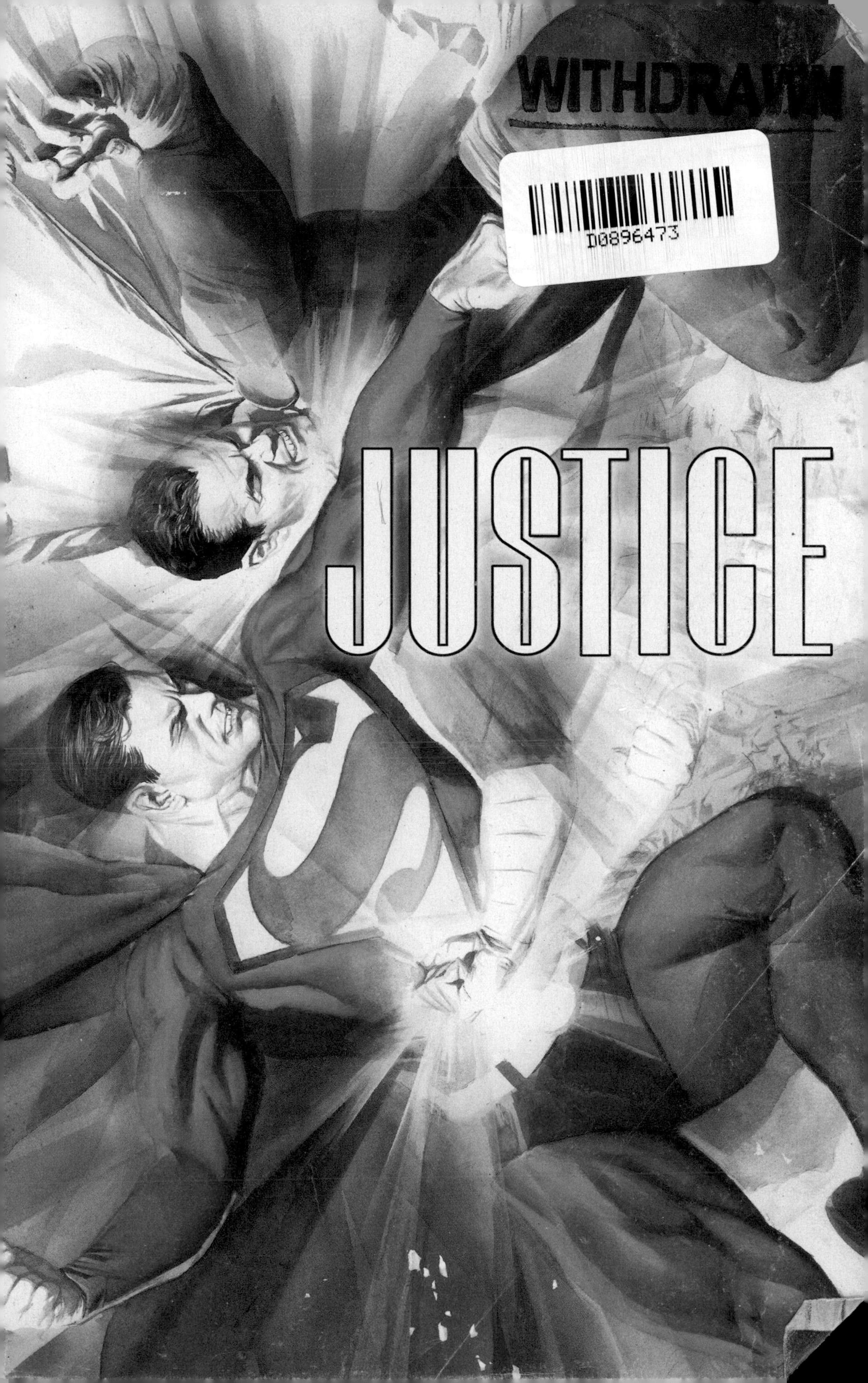
JUSTICE

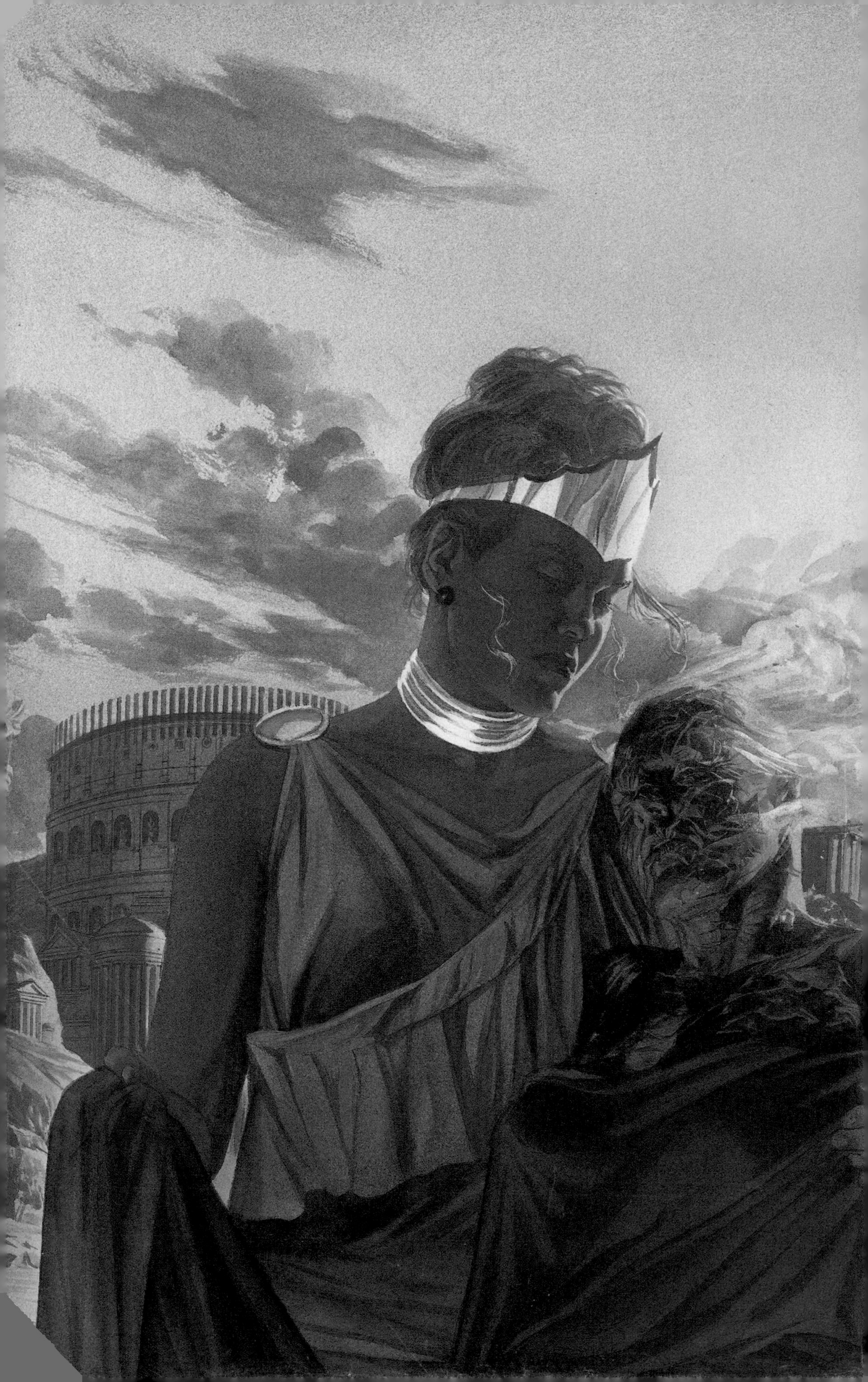

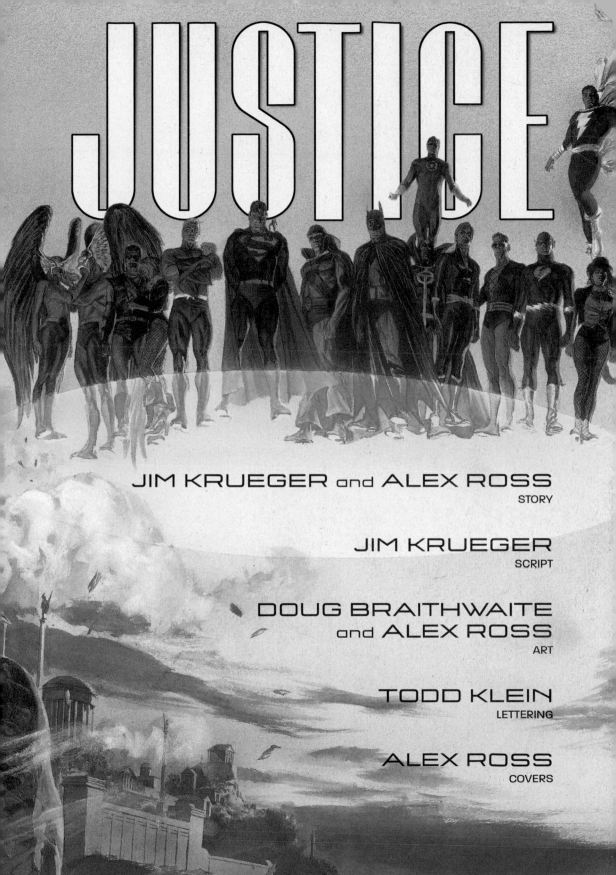

JUSTICE

JIM KRUEGER and **ALEX ROSS**
STORY

JIM KRUEGER
SCRIPT

DOUG BRAITHWAITE
and **ALEX ROSS**
ART

TODD KLEIN
LETTERING

ALEX ROSS
COVERS

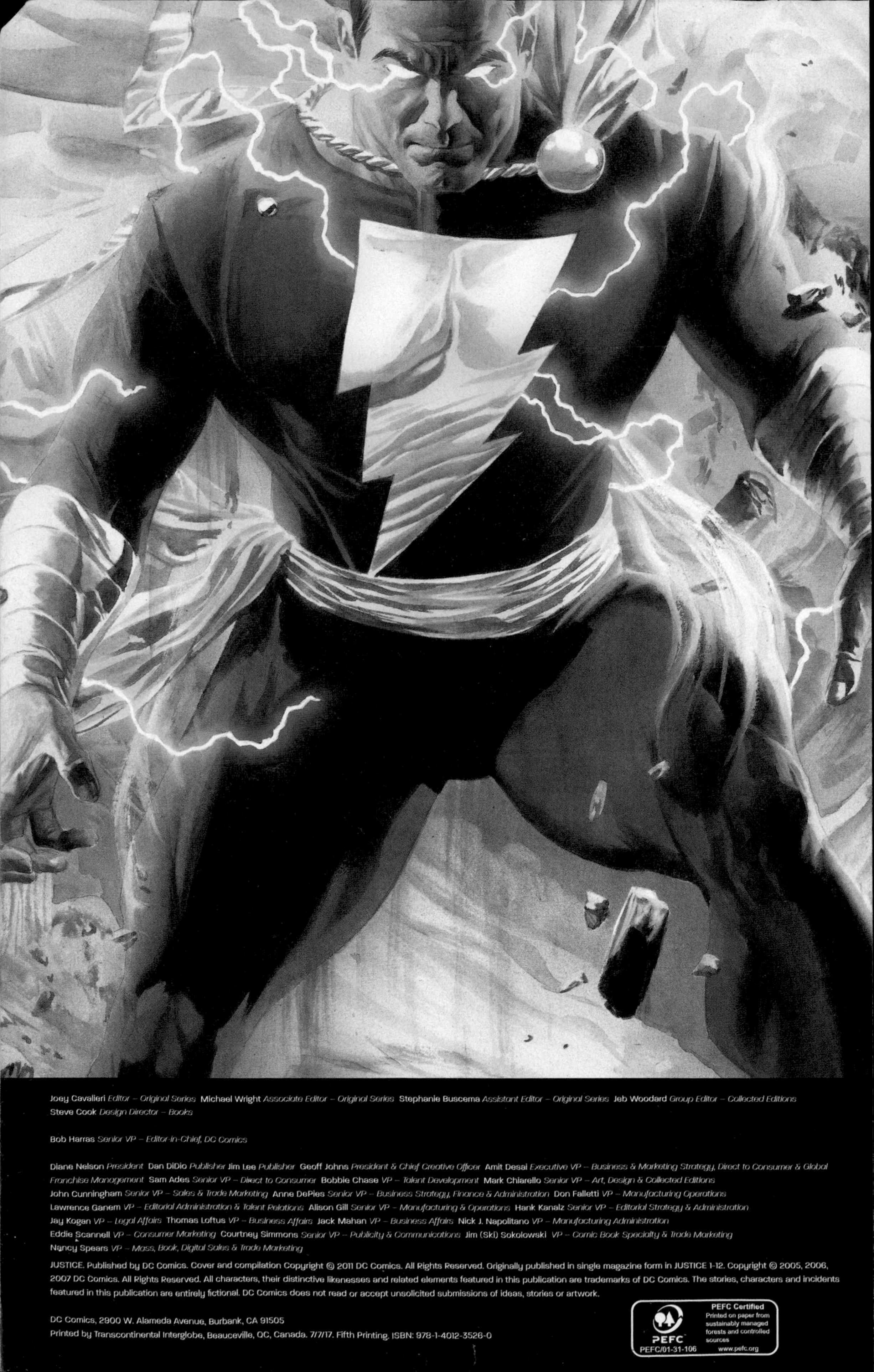

Joey Cavalieri *Editor – Original Series* **Michael Wright** *Associate Editor – Original Series* **Stephanie Buscema** *Assistant Editor – Original Series* **Jeb Woodard** *Group Editor – Collected Editions*
Steve Cook *Design Director – Books*

Bob Harras *Senior VP – Editor-in-Chief, DC Comics*

Diane Nelson *President* **Dan DiDio** *Publisher* **Jim Lee** *Publisher* **Geoff Johns** *President & Chief Creative Officer* **Amit Desai** *Executive VP – Business & Marketing Strategy, Direct to Consumer & Global Franchise Management* **Sam Ades** *Senior VP – Direct to Consumer* **Bobbie Chase** *VP – Talent Development* **Mark Chiarello** *Senior VP – Art, Design & Collected Editions*
John Cunningham *Senior VP – Sales & Trade Marketing* **Anne DePies** *Senior VP – Business Strategy, Finance & Administration* **Don Falletti** *VP – Manufacturing Operations*
Lawrence Ganem *VP – Editorial Administration & Talent Relations* **Alison Gill** *Senior VP – Manufacturing & Operations* **Hank Kanalz** *Senior VP – Editorial Strategy & Administration*
Jay Kogan *VP – Legal Affairs* **Thomas Loftus** *VP – Business Affairs* **Jack Mahan** *VP – Business Affairs* **Nick J. Napolitano** *VP – Manufacturing Administration*
Eddie Scannell *VP – Consumer Marketing* **Courtney Simmons** *Senior VP – Publicity & Communications* **Jim (Ski) Sokolowski** *VP – Comic Book Specialty & Trade Marketing*
Nancy Spears *VP – Mass, Book, Digital Sales & Trade Marketing*

DC Comics, 2900 W. Alameda Avenue, Burbank, CA 91505
Printed by Transcontinental Interglobe, Beauceville, QC, Canada. 7/7/17. Fifth Printing. ISBN: 978-1-4012-3526-0

PEFC Certified
Printed on paper from sustainably managed forests and controlled sources
PEFC
PEFC/01-31-106
www.pefc.org

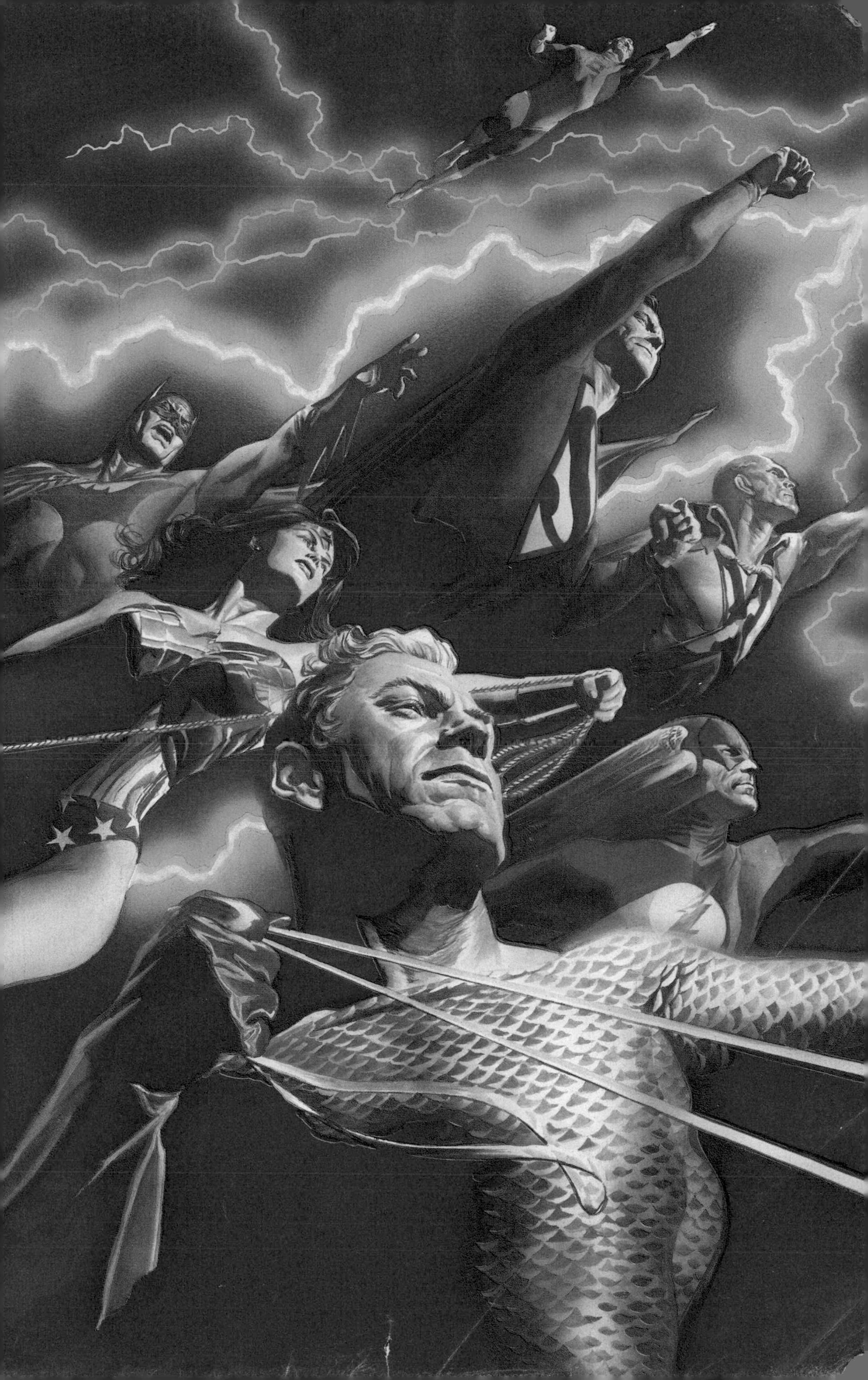

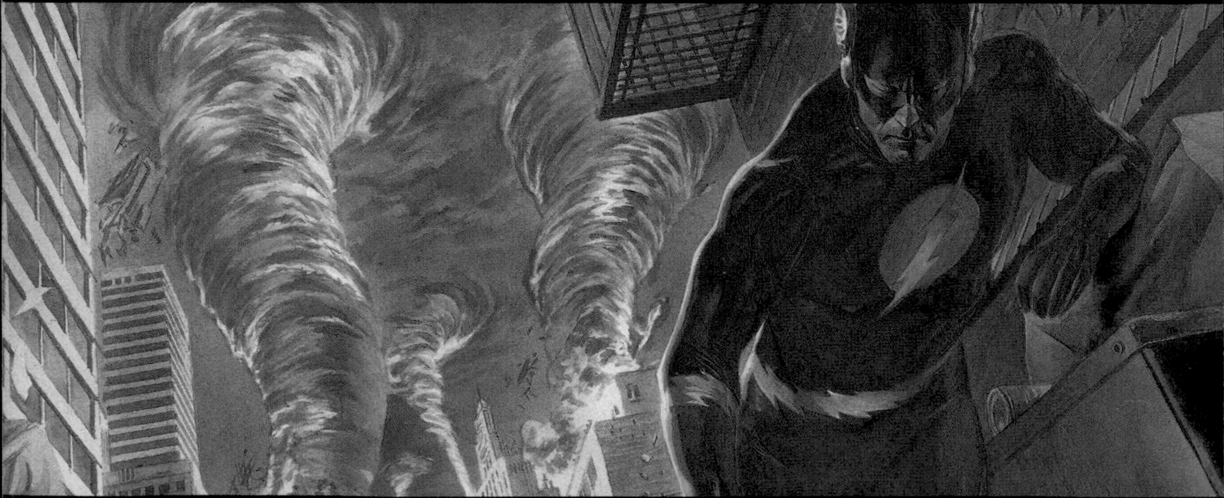

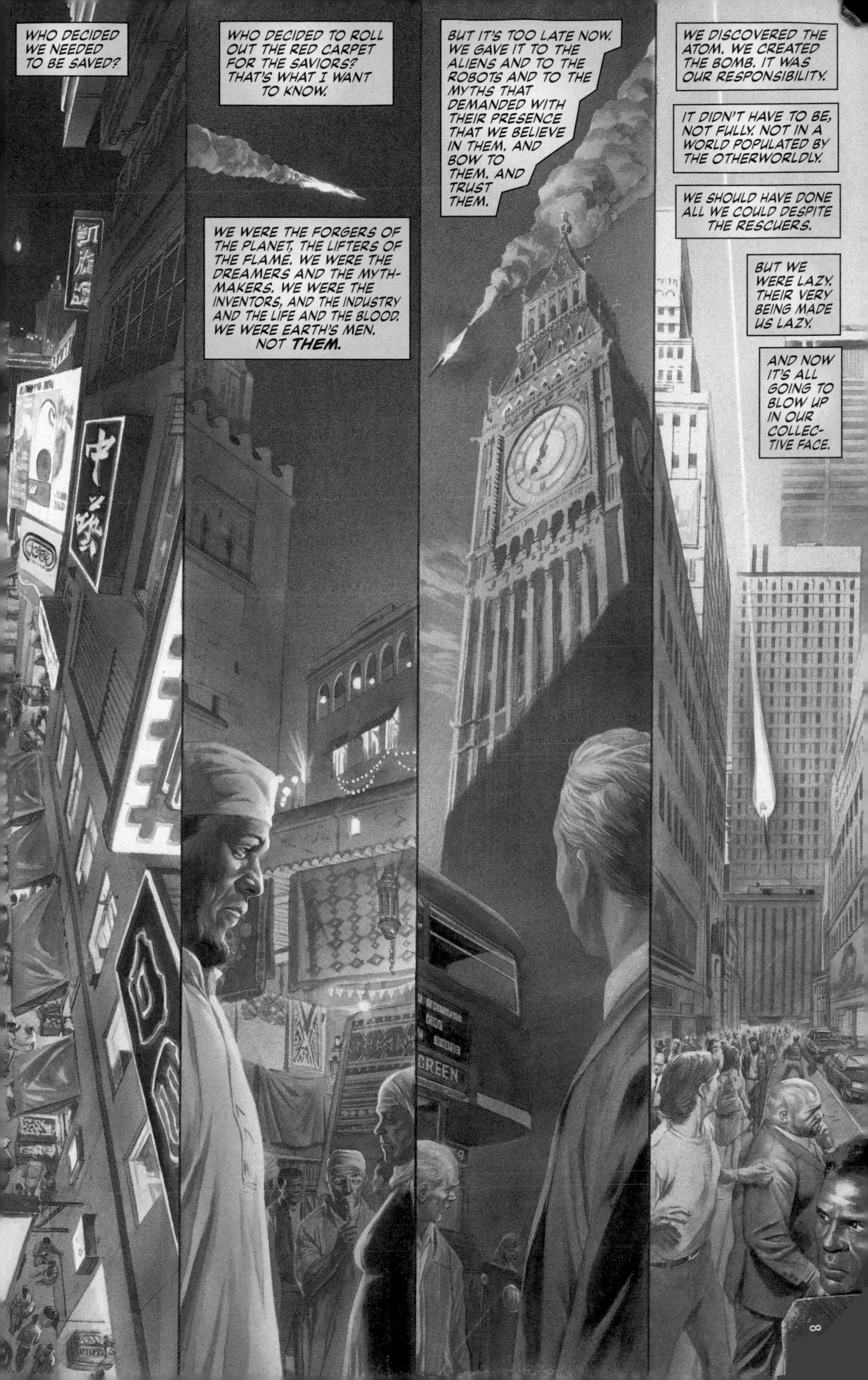
WHO DECIDED WE NEEDED TO BE SAVED?
WHO DECIDED TO ROLL OUT THE RED CARPET FOR THE SAVIORS? THAT'S WHAT I WANT TO KNOW.
WE WERE THE FORGERS OF THE PLANET, THE LIFTERS OF THE FLAME. WE WERE THE DREAMERS AND THE MYTH-MAKERS. WE WERE THE INVENTORS, AND THE INDUSTRY AND THE LIFE AND THE BLOOD. WE WERE EARTH'S MEN. NOT THEM.
BUT IT'S TOO LATE NOW. WE GAVE IT TO THE ALIENS AND TO THE ROBOTS AND TO THE MYTHS THAT DEMANDED WITH THEIR PRESENCE THAT WE BELIEVE IN THEM. AND BOW TO THEM. AND TRUST THEM.
WE DISCOVERED THE ATOM. WE CREATED THE BOMB. IT WAS OUR RESPONSIBILITY.
IT DIDN'T HAVE TO BE, NOT FULLY. NOT IN A WORLD POPULATED BY THE OTHERWORLDLY.
WE SHOULD HAVE DONE ALL WE COULD DESPITE THE RESCUERS.
BUT WE WERE LAZY. THEIR VERY BEING MADE US LAZY.
AND NOW IT'S ALL GOING TO BLOW UP IN OUR COLLECTIVE FACE.
GREEN

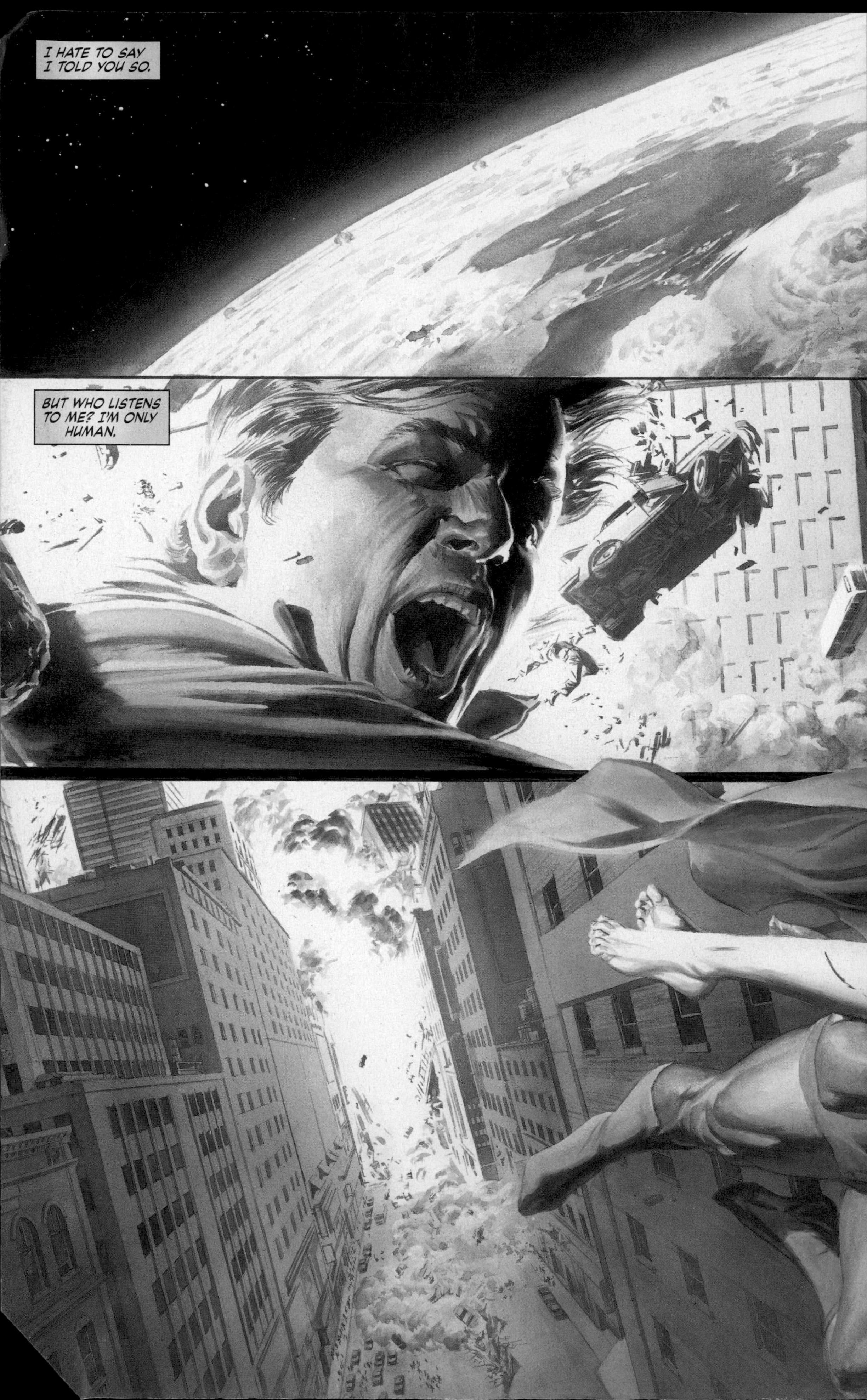
I HATE TO SAY I TOLD YOU SO.
BUT WHO LISTENS TO ME? I'M ONLY HUMAN.

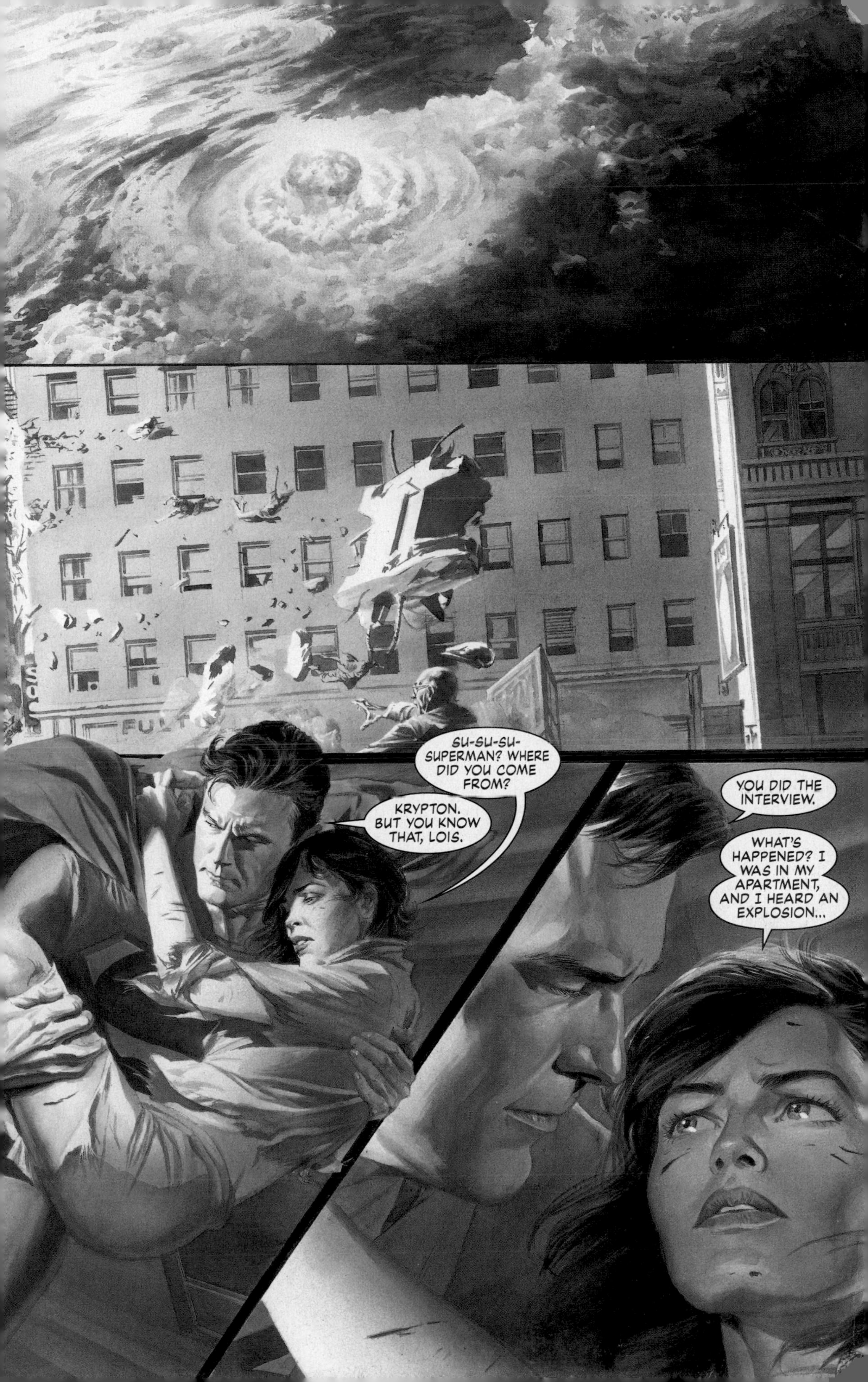
SU-SU-SU-SUPERMAN? WHERE DID YOU COME FROM?
KRYPTON. BUT YOU KNOW THAT, LOIS.
YOU DID THE INTERVIEW.
WHAT'S HAPPENED? I WAS IN MY APARTMENT, AND I HEARD AN EXPLOSION...

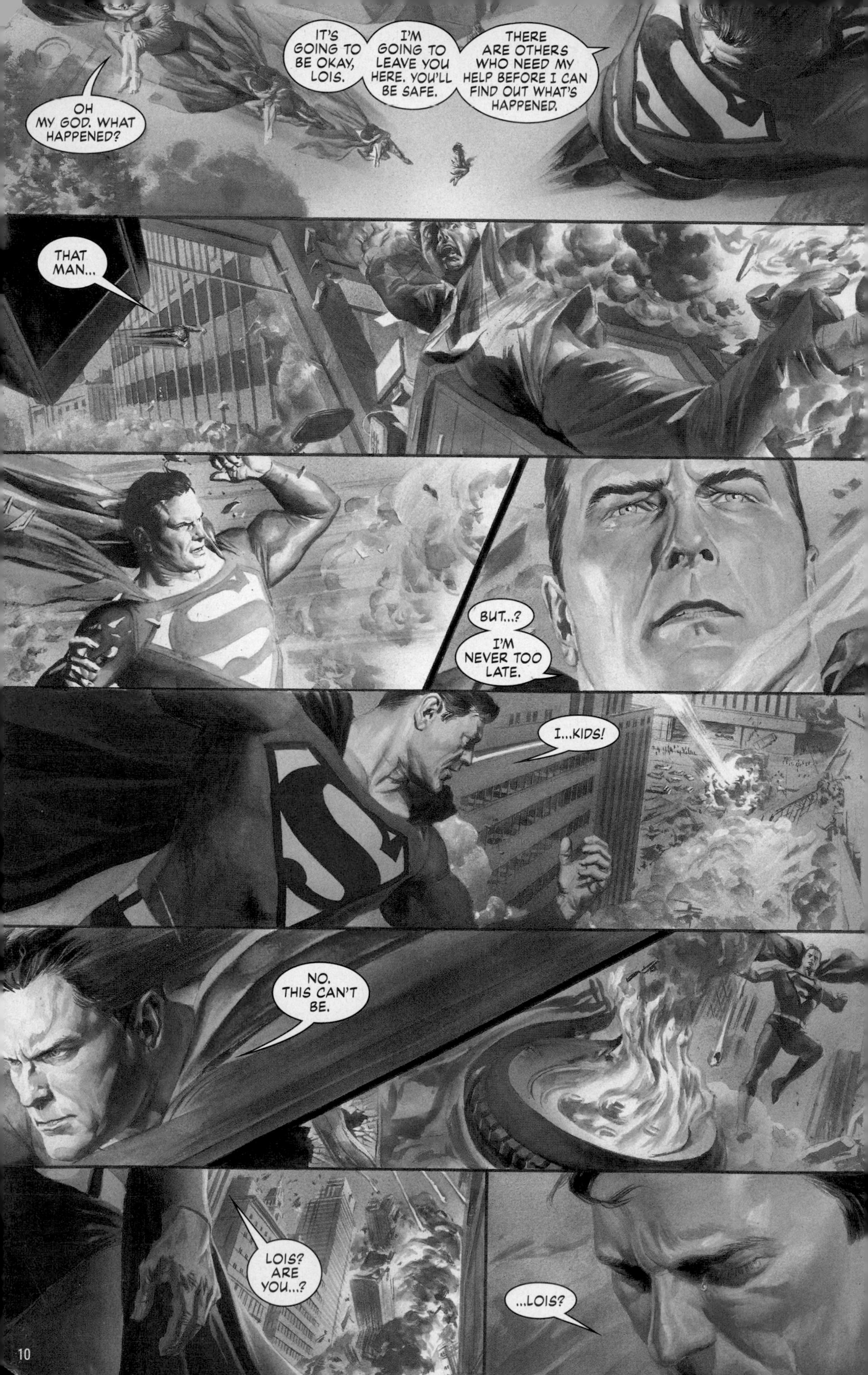

OH MY GOD. WHAT HAPPENED?
IT'S GOING TO BE OKAY, LOIS.
I'M GOING TO LEAVE YOU HERE. YOU'LL BE SAFE.
THERE ARE OTHERS WHO NEED MY HELP BEFORE I CAN FIND OUT WHAT'S HAPPENED.
THAT MAN...
BUT...?
I'M NEVER TOO LATE.
I...KIDS!
NO. THIS CAN'T BE.
LOIS? ARE YOU...?
...LOIS?

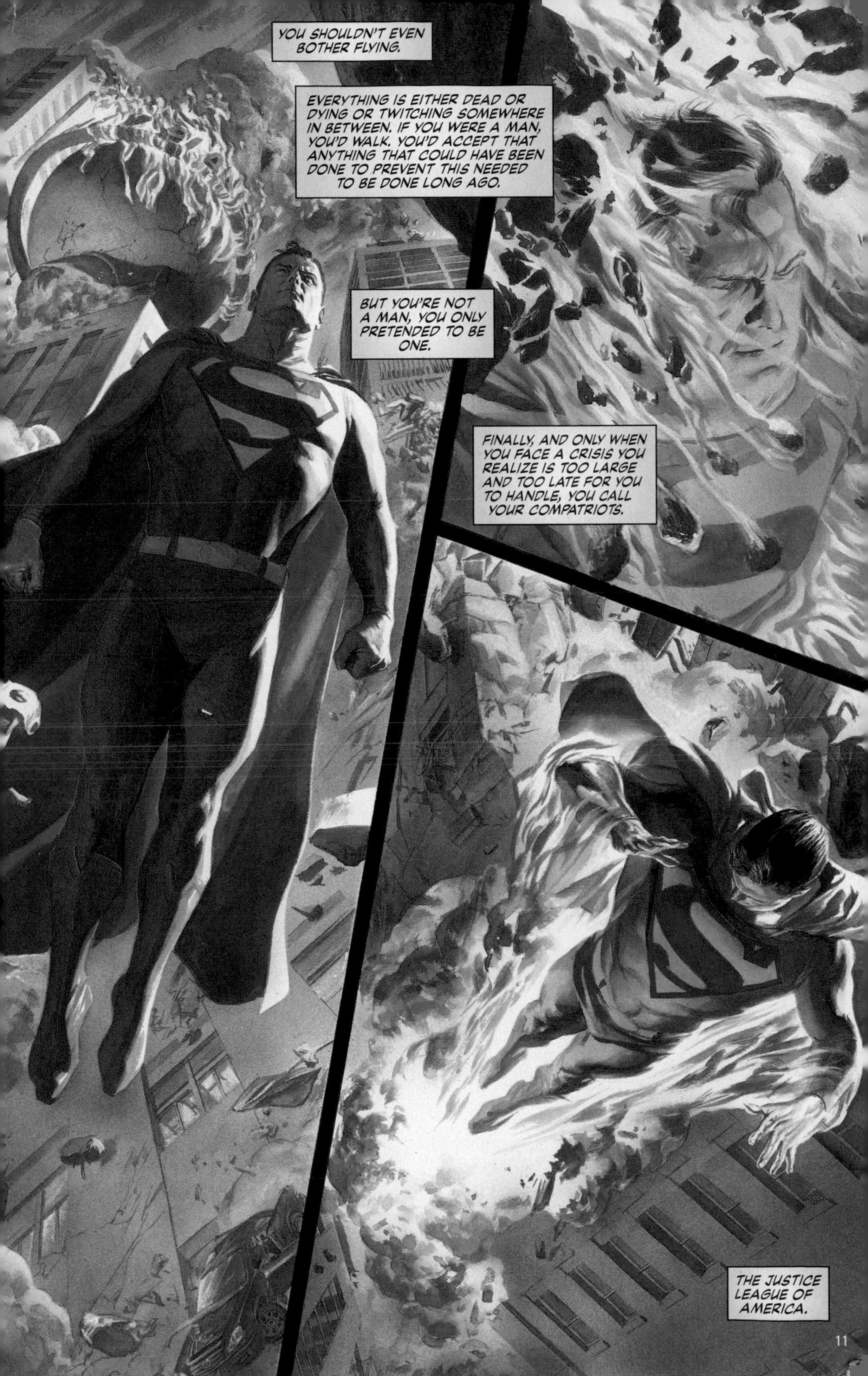
YOU SHOULDN'T EVEN BOTHER FLYING.
EVERYTHING IS EITHER DEAD OR DYING OR TWITCHING SOMEWHERE IN BETWEEN. IF YOU WERE A MAN, YOU'D WALK. YOU'D ACCEPT THAT ANYTHING THAT COULD HAVE BEEN DONE TO PREVENT THIS NEEDED TO BE DONE LONG AGO.
BUT YOU'RE NOT A MAN, YOU ONLY PRETENDED TO BE ONE.
FINALLY, AND ONLY WHEN YOU FACE A CRISIS YOU REALIZE IS TOO LARGE AND TOO LATE FOR YOU TO HANDLE, YOU CALL YOUR COMPATRIOTS.
THE JUSTICE LEAGUE OF AMERICA.

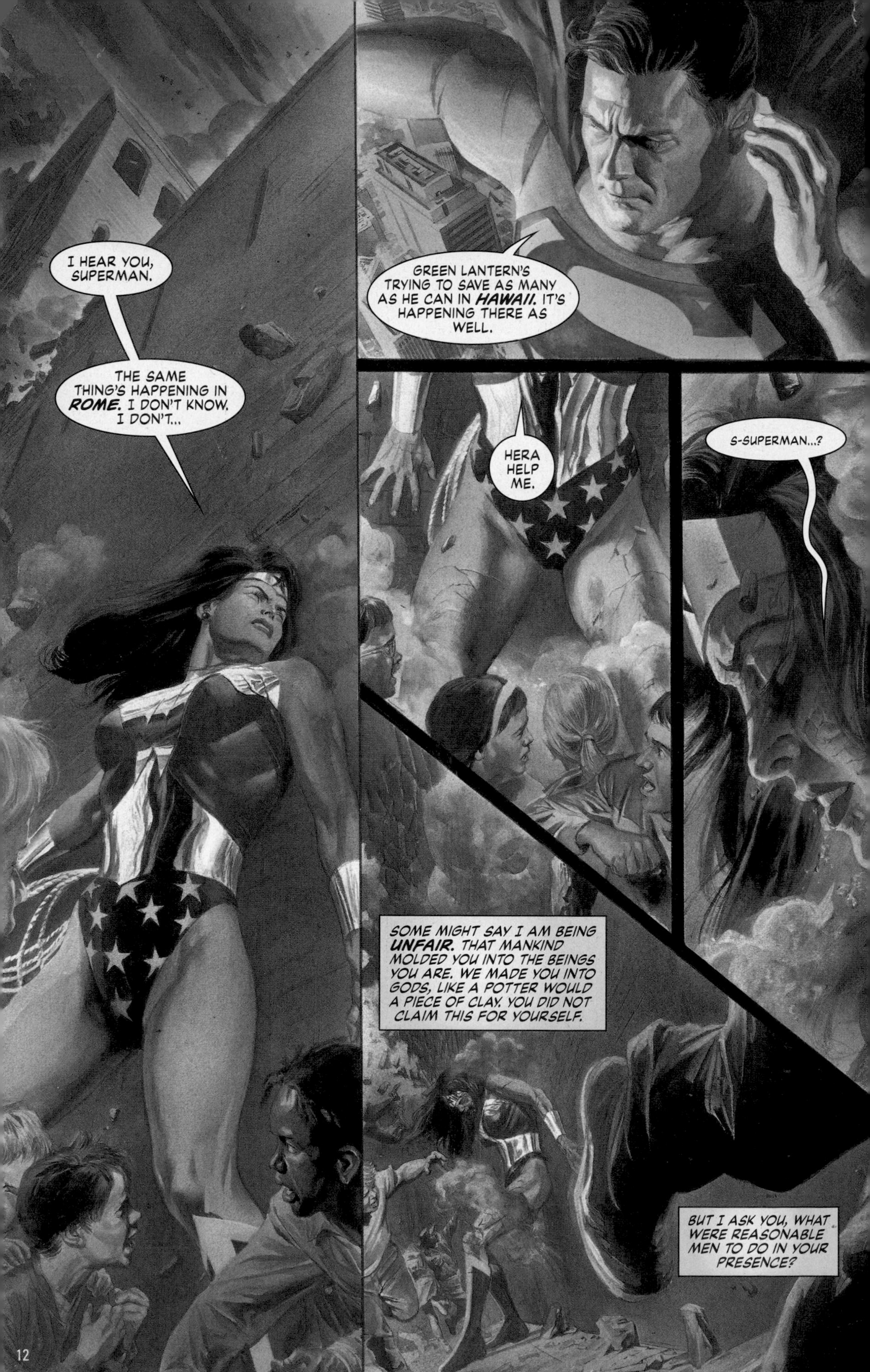
I HEAR YOU, SUPERMAN.
THE SAME THING'S HAPPENING IN ROME. I DON'T KNOW. I DON'T...
GREEN LANTERN'S TRYING TO SAVE AS MANY AS HE CAN IN HAWAII. IT'S HAPPENING THERE AS WELL.
HERA HELP ME.
S-SUPERMAN...?
SOME MIGHT SAY I AM BEING UNFAIR. THAT MANKIND MOLDED YOU INTO THE BEINGS YOU ARE. WE MADE YOU INTO GODS, LIKE A POTTER WOULD A PIECE OF CLAY. YOU DID NOT CLAIM THIS FOR YOURSELF.
BUT I ASK YOU, WHAT WERE REASONABLE MEN TO DO IN YOUR PRESENCE?

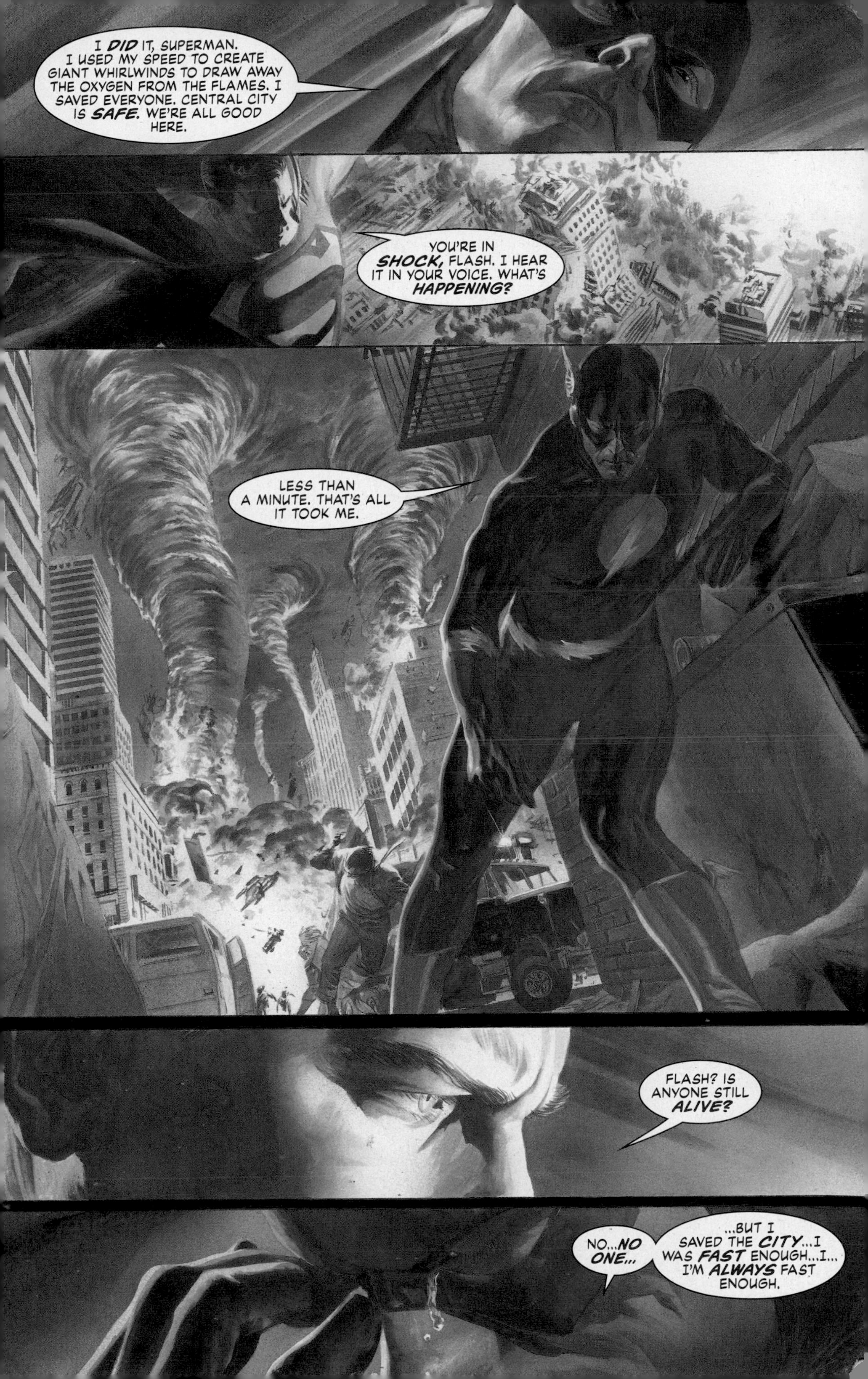
I DID IT, SUPERMAN. I USED MY SPEED TO CREATE GIANT WHIRLWINDS TO DRAW AWAY THE OXYGEN FROM THE FLAMES. I SAVED EVERYONE. CENTRAL CITY IS SAFE. WE'RE ALL GOOD HERE.
YOU'RE IN SHOCK, FLASH. I HEAR IT IN YOUR VOICE. WHAT'S HAPPENING?
LESS THAN A MINUTE. THAT'S ALL IT TOOK ME.
FLASH? IS ANYONE STILL ALIVE?
NO...NO ONE...
...BUT I SAVED THE CITY...I WAS FAST ENOUGH...I... I'M ALWAYS FAST ENOUGH.

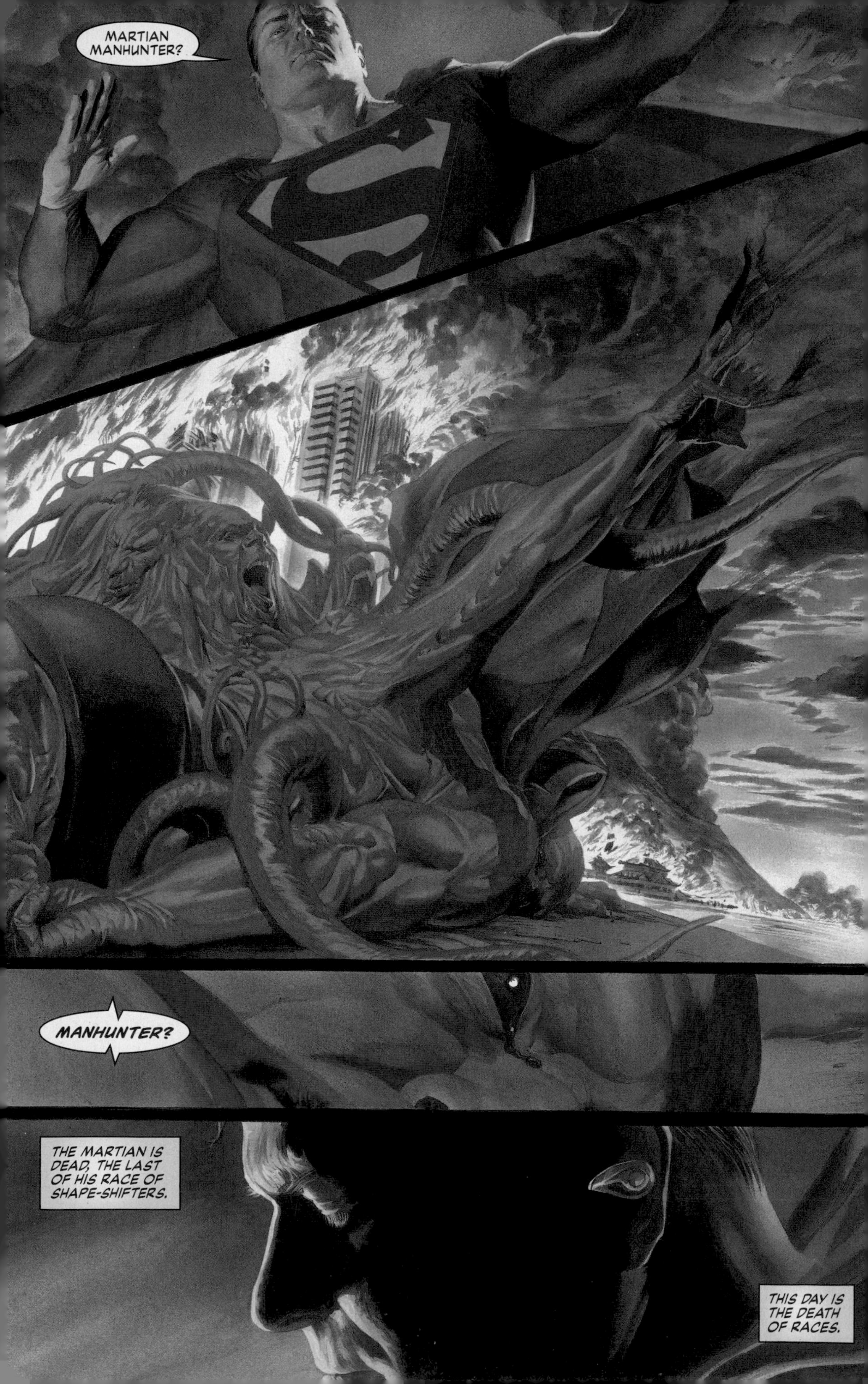
MARTIAN MANHUNTER?
MANHUNTER?
THE MARTIAN IS DEAD, THE LAST OF HIS RACE OF SHAPE-SHIFTERS.
THIS DAY IS THE DEATH OF RACES.

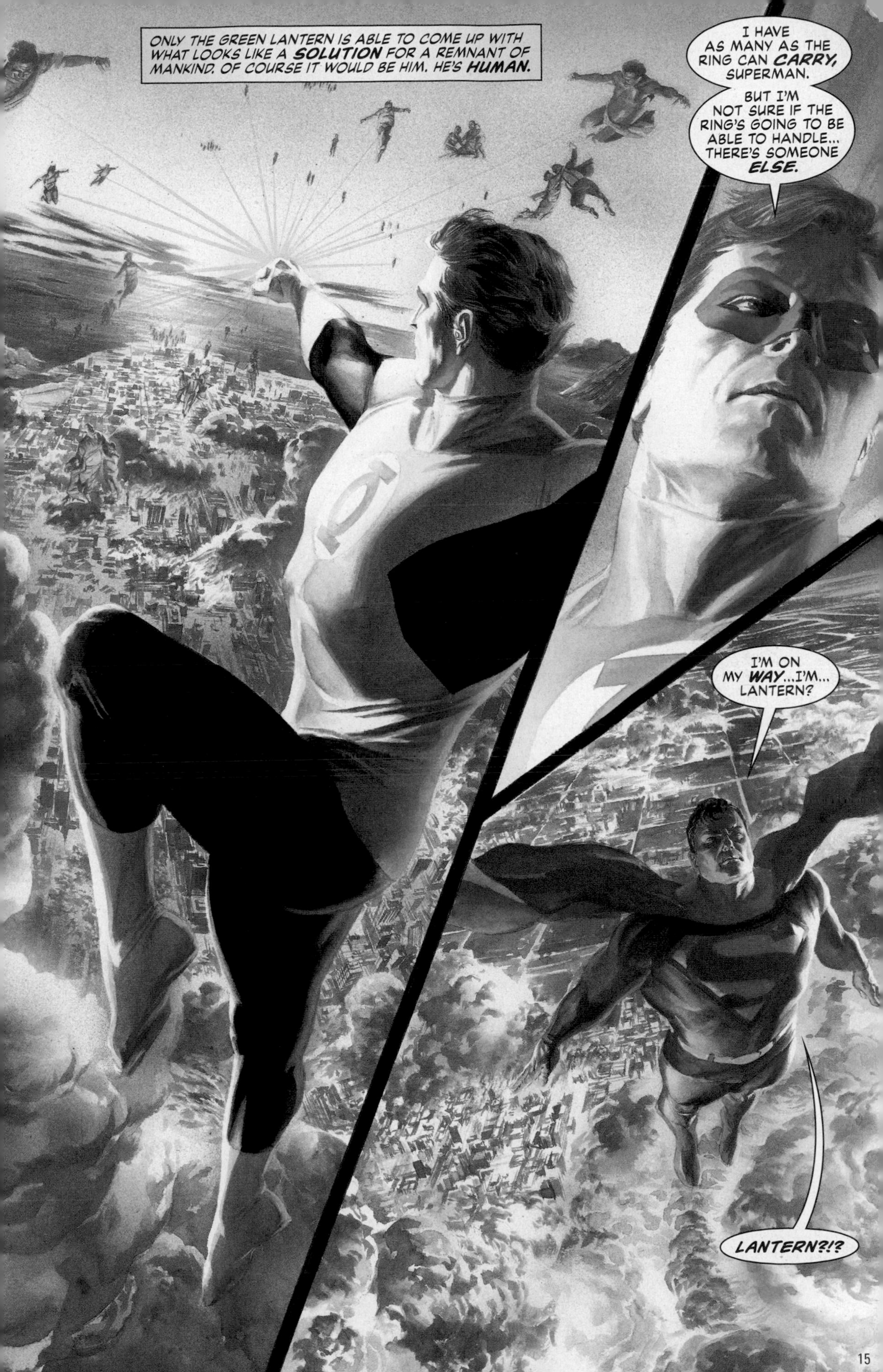
ONLY THE GREEN LANTERN IS ABLE TO COME UP WITH WHAT LOOKS LIKE A SOLUTION FOR A REMNANT OF MANKIND. OF COURSE IT WOULD BE HIM. HE'S HUMAN.
I HAVE AS MANY AS THE RING CAN CARRY, SUPERMAN.
BUT I'M NOT SURE IF THE RING'S GOING TO BE ABLE TO HANDLE... THERE'S SOMEONE ELSE.
I'M ON MY WAY...I'M... LANTERN?
LANTERN?!?

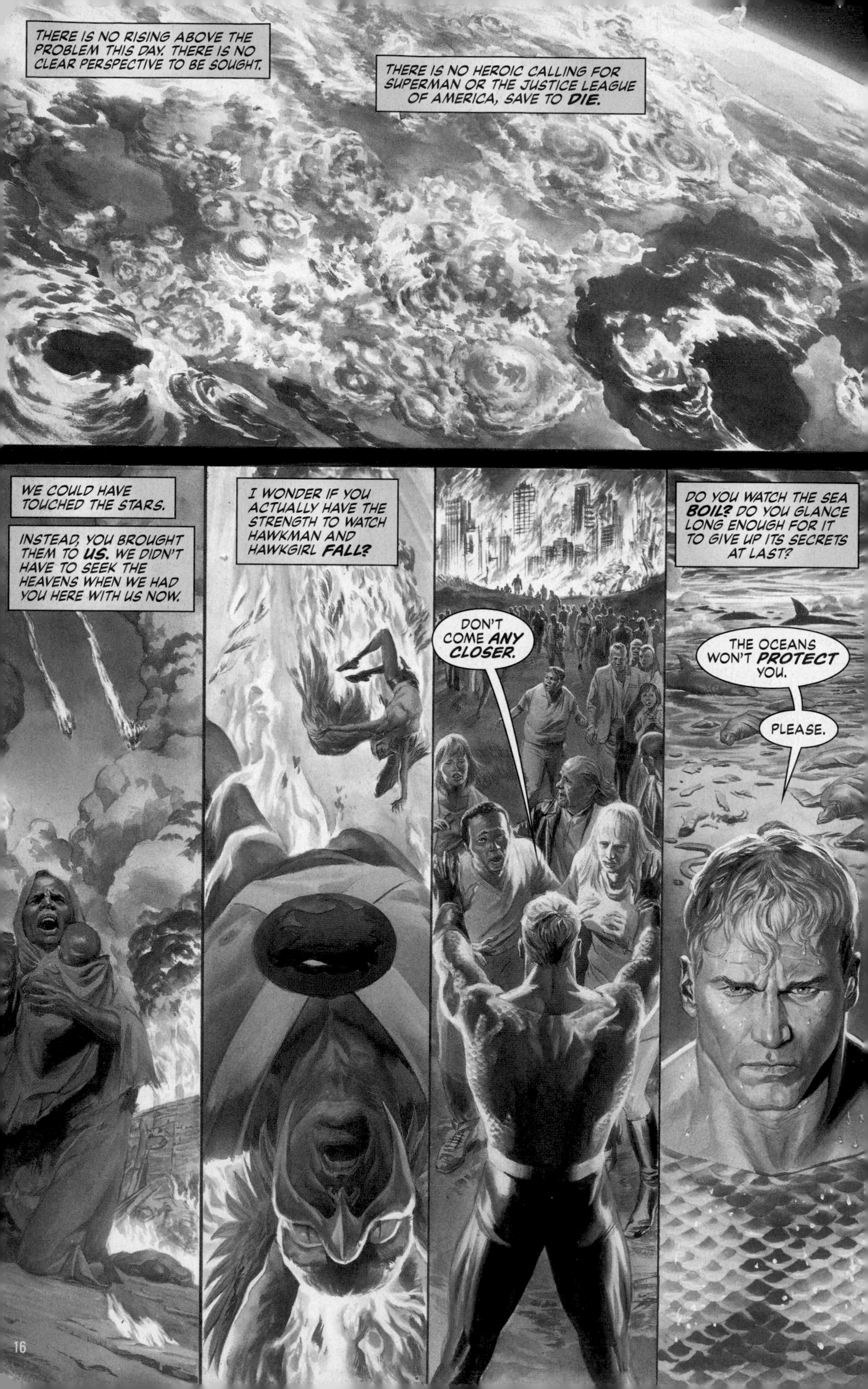
THERE IS NO RISING ABOVE THE PROBLEM THIS DAY. THERE IS NO CLEAR PERSPECTIVE TO BE SOUGHT.
THERE IS NO HEROIC CALLING FOR SUPERMAN OR THE JUSTICE LEAGUE OF AMERICA, SAVE TO DIE.
WE COULD HAVE TOUCHED THE STARS.
INSTEAD, YOU BROUGHT THEM TO US. WE DIDN'T HAVE TO SEEK THE HEAVENS WHEN WE HAD YOU HERE WITH US NOW.
I WONDER IF YOU ACTUALLY HAVE THE STRENGTH TO WATCH HAWKMAN AND HAWKGIRL FALL?
DON'T COME ANY CLOSER.
DO YOU WATCH THE SEA BOIL? DO YOU GLANCE LONG ENOUGH FOR IT TO GIVE UP ITS SECRETS AT LAST?
THE OCEANS WON'T PROTECT YOU.
PLEASE.

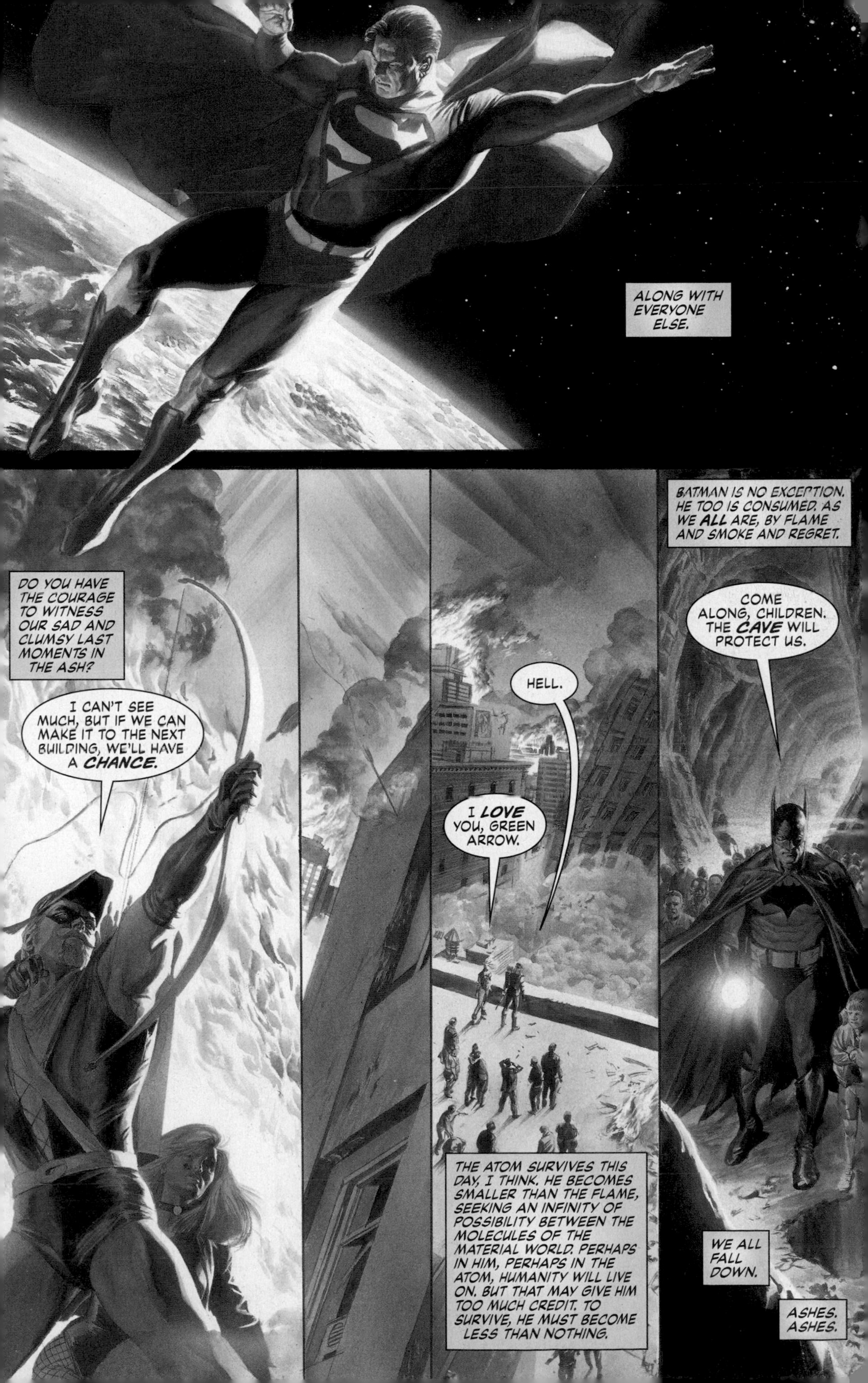
ALONG WITH EVERYONE ELSE.
DO YOU HAVE THE COURAGE TO WITNESS OUR SAD AND CLUMSY LAST MOMENTS IN THE ASH?
I CAN'T SEE MUCH, BUT IF WE CAN MAKE IT TO THE NEXT BUILDING, WE'LL HAVE A CHANCE.
HELL.
I LOVE YOU, GREEN ARROW.
THE ATOM SURVIVES THIS DAY, I THINK. HE BECOMES SMALLER THAN THE FLAME, SEEKING AN INFINITY OF POSSIBILITY BETWEEN THE MOLECULES OF THE MATERIAL WORLD. PERHAPS IN HIM, PERHAPS IN THE ATOM, HUMANITY WILL LIVE ON. BUT THAT MAY GIVE HIM TOO MUCH CREDIT. TO SURVIVE, HE MUST BECOME LESS THAN NOTHING.
BATMAN IS NO EXCEPTION. HE TOO IS CONSUMED. AS WE ALL ARE, BY FLAME AND SMOKE AND REGRET.
COME ALONG, CHILDREN. THE CAVE WILL PROTECT US.
WE ALL FALL DOWN.
ASHES. ASHES.

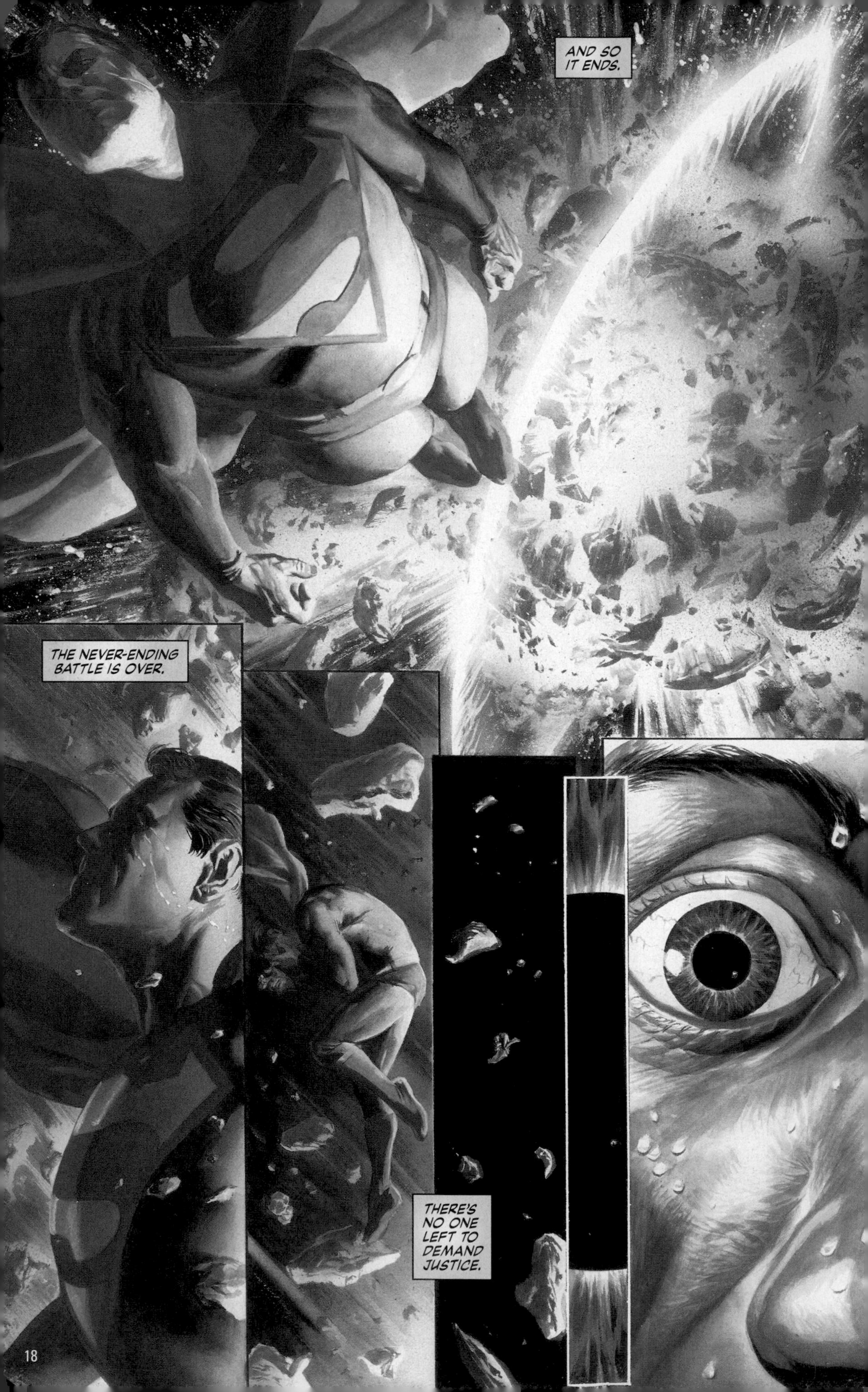
AND SO IT ENDS.
THE NEVER-ENDING BATTLE IS OVER.
THERE'S NO ONE LEFT TO DEMAND JUSTICE.

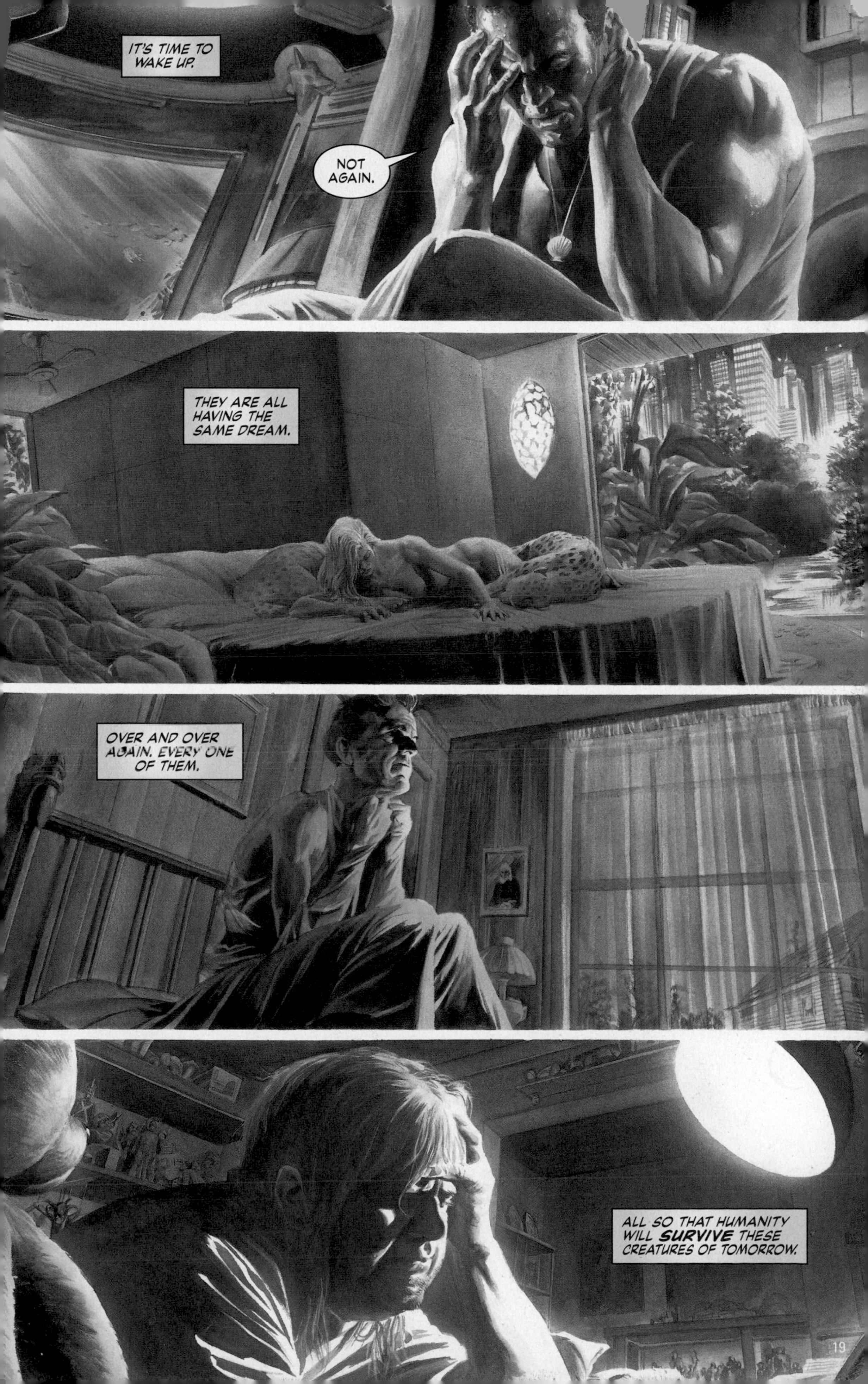
IT'S TIME TO WAKE UP.
NOT AGAIN.
THEY ARE ALL HAVING THE SAME DREAM.
OVER AND OVER AGAIN. EVERY ONE OF THEM.
ALL SO THAT HUMANITY WILL **SURVIVE** THESE CREATURES OF TOMORROW.

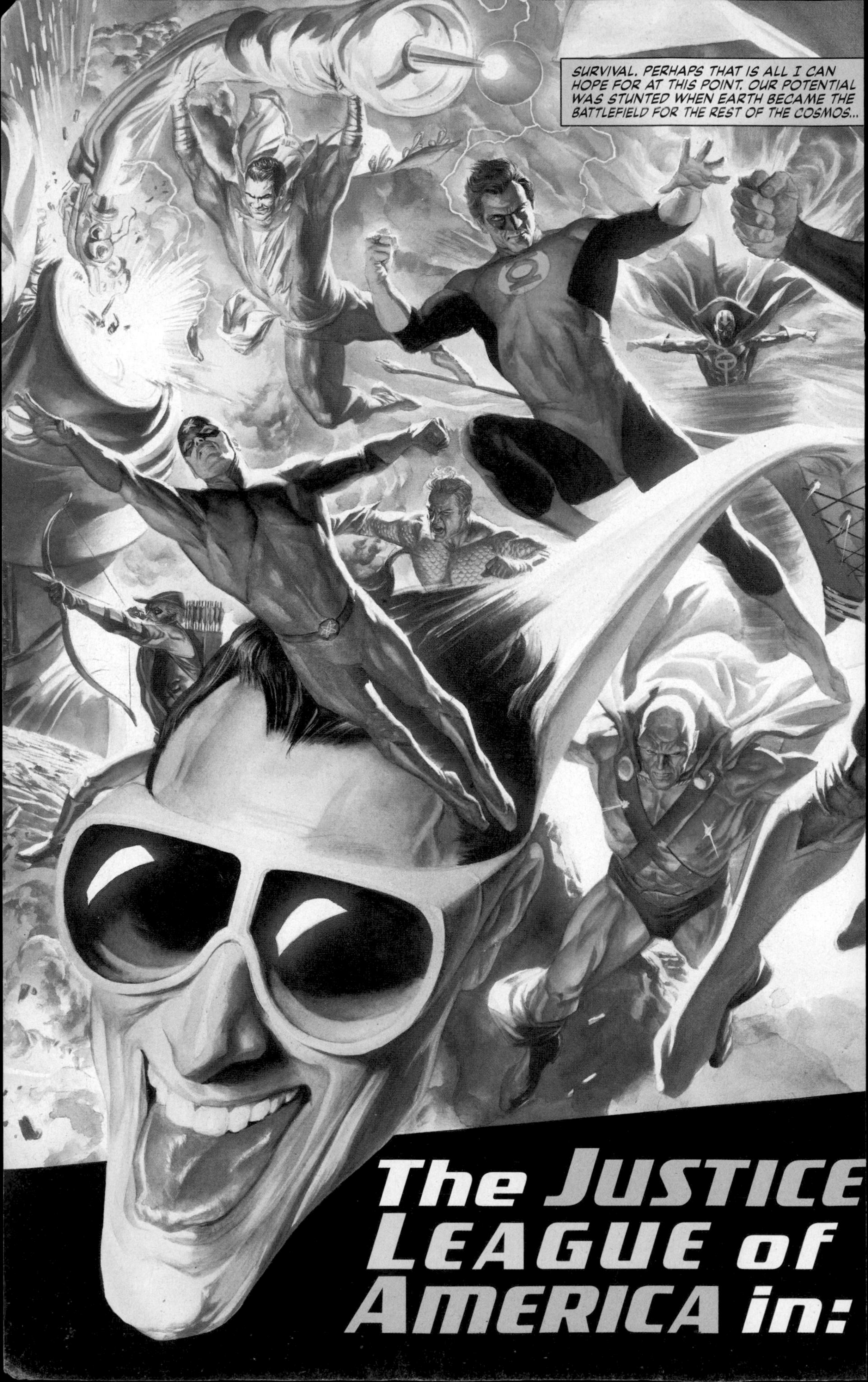
SURVIVAL. PERHAPS THAT IS ALL I CAN HOPE FOR AT THIS POINT. OUR POTENTIAL WAS STUNTED WHEN EARTH BECAME THE BATTLEFIELD FOR THE REST OF THE COSMOS...
The JUSTICE LEAGUE of AMERICA in:

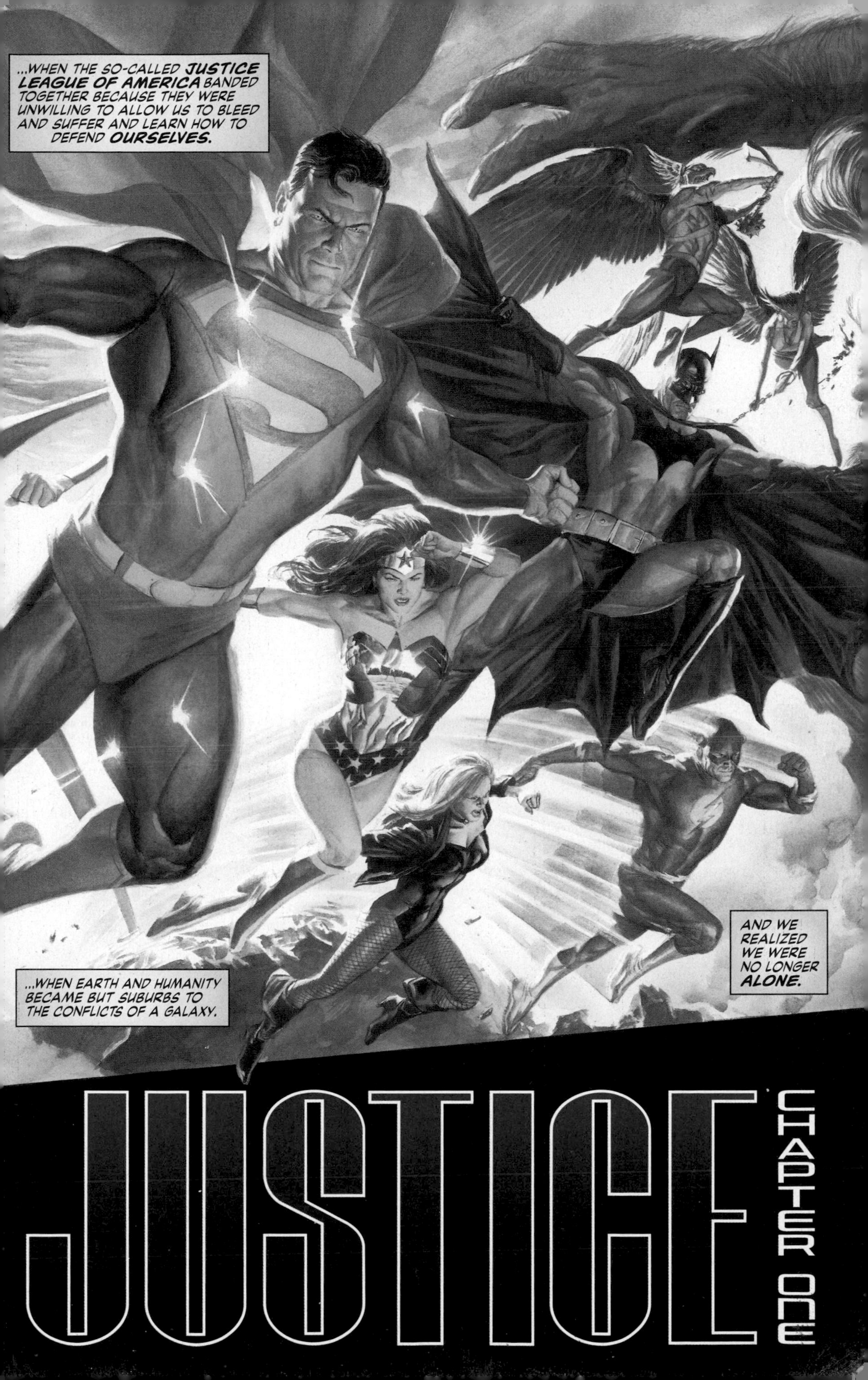
...WHEN THE SO-CALLED JUSTICE LEAGUE OF AMERICA BANDED TOGETHER BECAUSE THEY WERE UNWILLING TO ALLOW US TO BLEED AND SUFFER AND LEARN HOW TO DEFEND OURSELVES.
...WHEN EARTH AND HUMANITY BECAME BUT SUBURBS TO THE CONFLICTS OF A GALAXY.
AND WE REALIZED WE WERE NO LONGER ALONE.
JUSTICE
CHAPTER ONE

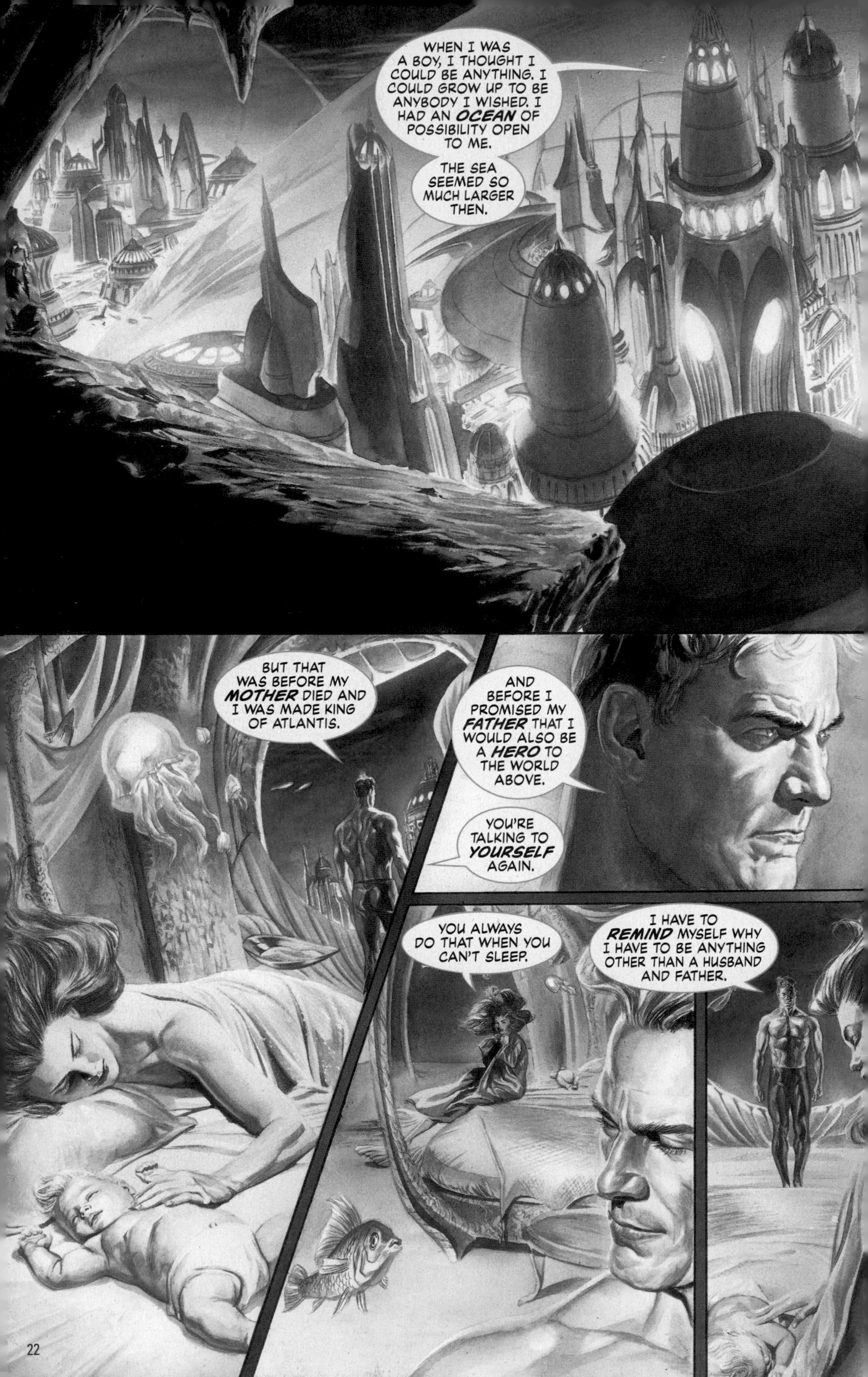

WHEN I WAS A BOY, I THOUGHT I COULD BE ANYTHING. I COULD GROW UP TO BE ANYBODY I WISHED. I HAD AN **OCEAN** OF POSSIBILITY OPEN TO ME.
THE SEA SEEMED SO MUCH LARGER THEN.
BUT THAT WAS BEFORE MY **MOTHER** DIED AND I WAS MADE KING OF ATLANTIS.
AND BEFORE I PROMISED MY **FATHER** THAT I WOULD ALSO BE A **HERO** TO THE WORLD ABOVE.
YOU'RE TALKING TO **YOURSELF** AGAIN.
YOU ALWAYS DO THAT WHEN YOU CAN'T SLEEP.
I HAVE TO **REMIND** MYSELF WHY I HAVE TO BE ANYTHING OTHER THAN A HUSBAND AND FATHER.

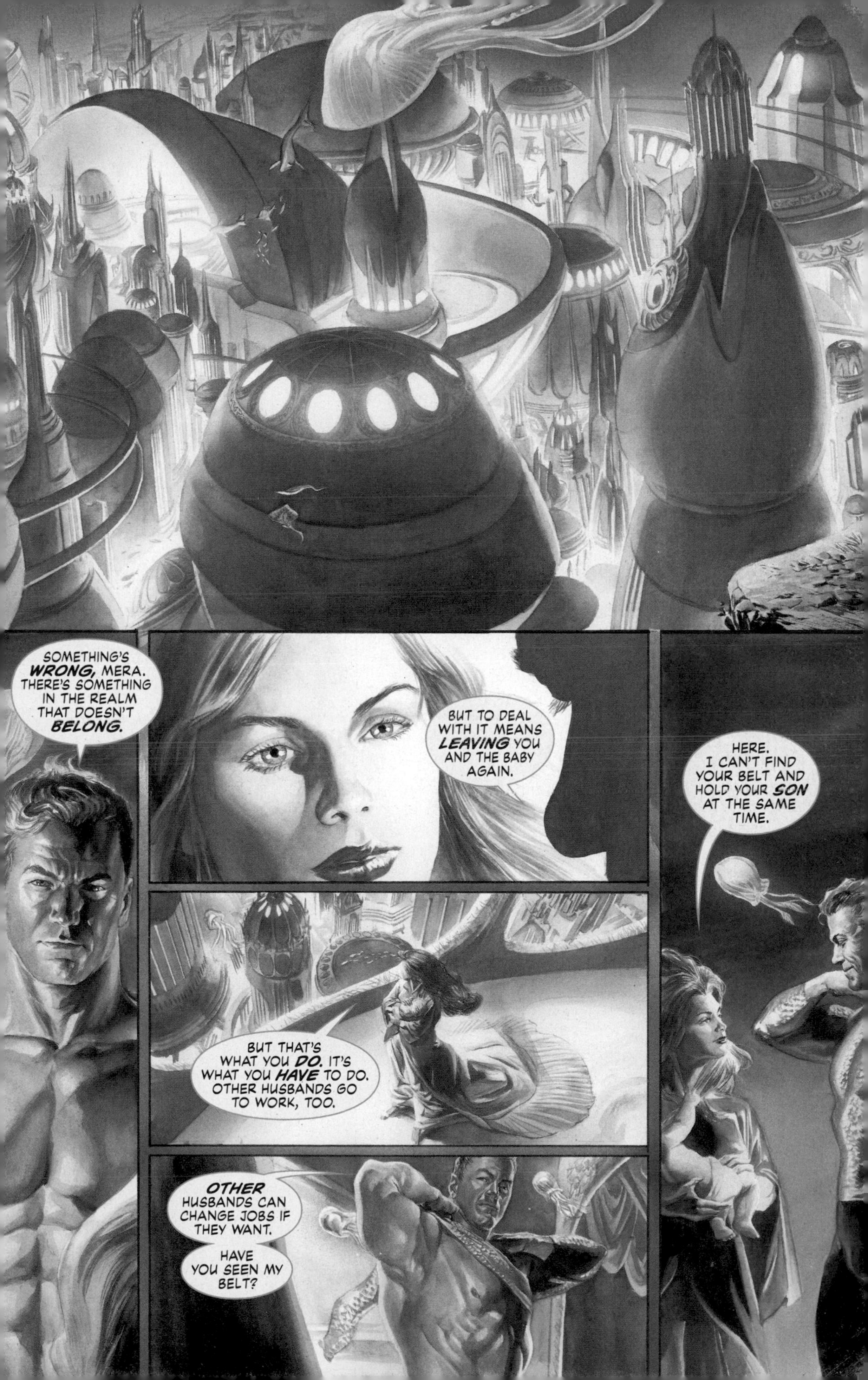
SOMETHING'S WRONG, MERA. THERE'S SOMETHING IN THE REALM THAT DOESN'T BELONG.
BUT TO DEAL WITH IT MEANS LEAVING YOU AND THE BABY AGAIN.
BUT THAT'S WHAT YOU DO. IT'S WHAT YOU HAVE TO DO. OTHER HUSBANDS GO TO WORK, TOO.
OTHER HUSBANDS CAN CHANGE JOBS IF THEY WANT.
HAVE YOU SEEN MY BELT?
HERE. I CAN'T FIND YOUR BELT AND HOLD YOUR SON AT THE SAME TIME.

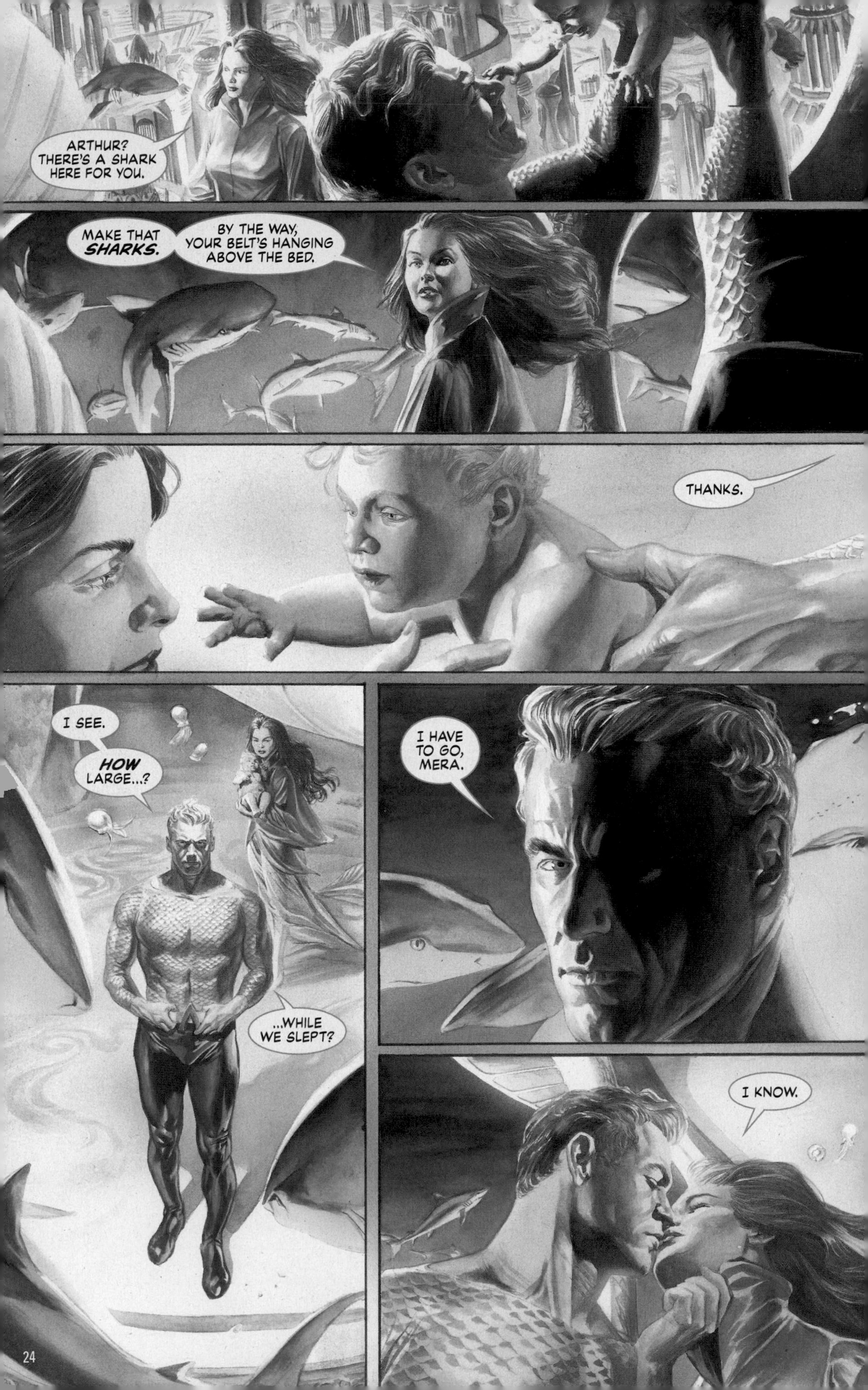
ARTHUR? THERE'S A SHARK HERE FOR YOU.
MAKE THAT *SHARKS.*
BY THE WAY, YOUR BELT'S HANGING ABOVE THE BED.
THANKS.
I SEE.
HOW LARGE...?
...WHILE WE SLEPT?
I HAVE TO GO, MERA.
I KNOW.

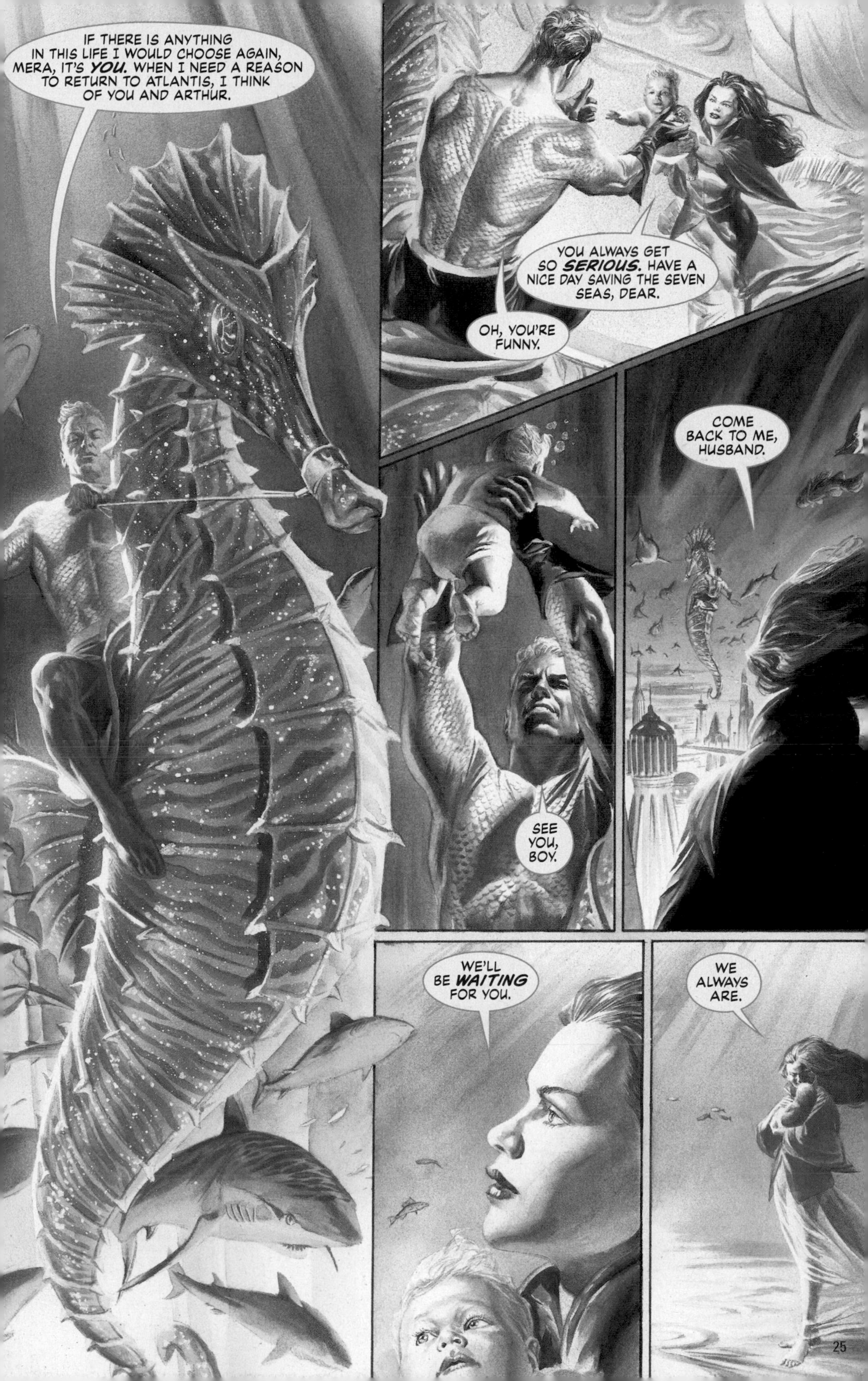
IF THERE IS ANYTHING IN THIS LIFE I WOULD CHOOSE AGAIN, MERA, IT'S YOU. WHEN I NEED A REASON TO RETURN TO ATLANTIS, I THINK OF YOU AND ARTHUR.
YOU ALWAYS GET SO SERIOUS. HAVE A NICE DAY SAVING THE SEVEN SEAS, DEAR.
OH, YOU'RE FUNNY.
SEE YOU, BOY.
COME BACK TO ME, HUSBAND.
WE'LL BE WAITING FOR YOU.
WE ALWAYS ARE.

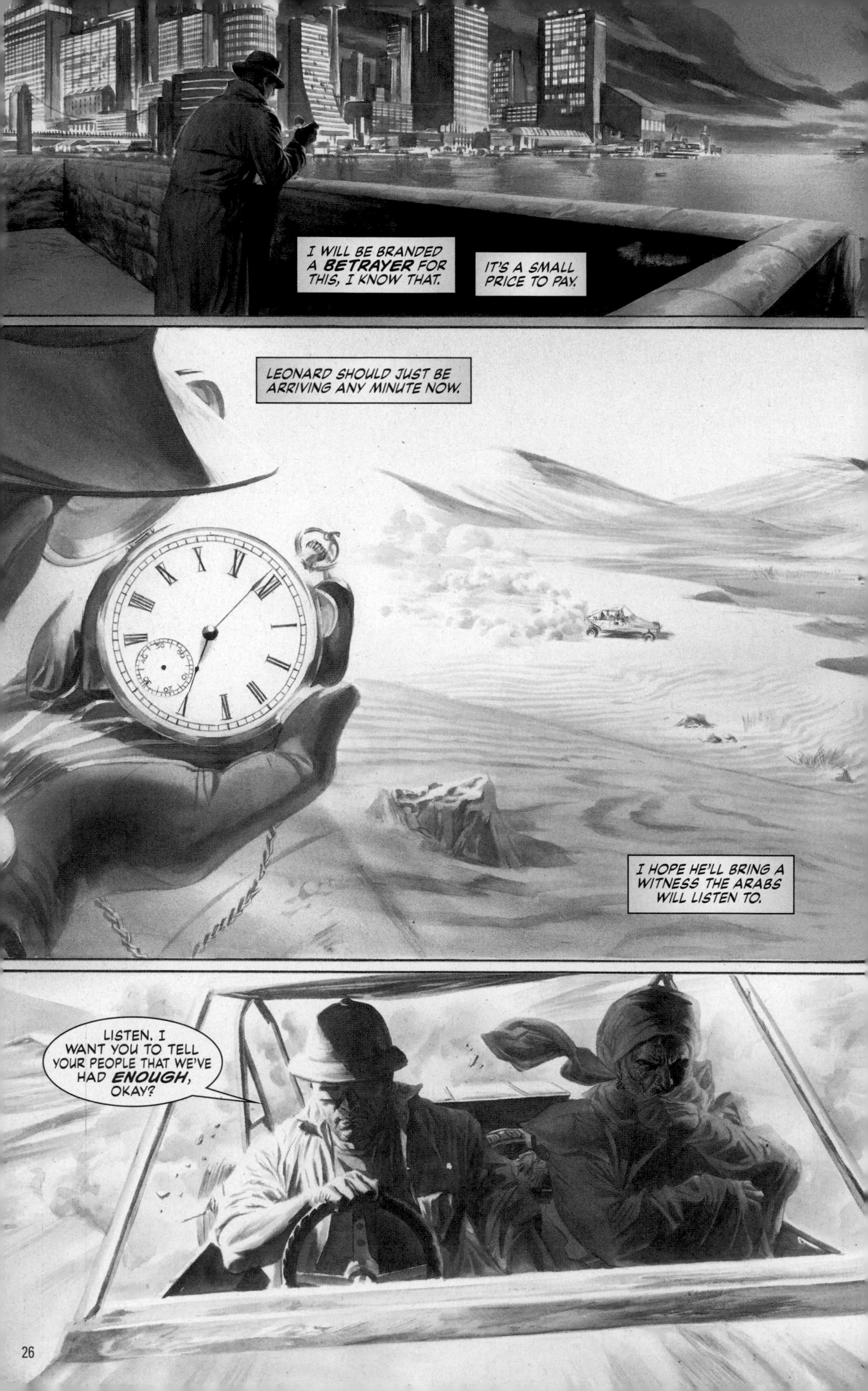

I WILL BE BRANDED A **BETRAYER** FOR THIS, I KNOW THAT.
IT'S A SMALL PRICE TO PAY.
LEONARD SHOULD JUST BE ARRIVING ANY MINUTE NOW.
I HOPE HE'LL BRING A WITNESS THE ARABS WILL LISTEN TO.
LISTEN. I WANT YOU TO TELL YOUR PEOPLE THAT WE'VE HAD **ENOUGH**, OKAY?

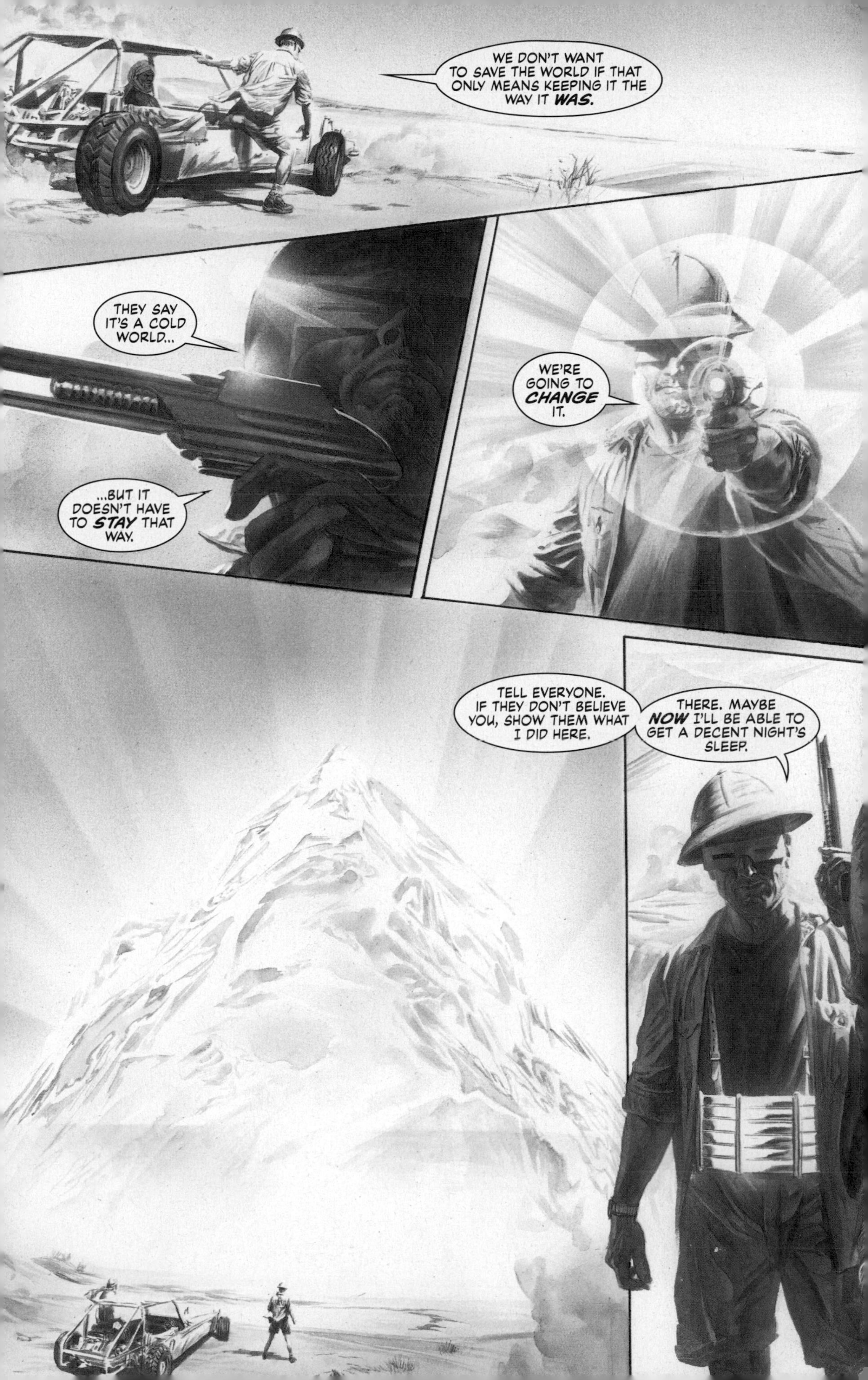
WE DON'T WANT TO SAVE THE WORLD IF THAT ONLY MEANS KEEPING IT THE WAY IT **WAS.**
THEY SAY IT'S A COLD WORLD...
...BUT IT DOESN'T HAVE TO **STAY** THAT WAY.
WE'RE GOING TO **CHANGE** IT.
TELL EVERYONE. IF THEY DON'T BELIEVE YOU, SHOW THEM WHAT I DID HERE.
THERE. MAYBE **NOW** I'LL BE ABLE TO GET A DECENT NIGHT'S SLEEP.

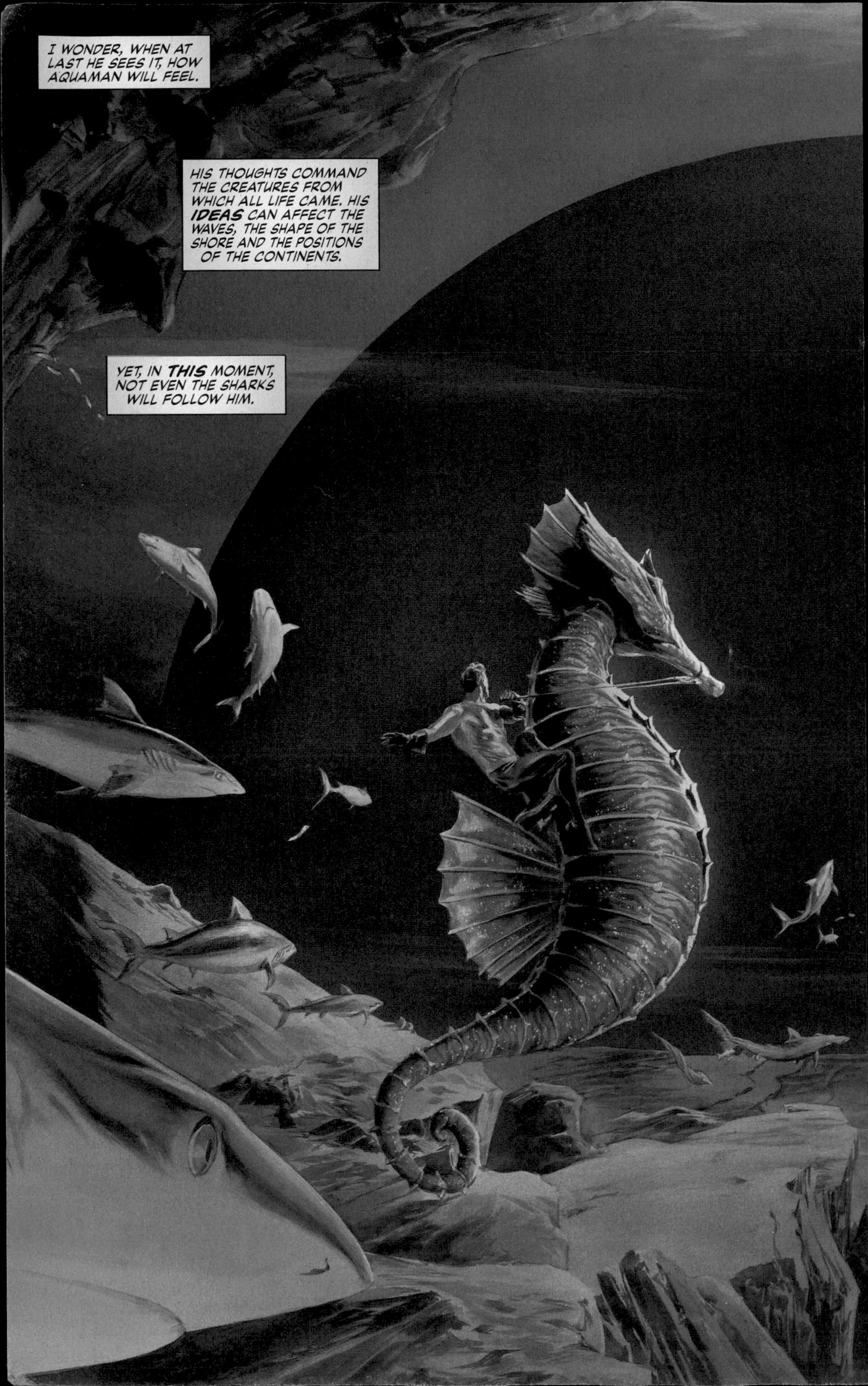
I WONDER, WHEN AT LAST HE SEES IT, HOW AQUAMAN WILL FEEL.
HIS THOUGHTS COMMAND THE CREATURES FROM WHICH ALL LIFE CAME. HIS IDEAS CAN AFFECT THE WAVES, THE SHAPE OF THE SHORE AND THE POSITIONS OF THE CONTINENTS.
YET, IN THIS MOMENT, NOT EVEN THE SHARKS WILL FOLLOW HIM.

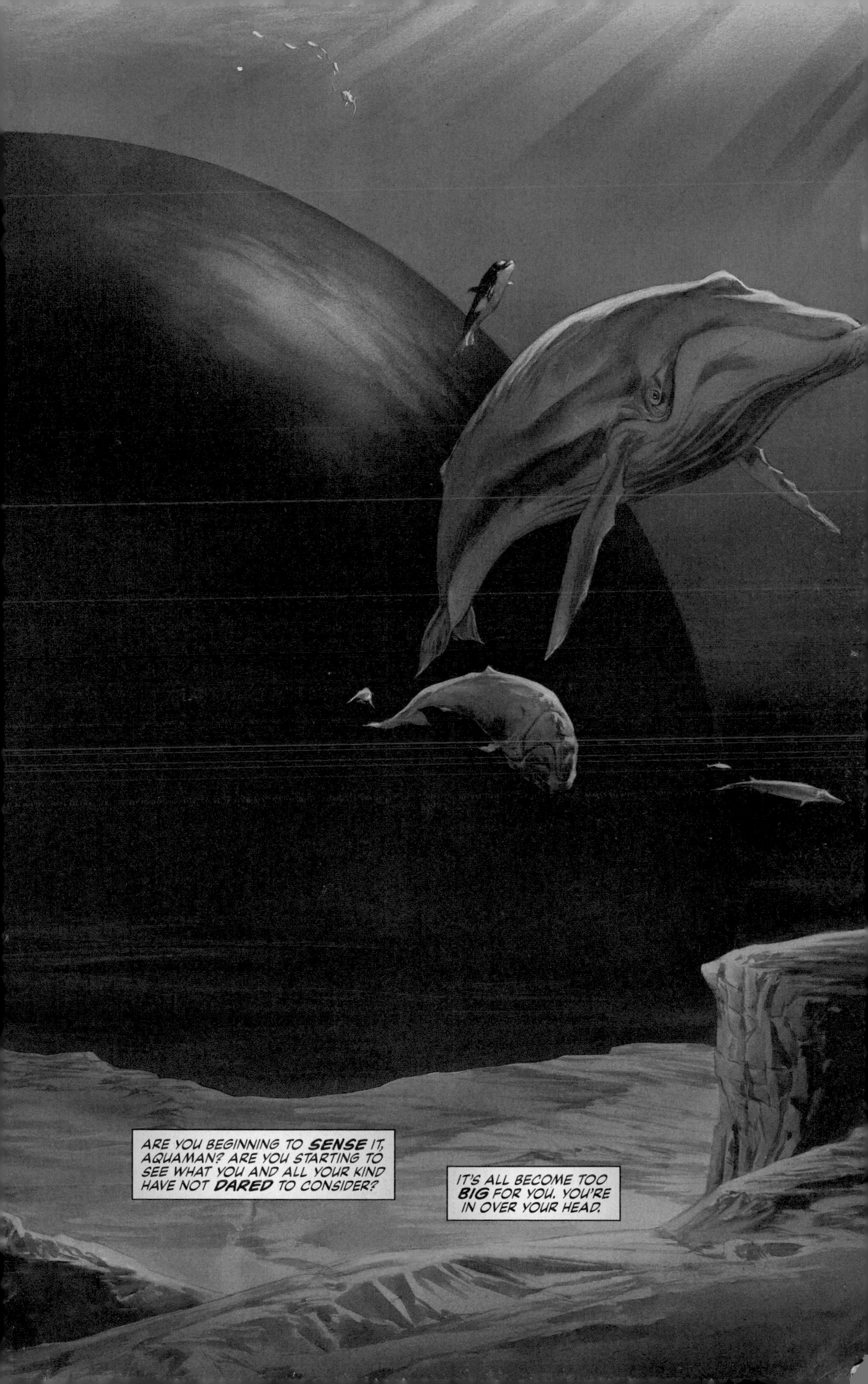
ARE YOU BEGINNING TO SENSE IT, AQUAMAN? ARE YOU STARTING TO SEE WHAT YOU AND ALL YOUR KIND HAVE NOT DARED TO CONSIDER?
IT'S ALL BECOME TOO BIG FOR YOU. YOU'RE IN OVER YOUR HEAD.

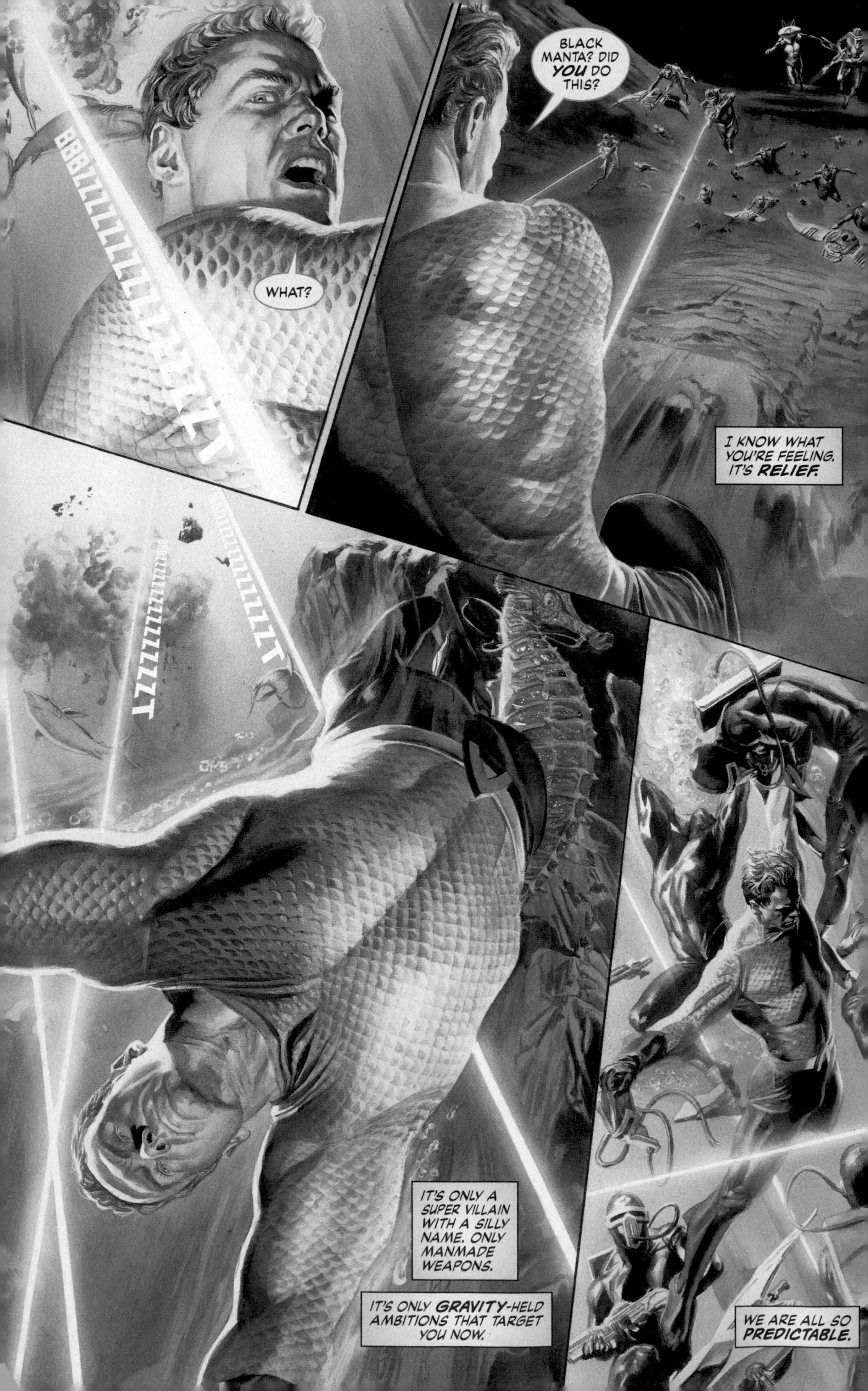
WHAT?
BLACK MANTA? DID YOU DO THIS?
I KNOW WHAT YOU'RE FEELING. IT'S RELIEF.
IT'S ONLY A SUPER VILLAIN WITH A SILLY NAME. ONLY MANMADE WEAPONS.
IT'S ONLY GRAVITY-HELD AMBITIONS THAT TARGET YOU NOW.
WE ARE ALL SO PREDICTABLE.

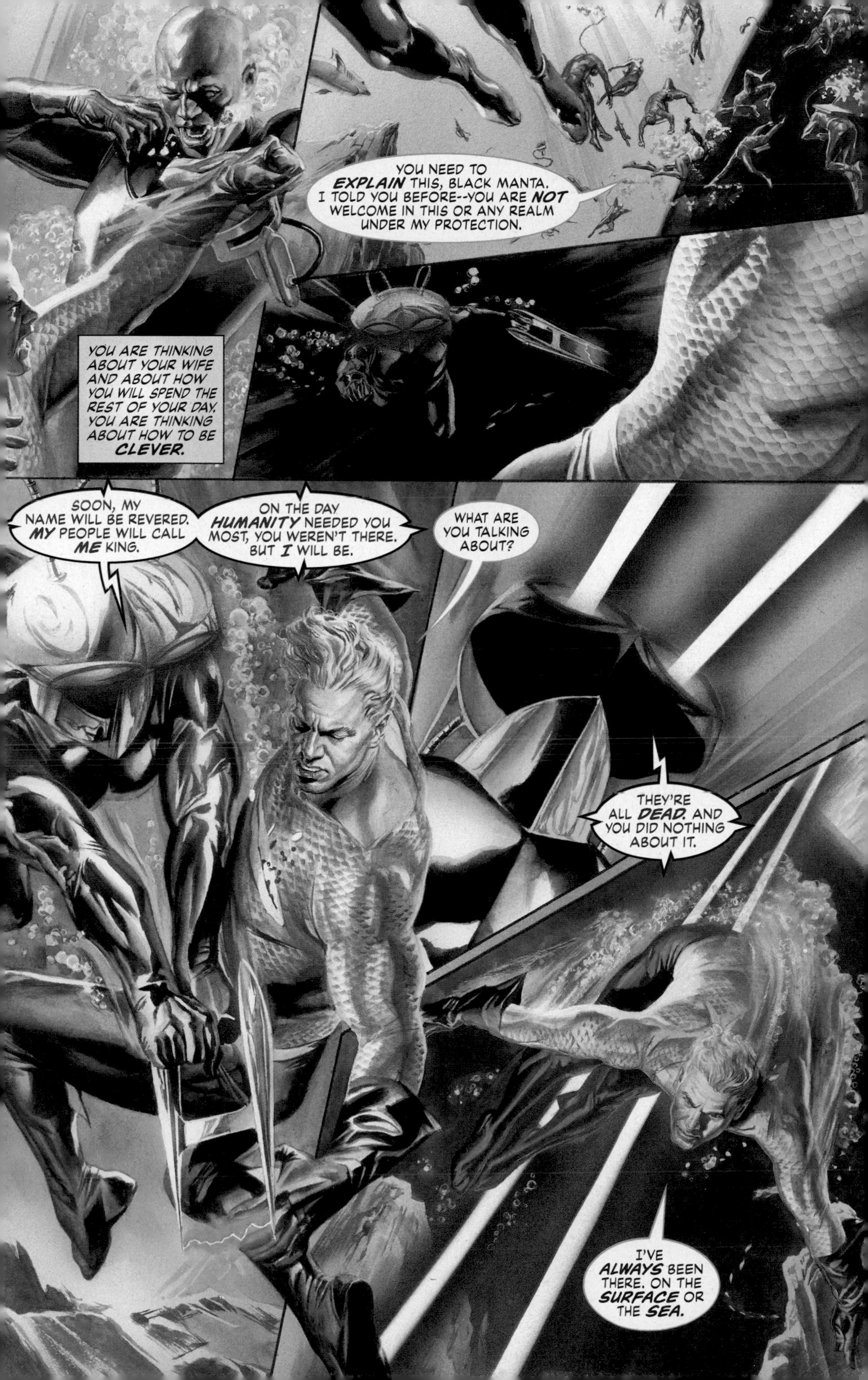

YOU NEED TO EXPLAIN THIS, BLACK MANTA. I TOLD YOU BEFORE--YOU ARE NOT WELCOME IN THIS OR ANY REALM UNDER MY PROTECTION.
YOU ARE THINKING ABOUT YOUR WIFE AND ABOUT HOW YOU WILL SPEND THE REST OF YOUR DAY. YOU ARE THINKING ABOUT HOW TO BE CLEVER.
SOON, MY NAME WILL BE REVERED. MY PEOPLE WILL CALL ME KING.
ON THE DAY HUMANITY NEEDED YOU MOST, YOU WEREN'T THERE. BUT I WILL BE.
WHAT ARE YOU TALKING ABOUT?
THEY'RE ALL DEAD, AND YOU DID NOTHING ABOUT IT.
I'VE ALWAYS BEEN THERE. ON THE SURFACE OR THE SEA.

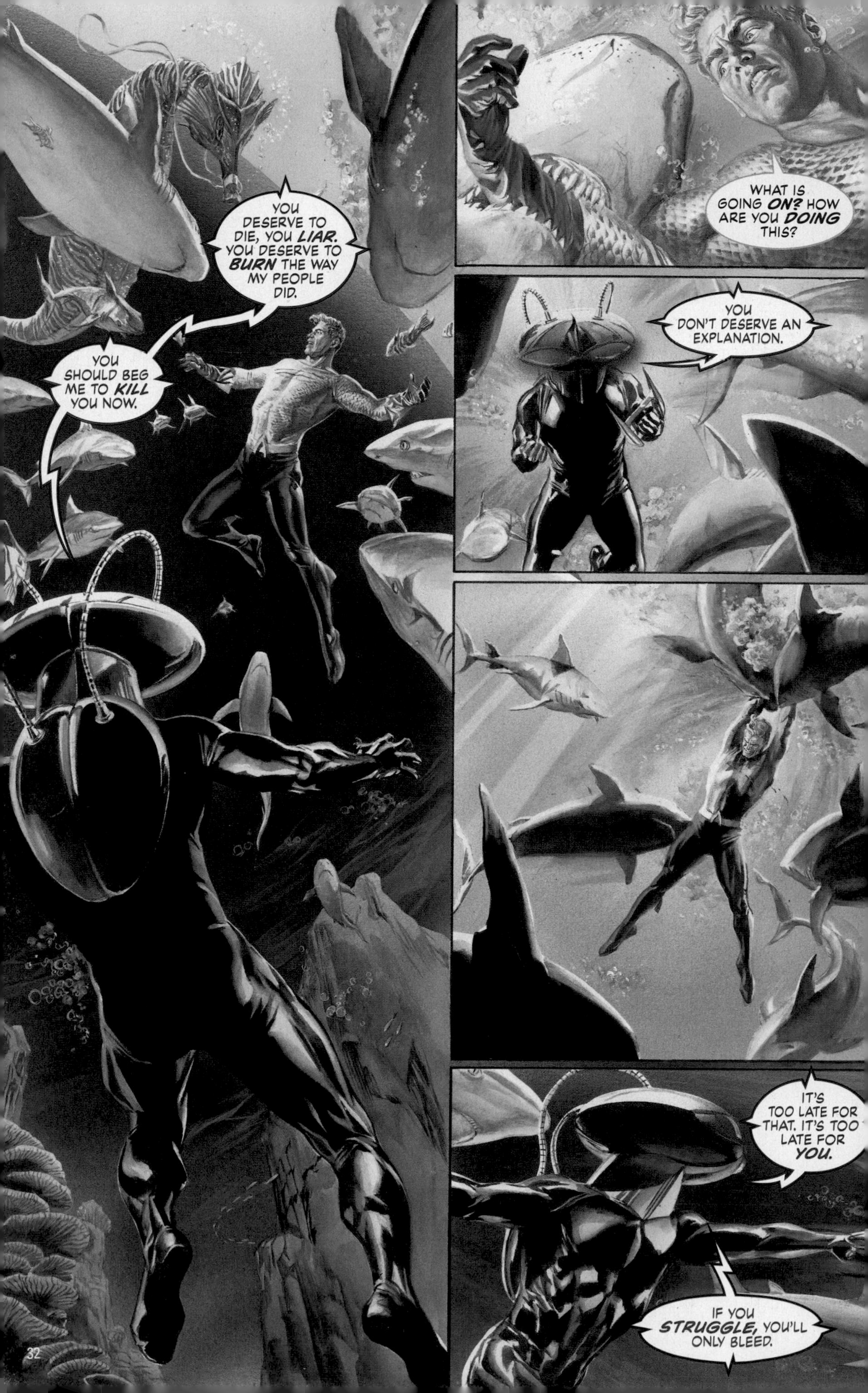

YOU DESERVE TO DIE, YOU LIAR. YOU DESERVE TO BURN THE WAY MY PEOPLE DID.
YOU SHOULD BEG ME TO KILL YOU NOW.
WHAT IS GOING ON? HOW ARE YOU DOING THIS?
YOU DON'T DESERVE AN EXPLANATION.
IT'S TOO LATE FOR THAT. IT'S TOO LATE FOR YOU.
IF YOU STRUGGLE, YOU'LL ONLY BLEED.

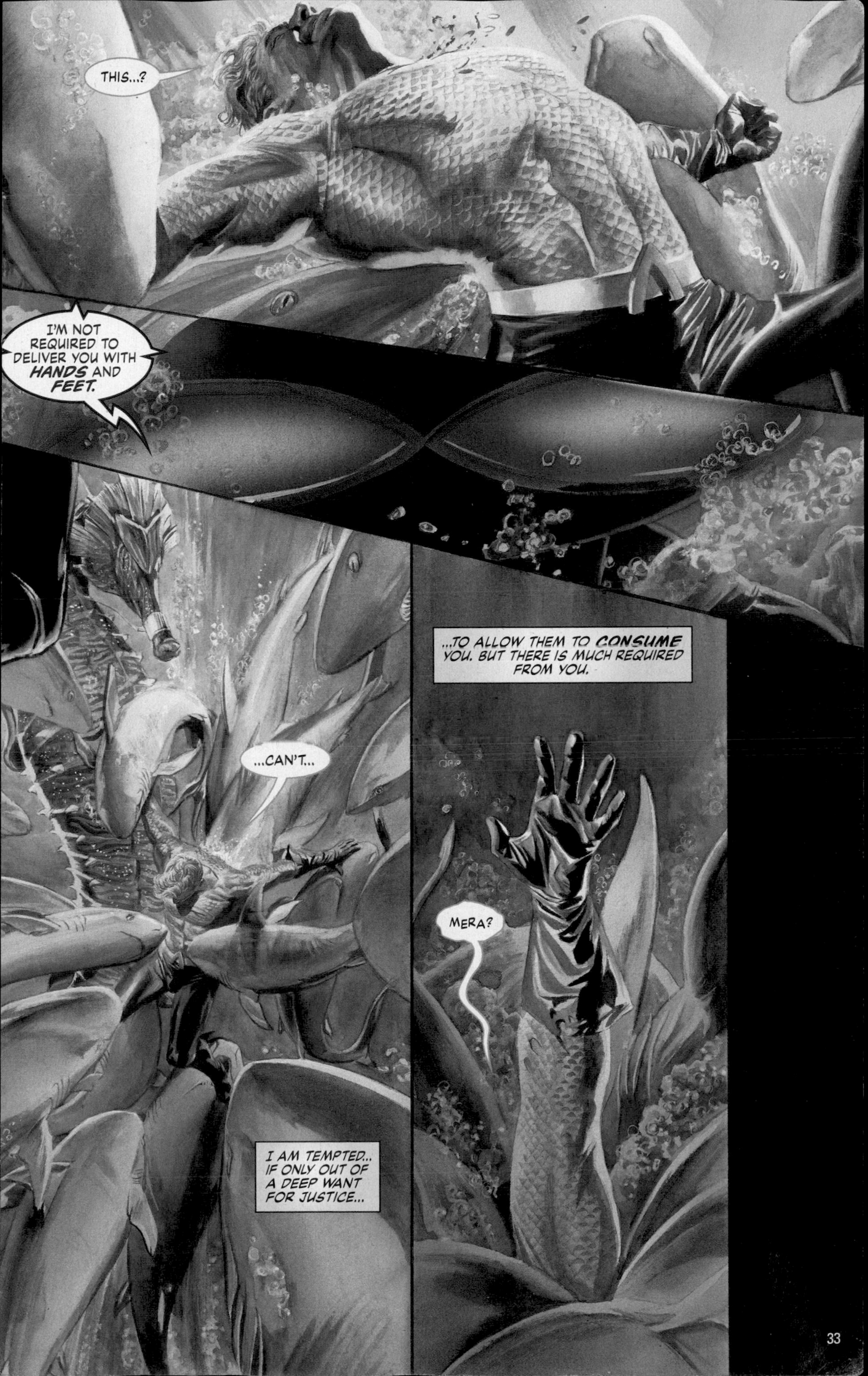

THIS...?
I'M NOT REQUIRED TO DELIVER YOU WITH HANDS AND FEET.
...TO ALLOW THEM TO CONSUME YOU. BUT THERE IS MUCH REQUIRED FROM YOU.
...CAN'T...
MERA?
I AM TEMPTED... IF ONLY OUT OF A DEEP WANT FOR JUSTICE...

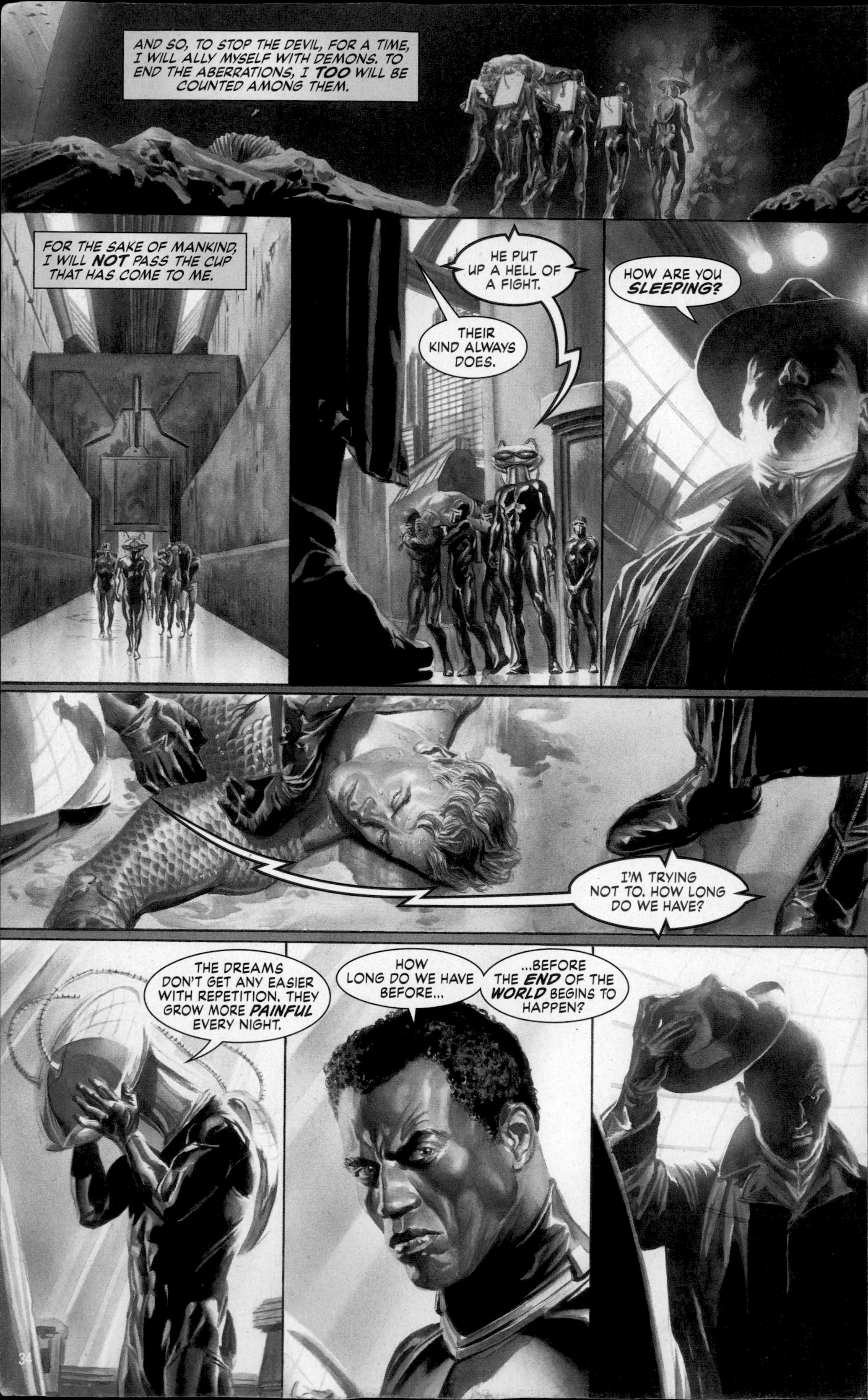

AND SO, TO STOP THE DEVIL, FOR A TIME, I WILL ALLY MYSELF WITH DEMONS. TO END THE ABERRATIONS, I TOO WILL BE COUNTED AMONG THEM.
FOR THE SAKE OF MANKIND, I WILL NOT PASS THE CUP THAT HAS COME TO ME.
HE PUT UP A HELL OF A FIGHT.
THEIR KIND ALWAYS DOES.
HOW ARE YOU SLEEPING?
I'M TRYING NOT TO. HOW LONG DO WE HAVE?
THE DREAMS DON'T GET ANY EASIER WITH REPETITION. THEY GROW MORE PAINFUL EVERY NIGHT.
HOW LONG DO WE HAVE BEFORE...
...BEFORE THE END OF THE WORLD BEGINS TO HAPPEN?

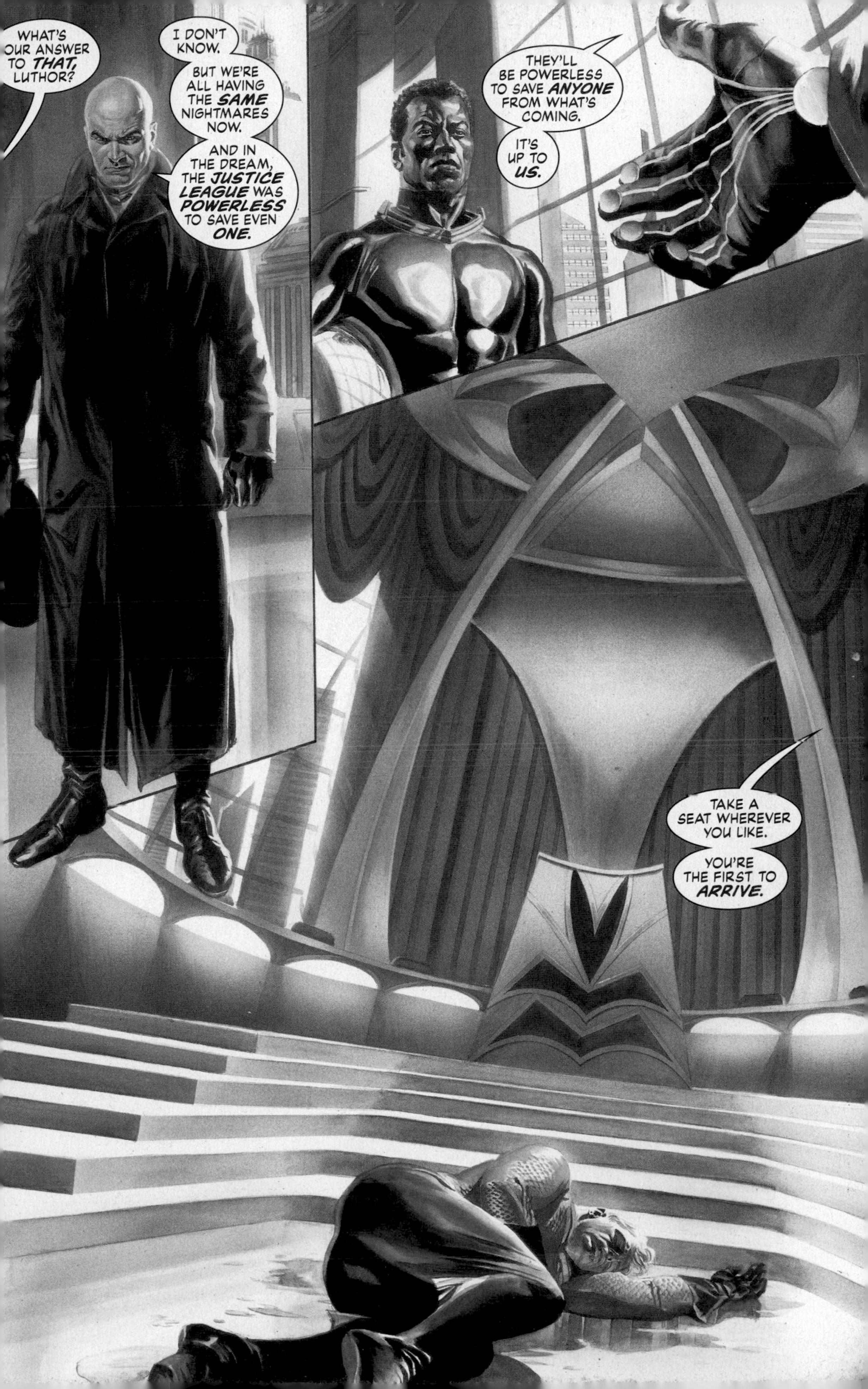
WHAT'S OUR ANSWER TO THAT, LUTHOR?
I DON'T KNOW.
BUT WE'RE ALL HAVING THE SAME NIGHTMARES NOW.
AND IN THE DREAM, THE JUSTICE LEAGUE WAS POWERLESS TO SAVE EVEN ONE.
THEY'LL BE POWERLESS TO SAVE ANYONE FROM WHAT'S COMING.
IT'S UP TO US.
TAKE A SEAT WHEREVER YOU LIKE.
YOU'RE THE FIRST TO ARRIVE.

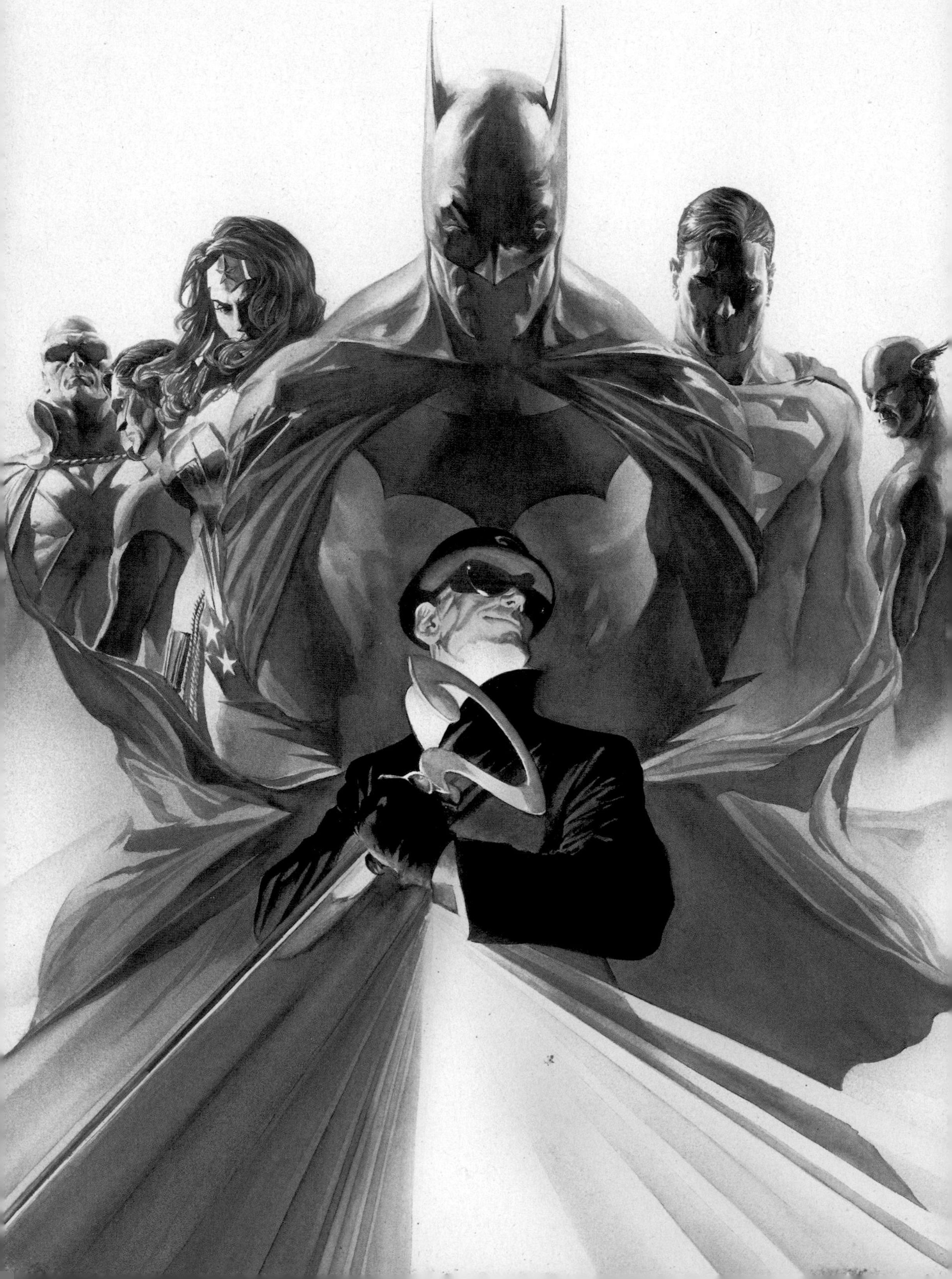

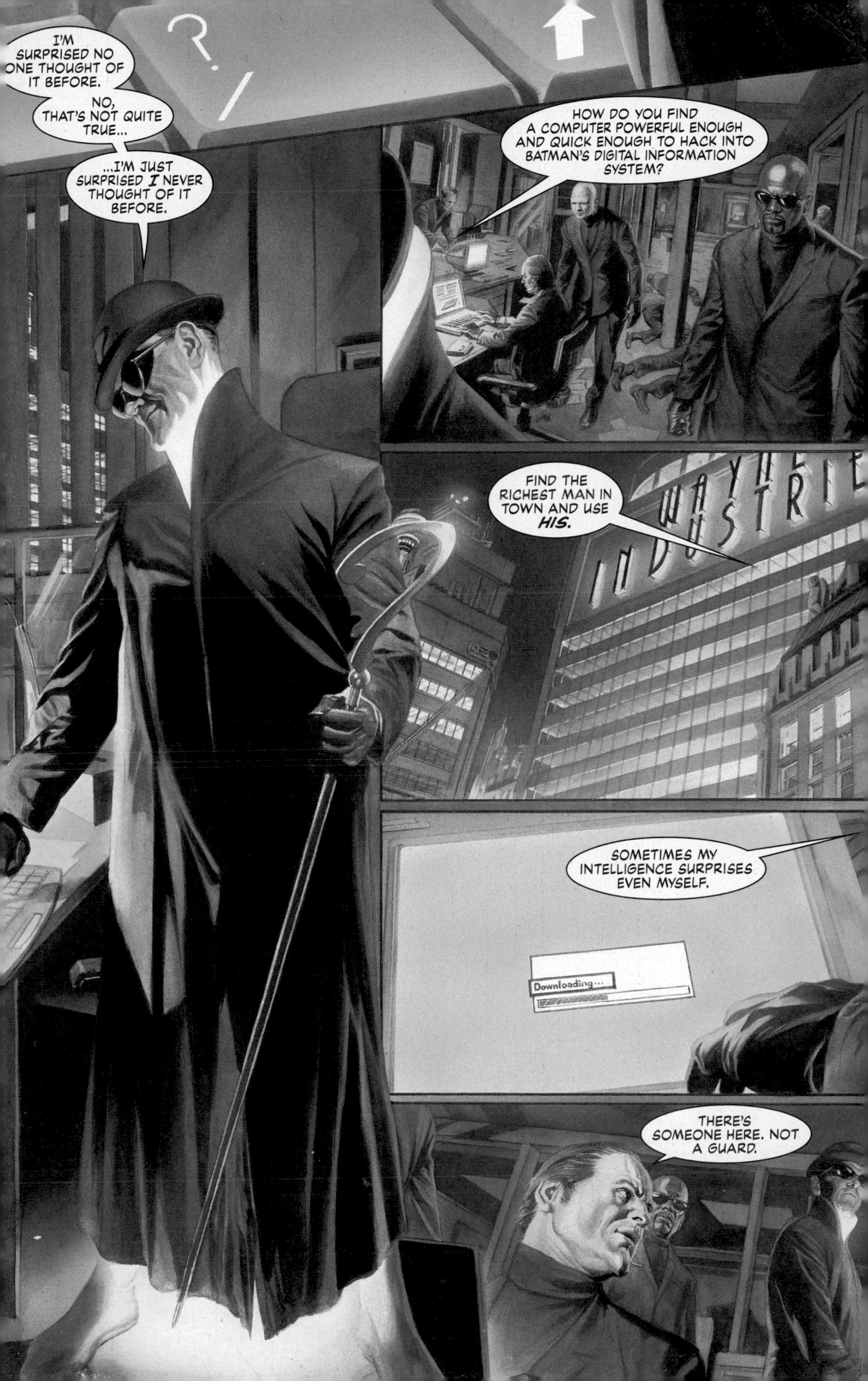
I'M SURPRISED NO ONE THOUGHT OF IT BEFORE.
NO, THAT'S NOT QUITE TRUE...
...I'M JUST SURPRISED *I* NEVER THOUGHT OF IT BEFORE.
HOW DO YOU FIND A COMPUTER POWERFUL ENOUGH AND QUICK ENOUGH TO HACK INTO BATMAN'S DIGITAL INFORMATION SYSTEM?
FIND THE RICHEST MAN IN TOWN AND USE ***HIS***.
WAYNE INDUSTRIE
SOMETIMES MY INTELLIGENCE SURPRISES EVEN MYSELF.
Downloading...
THERE'S SOMEONE HERE. NOT A GUARD.

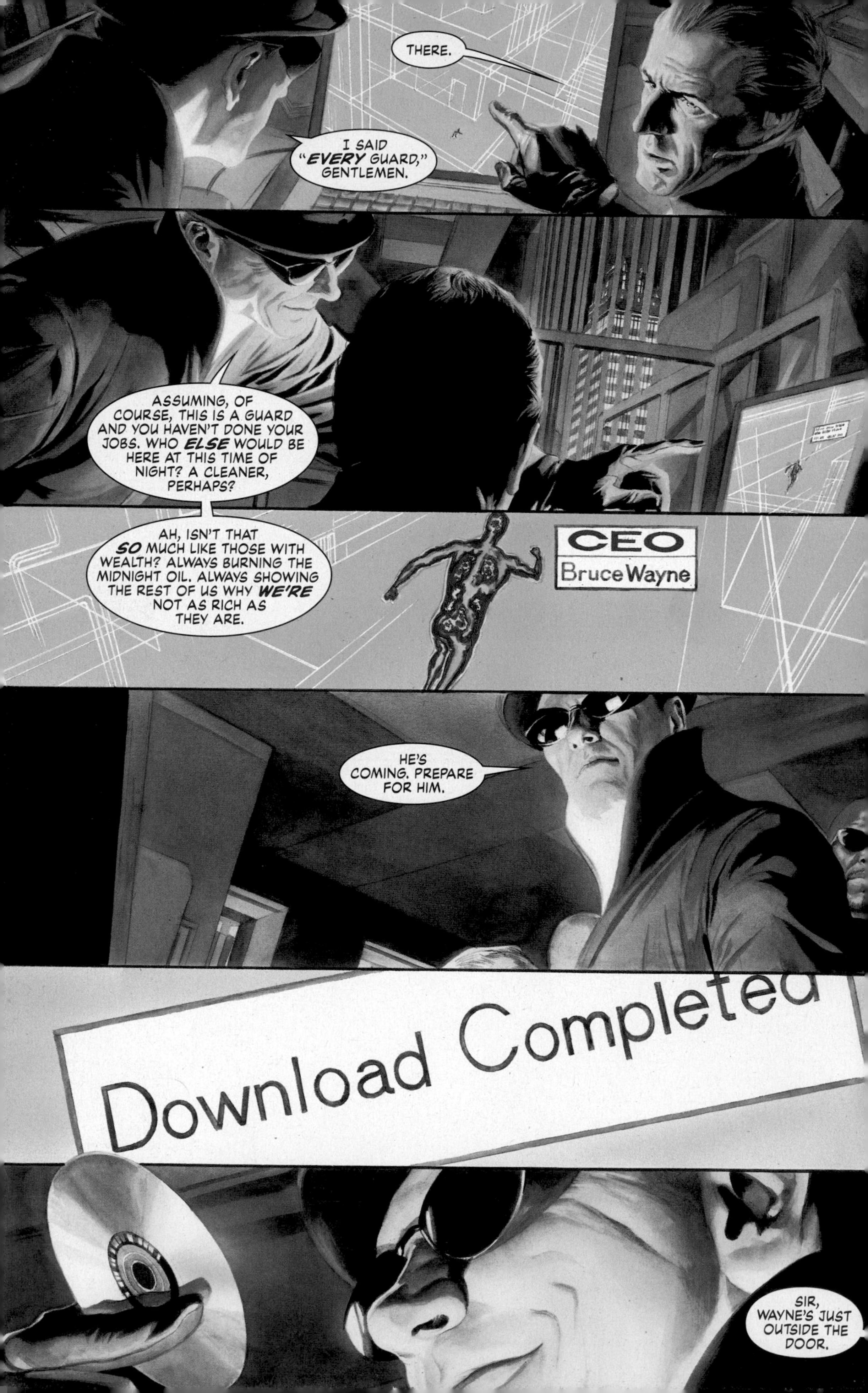
THERE.
I SAID "EVERY GUARD," GENTLEMEN.
ASSUMING, OF COURSE, THIS IS A GUARD AND YOU HAVEN'T DONE YOUR JOBS. WHO ELSE WOULD BE HERE AT THIS TIME OF NIGHT? A CLEANER, PERHAPS?
AH, ISN'T THAT SO MUCH LIKE THOSE WITH WEALTH? ALWAYS BURNING THE MIDNIGHT OIL. ALWAYS SHOWING THE REST OF US WHY WE'RE NOT AS RICH AS THEY ARE.
CEO
Bruce Wayne
HE'S COMING. PREPARE FOR HIM.
Download Completed
SIR, WAYNE'S JUST OUTSIDE THE DOOR.

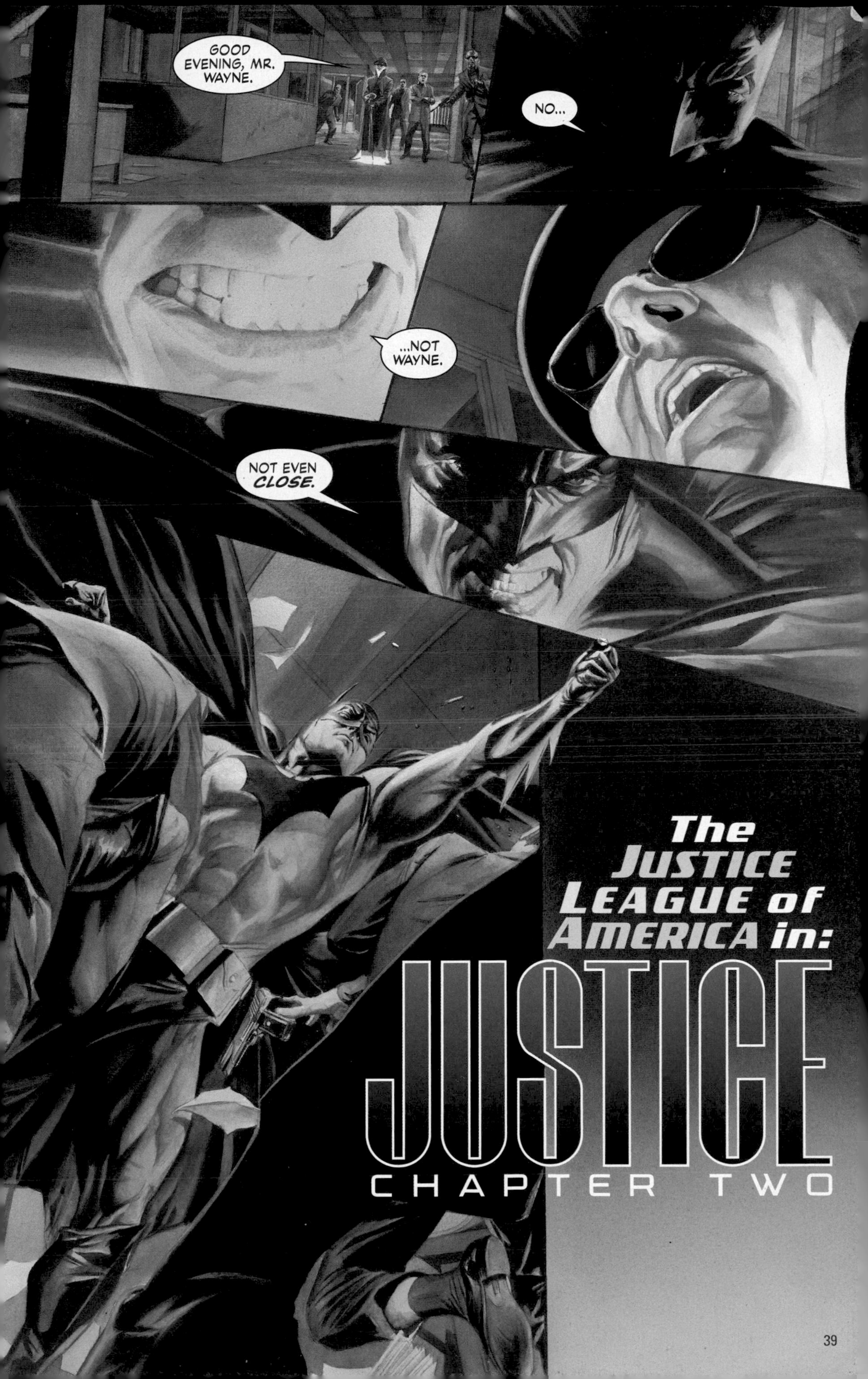
GOOD EVENING, MR. WAYNE.
NO...
...NOT WAYNE.
NOT EVEN CLOSE.
The JUSTICE LEAGUE of AMERICA in:
JUSTICE
CHAPTER TWO

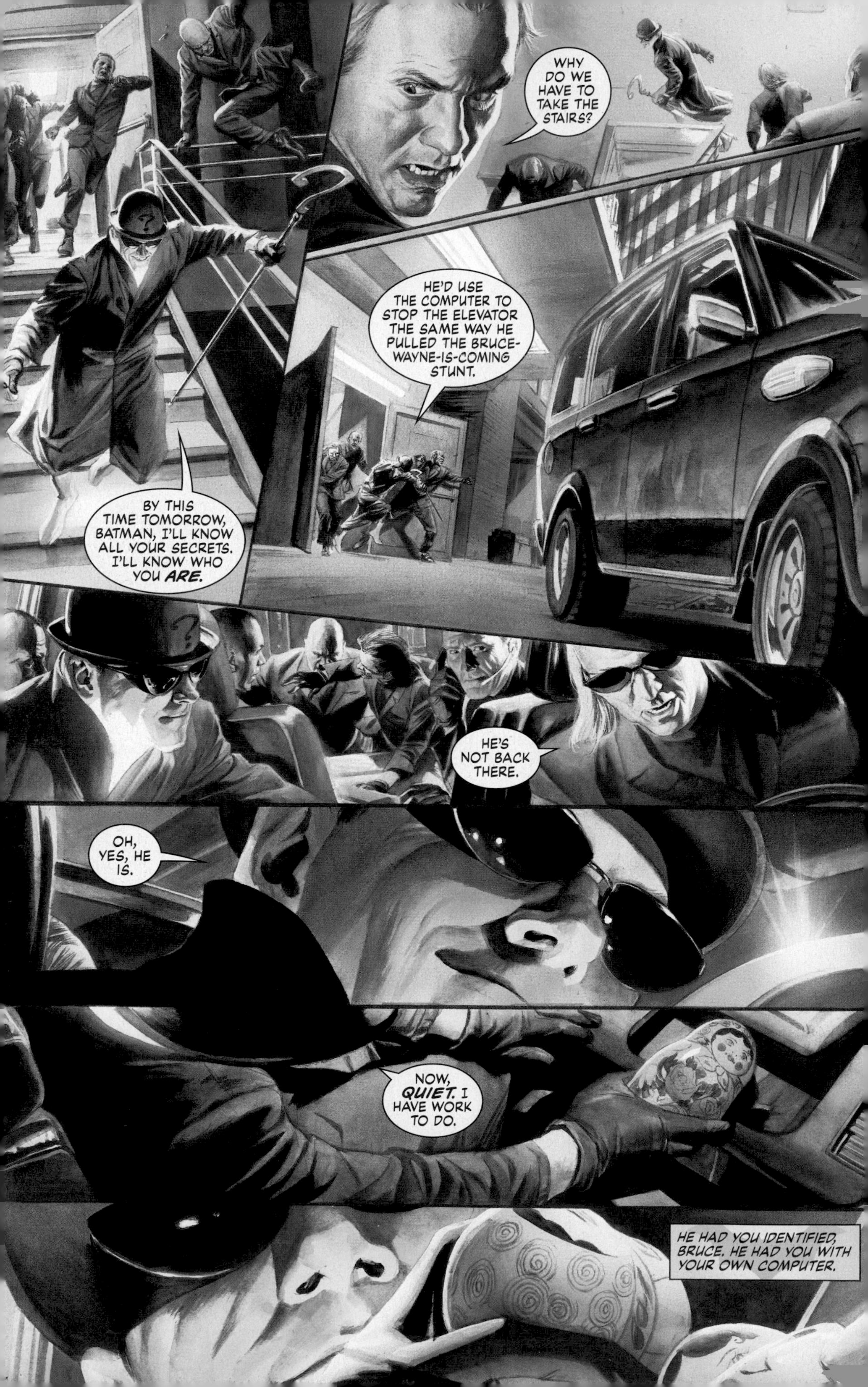
WHY DO WE HAVE TO TAKE THE STAIRS?
BY THIS TIME TOMORROW, BATMAN, I'LL KNOW ALL YOUR SECRETS. I'LL KNOW WHO YOU **ARE.**
HE'D USE THE COMPUTER TO STOP THE ELEVATOR THE SAME WAY HE PULLED THE BRUCE-WAYNE-IS-COMING STUNT.
HE'S NOT BACK THERE.
OH, YES, HE IS.
NOW, ***QUIET.*** I HAVE WORK TO DO.
HE HAD YOU IDENTIFIED, BRUCE. HE HAD YOU WITH YOUR OWN COMPUTER.

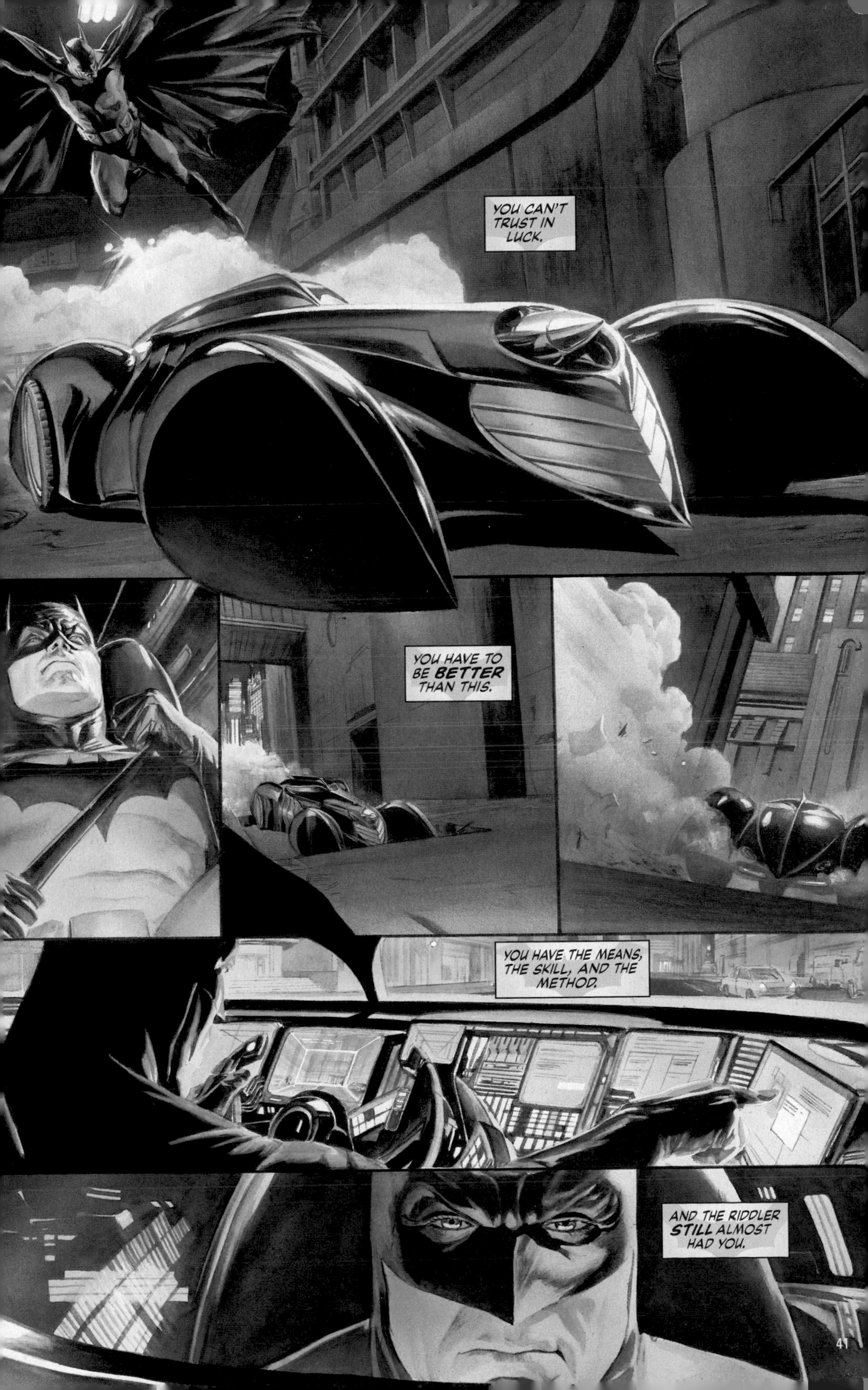
YOU CAN'T TRUST IN LUCK.
YOU HAVE TO BE BETTER THAN THIS.
YOU HAVE THE MEANS, THE SKILL, AND THE METHOD.
AND THE RIDDLER STILL ALMOST HAD YOU.

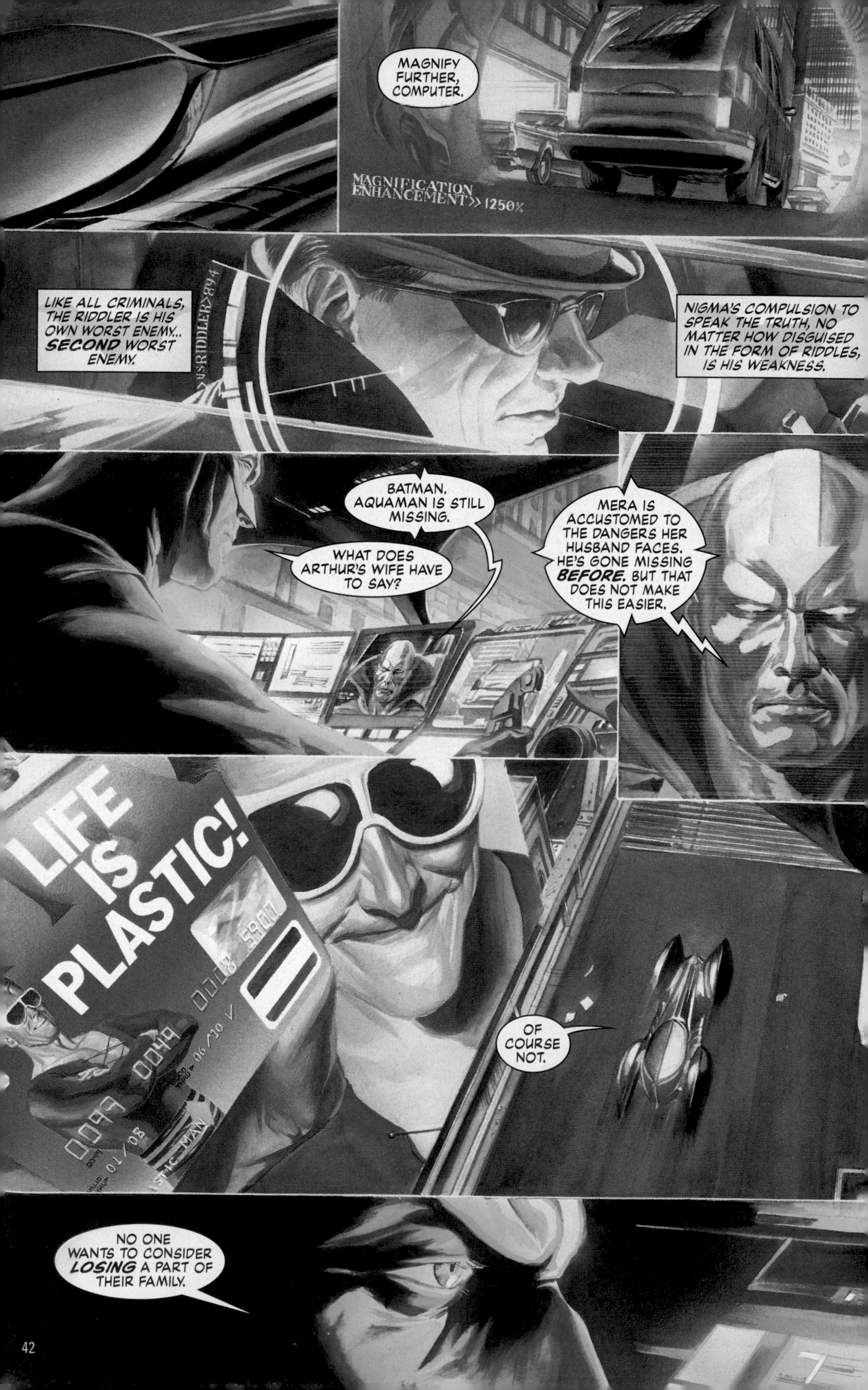
MAGNIFY FURTHER, COMPUTER.
MAGNIFICATION ENHANCEMENT>> 1250%
LIKE ALL CRIMINALS, THE RIDDLER IS HIS OWN WORST ENEMY... SECOND WORST ENEMY.
>US RIDDLER>894
NIGMA'S COMPULSION TO SPEAK THE TRUTH, NO MATTER HOW DISGUISED IN THE FORM OF RIDDLES, IS HIS WEAKNESS.
BATMAN. AQUAMAN IS STILL MISSING.
WHAT DOES ARTHUR'S WIFE HAVE TO SAY?
MERA IS ACCUSTOMED TO THE DANGERS HER HUSBAND FACES. HE'S GONE MISSING BEFORE. BUT THAT DOES NOT MAKE THIS EASIER.
LIFE IS PLASTIC!
OF COURSE NOT.
NO ONE WANTS TO CONSIDER LOSING A PART OF THEIR FAMILY.

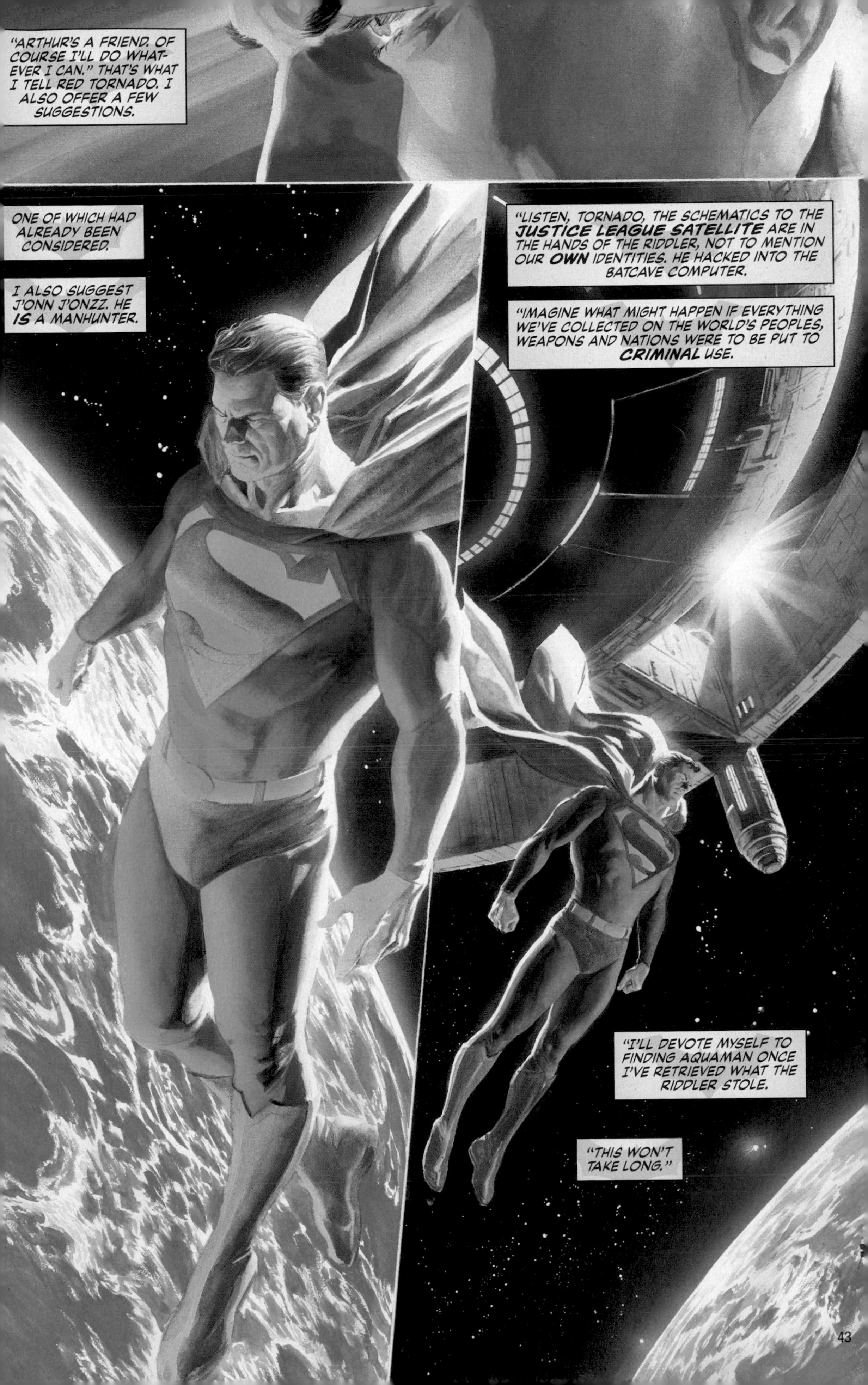
"ARTHUR'S A FRIEND. OF COURSE I'LL DO WHATEVER I CAN." THAT'S WHAT I TELL RED TORNADO. I ALSO OFFER A FEW SUGGESTIONS.
ONE OF WHICH HAD ALREADY BEEN CONSIDERED.
I ALSO SUGGEST J'ONN J'ONZZ. HE **IS** A MANHUNTER.
"LISTEN, TORNADO, THE SCHEMATICS TO THE **JUSTICE LEAGUE SATELLITE** ARE IN THE HANDS OF THE RIDDLER, NOT TO MENTION OUR **OWN** IDENTITIES. HE HACKED INTO THE BATCAVE COMPUTER.
"IMAGINE WHAT MIGHT HAPPEN IF EVERYTHING WE'VE COLLECTED ON THE WORLD'S PEOPLES, WEAPONS AND NATIONS WERE TO BE PUT TO **CRIMINAL** USE.
"I'LL DEVOTE MYSELF TO FINDING AQUAMAN ONCE I'VE RETRIEVED WHAT THE RIDDLER STOLE.
"THIS WON'T TAKE LONG."

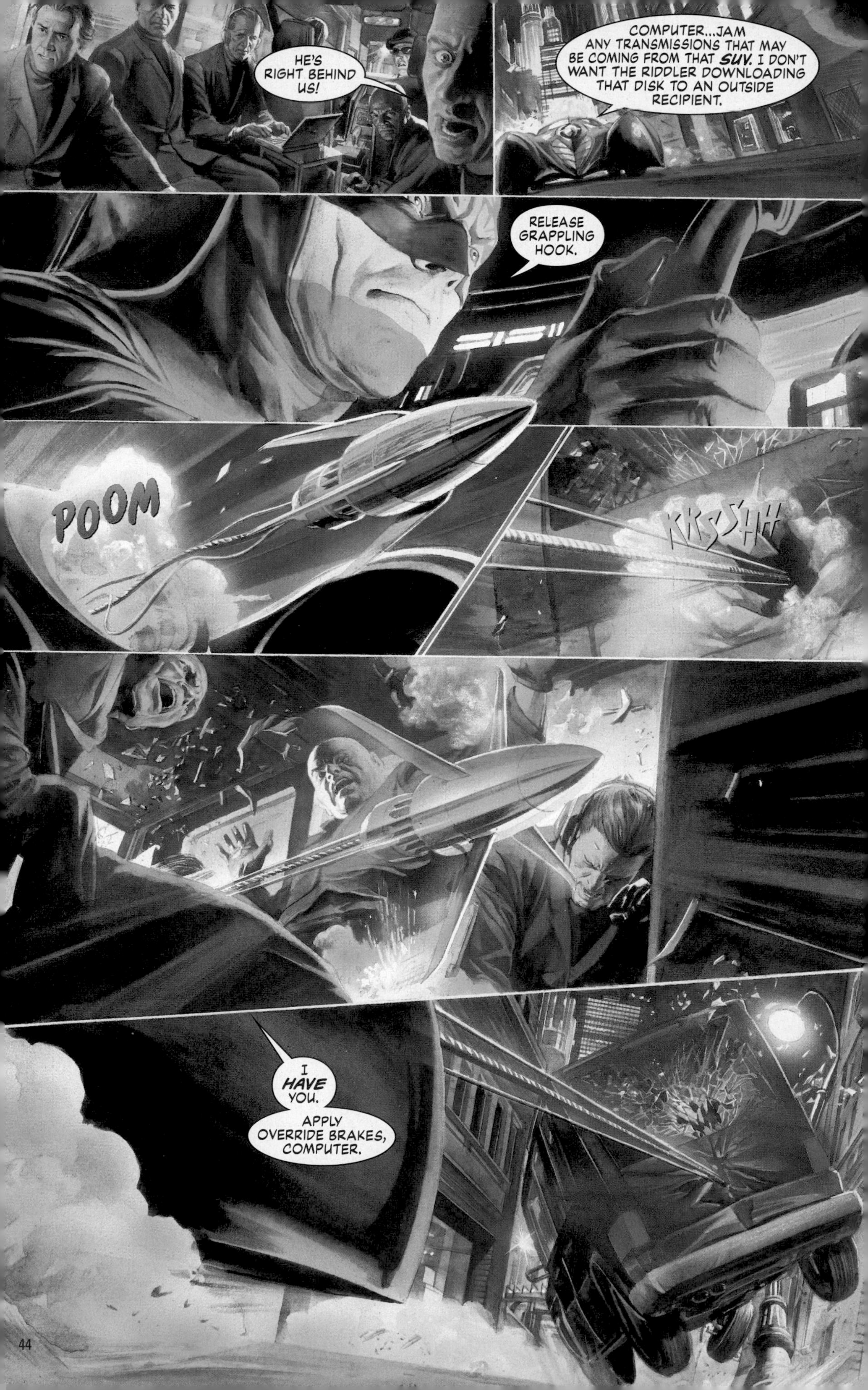
HE'S RIGHT BEHIND US!
COMPUTER...JAM ANY TRANSMISSIONS THAT MAY BE COMING FROM THAT SUV. I DON'T WANT THE RIDDLER DOWNLOADING THAT DISK TO AN OUTSIDE RECIPIENT.
RELEASE GRAPPLING HOOK.
POOM
KRSSHH
I HAVE YOU.
APPLY OVERRIDE BRAKES, COMPUTER.

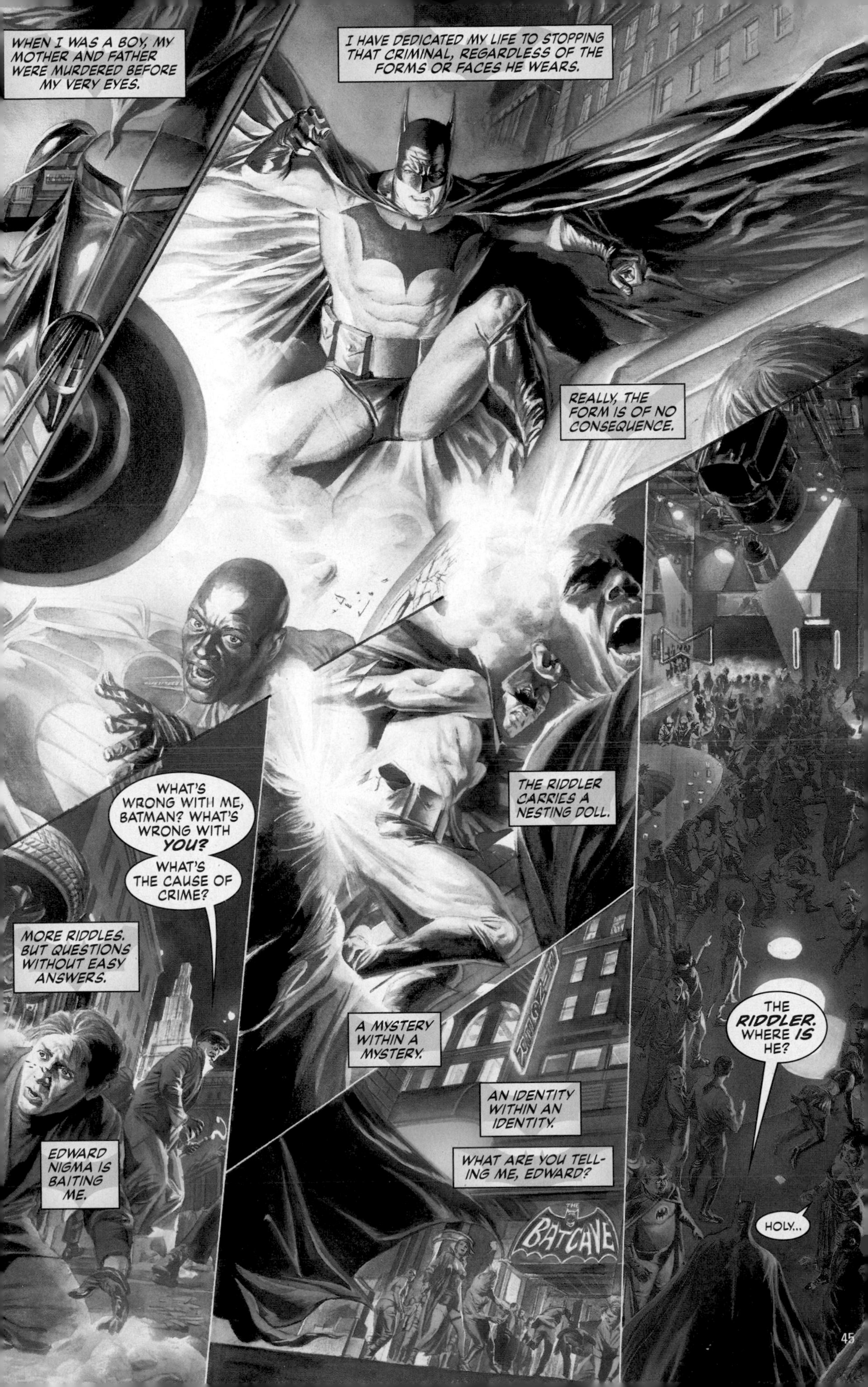
WHEN I WAS A BOY, MY MOTHER AND FATHER WERE MURDERED BEFORE MY VERY EYES.
I HAVE DEDICATED MY LIFE TO STOPPING THAT CRIMINAL, REGARDLESS OF THE FORMS OR FACES HE WEARS.
REALLY, THE FORM IS OF NO CONSEQUENCE.
THE RIDDLER CARRIES A NESTING DOLL.
WHAT'S WRONG WITH ME, BATMAN? WHAT'S WRONG WITH YOU?
WHAT'S THE CAUSE OF CRIME?
MORE RIDDLES. BUT QUESTIONS WITHOUT EASY ANSWERS.
A MYSTERY WITHIN A MYSTERY.
AN IDENTITY WITHIN AN IDENTITY.
WHAT ARE YOU TELL-ING ME, EDWARD?
EDWARD NIGMA IS BAITING ME.
THE BATCAVE
THE RIDDLER. WHERE IS HE?
HOLY...

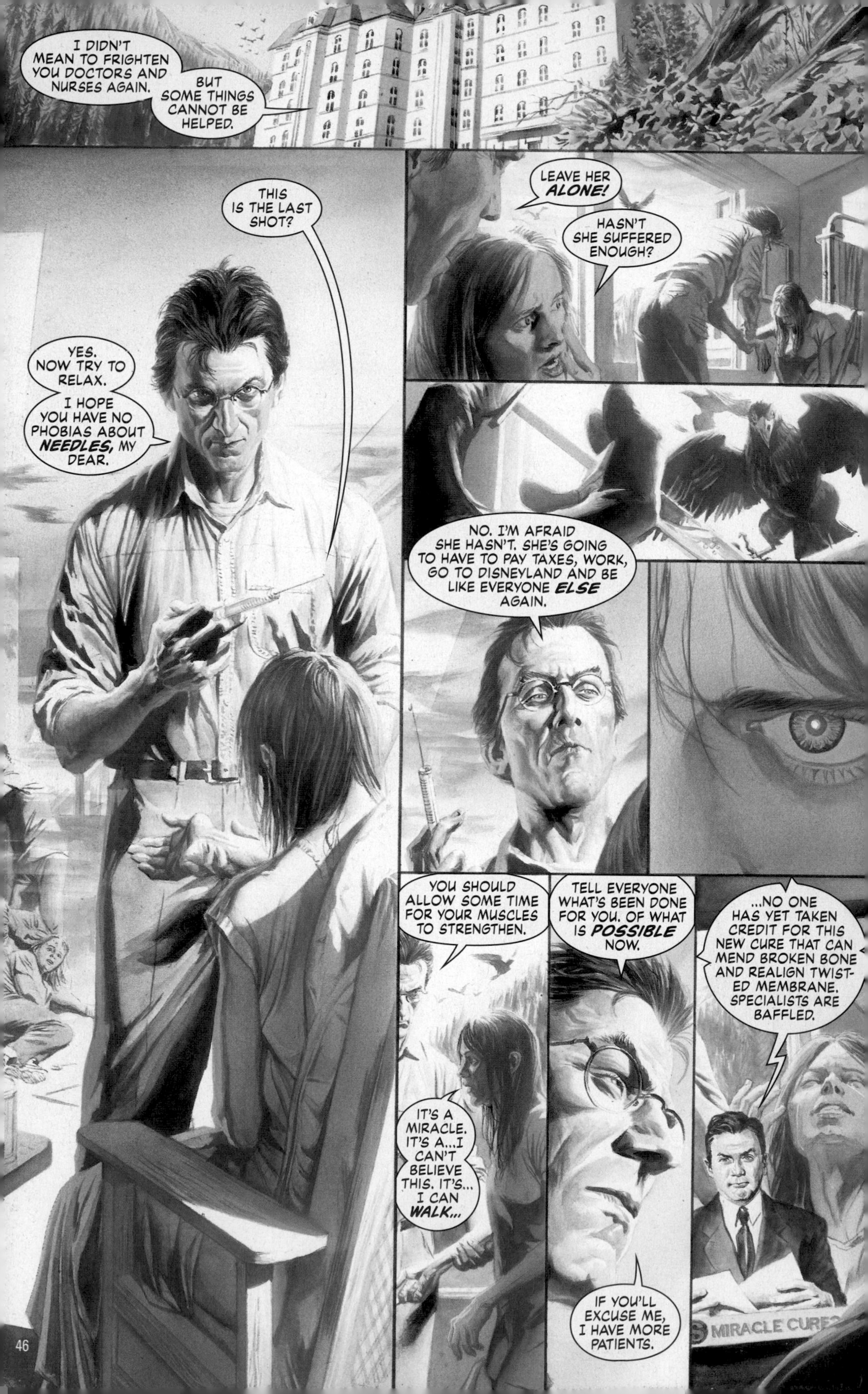
I DIDN'T MEAN TO FRIGHTEN YOU DOCTORS AND NURSES AGAIN.
BUT SOME THINGS CANNOT BE HELPED.
THIS IS THE LAST SHOT?
YES. NOW TRY TO RELAX.
I HOPE YOU HAVE NO PHOBIAS ABOUT *NEEDLES,* MY DEAR.
LEAVE HER *ALONE!*
HASN'T SHE SUFFERED ENOUGH?
NO. I'M AFRAID SHE HASN'T. SHE'S GOING TO HAVE TO PAY TAXES, WORK, GO TO DISNEYLAND AND BE LIKE EVERYONE *ELSE* AGAIN.
YOU SHOULD ALLOW SOME TIME FOR YOUR MUSCLES TO STRENGTHEN.
IT'S A MIRACLE. IT'S A...I CAN'T BELIEVE THIS. IT'S... I CAN *WALK...*
TELL EVERYONE WHAT'S BEEN DONE FOR YOU. OF WHAT IS *POSSIBLE* NOW.
IF YOU'LL EXCUSE ME, I HAVE MORE PATIENTS.
...NO ONE HAS YET TAKEN CREDIT FOR THIS NEW CURE THAT CAN MEND BROKEN BONE AND REALIGN TWISTED MEMBRANE. SPECIALISTS ARE BAFFLED.
MIRACLE CURE

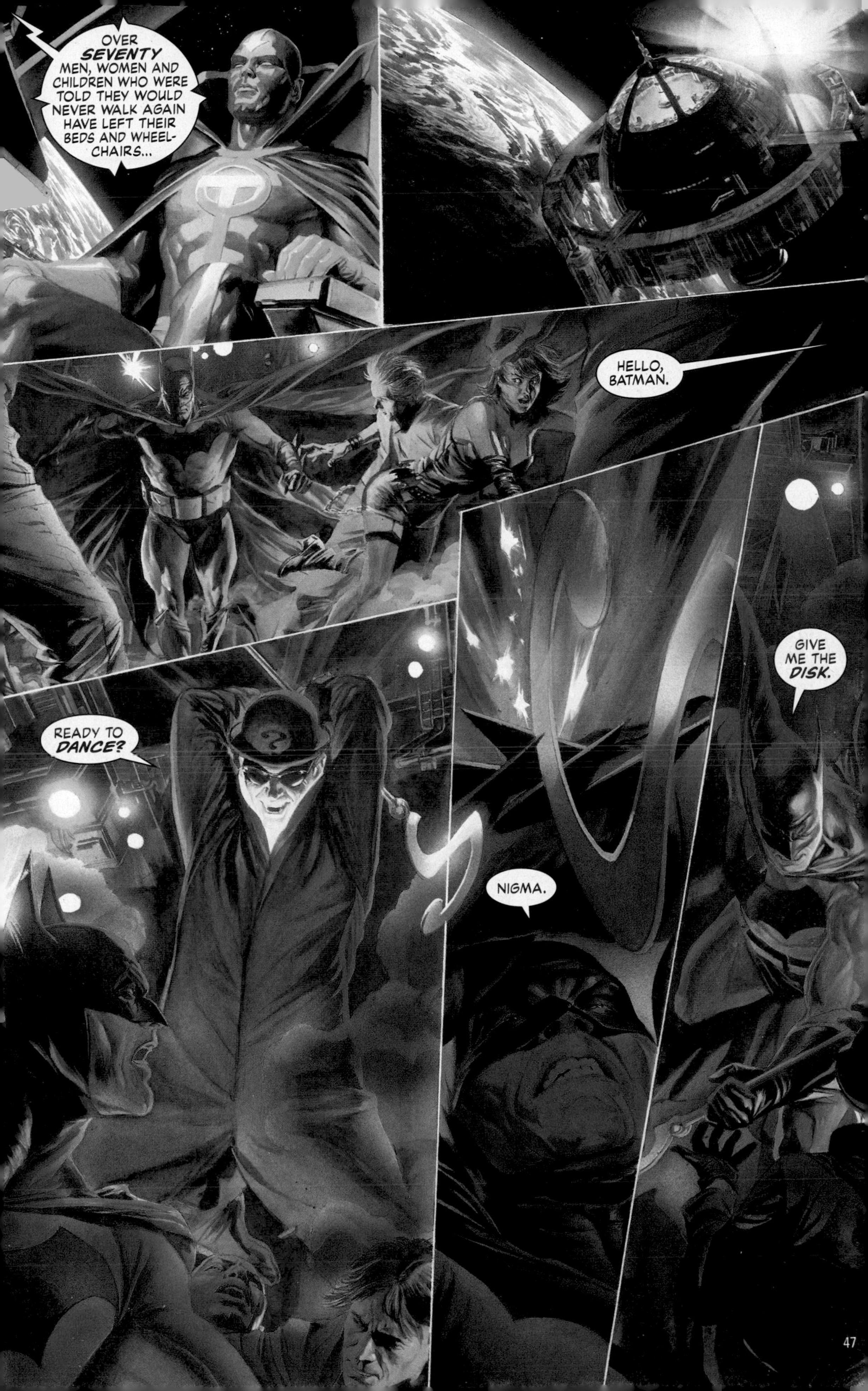
OVER SEVENTY MEN, WOMEN AND CHILDREN WHO WERE TOLD THEY WOULD NEVER WALK AGAIN HAVE LEFT THEIR BEDS AND WHEEL-CHAIRS...
HELLO, BATMAN.
READY TO DANCE?
GIVE ME THE DISK.
NIGMA.

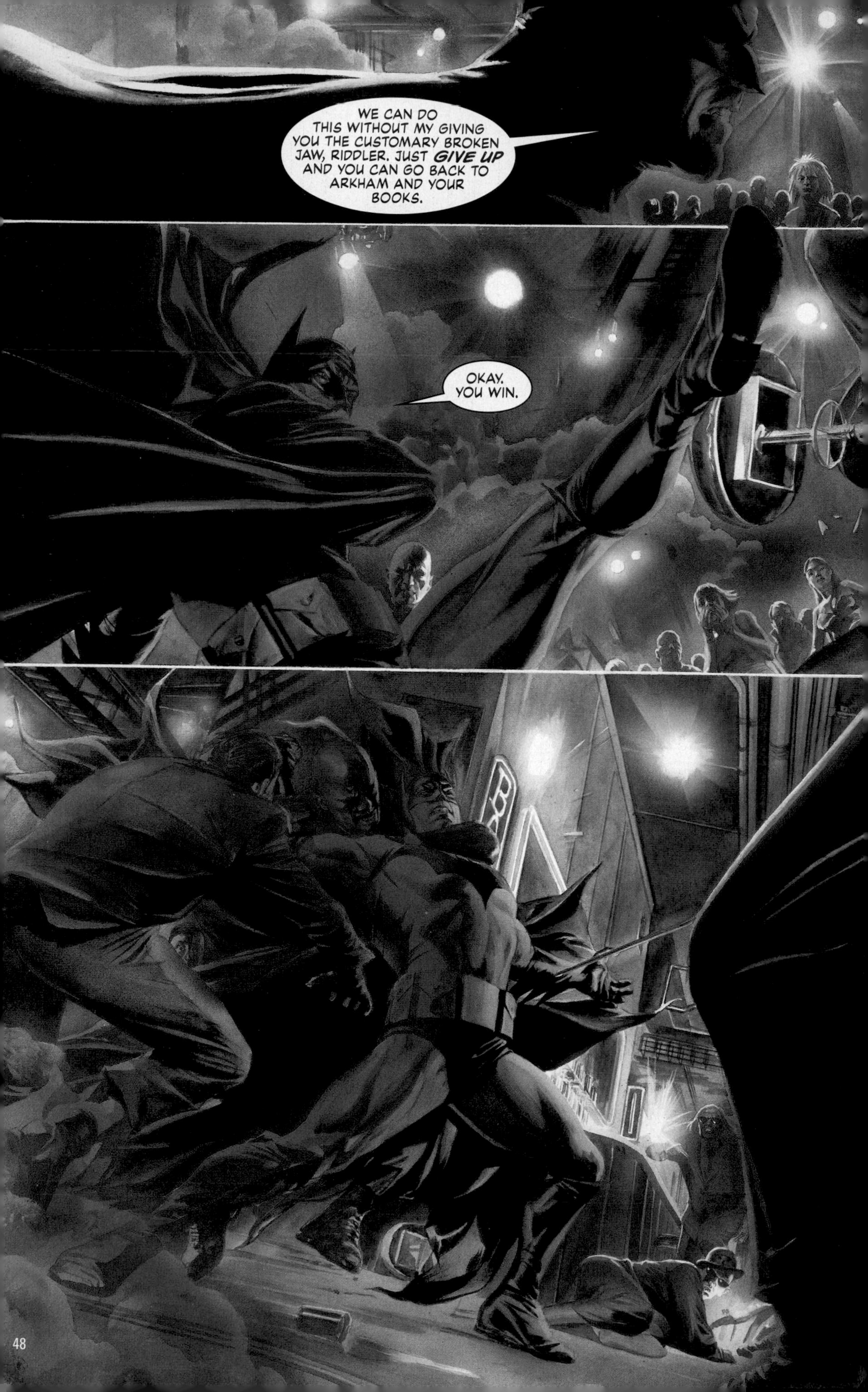
WE CAN DO THIS WITHOUT MY GIVING YOU THE CUSTOMARY BROKEN JAW, RIDDLER. JUST **GIVE UP** AND YOU CAN GO BACK TO ARKHAM AND YOUR BOOKS.
OKAY. YOU WIN.

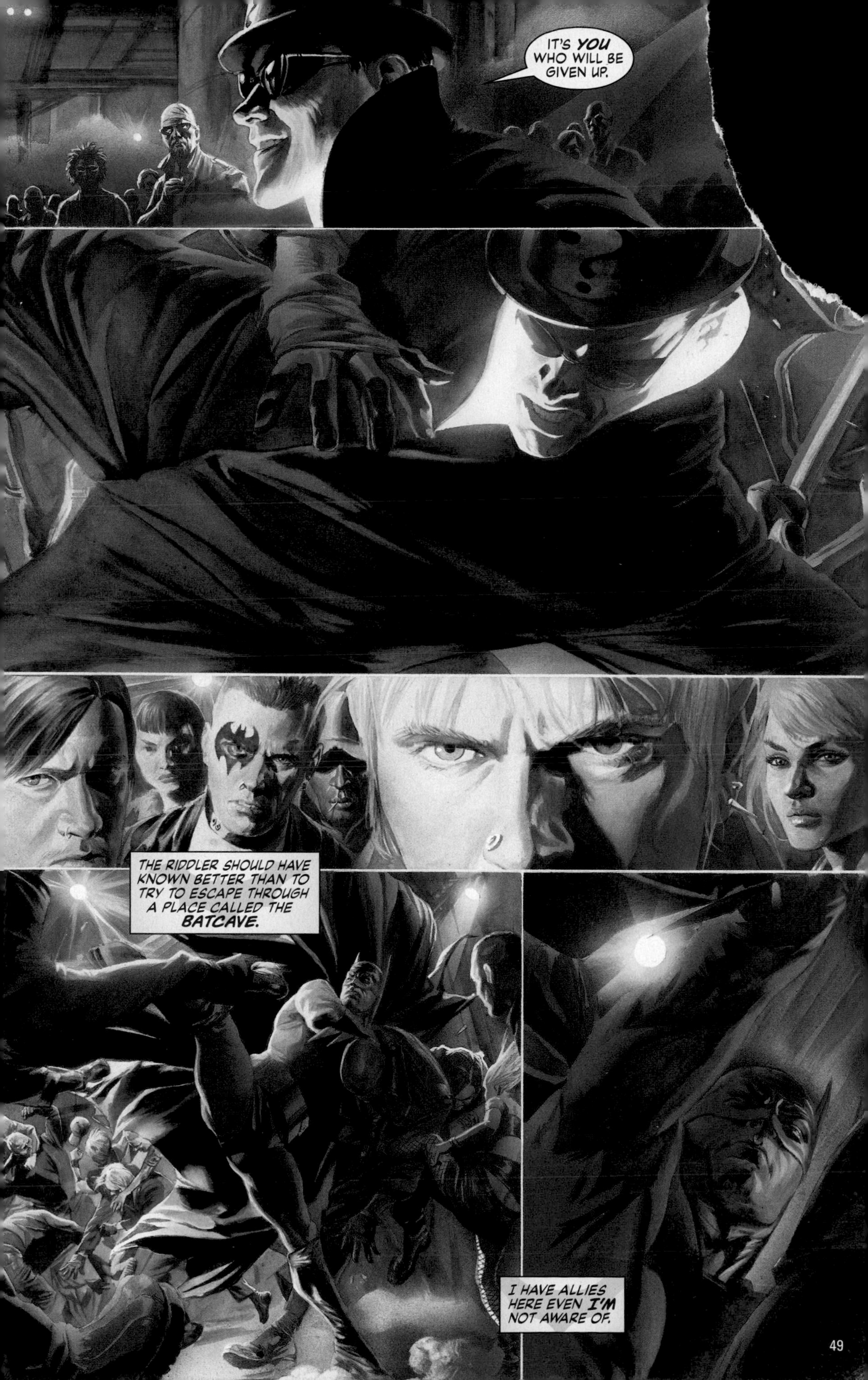
IT'S YOU WHO WILL BE GIVEN UP.
THE RIDDLER SHOULD HAVE KNOWN BETTER THAN TO TRY TO ESCAPE THROUGH A PLACE CALLED THE BATCAVE.
I HAVE ALLIES HERE EVEN I'M NOT AWARE OF.

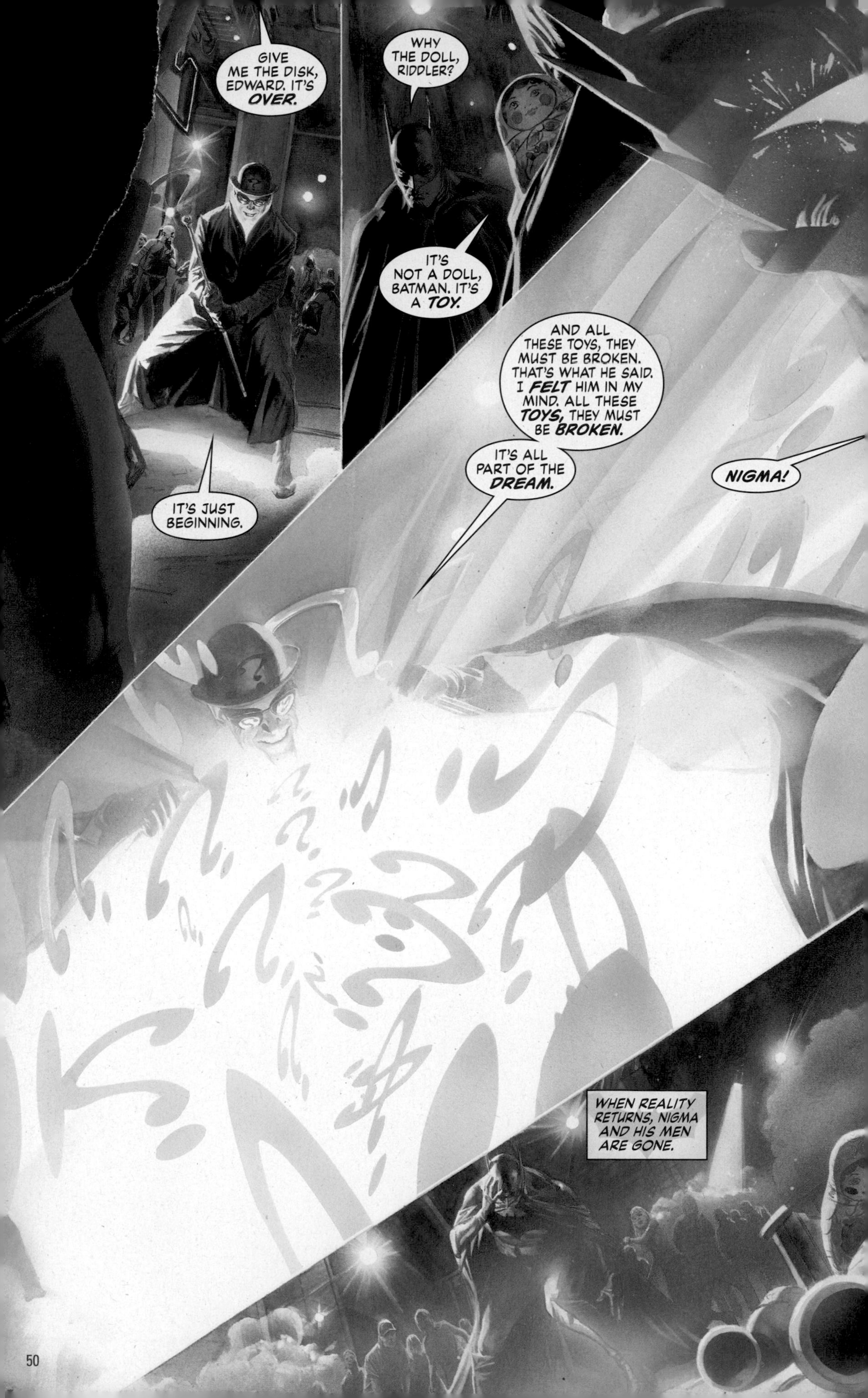

GIVE ME THE DISK, EDWARD. IT'S **OVER.**
IT'S JUST BEGINNING.
WHY THE DOLL, RIDDLER?
IT'S NOT A DOLL, BATMAN. IT'S A **TOY.**
AND ALL THESE TOYS, THEY MUST BE BROKEN. THAT'S WHAT HE SAID. I **FELT** HIM IN MY MIND. ALL THESE **TOYS,** THEY MUST BE **BROKEN.**
IT'S ALL PART OF THE **DREAM.**
NIGMA!
WHEN REALITY RETURNS, NIGMA AND HIS MEN ARE GONE.

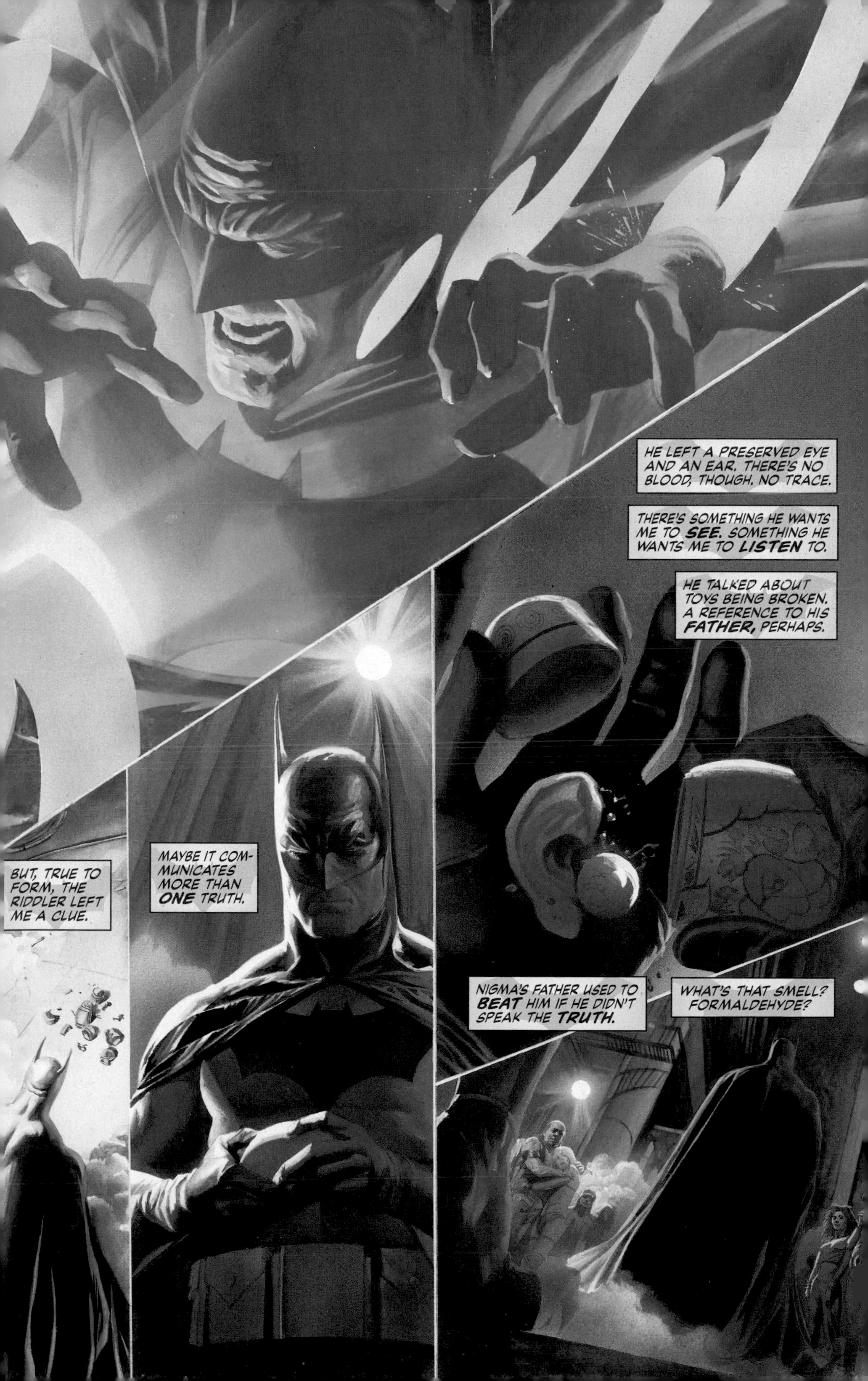
HE LEFT A PRESERVED EYE AND AN EAR. THERE'S NO BLOOD, THOUGH. NO TRACE.
THERE'S SOMETHING HE WANTS ME TO SEE. SOMETHING HE WANTS ME TO LISTEN TO.
HE TALKED ABOUT TOYS BEING BROKEN. A REFERENCE TO HIS FATHER, PERHAPS.
BUT, TRUE TO FORM, THE RIDDLER LEFT ME A CLUE.
MAYBE IT COMMUNICATES MORE THAN ONE TRUTH.
NIGMA'S FATHER USED TO BEAT HIM IF HE DIDN'T SPEAK THE TRUTH.
WHAT'S THAT SMELL? FORMALDEHYDE?

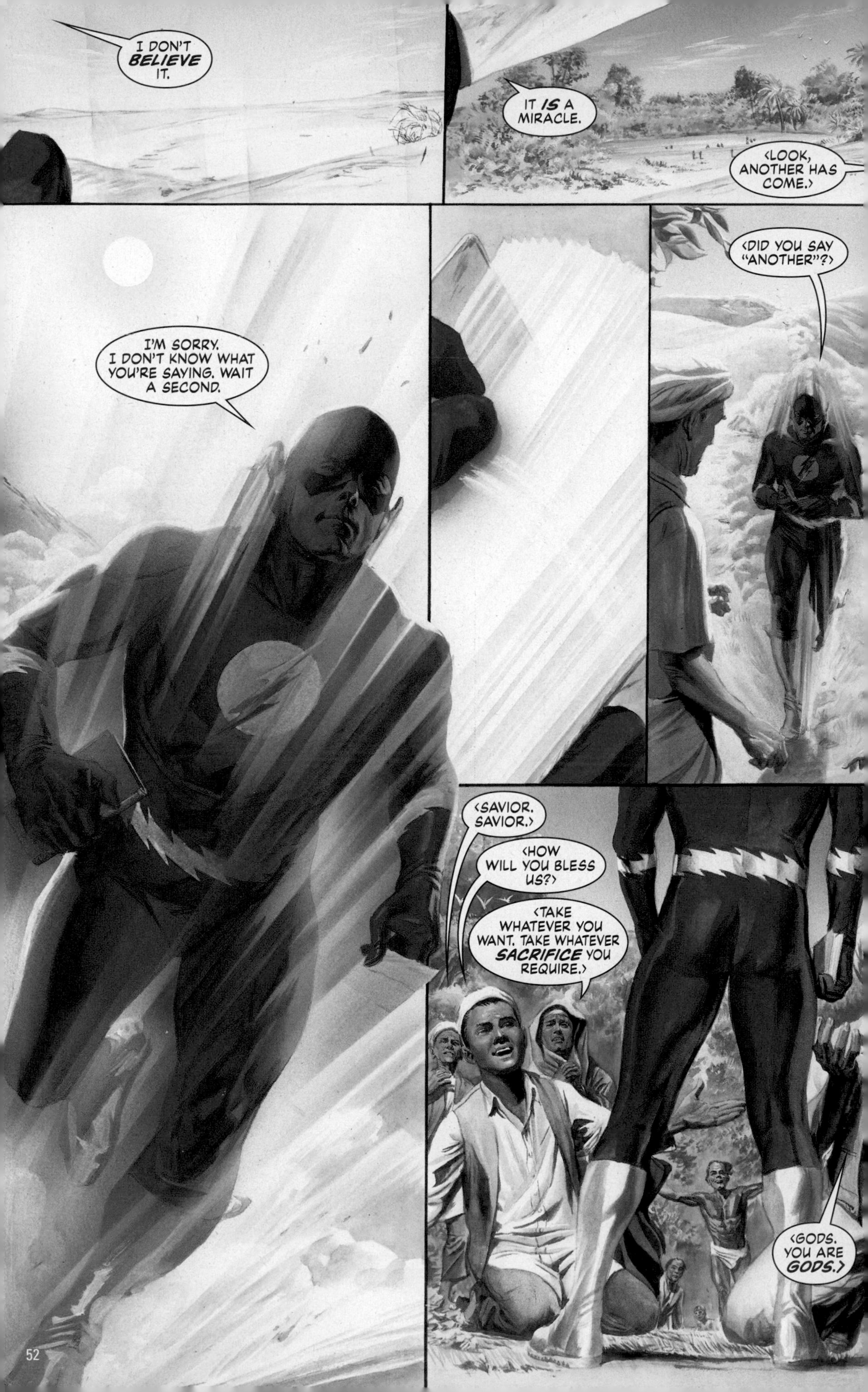
I DON'T BELIEVE IT.
IT IS A MIRACLE.
<LOOK, ANOTHER HAS COME.>
I'M SORRY. I DON'T KNOW WHAT YOU'RE SAYING. WAIT A SECOND.
<DID YOU SAY "ANOTHER"?>
<SAVIOR. SAVIOR.>
<HOW WILL YOU BLESS US?>
<TAKE WHATEVER YOU WANT. TAKE WHATEVER SACRIFICE YOU REQUIRE.>
<GODS. YOU ARE GODS.>

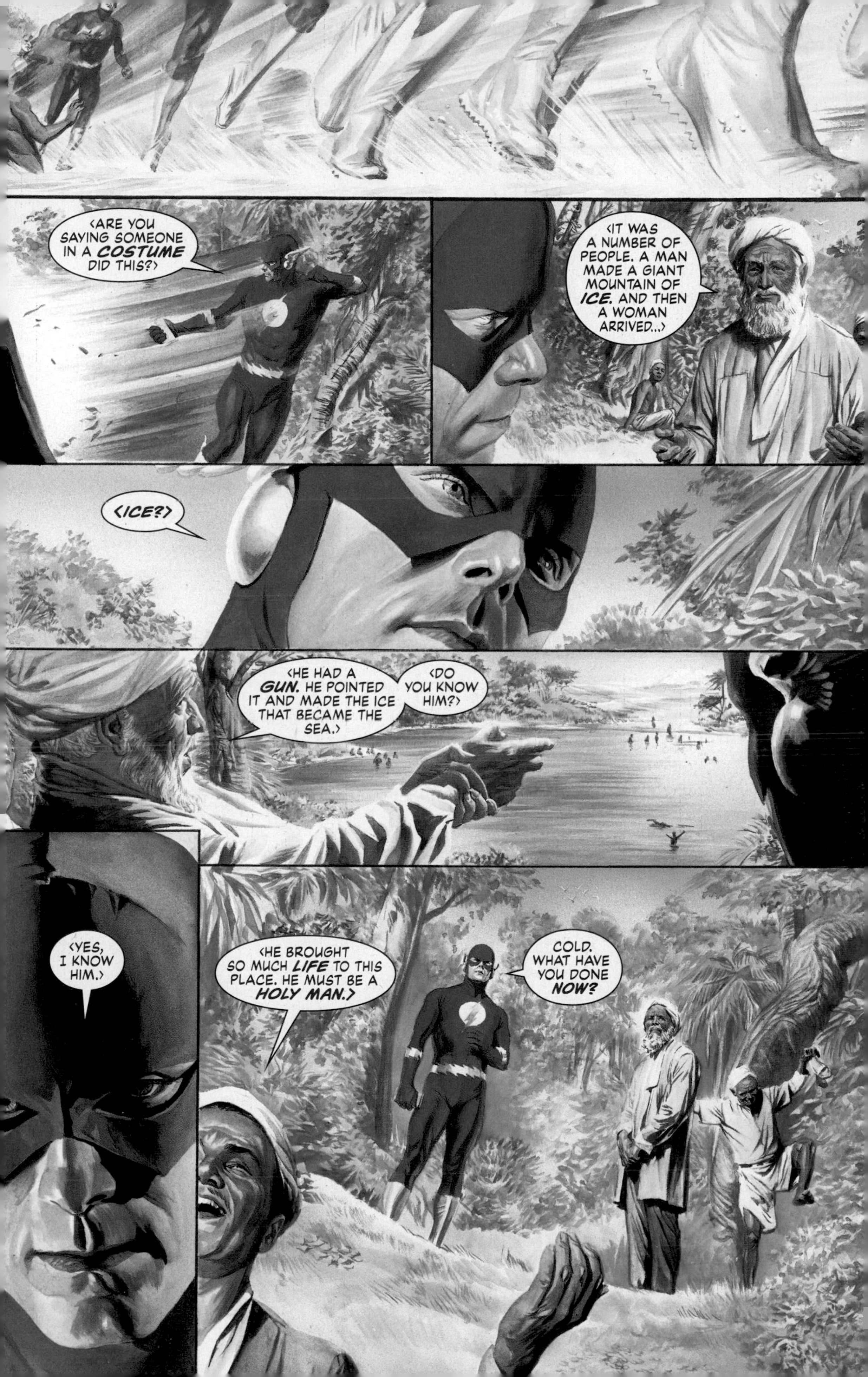

‹ARE YOU SAYING SOMEONE IN A **COSTUME** DID THIS?›
‹IT WAS A NUMBER OF PEOPLE. A MAN MADE A GIANT MOUNTAIN OF **ICE.** AND THEN A WOMAN ARRIVED...›
‹ICE?›
‹HE HAD A **GUN.** HE POINTED IT AND MADE THE ICE THAT BECAME THE SEA.›
‹DO YOU KNOW HIM?›
‹YES, I KNOW HIM.›
‹HE BROUGHT SO MUCH **LIFE** TO THIS PLACE. HE MUST BE A **HOLY MAN.**›
COLD. WHAT HAVE YOU DONE **NOW?**

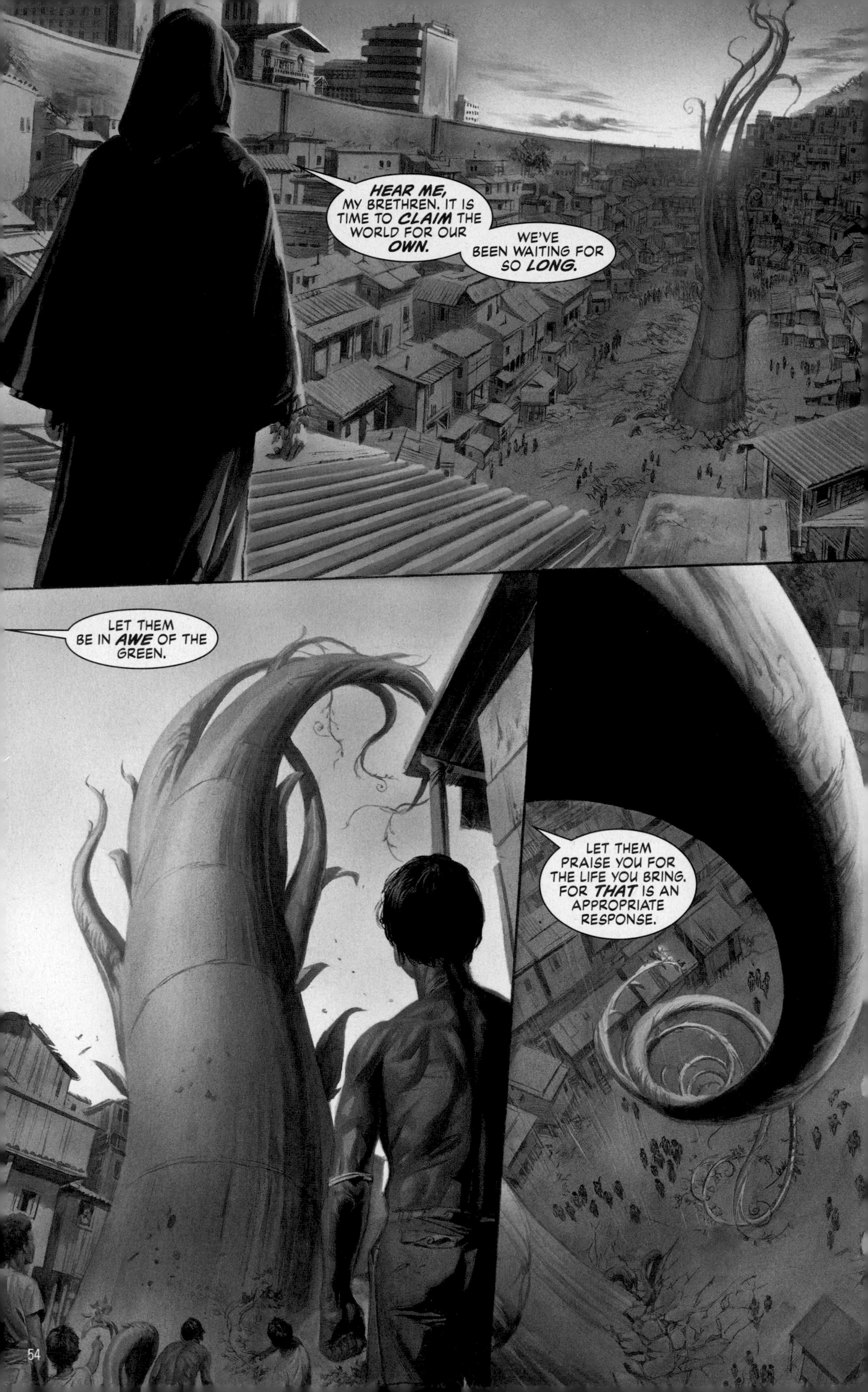
HEAR ME, MY BRETHREN. IT IS TIME TO CLAIM THE WORLD FOR OUR OWN.
WE'VE BEEN WAITING FOR SO LONG.
LET THEM BE IN AWE OF THE GREEN.
LET THEM PRAISE YOU FOR THE LIFE YOU BRING. FOR THAT IS AN APPROPRIATE RESPONSE.

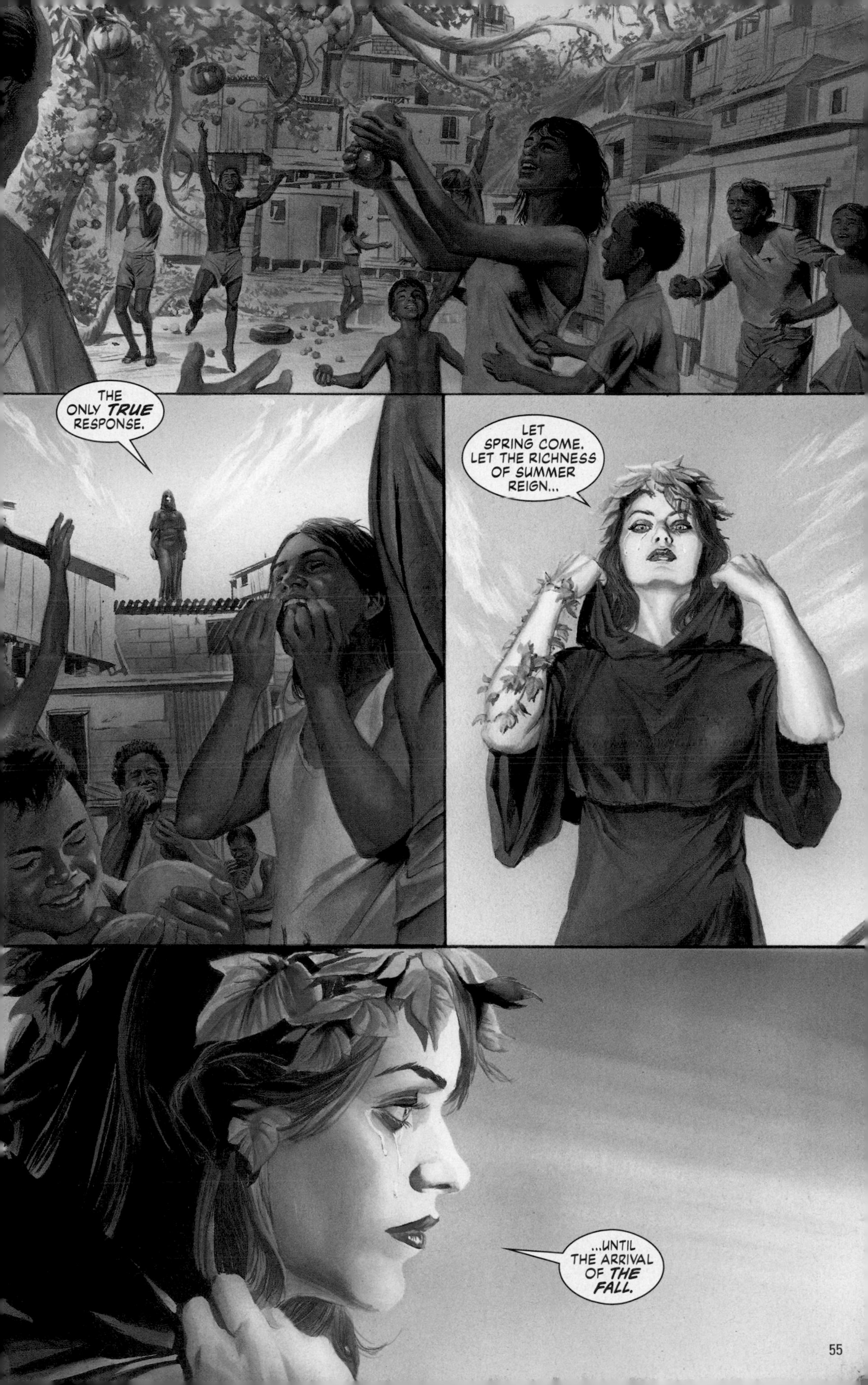
THE ONLY TRUE RESPONSE.
LET SPRING COME. LET THE RICHNESS OF SUMMER REIGN...
...UNTIL THE ARRIVAL OF THE FALL.

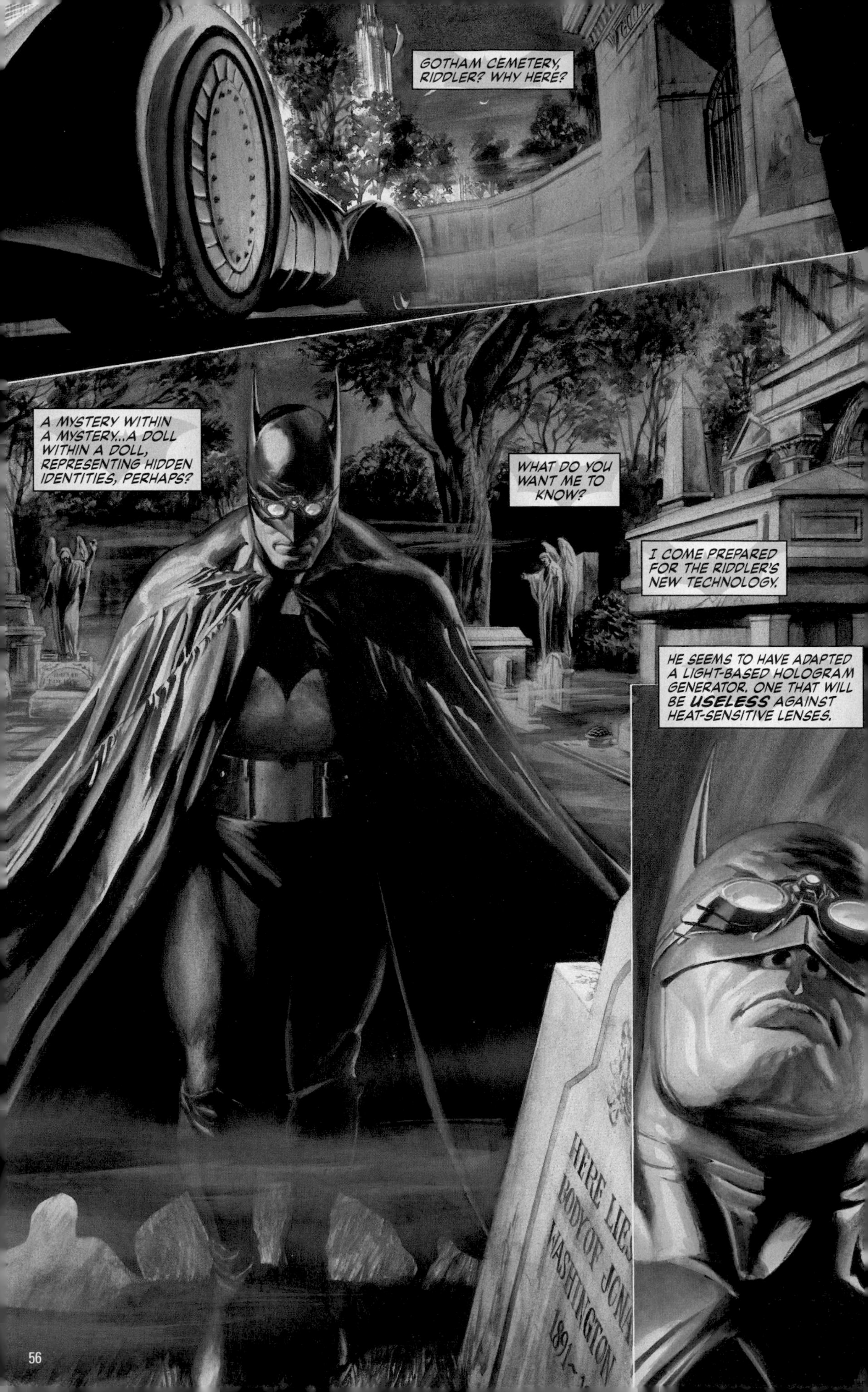
GOTHAM CEMETERY, RIDDLER? WHY HERE?
A MYSTERY WITHIN A MYSTERY...A DOLL WITHIN A DOLL, REPRESENTING HIDDEN IDENTITIES, PERHAPS?
WHAT DO YOU WANT ME TO KNOW?
I COME PREPARED FOR THE RIDDLER'S NEW TECHNOLOGY.
HE SEEMS TO HAVE ADAPTED A LIGHT-BASED HOLOGRAM GENERATOR. ONE THAT WILL BE **USELESS** AGAINST HEAT-SENSITIVE LENSES.

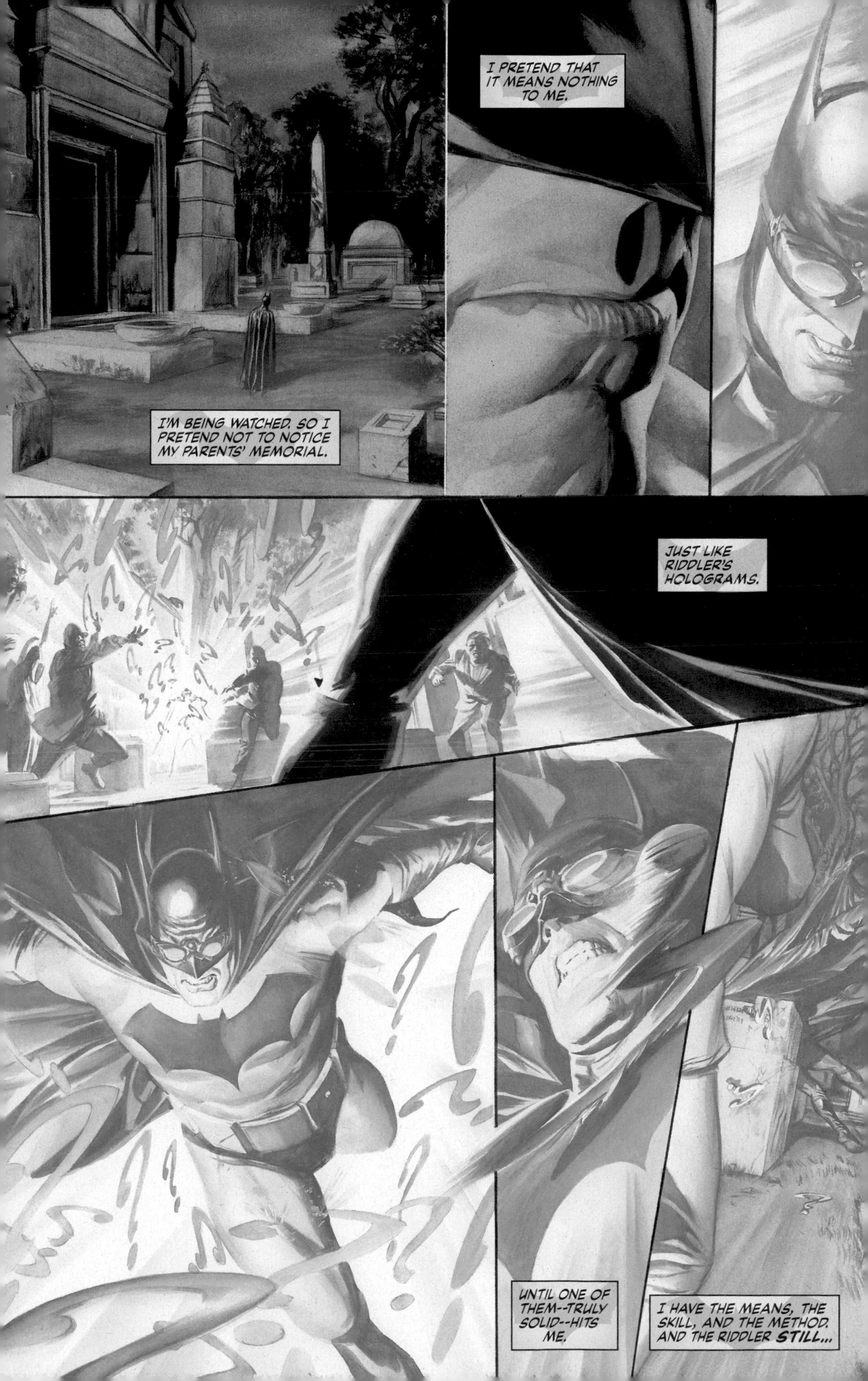
I'M BEING WATCHED. SO I PRETEND NOT TO NOTICE MY PARENTS' MEMORIAL.
I PRETEND THAT IT MEANS NOTHING TO ME.
JUST LIKE RIDDLER'S HOLOGRAMS.
UNTIL ONE OF THEM--TRULY SOLID--HITS ME.
I HAVE THE MEANS, THE SKILL, AND THE METHOD. AND THE RIDDLER STILL...

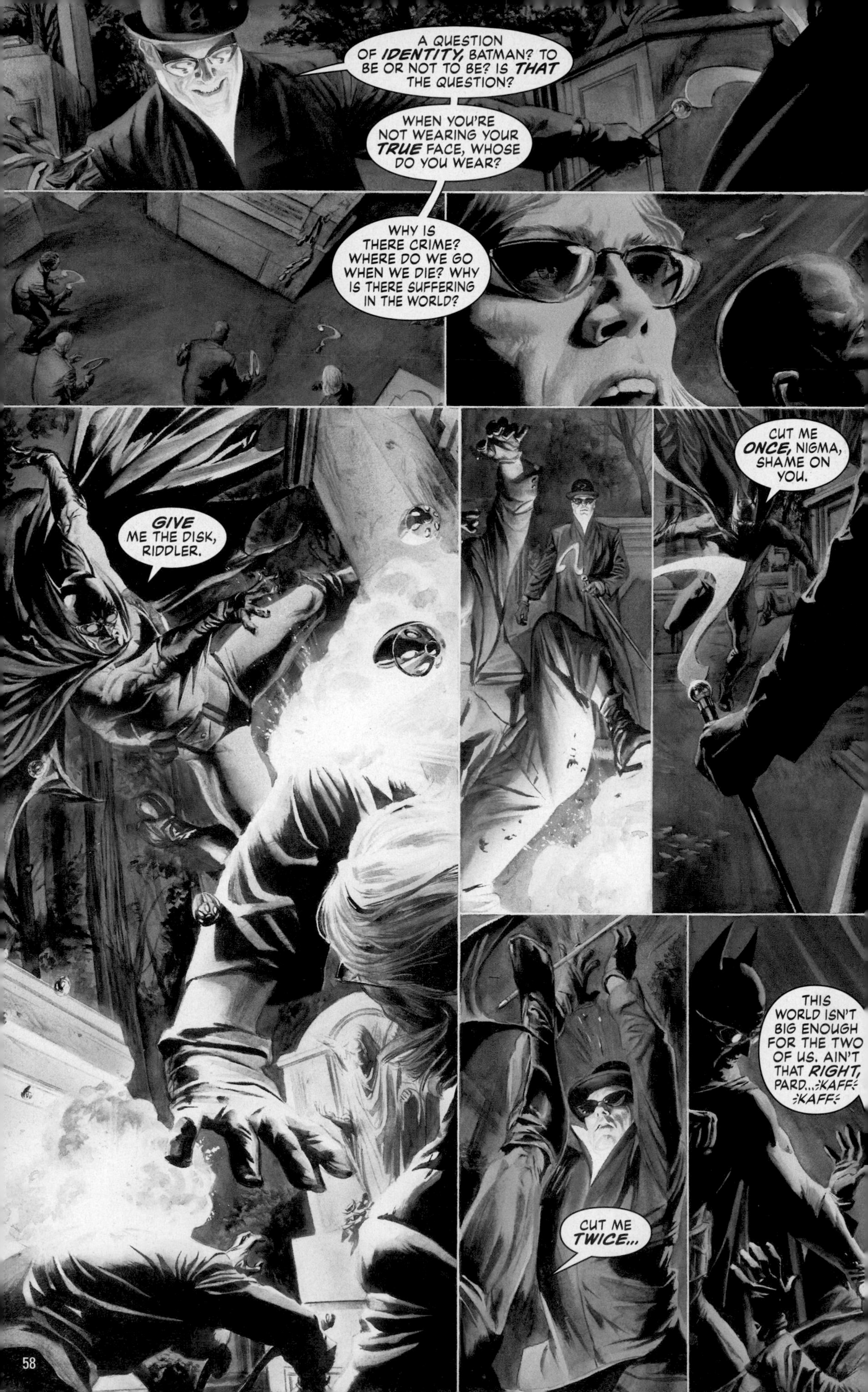
A QUESTION OF IDENTITY, BATMAN? TO BE OR NOT TO BE? IS THAT THE QUESTION?
WHEN YOU'RE NOT WEARING YOUR TRUE FACE, WHOSE DO YOU WEAR?
WHY IS THERE CRIME? WHERE DO WE GO WHEN WE DIE? WHY IS THERE SUFFERING IN THE WORLD?
GIVE ME THE DISK, RIDDLER.
CUT ME ONCE, NIGMA, SHAME ON YOU.
CUT ME TWICE...
THIS WORLD ISN'T BIG ENOUGH FOR THE TWO OF US. AIN'T THAT RIGHT, PARD...KAFF KAFF

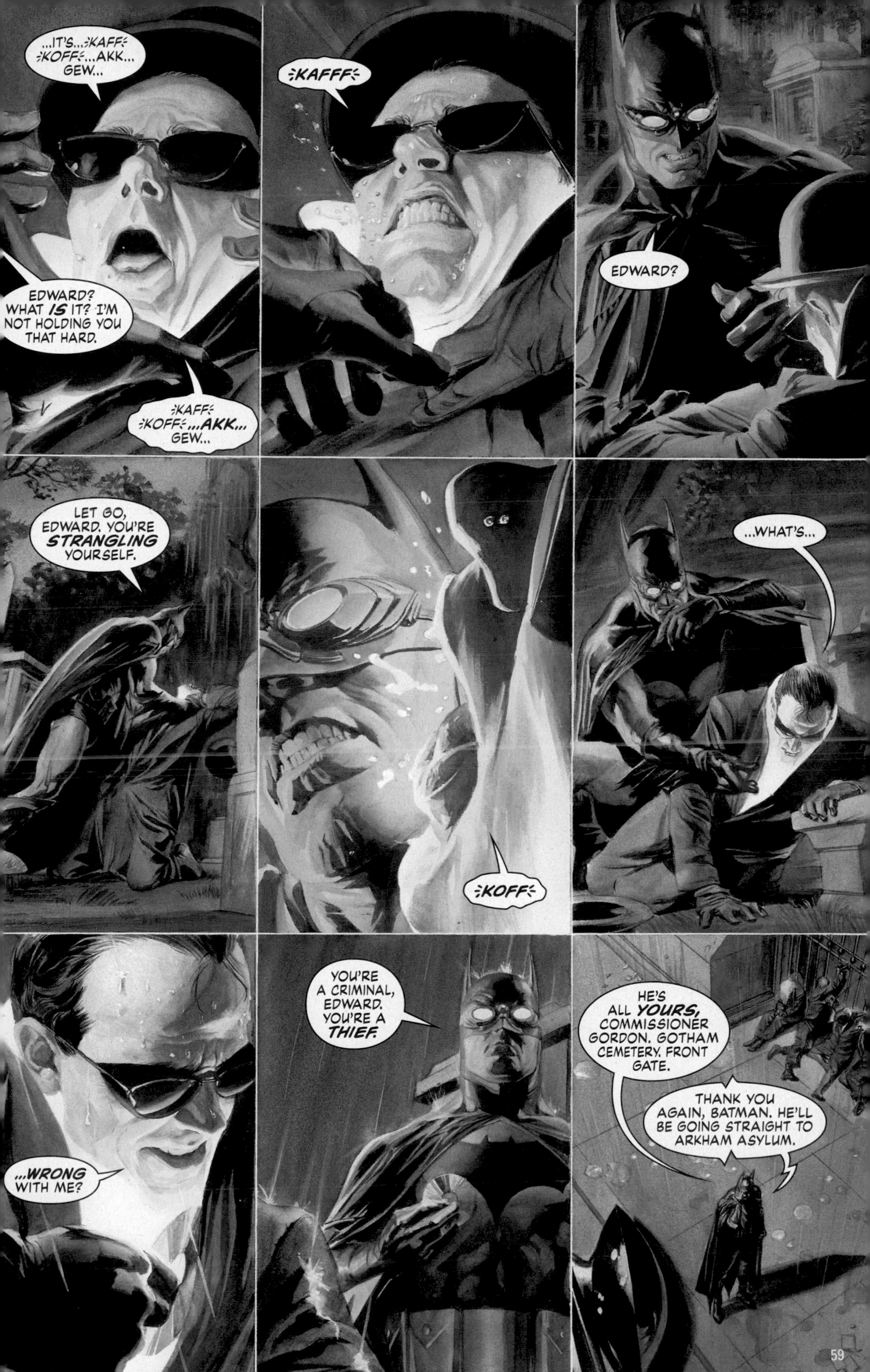

...IT'S...KAFF KOFF...AKK... GEW...
EDWARD? WHAT IS IT? I'M NOT HOLDING YOU THAT HARD.
KAFF KOFF ...AKK... GEW...
KAFFF
EDWARD?
LET GO, EDWARD. YOU'RE STRANGLING YOURSELF.
KOFF
...WHAT'S...
...WRONG WITH ME?
YOU'RE A CRIMINAL, EDWARD. YOU'RE A THIEF.
HE'S ALL YOURS, COMMISSIONER GORDON. GOTHAM CEMETERY. FRONT GATE.
THANK YOU AGAIN, BATMAN. HE'LL BE GOING STRAIGHT TO ARKHAM ASYLUM.

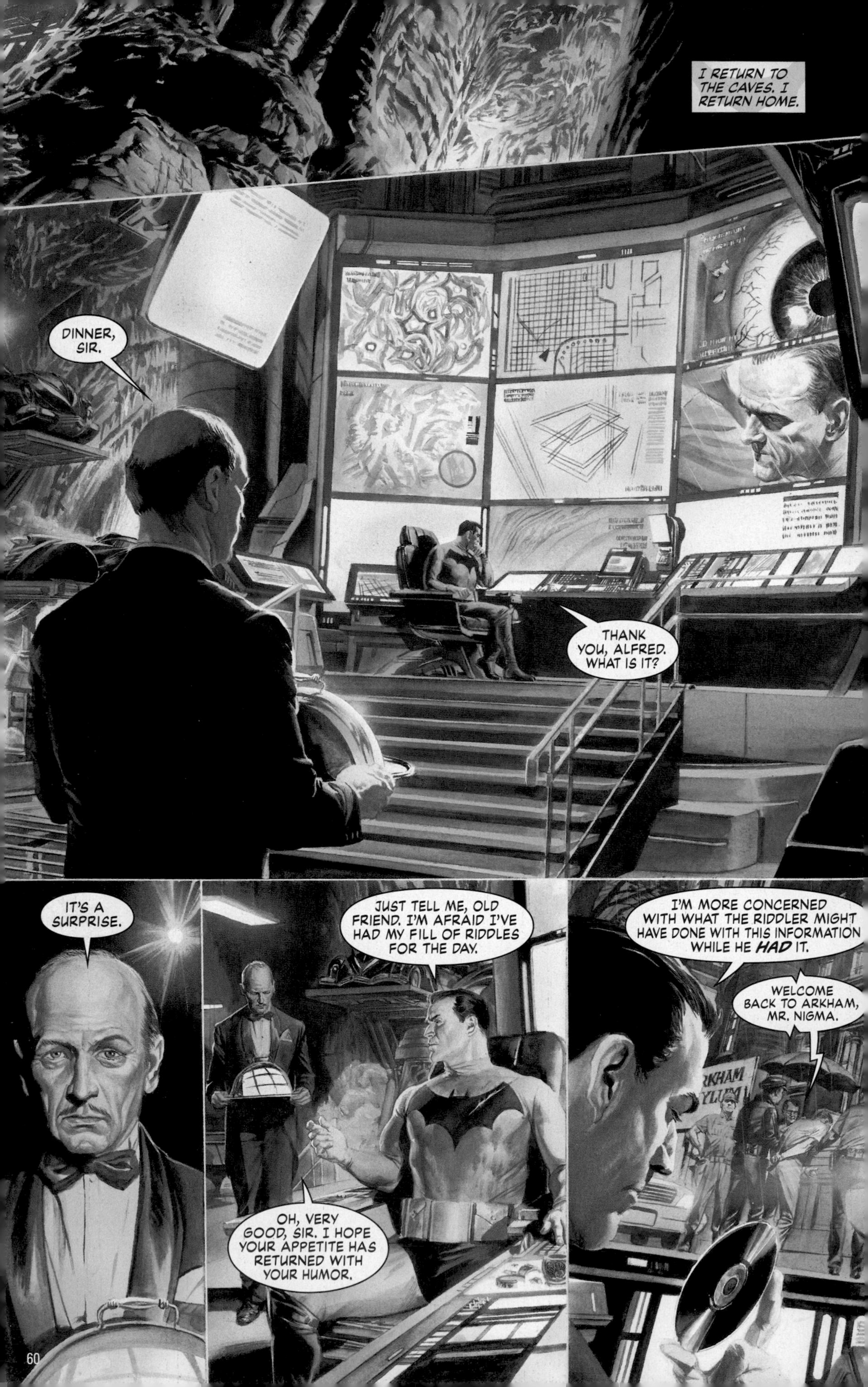
I RETURN TO THE CAVES. I RETURN HOME.
DINNER, SIR.
THANK YOU, ALFRED. WHAT IS IT?
IT'S A SURPRISE.
JUST TELL ME, OLD FRIEND. I'M AFRAID I'VE HAD MY FILL OF RIDDLES FOR THE DAY.
OH, VERY GOOD, SIR. I HOPE YOUR APPETITE HAS RETURNED WITH YOUR HUMOR.
I'M MORE CONCERNED WITH WHAT THE RIDDLER MIGHT HAVE DONE WITH THIS INFORMATION WHILE HE ***HAD*** IT.
WELCOME BACK TO ARKHAM, MR. NIGMA.

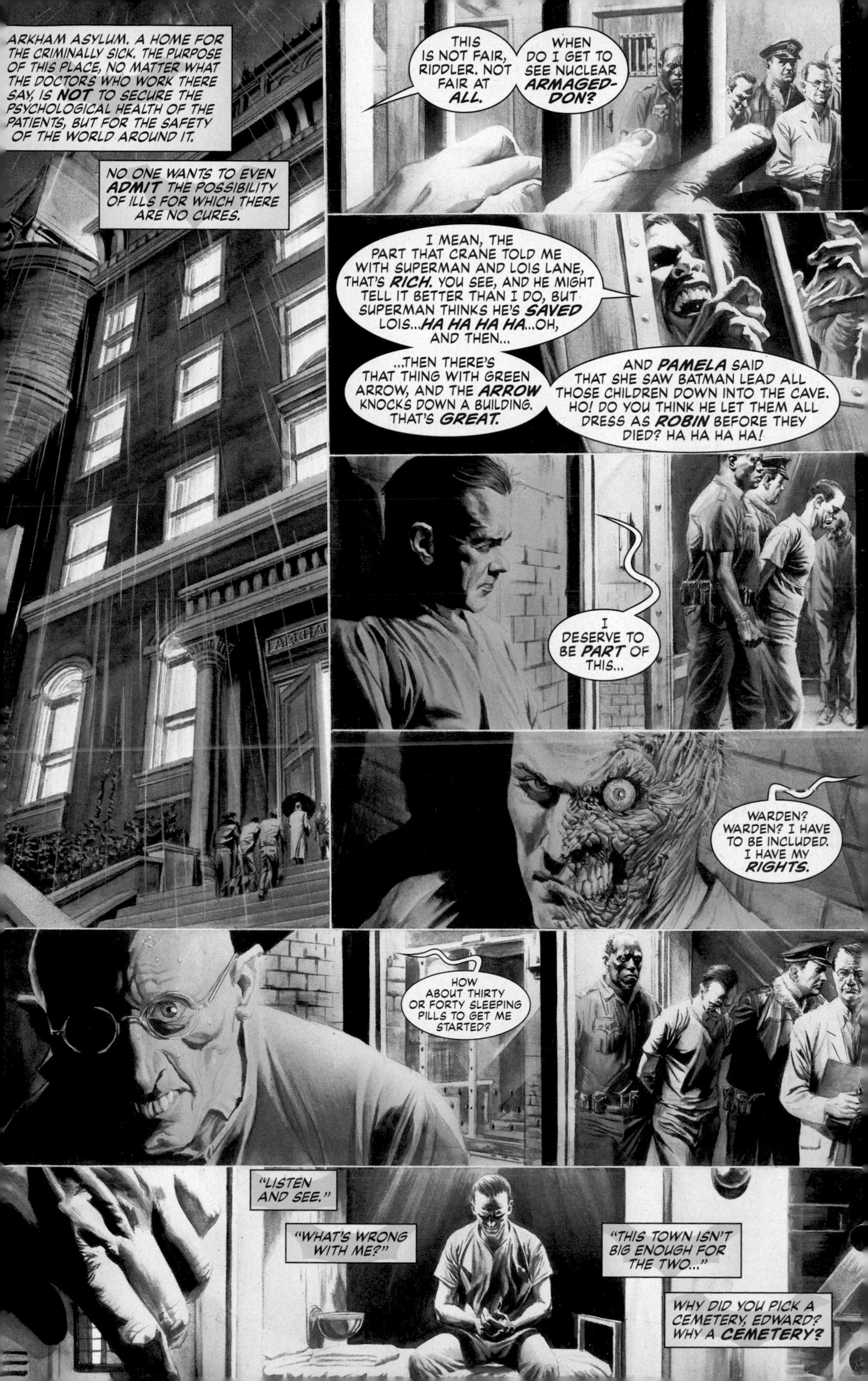
ARKHAM ASYLUM. A HOME FOR THE CRIMINALLY SICK. THE PURPOSE OF THIS PLACE, NO MATTER WHAT THE DOCTORS WHO WORK THERE SAY, IS NOT TO SECURE THE PSYCHOLOGICAL HEALTH OF THE PATIENTS, BUT FOR THE SAFETY OF THE WORLD AROUND IT.
NO ONE WANTS TO EVEN ADMIT THE POSSIBILITY OF ILLS FOR WHICH THERE ARE NO CURES.
ARKHAM
THIS IS NOT FAIR, RIDDLER. NOT FAIR AT ALL.
WHEN DO I GET TO SEE NUCLEAR ARMAGED-DON?
I MEAN, THE PART THAT CRANE TOLD ME WITH SUPERMAN AND LOIS LANE, THAT'S RICH. YOU SEE, AND HE MIGHT TELL IT BETTER THAN I DO, BUT SUPERMAN THINKS HE'S SAVED LOIS...HA HA HA HA...OH, AND THEN...
...THEN THERE'S THAT THING WITH GREEN ARROW, AND THE ARROW KNOCKS DOWN A BUILDING. THAT'S GREAT.
AND PAMELA SAID THAT SHE SAW BATMAN LEAD ALL THOSE CHILDREN DOWN INTO THE CAVE. HO! DO YOU THINK HE LET THEM ALL DRESS AS ROBIN BEFORE THEY DIED? HA HA HA HA!
I DESERVE TO BE PART OF THIS...
WARDEN? WARDEN? I HAVE TO BE INCLUDED. I HAVE MY RIGHTS.
HOW ABOUT THIRTY OR FORTY SLEEPING PILLS TO GET ME STARTED?
"LISTEN AND SEE."
"WHAT'S WRONG WITH ME?"
"THIS TOWN ISN'T BIG ENOUGH FOR THE TWO..."
WHY DID YOU PICK A CEMETERY, EDWARD? WHY A CEMETERY?

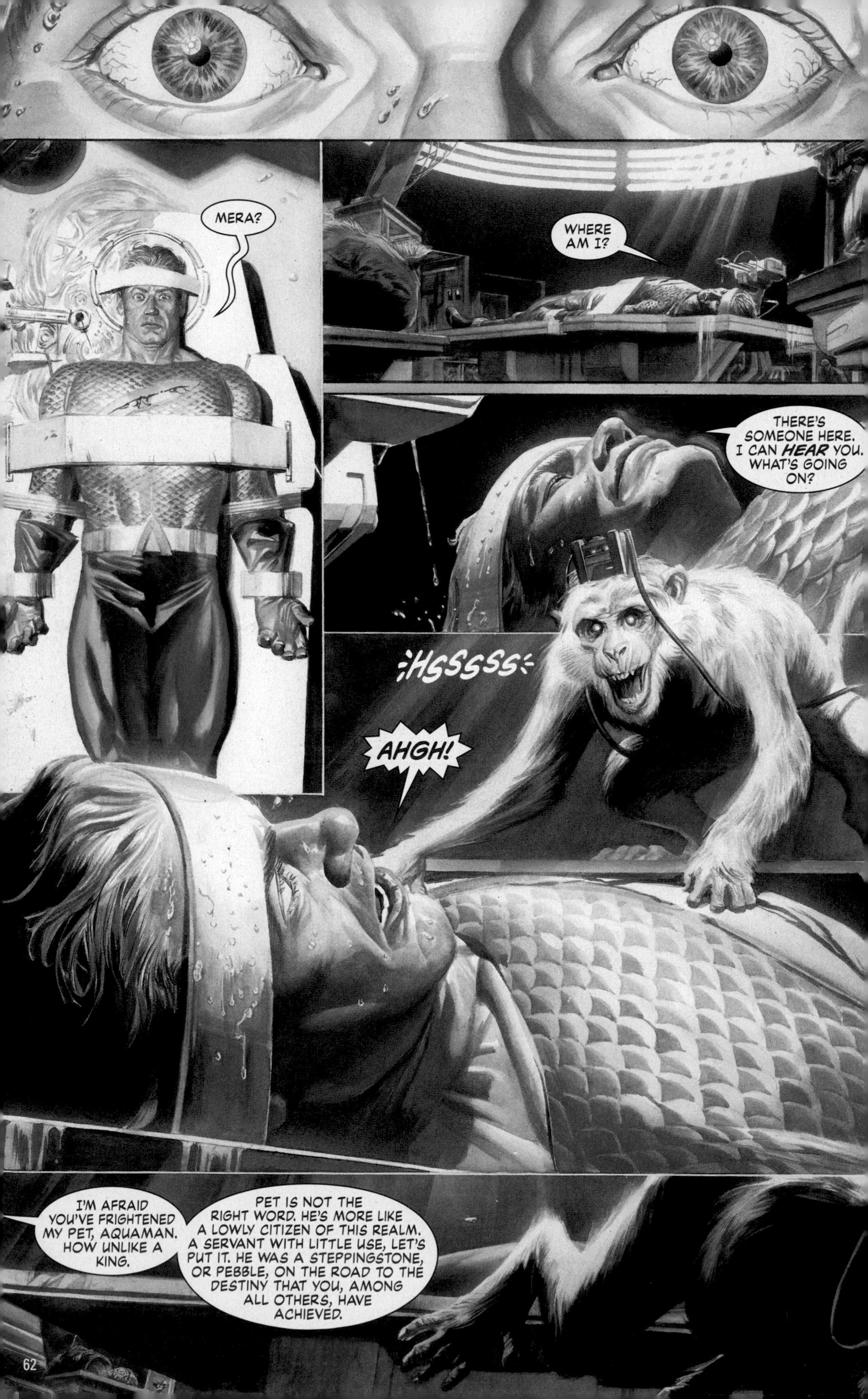
MERA?
WHERE AM I?
THERE'S SOMEONE HERE. I CAN HEAR YOU. WHAT'S GOING ON?
HSSSSS
AHGH!
I'M AFRAID YOU'VE FRIGHTENED MY PET, AQUAMAN. HOW UNLIKE A KING.
PET IS NOT THE RIGHT WORD. HE'S MORE LIKE A LOWLY CITIZEN OF THIS REALM. A SERVANT WITH LITTLE USE, LET'S PUT IT. HE WAS A STEPPINGSTONE, OR PEBBLE, ON THE ROAD TO THE DESTINY THAT YOU, AMONG ALL OTHERS, HAVE ACHIEVED.

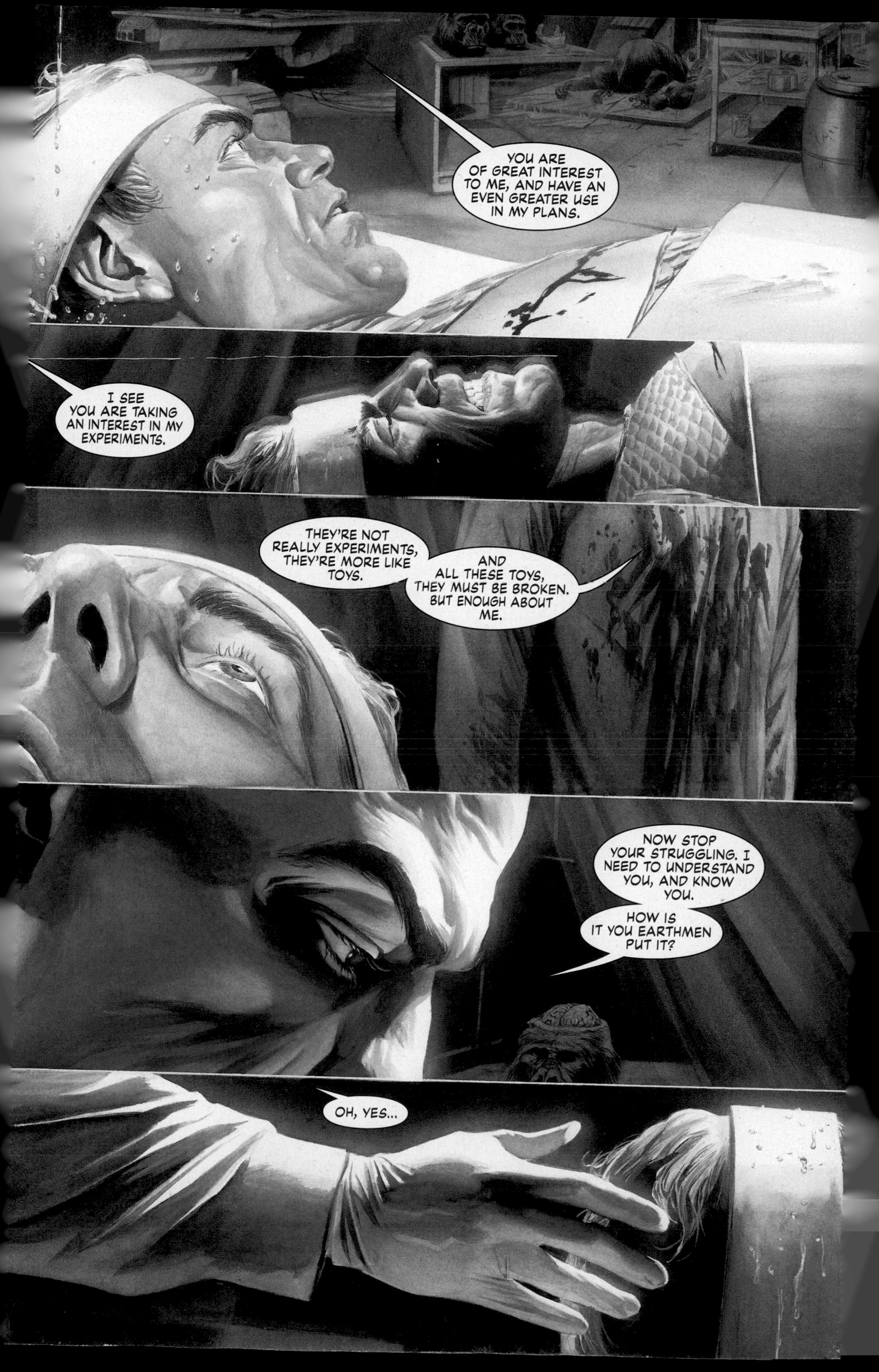
YOU ARE OF GREAT INTEREST TO ME, AND HAVE AN EVEN GREATER USE IN MY PLANS.
I SEE YOU ARE TAKING AN INTEREST IN MY EXPERIMENTS.
THEY'RE NOT REALLY EXPERIMENTS, THEY'RE MORE LIKE TOYS.
AND ALL THESE TOYS, THEY MUST BE BROKEN. BUT ENOUGH ABOUT ME.
NOW STOP YOUR STRUGGLING. I NEED TO UNDERSTAND YOU, AND KNOW YOU.
HOW IS IT YOU EARTHMEN PUT IT?
OH, YES...

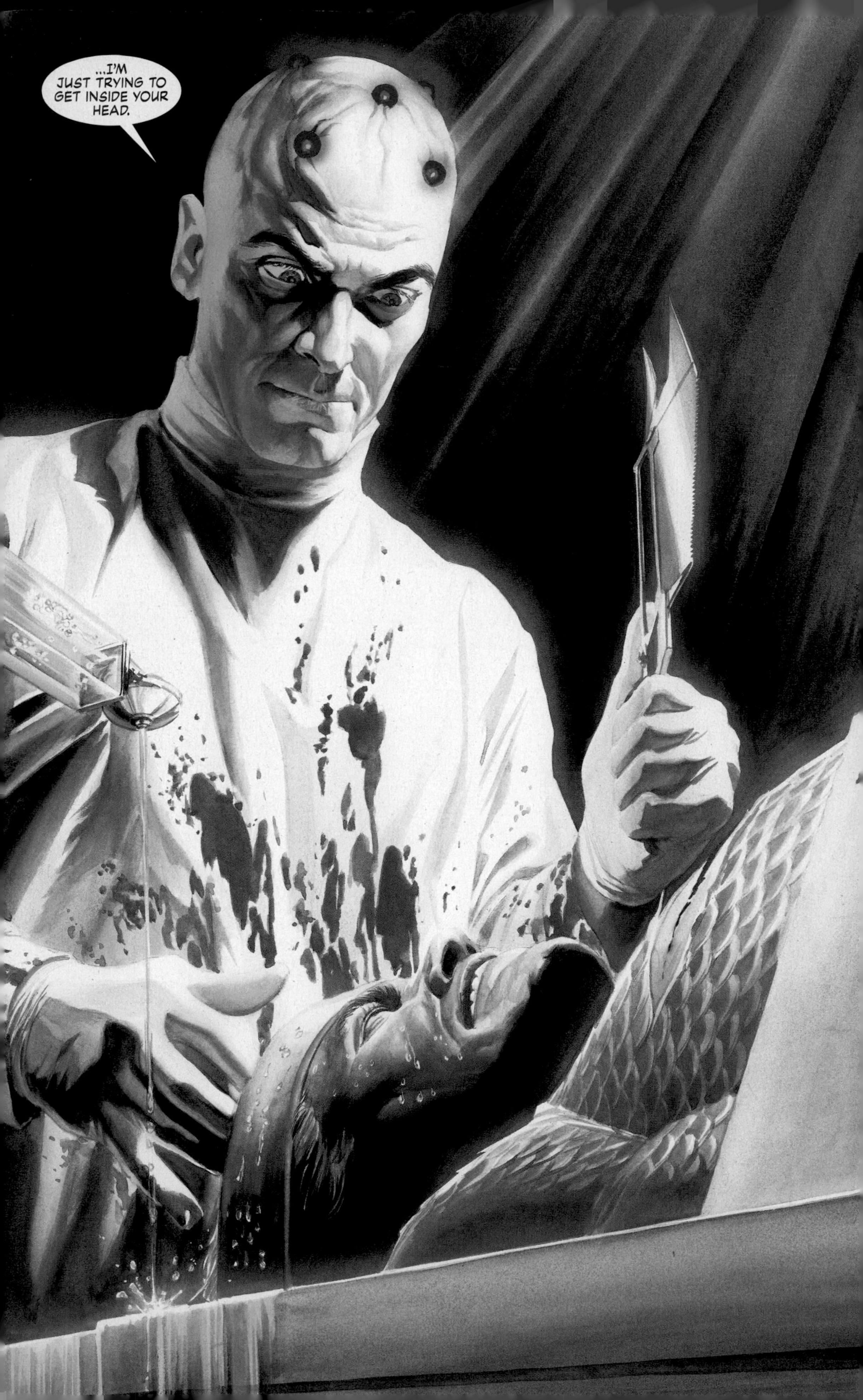
...I'M JUST TRYING TO GET INSIDE YOUR HEAD.

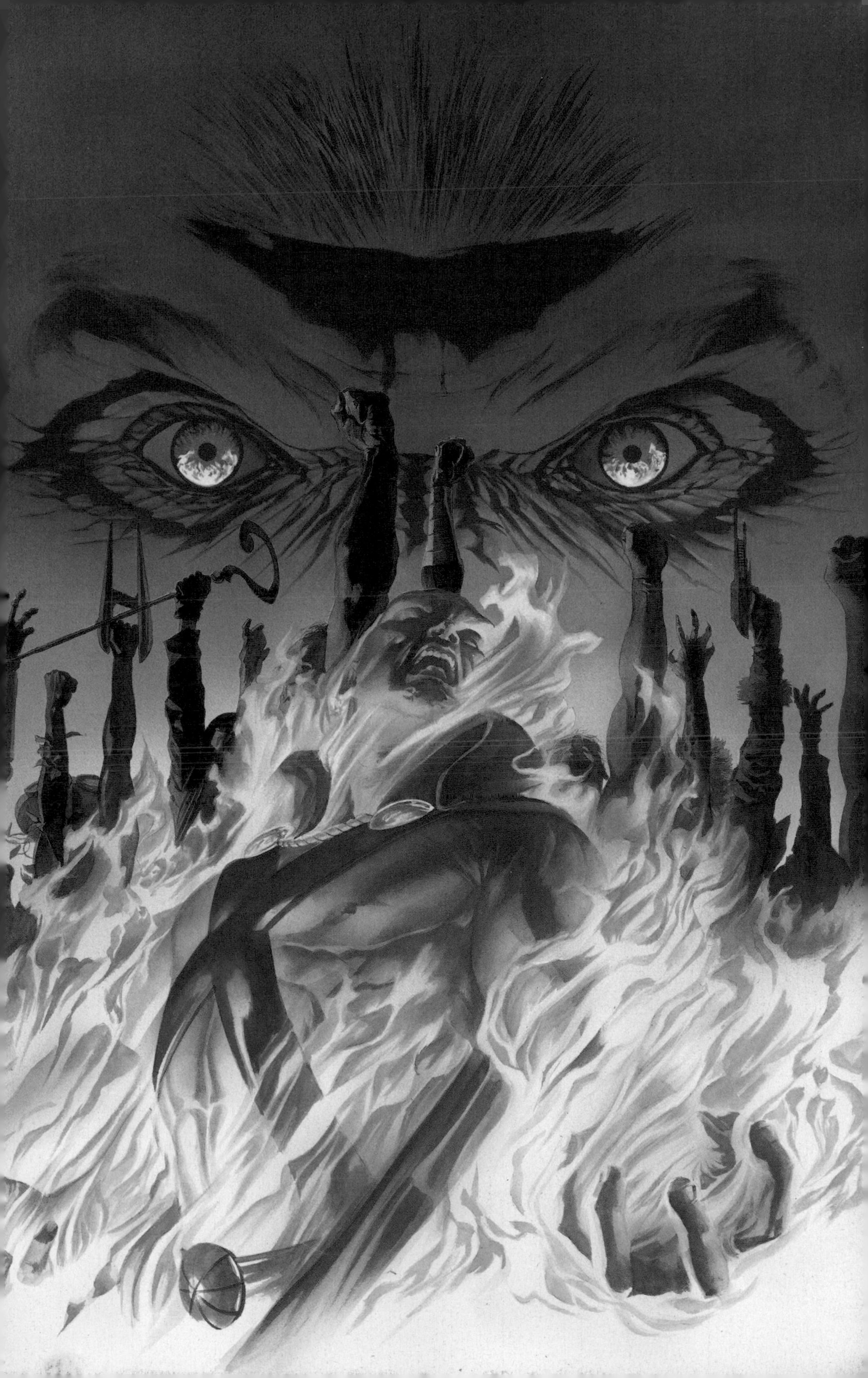

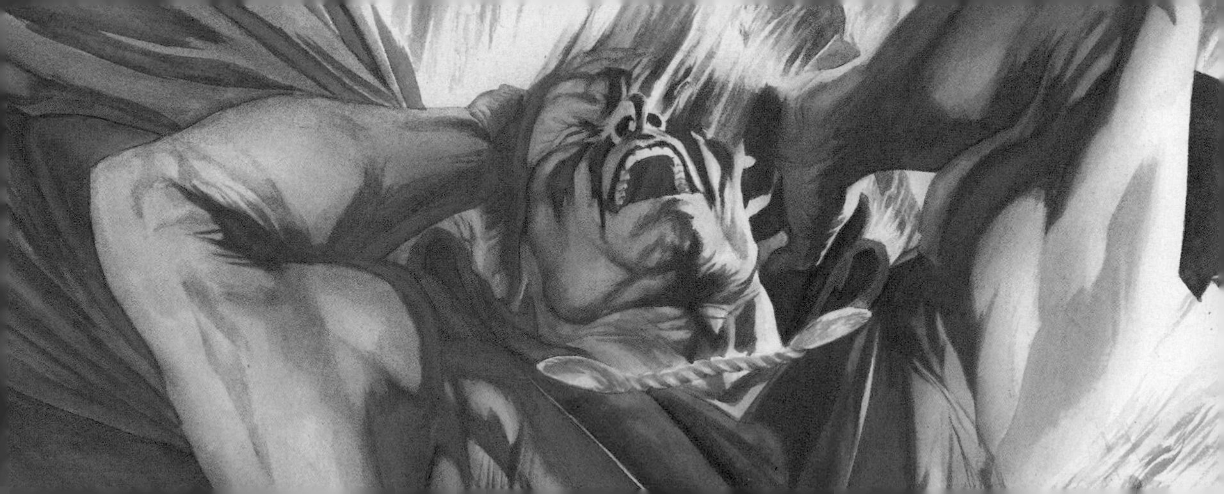

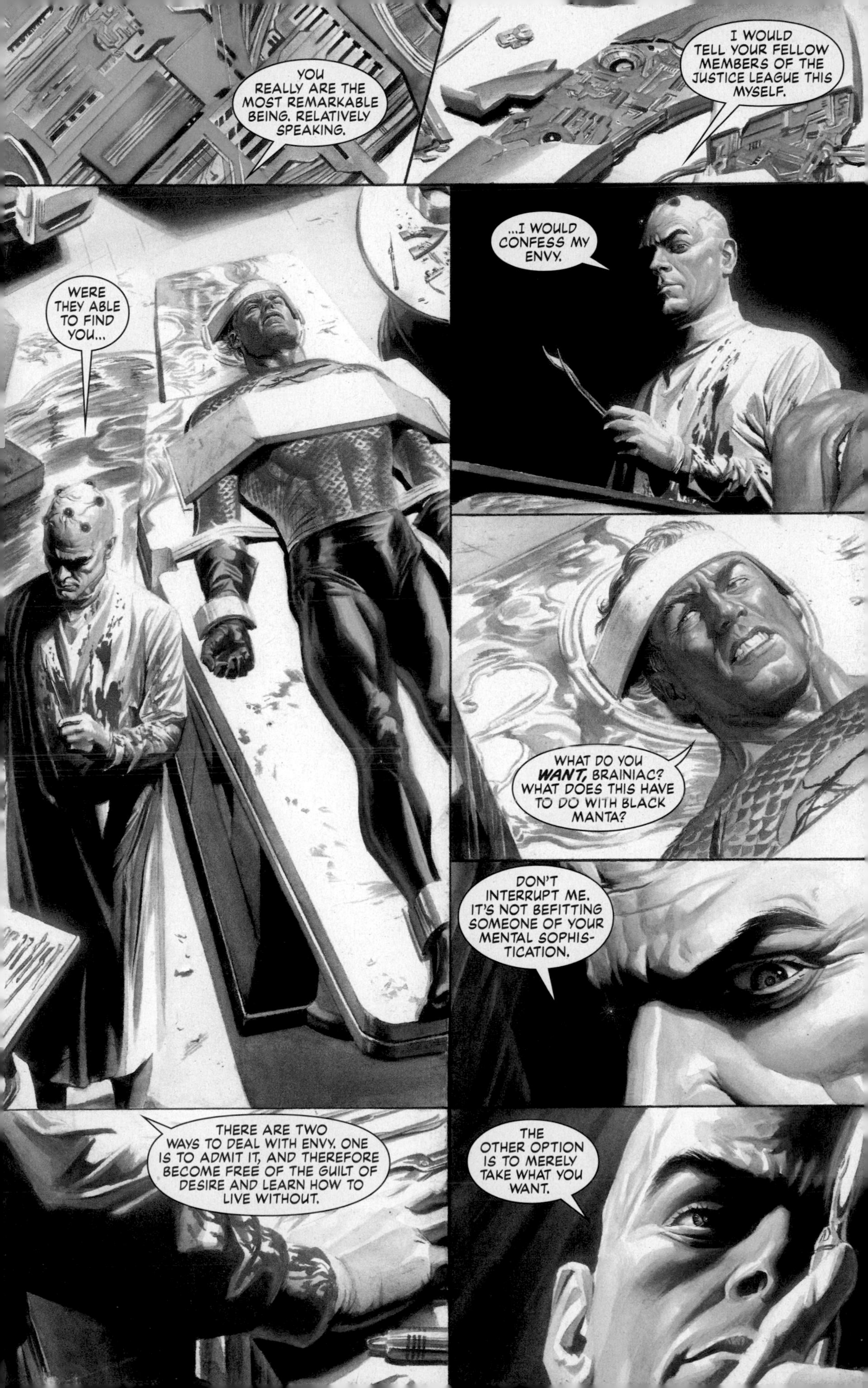
YOU REALLY ARE THE MOST REMARKABLE BEING. RELATIVELY SPEAKING.
I WOULD TELL YOUR FELLOW MEMBERS OF THE JUSTICE LEAGUE THIS MYSELF.
WERE THEY ABLE TO FIND YOU...
...I WOULD CONFESS MY ENVY.
WHAT DO YOU *WANT,* BRAINIAC? WHAT DOES THIS HAVE TO DO WITH BLACK MANTA?
DON'T INTERRUPT ME. IT'S NOT BEFITTING SOMEONE OF YOUR MENTAL SOPHIS-TICATION.
THERE ARE TWO WAYS TO DEAL WITH ENVY. ONE IS TO ADMIT IT, AND THEREFORE BECOME FREE OF THE GUILT OF DESIRE AND LEARN HOW TO LIVE WITHOUT.
THE OTHER OPTION IS TO MERELY TAKE WHAT YOU WANT.

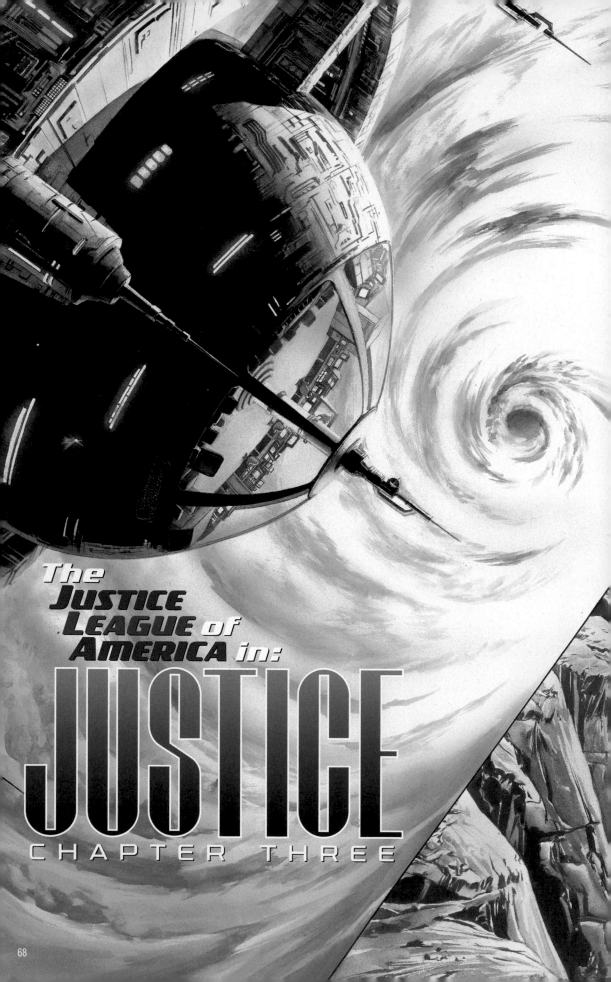

The **JUSTICE LEAGUE** of **AMERICA** in:

JUSTICE

CHAPTER THREE

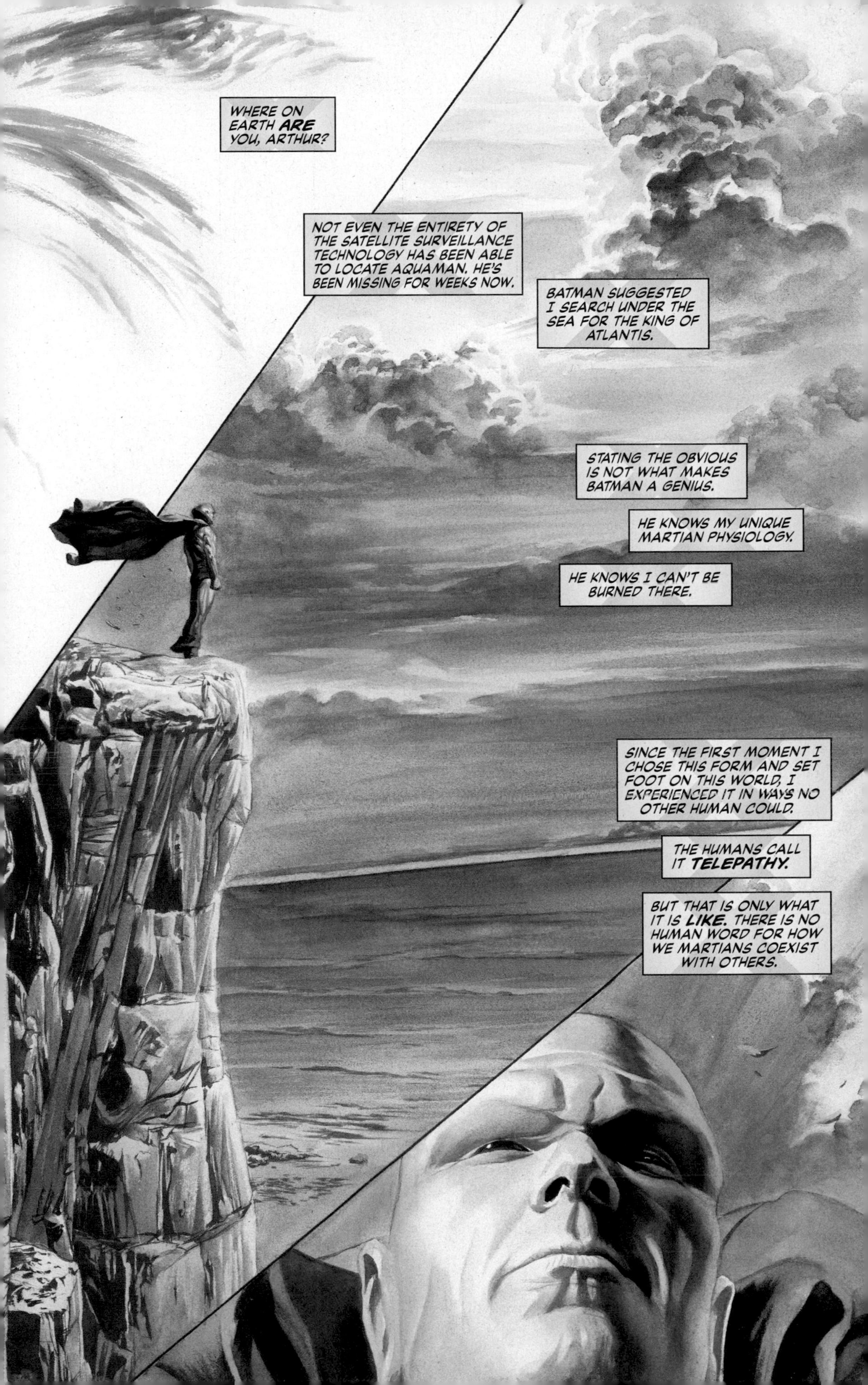
WHERE ON EARTH **ARE** YOU, ARTHUR?
NOT EVEN THE ENTIRETY OF THE SATELLITE SURVEILLANCE TECHNOLOGY HAS BEEN ABLE TO LOCATE AQUAMAN. HE'S BEEN MISSING FOR WEEKS NOW.
BATMAN SUGGESTED I SEARCH UNDER THE SEA FOR THE KING OF ATLANTIS.
STATING THE OBVIOUS IS NOT WHAT MAKES BATMAN A GENIUS.
HE KNOWS MY UNIQUE MARTIAN PHYSIOLOGY.
HE KNOWS I CAN'T BE BURNED THERE.
SINCE THE FIRST MOMENT I CHOSE THIS FORM AND SET FOOT ON THIS WORLD, I EXPERIENCED IT IN WAYS NO OTHER HUMAN COULD.
THE HUMANS CALL IT **TELEPATHY.**
BUT THAT IS ONLY WHAT IT IS **LIKE.** THERE IS NO HUMAN WORD FOR HOW WE MARTIANS COEXIST WITH OTHERS.

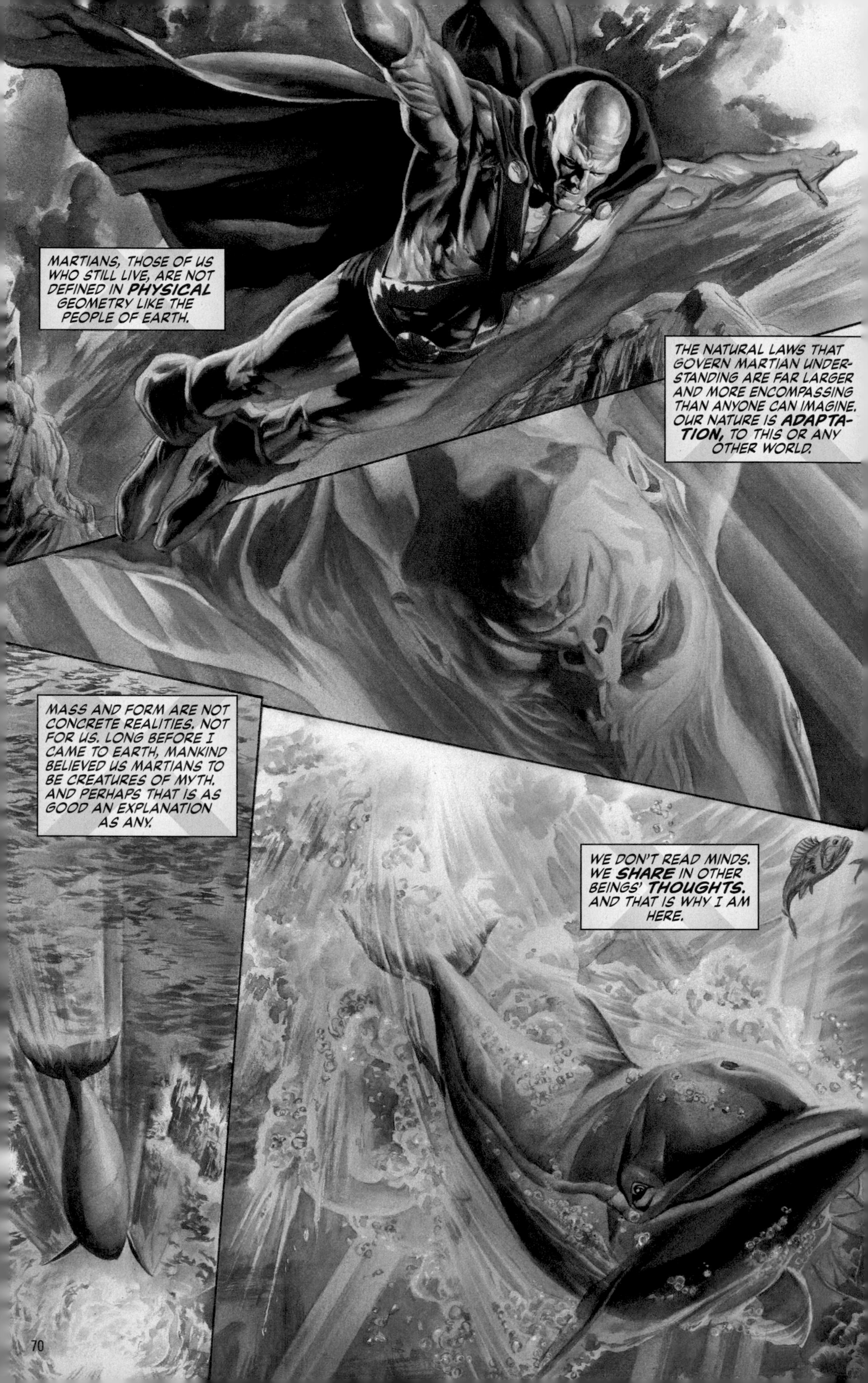
MARTIANS, THOSE OF US WHO STILL LIVE, ARE NOT DEFINED IN PHYSICAL GEOMETRY LIKE THE PEOPLE OF EARTH.
THE NATURAL LAWS THAT GOVERN MARTIAN UNDERSTANDING ARE FAR LARGER AND MORE ENCOMPASSING THAN ANYONE CAN IMAGINE. OUR NATURE IS ADAPTATION, TO THIS OR ANY OTHER WORLD.
MASS AND FORM ARE NOT CONCRETE REALITIES. NOT FOR US. LONG BEFORE I CAME TO EARTH, MANKIND BELIEVED US MARTIANS TO BE CREATURES OF MYTH. AND PERHAPS THAT IS AS GOOD AN EXPLANATION AS ANY.
WE DON'T READ MINDS. WE SHARE IN OTHER BEINGS' THOUGHTS. AND THAT IS WHY I AM HERE.

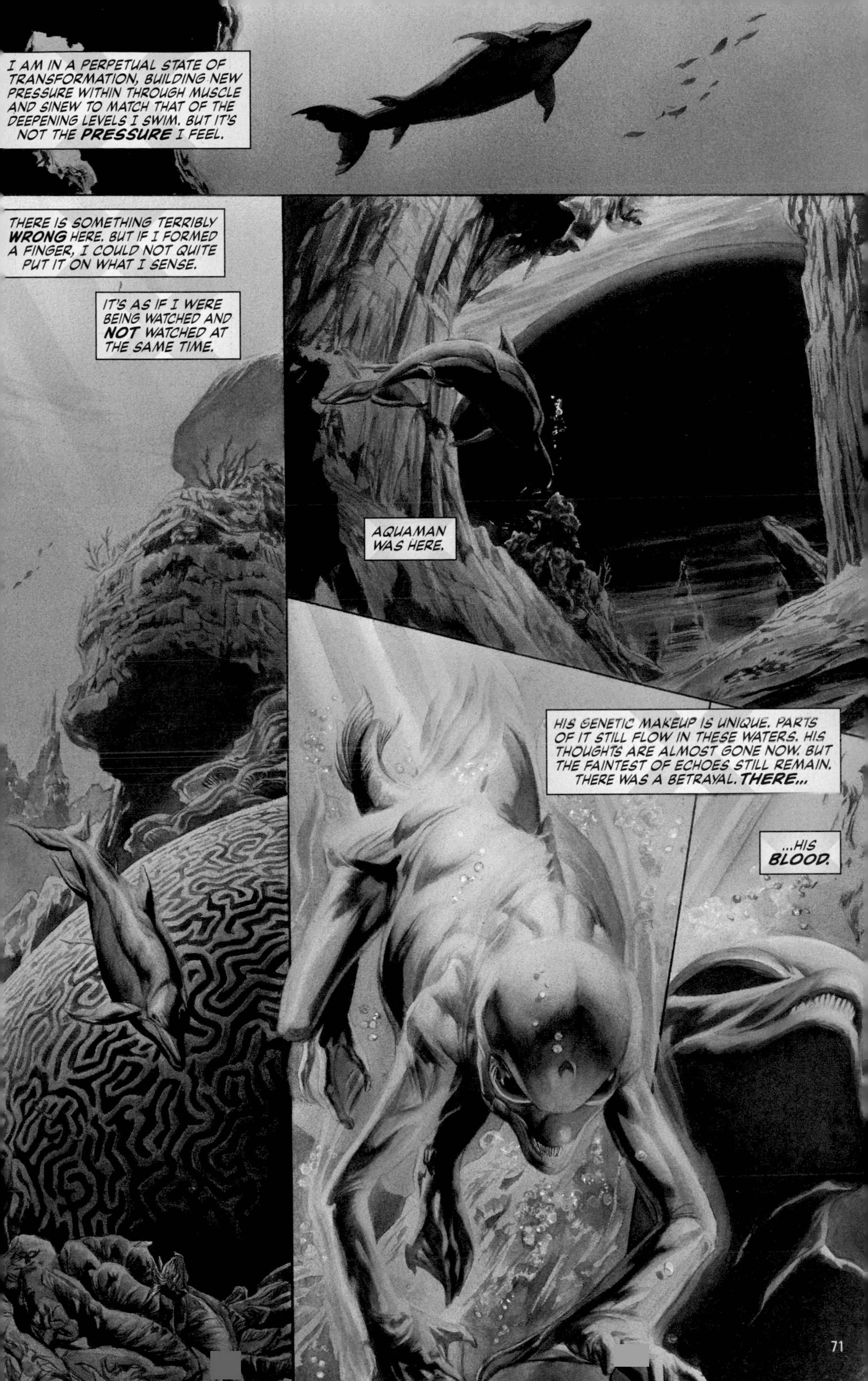

I AM IN A PERPETUAL STATE OF TRANSFORMATION, BUILDING NEW PRESSURE WITHIN THROUGH MUSCLE AND SINEW TO MATCH THAT OF THE DEEPENING LEVELS I SWIM. BUT IT'S NOT THE **PRESSURE** I FEEL.
THERE IS SOMETHING TERRIBLY **WRONG** HERE. BUT IF I FORMED A FINGER, I COULD NOT QUITE PUT IT ON WHAT I SENSE.
IT'S AS IF I WERE BEING WATCHED AND **NOT** WATCHED AT THE SAME TIME.
AQUAMAN WAS HERE.
HIS GENETIC MAKEUP IS UNIQUE. PARTS OF IT STILL FLOW IN THESE WATERS. HIS THOUGHTS ARE ALMOST GONE NOW. BUT THE FAINTEST OF ECHOES STILL REMAIN. THERE WAS A BETRAYAL. **THERE...**
...HIS **BLOOD.**

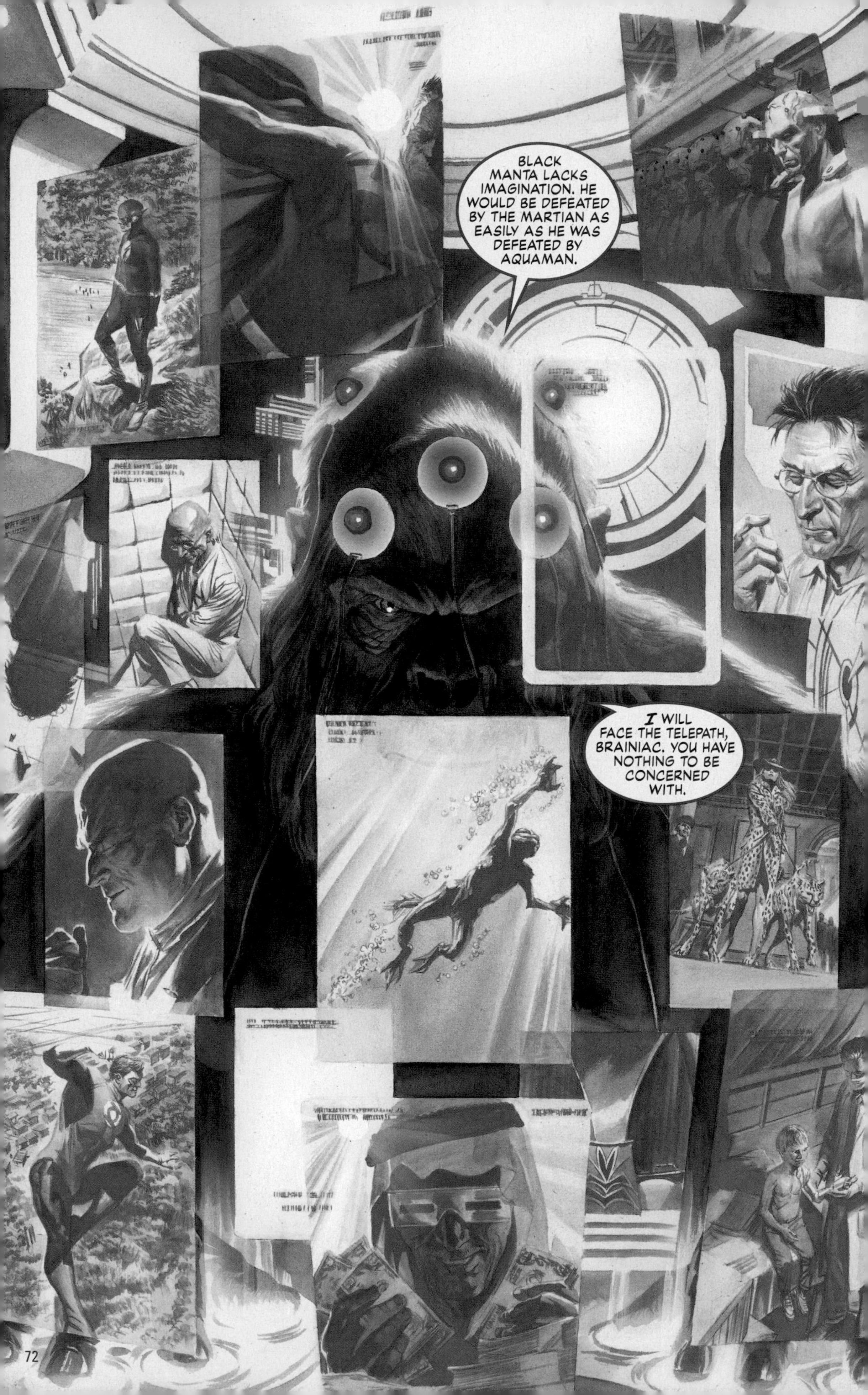
BLACK MANTA LACKS IMAGINATION. HE WOULD BE DEFEATED BY THE MARTIAN AS EASILY AS HE WAS DEFEATED BY AQUAMAN.
I WILL FACE THE TELEPATH, BRAINIAC. YOU HAVE NOTHING TO BE CONCERNED WITH.

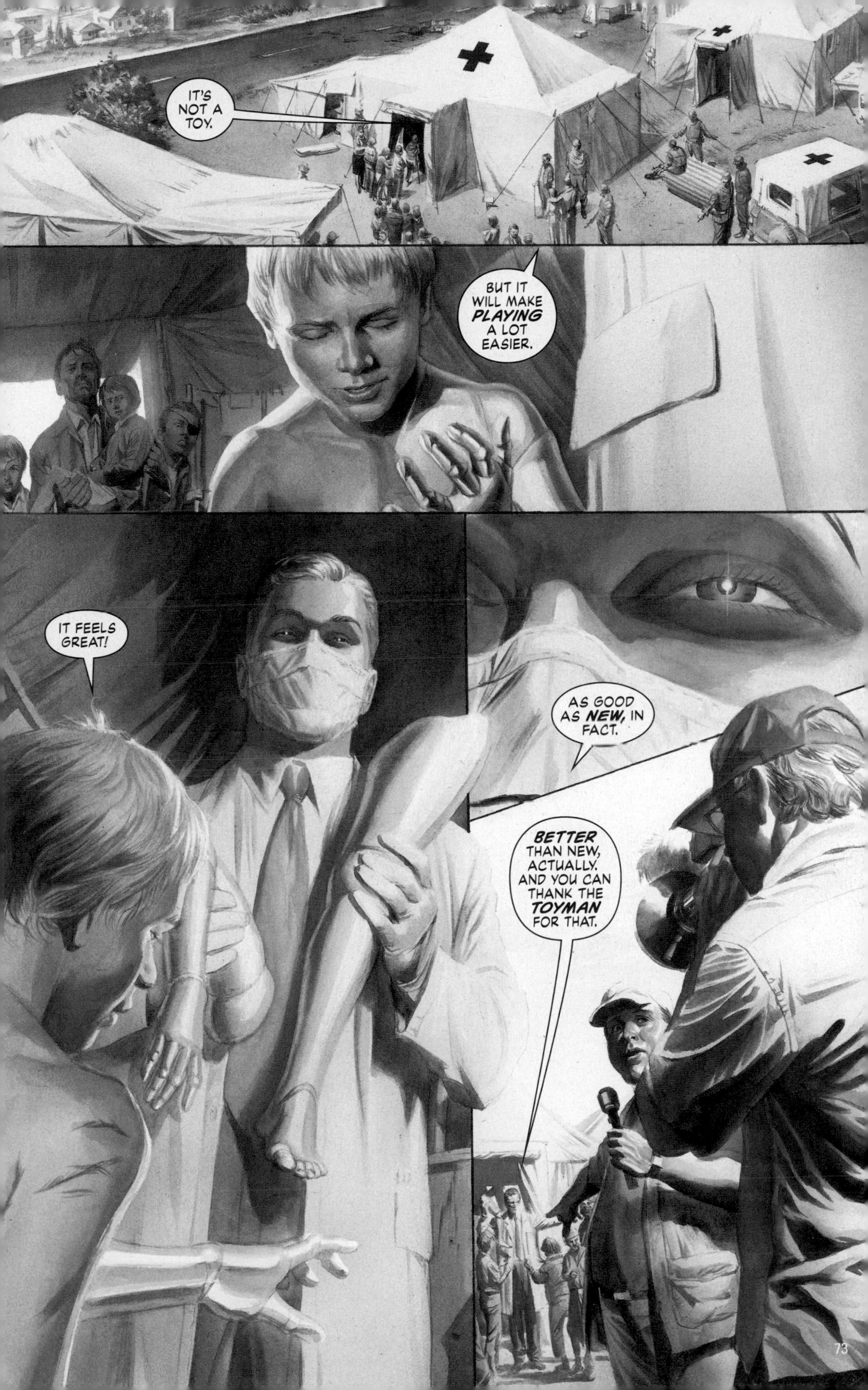
IT'S NOT A TOY.
BUT IT WILL MAKE PLAYING A LOT EASIER.
IT FEELS GREAT!
AS GOOD AS NEW, IN FACT.
BETTER THAN NEW, ACTUALLY. AND YOU CAN THANK THE TOYMAN FOR THAT.

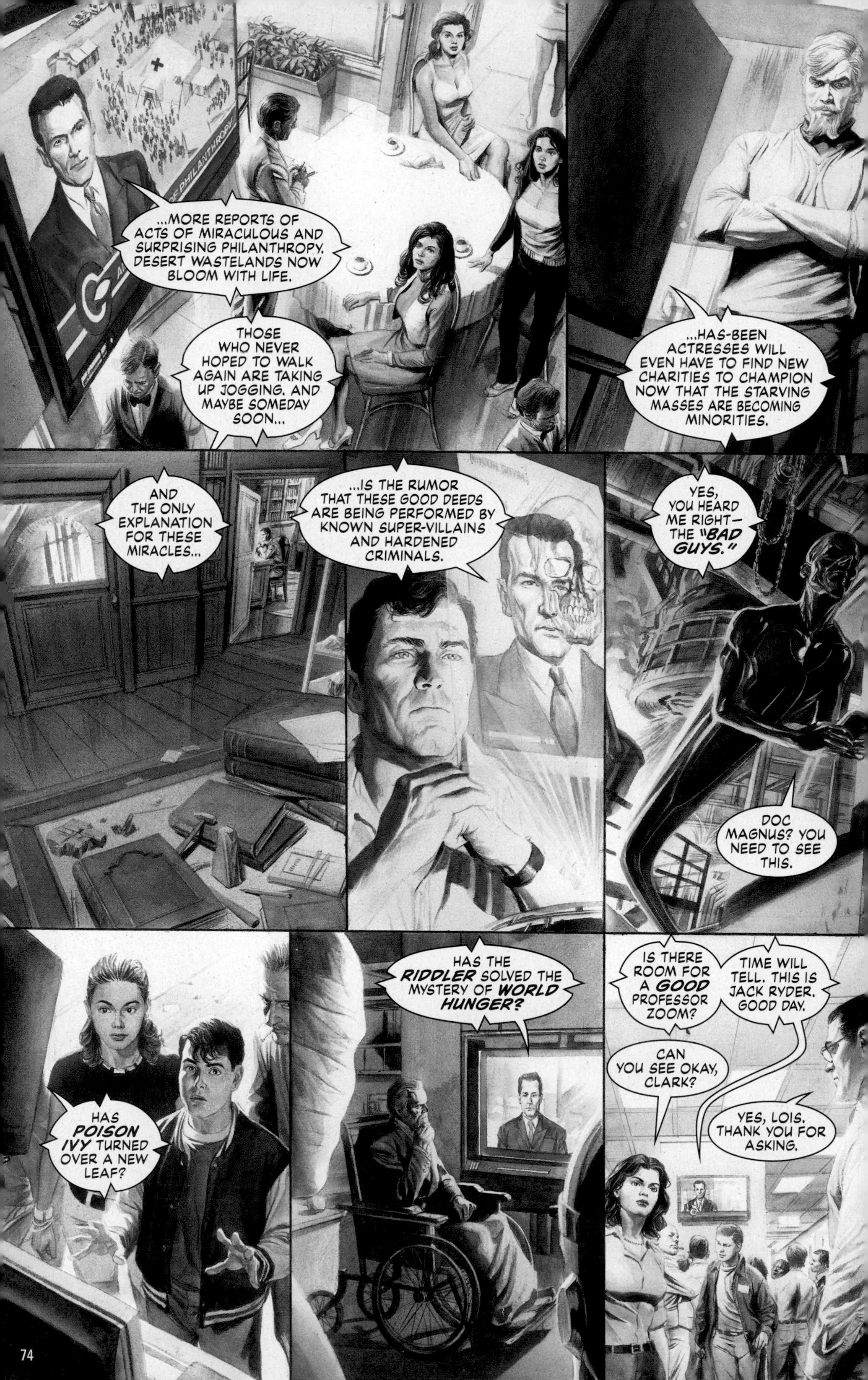
...MORE REPORTS OF ACTS OF MIRACULOUS AND SURPRISING PHILANTHROPY. DESERT WASTELANDS NOW BLOOM WITH LIFE.
THOSE WHO NEVER HOPED TO WALK AGAIN ARE TAKING UP JOGGING. AND MAYBE SOMEDAY SOON...
...HAS-BEEN ACTRESSES WILL EVEN HAVE TO FIND NEW CHARITIES TO CHAMPION NOW THAT THE STARVING MASSES ARE BECOMING MINORITIES.
AND THE ONLY EXPLANATION FOR THESE MIRACLES...
...IS THE RUMOR THAT THESE GOOD DEEDS ARE BEING PERFORMED BY KNOWN SUPER-VILLAINS AND HARDENED CRIMINALS.
YES, YOU HEARD ME RIGHT— THE "BAD GUYS."
DOC MAGNUS? YOU NEED TO SEE THIS.
HAS POISON IVY TURNED OVER A NEW LEAF?
HAS THE RIDDLER SOLVED THE MYSTERY OF WORLD HUNGER?
IS THERE ROOM FOR A GOOD PROFESSOR ZOOM?
TIME WILL TELL. THIS IS JACK RYDER. GOOD DAY.
CAN YOU SEE OKAY, CLARK?
YES, LOIS. THANK YOU FOR ASKING.

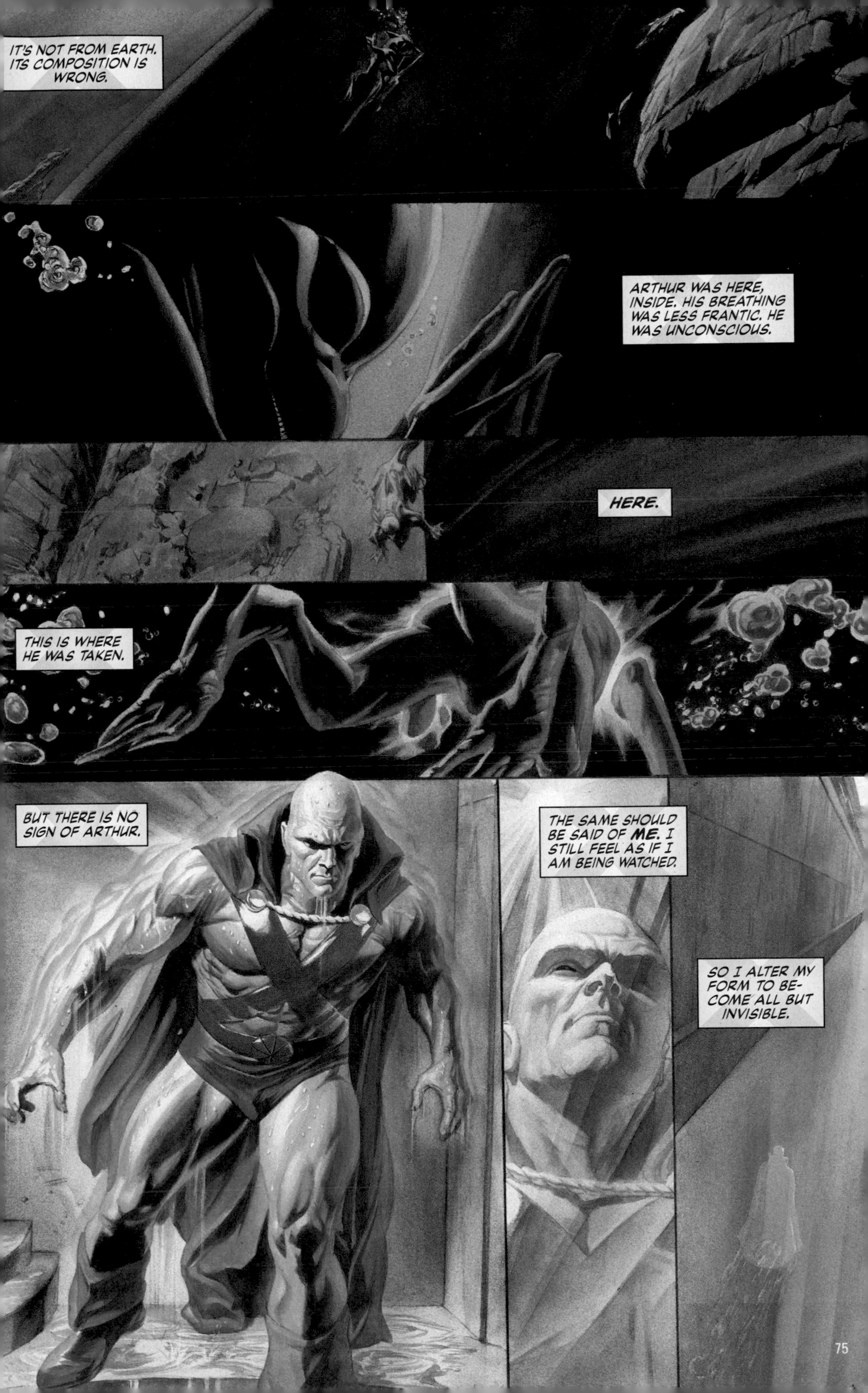
IT'S NOT FROM EARTH. ITS COMPOSITION IS WRONG.
ARTHUR WAS HERE, INSIDE. HIS BREATHING WAS LESS FRANTIC. HE WAS UNCONSCIOUS.
HERE.
THIS IS WHERE HE WAS TAKEN.
BUT THERE IS NO SIGN OF ARTHUR.
THE SAME SHOULD BE SAID OF **ME.** I STILL FEEL AS IF I AM BEING WATCHED.
SO I ALTER MY FORM TO BECOME ALL BUT INVISIBLE.

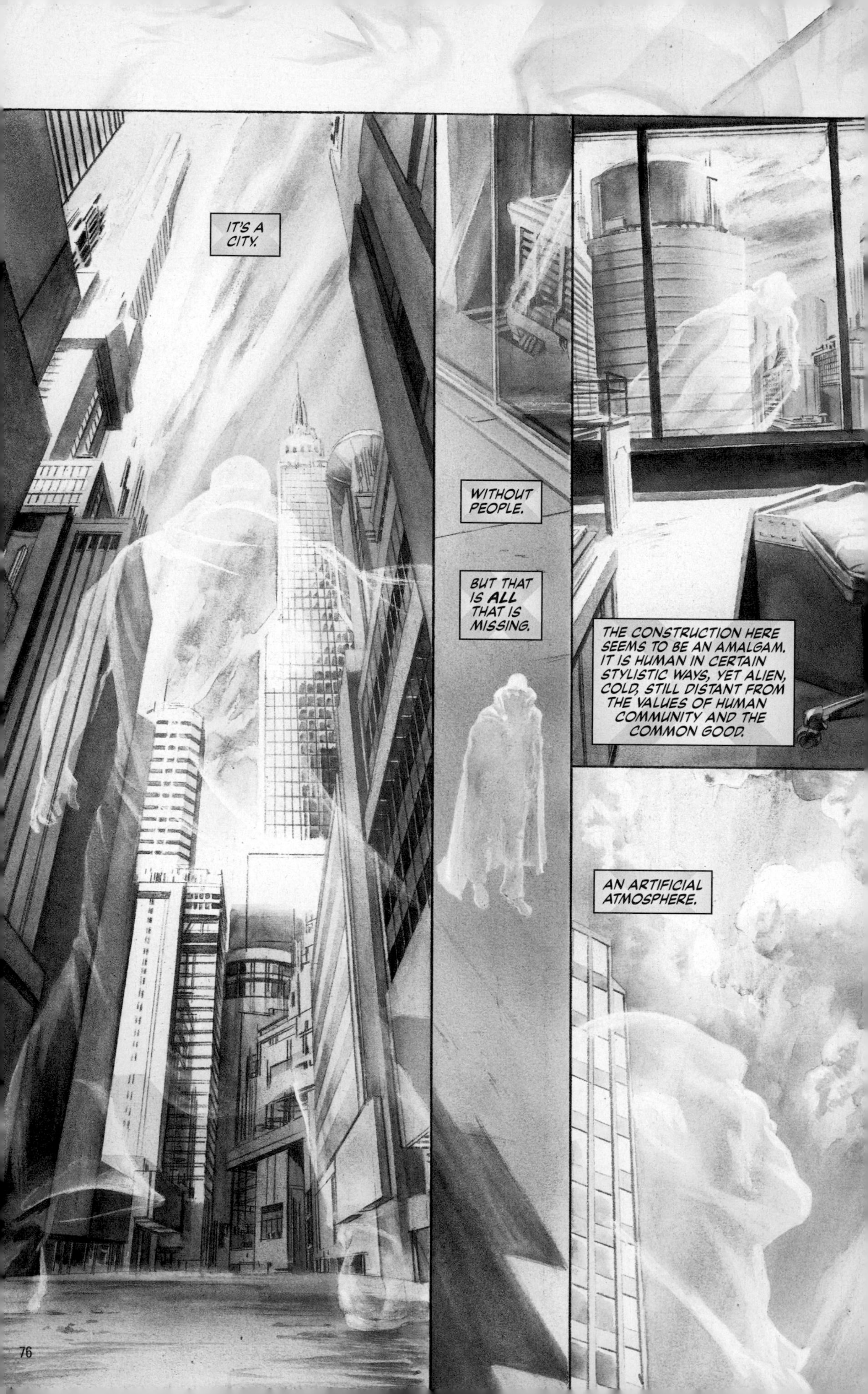
IT'S A CITY.
WITHOUT PEOPLE.
BUT THAT IS ALL THAT IS MISSING.
THE CONSTRUCTION HERE SEEMS TO BE AN AMALGAM. IT IS HUMAN IN CERTAIN STYLISTIC WAYS, YET ALIEN, COLD, STILL DISTANT FROM THE VALUES OF HUMAN COMMUNITY AND THE COMMON GOOD.
AN ARTIFICIAL ATMOSPHERE.

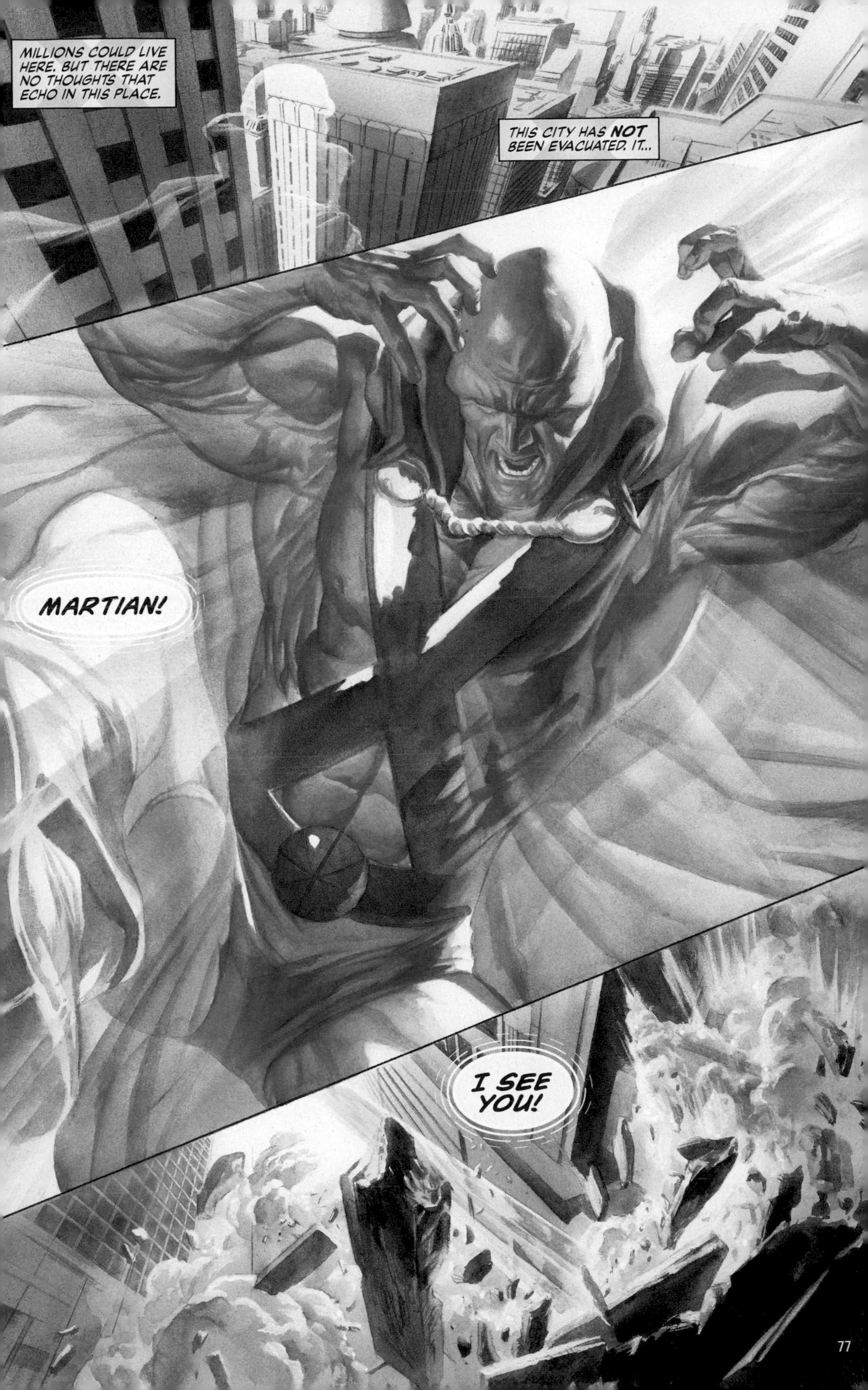
MILLIONS COULD LIVE HERE. BUT THERE ARE NO THOUGHTS THAT ECHO IN THIS PLACE.
THIS CITY HAS NOT BEEN EVACUATED. IT...
MARTIAN!
I SEE YOU!

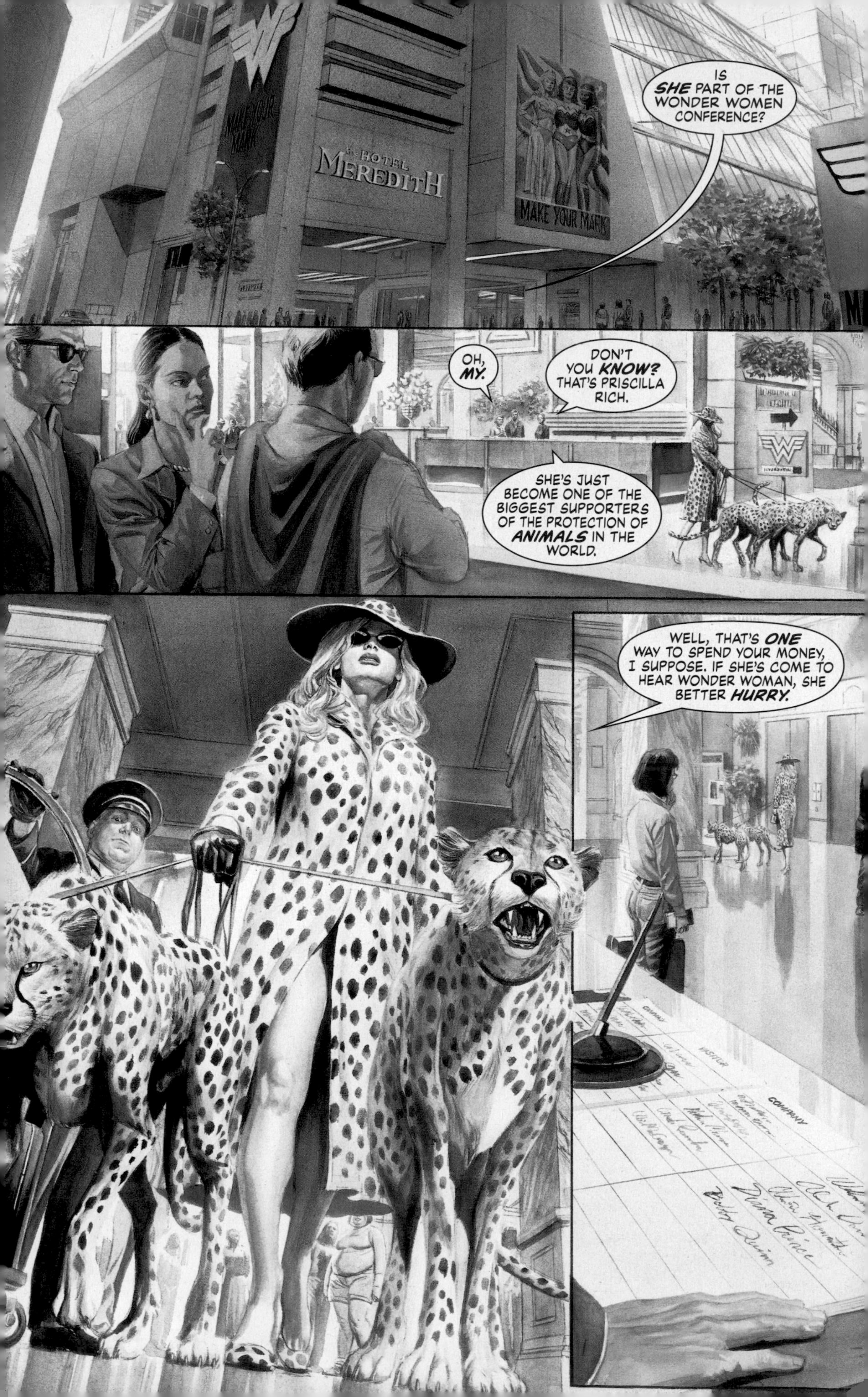

HOTEL MEREDITH
MAKE YOUR MARK
MAKE YOUR MARK
IS *SHE* PART OF THE WONDER WOMEN CONFERENCE?
OH, *MY.*
DON'T YOU *KNOW?* THAT'S PRISCILLA RICH.
SHE'S JUST BECOME ONE OF THE BIGGEST SUPPORTERS OF THE PROTECTION OF *ANIMALS* IN THE WORLD.
WELL, THAT'S *ONE* WAY TO SPEND YOUR MONEY, I SUPPOSE. IF SHE'S COME TO HEAR WONDER WOMAN, SHE BETTER *HURRY.*
VISITOR
COMPANY

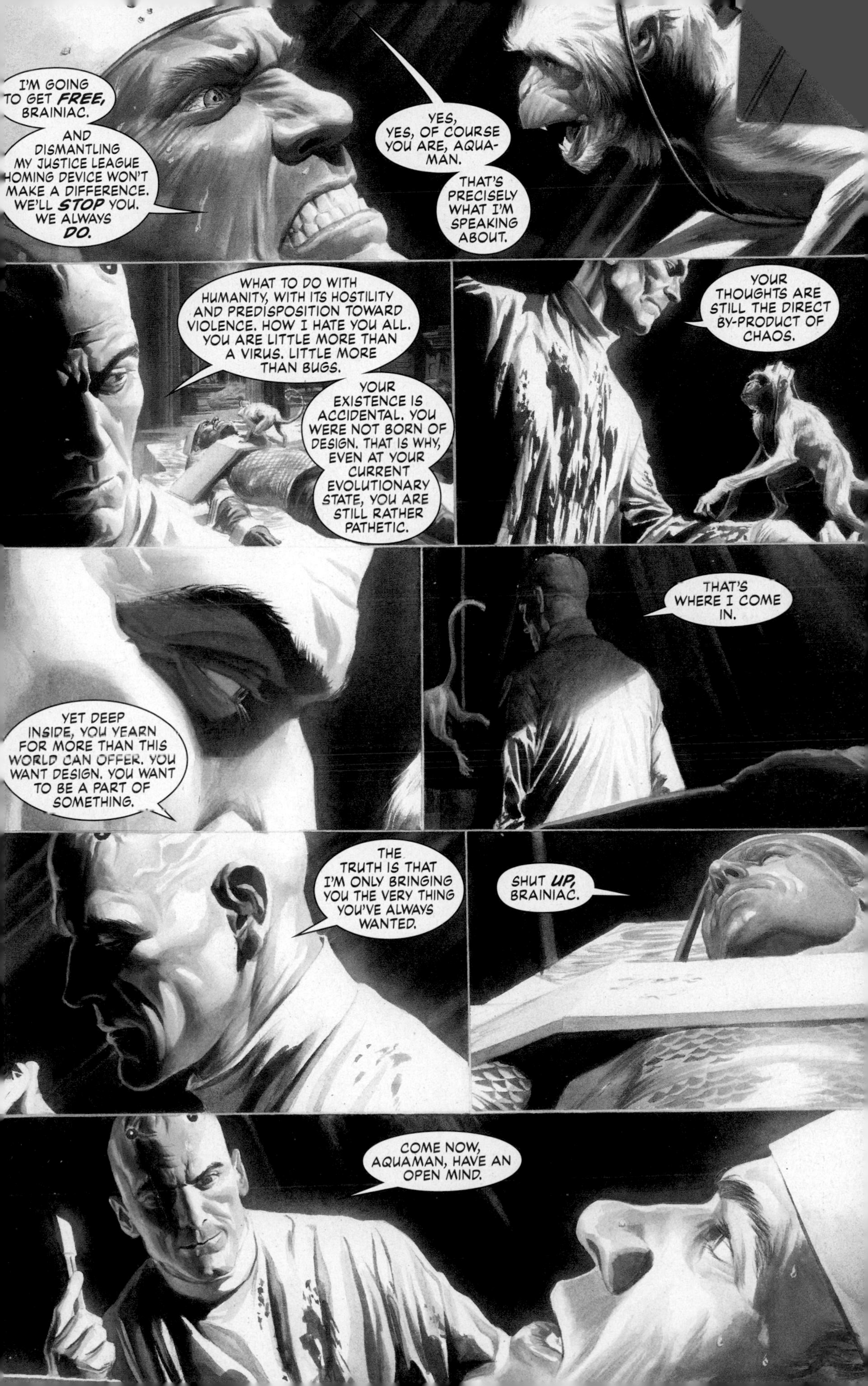
I'M GOING TO GET FREE, BRAINIAC.
AND DISMANTLING MY JUSTICE LEAGUE HOMING DEVICE WON'T MAKE A DIFFERENCE. WE'LL STOP YOU. WE ALWAYS DO.
YES, YES, OF COURSE YOU ARE, AQUA-MAN.
THAT'S PRECISELY WHAT I'M SPEAKING ABOUT.
WHAT TO DO WITH HUMANITY, WITH ITS HOSTILITY AND PREDISPOSITION TOWARD VIOLENCE. HOW I HATE YOU ALL. YOU ARE LITTLE MORE THAN A VIRUS. LITTLE MORE THAN BUGS.
YOUR EXISTENCE IS ACCIDENTAL. YOU WERE NOT BORN OF DESIGN. THAT IS WHY, EVEN AT YOUR CURRENT EVOLUTIONARY STATE, YOU ARE STILL RATHER PATHETIC.
YOUR THOUGHTS ARE STILL THE DIRECT BY-PRODUCT OF CHAOS.
YET DEEP INSIDE, YOU YEARN FOR MORE THAN THIS WORLD CAN OFFER. YOU WANT DESIGN. YOU WANT TO BE A PART OF SOMETHING.
THAT'S WHERE I COME IN.
THE TRUTH IS THAT I'M ONLY BRINGING YOU THE VERY THING YOU'VE ALWAYS WANTED.
SHUT UP, BRAINIAC.
COME NOW, AQUAMAN, HAVE AN OPEN MIND.

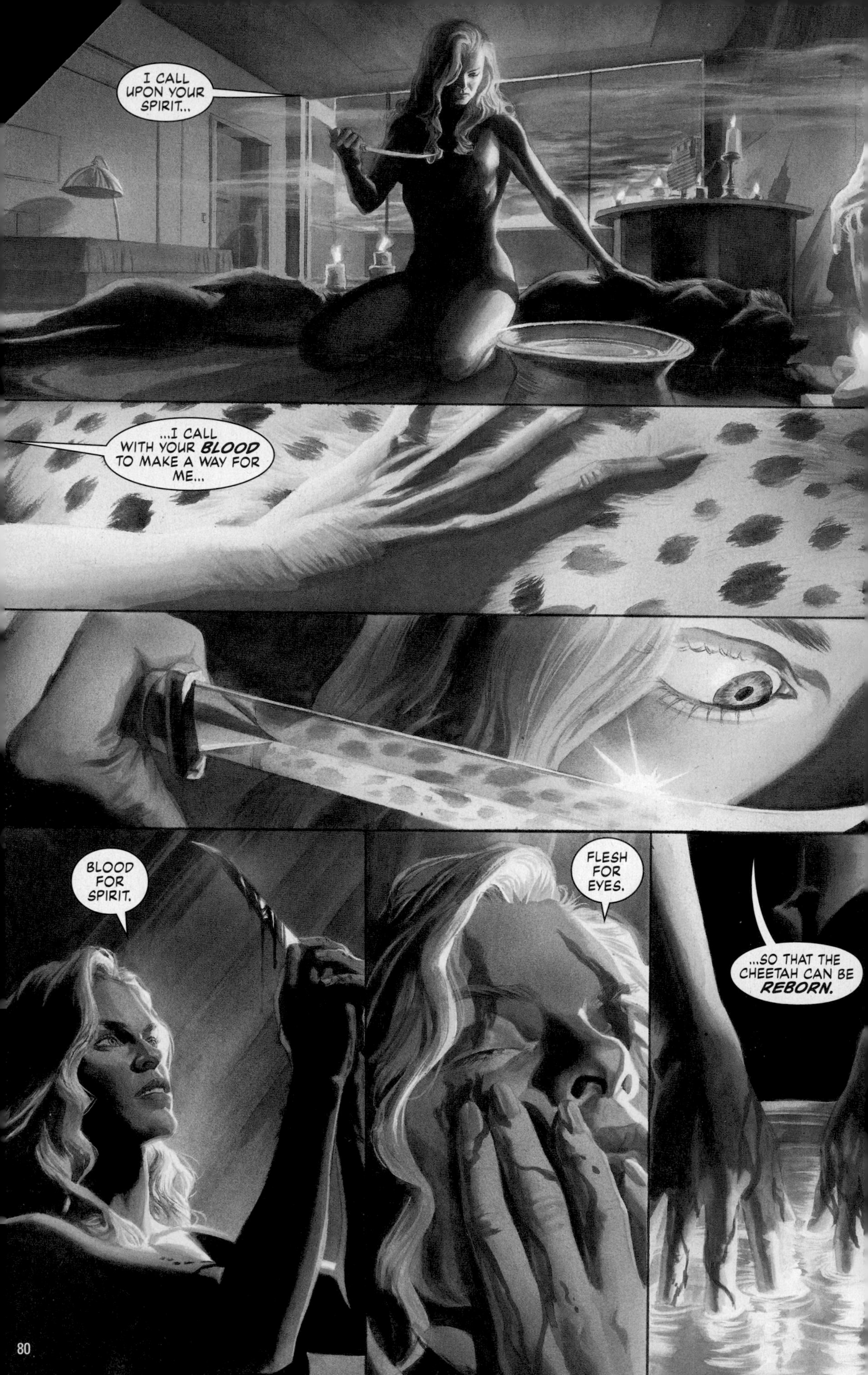
I CALL UPON YOUR SPIRIT...
...I CALL WITH YOUR *BLOOD* TO MAKE A WAY FOR ME...
BLOOD FOR SPIRIT.
FLESH FOR EYES.
...SO THAT THE CHEETAH CAN BE ***REBORN.***

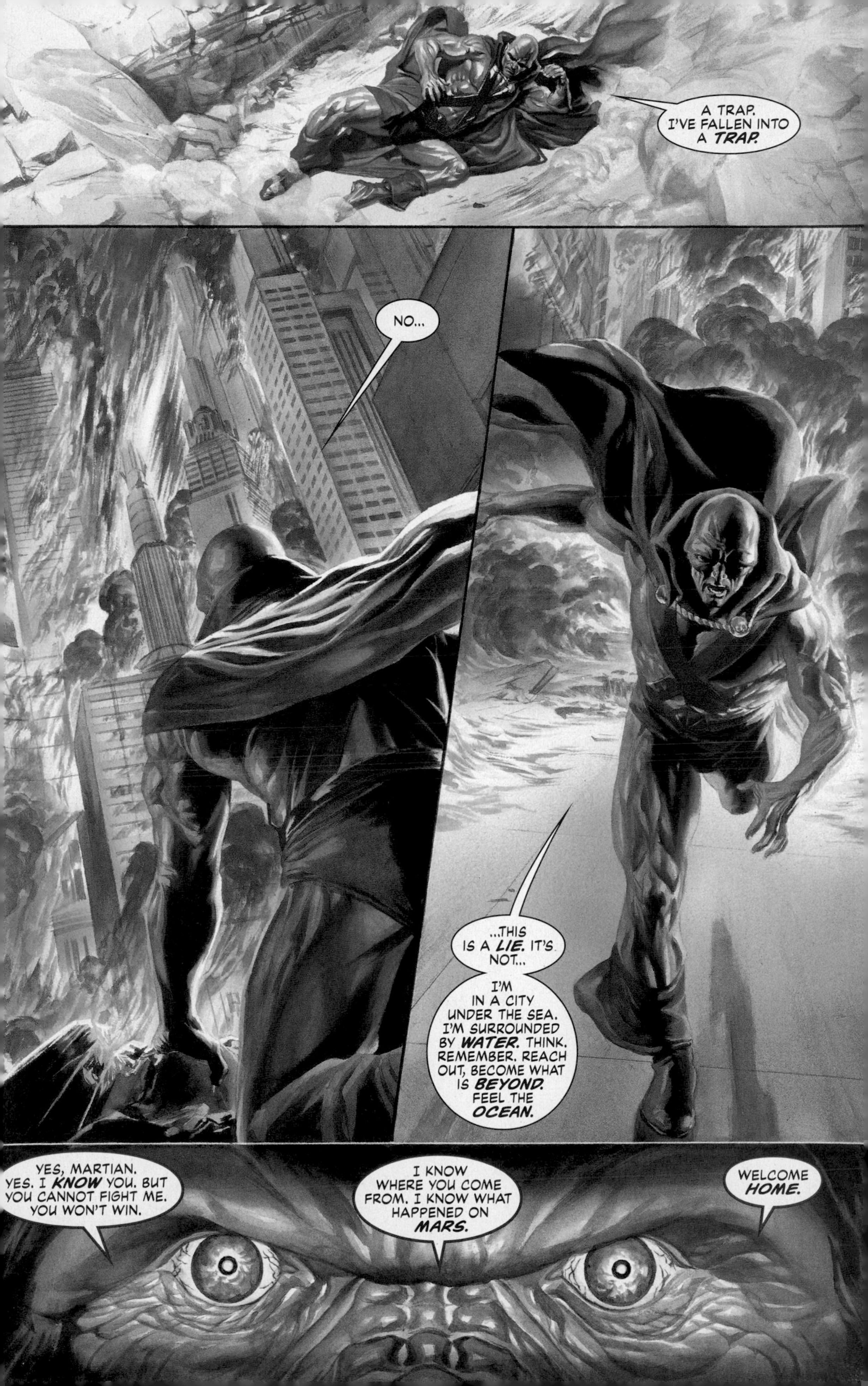
A TRAP. I'VE FALLEN INTO A *TRAP.*
NO...
...THIS IS A *LIE.* IT'S NOT...
I'M IN A CITY UNDER THE SEA. I'M SURROUNDED BY *WATER.* THINK. REMEMBER. REACH OUT, BECOME WHAT IS *BEYOND.* FEEL THE *OCEAN.*
YES, MARTIAN. YES. I *KNOW* YOU. BUT YOU CANNOT FIGHT ME. YOU WON'T WIN.
I KNOW WHERE YOU COME FROM. I KNOW WHAT HAPPENED ON *MARS.*
WELCOME *HOME.*

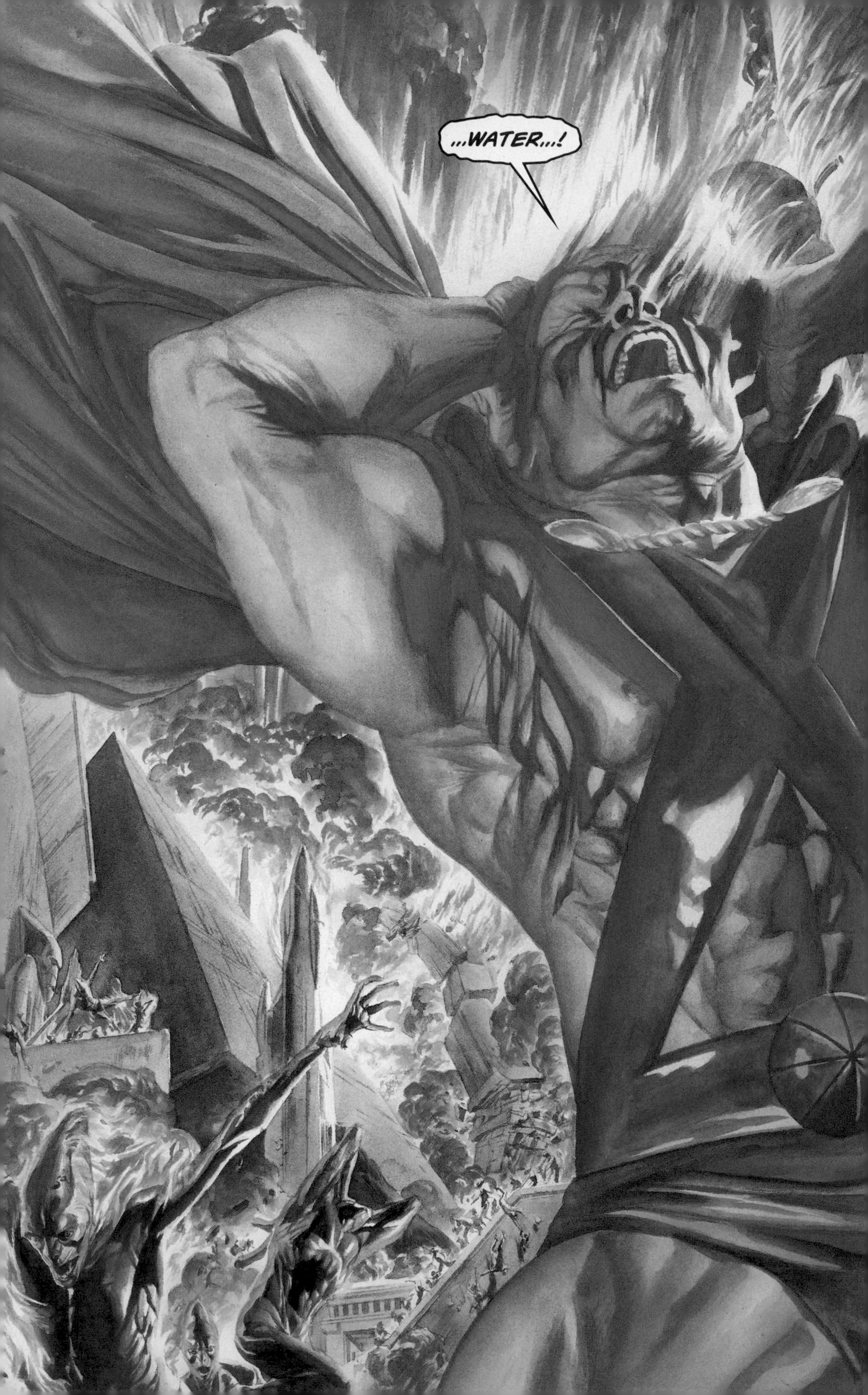
...WATER...!

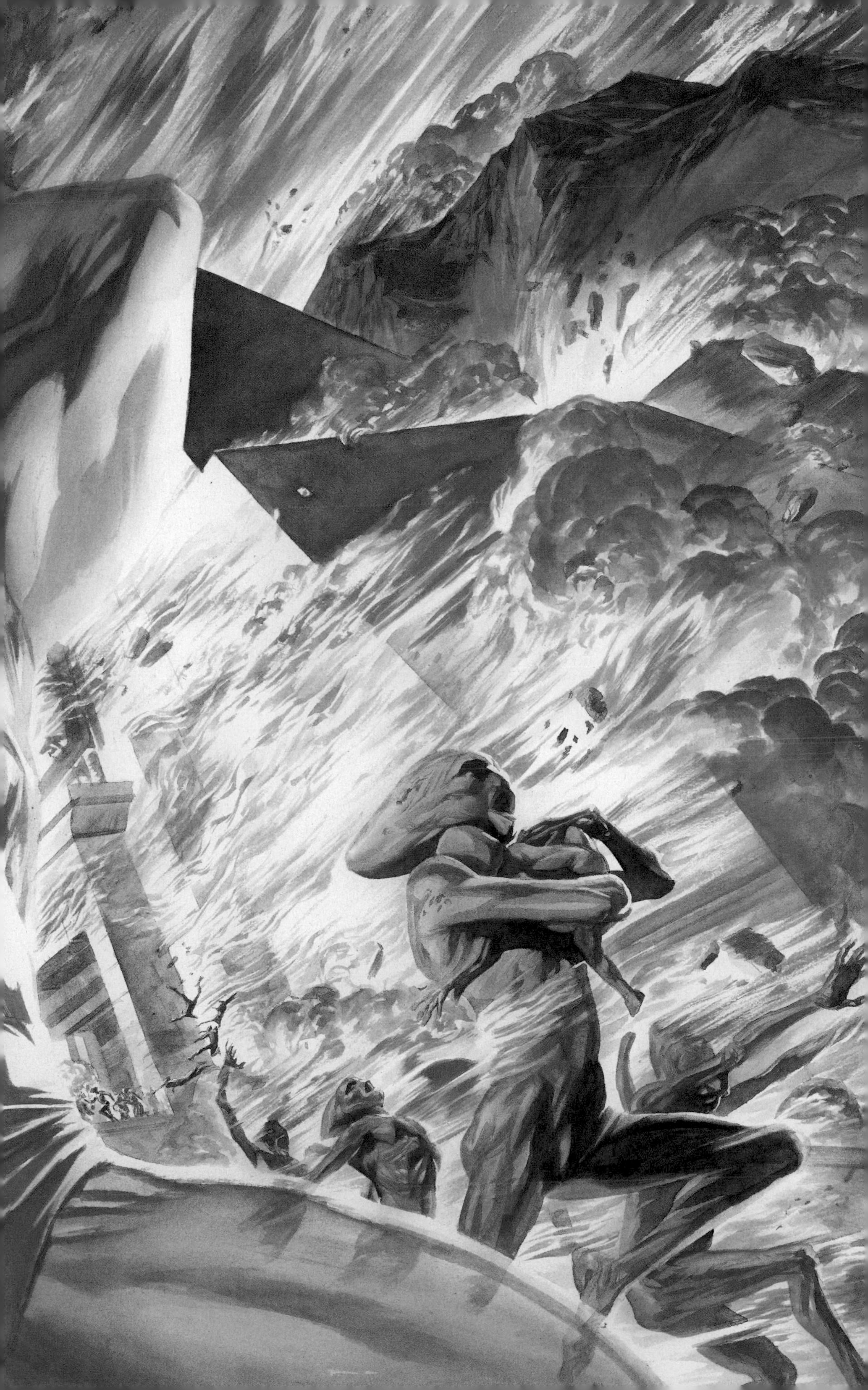

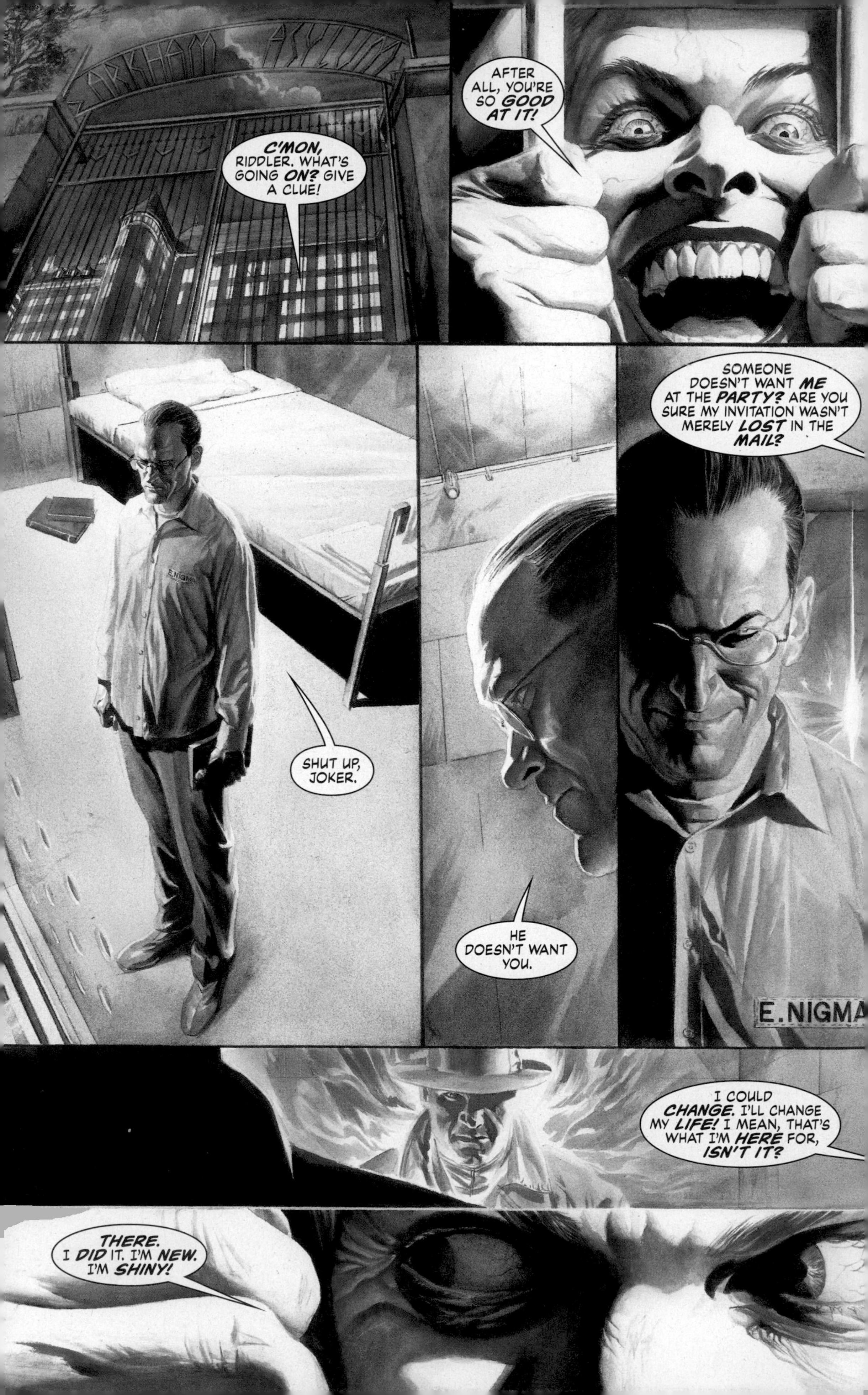
ARKHAM ASYLUM
C'MON, RIDDLER. WHAT'S GOING ON? GIVE A CLUE!
AFTER ALL, YOU'RE SO GOOD AT IT!
E.NIGMA
SHUT UP, JOKER.
SOMEONE DOESN'T WANT ME AT THE PARTY? ARE YOU SURE MY INVITATION WASN'T MERELY LOST IN THE MAIL?
HE DOESN'T WANT YOU.
E.NIGMA
I COULD CHANGE. I'LL CHANGE MY LIFE! I MEAN, THAT'S WHAT I'M HERE FOR, ISN'T IT?
THERE. I DID IT. I'M NEW. I'M SHINY!

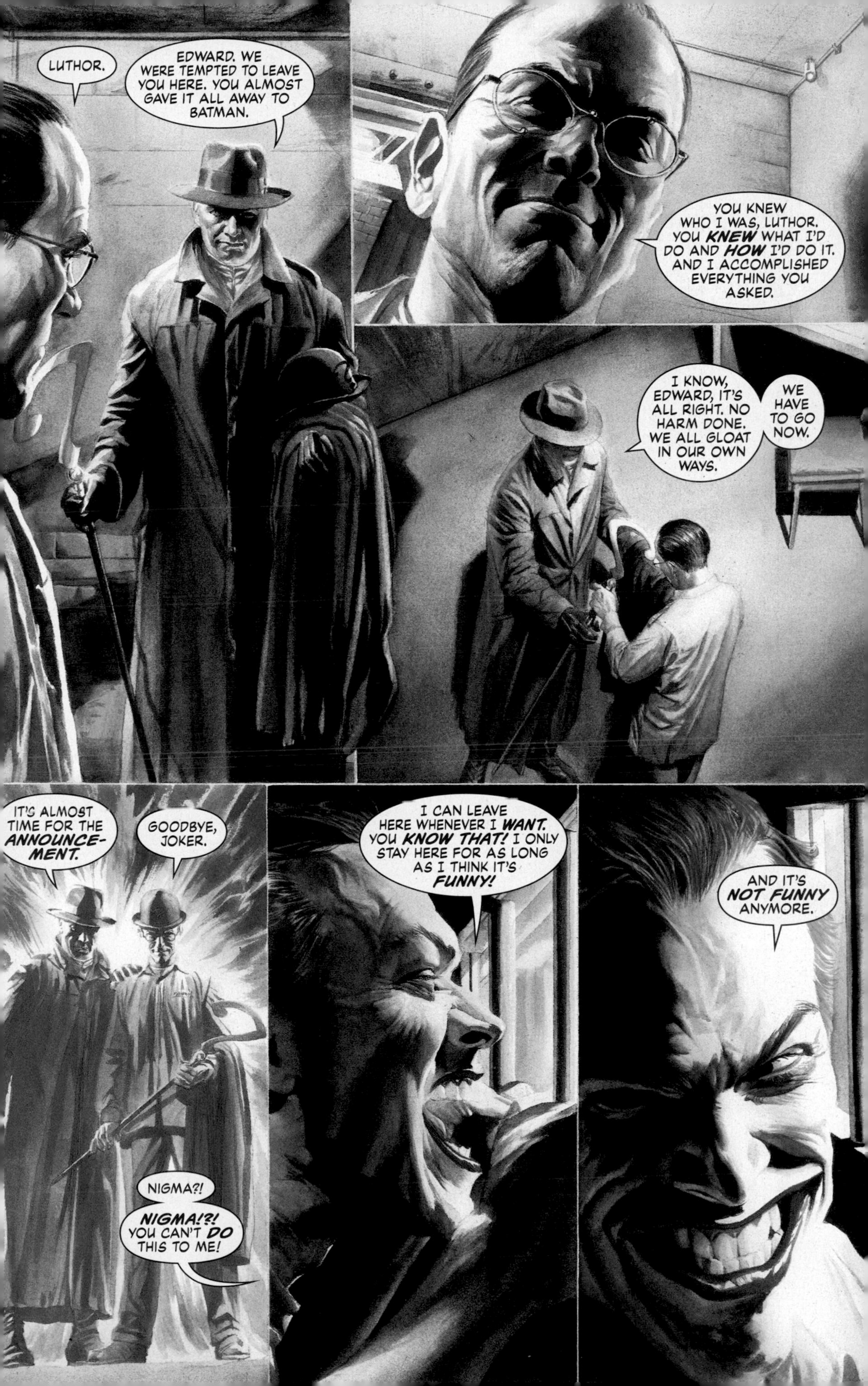
LUTHOR.
EDWARD. WE WERE TEMPTED TO LEAVE YOU HERE. YOU ALMOST GAVE IT ALL AWAY TO BATMAN.
YOU KNEW WHO I WAS, LUTHOR. YOU KNEW WHAT I'D DO AND HOW I'D DO IT. AND I ACCOMPLISHED EVERYTHING YOU ASKED.
I KNOW, EDWARD, IT'S ALL RIGHT. NO HARM DONE. WE ALL GLOAT IN OUR OWN WAYS.
WE HAVE TO GO NOW.
IT'S ALMOST TIME FOR THE ANNOUNCE-MENT.
GOODBYE, JOKER.
NIGMA?!
NIGMA!?! YOU CAN'T DO THIS TO ME!
I CAN LEAVE HERE WHENEVER I WANT. YOU KNOW THAT! I ONLY STAY HERE FOR AS LONG AS I THINK IT'S FUNNY!
AND IT'S NOT FUNNY ANYMORE.

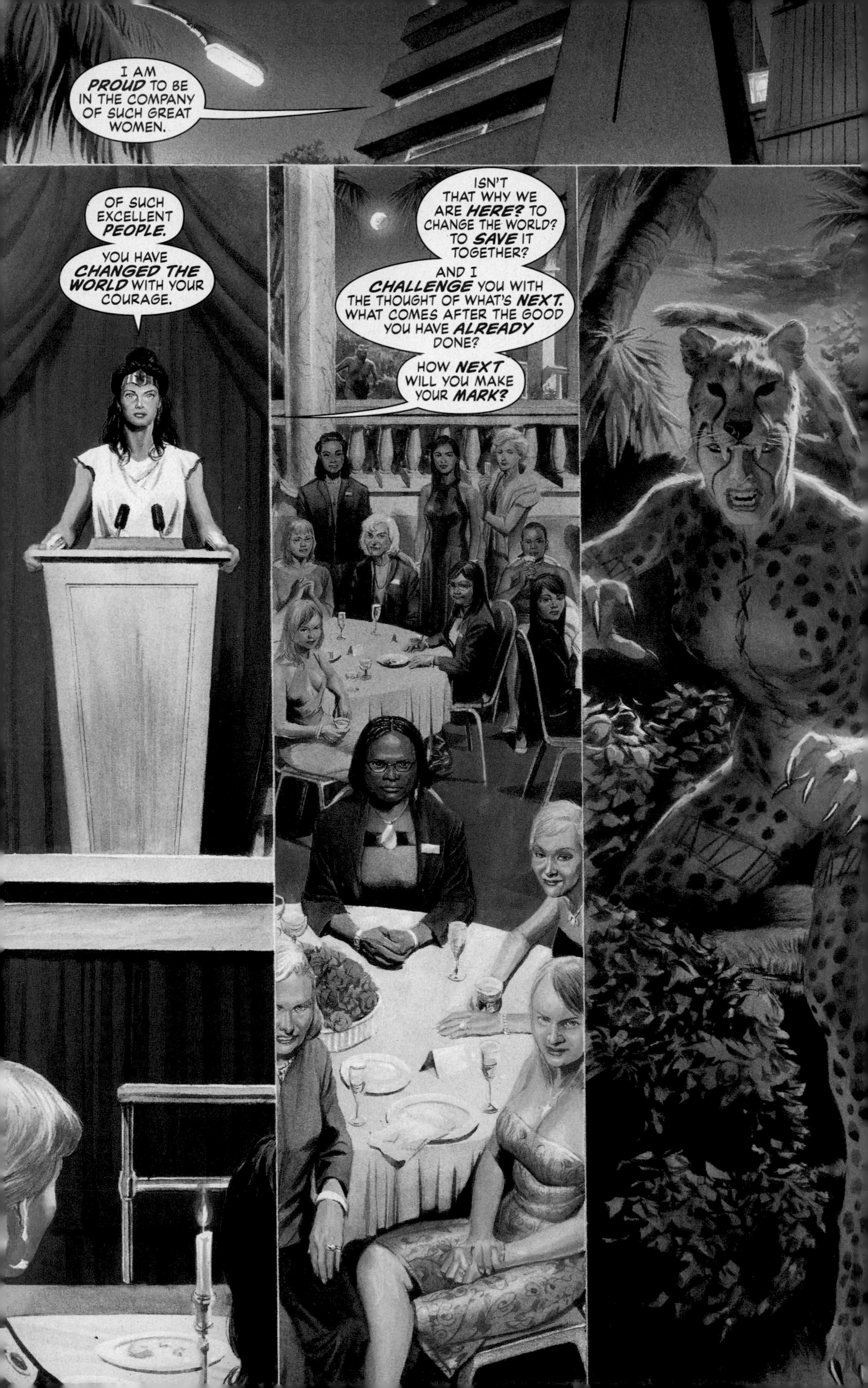
I AM PROUD TO BE IN THE COMPANY OF SUCH GREAT WOMEN.
OF SUCH EXCELLENT PEOPLE.
YOU HAVE CHANGED THE WORLD WITH YOUR COURAGE.
ISN'T THAT WHY WE ARE HERE? TO CHANGE THE WORLD? TO SAVE IT TOGETHER?
AND I CHALLENGE YOU WITH THE THOUGHT OF WHAT'S NEXT. WHAT COMES AFTER THE GOOD YOU HAVE ALREADY DONE?
HOW NEXT WILL YOU MAKE YOUR MARK?

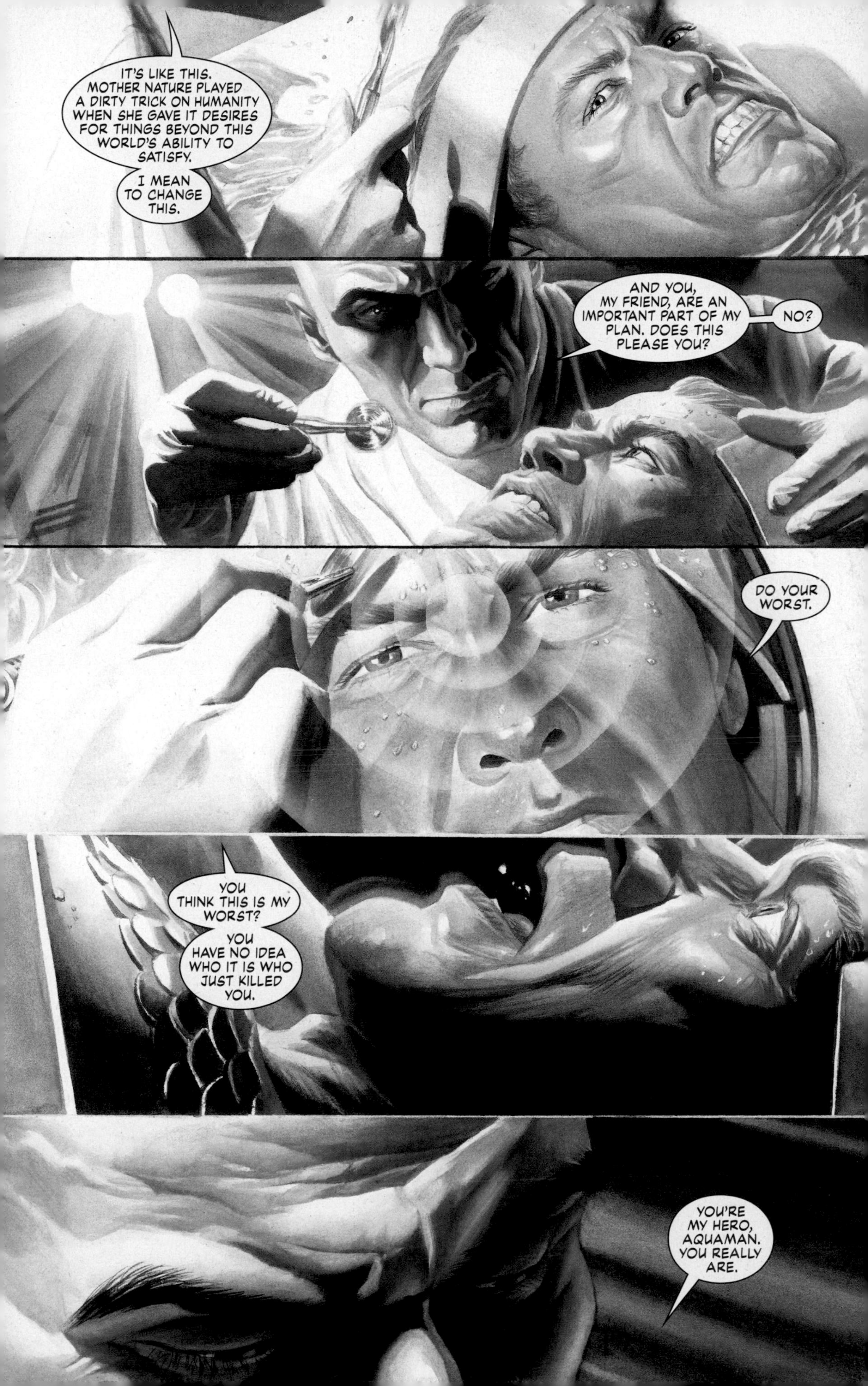
IT'S LIKE THIS. MOTHER NATURE PLAYED A DIRTY TRICK ON HUMANITY WHEN SHE GAVE IT DESIRES FOR THINGS BEYOND THIS WORLD'S ABILITY TO SATISFY.
I MEAN TO CHANGE THIS.
AND YOU, MY FRIEND, ARE AN IMPORTANT PART OF MY PLAN. DOES THIS PLEASE YOU?
NO?
DO YOUR WORST.
YOU THINK THIS IS MY WORST?
YOU HAVE NO IDEA WHO IT IS WHO JUST KILLED YOU.
YOU'RE MY HERO, AQUAMAN. YOU REALLY ARE.

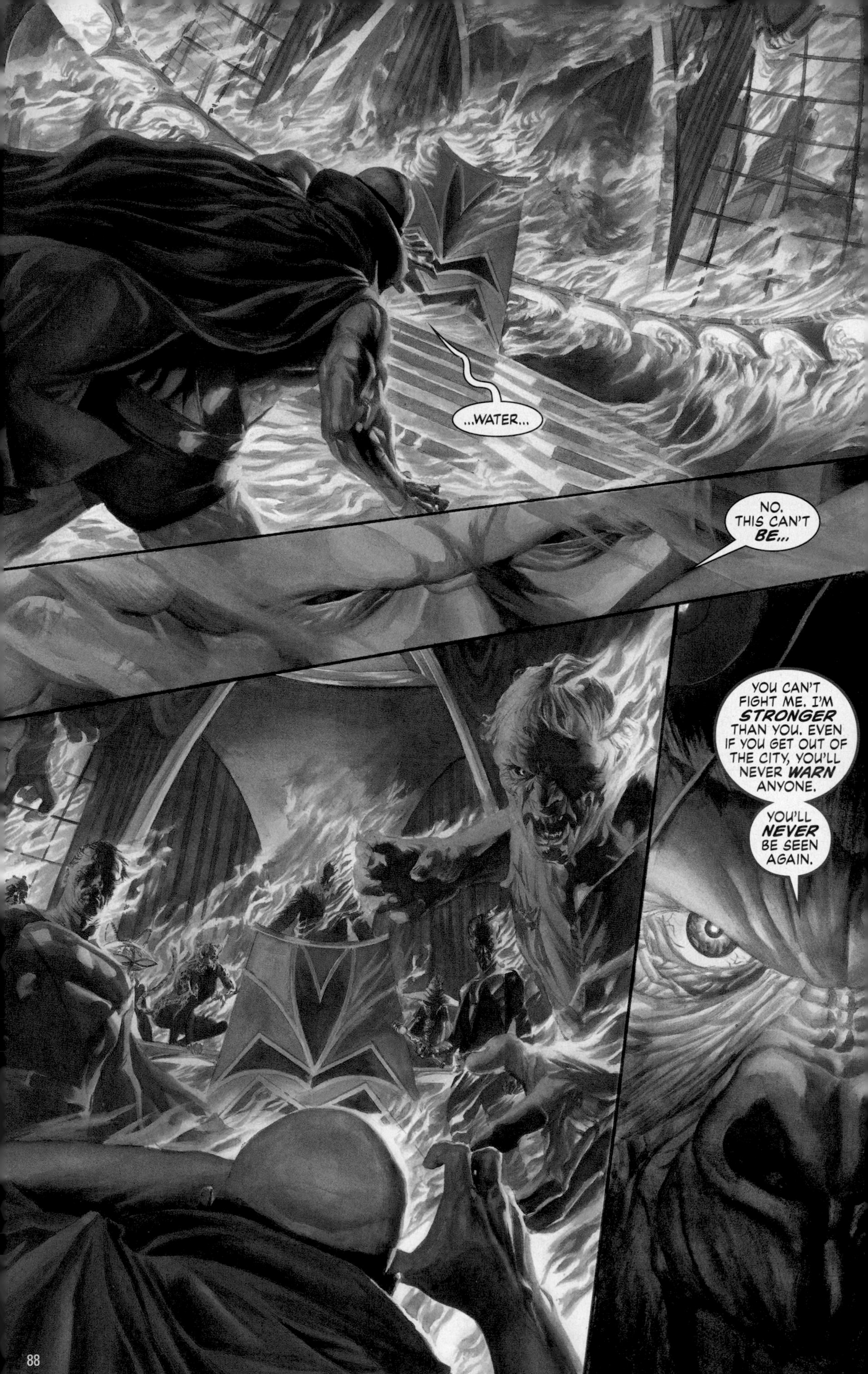
...WATER...
NO. THIS CAN'T BE...
YOU CAN'T FIGHT ME. I'M STRONGER THAN YOU. EVEN IF YOU GET OUT OF THE CITY, YOU'LL NEVER WARN ANYONE.
YOU'LL NEVER BE SEEN AGAIN.

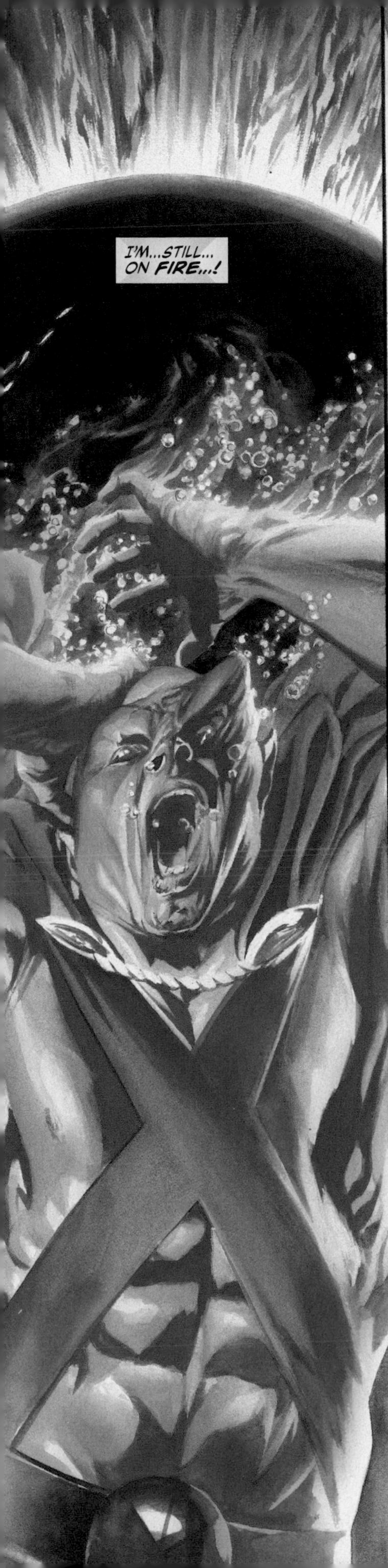
I'M...STILL...
ON FIRE...!
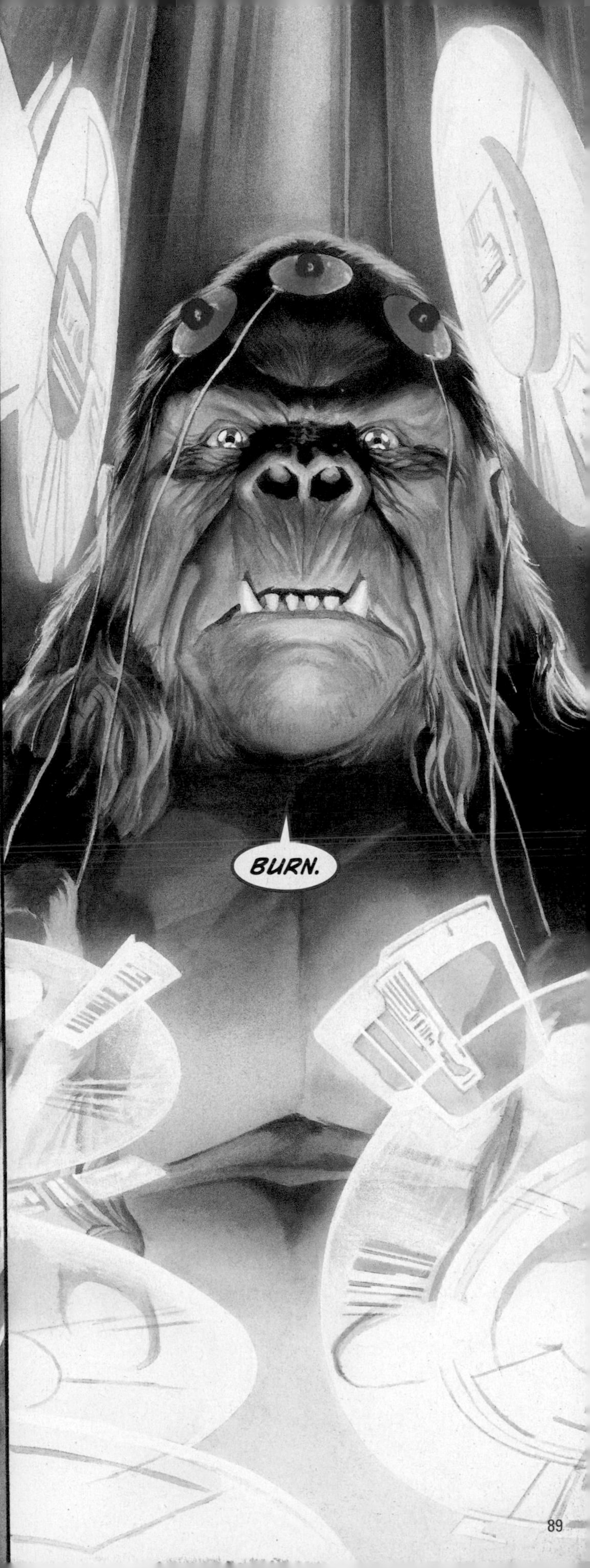
BURN.

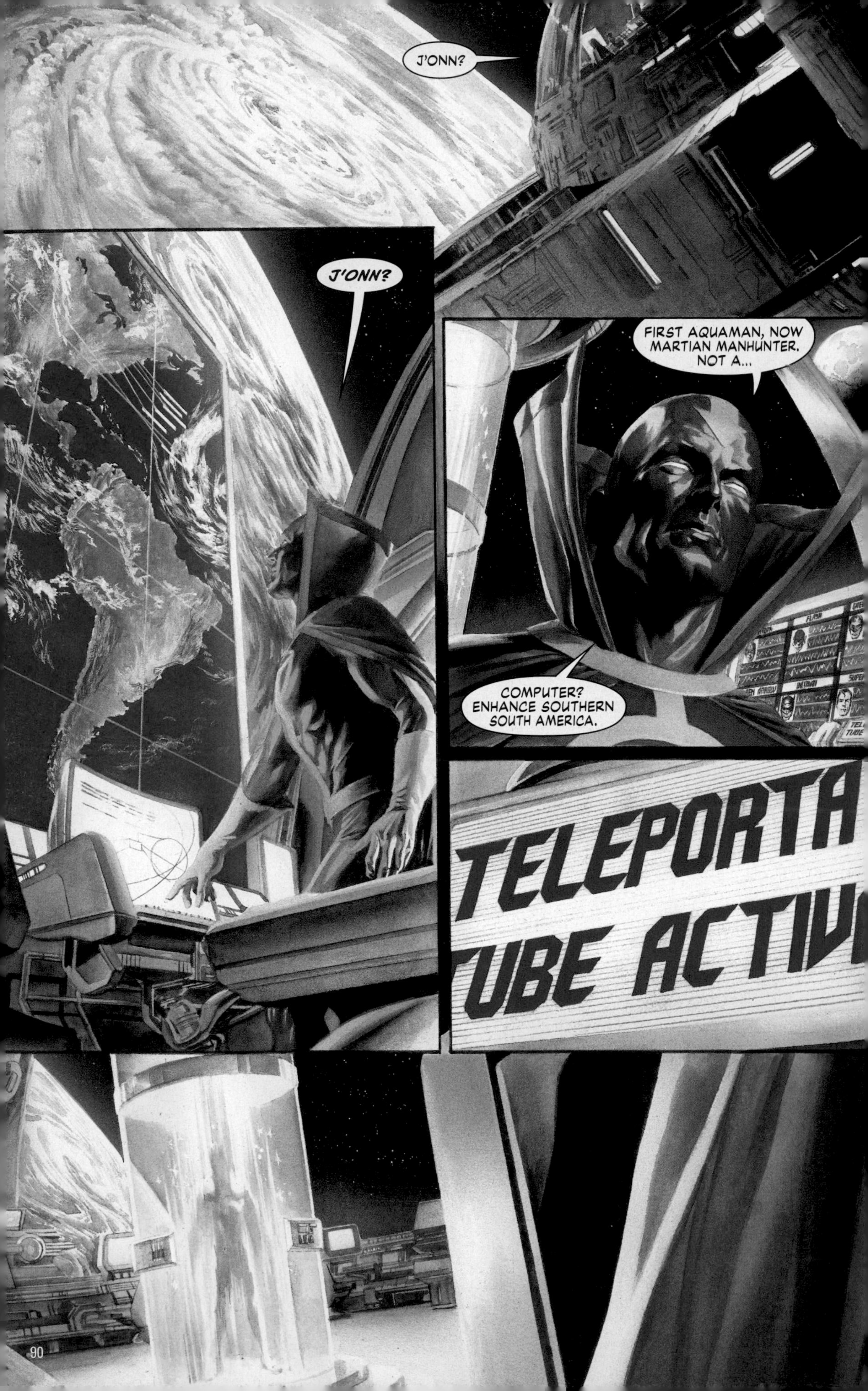
J'ONN?
J'ONN?
FIRST AQUAMAN, NOW MARTIAN MANHUNTER. NOT A...
COMPUTER? ENHANCE SOUTHERN SOUTH AMERICA.
TELEPORTA
TUBE ACTIV

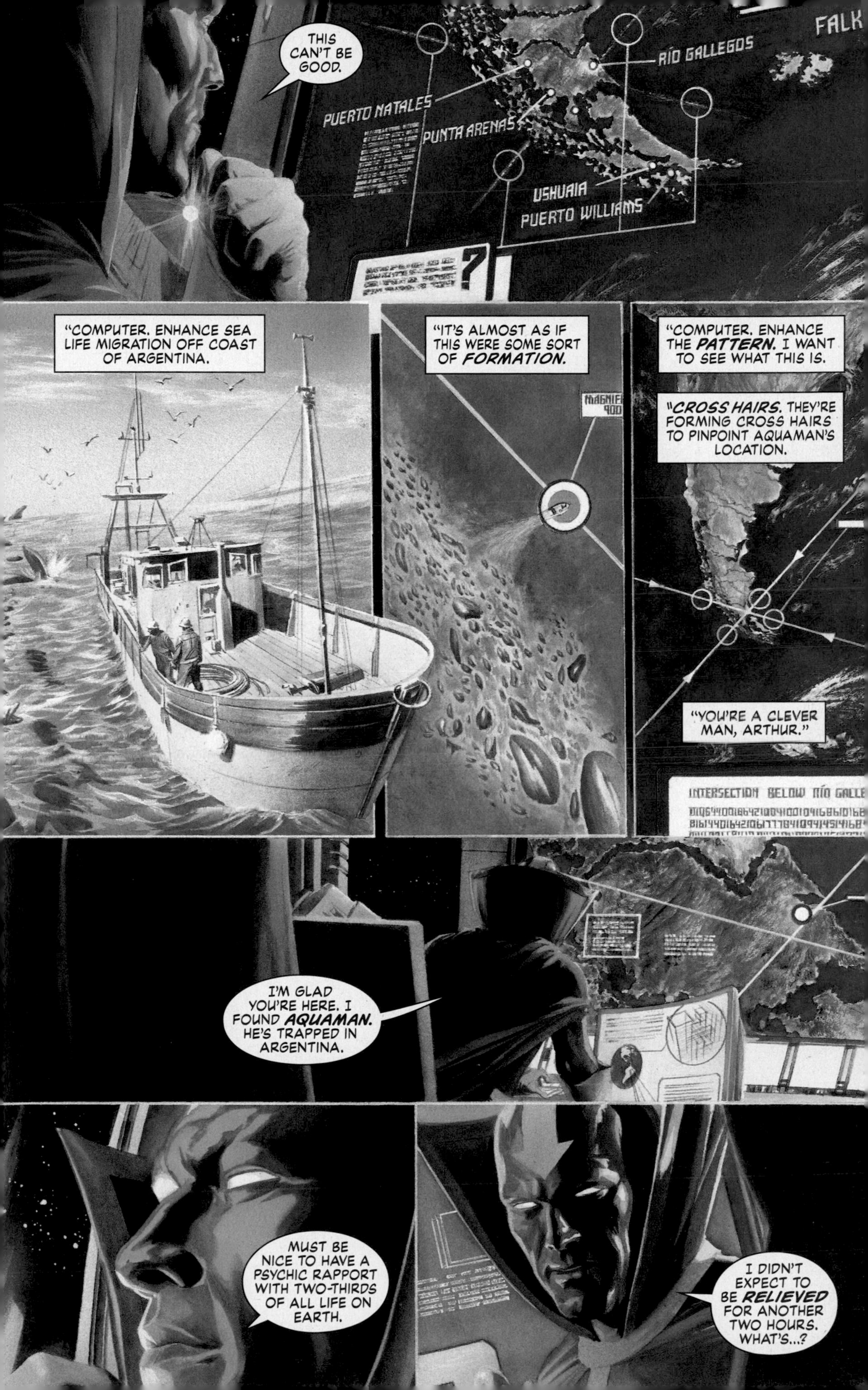

THIS CAN'T BE GOOD.
FALK
RÍO GALLEGOS
PUERTO NATALES
PUNTA ARENAS
USHUAIA
PUERTO WILLIAMS
?
"COMPUTER. ENHANCE SEA LIFE MIGRATION OFF COAST OF ARGENTINA.
"IT'S ALMOST AS IF THIS WERE SOME SORT OF FORMATION.
"COMPUTER. ENHANCE THE PATTERN. I WANT TO SEE WHAT THIS IS.
"CROSS HAIRS. THEY'RE FORMING CROSS HAIRS TO PINPOINT AQUAMAN'S LOCATION.
"YOU'RE A CLEVER MAN, ARTHUR."
INTERSECTION BELOW RÍO GALLE
I'M GLAD YOU'RE HERE. I FOUND AQUAMAN. HE'S TRAPPED IN ARGENTINA.
MUST BE NICE TO HAVE A PSYCHIC RAPPORT WITH TWO-THIRDS OF ALL LIFE ON EARTH.
I DIDN'T EXPECT TO BE RELIEVED FOR ANOTHER TWO HOURS. WHAT'S...?

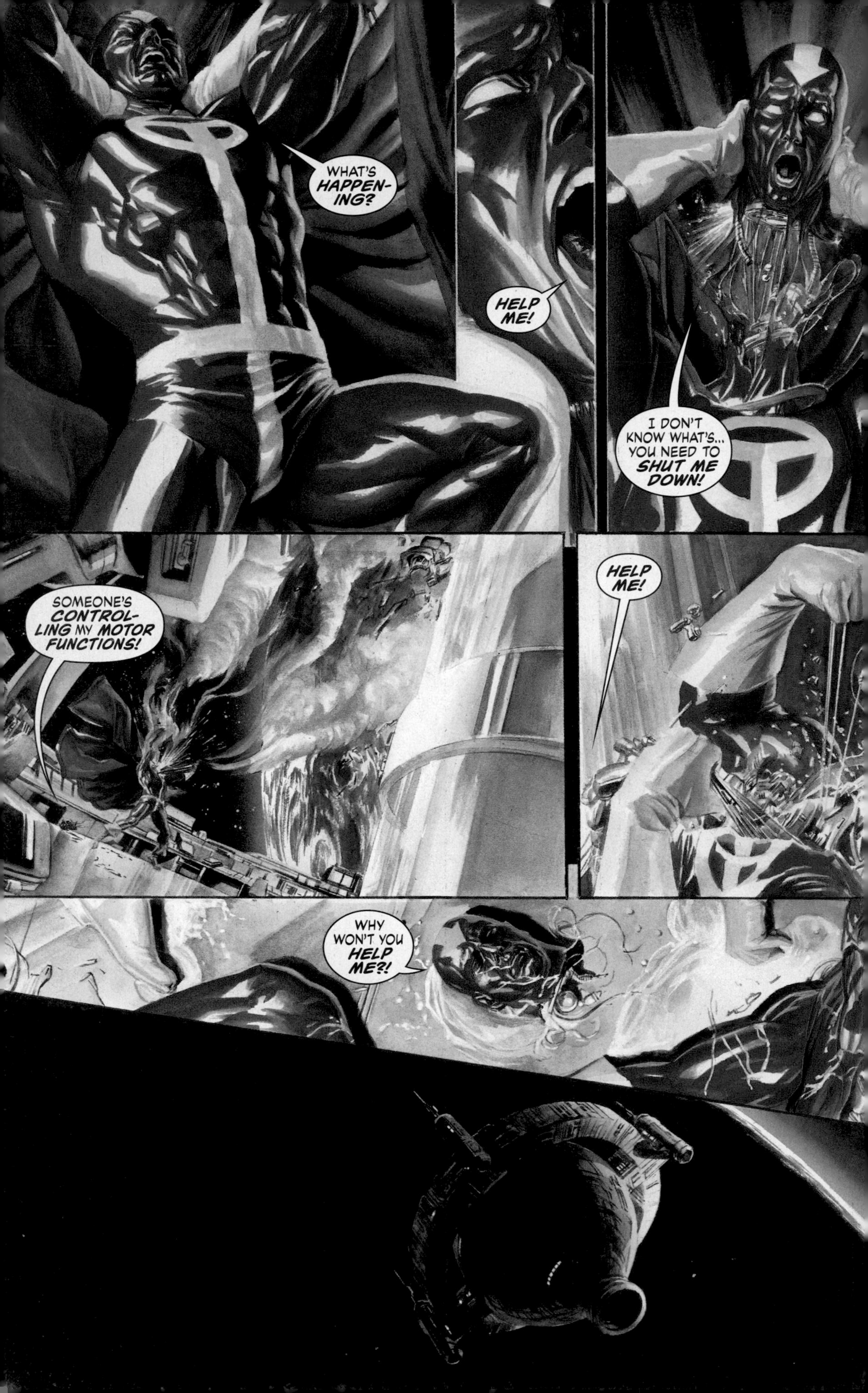
WHAT'S HAPPEN-ING?
HELP ME!
I DON'T KNOW WHAT'S... YOU NEED TO SHUT ME DOWN!
SOMEONE'S CONTROL-LING MY MOTOR FUNCTIONS!
HELP ME!
WHY WON'T YOU HELP ME?!

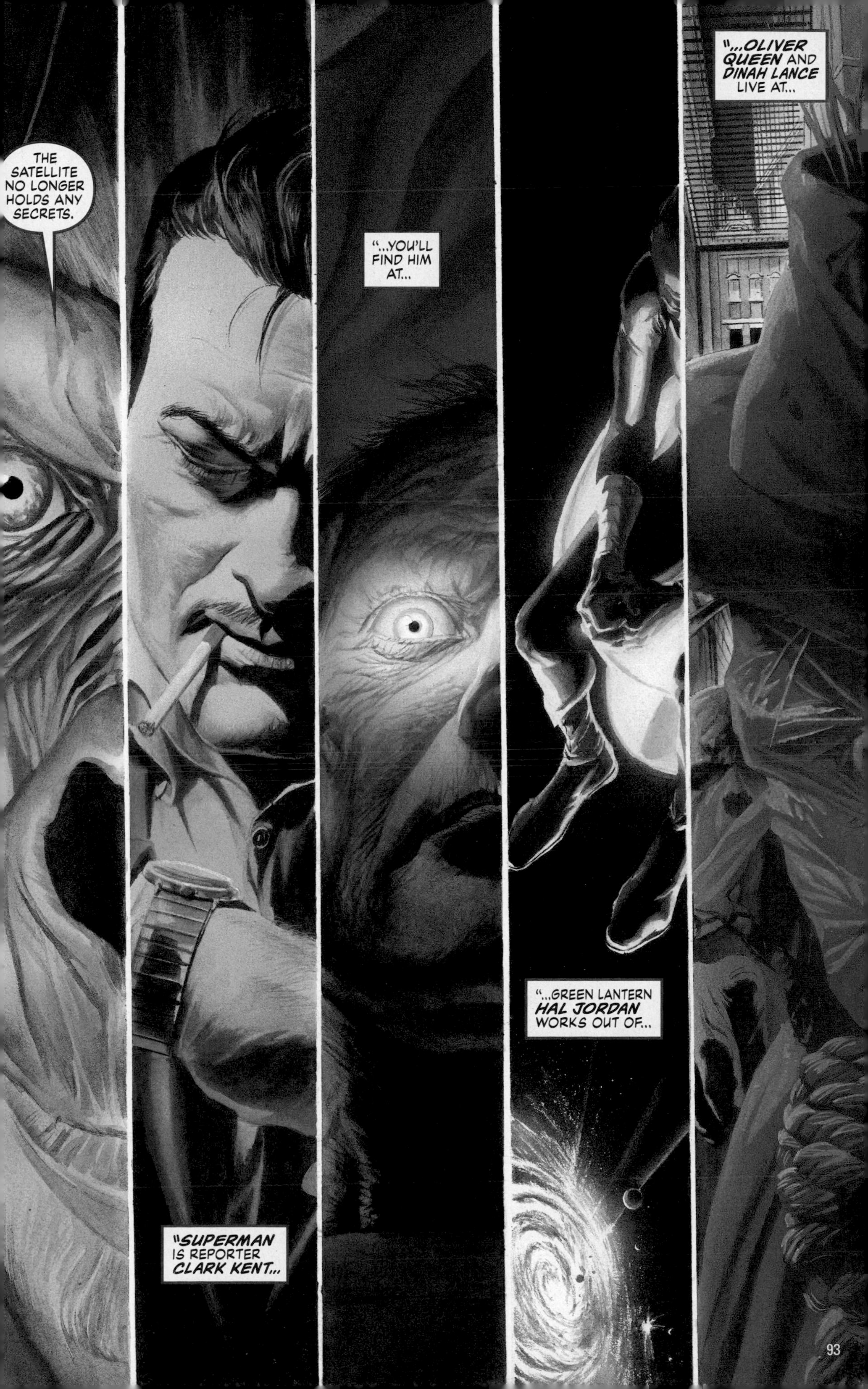
THE SATELLITE NO LONGER HOLDS ANY SECRETS.
"SUPERMAN IS REPORTER CLARK KENT...
"...YOU'LL FIND HIM AT...
"...GREEN LANTERN HAL JORDAN WORKS OUT OF...
"...OLIVER QUEEN AND DINAH LANCE LIVE AT...

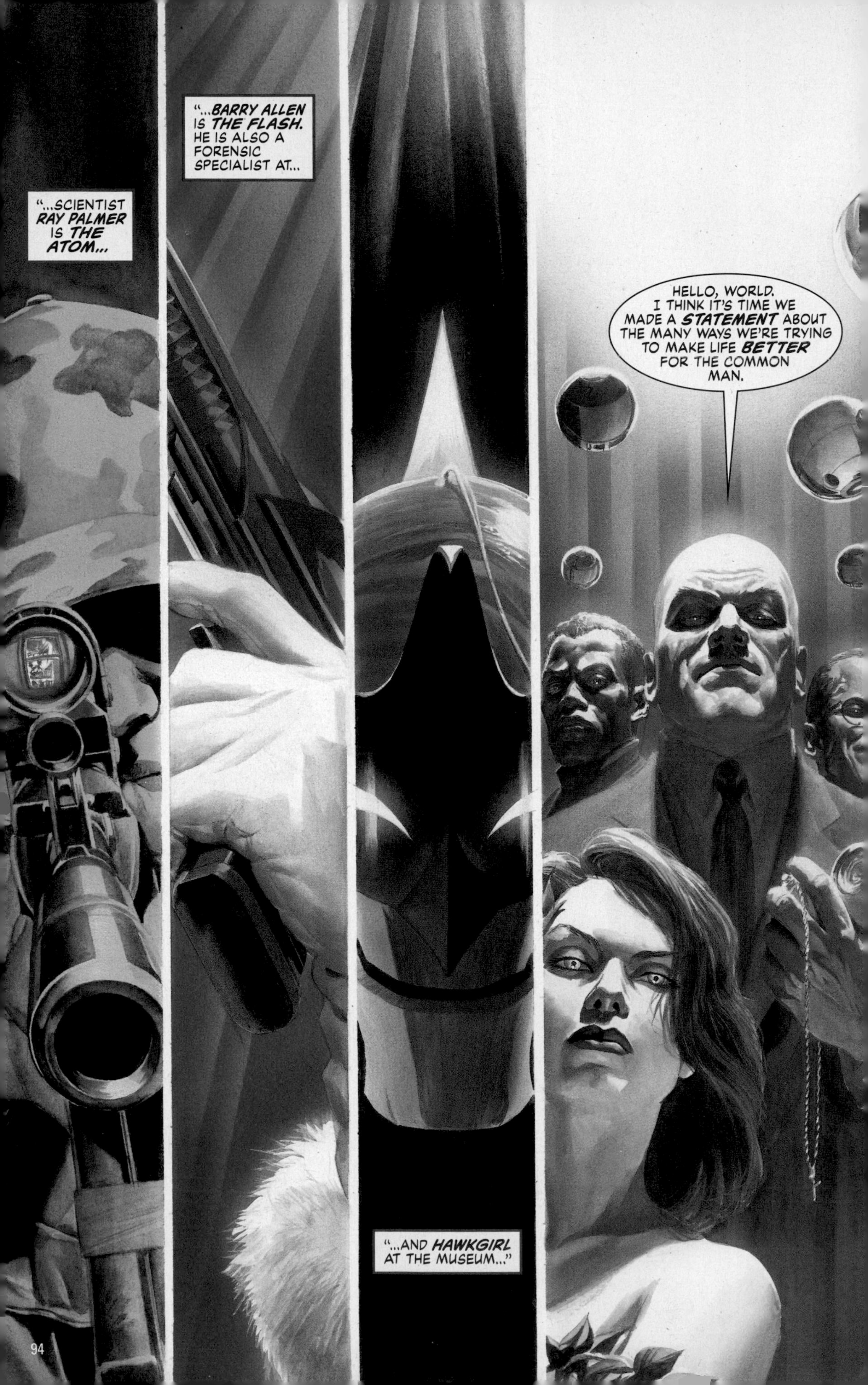
"...SCIENTIST RAY PALMER IS THE ATOM...
"...BARRY ALLEN IS THE FLASH. HE IS ALSO A FORENSIC SPECIALIST AT...
"...AND HAWKGIRL AT THE MUSEUM..."
HELLO, WORLD. I THINK IT'S TIME WE MADE A STATEMENT ABOUT THE MANY WAYS WE'RE TRYING TO MAKE LIFE BETTER FOR THE COMMON MAN.

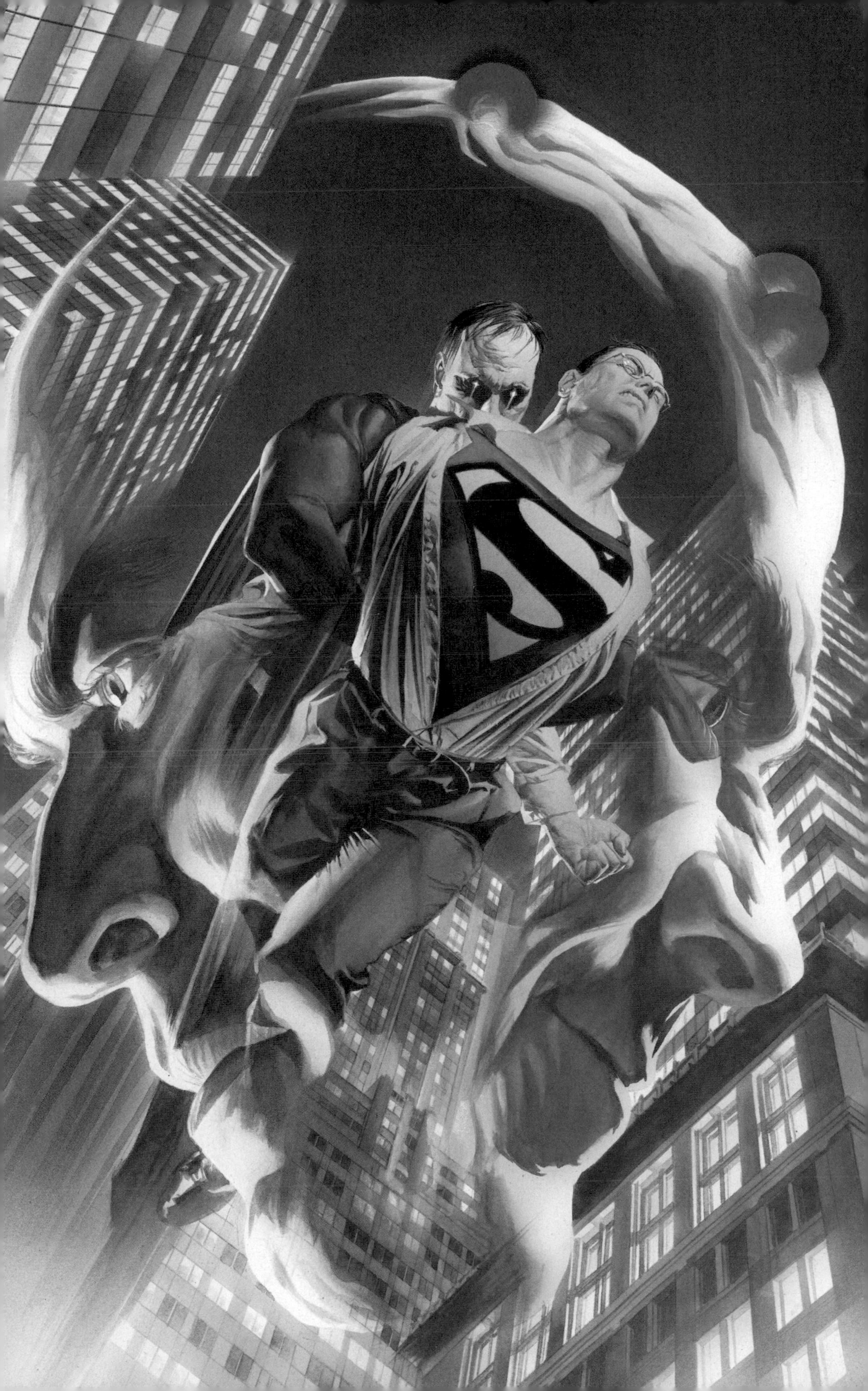

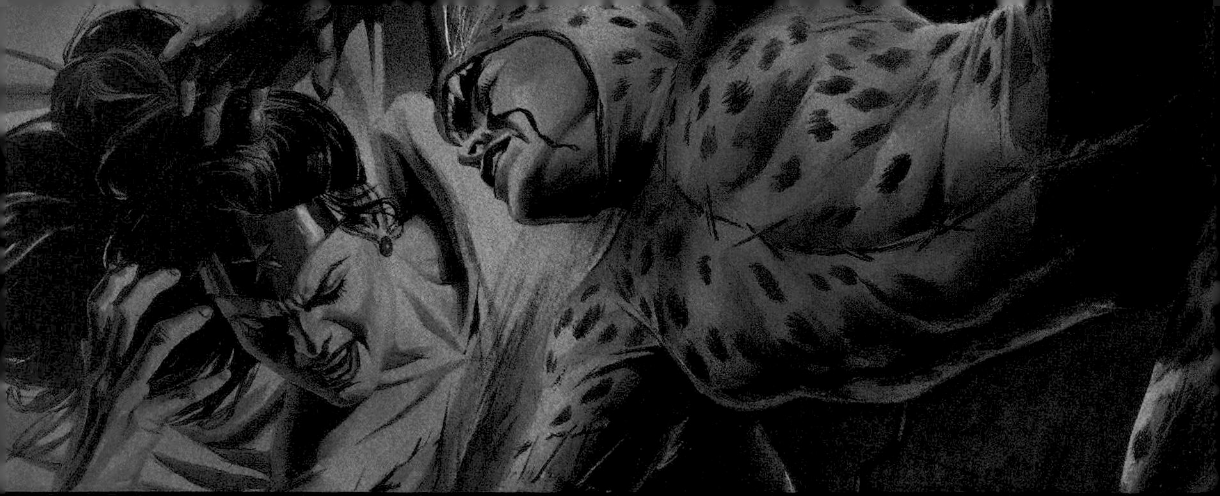

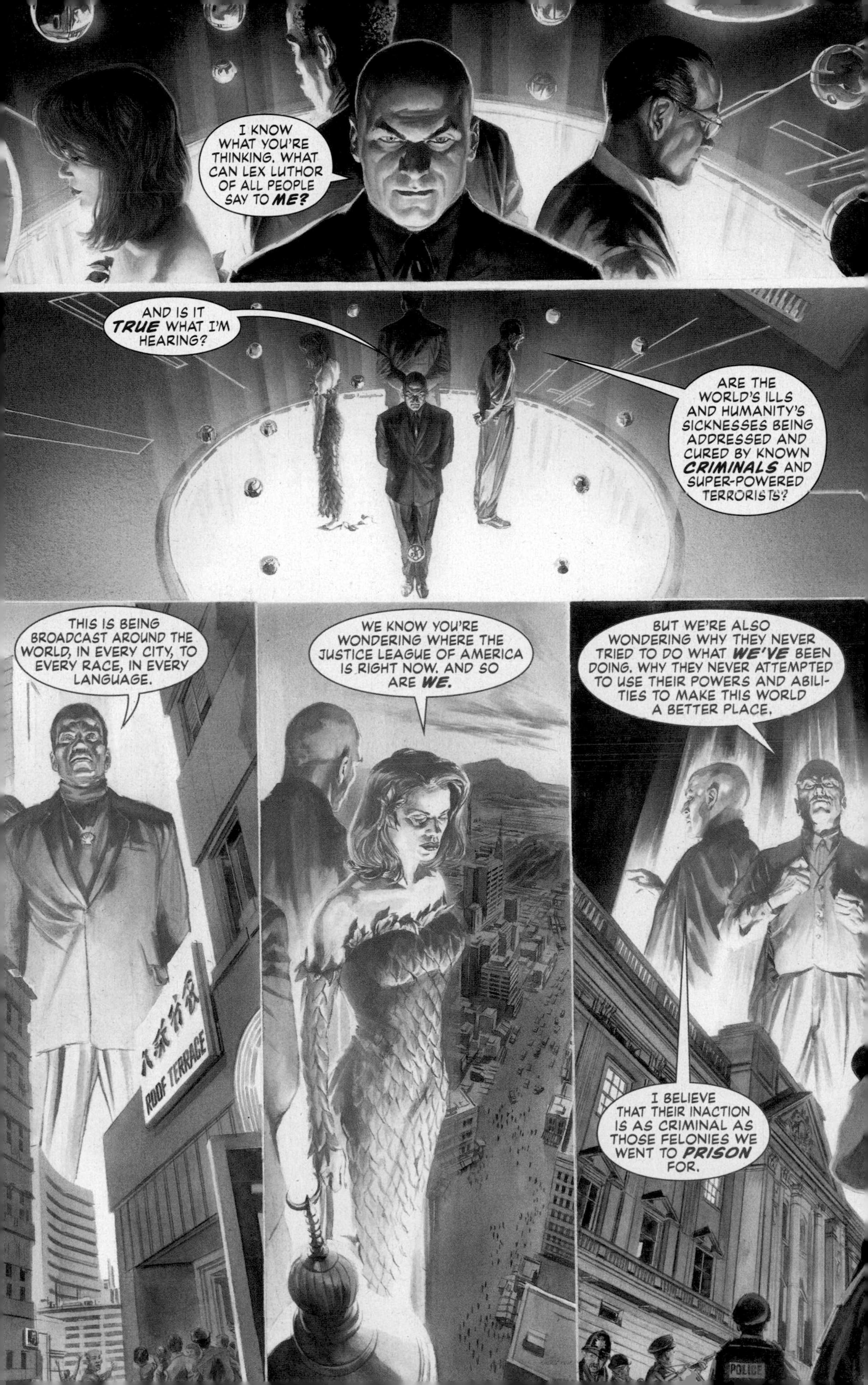
I KNOW WHAT YOU'RE THINKING. WHAT CAN LEX LUTHOR OF ALL PEOPLE SAY TO ME?
AND IS IT TRUE WHAT I'M HEARING?
ARE THE WORLD'S ILLS AND HUMANITY'S SICKNESSES BEING ADDRESSED AND CURED BY KNOWN CRIMINALS AND SUPER-POWERED TERRORISTS?
THIS IS BEING BROADCAST AROUND THE WORLD, IN EVERY CITY, TO EVERY RACE, IN EVERY LANGUAGE.
ROOF TERRACE
WE KNOW YOU'RE WONDERING WHERE THE JUSTICE LEAGUE OF AMERICA IS RIGHT NOW. AND SO ARE WE.
BUT WE'RE ALSO WONDERING WHY THEY NEVER TRIED TO DO WHAT WE'VE BEEN DOING. WHY THEY NEVER ATTEMPTED TO USE THEIR POWERS AND ABILITIES TO MAKE THIS WORLD A BETTER PLACE.
I BELIEVE THAT THEIR INACTION IS AS CRIMINAL AS THOSE FELONIES WE WENT TO PRISON FOR.
POLICE

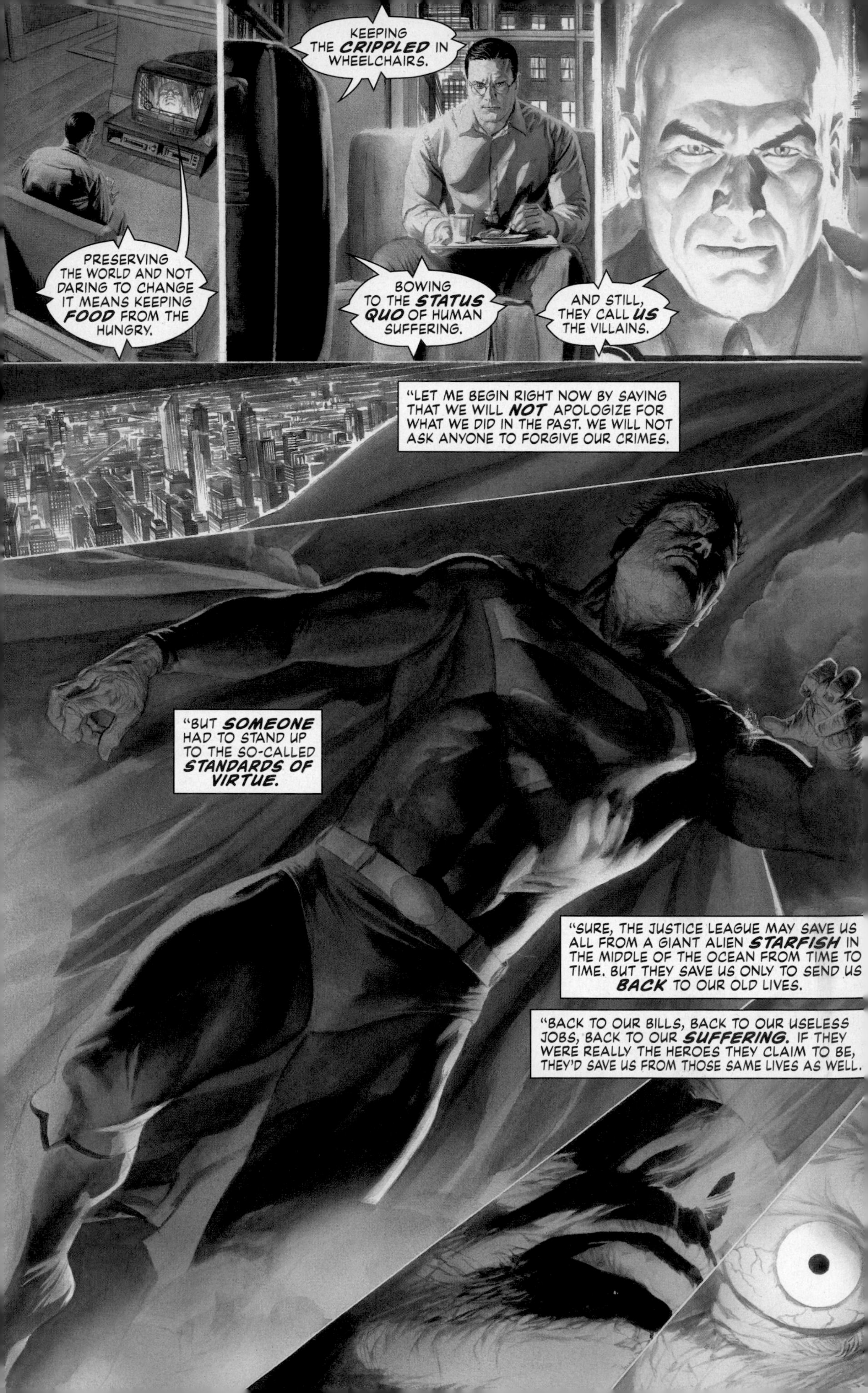
PRESERVING THE WORLD AND NOT DARING TO CHANGE IT MEANS KEEPING FOOD FROM THE HUNGRY.
KEEPING THE CRIPPLED IN WHEELCHAIRS.
BOWING TO THE STATUS QUO OF HUMAN SUFFERING.
AND STILL, THEY CALL US THE VILLAINS.
"LET ME BEGIN RIGHT NOW BY SAYING THAT WE WILL NOT APOLOGIZE FOR WHAT WE DID IN THE PAST. WE WILL NOT ASK ANYONE TO FORGIVE OUR CRIMES.
"BUT SOMEONE HAD TO STAND UP TO THE SO-CALLED STANDARDS OF VIRTUE.
"SURE, THE JUSTICE LEAGUE MAY SAVE US ALL FROM A GIANT ALIEN STARFISH IN THE MIDDLE OF THE OCEAN FROM TIME TO TIME. BUT THEY SAVE US ONLY TO SEND US BACK TO OUR OLD LIVES.
"BACK TO OUR BILLS, BACK TO OUR USELESS JOBS, BACK TO OUR SUFFERING. IF THEY WERE REALLY THE HEROES THEY CLAIM TO BE, THEY'D SAVE US FROM THOSE SAME LIVES AS WELL.

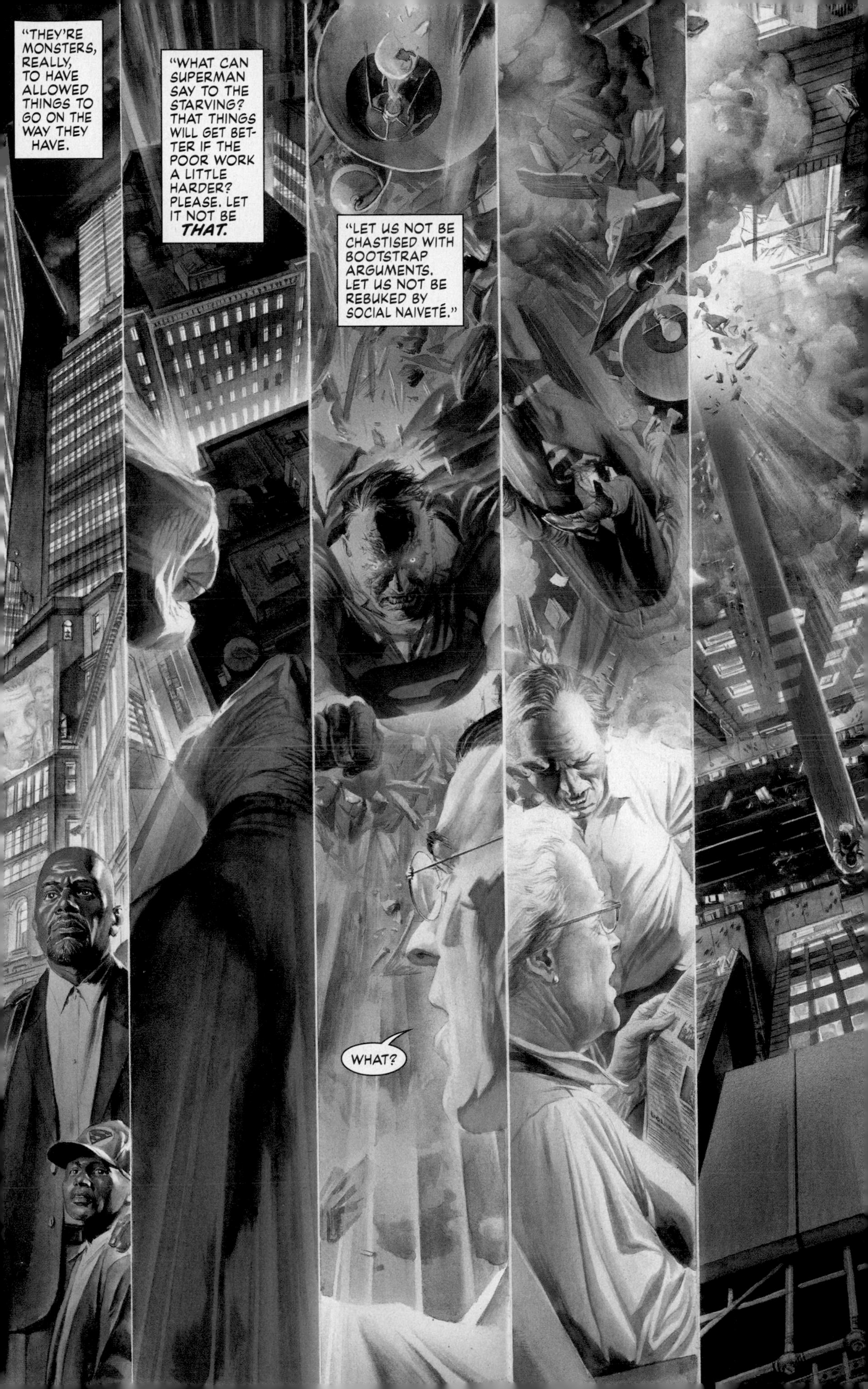
"THEY'RE MONSTERS, REALLY, TO HAVE ALLOWED THINGS TO GO ON THE WAY THEY HAVE.
"WHAT CAN SUPERMAN SAY TO THE STARVING? THAT THINGS WILL GET BETTER IF THE POOR WORK A LITTLE HARDER? PLEASE. LET IT NOT BE *THAT.*
"LET US NOT BE CHASTISED WITH BOOTSTRAP ARGUMENTS. LET US NOT BE REBUKED BY SOCIAL NAIVETÉ."
WHAT?

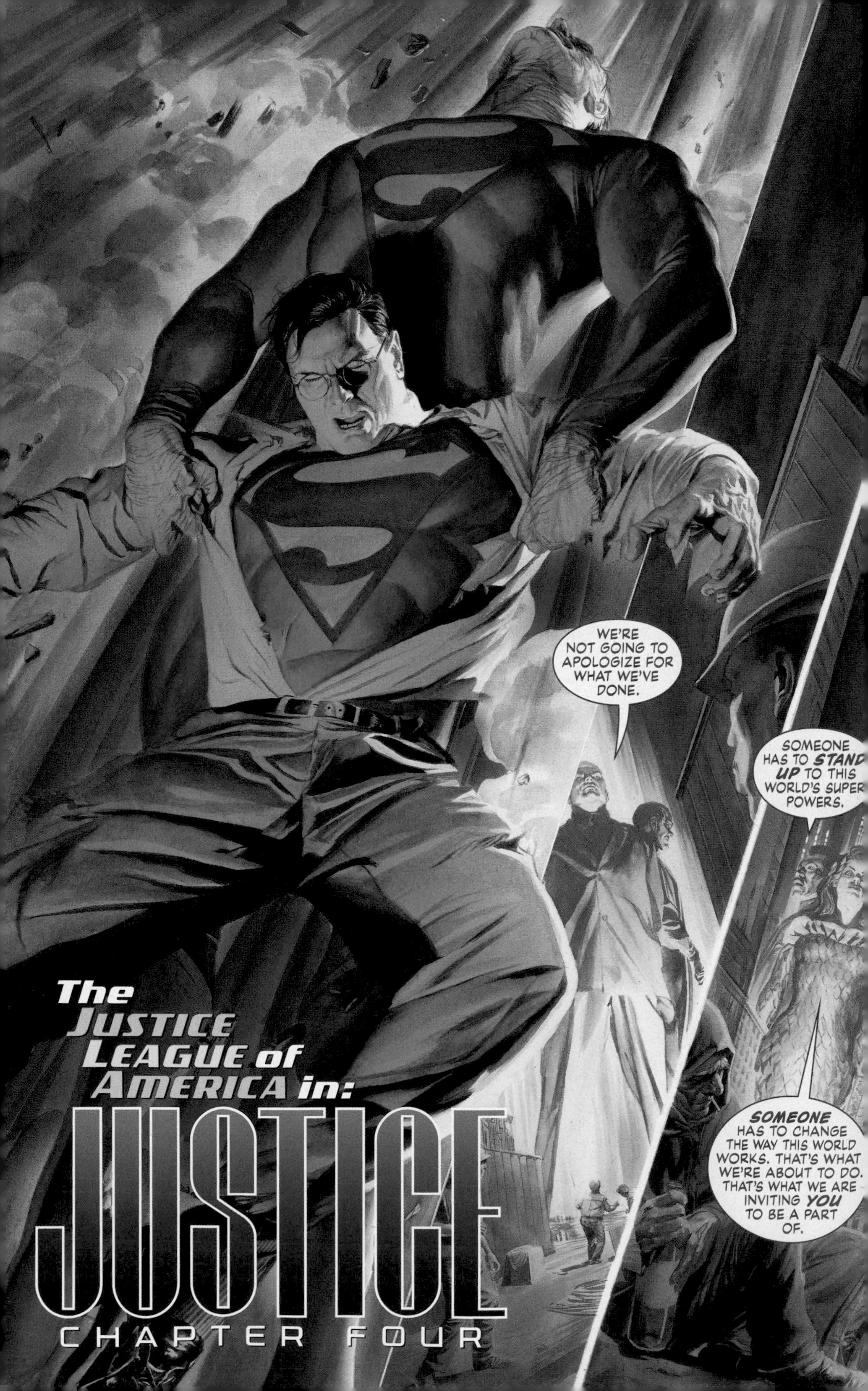
WE'RE NOT GOING TO APOLOGIZE FOR WHAT WE'VE DONE.
SOMEONE HAS TO STAND UP TO THIS WORLD'S SUPER POWERS.
SOMEONE HAS TO CHANGE THE WAY THIS WORLD WORKS. THAT'S WHAT WE'RE ABOUT TO DO. THAT'S WHAT WE ARE INVITING YOU TO BE A PART OF.
The JUSTICE LEAGUE of AMERICA in:
JUSTICE
CHAPTER FOUR

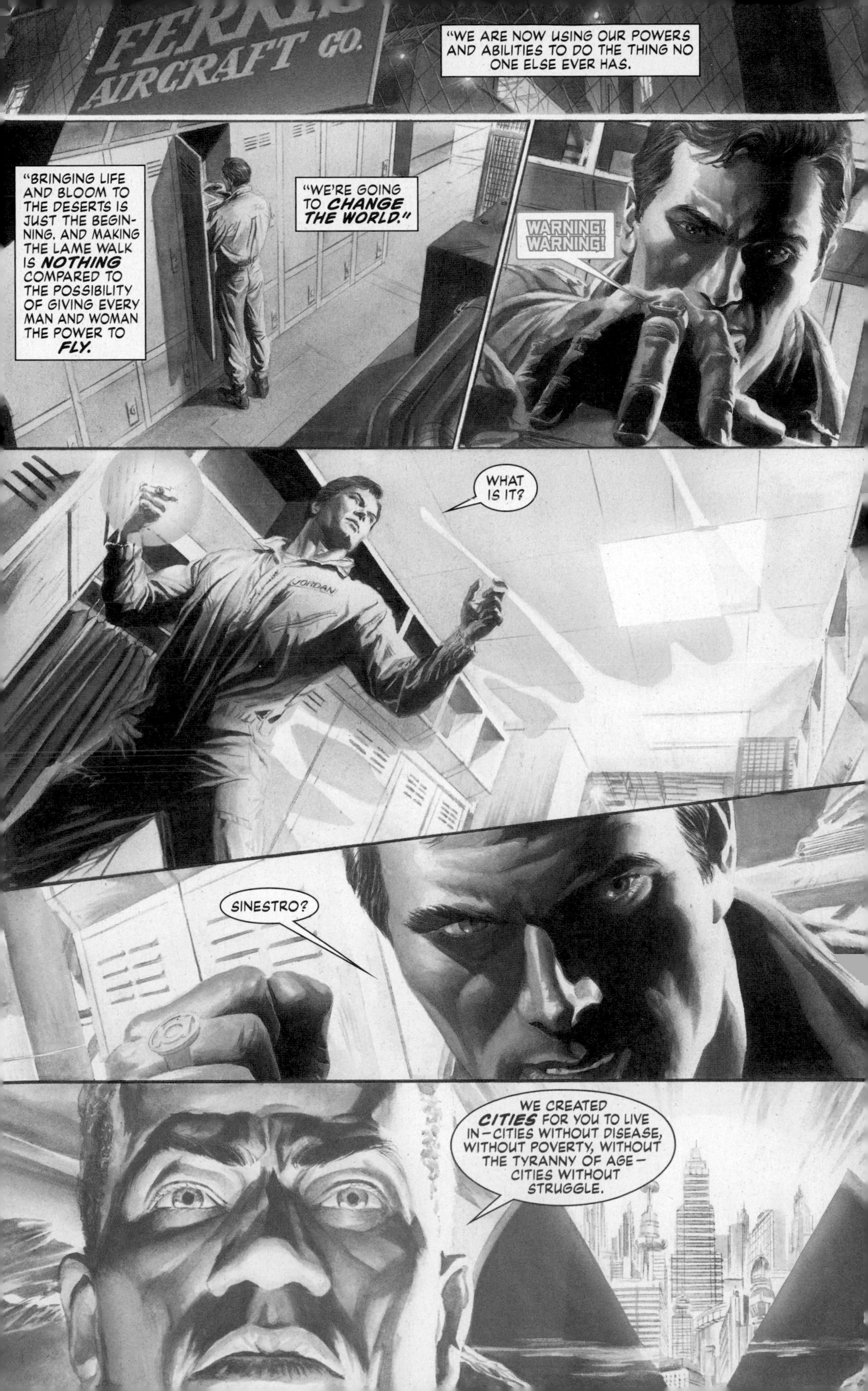
FERRIS AIRCRAFT CO.
"WE ARE NOW USING OUR POWERS AND ABILITIES TO DO THE THING NO ONE ELSE EVER HAS.
"BRINGING LIFE AND BLOOM TO THE DESERTS IS JUST THE BEGINNING, AND MAKING THE LAME WALK IS NOTHING COMPARED TO THE POSSIBILITY OF GIVING EVERY MAN AND WOMAN THE POWER TO FLY.
"WE'RE GOING TO CHANGE THE WORLD."
WARNING! WARNING!
WHAT IS IT?
JORDAN
SINESTRO?
WE CREATED CITIES FOR YOU TO LIVE IN—CITIES WITHOUT DISEASE, WITHOUT POVERTY, WITHOUT THE TYRANNY OF AGE—CITIES WITHOUT STRUGGLE.

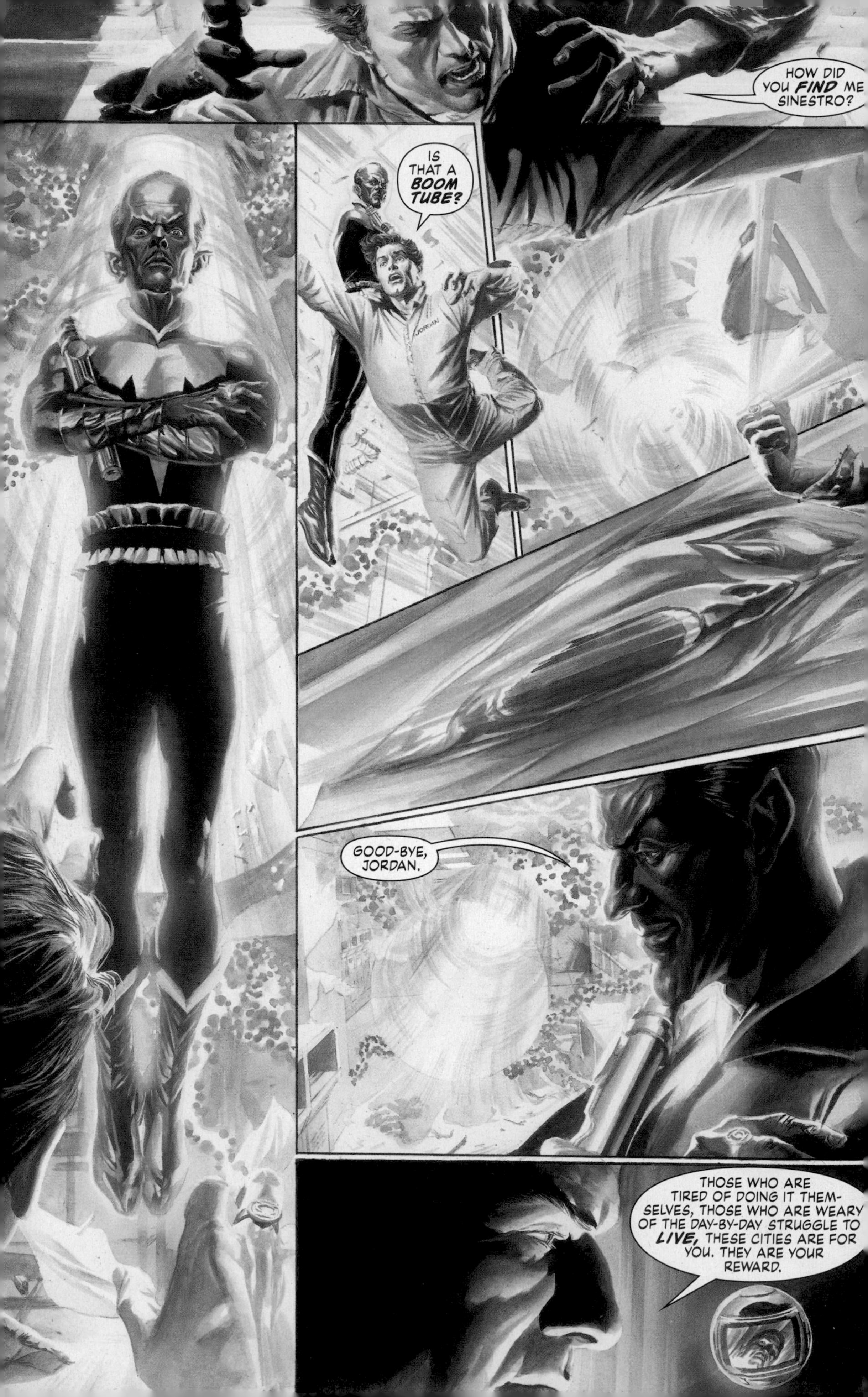
HOW DID YOU FIND ME SINESTRO?
IS THAT A BOOM TUBE?
GOOD-BYE, JORDAN.
THOSE WHO ARE TIRED OF DOING IT THEM-SELVES, THOSE WHO ARE WEARY OF THE DAY-BY-DAY STRUGGLE TO LIVE, THESE CITIES ARE FOR YOU. THEY ARE YOUR REWARD.

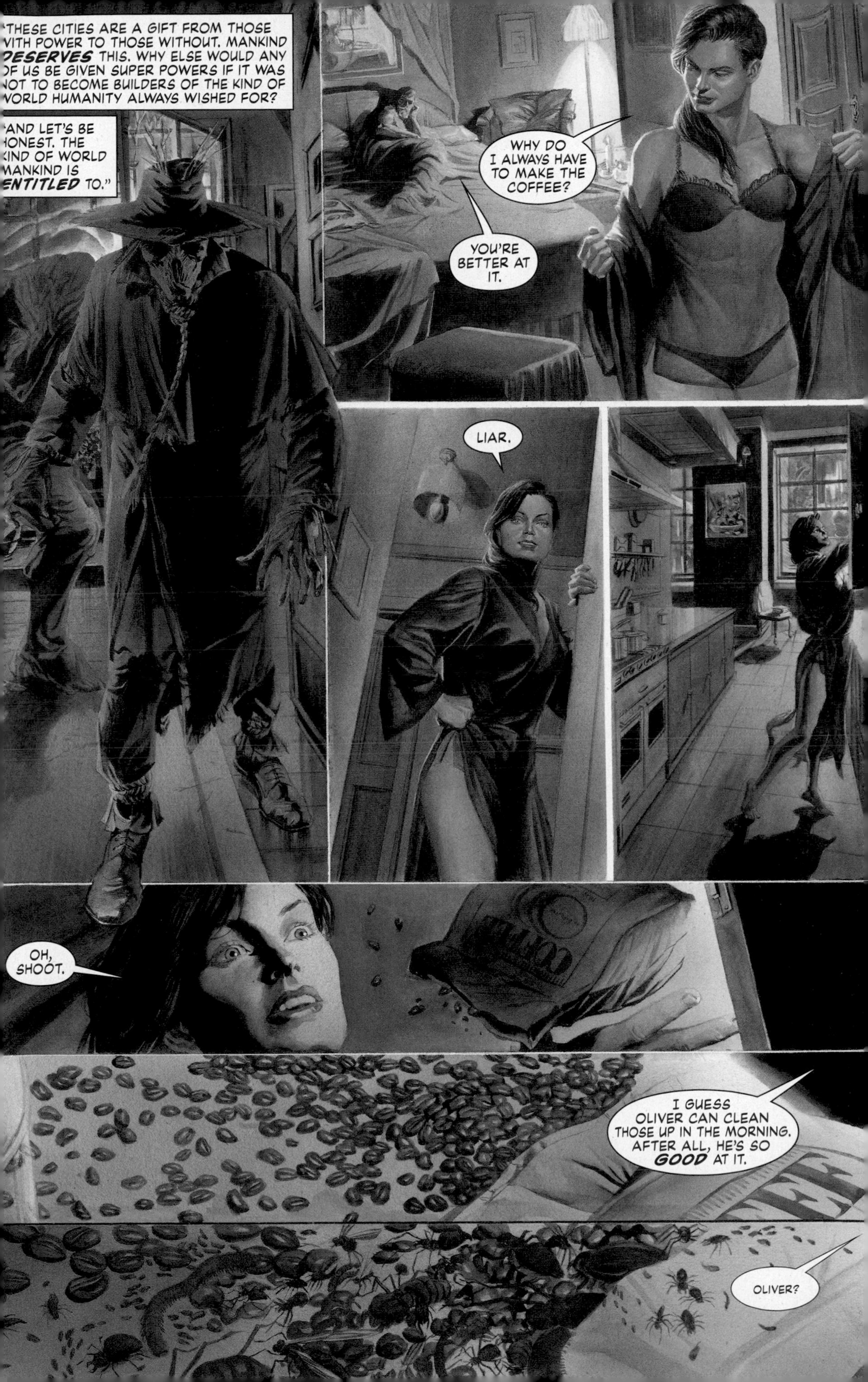
"THESE CITIES ARE A GIFT FROM THOSE WITH POWER TO THOSE WITHOUT. MANKIND DESERVES THIS. WHY ELSE WOULD ANY OF US BE GIVEN SUPER POWERS IF IT WAS NOT TO BECOME BUILDERS OF THE KIND OF WORLD HUMANITY ALWAYS WISHED FOR?
"AND LET'S BE HONEST. THE KIND OF WORLD MANKIND IS ENTITLED TO."
WHY DO I ALWAYS HAVE TO MAKE THE COFFEE?
YOU'RE BETTER AT IT.
LIAR.
OH, SHOOT.
I GUESS OLIVER CAN CLEAN THOSE UP IN THE MORNING. AFTER ALL, HE'S SO GOOD AT IT.
OLIVER?

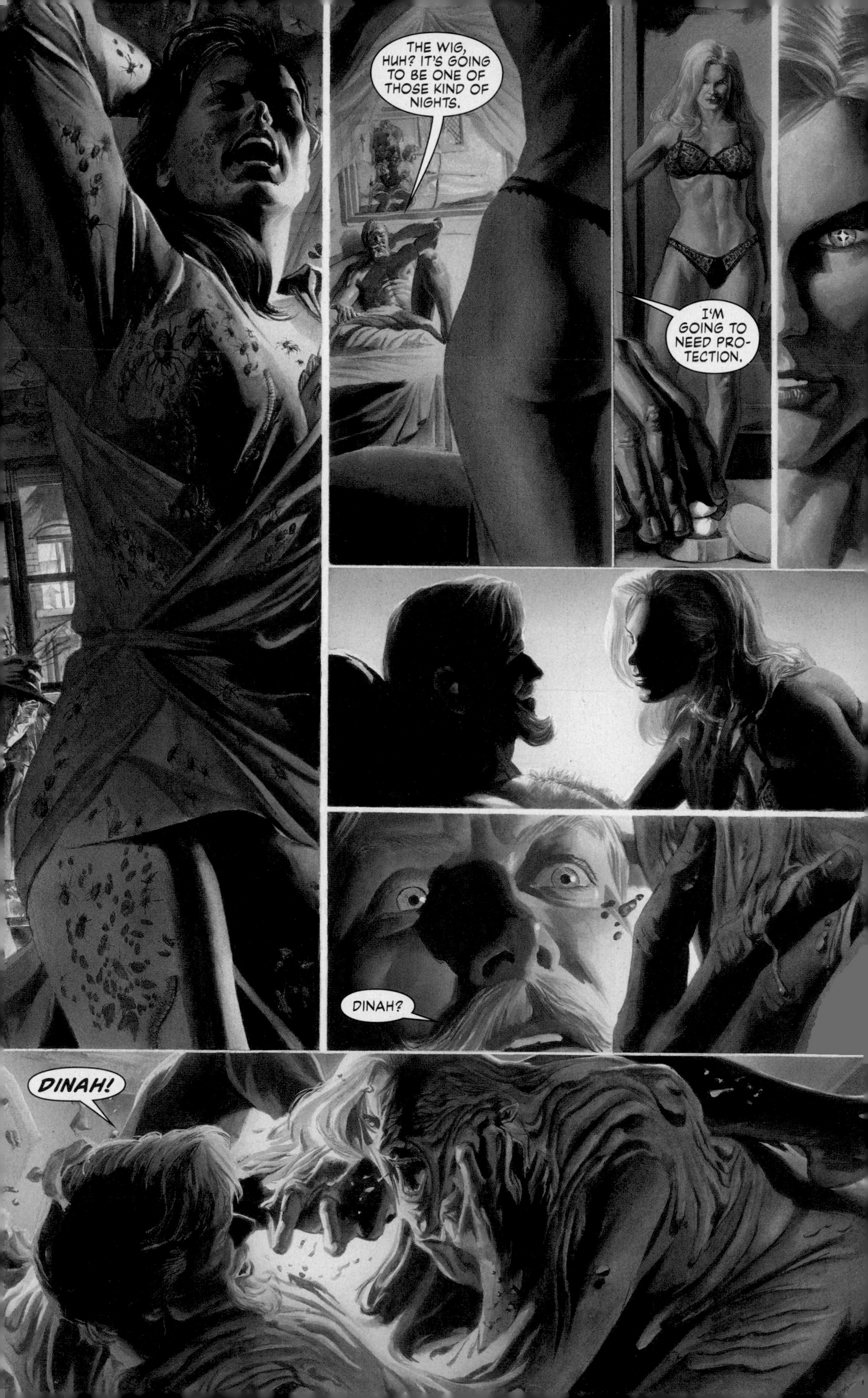
THE WIG, HUH? IT'S GOING TO BE ONE OF THOSE KIND OF NIGHTS.
I'M GOING TO NEED PRO-TECTION.
DINAH?
DINAH!

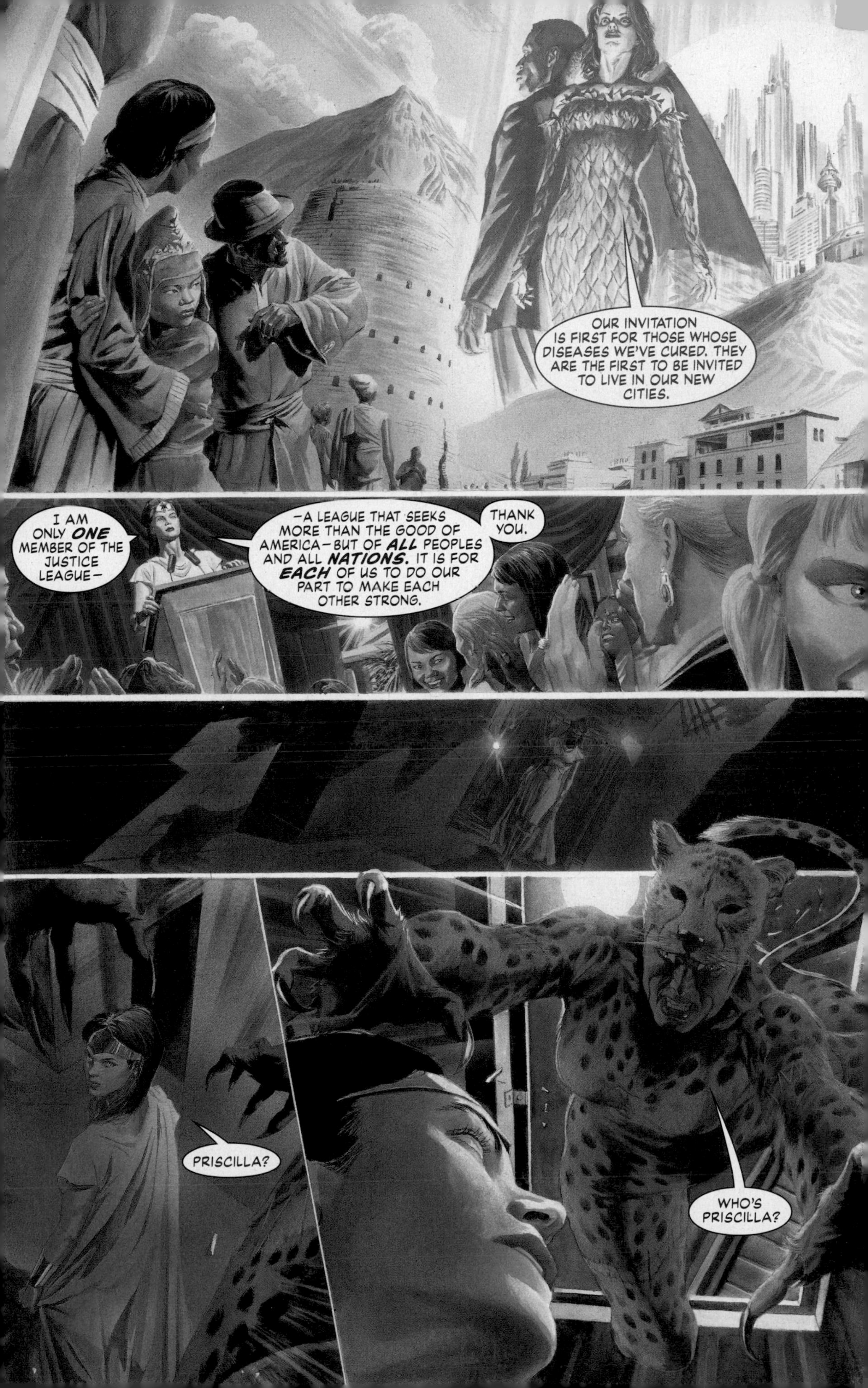
OUR INVITATION IS FIRST FOR THOSE WHOSE DISEASES WE'VE CURED. THEY ARE THE FIRST TO BE INVITED TO LIVE IN OUR NEW CITIES.
I AM ONLY ONE MEMBER OF THE JUSTICE LEAGUE—
—A LEAGUE THAT SEEKS MORE THAN THE GOOD OF AMERICA—BUT OF ALL PEOPLES AND ALL NATIONS. IT IS FOR EACH OF US TO DO OUR PART TO MAKE EACH OTHER STRONG.
THANK YOU.
PRISCILLA?
WHO'S PRISCILLA?

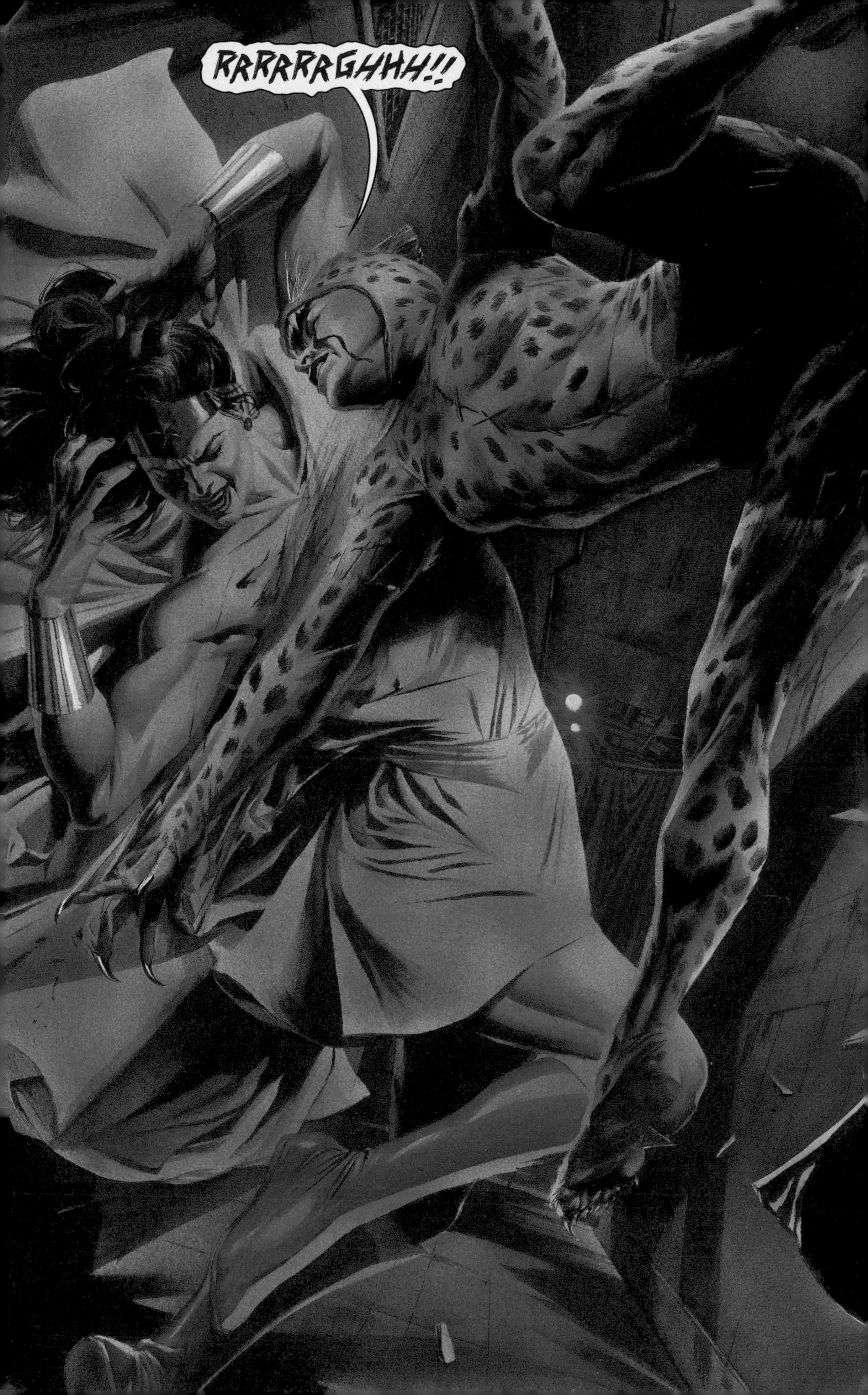
RRRRRRGHHH!!

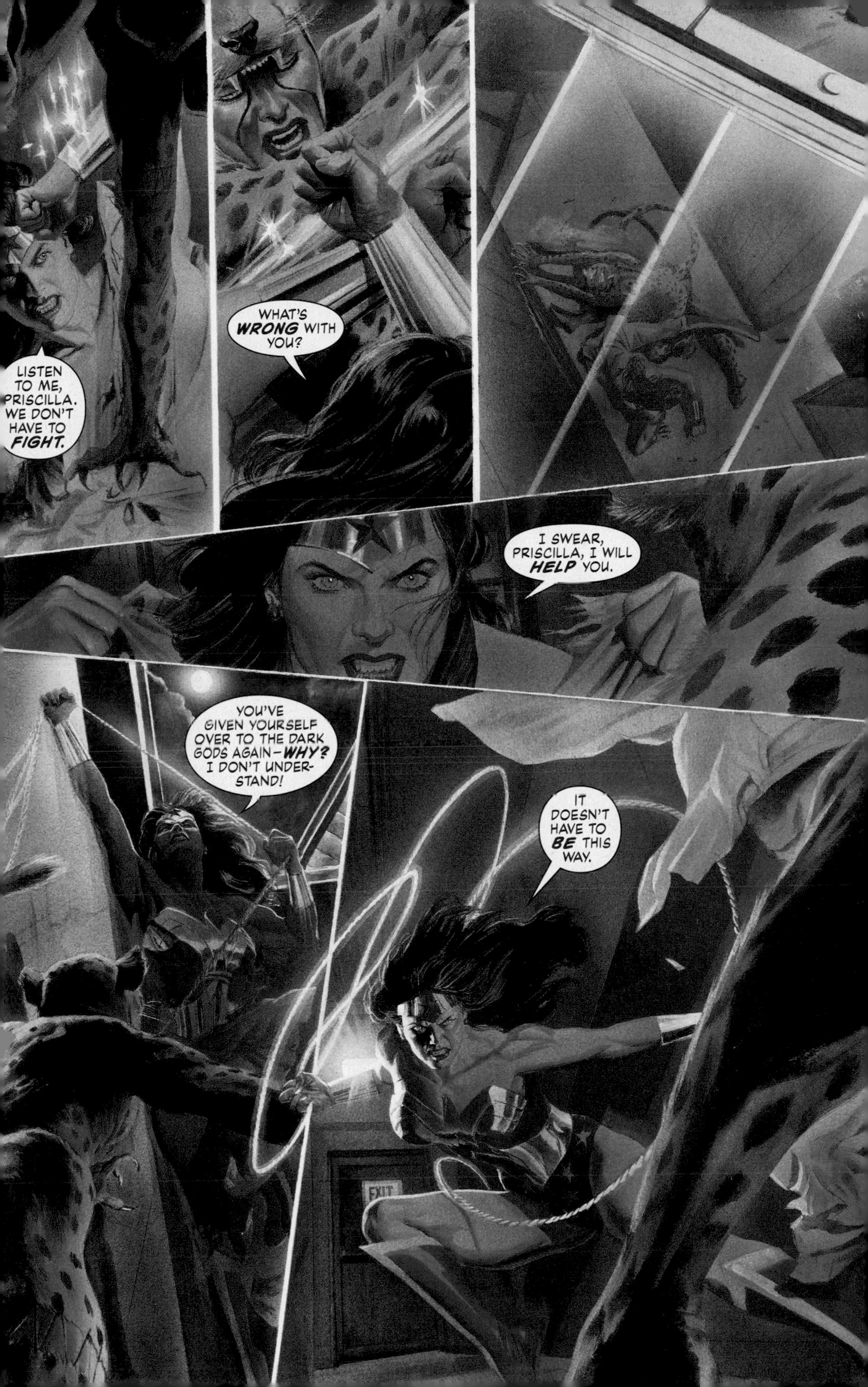
LISTEN TO ME, PRISCILLA. WE DON'T HAVE TO **FIGHT**.
WHAT'S **WRONG** WITH YOU?
I SWEAR, PRISCILLA, I WILL **HELP** YOU.
YOU'VE GIVEN YOURSELF OVER TO THE DARK GODS AGAIN--**WHY?** I DON'T UNDERSTAND!
IT DOESN'T HAVE TO **BE** THIS WAY.
EXIT

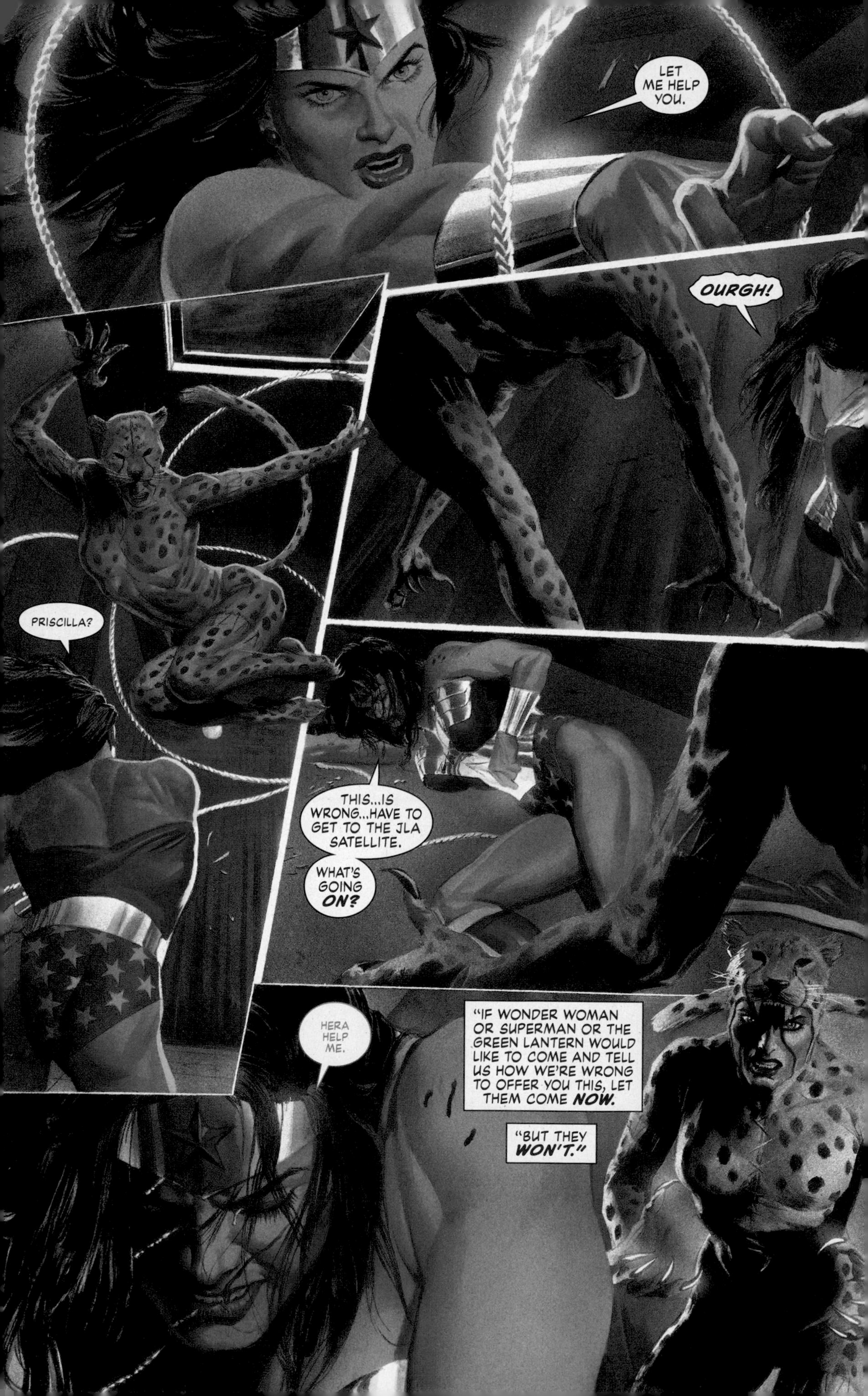
LET ME HELP YOU.
OURGH!
PRISCILLA?
THIS...IS WRONG...HAVE TO GET TO THE JLA SATELLITE.
WHAT'S GOING ON?
HERA HELP ME.
"IF WONDER WOMAN OR SUPERMAN OR THE GREEN LANTERN WOULD LIKE TO COME AND TELL US HOW WE'RE WRONG TO OFFER YOU THIS, LET THEM COME NOW.
"BUT THEY WON'T."

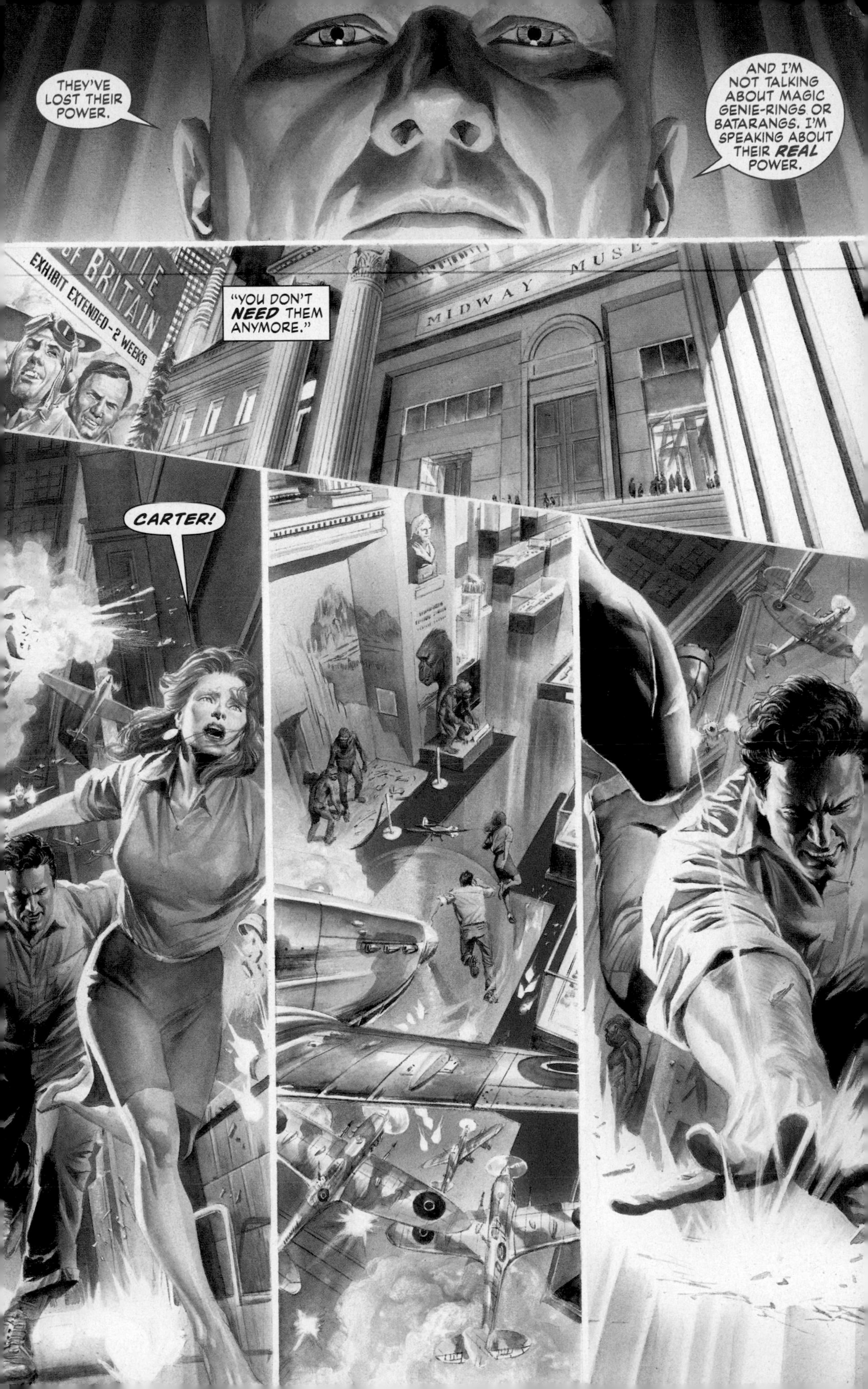
THEY'VE LOST THEIR POWER.
AND I'M NOT TALKING ABOUT MAGIC GENIE-RINGS OR BATARANGS. I'M SPEAKING ABOUT THEIR *REAL* POWER.
BRITAIN
EXHIBIT EXTENDED - 2 WEEKS
"YOU DON'T *NEED* THEM ANYMORE."
MIDWAY MUSE
CARTER!

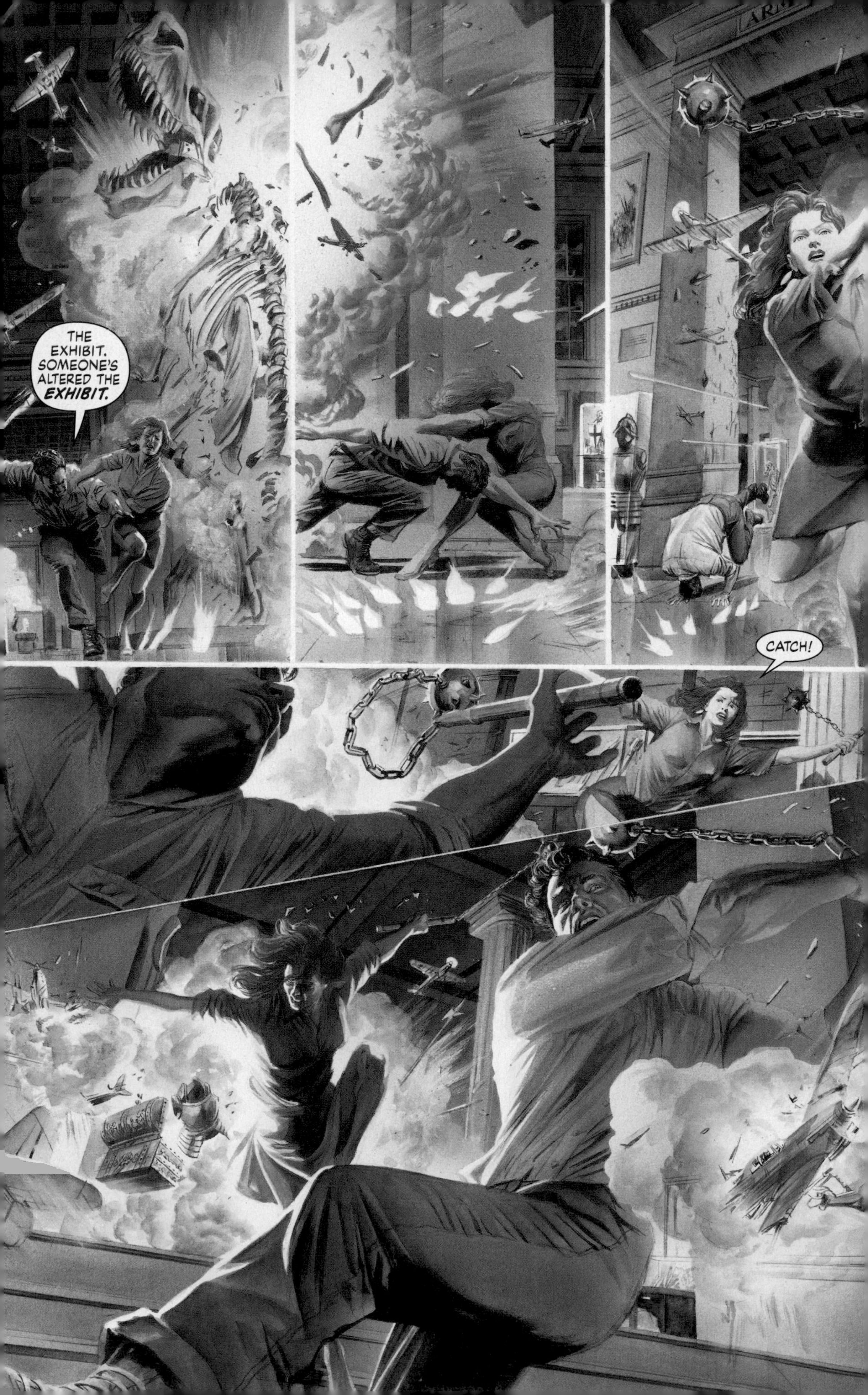
THE EXHIBIT. SOMEONE'S ALTERED THE ***EXHIBIT.***
CATCH!

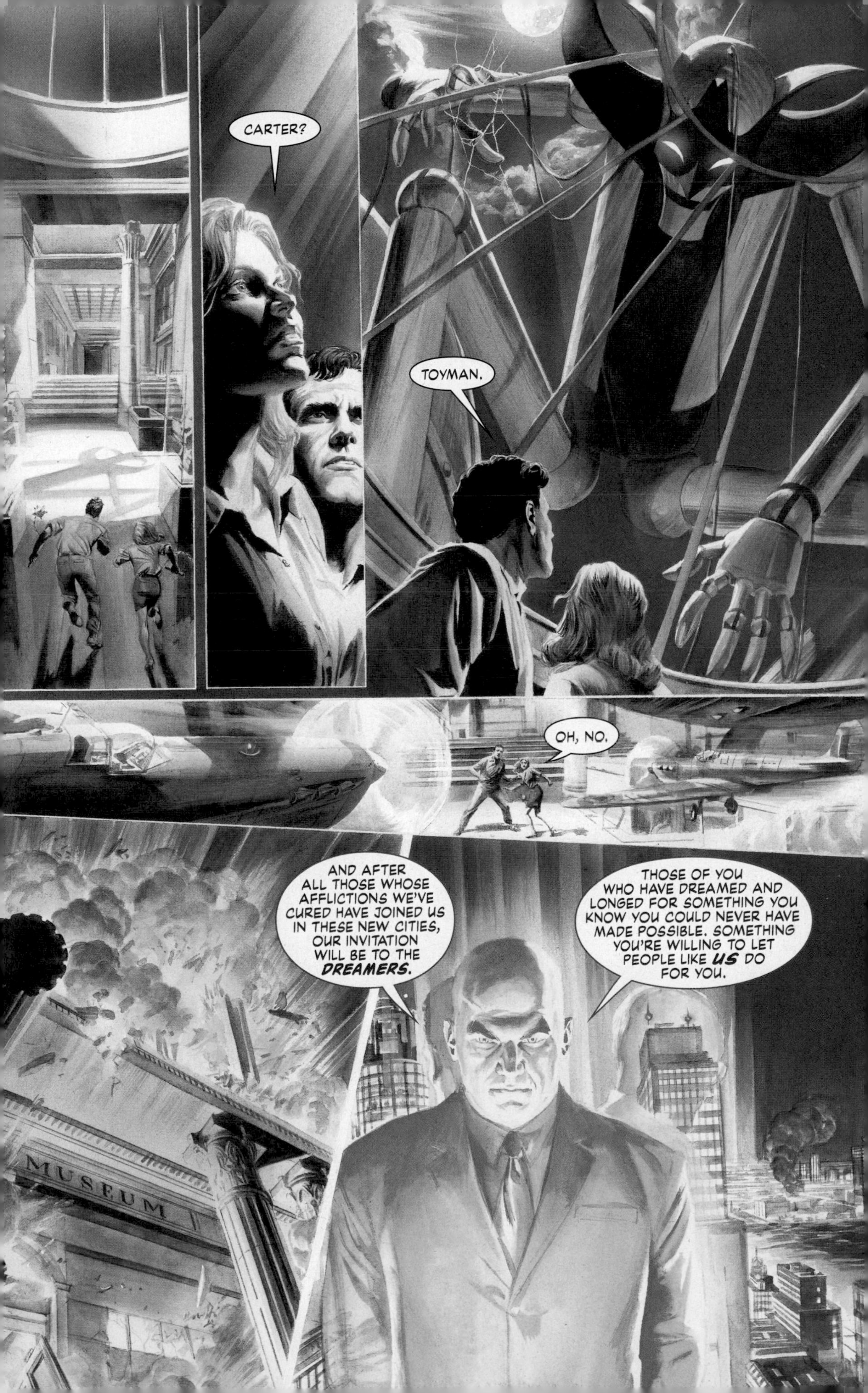
CARTER?
TOYMAN.
OH, NO.
AND AFTER ALL THOSE WHOSE AFFLICTIONS WE'VE CURED HAVE JOINED US IN THESE NEW CITIES, OUR INVITATION WILL BE TO THE ***DREAMERS.***
THOSE OF YOU WHO HAVE DREAMED AND LONGED FOR SOMETHING YOU KNOW YOU COULD NEVER HAVE MADE POSSIBLE. SOMETHING YOU'RE WILLING TO LET PEOPLE LIKE ***US*** DO FOR YOU.
MUSEUM

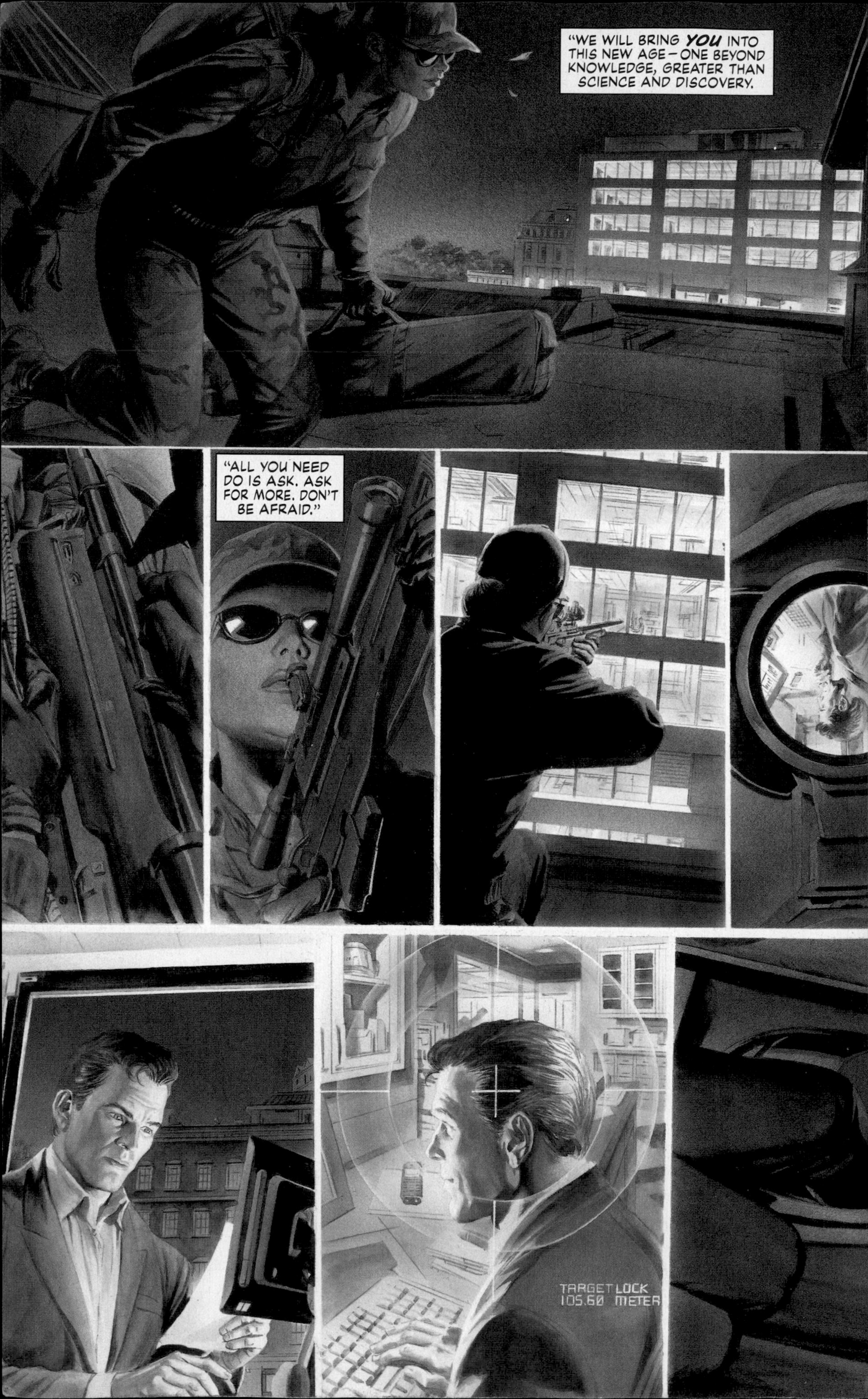
"WE WILL BRING YOU INTO THIS NEW AGE—ONE BEYOND KNOWLEDGE, GREATER THAN SCIENCE AND DISCOVERY.
"ALL YOU NEED DO IS ASK. ASK FOR MORE. DON'T BE AFRAID."
TARGET LOCK
105.60 METER

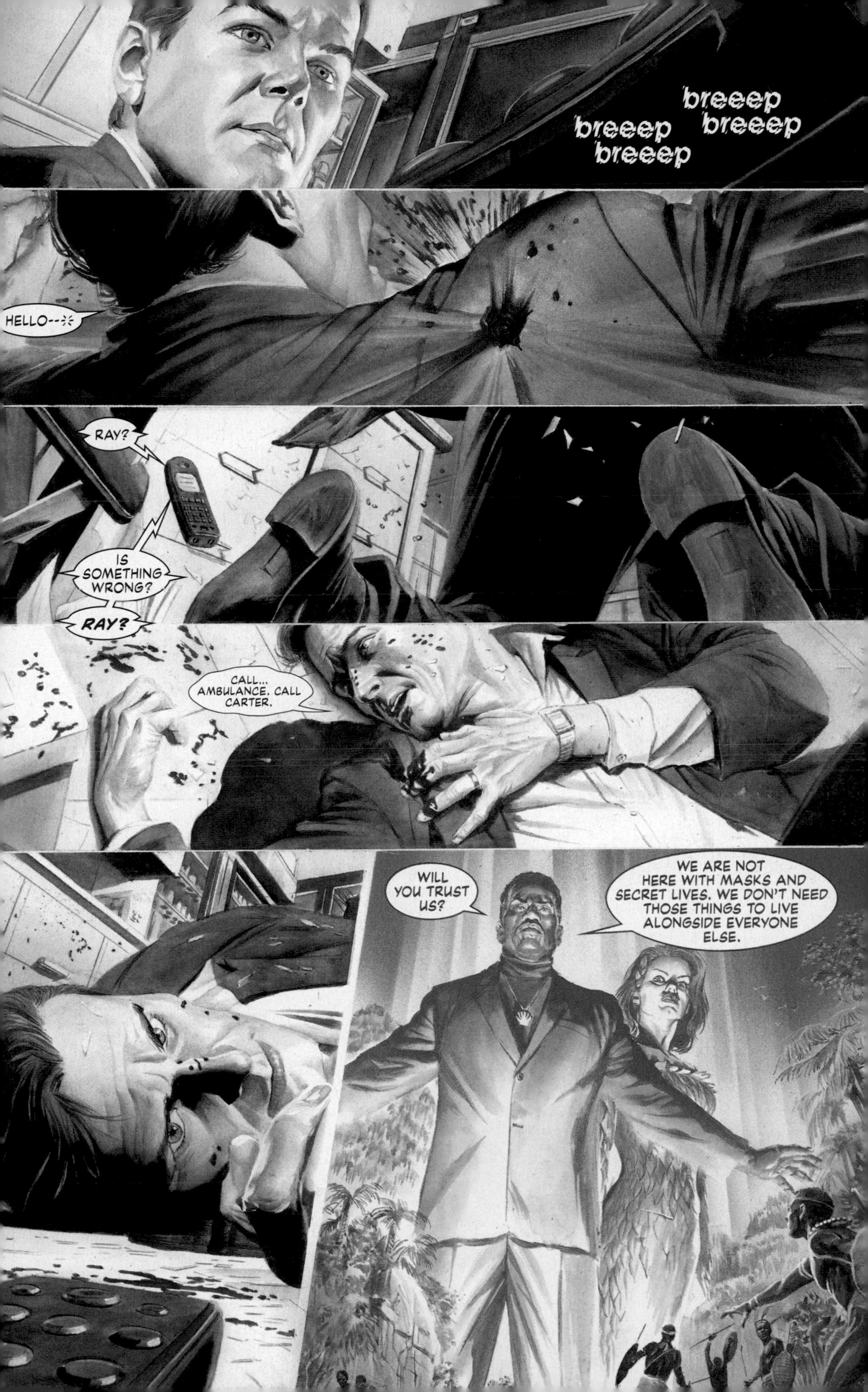
breeep
breeep breeep
breeep
HELLO--
RAY?
IS SOMETHING WRONG?
RAY?
CALL... AMBULANCE. CALL CARTER.
WILL YOU TRUST US?
WE ARE NOT HERE WITH MASKS AND SECRET LIVES. WE DON'T NEED THOSE THINGS TO LIVE ALONGSIDE EVERYONE ELSE.

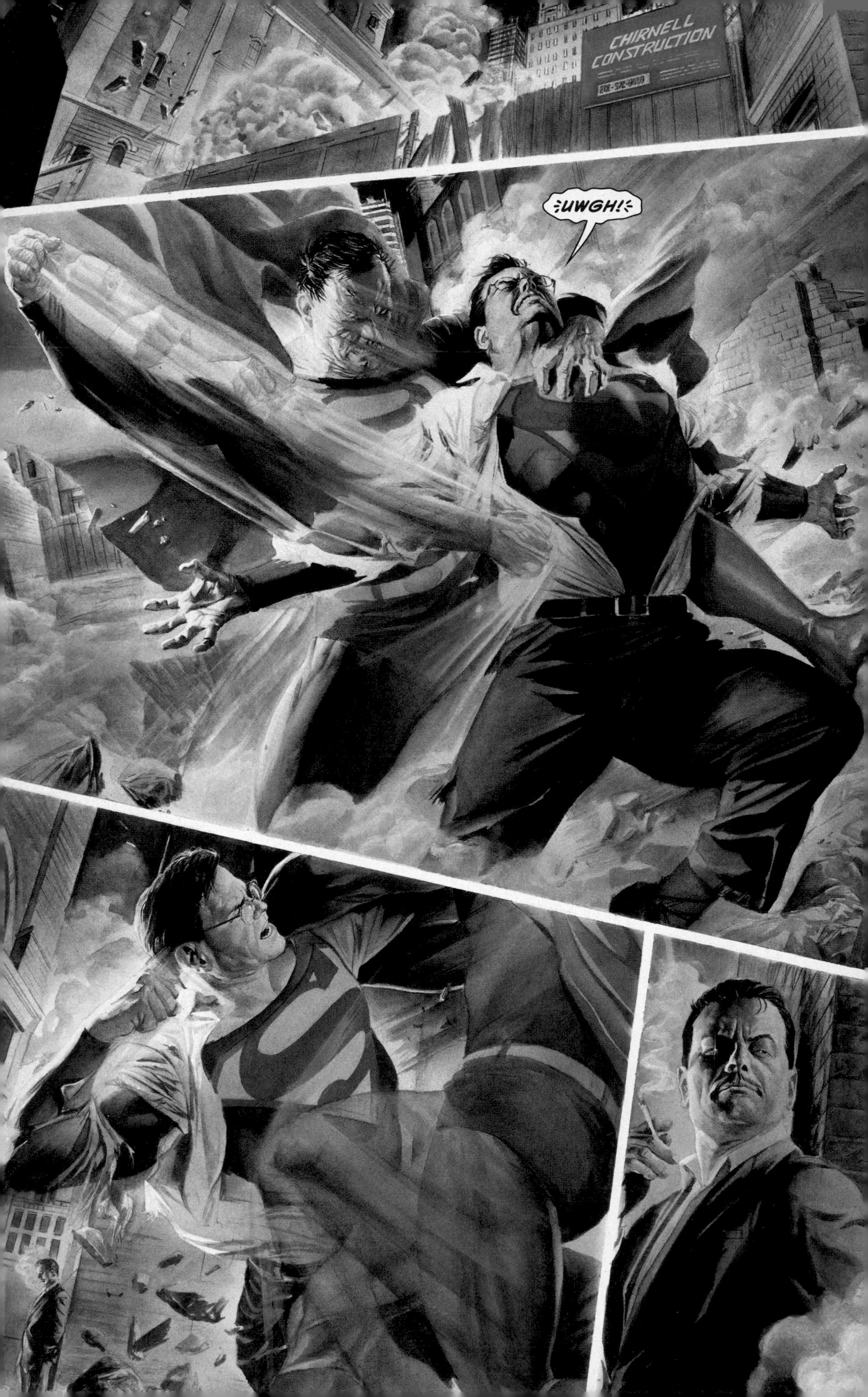
CHIRNELL CONSTRUCTION
¡UWGH!

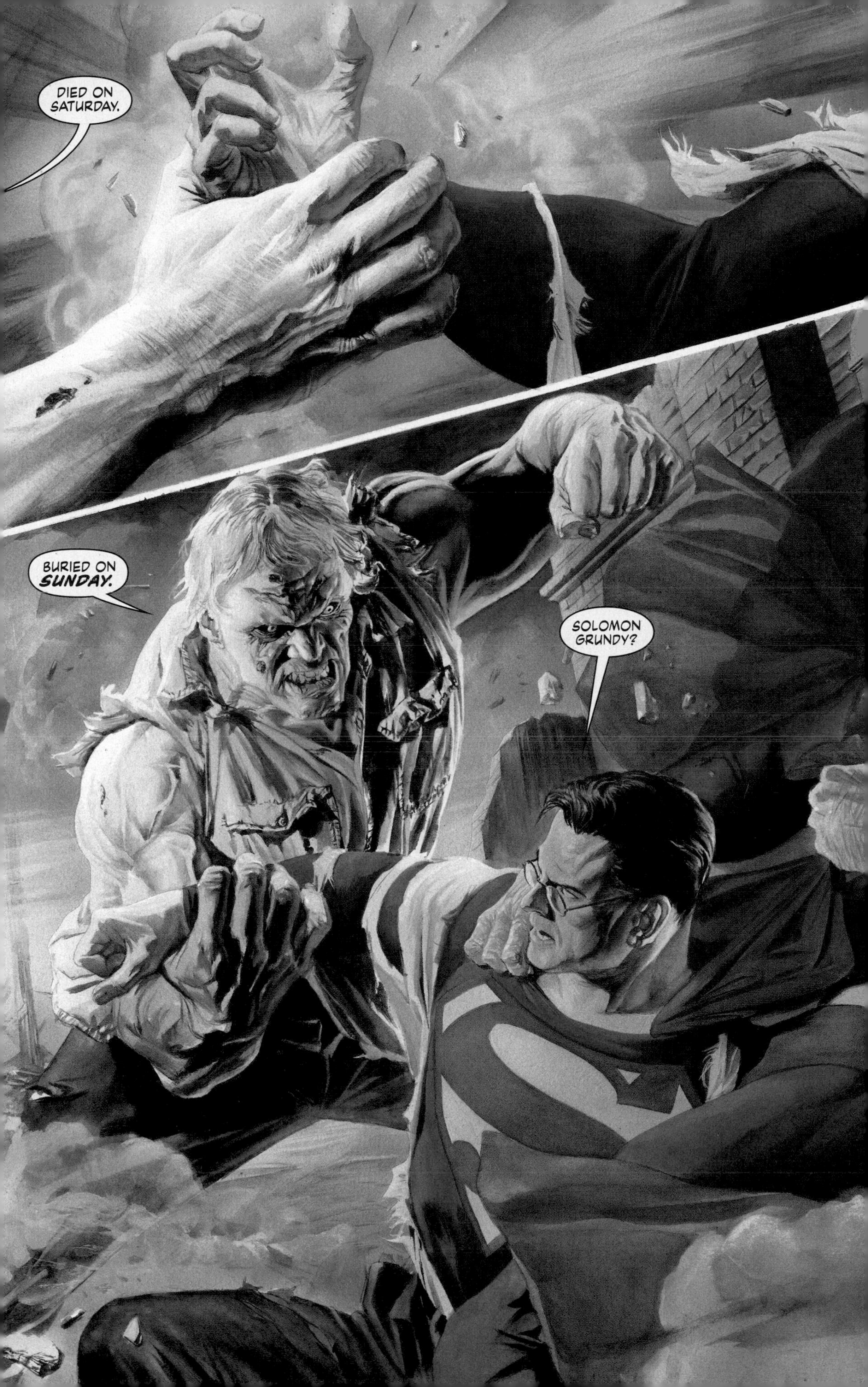
DIED ON SATURDAY.
BURIED ON **SUNDAY.**
SOLOMON GRUNDY?

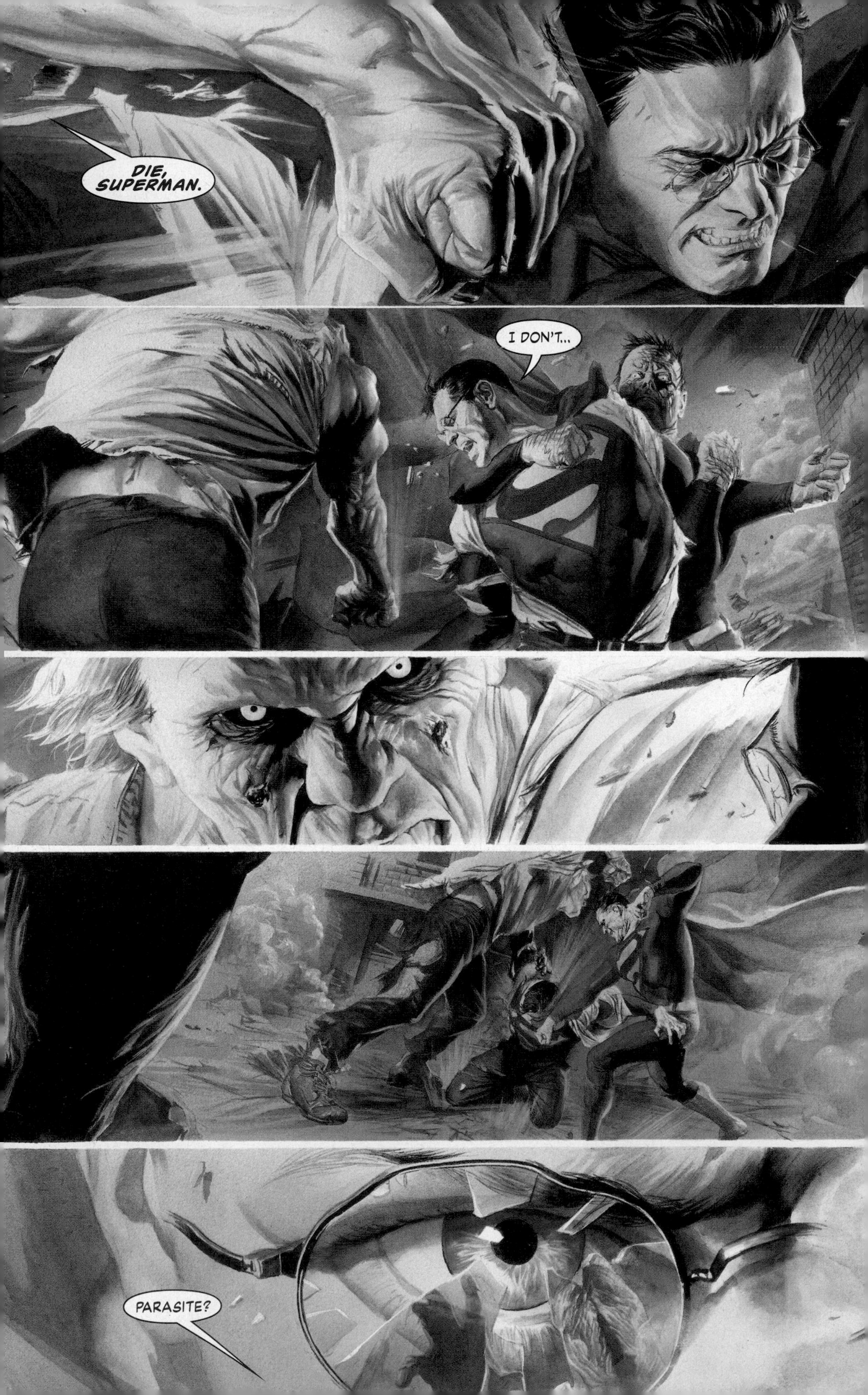
DIE, SUPERMAN.
I DON'T...
PARASITE?

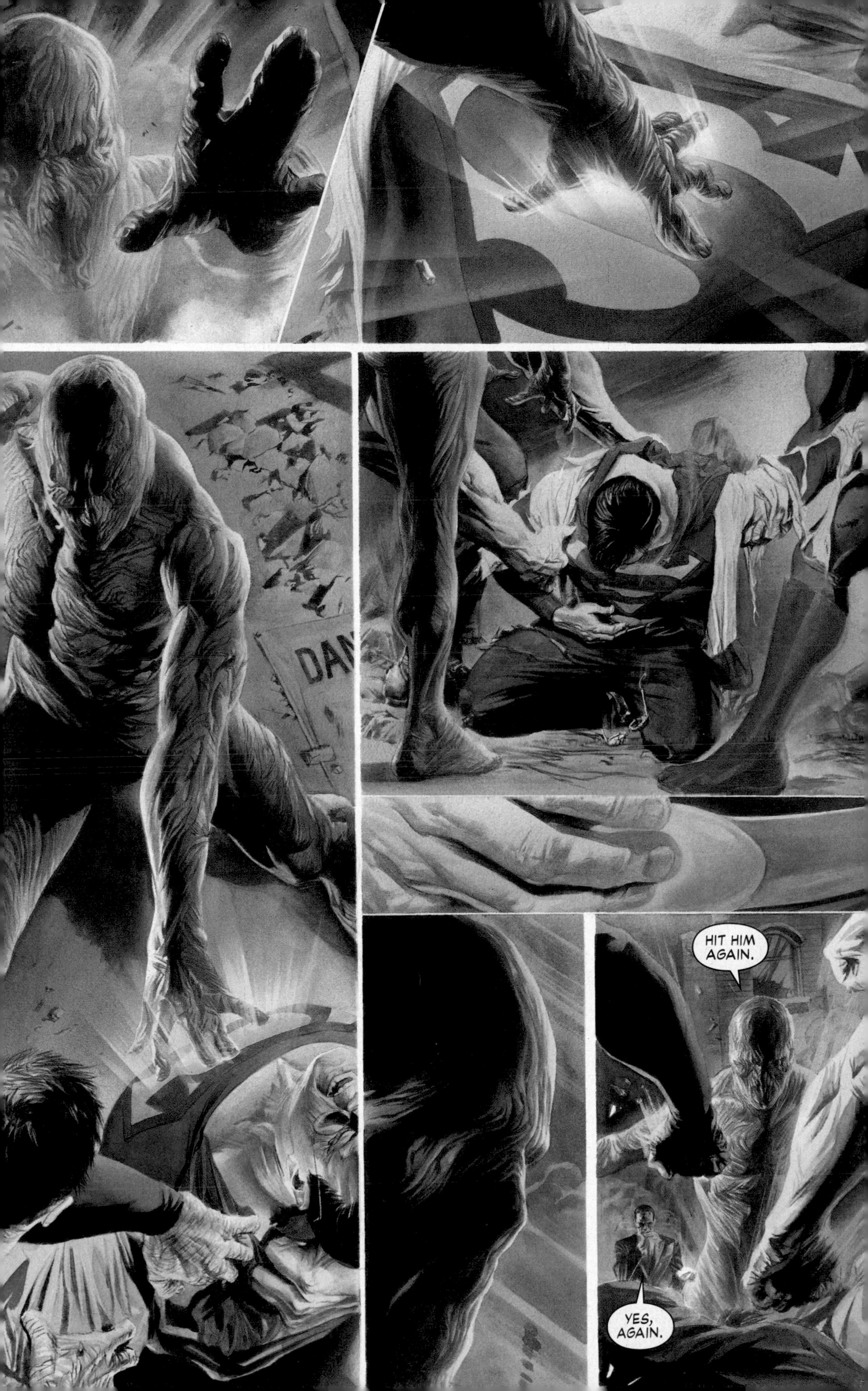
HIT HIM AGAIN.
YES, AGAIN.

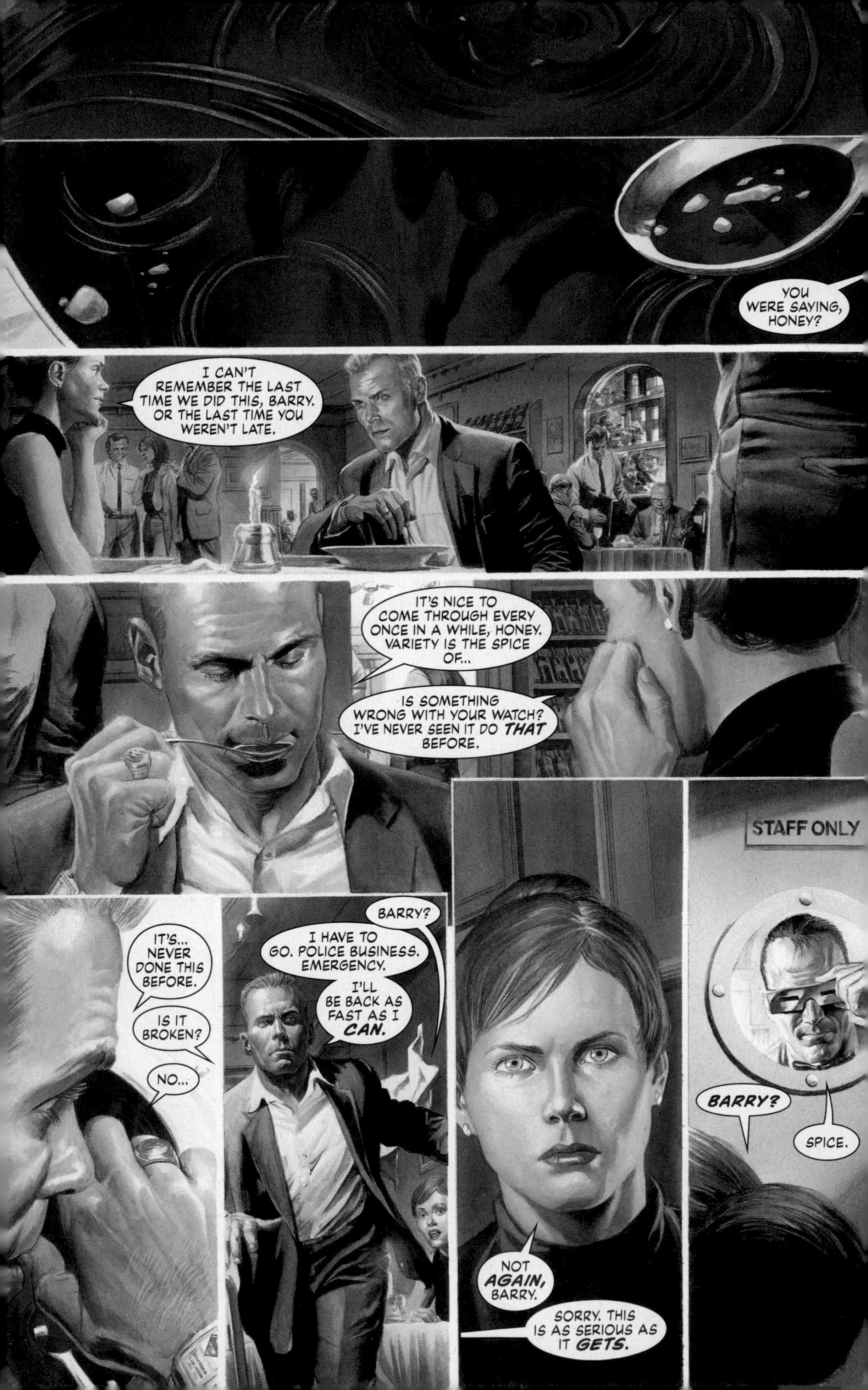
YOU WERE SAYING, HONEY?
I CAN'T REMEMBER THE LAST TIME WE DID THIS, BARRY. OR THE LAST TIME YOU WEREN'T LATE.
IT'S NICE TO COME THROUGH EVERY ONCE IN A WHILE, HONEY. VARIETY IS THE SPICE OF...
IS SOMETHING WRONG WITH YOUR WATCH? I'VE NEVER SEEN IT DO THAT BEFORE.
IT'S... NEVER DONE THIS BEFORE.
IS IT BROKEN?
NO...
BARRY?
I HAVE TO GO. POLICE BUSINESS. EMERGENCY.
I'LL BE BACK AS FAST AS I CAN.
NOT AGAIN, BARRY.
SORRY. THIS IS AS SERIOUS AS IT GETS.
STAFF ONLY
BARRY?
SPICE.

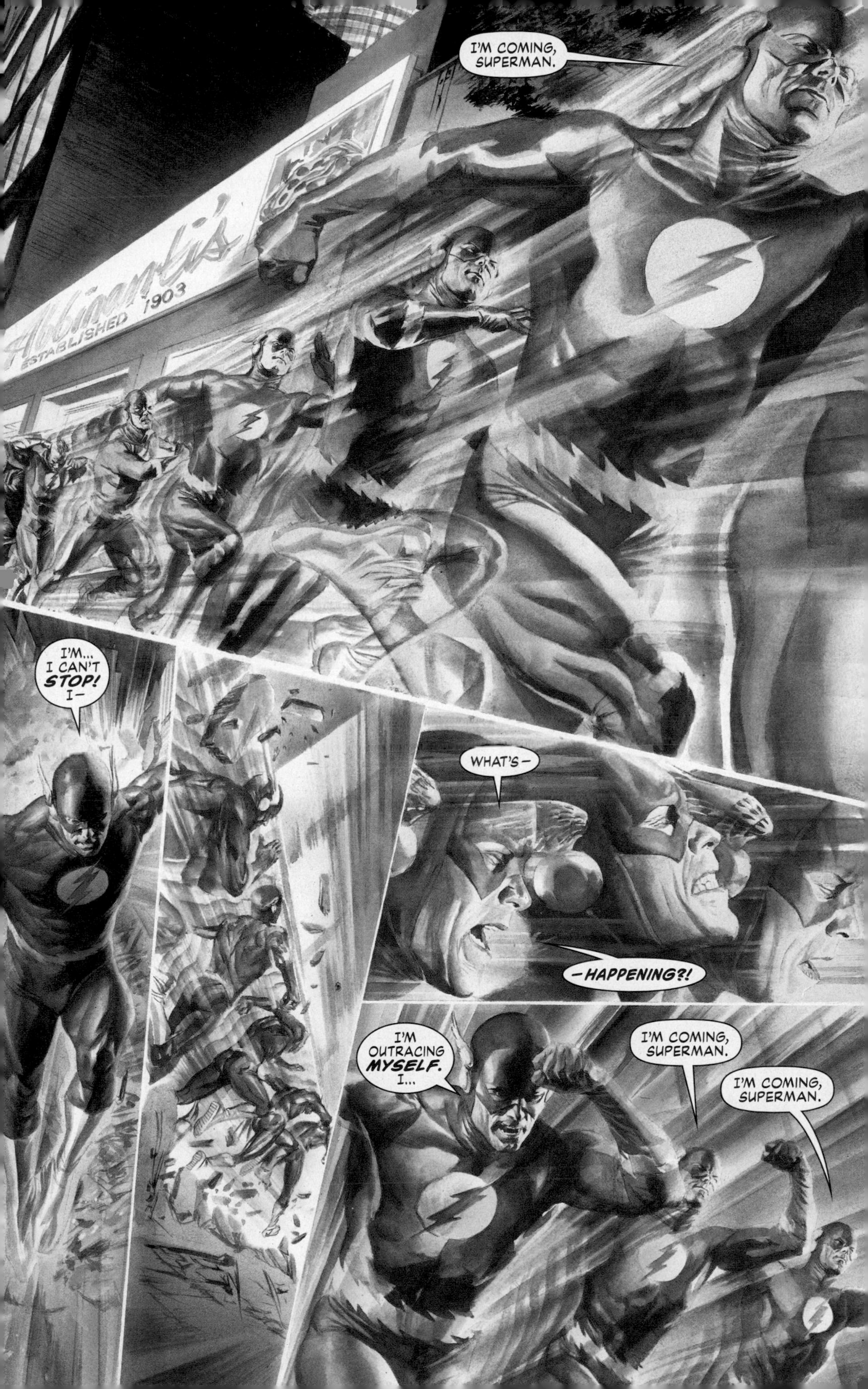

I'M COMING, SUPERMAN.
I'M... I CAN'T STOP! I–
WHAT'S–
–HAPPENING?!
I'M OUTRACING MYSELF. I...
I'M COMING, SUPERMAN.
I'M COMING, SUPERMAN.

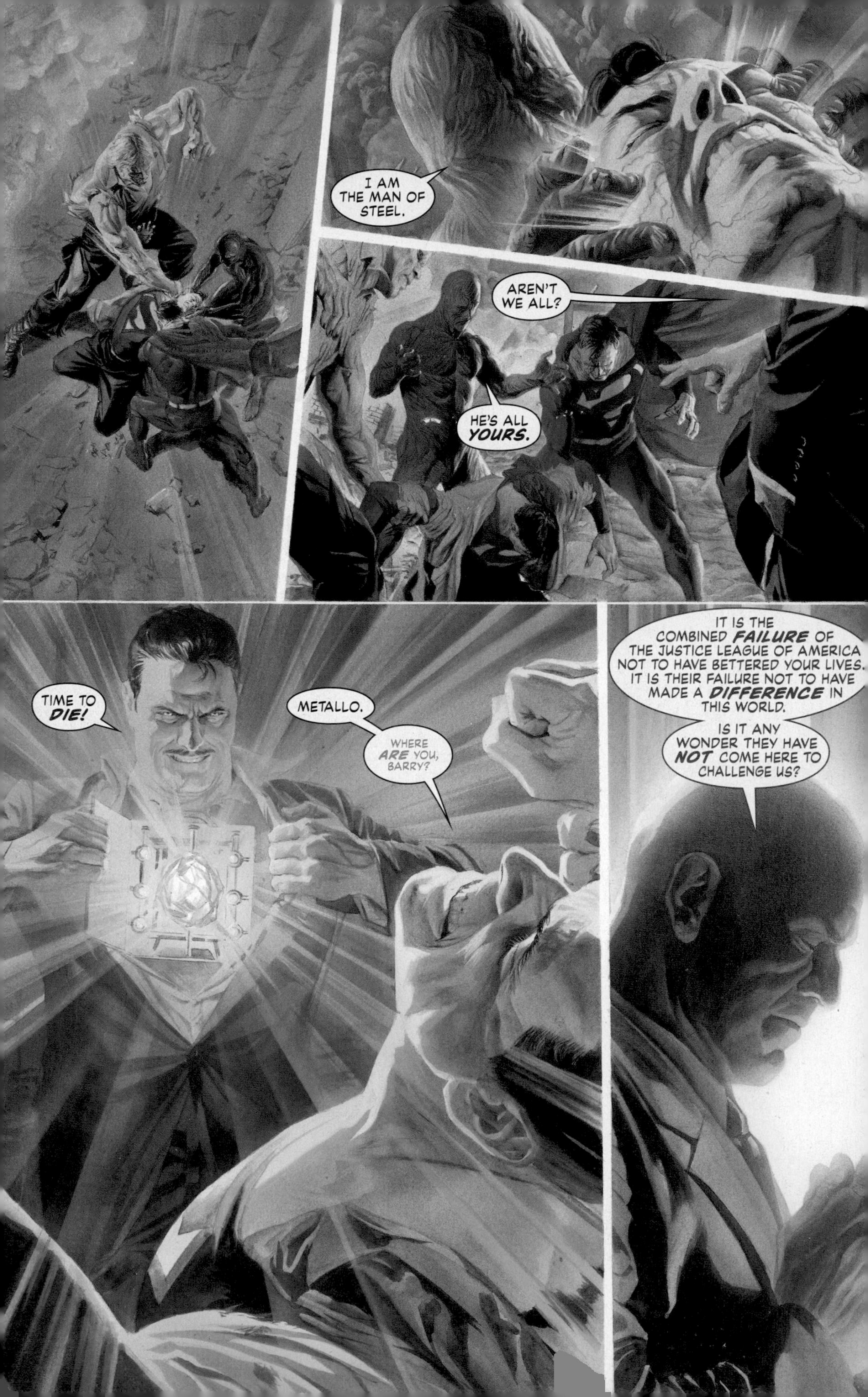
I AM THE MAN OF STEEL.
AREN'T WE ALL?
HE'S ALL *YOURS.*
TIME TO *DIE!*
METALLO.
WHERE *ARE* YOU, BARRY?
IT IS THE COMBINED *FAILURE* OF THE JUSTICE LEAGUE OF AMERICA NOT TO HAVE BETTERED YOUR LIVES. IT IS THEIR FAILURE NOT TO HAVE MADE A *DIFFERENCE* IN THIS WORLD.
IS IT ANY WONDER THEY HAVE *NOT* COME HERE TO CHALLENGE US?

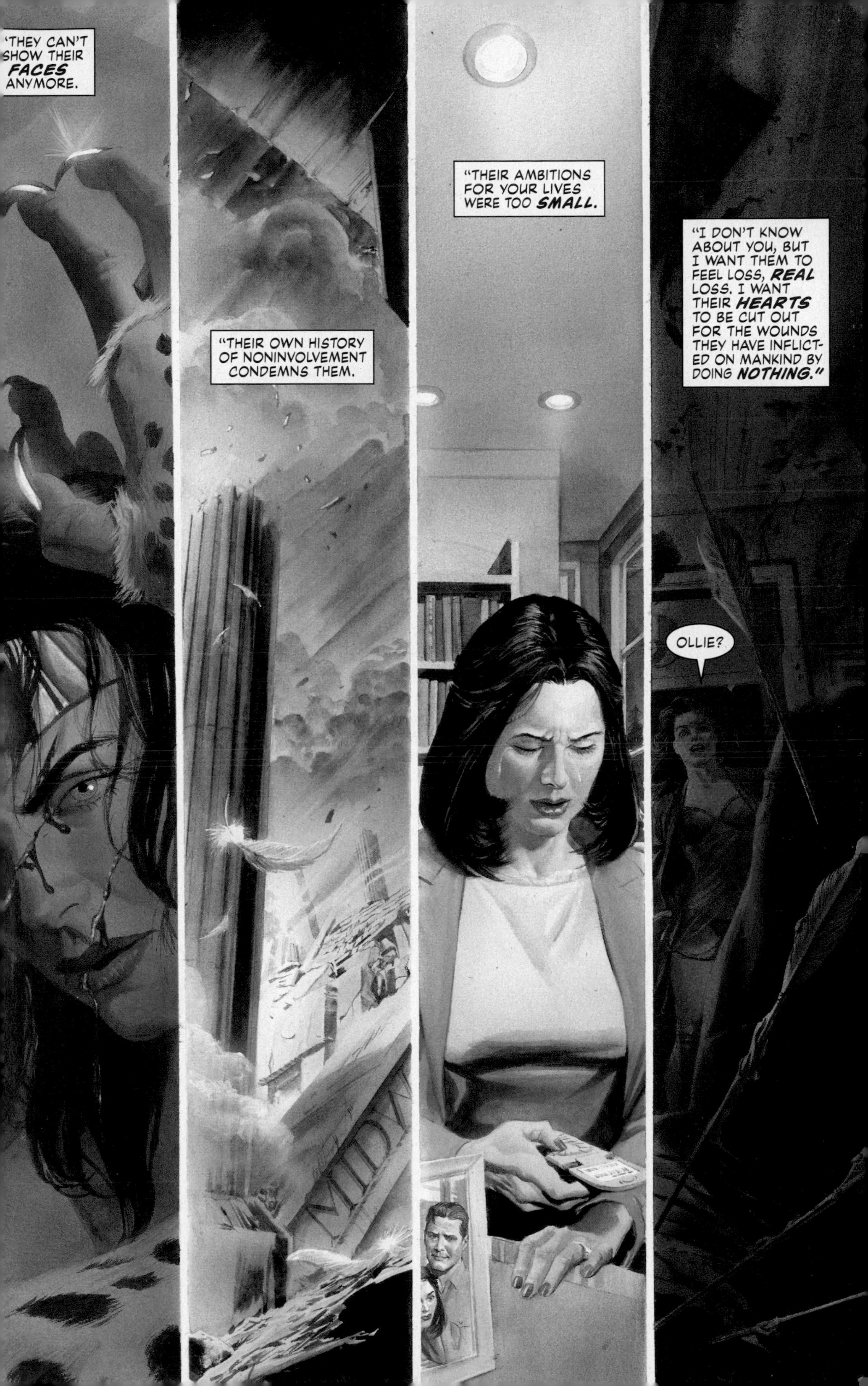
'THEY CAN'T SHOW THEIR FACES ANYMORE.
"THEIR OWN HISTORY OF NONINVOLVEMENT CONDEMNS THEM.
"THEIR AMBITIONS FOR YOUR LIVES WERE TOO SMALL.
"I DON'T KNOW ABOUT YOU, BUT I WANT THEM TO FEEL LOSS, REAL LOSS. I WANT THEIR HEARTS TO BE CUT OUT FOR THE WOUNDS THEY HAVE INFLICTED ON MANKIND BY DOING NOTHING."
OLLIE?

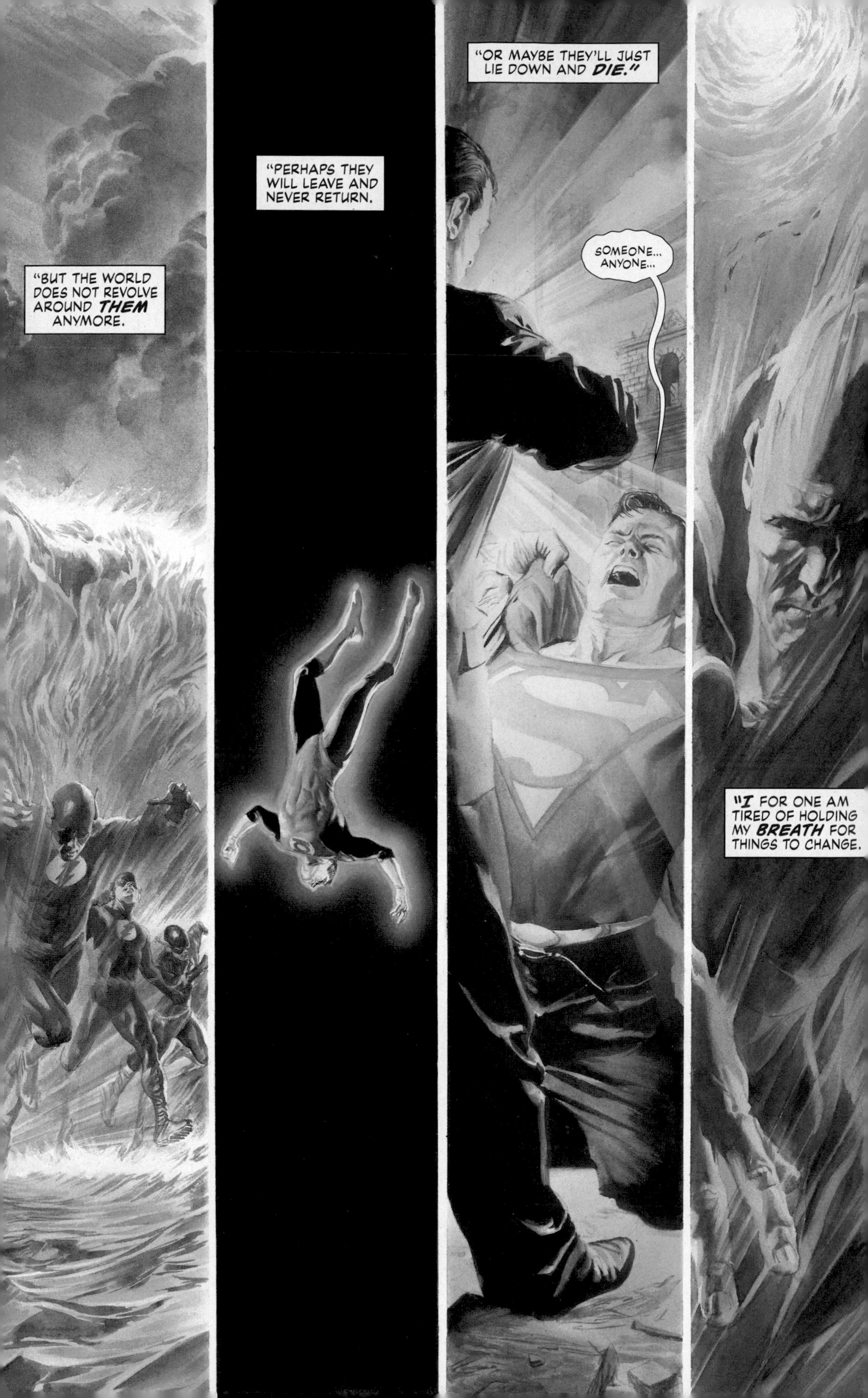
"BUT THE WORLD DOES NOT REVOLVE AROUND THEM ANYMORE.
"PERHAPS THEY WILL LEAVE AND NEVER RETURN.
"OR MAYBE THEY'LL JUST LIE DOWN AND DIE."
SOMEONE... ANYONE...
"I FOR ONE AM TIRED OF HOLDING MY BREATH FOR THINGS TO CHANGE.

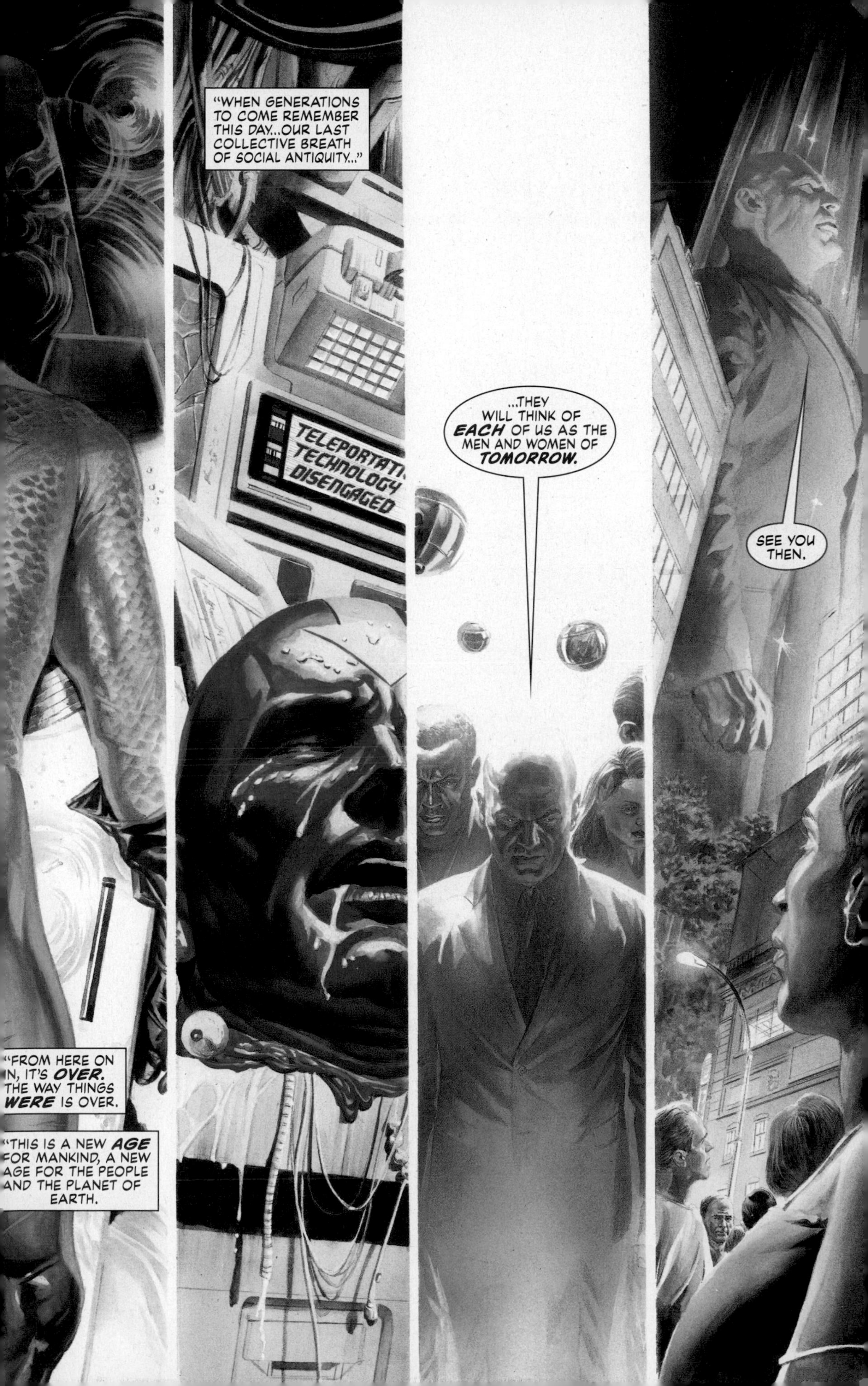
"WHEN GENERATIONS TO COME REMEMBER THIS DAY...OUR LAST COLLECTIVE BREATH OF SOCIAL ANTIQUITY..."
TELEPORTATI TECHNOLOGY DISENGAGED
...THEY WILL THINK OF EACH OF US AS THE MEN AND WOMEN OF TOMORROW.
SEE YOU THEN.
"FROM HERE ON IN, IT'S OVER. THE WAY THINGS WERE IS OVER.
"THIS IS A NEW AGE FOR MANKIND, A NEW AGE FOR THE PEOPLE AND THE PLANET OF EARTH.

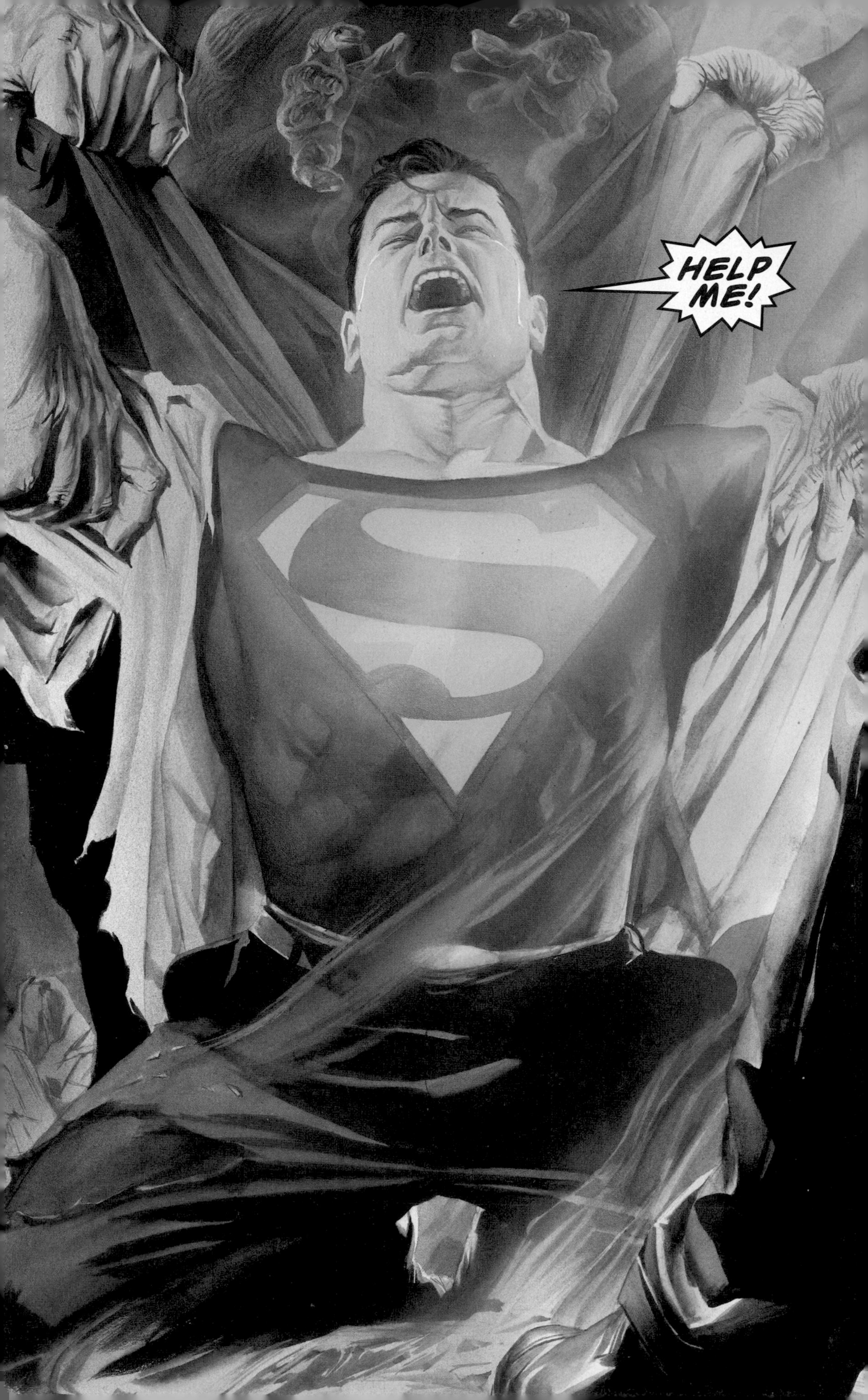
HELP ME!

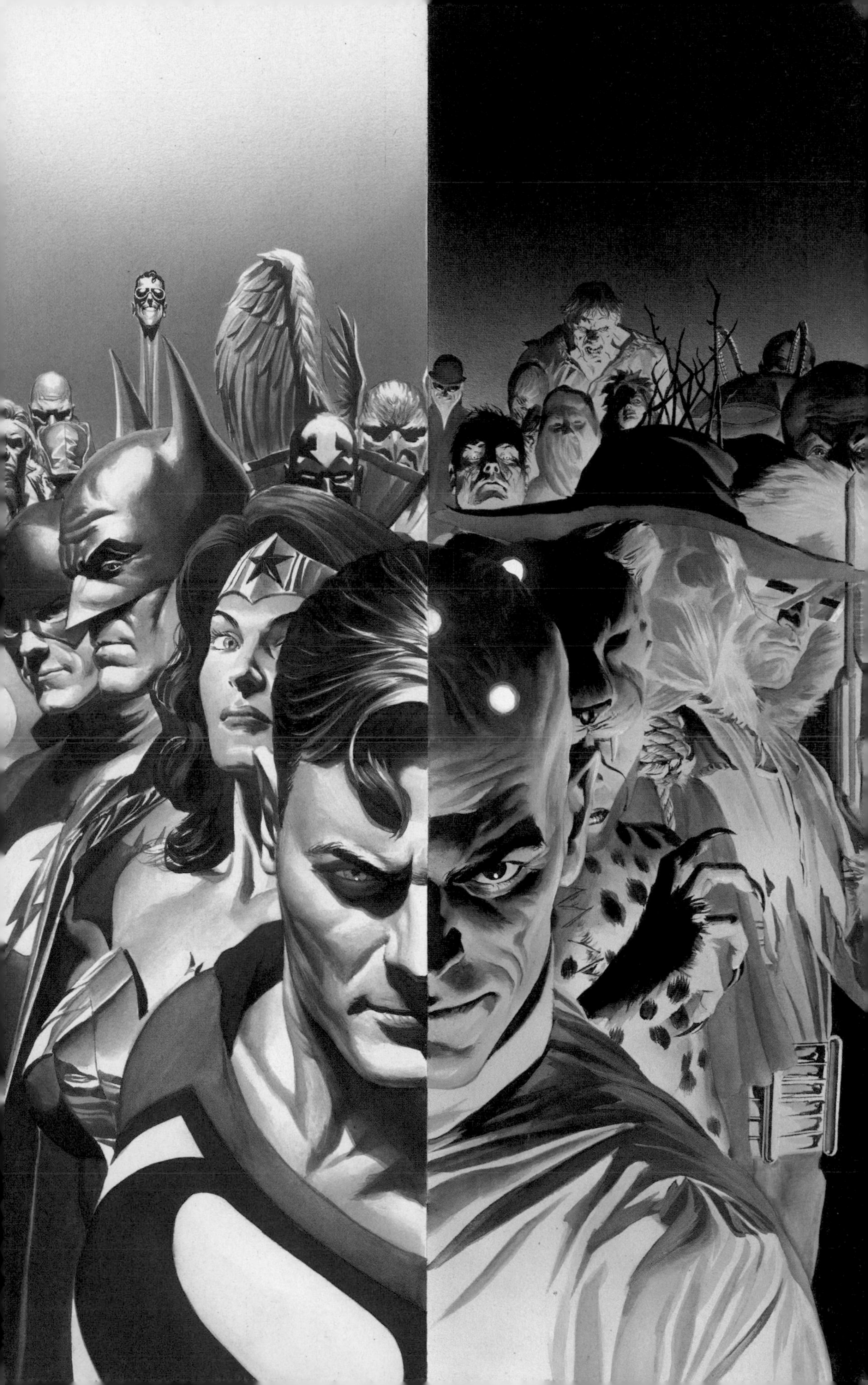

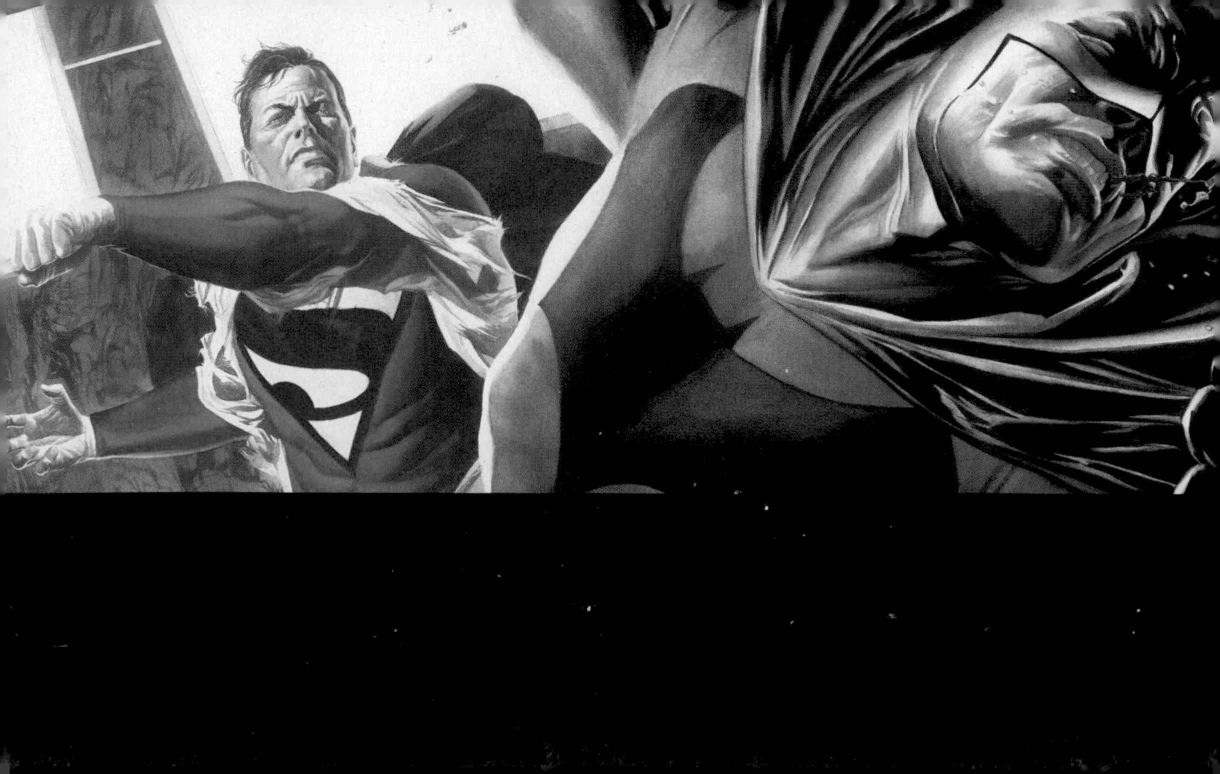

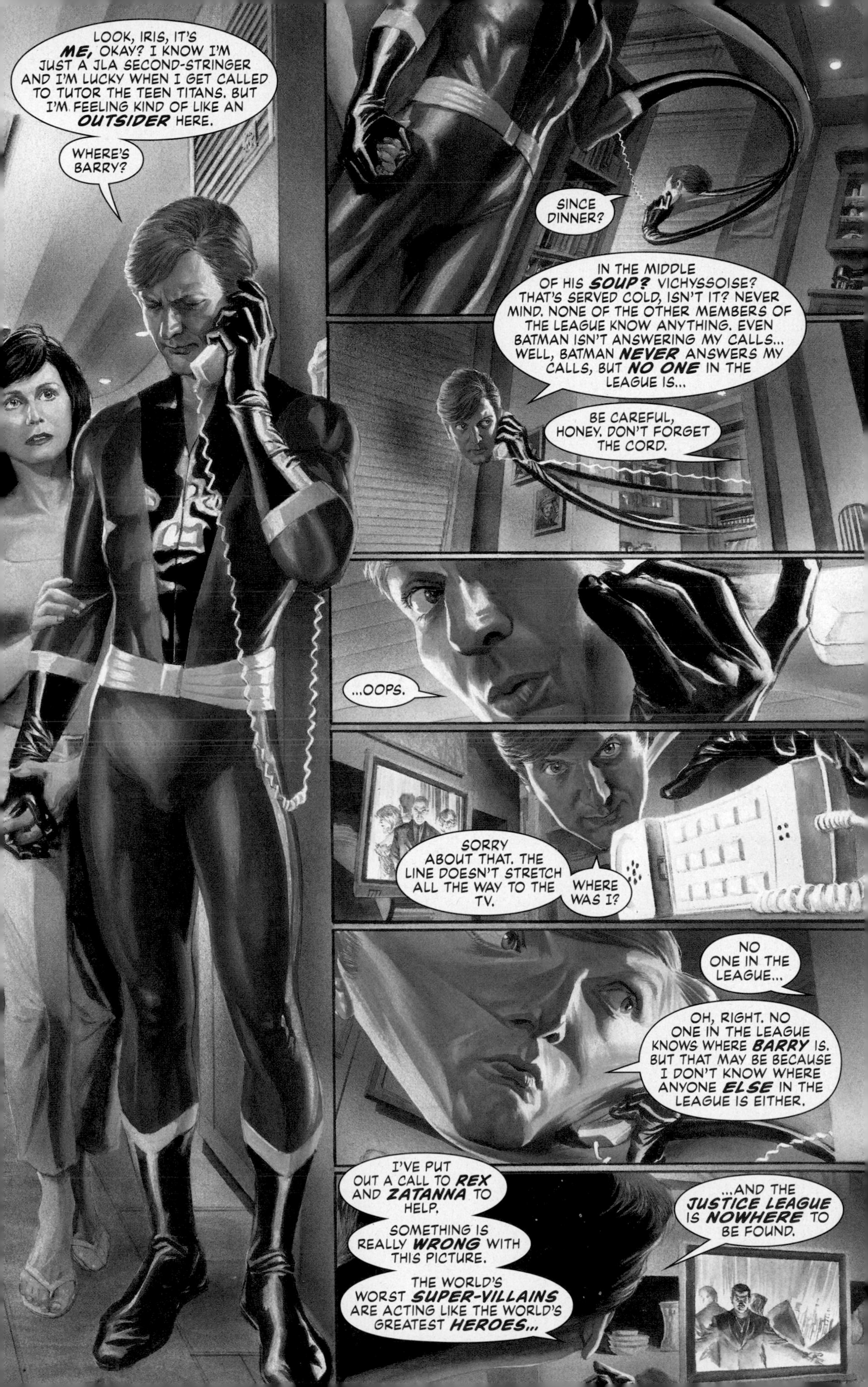
LOOK, IRIS, IT'S **ME,** OKAY? I KNOW I'M JUST A JLA SECOND-STRINGER AND I'M LUCKY WHEN I GET CALLED TO TUTOR THE TEEN TITANS. BUT I'M FEELING KIND OF LIKE AN **OUTSIDER** HERE.
WHERE'S BARRY?
SINCE DINNER?
IN THE MIDDLE OF HIS **SOUP?** VICHYSSOISE? THAT'S SERVED COLD, ISN'T IT? NEVER MIND. NONE OF THE OTHER MEMBERS OF THE LEAGUE KNOW ANYTHING. EVEN BATMAN ISN'T ANSWERING MY CALLS... WELL, BATMAN **NEVER** ANSWERS MY CALLS, BUT **NO ONE** IN THE LEAGUE IS...
BE CAREFUL, HONEY. DON'T FORGET THE CORD.
...OOPS.
SORRY ABOUT THAT. THE LINE DOESN'T STRETCH ALL THE WAY TO THE TV.
WHERE WAS I?
NO ONE IN THE LEAGUE...
OH, RIGHT. NO ONE IN THE LEAGUE KNOWS WHERE **BARRY** IS. BUT THAT MAY BE BECAUSE I DON'T KNOW WHERE ANYONE **ELSE** IN THE LEAGUE IS EITHER.
I'VE PUT OUT A CALL TO **REX** AND **ZATANNA** TO HELP.
SOMETHING IS REALLY **WRONG** WITH THIS PICTURE.
THE WORLD'S WORST **SUPER-VILLAINS** ARE ACTING LIKE THE WORLD'S GREATEST **HEROES...**
...AND THE **JUSTICE LEAGUE** IS **NOWHERE** TO BE FOUND.

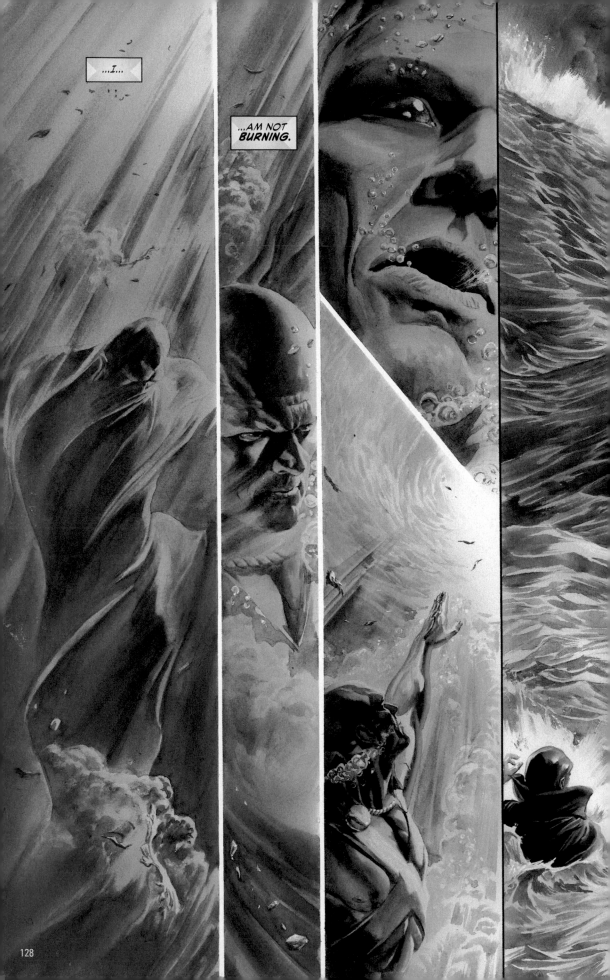

...I...

...AM NOT
BURNING.

CONSPIRACY...IT'S A **CONSPIRACY.** THEY ALL STRUCK AT ONCE...
...ALL AT **ONCE.**
I'M COMING, SUPERMAN.
I'M COMING, SUPERMAN.
I'M COMING, SUPERMAN.
I'M COMING, SUPERMAN.
The JUSTICE LEAGUE of AMERICA in:
JUSTICE
CHAPTER FIVE

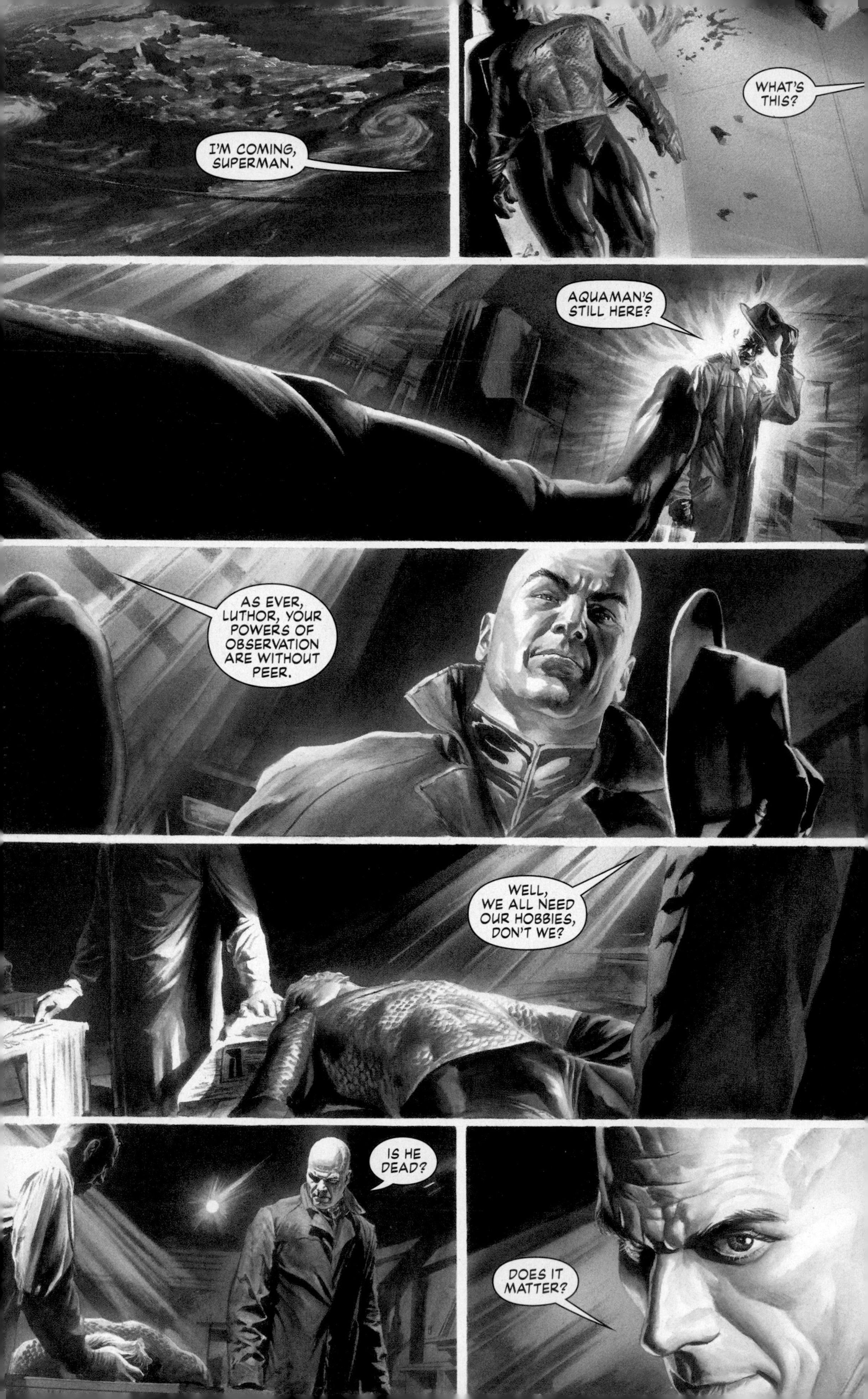
I'M COMING, SUPERMAN.
WHAT'S THIS?
AQUAMAN'S STILL HERE?
AS EVER, LUTHOR, YOUR POWERS OF OBSERVATION ARE WITHOUT PEER.
WELL, WE ALL NEED OUR HOBBIES, DON'T WE?
IS HE DEAD?
DOES IT MATTER?

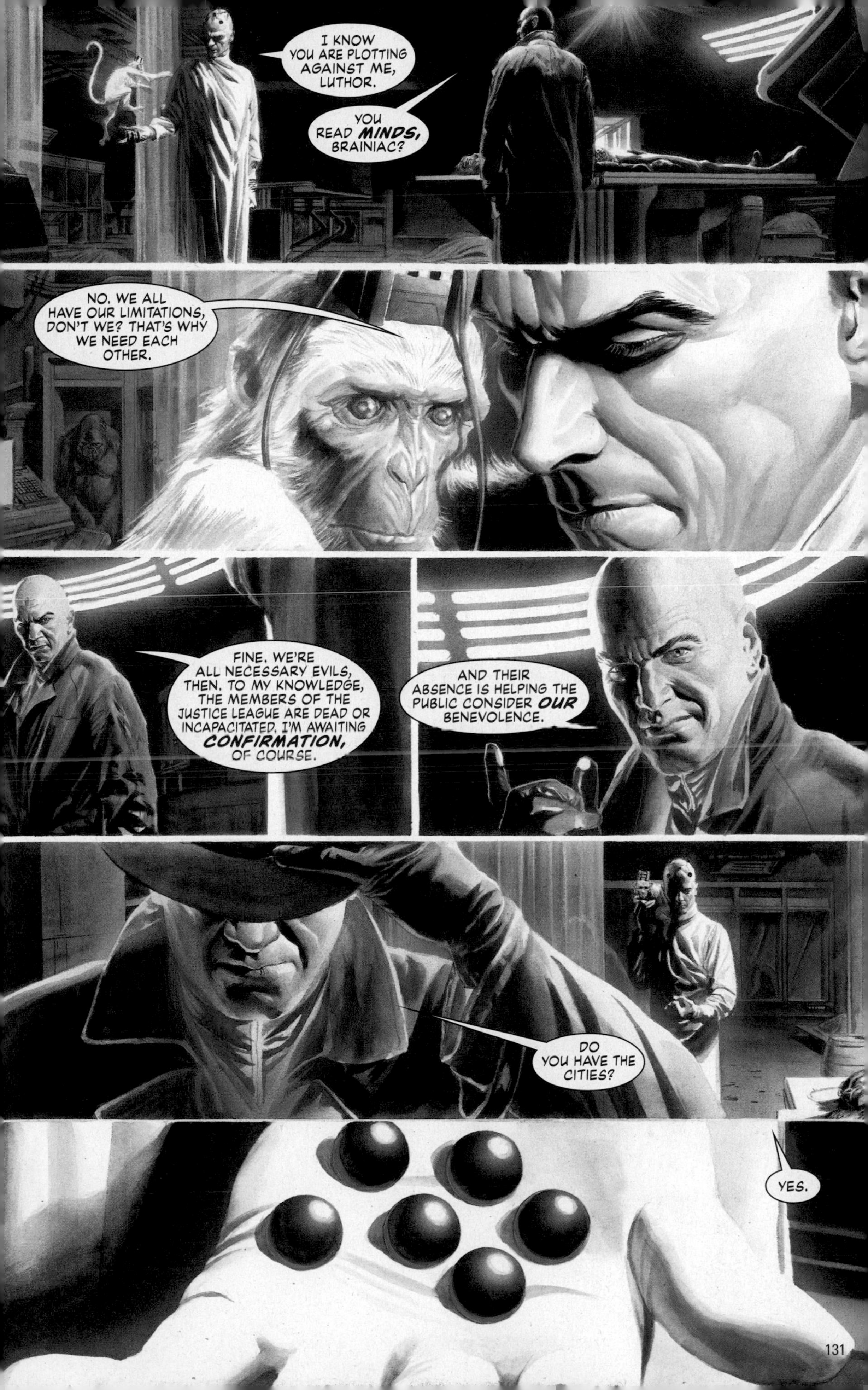
I KNOW YOU ARE PLOTTING AGAINST ME, LUTHOR.
YOU READ MINDS, BRAINIAC?
NO. WE ALL HAVE OUR LIMITATIONS, DON'T WE? THAT'S WHY WE NEED EACH OTHER.
FINE. WE'RE ALL NECESSARY EVILS, THEN. TO MY KNOWLEDGE, THE MEMBERS OF THE JUSTICE LEAGUE ARE DEAD OR INCAPACITATED. I'M AWAITING CONFIRMATION, OF COURSE.
AND THEIR ABSENCE IS HELPING THE PUBLIC CONSIDER OUR BENEVOLENCE.
DO YOU HAVE THE CITIES?
YES.

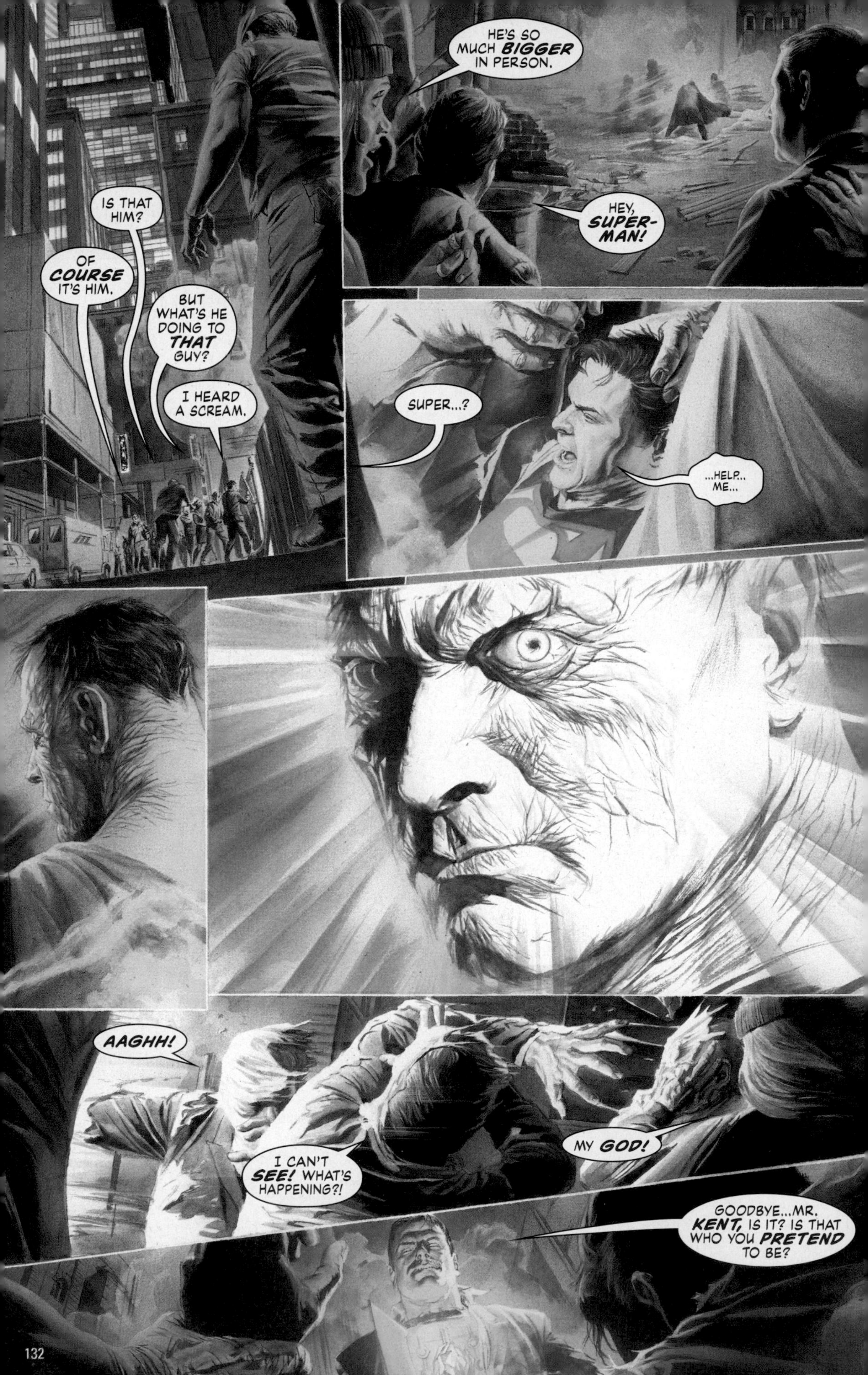
IS THAT HIM?
OF COURSE IT'S HIM.
BUT WHAT'S HE DOING TO THAT GUY?
I HEARD A SCREAM.
HE'S SO MUCH BIGGER IN PERSON.
HEY, SUPER-MAN!
SUPER...?
...HELP... ME...
AAGHH!
I CAN'T SEE! WHAT'S HAPPENING?!
MY GOD!
GOODBYE...MR. KENT, IS IT? IS THAT WHO YOU PRETEND TO BE?

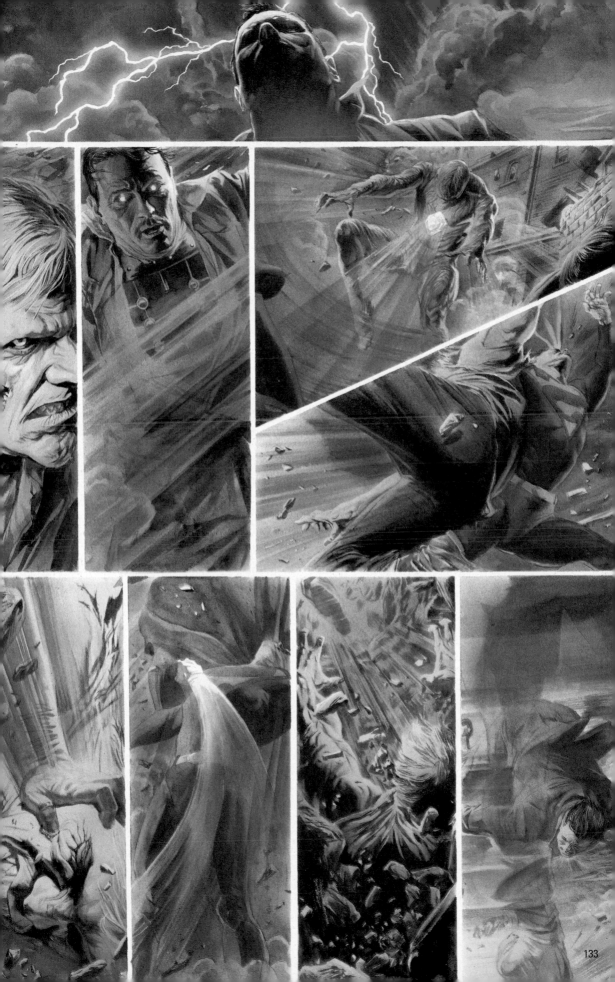

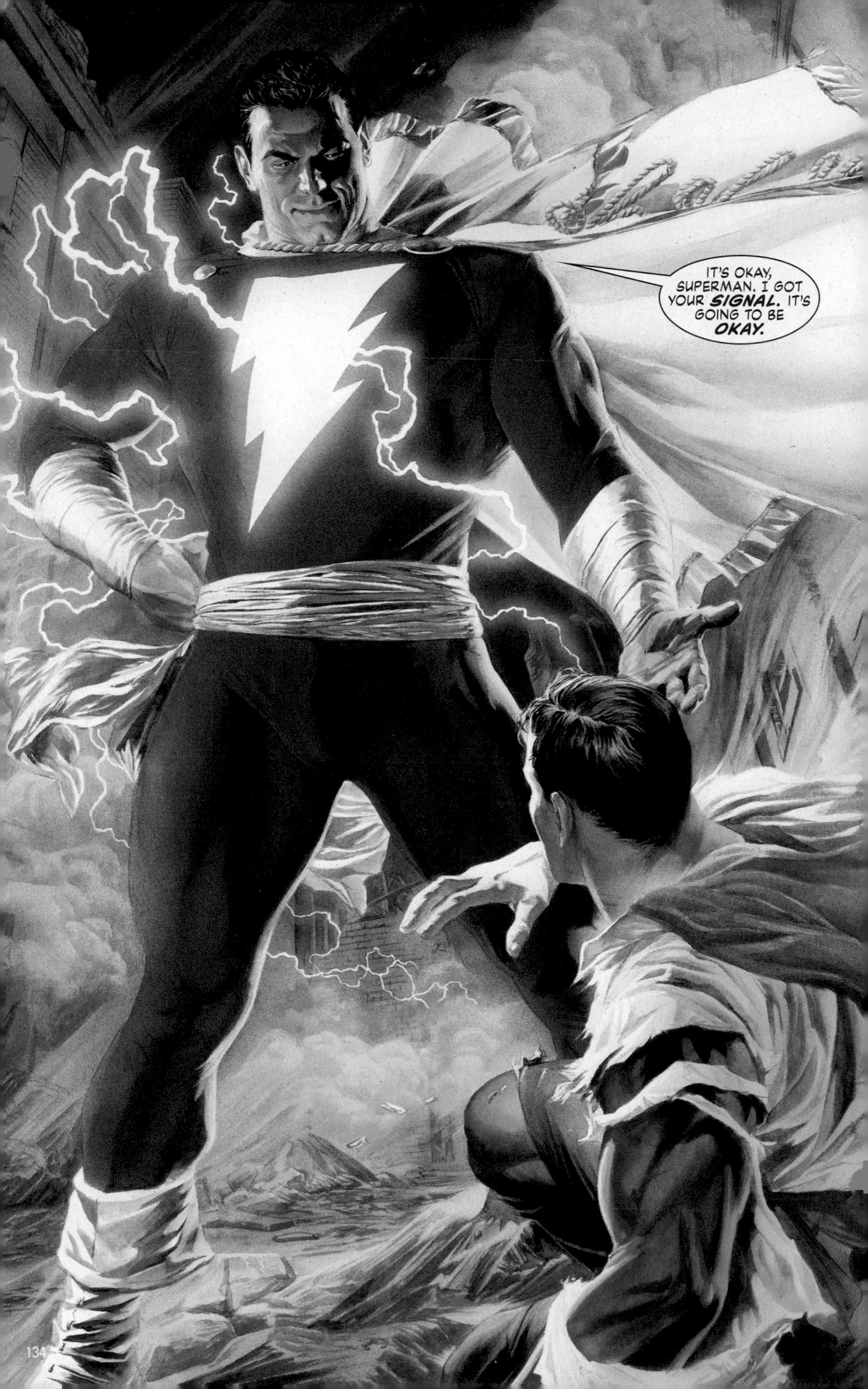
IT'S OKAY, SUPERMAN. I GOT YOUR **SIGNAL**. IT'S GOING TO BE **OKAY**.

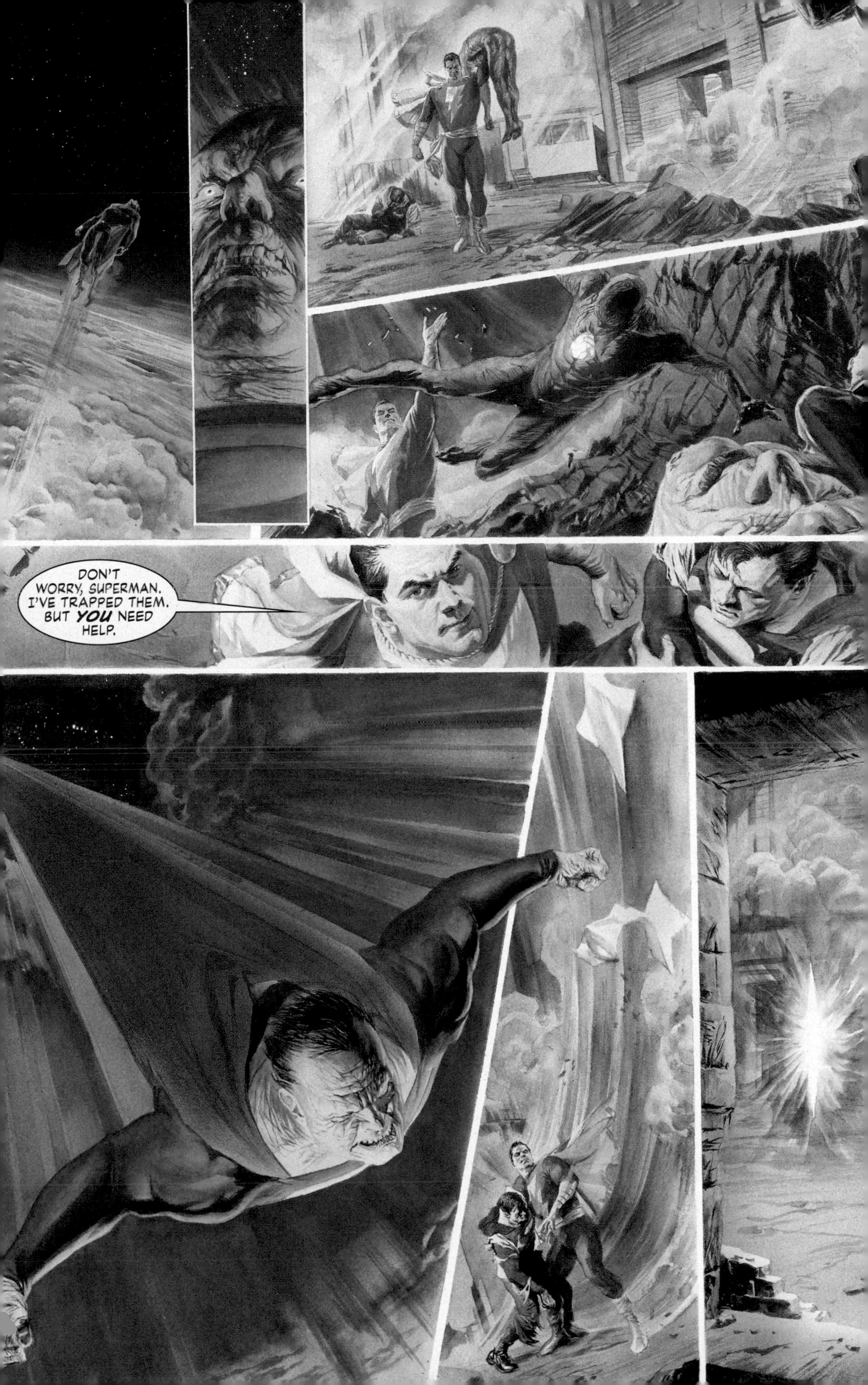
DON'T WORRY, SUPERMAN. I'VE TRAPPED THEM. BUT YOU NEED HELP.

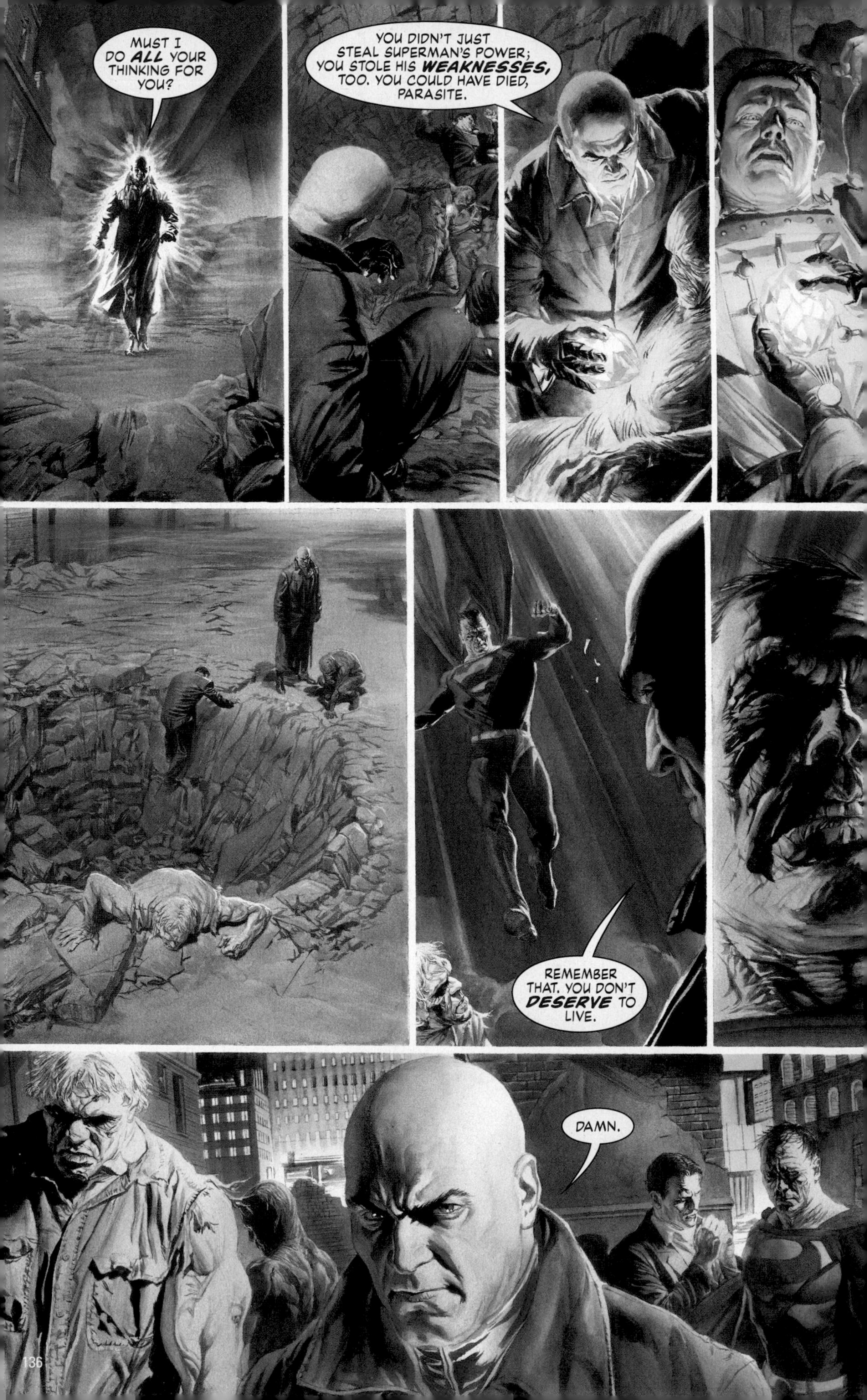
MUST I DO ALL YOUR THINKING FOR YOU?
YOU DIDN'T JUST STEAL SUPERMAN'S POWER; YOU STOLE HIS WEAKNESSES, TOO. YOU COULD HAVE DIED, PARASITE.
REMEMBER THAT. YOU DON'T DESERVE TO LIVE.
DAMN.

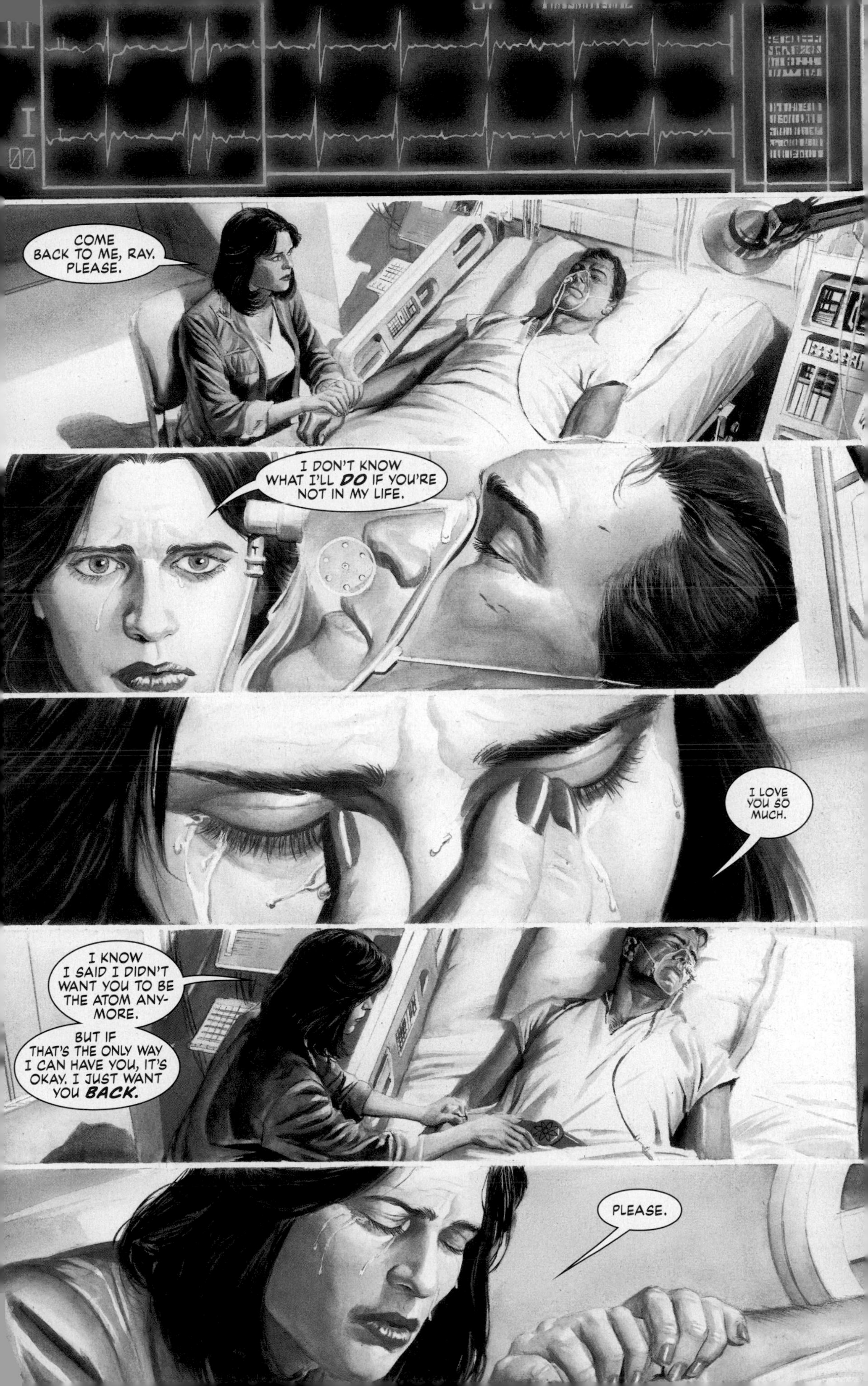
COME BACK TO ME, RAY. PLEASE.
I DON'T KNOW WHAT I'LL DO IF YOU'RE NOT IN MY LIFE.
I LOVE YOU SO MUCH.
I KNOW I SAID I DIDN'T WANT YOU TO BE THE ATOM ANY-MORE.
BUT IF THAT'S THE ONLY WAY I CAN HAVE YOU, IT'S OKAY. I JUST WANT YOU BACK.
PLEASE.

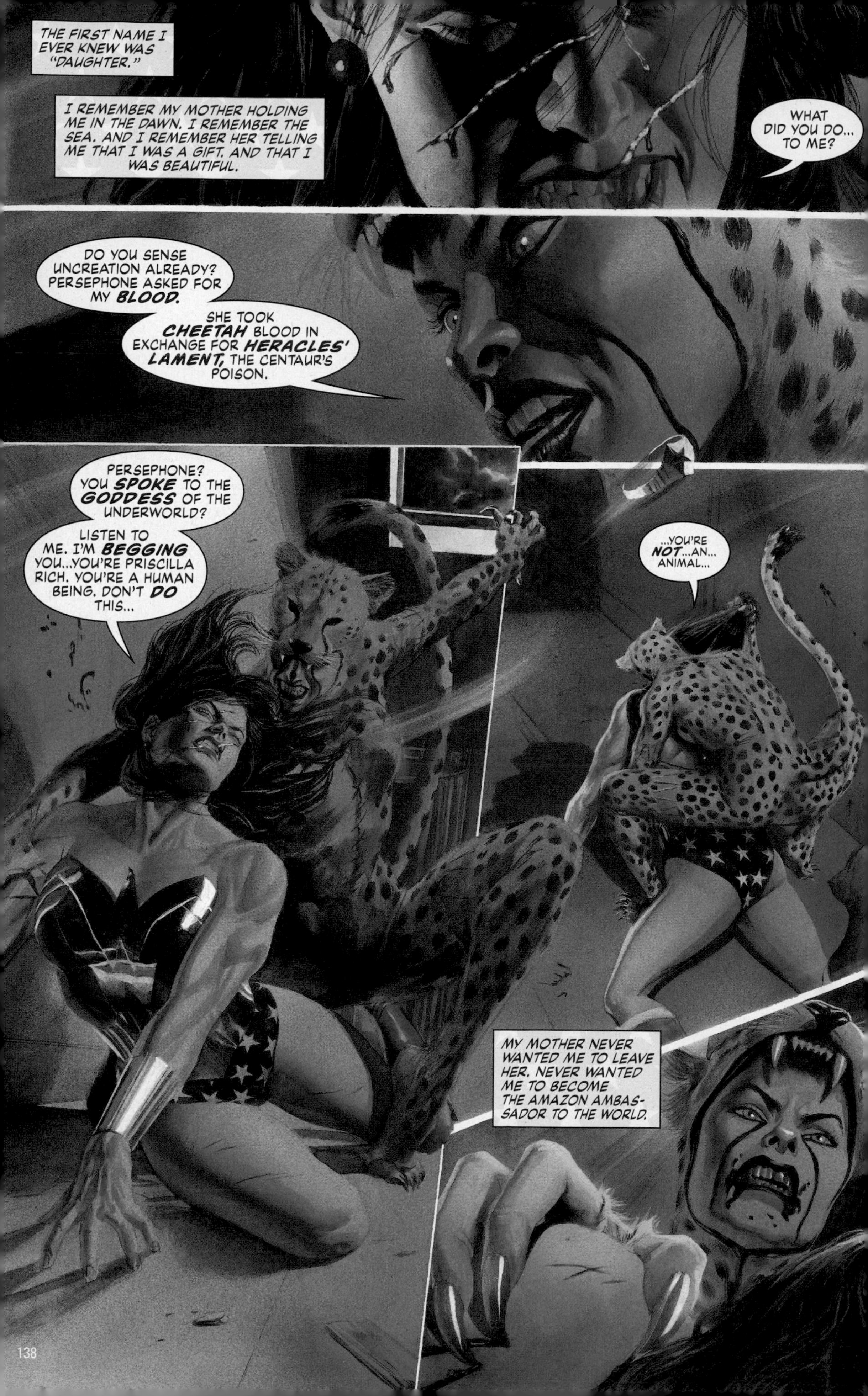

THE FIRST NAME I EVER KNEW WAS "DAUGHTER."
I REMEMBER MY MOTHER HOLDING ME IN THE DAWN. I REMEMBER THE SEA. AND I REMEMBER HER TELLING ME THAT I WAS A GIFT. AND THAT I WAS BEAUTIFUL.
WHAT DID YOU DO... TO ME?
DO YOU SENSE UNCREATION ALREADY? PERSEPHONE ASKED FOR MY BLOOD.
SHE TOOK CHEETAH BLOOD IN EXCHANGE FOR HERACLES' LAMENT, THE CENTAUR'S POISON.
PERSEPHONE? YOU SPOKE TO THE GODDESS OF THE UNDERWORLD?
LISTEN TO ME. I'M BEGGING YOU...YOU'RE PRISCILLA RICH. YOU'RE A HUMAN BEING. DON'T DO THIS...
...YOU'RE NOT...AN... ANIMAL...
MY MOTHER NEVER WANTED ME TO LEAVE HER. NEVER WANTED ME TO BECOME THE AMAZON AMBASSADOR TO THE WORLD.

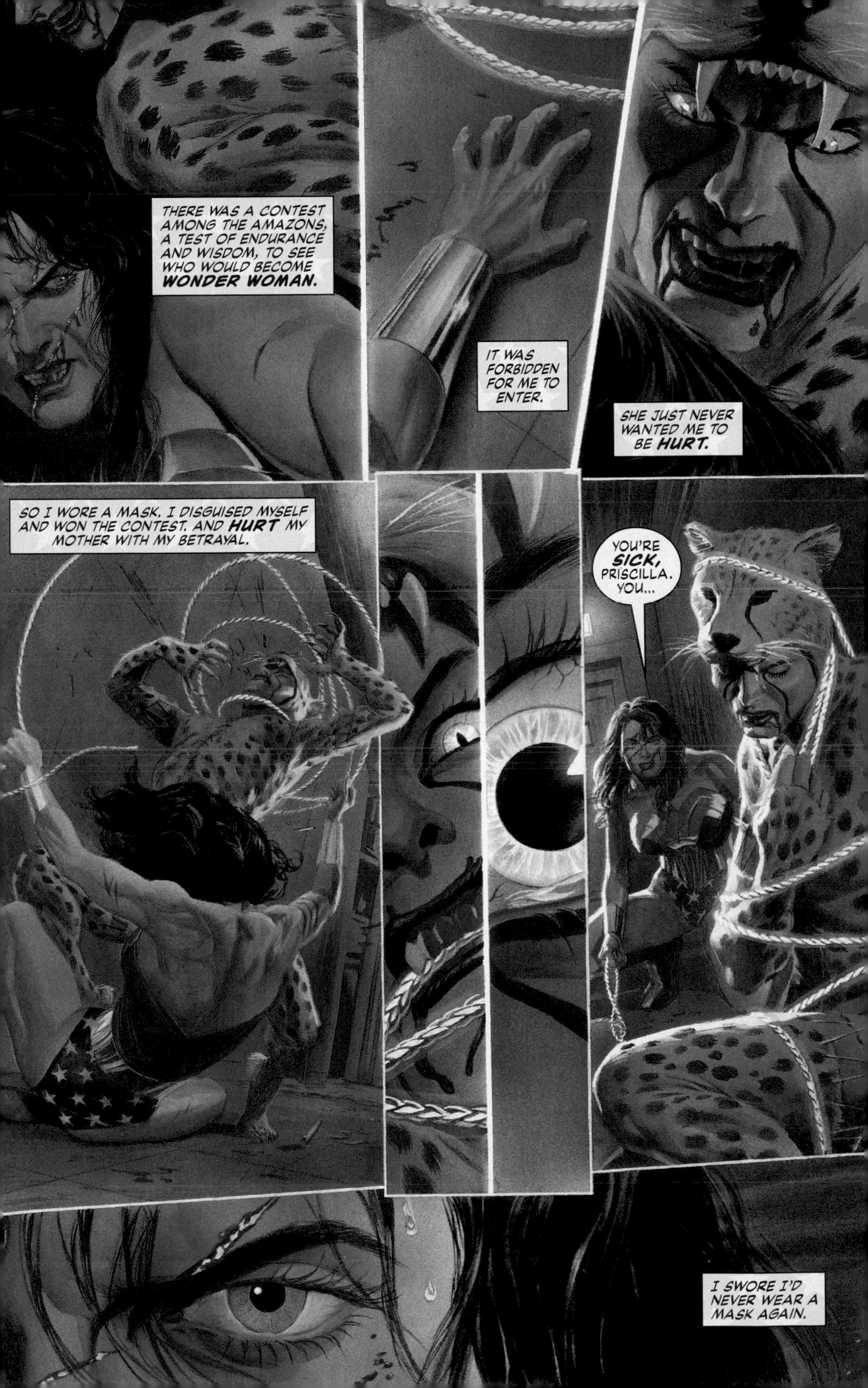
THERE WAS A CONTEST AMONG THE AMAZONS, A TEST OF ENDURANCE AND WISDOM, TO SEE WHO WOULD BECOME **WONDER WOMAN.**
IT WAS FORBIDDEN FOR ME TO ENTER.
SHE JUST NEVER WANTED ME TO BE **HURT.**
SO I WORE A MASK. I DISGUISED MYSELF AND WON THE CONTEST. AND **HURT** MY MOTHER WITH MY BETRAYAL.
YOU'RE **SICK,** PRISCILLA. YOU...
I SWORE I'D NEVER WEAR A MASK AGAIN.

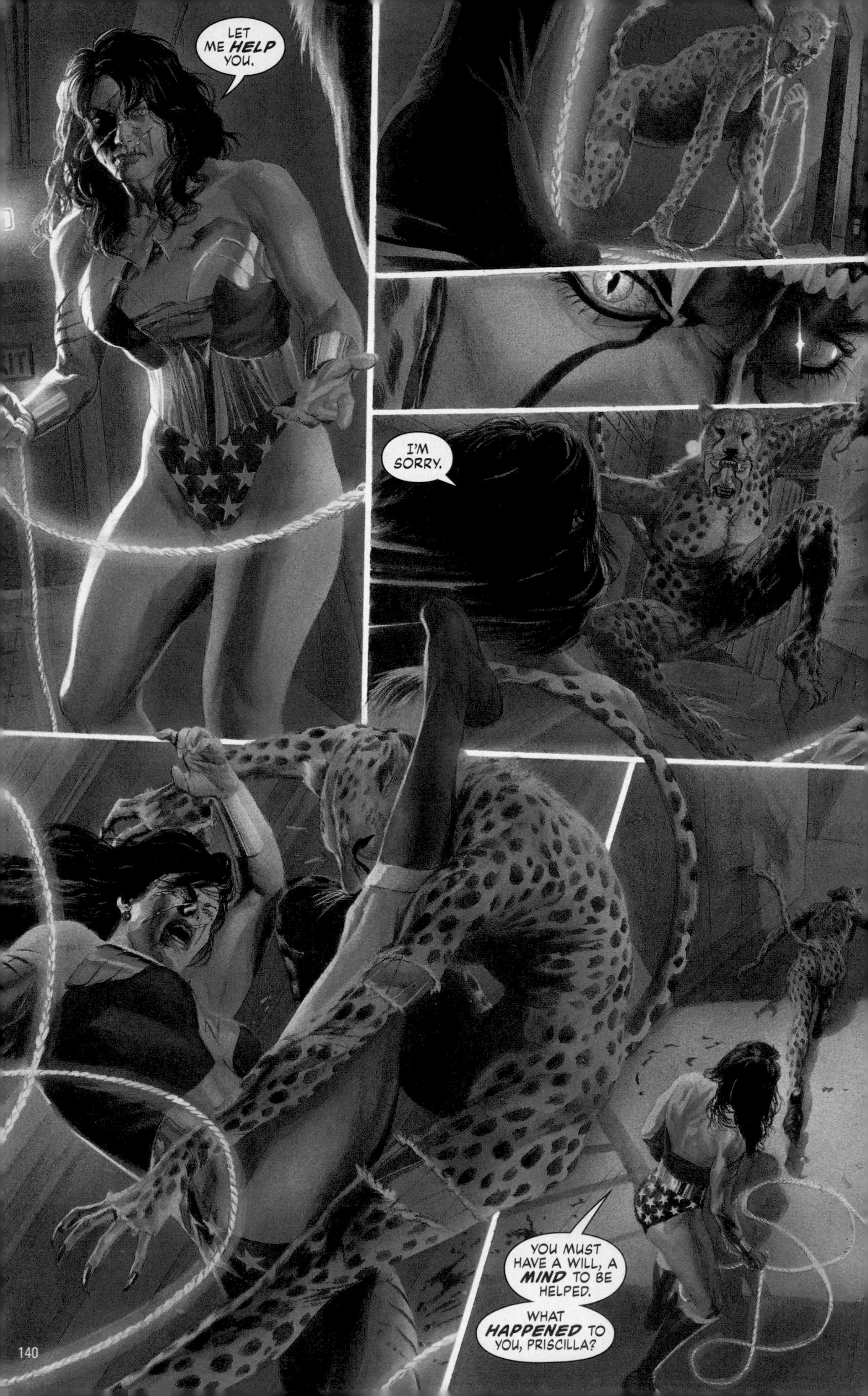
LET ME HELP YOU.
I'M SORRY.
YOU MUST HAVE A WILL, A MIND TO BE HELPED.
WHAT HAPPENED TO YOU, PRISCILLA?

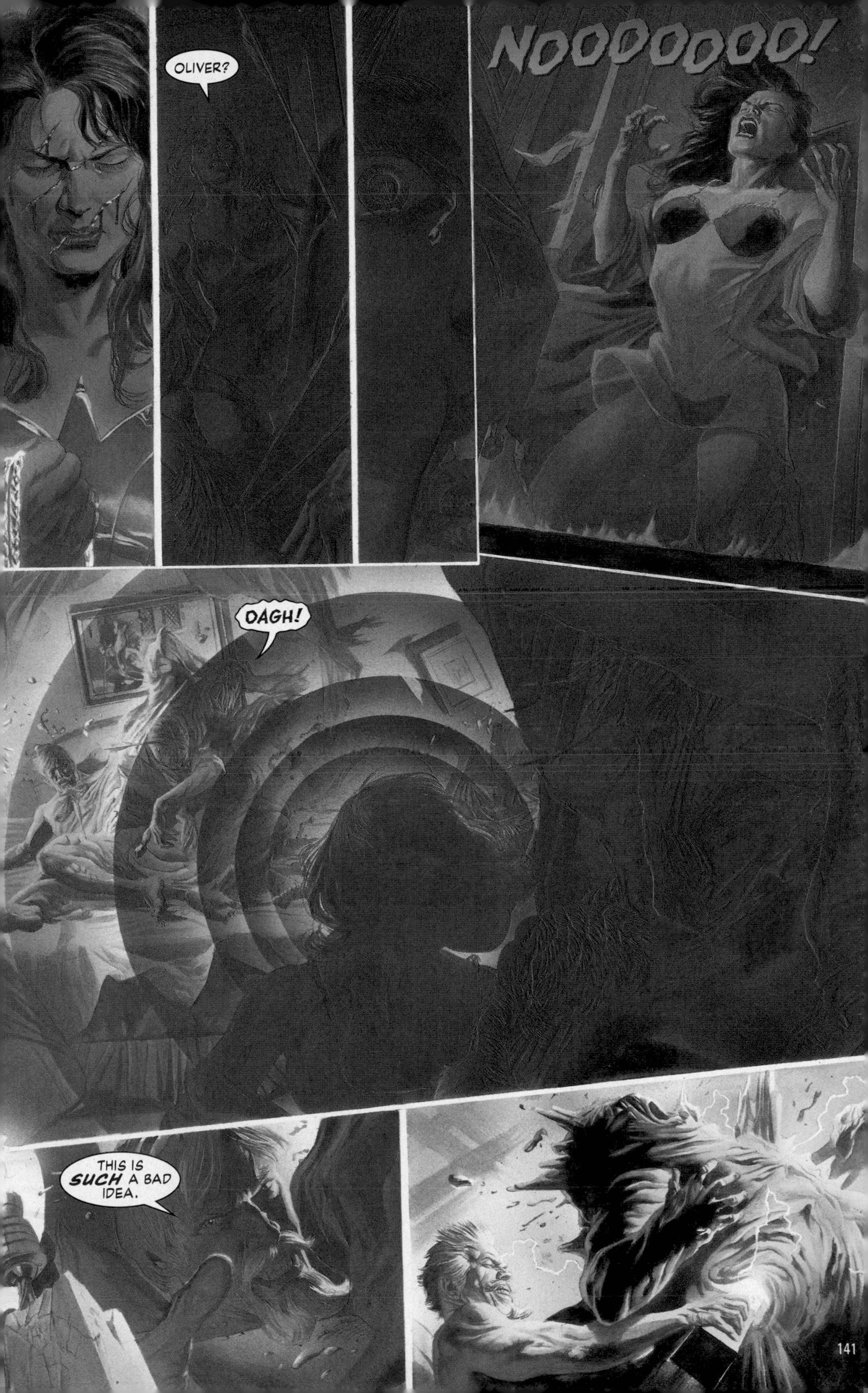
OLIVER?
NOOOOOOO!
OAGH!
THIS IS SUCH A BAD IDEA.

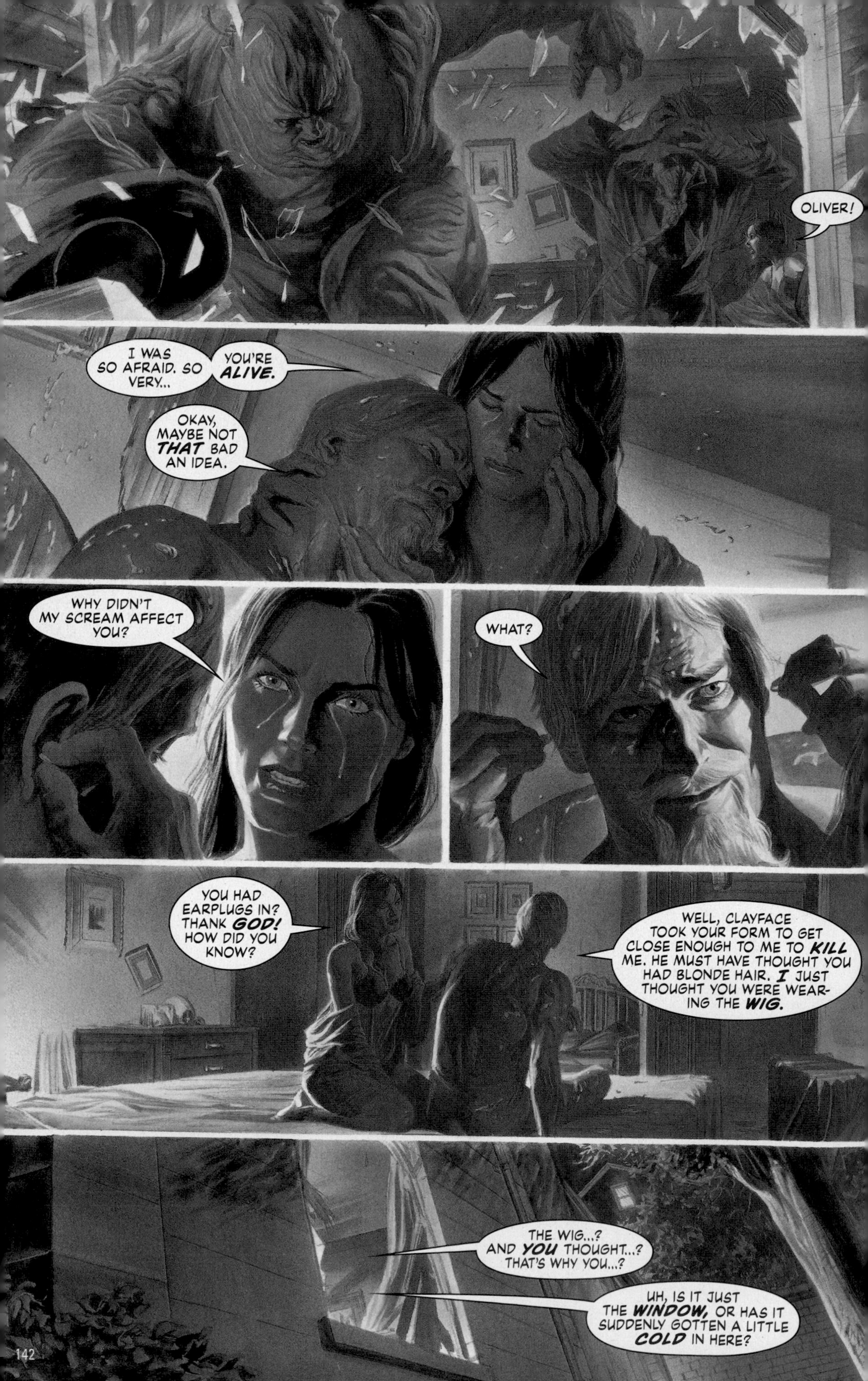
OLIVER!
YOU'RE ALIVE.
I WAS SO AFRAID. SO VERY...
OKAY, MAYBE NOT THAT BAD AN IDEA.
WHY DIDN'T MY SCREAM AFFECT YOU?
WHAT?
YOU HAD EARPLUGS IN? THANK GOD! HOW DID YOU KNOW?
WELL, CLAYFACE TOOK YOUR FORM TO GET CLOSE ENOUGH TO ME TO KILL ME. HE MUST HAVE THOUGHT YOU HAD BLONDE HAIR. I JUST THOUGHT YOU WERE WEARING THE WIG.
THE WIG...? AND YOU THOUGHT...? THAT'S WHY YOU...?
UH, IS IT JUST THE WINDOW, OR HAS IT SUDDENLY GOTTEN A LITTLE COLD IN HERE?

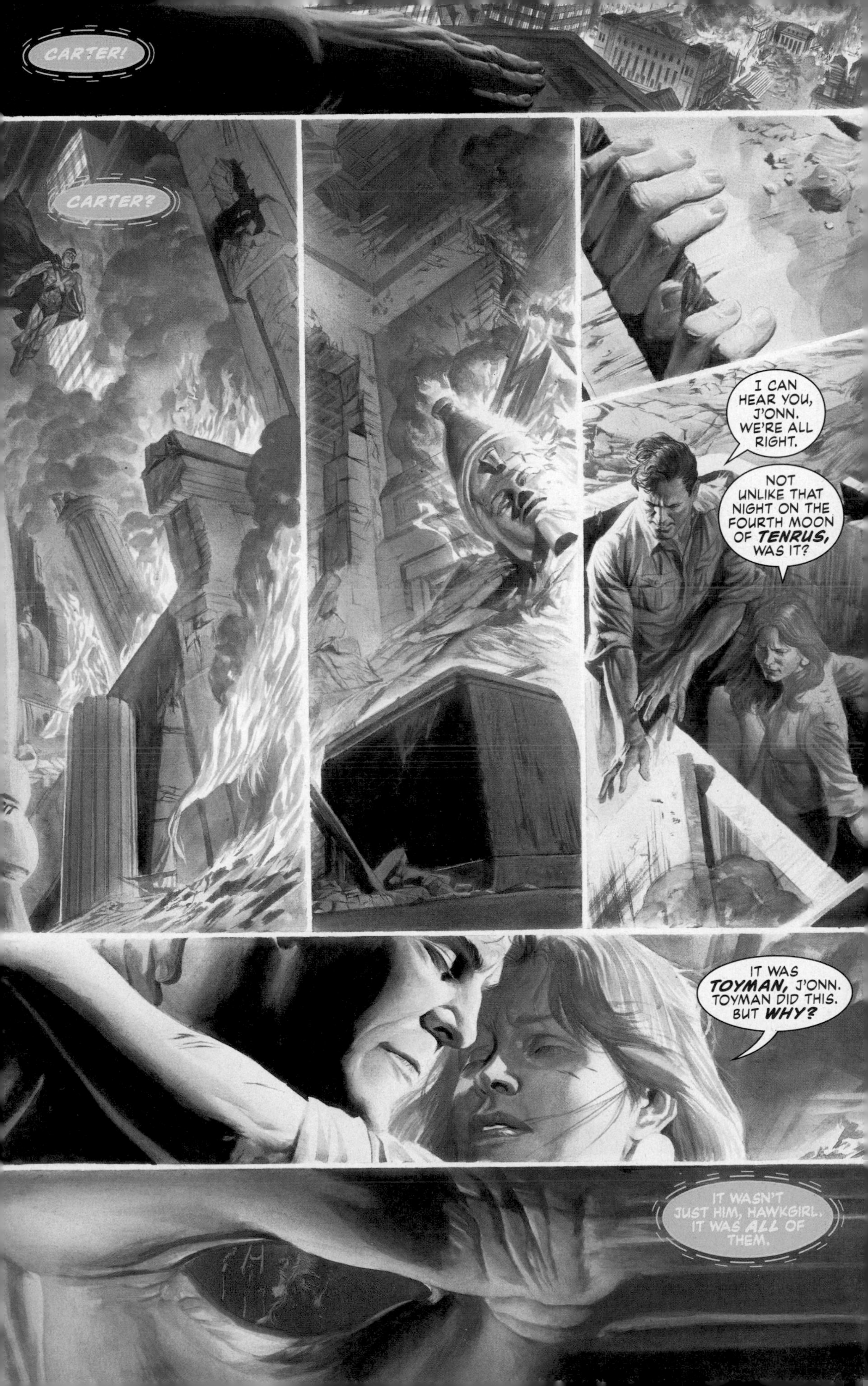
CARTER!
CARTER?
I CAN HEAR YOU, J'ONN. WE'RE ALL RIGHT.
NOT UNLIKE THAT NIGHT ON THE FOURTH MOON OF TENRUS, WAS IT?
IT WAS TOYMAN, J'ONN. TOYMAN DID THIS. BUT WHY?
IT WASN'T JUST HIM, HAWKGIRL. IT WAS ALL OF THEM.

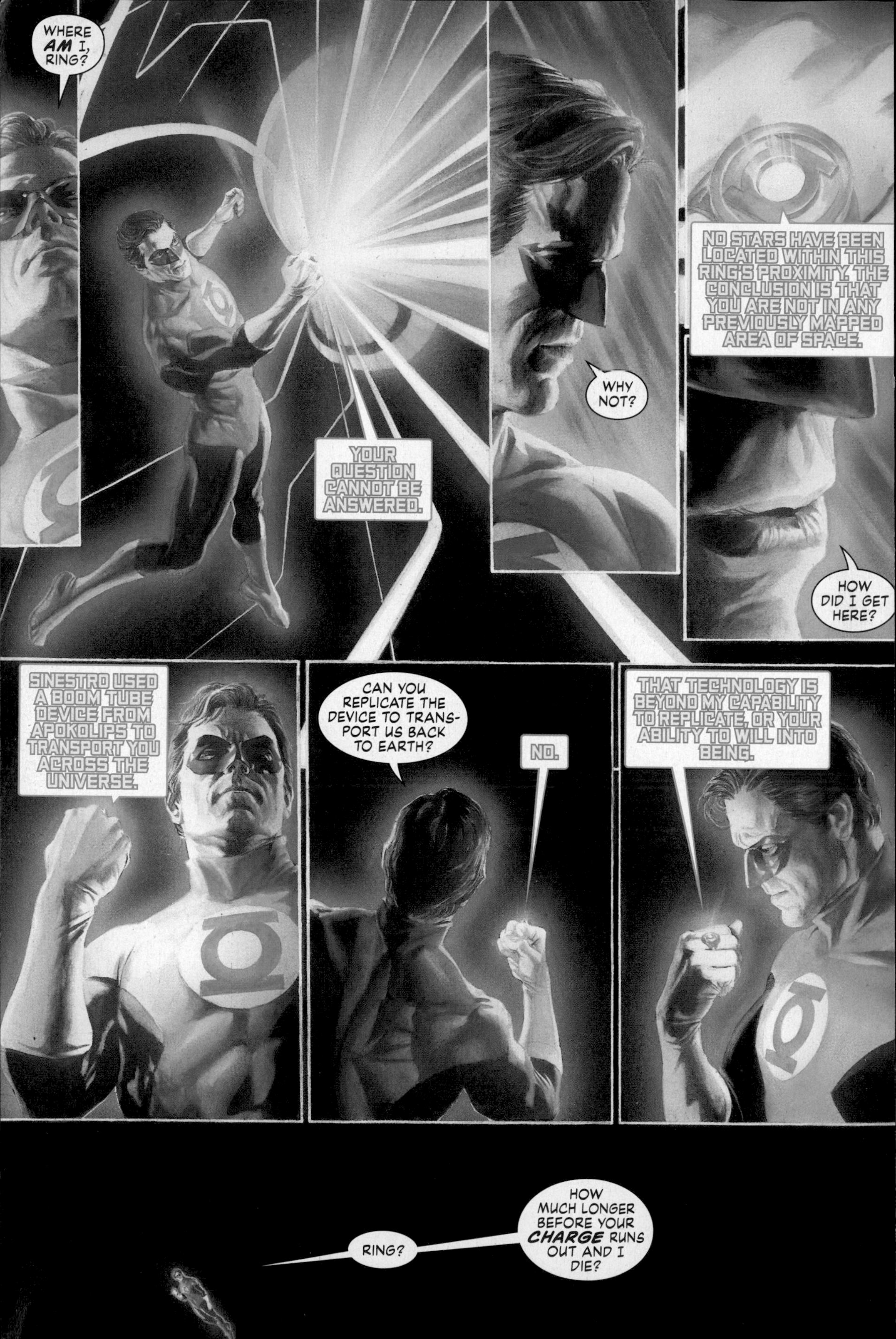
WHERE AM I, RING?
YOUR QUESTION CANNOT BE ANSWERED.
WHY NOT?
NO STARS HAVE BEEN LOCATED WITHIN THIS RING'S PROXIMITY. THE CONCLUSION IS THAT YOU ARE NOT IN ANY PREVIOUSLY MAPPED AREA OF SPACE.
HOW DID I GET HERE?
SINESTRO USED A BOOM TUBE DEVICE FROM APOKOLIPS TO TRANSPORT YOU ACROSS THE UNIVERSE.
CAN YOU REPLICATE THE DEVICE TO TRANSPORT US BACK TO EARTH?
NO.
THAT TECHNOLOGY IS BEYOND MY CAPABILITY TO REPLICATE, OR YOUR ABILITY TO WILL INTO BEING.
RING?
HOW MUCH LONGER BEFORE YOUR CHARGE RUNS OUT AND I DIE?

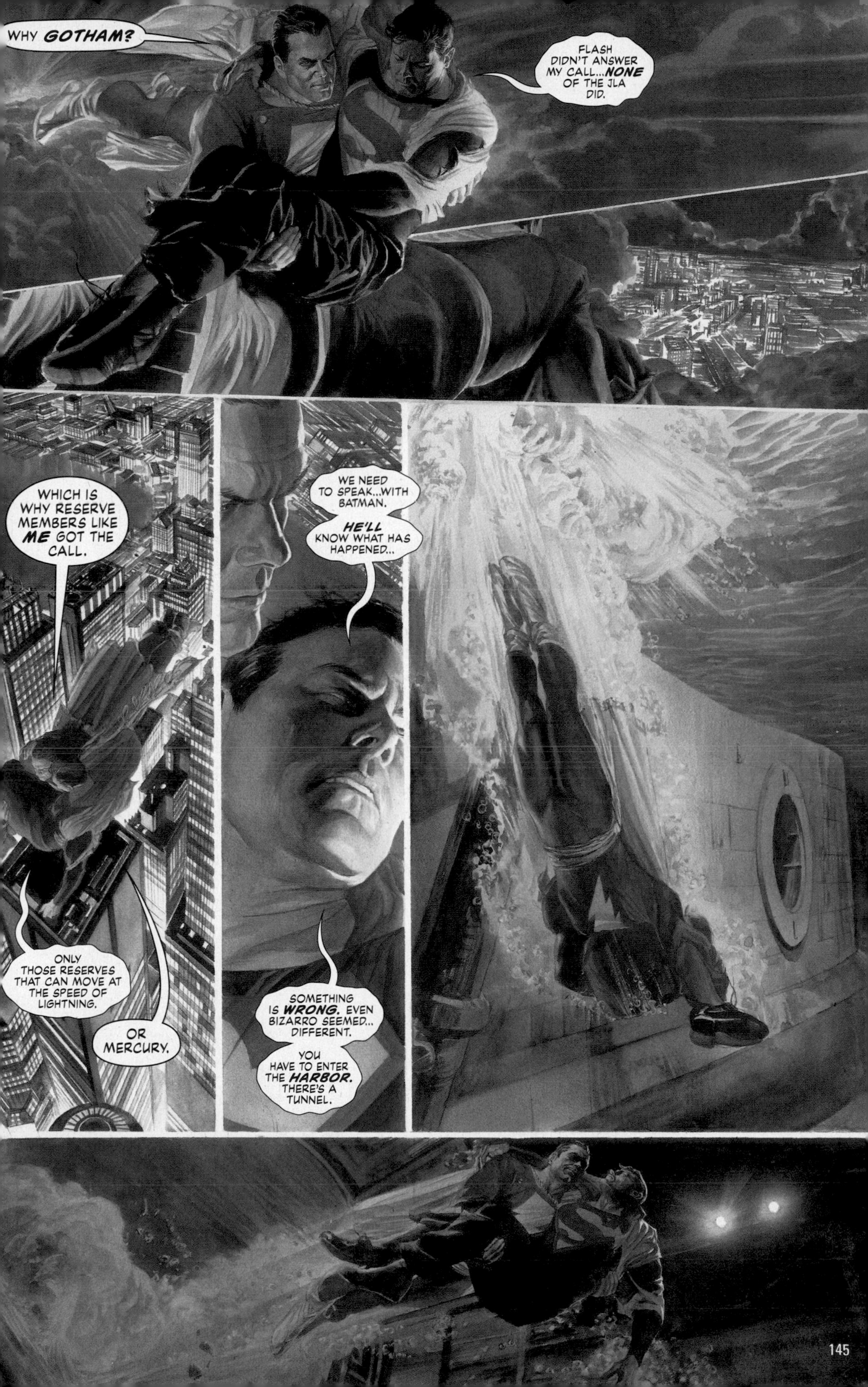
WHY GOTHAM?
FLASH DIDN'T ANSWER MY CALL...NONE OF THE JLA DID.
WHICH IS WHY RESERVE MEMBERS LIKE ME GOT THE CALL.
ONLY THOSE RESERVES THAT CAN MOVE AT THE SPEED OF LIGHTNING.
OR MERCURY.
WE NEED TO SPEAK...WITH BATMAN.
HE'LL KNOW WHAT HAS HAPPENED...
SOMETHING IS WRONG. EVEN BIZARRO SEEMED... DIFFERENT.
YOU HAVE TO ENTER THE HARBOR. THERE'S A TUNNEL.

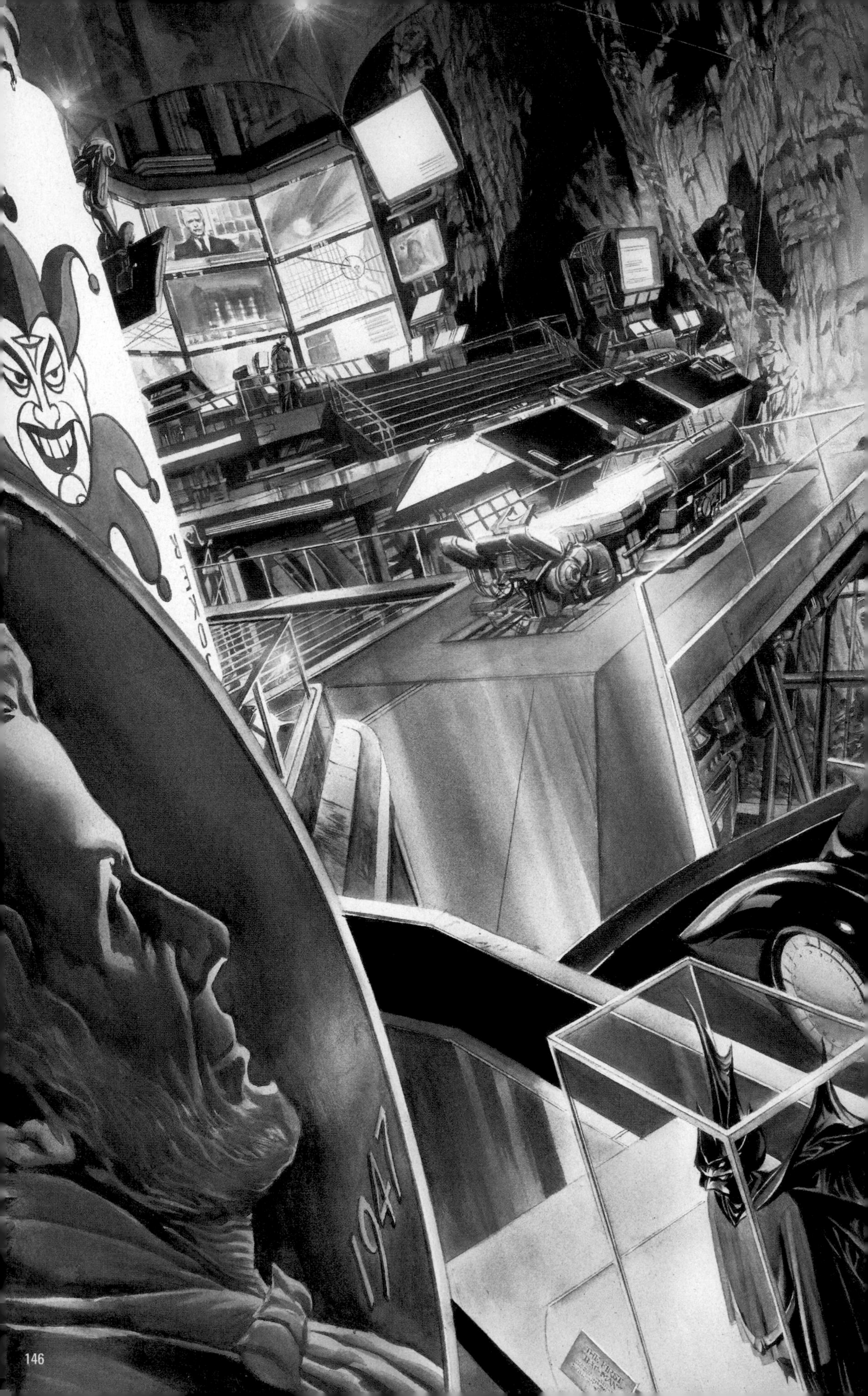
1947

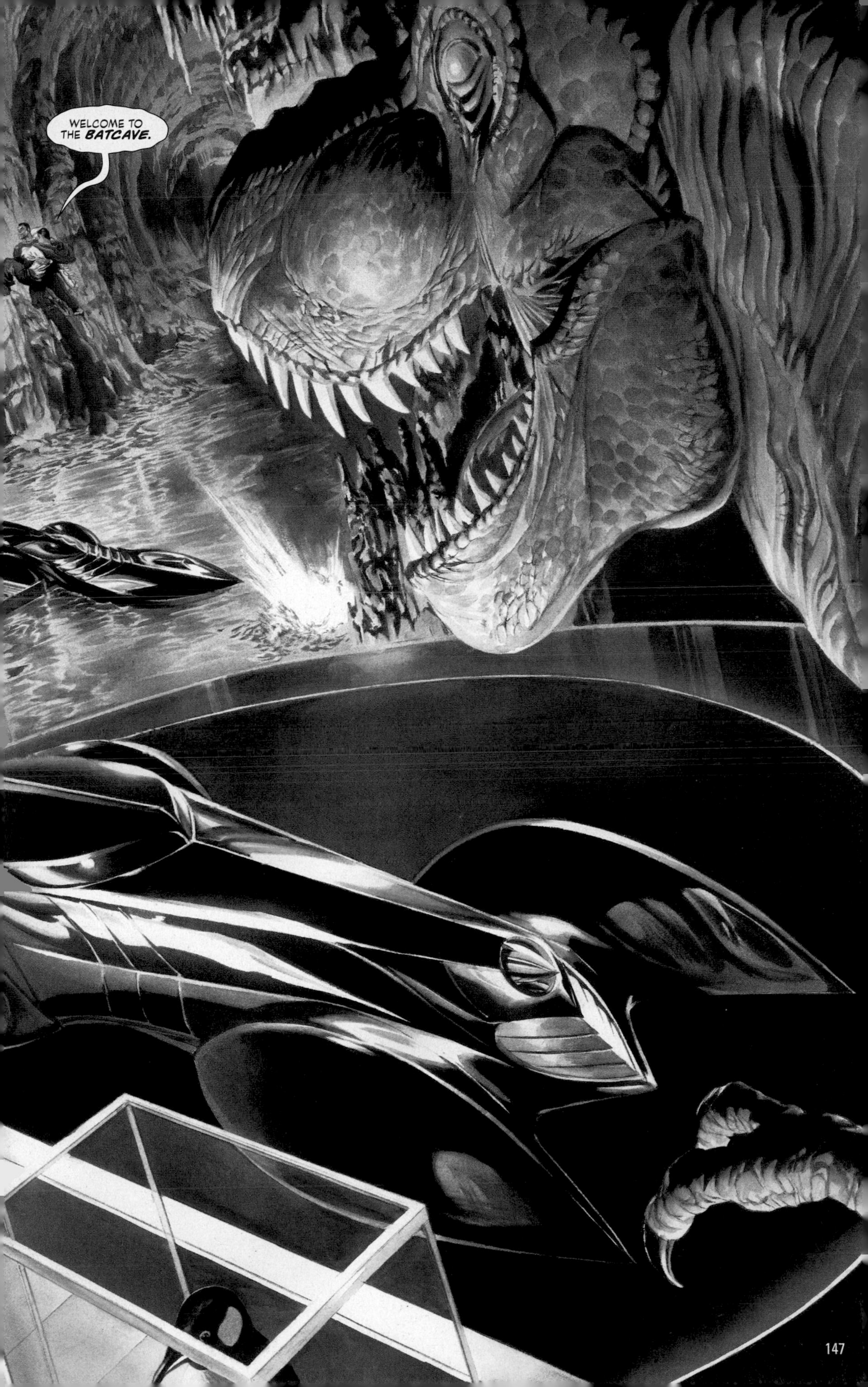
WELCOME TO THE BATCAVE.

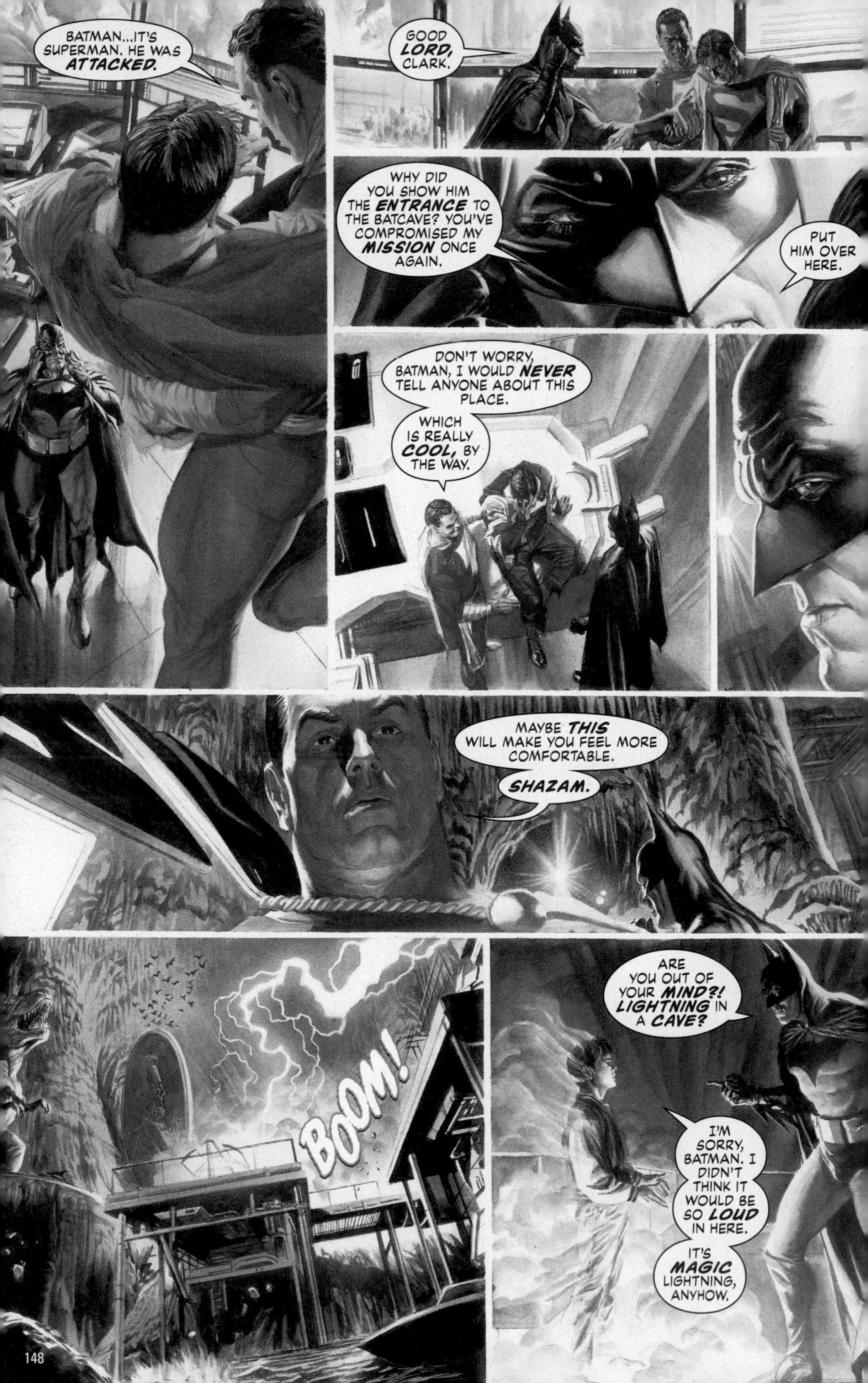
BATMAN...IT'S SUPERMAN. HE WAS ATTACKED.
GOOD LORD, CLARK.
WHY DID YOU SHOW HIM THE ENTRANCE TO THE BATCAVE? YOU'VE COMPROMISED MY MISSION ONCE AGAIN.
PUT HIM OVER HERE.
DON'T WORRY, BATMAN, I WOULD NEVER TELL ANYONE ABOUT THIS PLACE.
WHICH IS REALLY COOL, BY THE WAY.
MAYBE THIS WILL MAKE YOU FEEL MORE COMFORTABLE.
SHAZAM.
BOOM!
ARE YOU OUT OF YOUR MIND?! LIGHTNING IN A CAVE?
I'M SORRY, BATMAN. I DIDN'T THINK IT WOULD BE SO LOUD IN HERE.
IT'S MAGIC LIGHTNING, ANYHOW.

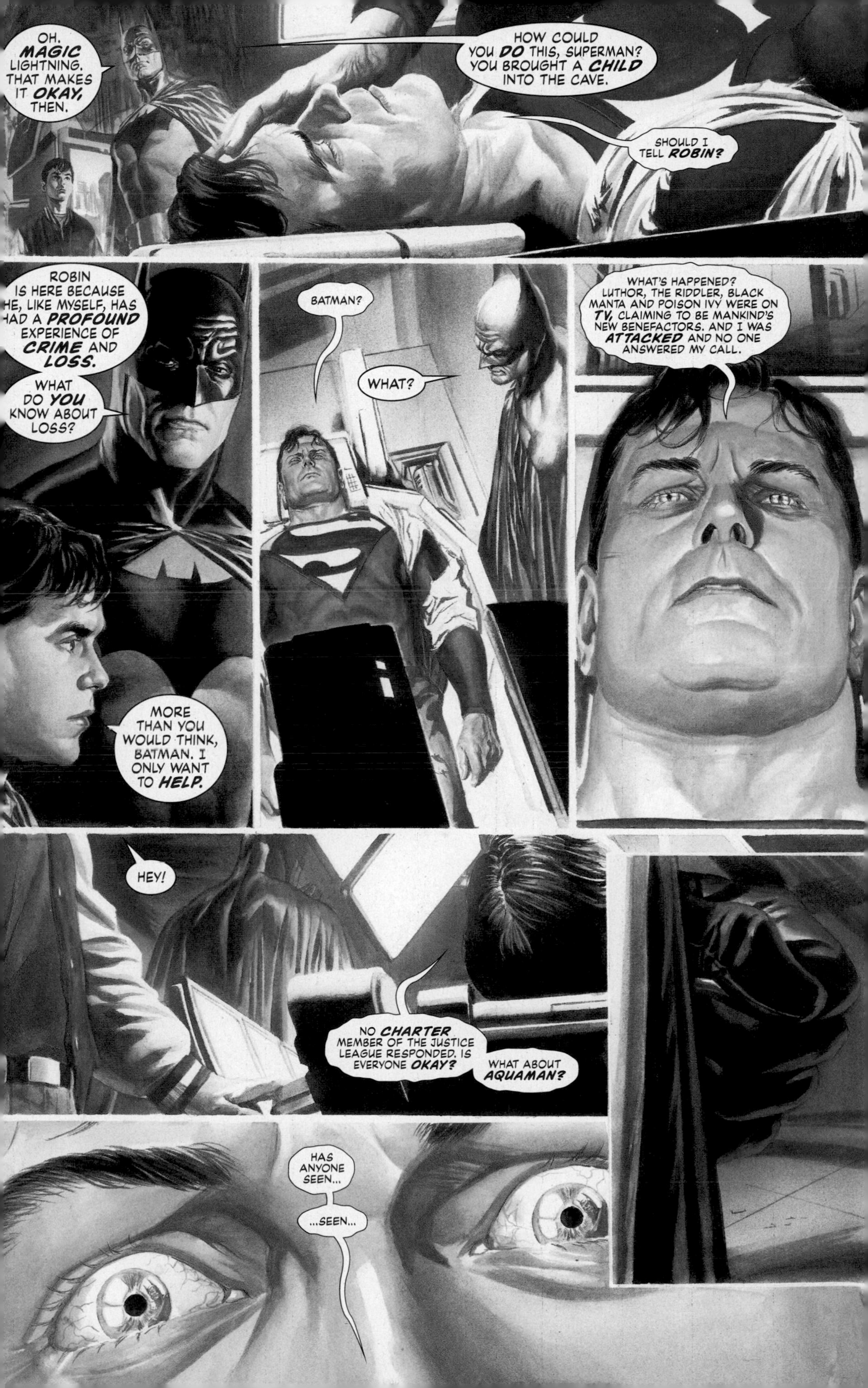

OH. MAGIC LIGHTNING. THAT MAKES IT OKAY, THEN.
HOW COULD YOU DO THIS, SUPERMAN? YOU BROUGHT A CHILD INTO THE CAVE.
SHOULD I TELL ROBIN?
ROBIN IS HERE BECAUSE HE, LIKE MYSELF, HAS HAD A PROFOUND EXPERIENCE OF CRIME AND LOSS.
WHAT DO YOU KNOW ABOUT LOSS?
MORE THAN YOU WOULD THINK, BATMAN. I ONLY WANT TO HELP.
BATMAN?
WHAT?
WHAT'S HAPPENED? LUTHOR, THE RIDDLER, BLACK MANTA AND POISON IVY WERE ON TV, CLAIMING TO BE MANKIND'S NEW BENEFACTORS. AND I WAS ATTACKED AND NO ONE ANSWERED MY CALL.
HEY!
NO CHARTER MEMBER OF THE JUSTICE LEAGUE RESPONDED. IS EVERYONE OKAY?
WHAT ABOUT AQUAMAN?
HAS ANYONE SEEN...
...SEEN...

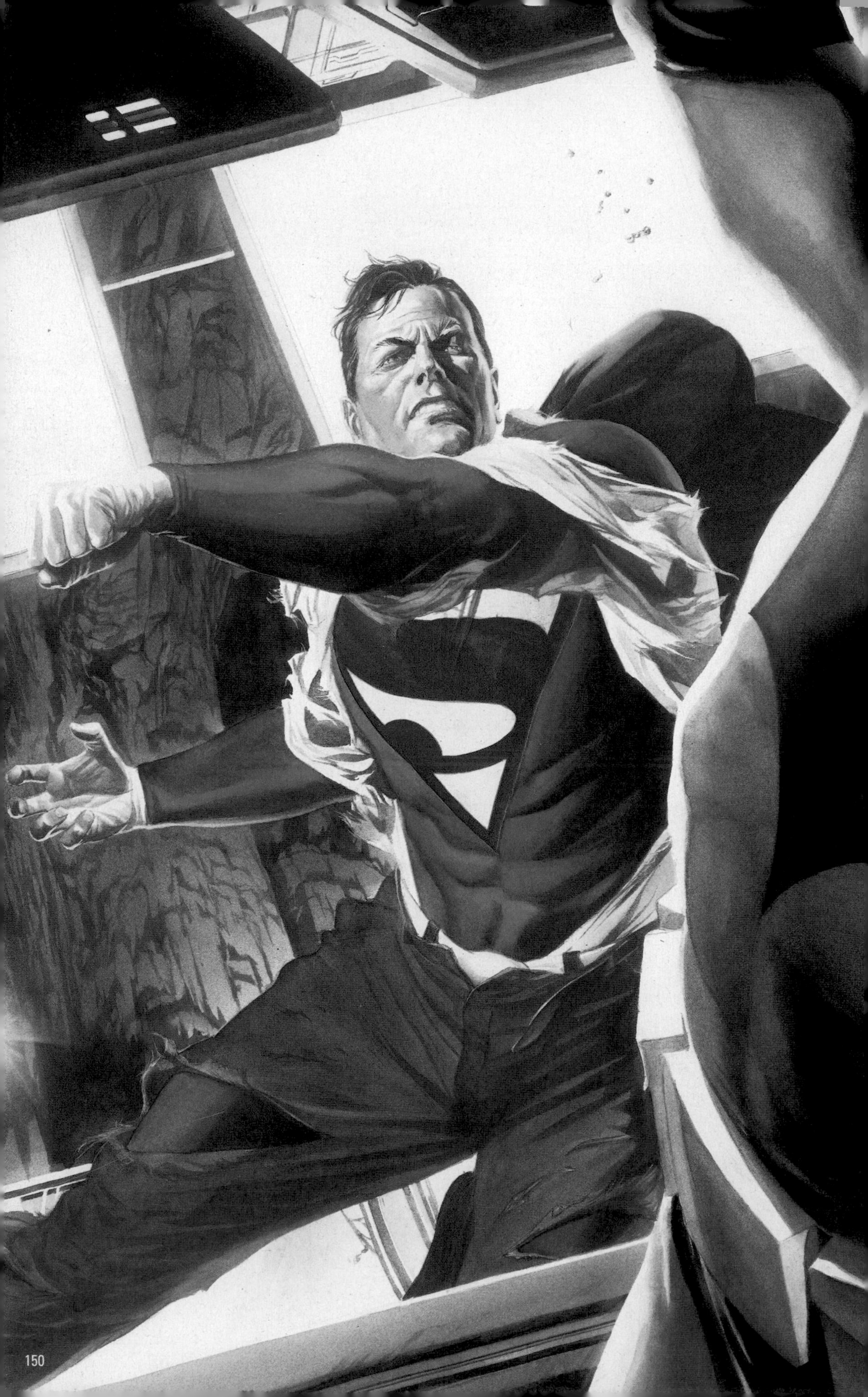

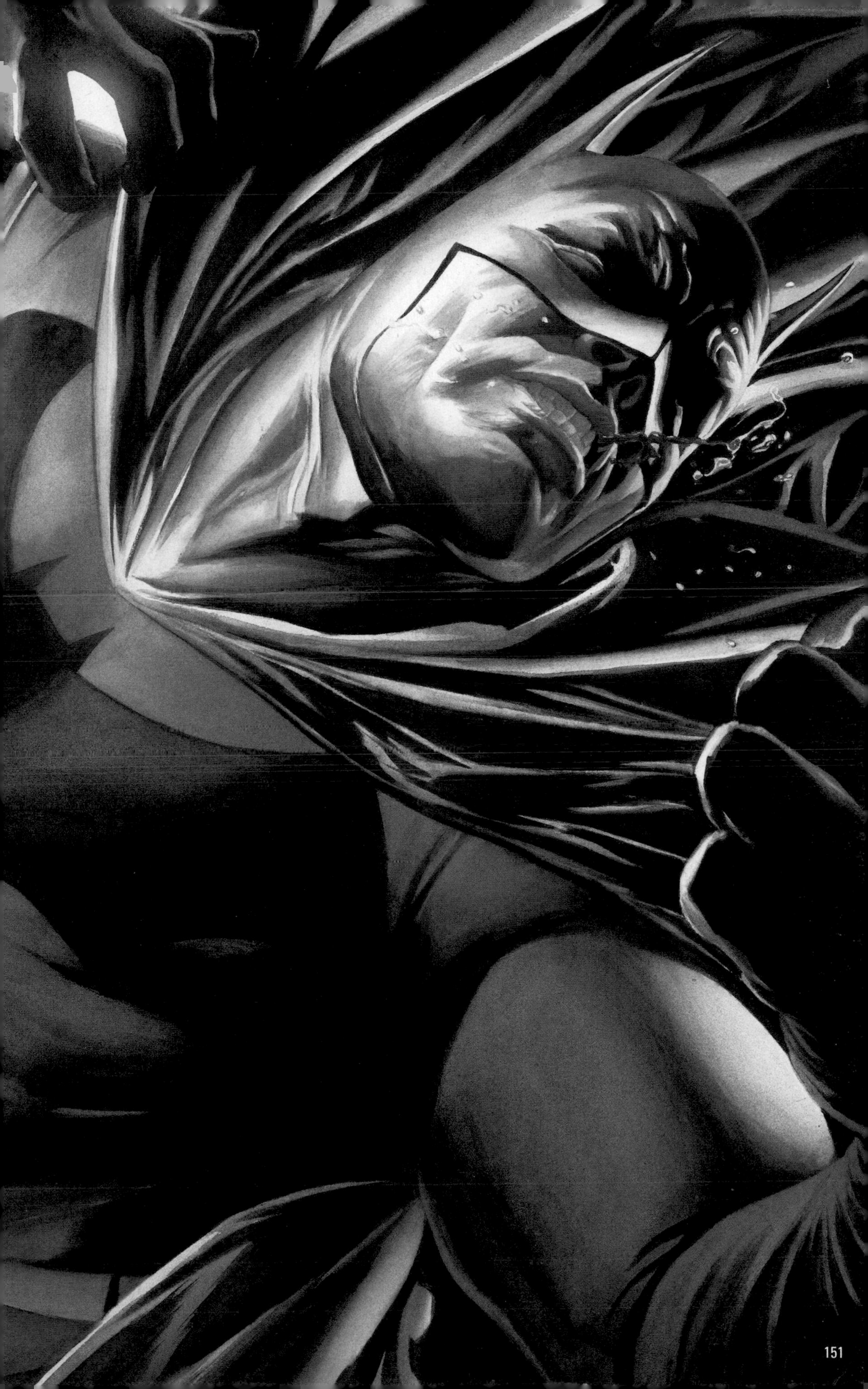

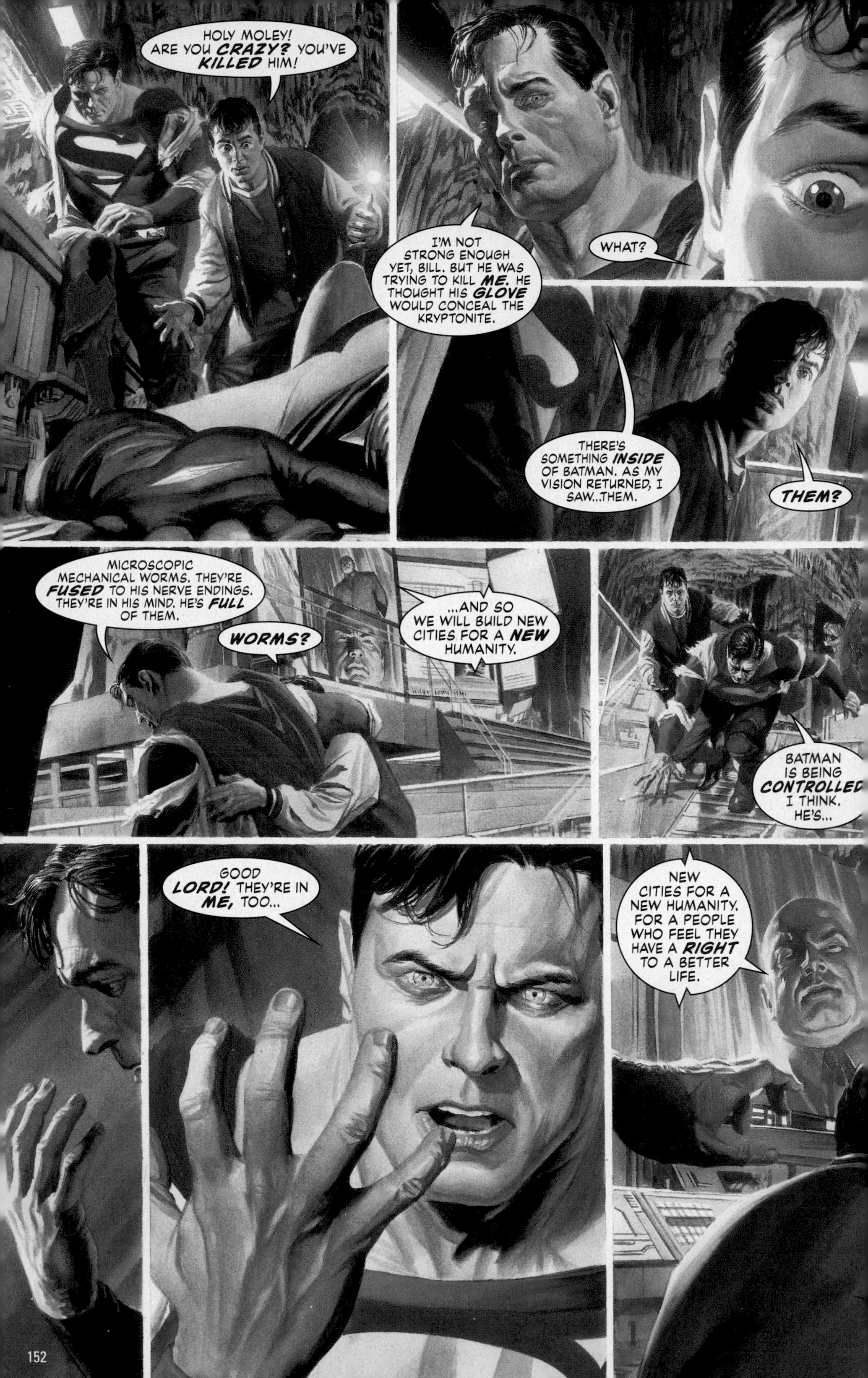
HOLY MOLEY! ARE YOU CRAZY? YOU'VE KILLED HIM!
I'M NOT STRONG ENOUGH YET, BILL. BUT HE WAS TRYING TO KILL ME. HE THOUGHT HIS GLOVE WOULD CONCEAL THE KRYPTONITE.
WHAT?
THERE'S SOMETHING INSIDE OF BATMAN. AS MY VISION RETURNED, I SAW...THEM.
THEM?
MICROSCOPIC MECHANICAL WORMS. THEY'RE FUSED TO HIS NERVE ENDINGS. THEY'RE IN HIS MIND. HE'S FULL OF THEM.
WORMS?
...AND SO WE WILL BUILD NEW CITIES FOR A NEW HUMANITY.
BATMAN IS BEING CONTROLLED I THINK. HE'S...
GOOD LORD! THEY'RE IN ME, TOO...
NEW CITIES FOR A NEW HUMANITY. FOR A PEOPLE WHO FEEL THEY HAVE A RIGHT TO A BETTER LIFE.

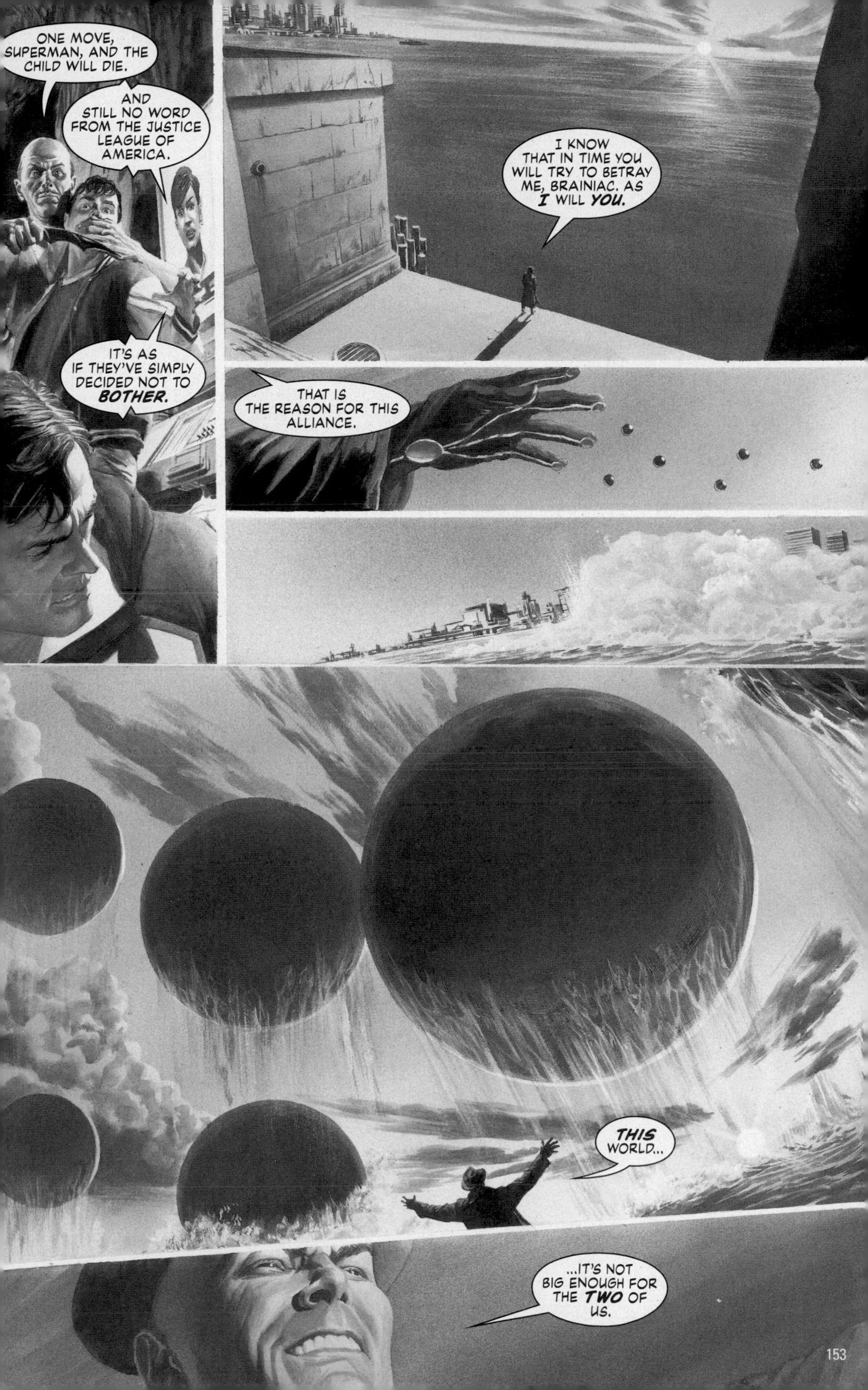
ONE MOVE, SUPERMAN, AND THE CHILD WILL DIE.
AND STILL NO WORD FROM THE JUSTICE LEAGUE OF AMERICA.
IT'S AS IF THEY'VE SIMPLY DECIDED NOT TO **BOTHER.**
I KNOW THAT IN TIME YOU WILL TRY TO BETRAY ME, BRAINIAC. AS ***I*** WILL ***YOU.***
THAT IS THE REASON FOR THIS ALLIANCE.
THIS WORLD...
...IT'S NOT BIG ENOUGH FOR THE ***TWO*** OF US.

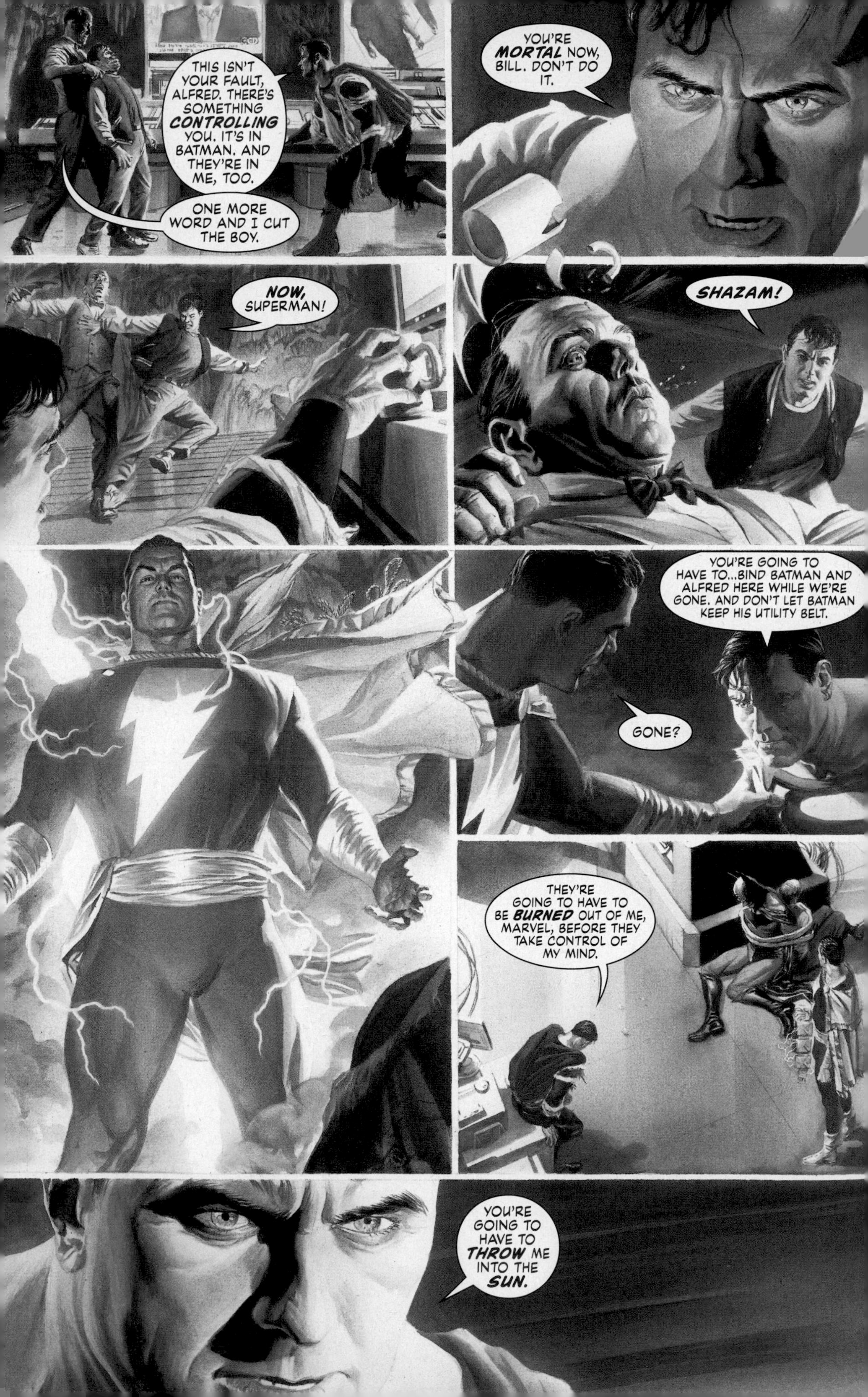
THIS ISN'T YOUR FAULT, ALFRED. THERE'S SOMETHING CONTROLLING YOU. IT'S IN BATMAN. AND THEY'RE IN ME, TOO.
ONE MORE WORD AND I CUT THE BOY.
YOU'RE MORTAL NOW, BILL. DON'T DO IT.
NOW, SUPERMAN!
SHAZAM!
YOU'RE GOING TO HAVE TO...BIND BATMAN AND ALFRED HERE WHILE WE'RE GONE. AND DON'T LET BATMAN KEEP HIS UTILITY BELT.
GONE?
THEY'RE GOING TO HAVE TO BE BURNED OUT OF ME, MARVEL, BEFORE THEY TAKE CONTROL OF MY MIND.
YOU'RE GOING TO HAVE TO THROW ME INTO THE SUN.

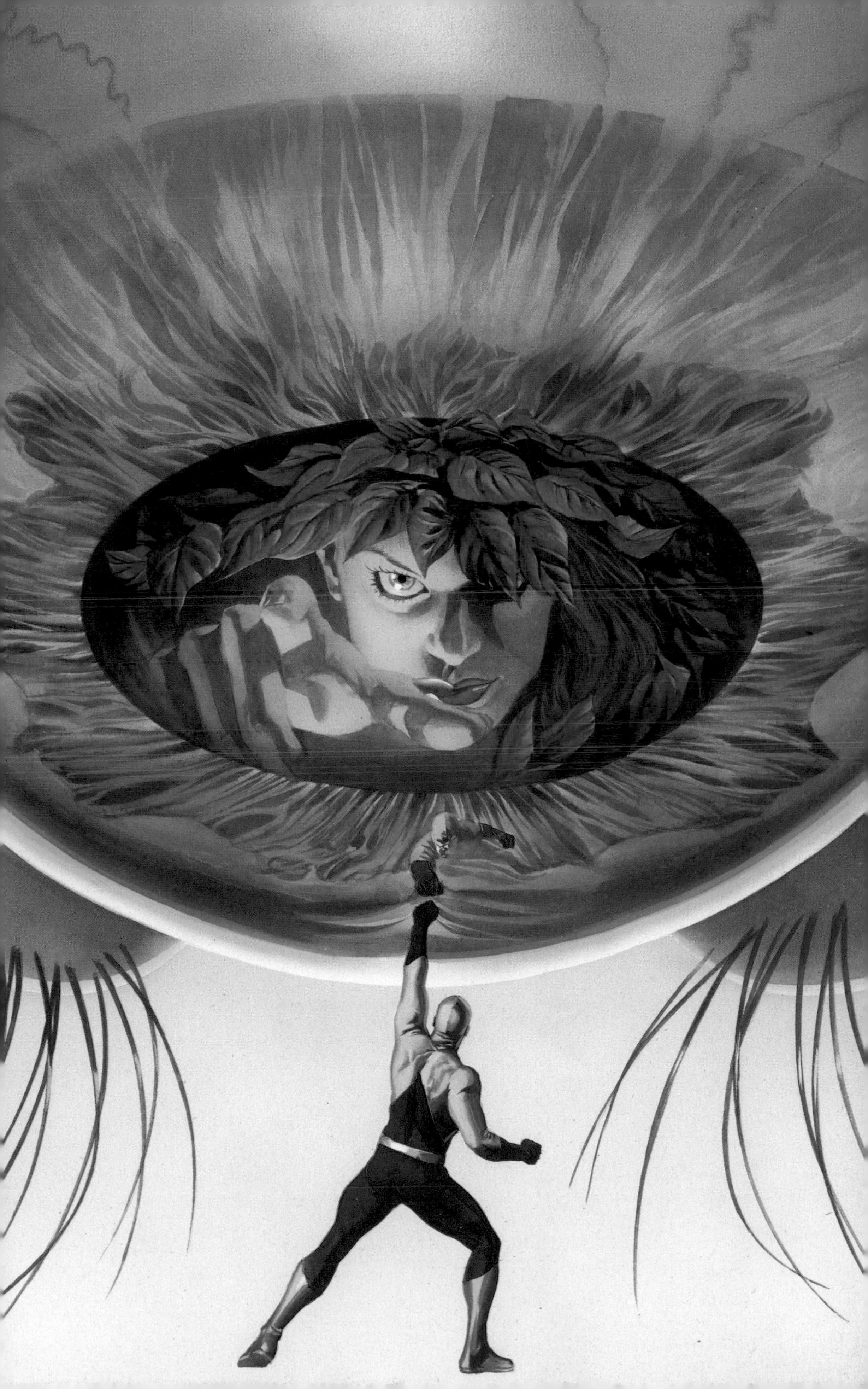

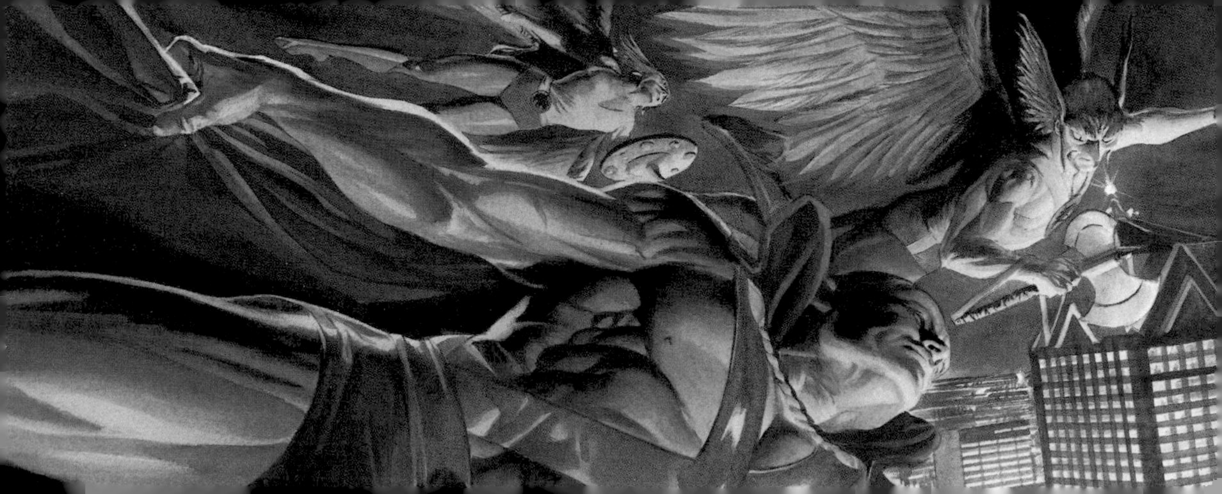

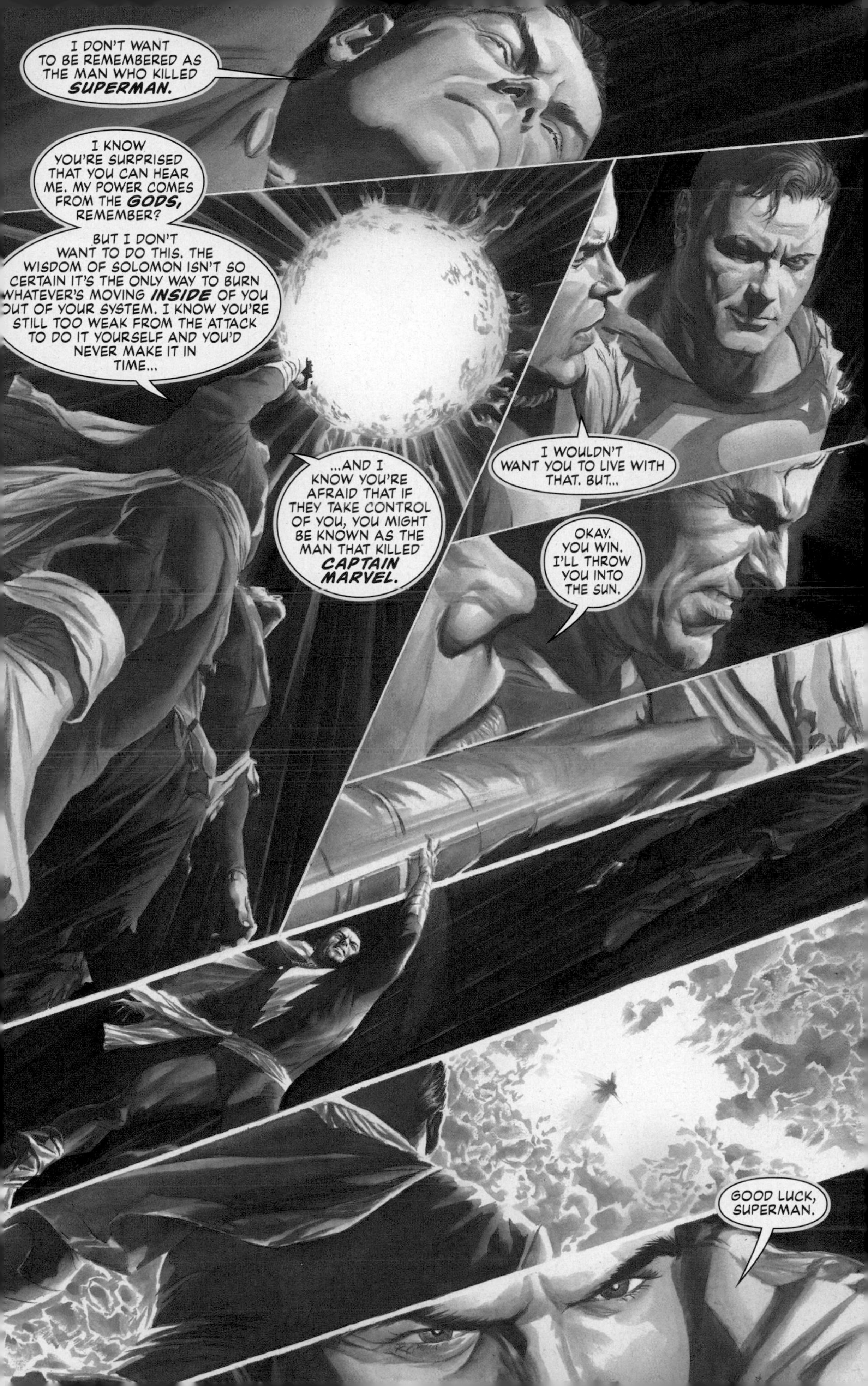
I DON'T WANT TO BE REMEMBERED AS THE MAN WHO KILLED SUPERMAN.
I KNOW YOU'RE SURPRISED THAT YOU CAN HEAR ME. MY POWER COMES FROM THE GODS, REMEMBER?
BUT I DON'T WANT TO DO THIS. THE WISDOM OF SOLOMON ISN'T SO CERTAIN IT'S THE ONLY WAY TO BURN WHATEVER'S MOVING INSIDE OF YOU OUT OF YOUR SYSTEM. I KNOW YOU'RE STILL TOO WEAK FROM THE ATTACK TO DO IT YOURSELF AND YOU'D NEVER MAKE IT IN TIME...
...AND I KNOW YOU'RE AFRAID THAT IF THEY TAKE CONTROL OF YOU, YOU MIGHT BE KNOWN AS THE MAN THAT KILLED CAPTAIN MARVEL.
I WOULDN'T WANT YOU TO LIVE WITH THAT. BUT...
OKAY. YOU WIN. I'LL THROW YOU INTO THE SUN.
GOOD LUCK, SUPERMAN.

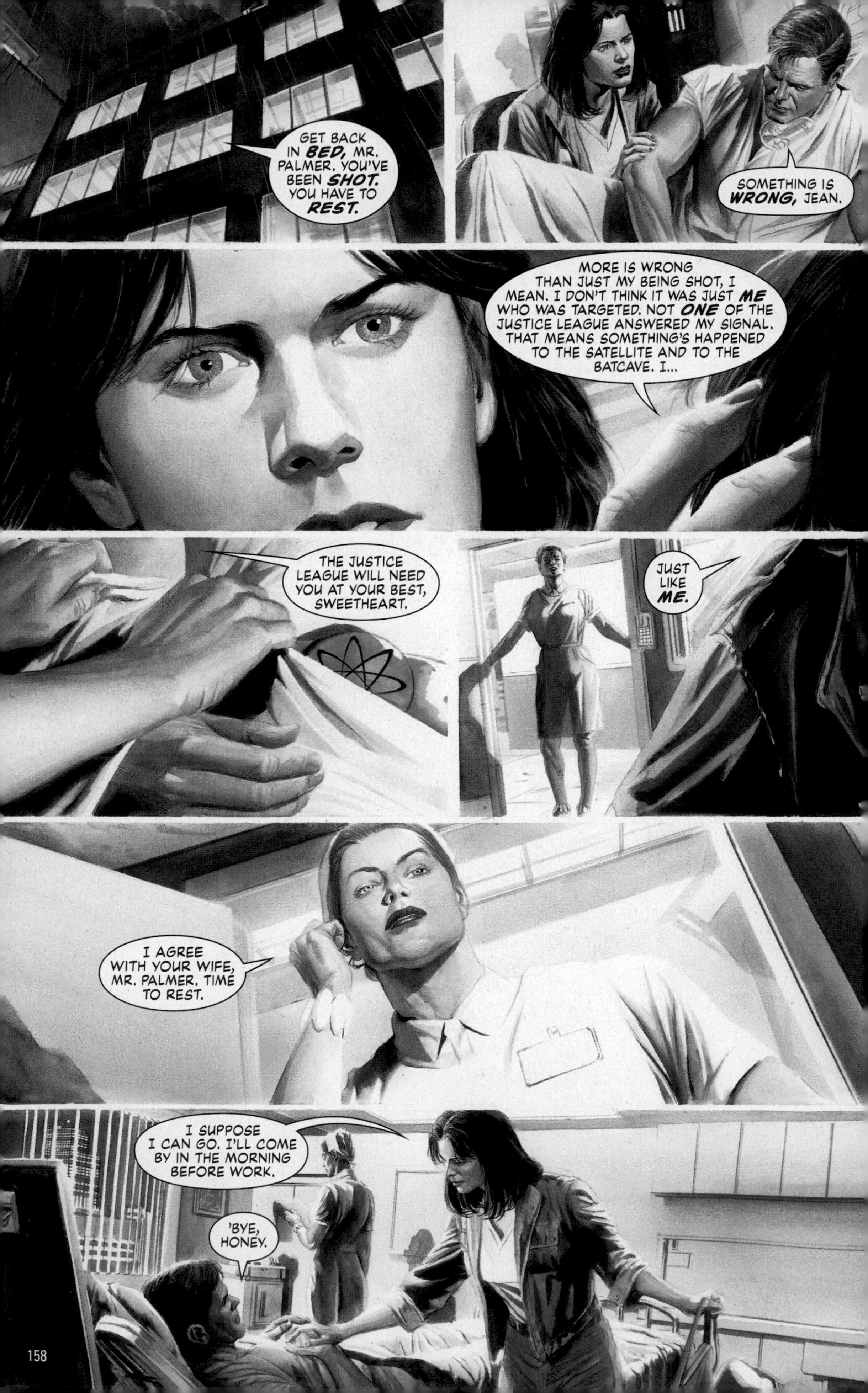
GET BACK IN BED, MR. PALMER. YOU'VE BEEN SHOT. YOU HAVE TO REST.
SOMETHING IS WRONG, JEAN.
MORE IS WRONG THAN JUST MY BEING SHOT, I MEAN. I DON'T THINK IT WAS JUST ME WHO WAS TARGETED. NOT ONE OF THE JUSTICE LEAGUE ANSWERED MY SIGNAL. THAT MEANS SOMETHING'S HAPPENED TO THE SATELLITE AND TO THE BATCAVE. I...
THE JUSTICE LEAGUE WILL NEED YOU AT YOUR BEST, SWEETHEART.
JUST LIKE ME.
I AGREE WITH YOUR WIFE, MR. PALMER. TIME TO REST.
I SUPPOSE I CAN GO. I'LL COME BY IN THE MORNING BEFORE WORK.
'BYE, HONEY.

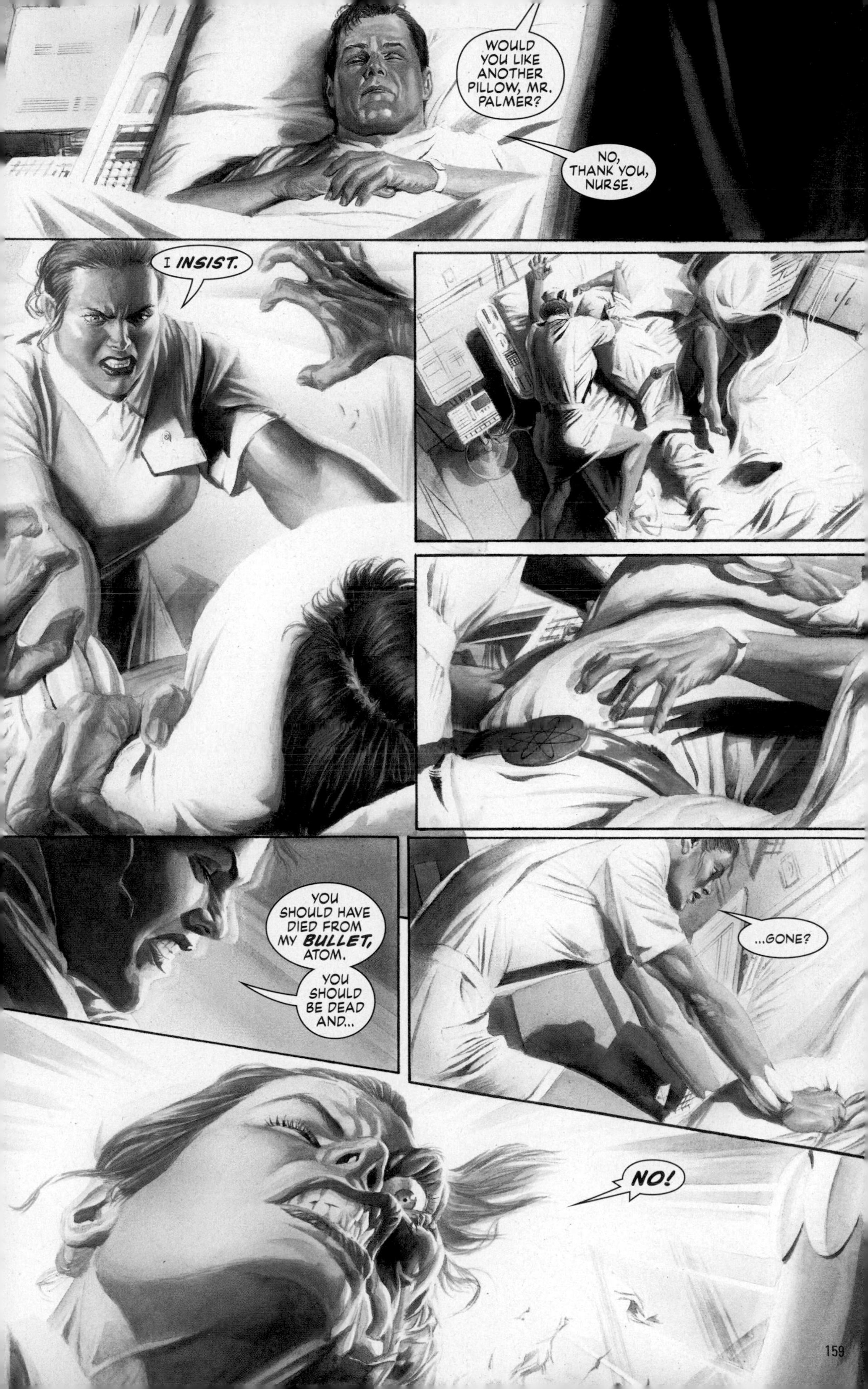
WOULD YOU LIKE ANOTHER PILLOW, MR. PALMER?
NO, THANK YOU, NURSE.
I INSIST.
YOU SHOULD HAVE DIED FROM MY BULLET, ATOM.
YOU SHOULD BE DEAD AND...
...GONE?
NO!

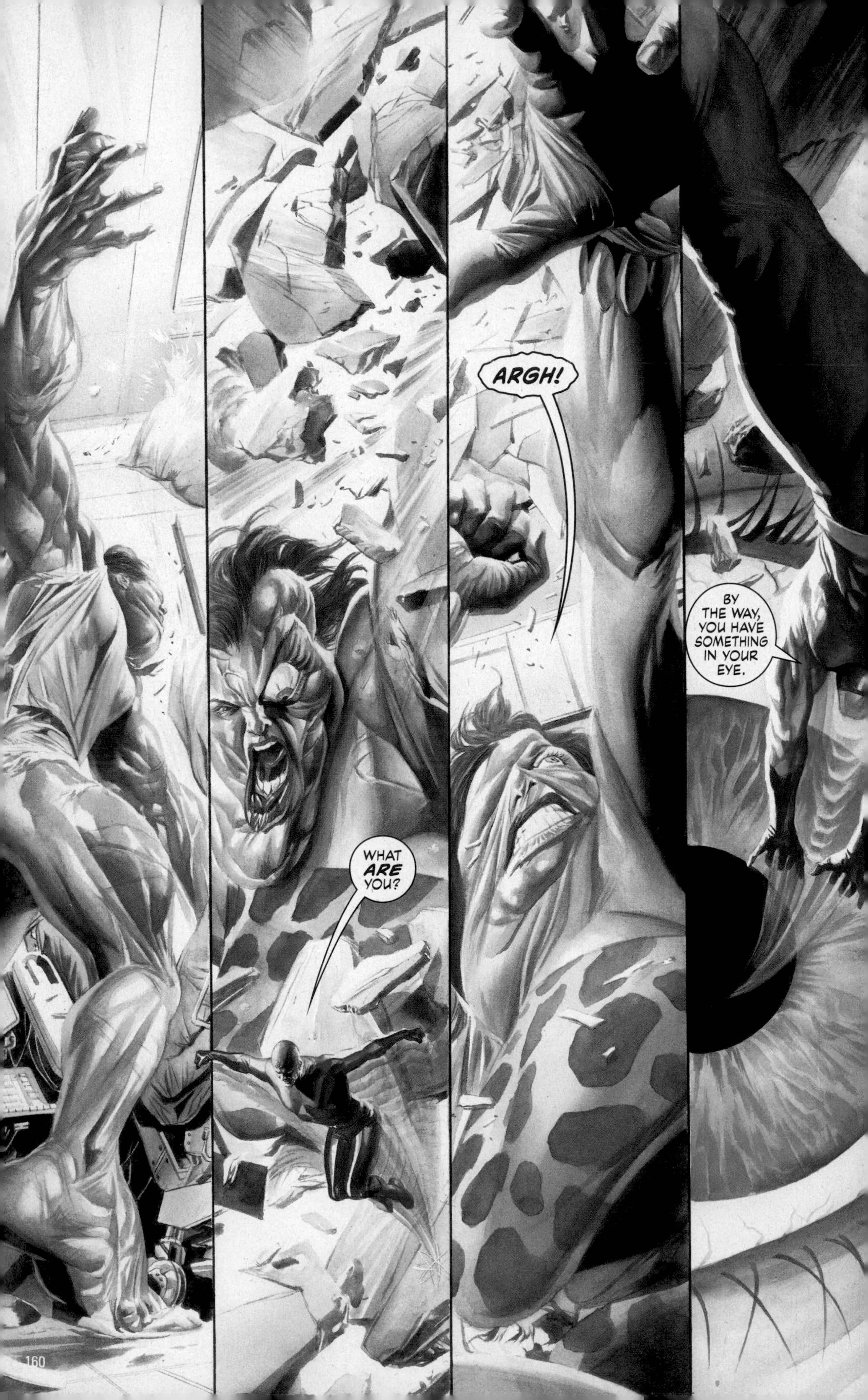

WHAT ARE YOU?
ARGH!
BY THE WAY, YOU HAVE SOMETHING IN YOUR EYE.

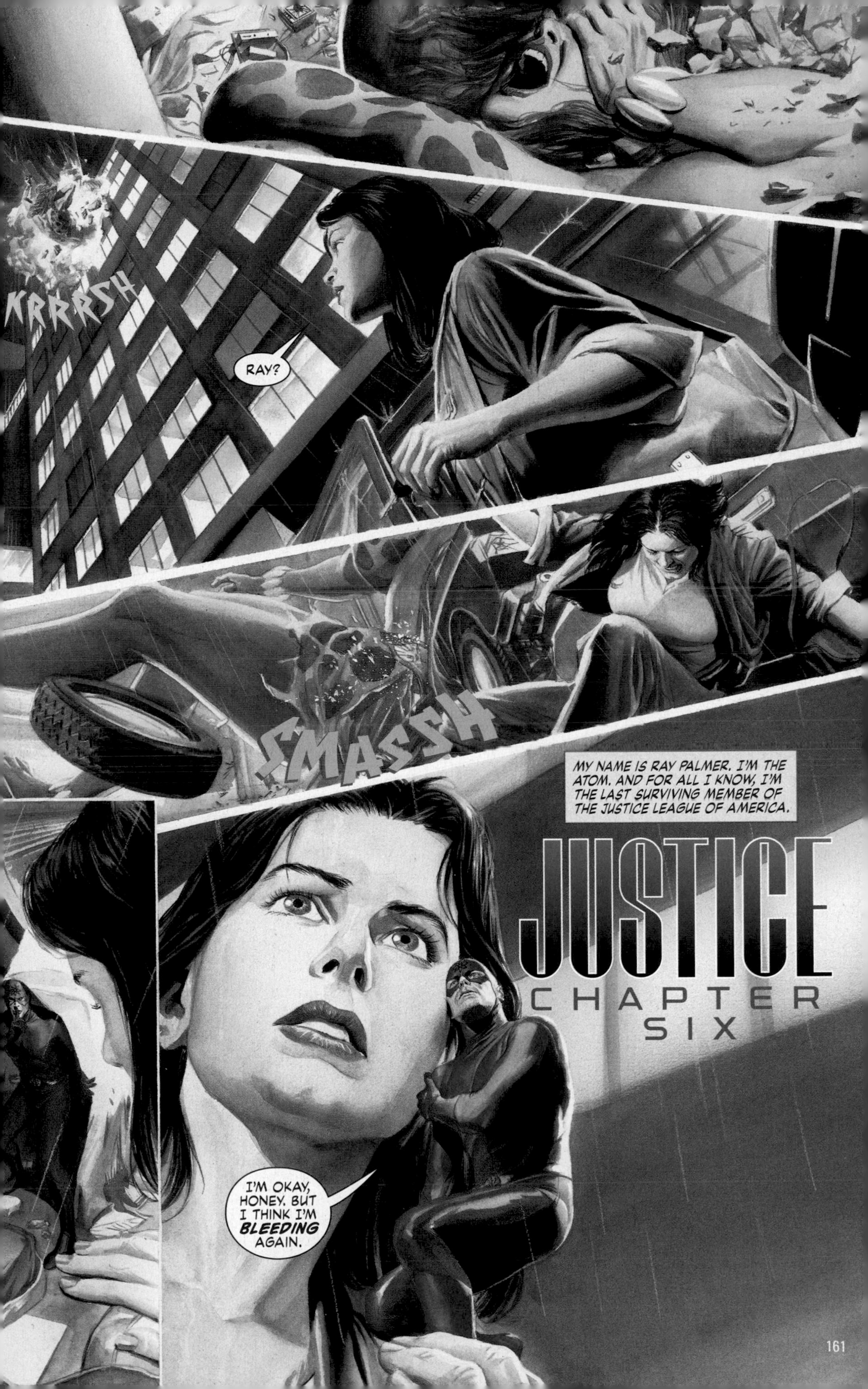
KRRRSH
RAY?
SMASSH
MY NAME IS RAY PALMER. I'M THE ATOM. AND FOR ALL I KNOW, I'M THE LAST SURVIVING MEMBER OF THE JUSTICE LEAGUE OF AMERICA.
JUSTICE
CHAPTER SIX
I'M OKAY, HONEY. BUT I THINK I'M ***BLEEDING*** AGAIN.

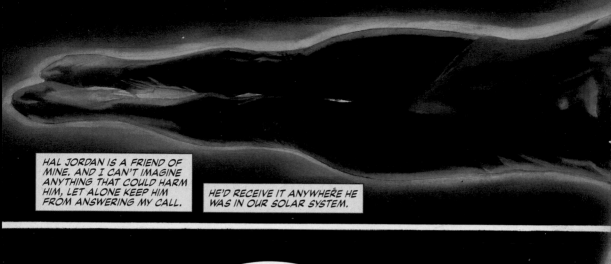

HAL JORDAN IS A FRIEND OF MINE. AND I CAN'T IMAGINE ANYTHING THAT COULD HARM HIM, LET ALONE KEEP HIM FROM ANSWERING MY CALL.

HE'D RECEIVE IT ANYWHERE HE WAS IN OUR SOLAR SYSTEM.

YOU DON'T KNOW HOW **LONG** I'VE WANTED TO HEAR THAT THEY DON'T KNOW EVERYTHING.

DAMN. BE CAREFUL OF WHAT YOU **WISH** FOR. HOW LONG DO I HAVE BEFORE YOU RUN OUT OF CHARGE?

STILL, THERE IS NO GUARANTEE WE WILL EVER BE FOUND.

DEAD IN SEVEN HOURS OR LOST FOREVER? THAT'S THE **BEST** I CAN HOPE FOR?

VERY WELL. **DO** IT, RING.

AQUAMAN WENT MISSING WEEKS AGO. OUR SEARCHES FOR HIM HAVE FOUND NOTHING. I DON'T EVEN KNOW IF MANHUNTER'S RETURNED YET.

THEN I GET SHOT. AND BY SOMEONE WHO OBVIOUSLY KNOWS RAY PALMER IS THE ATOM.

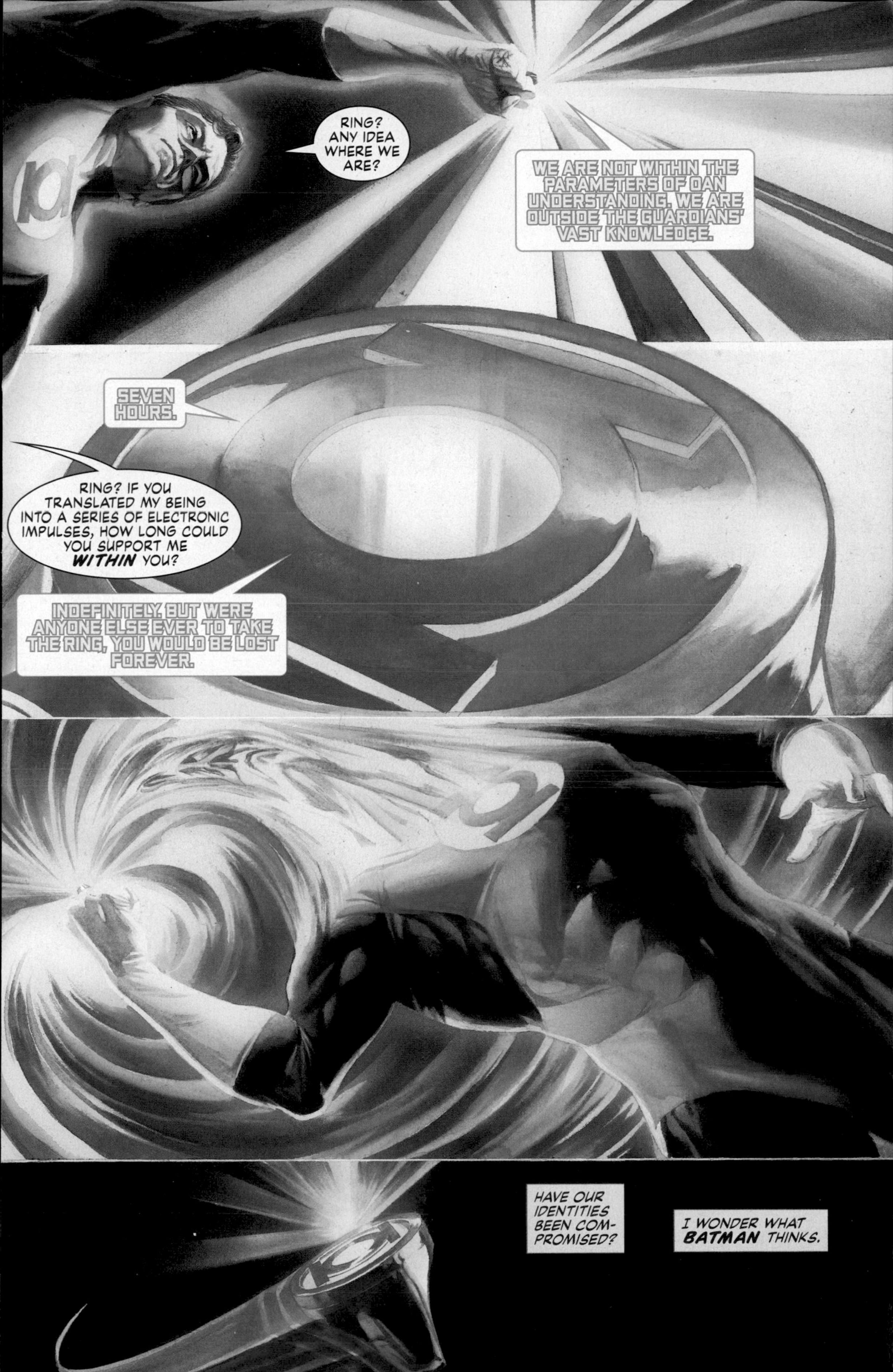
RING? ANY IDEA WHERE WE ARE?
WE ARE NOT WITHIN THE PARAMETERS OF OAN UNDERSTANDING. WE ARE OUTSIDE THE GUARDIANS' VAST KNOWLEDGE.
SEVEN HOURS.
RING? IF YOU TRANSLATED MY BEING INTO A SERIES OF ELECTRONIC IMPULSES, HOW LONG COULD YOU SUPPORT ME **WITHIN** YOU?
INDEFINITELY. BUT WERE ANYONE ELSE EVER TO TAKE THE RING, YOU WOULD BE LOST FOREVER.
HAVE OUR IDENTITIES BEEN COM-PROMISED?
*I WONDER WHAT **BATMAN** THINKS.*

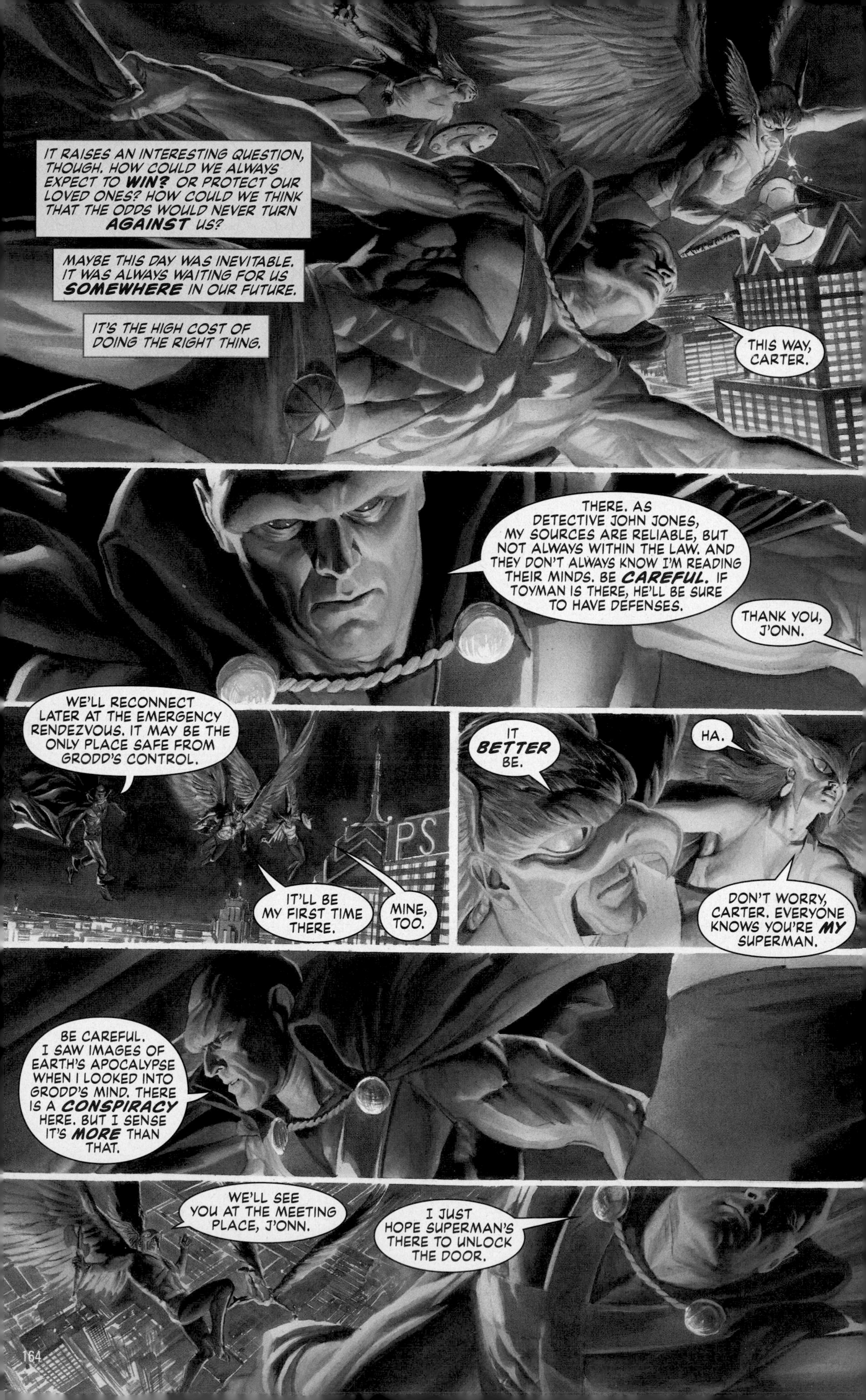
IT RAISES AN INTERESTING QUESTION, THOUGH. HOW COULD WE ALWAYS EXPECT TO WIN? OR PROTECT OUR LOVED ONES? HOW COULD WE THINK THAT THE ODDS WOULD NEVER TURN AGAINST US?
MAYBE THIS DAY WAS INEVITABLE. IT WAS ALWAYS WAITING FOR US SOMEWHERE IN OUR FUTURE.
IT'S THE HIGH COST OF DOING THE RIGHT THING.
THIS WAY, CARTER.
THERE. AS DETECTIVE JOHN JONES, MY SOURCES ARE RELIABLE, BUT NOT ALWAYS WITHIN THE LAW. AND THEY DON'T ALWAYS KNOW I'M READING THEIR MINDS. BE CAREFUL. IF TOYMAN IS THERE, HE'LL BE SURE TO HAVE DEFENSES.
THANK YOU, J'ONN.
WE'LL RECONNECT LATER AT THE EMERGENCY RENDEZVOUS. IT MAY BE THE ONLY PLACE SAFE FROM GRODD'S CONTROL.
IT'LL BE MY FIRST TIME THERE.
MINE, TOO.
IT BETTER BE.
HA.
DON'T WORRY, CARTER. EVERYONE KNOWS YOU'RE MY SUPERMAN.
BE CAREFUL. I SAW IMAGES OF EARTH'S APOCALYPSE WHEN I LOOKED INTO GRODD'S MIND. THERE IS A CONSPIRACY HERE. BUT I SENSE IT'S MORE THAN THAT.
WE'LL SEE YOU AT THE MEETING PLACE, J'ONN.
I JUST HOPE SUPERMAN'S THERE TO UNLOCK THE DOOR.

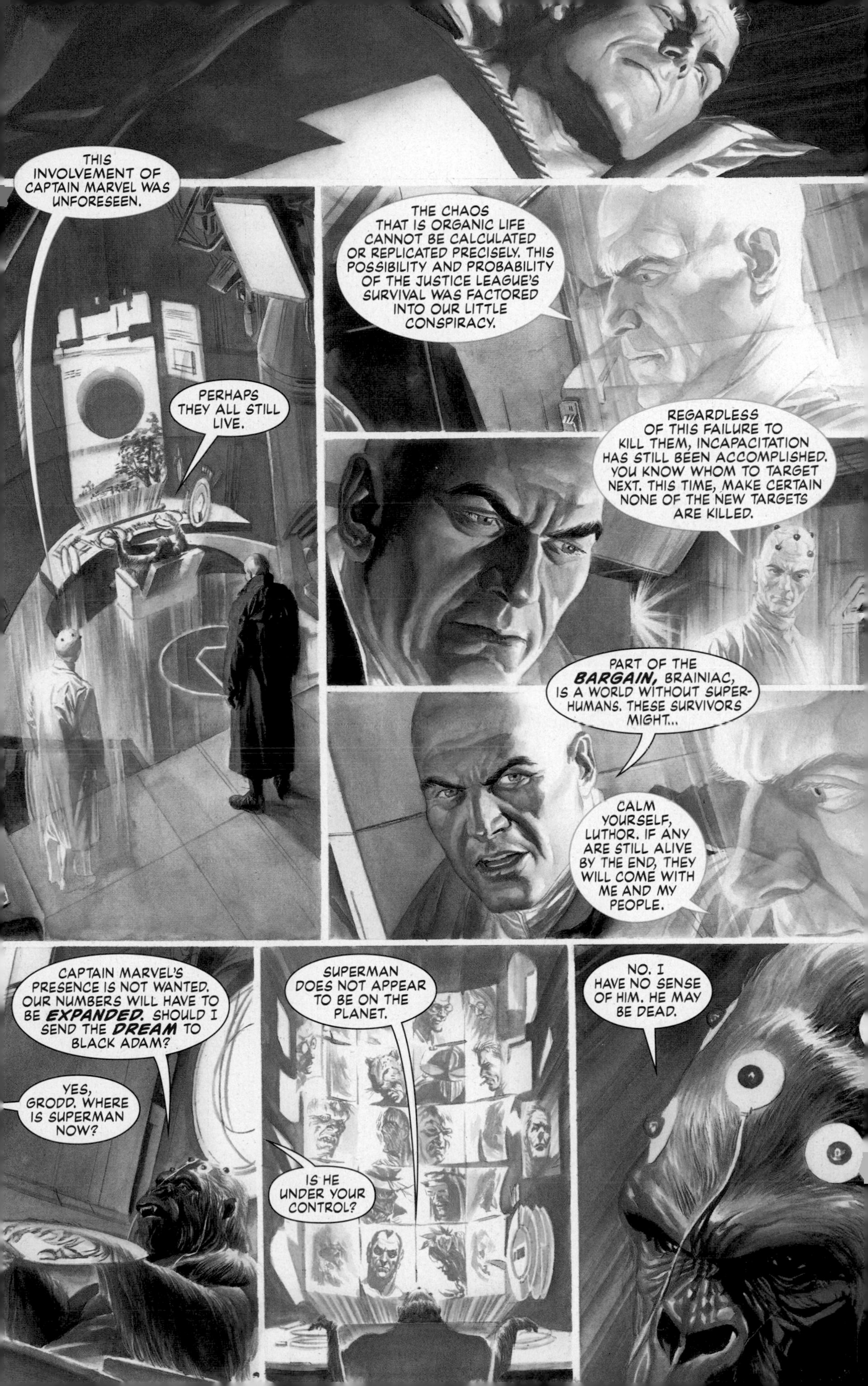
THIS INVOLVEMENT OF CAPTAIN MARVEL WAS UNFORESEEN.
THE CHAOS THAT IS ORGANIC LIFE CANNOT BE CALCULATED OR REPLICATED PRECISELY. THIS POSSIBILITY AND PROBABILITY OF THE JUSTICE LEAGUE'S SURVIVAL WAS FACTORED INTO OUR LITTLE CONSPIRACY.
PERHAPS THEY ALL STILL LIVE.
REGARDLESS OF THIS FAILURE TO KILL THEM, INCAPACITATION HAS STILL BEEN ACCOMPLISHED. YOU KNOW WHOM TO TARGET NEXT. THIS TIME, MAKE CERTAIN NONE OF THE NEW TARGETS ARE KILLED.
PART OF THE BARGAIN, BRAINIAC, IS A WORLD WITHOUT SUPER-HUMANS. THESE SURVIVORS MIGHT...
CALM YOURSELF, LUTHOR. IF ANY ARE STILL ALIVE BY THE END, THEY WILL COME WITH ME AND MY PEOPLE.
CAPTAIN MARVEL'S PRESENCE IS NOT WANTED. OUR NUMBERS WILL HAVE TO BE EXPANDED. SHOULD I SEND THE DREAM TO BLACK ADAM?
YES, GRODD. WHERE IS SUPERMAN NOW?
SUPERMAN DOES NOT APPEAR TO BE ON THE PLANET.
IS HE UNDER YOUR CONTROL?
NO. I HAVE NO SENSE OF HIM. HE MAY BE DEAD.

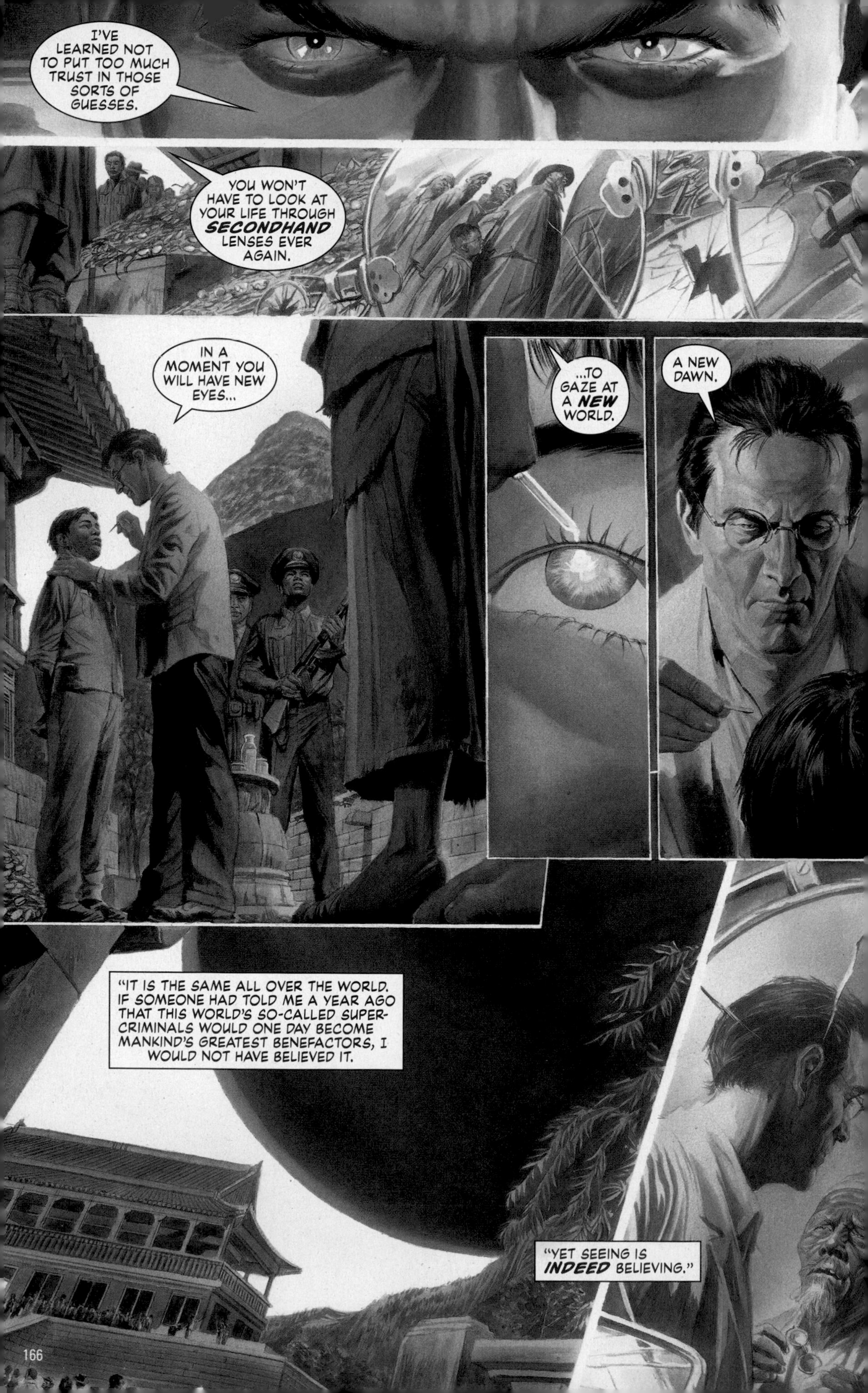
I'VE LEARNED NOT TO PUT TOO MUCH TRUST IN THOSE SORTS OF GUESSES.
YOU WON'T HAVE TO LOOK AT YOUR LIFE THROUGH SECONDHAND LENSES EVER AGAIN.
IN A MOMENT YOU WILL HAVE NEW EYES...
...TO GAZE AT A NEW WORLD.
A NEW DAWN.
"IT IS THE SAME ALL OVER THE WORLD. IF SOMEONE HAD TOLD ME A YEAR AGO THAT THIS WORLD'S SO-CALLED SUPER-CRIMINALS WOULD ONE DAY BECOME MANKIND'S GREATEST BENEFACTORS, I WOULD NOT HAVE BELIEVED IT.
"YET SEEING IS INDEED BELIEVING."

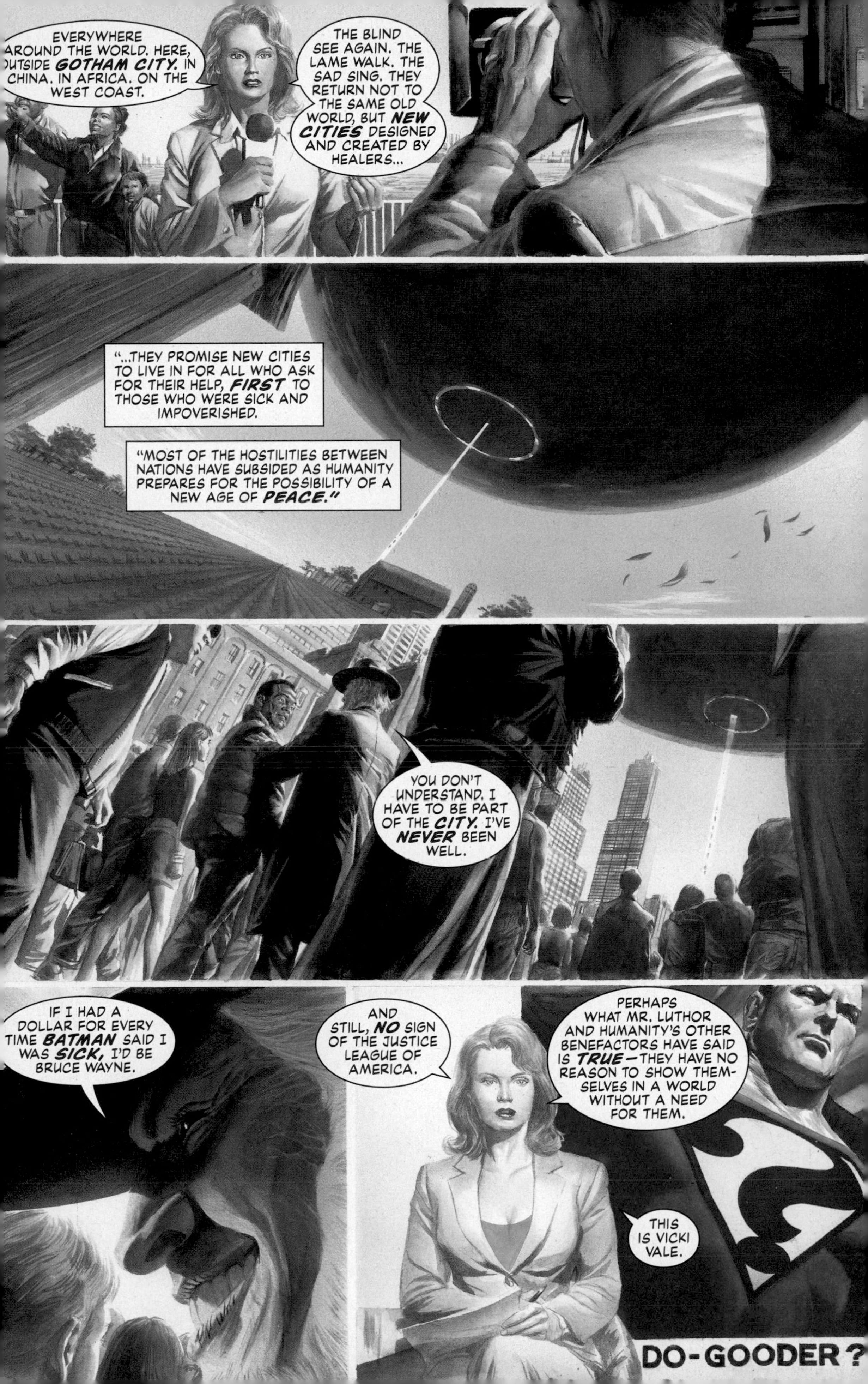
EVERYWHERE AROUND THE WORLD. HERE, OUTSIDE GOTHAM CITY. IN CHINA. IN AFRICA. ON THE WEST COAST.
THE BLIND SEE AGAIN. THE LAME WALK. THE SAD SING. THEY RETURN NOT TO THE SAME OLD WORLD, BUT NEW CITIES DESIGNED AND CREATED BY HEALERS...
"...THEY PROMISE NEW CITIES TO LIVE IN FOR ALL WHO ASK FOR THEIR HELP, FIRST TO THOSE WHO WERE SICK AND IMPOVERISHED.
"MOST OF THE HOSTILITIES BETWEEN NATIONS HAVE SUBSIDED AS HUMANITY PREPARES FOR THE POSSIBILITY OF A NEW AGE OF PEACE."
YOU DON'T UNDERSTAND. I HAVE TO BE PART OF THE CITY. I'VE NEVER BEEN WELL.
IF I HAD A DOLLAR FOR EVERY TIME BATMAN SAID I WAS SICK, I'D BE BRUCE WAYNE.
AND STILL, NO SIGN OF THE JUSTICE LEAGUE OF AMERICA.
PERHAPS WHAT MR. LUTHOR AND HUMANITY'S OTHER BENEFACTORS HAVE SAID IS TRUE—THEY HAVE NO REASON TO SHOW THEMSELVES IN A WORLD WITHOUT A NEED FOR THEM.
THIS IS VICKI VALE.
DO-GOODER?

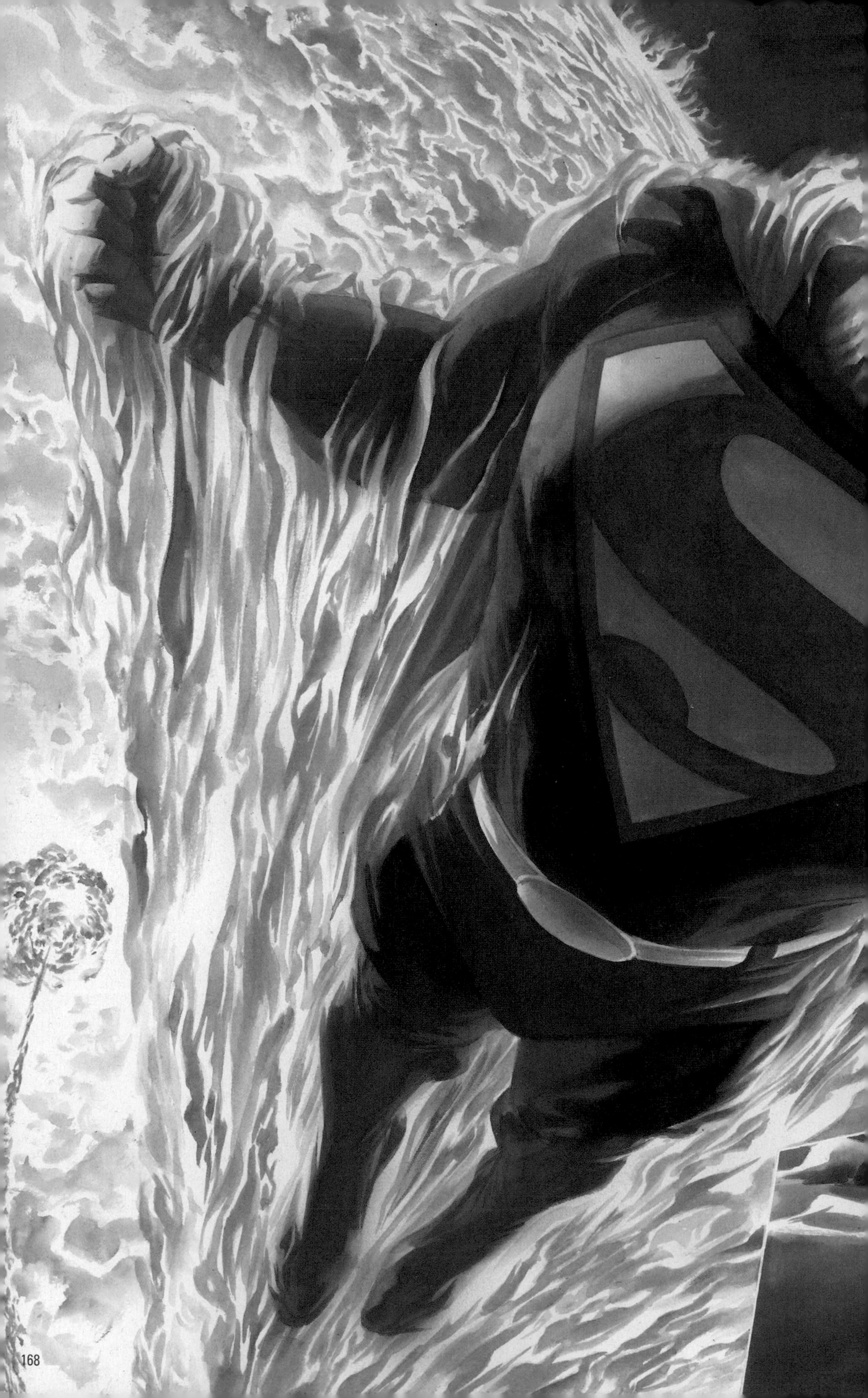

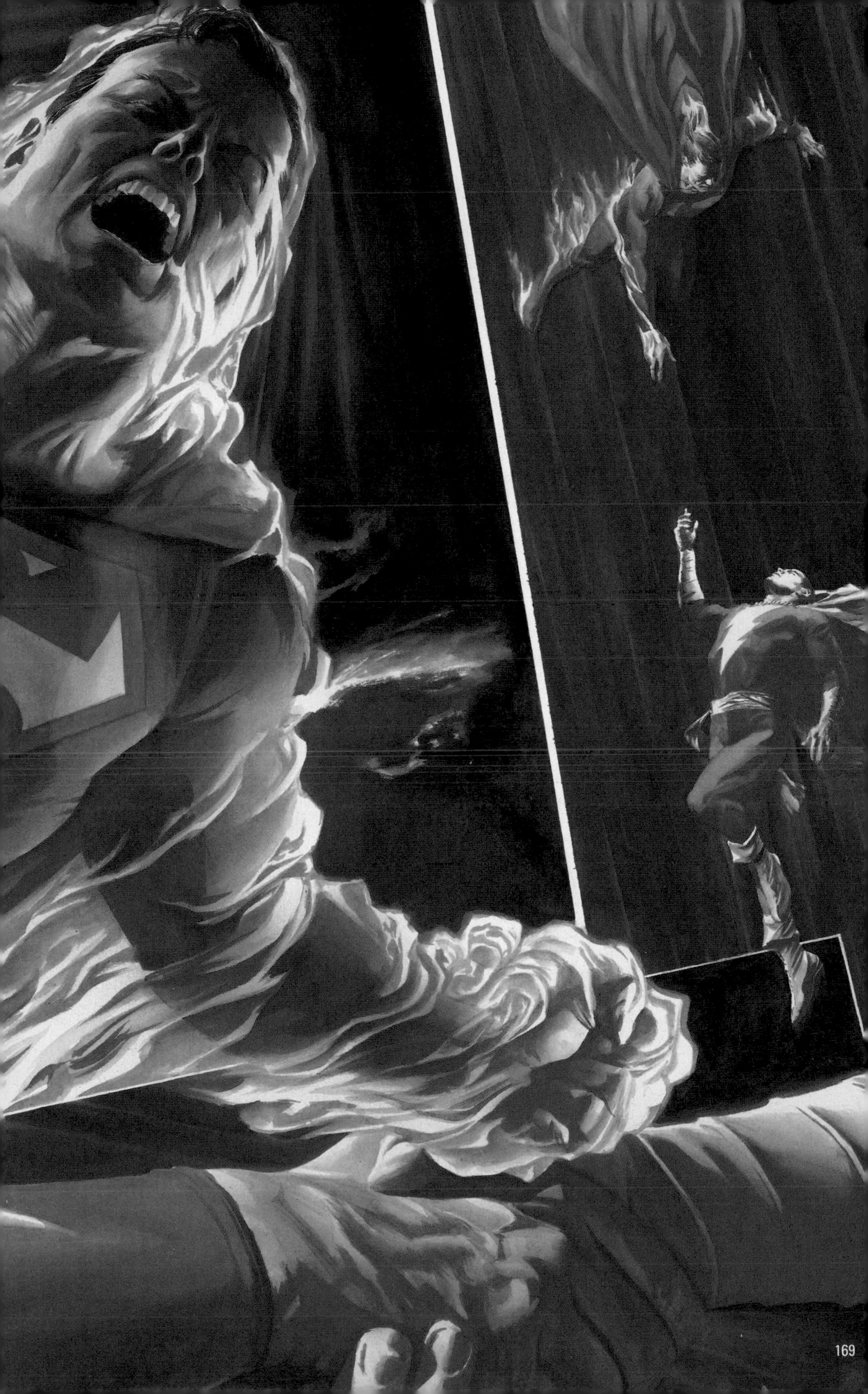

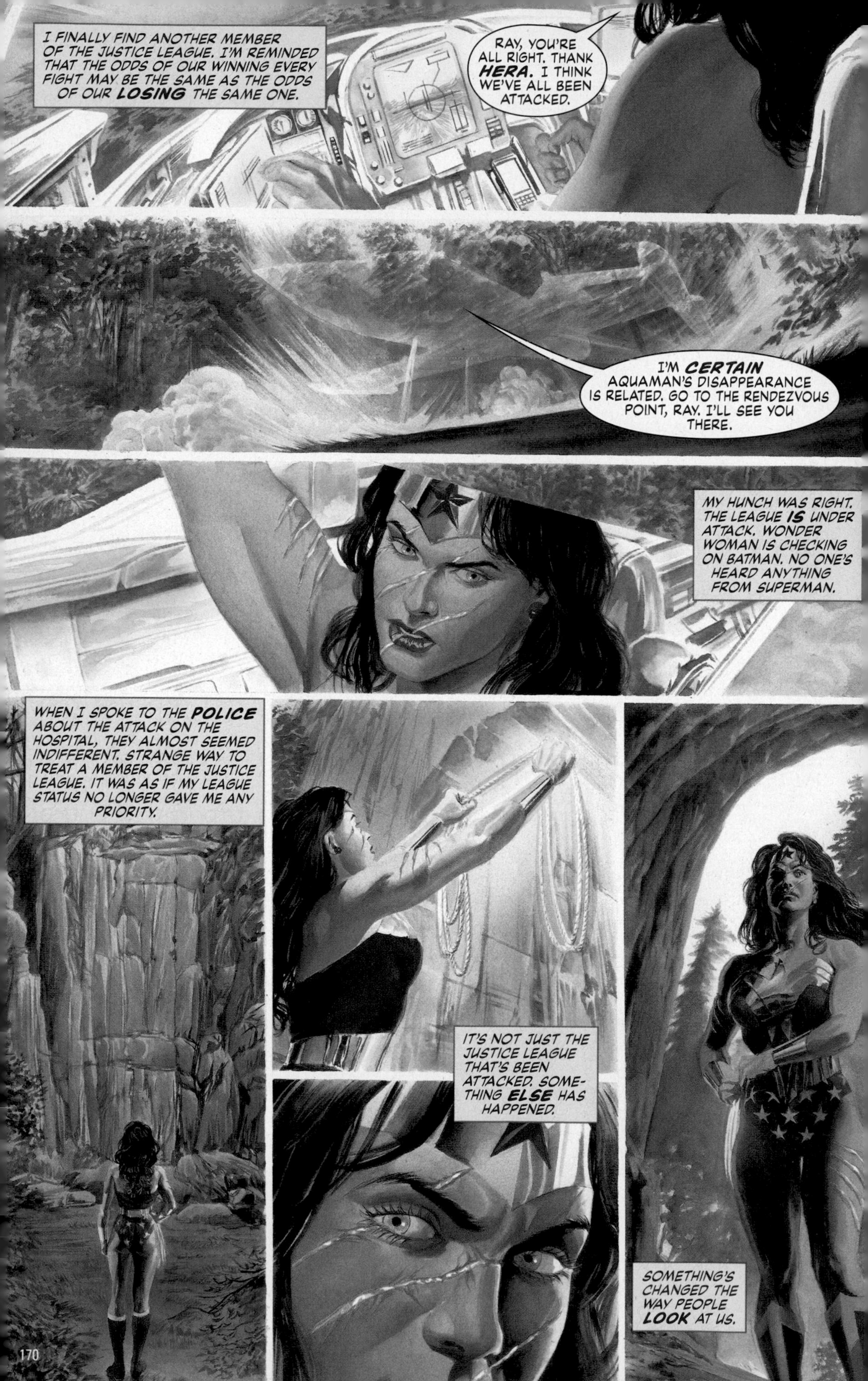
I FINALLY FIND ANOTHER MEMBER OF THE JUSTICE LEAGUE. I'M REMINDED THAT THE ODDS OF OUR WINNING EVERY FIGHT MAY BE THE SAME AS THE ODDS OF OUR LOSING THE SAME ONE.
RAY, YOU'RE ALL RIGHT. THANK HERA. I THINK WE'VE ALL BEEN ATTACKED.
I'M CERTAIN AQUAMAN'S DISAPPEARANCE IS RELATED. GO TO THE RENDEZVOUS POINT, RAY. I'LL SEE YOU THERE.
MY HUNCH WAS RIGHT. THE LEAGUE IS UNDER ATTACK. WONDER WOMAN IS CHECKING ON BATMAN. NO ONE'S HEARD ANYTHING FROM SUPERMAN.
WHEN I SPOKE TO THE POLICE ABOUT THE ATTACK ON THE HOSPITAL, THEY ALMOST SEEMED INDIFFERENT. STRANGE WAY TO TREAT A MEMBER OF THE JUSTICE LEAGUE. IT WAS AS IF MY LEAGUE STATUS NO LONGER GAVE ME ANY PRIORITY.
IT'S NOT JUST THE JUSTICE LEAGUE THAT'S BEEN ATTACKED. SOME-THING ELSE HAS HAPPENED.
SOMETHING'S CHANGED THE WAY PEOPLE LOOK AT US.

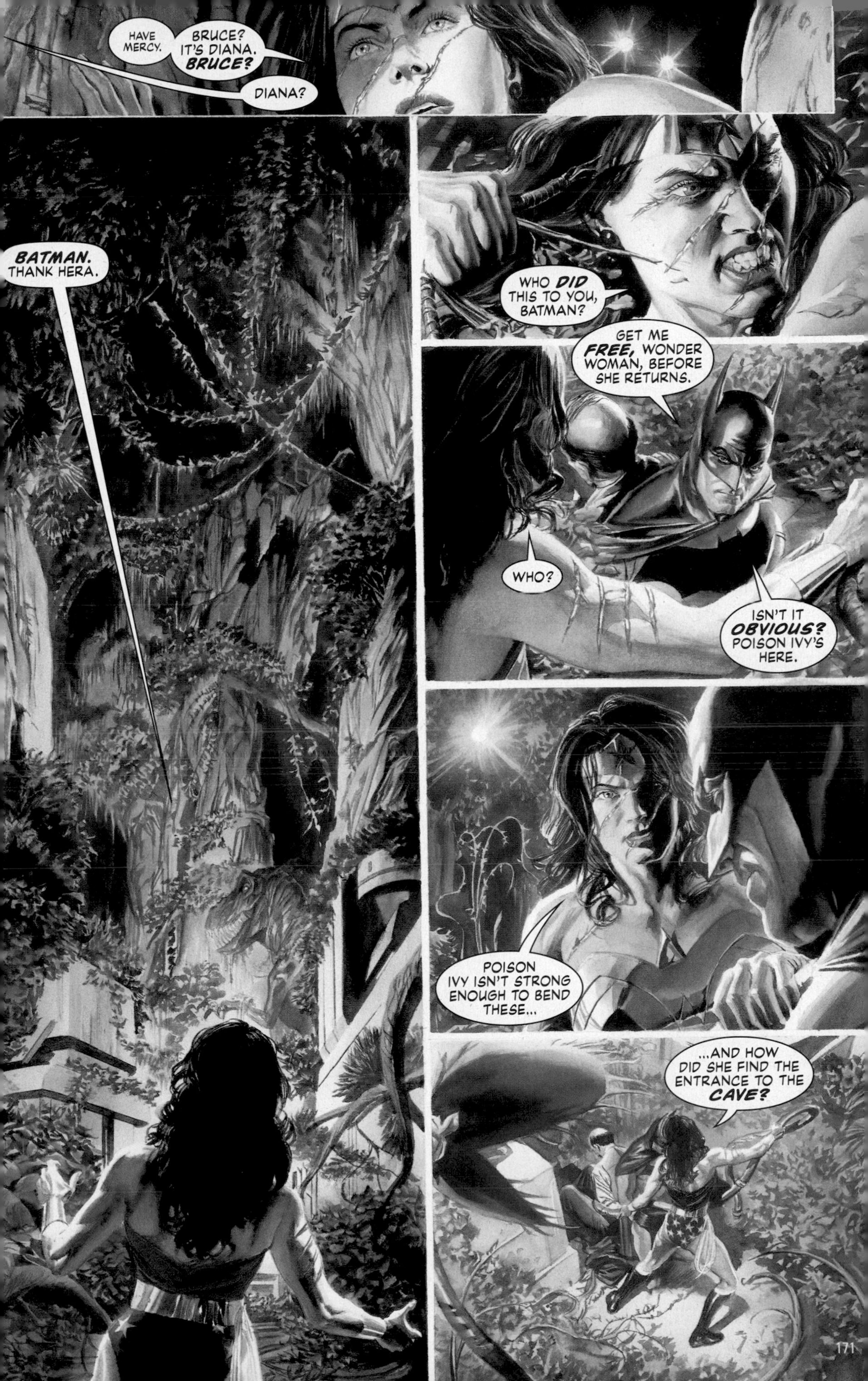
HAVE MERCY.
BRUCE? IT'S DIANA. BRUCE?
DIANA?
BATMAN. THANK HERA.
WHO DID THIS TO YOU, BATMAN?
GET ME FREE, WONDER WOMAN, BEFORE SHE RETURNS.
WHO?
ISN'T IT OBVIOUS? POISON IVY'S HERE.
POISON IVY ISN'T STRONG ENOUGH TO BEND THESE...
...AND HOW DID SHE FIND THE ENTRANCE TO THE CAVE?

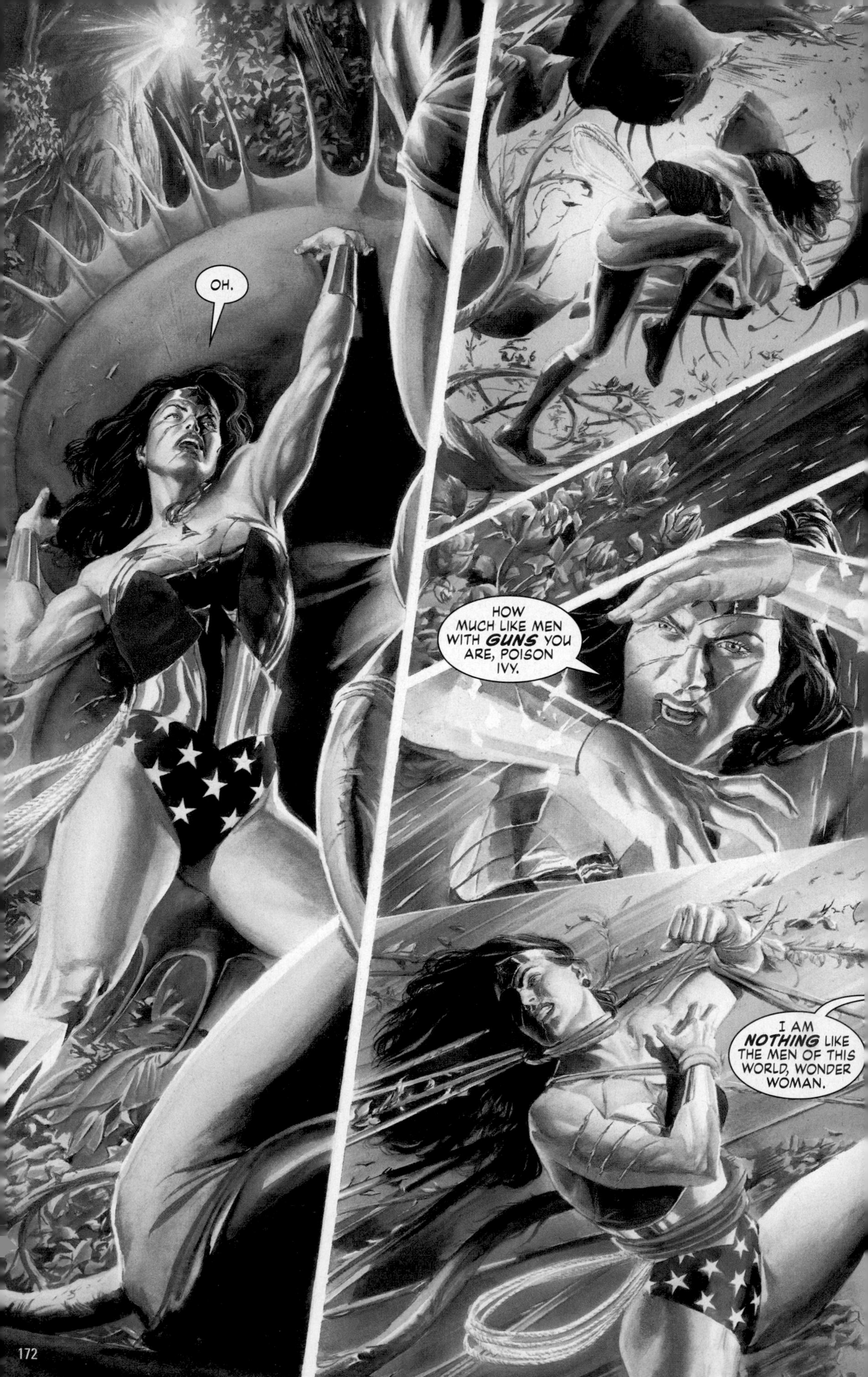
OH.
HOW MUCH LIKE MEN WITH GUNS YOU ARE, POISON IVY.
I AM NOTHING LIKE THE MEN OF THIS WORLD, WONDER WOMAN.

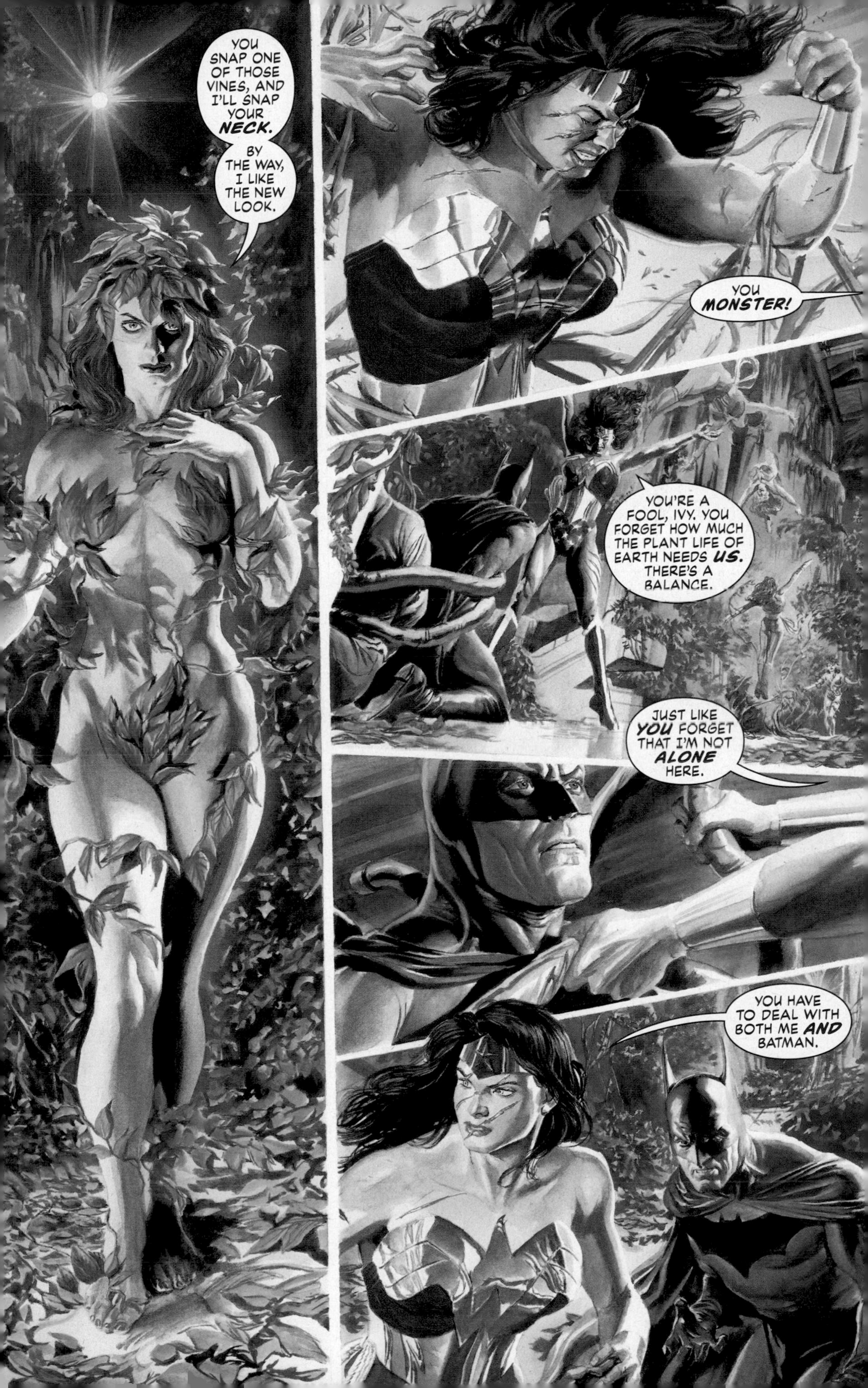
YOU SNAP ONE OF THOSE VINES, AND I'LL SNAP YOUR NECK.
BY THE WAY, I LIKE THE NEW LOOK.
YOU MONSTER!
YOU'RE A FOOL, IVY. YOU FORGET HOW MUCH THE PLANT LIFE OF EARTH NEEDS US. THERE'S A BALANCE.
JUST LIKE YOU FORGET THAT I'M NOT ALONE HERE.
YOU HAVE TO DEAL WITH BOTH ME AND BATMAN.

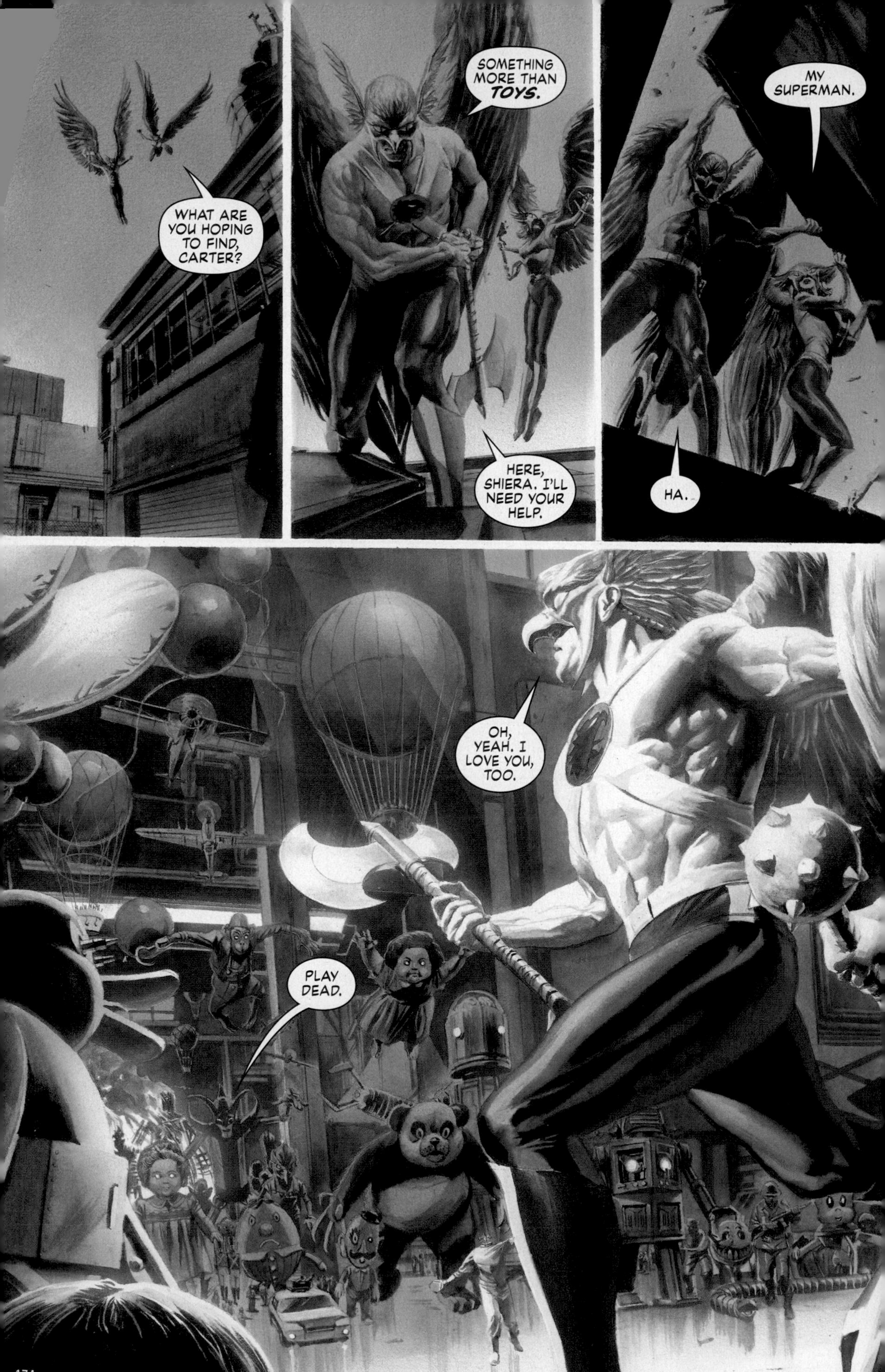
WHAT ARE YOU HOPING TO FIND, CARTER?
SOMETHING MORE THAN TOYS.
HERE, SHIERA. I'LL NEED YOUR HELP.
MY SUPERMAN.
HA.
OH, YEAH. I LOVE YOU, TOO.
PLAY DEAD.

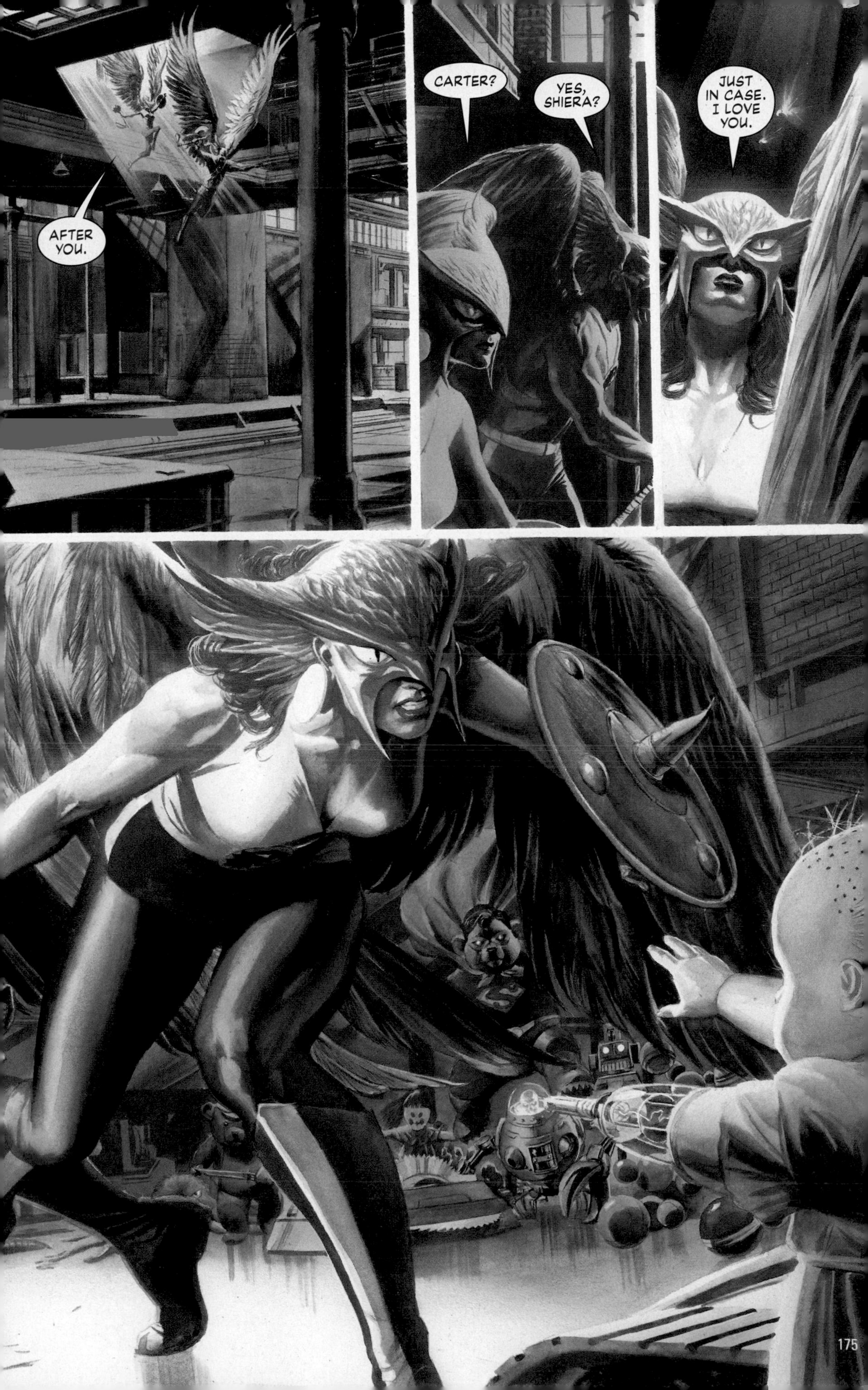
AFTER YOU.
CARTER?
YES, SHIERA?
JUST IN CASE. I LOVE YOU.

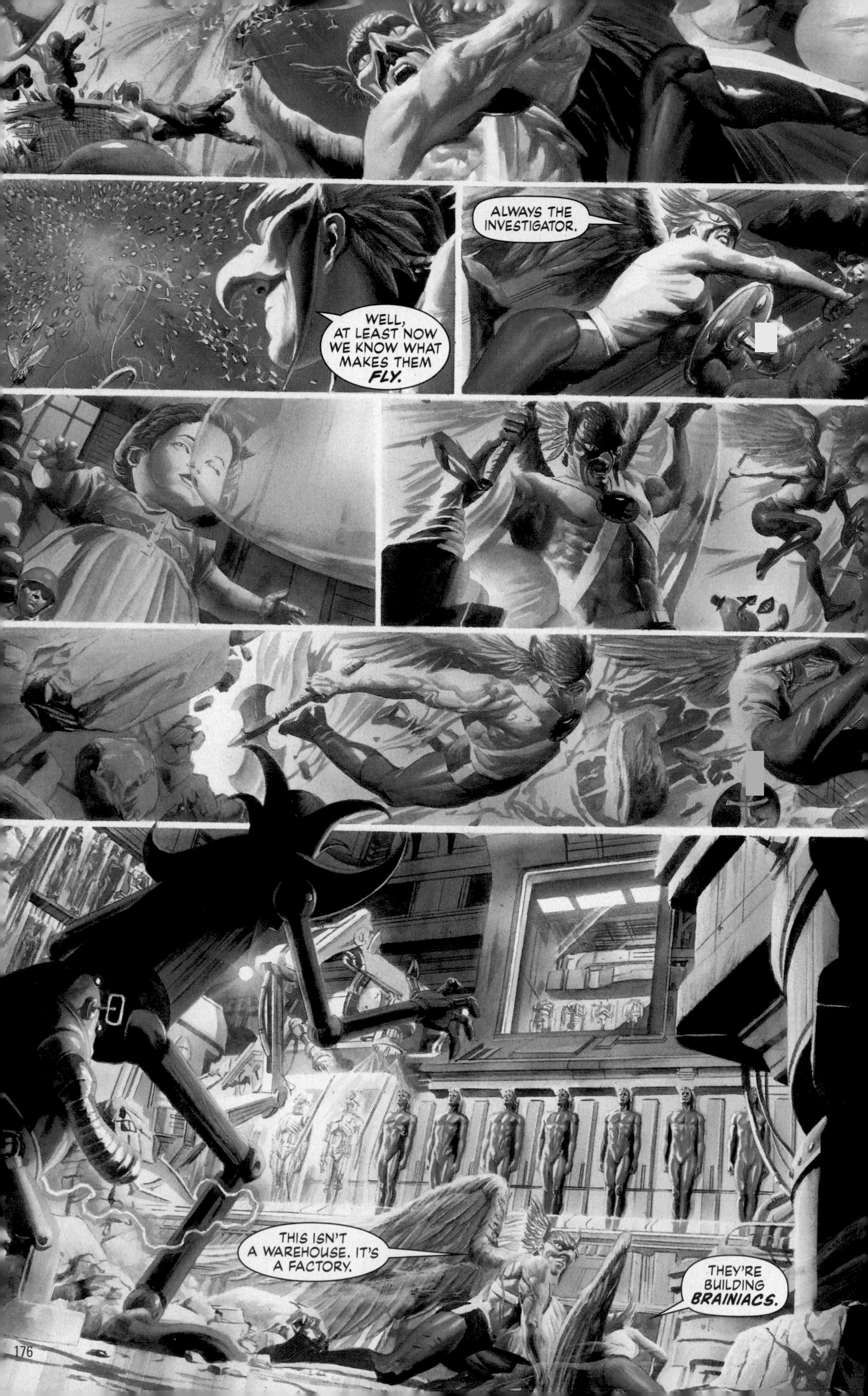
WELL, AT LEAST NOW WE KNOW WHAT MAKES THEM FLY.
ALWAYS THE INVESTIGATOR.
THIS ISN'T A WAREHOUSE. IT'S A FACTORY.
THEY'RE BUILDING BRAINIACS.

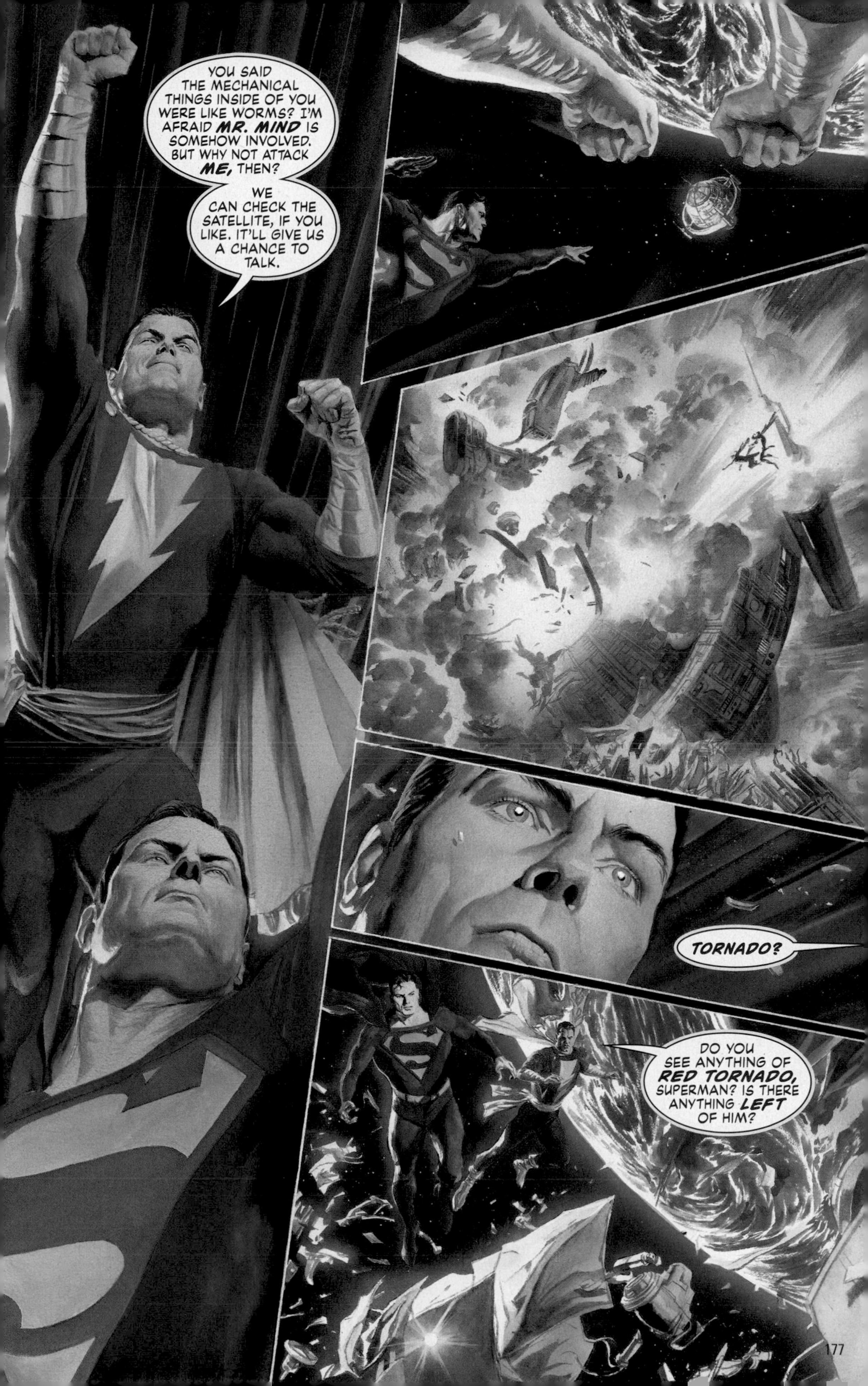
YOU SAID THE MECHANICAL THINGS INSIDE OF YOU WERE LIKE WORMS? I'M AFRAID MR. MIND IS SOMEHOW INVOLVED. BUT WHY NOT ATTACK ME, THEN?
WE CAN CHECK THE SATELLITE, IF YOU LIKE. IT'LL GIVE US A CHANCE TO TALK.
TORNADO?
DO YOU SEE ANYTHING OF RED TORNADO, SUPERMAN? IS THERE ANYTHING LEFT OF HIM?

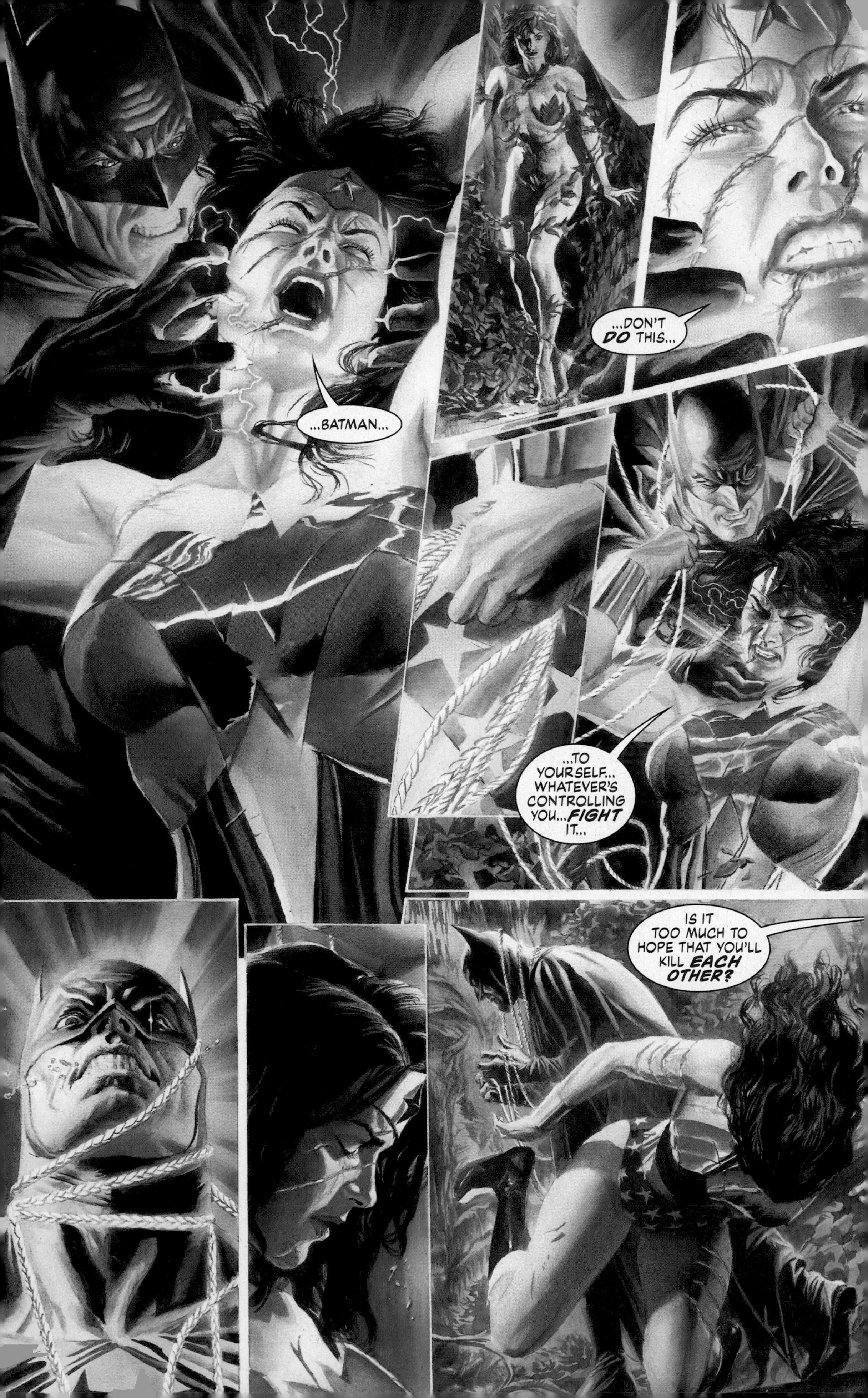
...BATMAN...
...DON'T DO THIS...
...TO YOURSELF... WHATEVER'S CONTROLLING YOU...FIGHT IT...
IS IT TOO MUCH TO HOPE THAT YOU'LL KILL EACH OTHER?

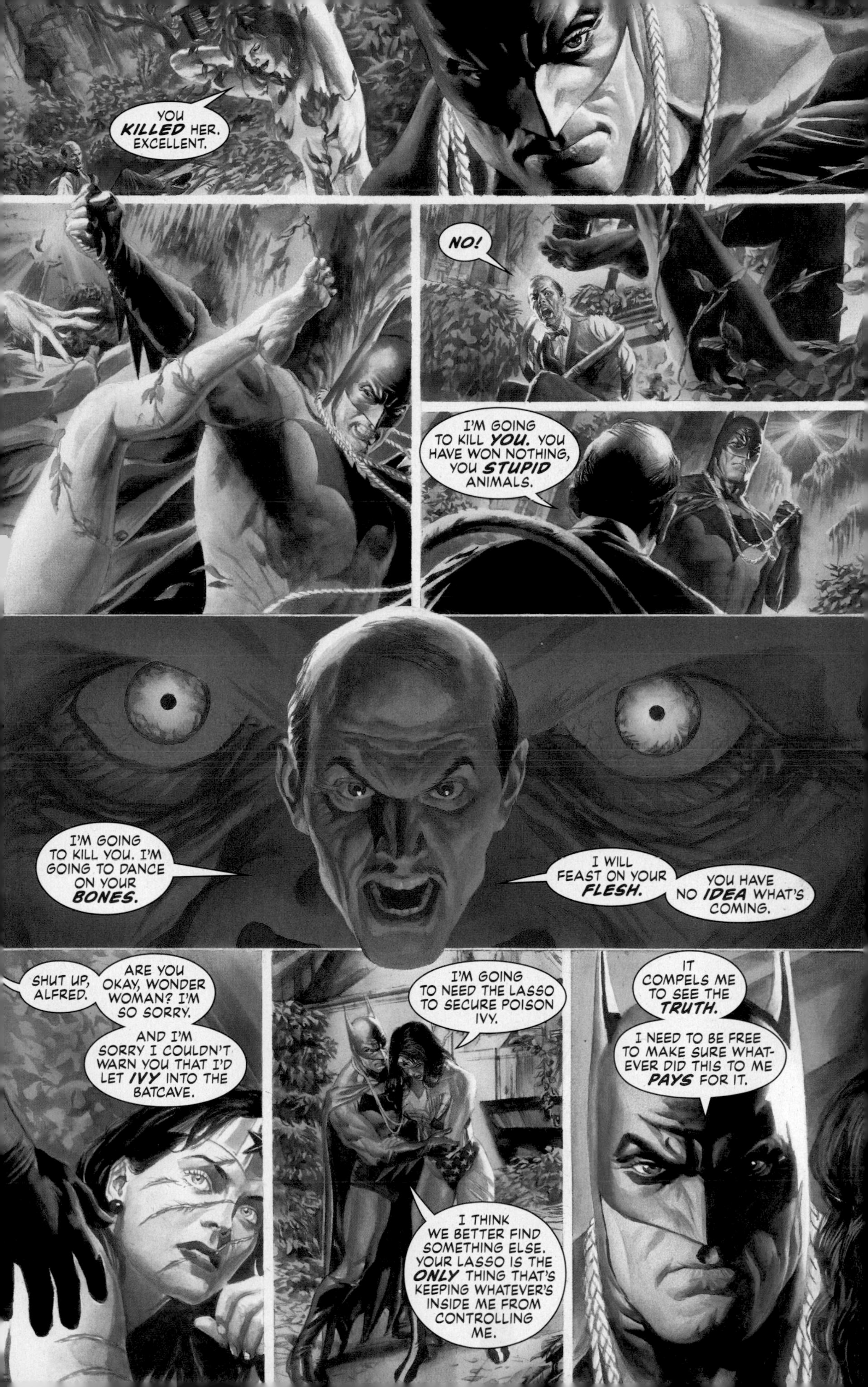

YOU KILLED HER. EXCELLENT.
NO!
I'M GOING TO KILL YOU. YOU HAVE WON NOTHING, YOU STUPID ANIMALS.
I'M GOING TO KILL YOU. I'M GOING TO DANCE ON YOUR BONES.
I WILL FEAST ON YOUR FLESH.
YOU HAVE NO IDEA WHAT'S COMING.
SHUT UP, ALFRED.
ARE YOU OKAY, WONDER WOMAN? I'M SO SORRY.
AND I'M SORRY I COULDN'T WARN YOU THAT I'D LET IVY INTO THE BATCAVE.
I'M GOING TO NEED THE LASSO TO SECURE POISON IVY.
I THINK WE BETTER FIND SOMETHING ELSE. YOUR LASSO IS THE ONLY THING THAT'S KEEPING WHATEVER'S INSIDE ME FROM CONTROLLING ME.
IT COMPELS ME TO SEE THE TRUTH.
I NEED TO BE FREE TO MAKE SURE WHATEVER DID THIS TO ME PAYS FOR IT.

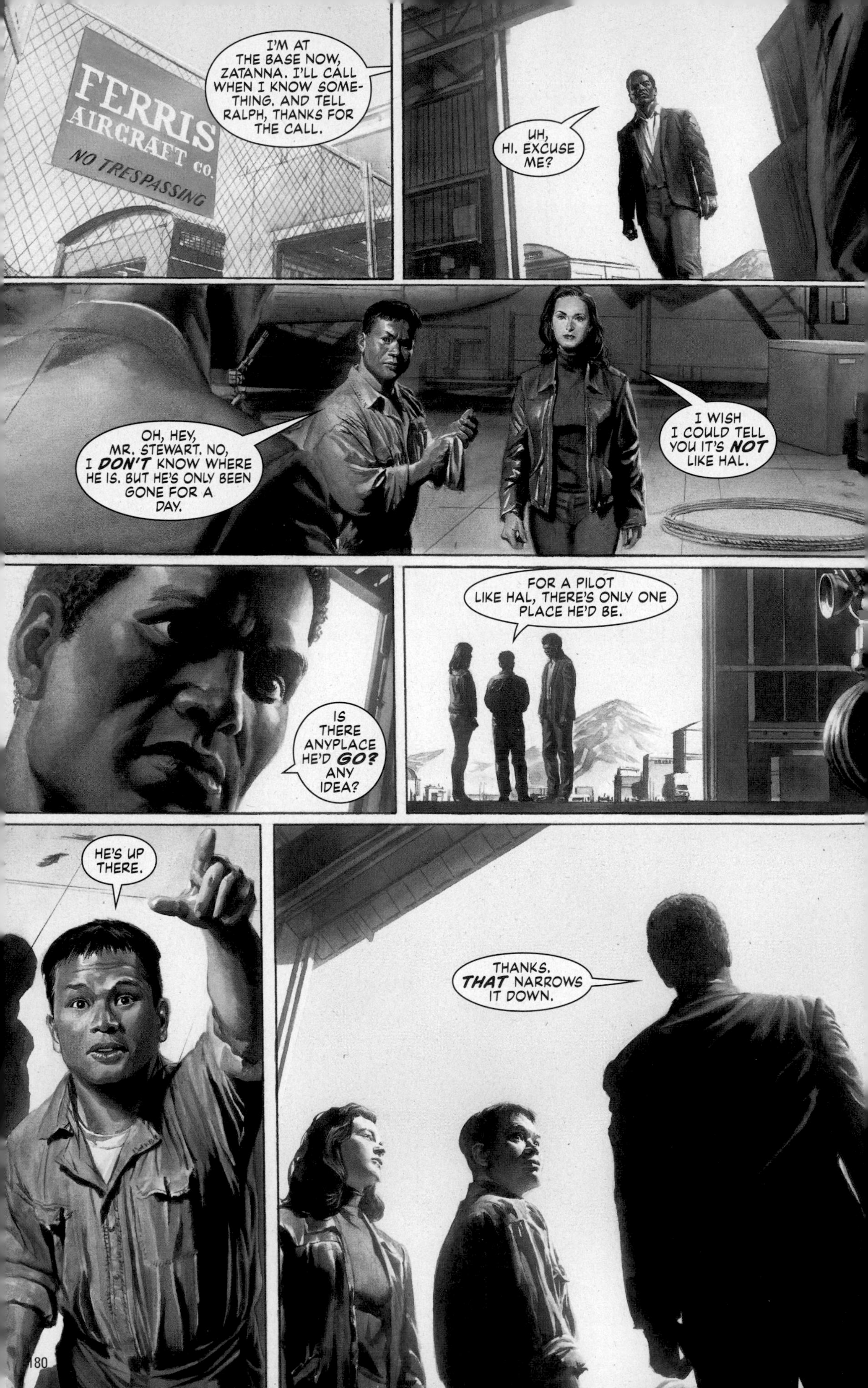
FERRIS AIRCRAFT CO.
NO TRESPASSING
I'M AT THE BASE NOW, ZATANNA. I'LL CALL WHEN I KNOW SOMETHING. AND TELL RALPH, THANKS FOR THE CALL.
UH, HI. EXCUSE ME?
OH, HEY, MR. STEWART. NO, I **DON'T** KNOW WHERE HE IS. BUT HE'S ONLY BEEN GONE FOR A DAY.
I WISH I COULD TELL YOU IT'S **NOT** LIKE HAL.
IS THERE ANYPLACE HE'D **GO?** ANY IDEA?
FOR A PILOT LIKE HAL, THERE'S ONLY ONE PLACE HE'D BE.
HE'S UP THERE.
THANKS. **THAT** NARROWS IT DOWN.

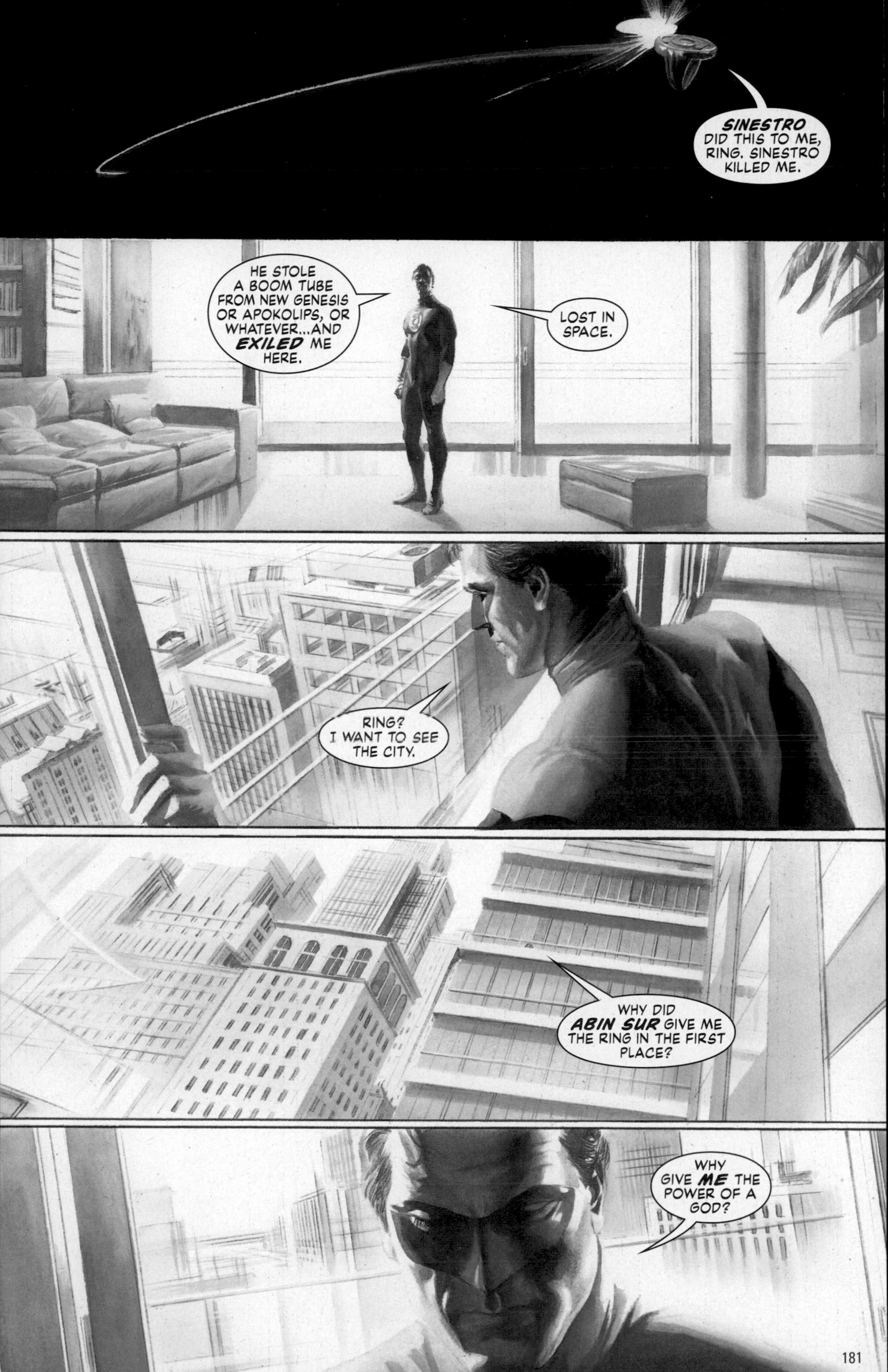
SINESTRO DID THIS TO ME, RING. SINESTRO KILLED ME.
HE STOLE A BOOM TUBE FROM NEW GENESIS OR APOKOLIPS, OR WHATEVER...AND EXILED ME HERE.
LOST IN SPACE.
RING? I WANT TO SEE THE CITY.
WHY DID ABIN SUR GIVE ME THE RING IN THE FIRST PLACE?
WHY GIVE ME THE POWER OF A GOD?

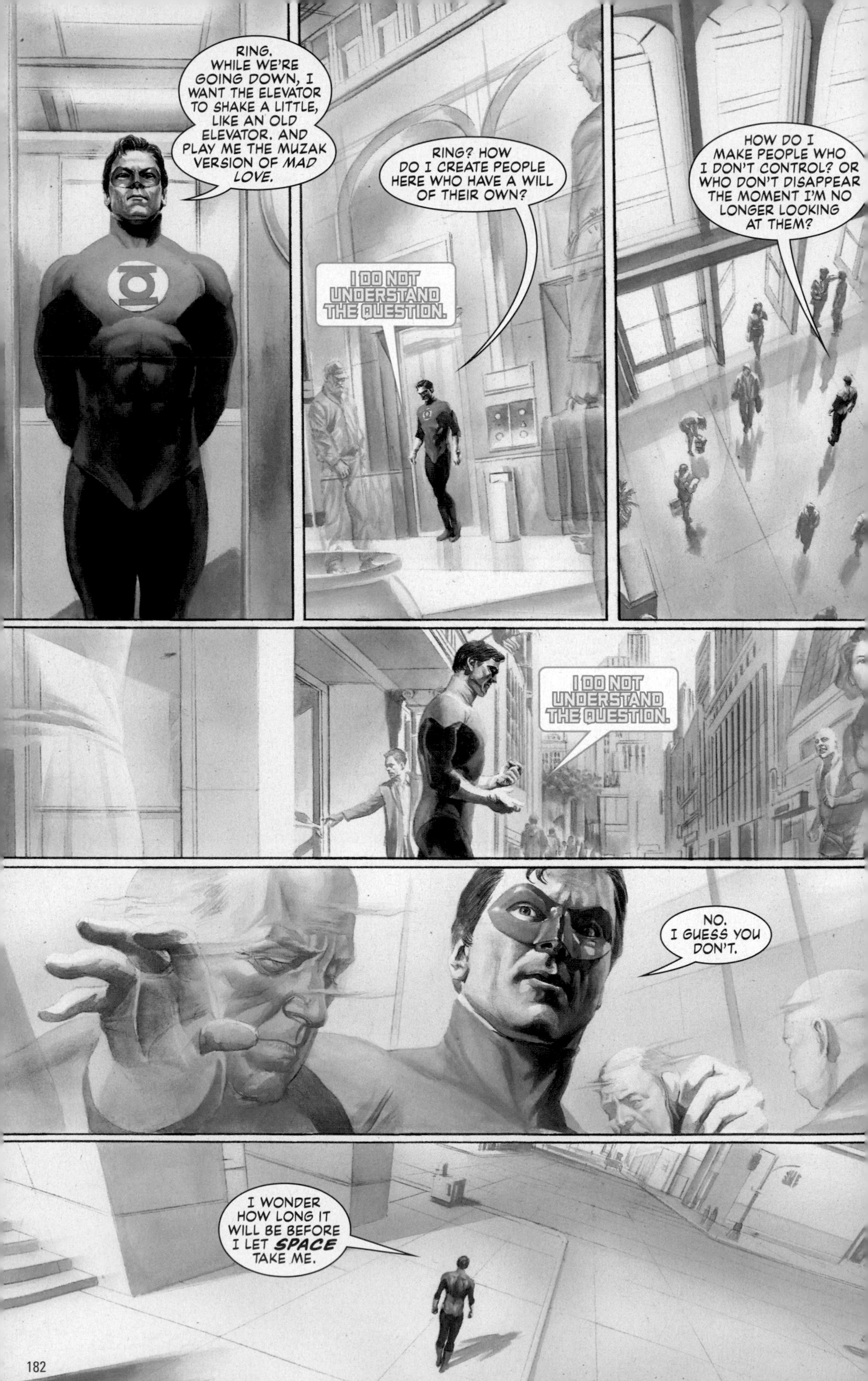

RING. WHILE WE'RE GOING DOWN, I WANT THE ELEVATOR TO SHAKE A LITTLE, LIKE AN OLD ELEVATOR. AND PLAY ME THE MUZAK VERSION OF *MAD LOVE.*
RING? HOW DO I CREATE PEOPLE HERE WHO HAVE A WILL OF THEIR OWN?
I DO NOT UNDERSTAND THE QUESTION.
HOW DO I MAKE PEOPLE WHO I DON'T CONTROL? OR WHO DON'T DISAPPEAR THE MOMENT I'M NO LONGER LOOKING AT THEM?
I DO NOT UNDERSTAND THE QUESTION.
NO. I GUESS YOU DON'T.
I WONDER HOW LONG IT WILL BE BEFORE I LET **SPACE** TAKE ME.

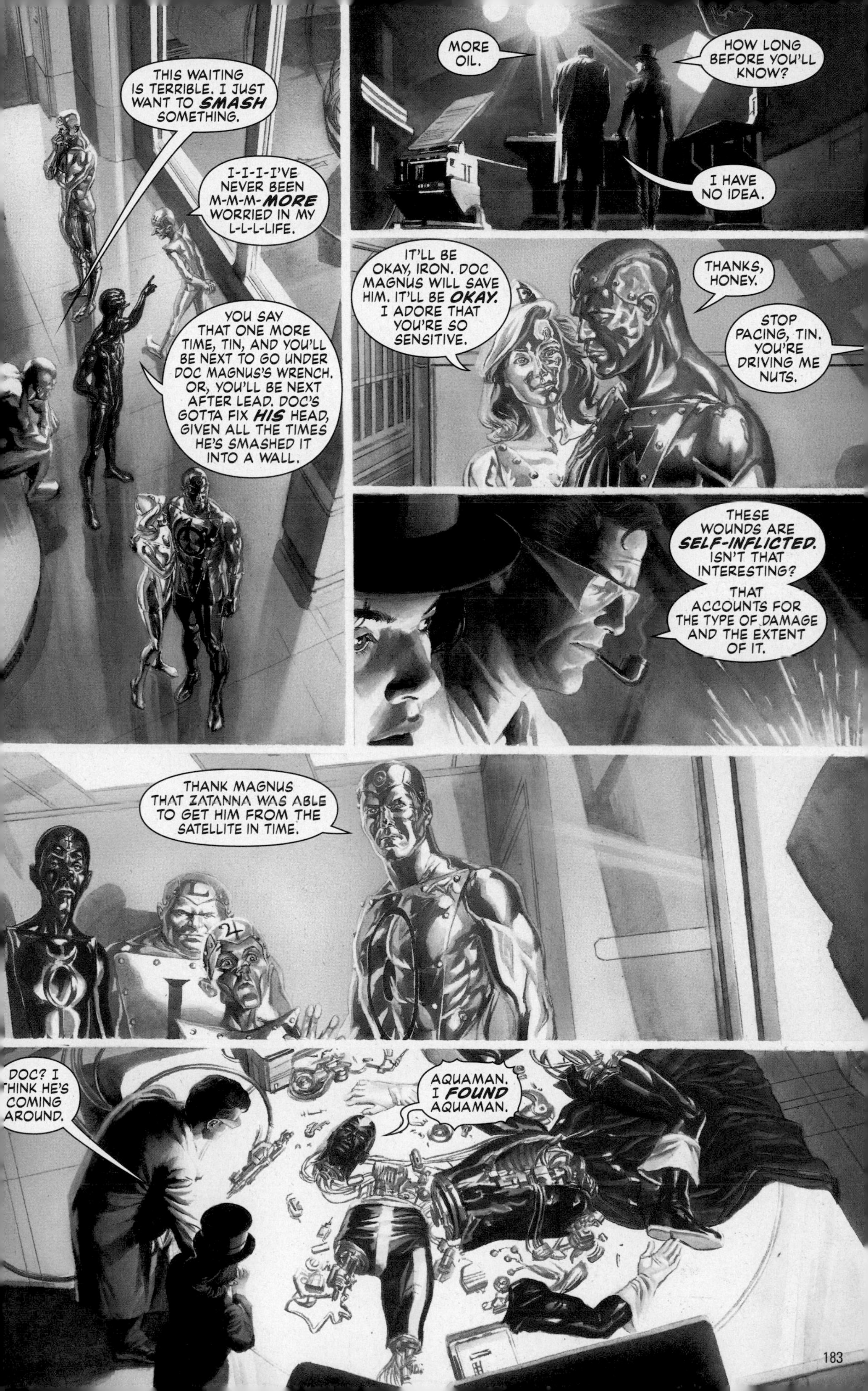
THIS WAITING IS TERRIBLE. I JUST WANT TO SMASH SOMETHING.
I-I-I-I'VE NEVER BEEN M-M-M-MORE WORRIED IN MY L-L-L-LIFE.
YOU SAY THAT ONE MORE TIME, TIN, AND YOU'LL BE NEXT TO GO UNDER DOC MAGNUS'S WRENCH. OR, YOU'LL BE NEXT AFTER LEAD. DOC'S GOTTA FIX HIS HEAD, GIVEN ALL THE TIMES HE'S SMASHED IT INTO A WALL.
MORE OIL.
HOW LONG BEFORE YOU'LL KNOW?
I HAVE NO IDEA.
IT'LL BE OKAY, IRON. DOC MAGNUS WILL SAVE HIM. IT'LL BE OKAY. I ADORE THAT YOU'RE SO SENSITIVE.
THANKS, HONEY.
STOP PACING, TIN. YOU'RE DRIVING ME NUTS.
THESE WOUNDS ARE SELF-INFLICTED. ISN'T THAT INTERESTING?
THAT ACCOUNTS FOR THE TYPE OF DAMAGE AND THE EXTENT OF IT.
THANK MAGNUS THAT ZATANNA WAS ABLE TO GET HIM FROM THE SATELLITE IN TIME.
DOC? I THINK HE'S COMING AROUND.
AQUAMAN. I FOUND AQUAMAN.

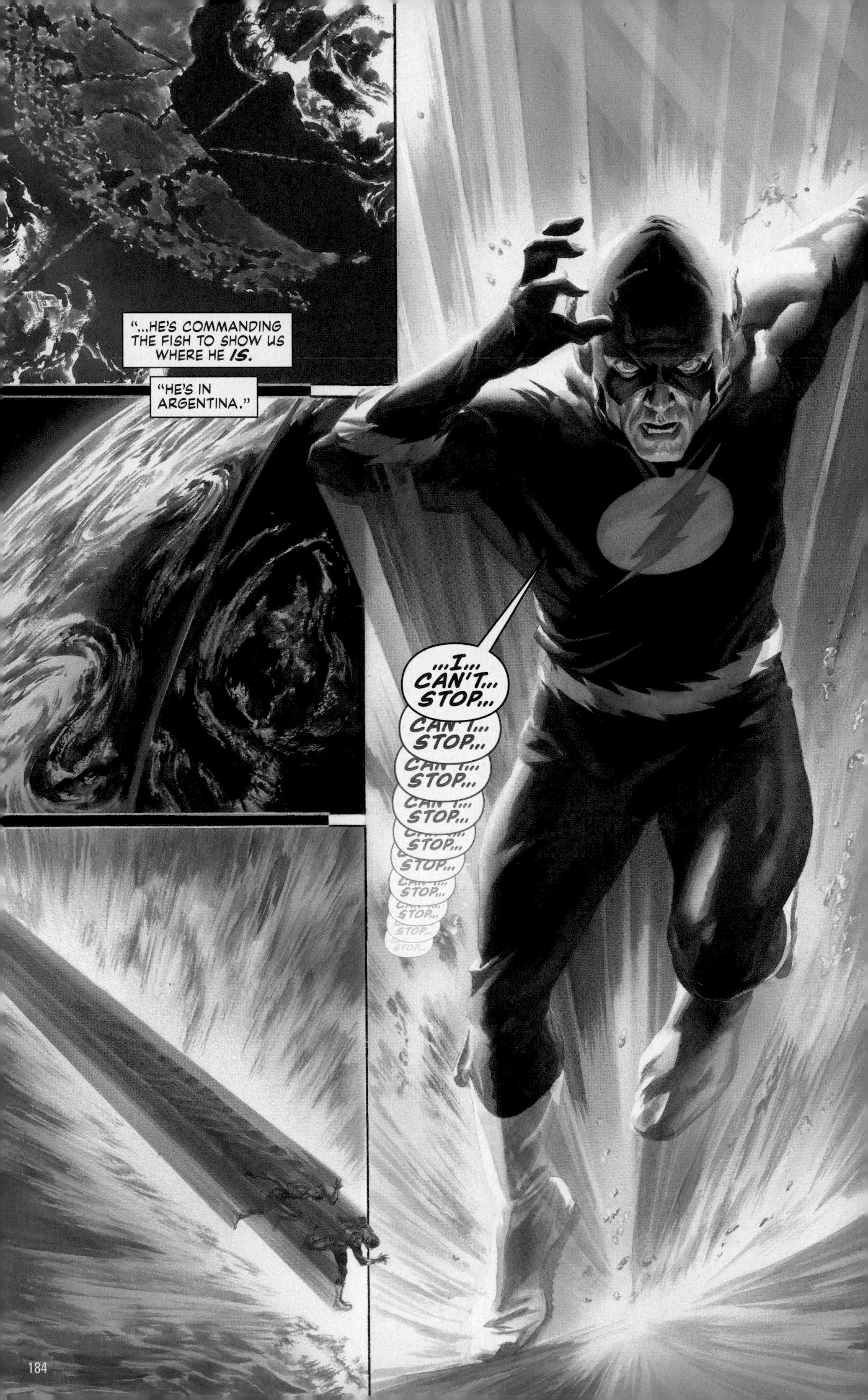
"...HE'S COMMANDING THE FISH TO SHOW US WHERE HE *IS*.
"HE'S IN ARGENTINA."
...I... CAN'T... STOP...
CAN'T... STOP...
CAN'T... STOP...
CAN'T... STOP...
STOP...
STOP...
STOP...
STOP...
STOP...
STOP...

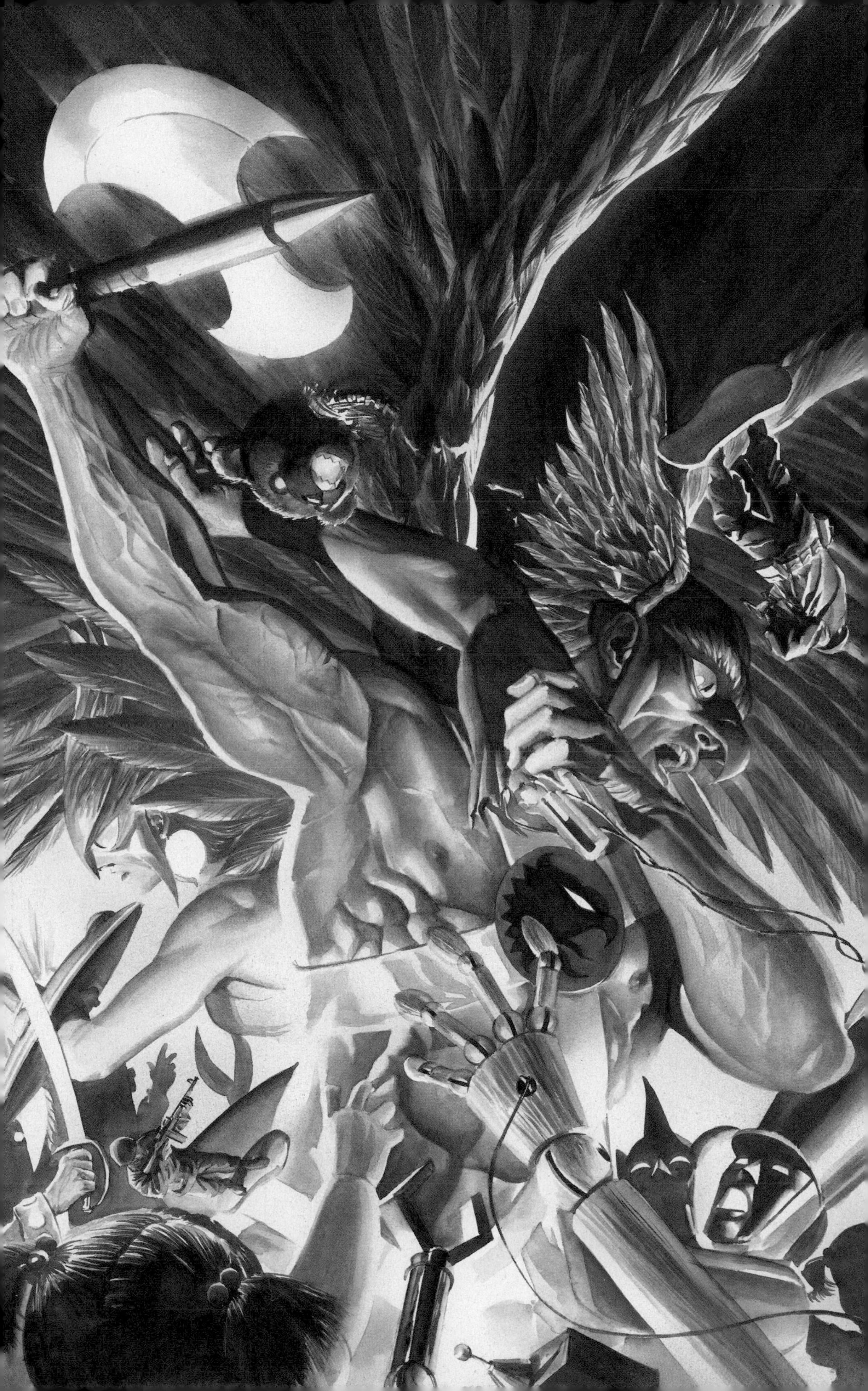

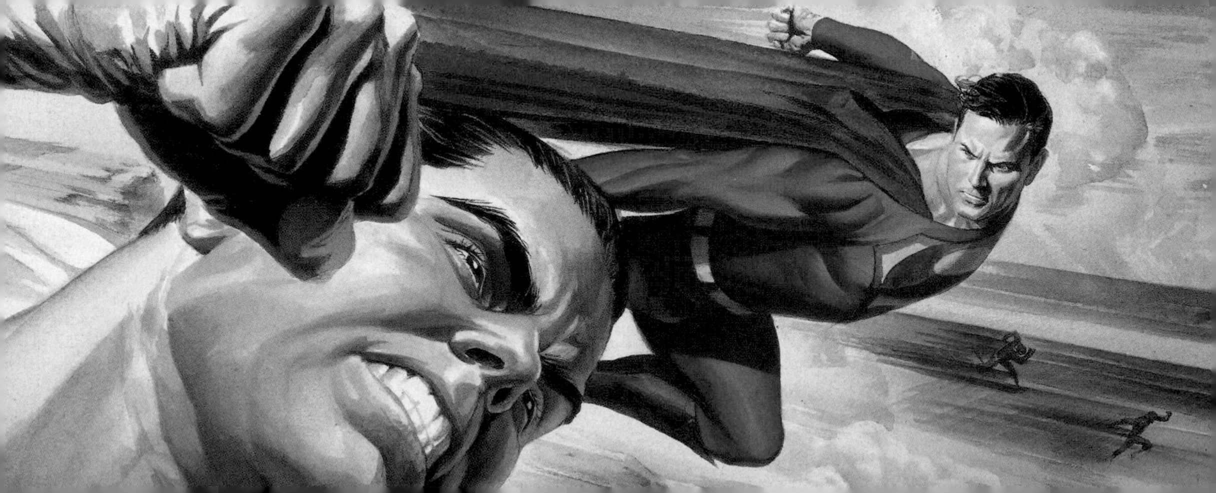

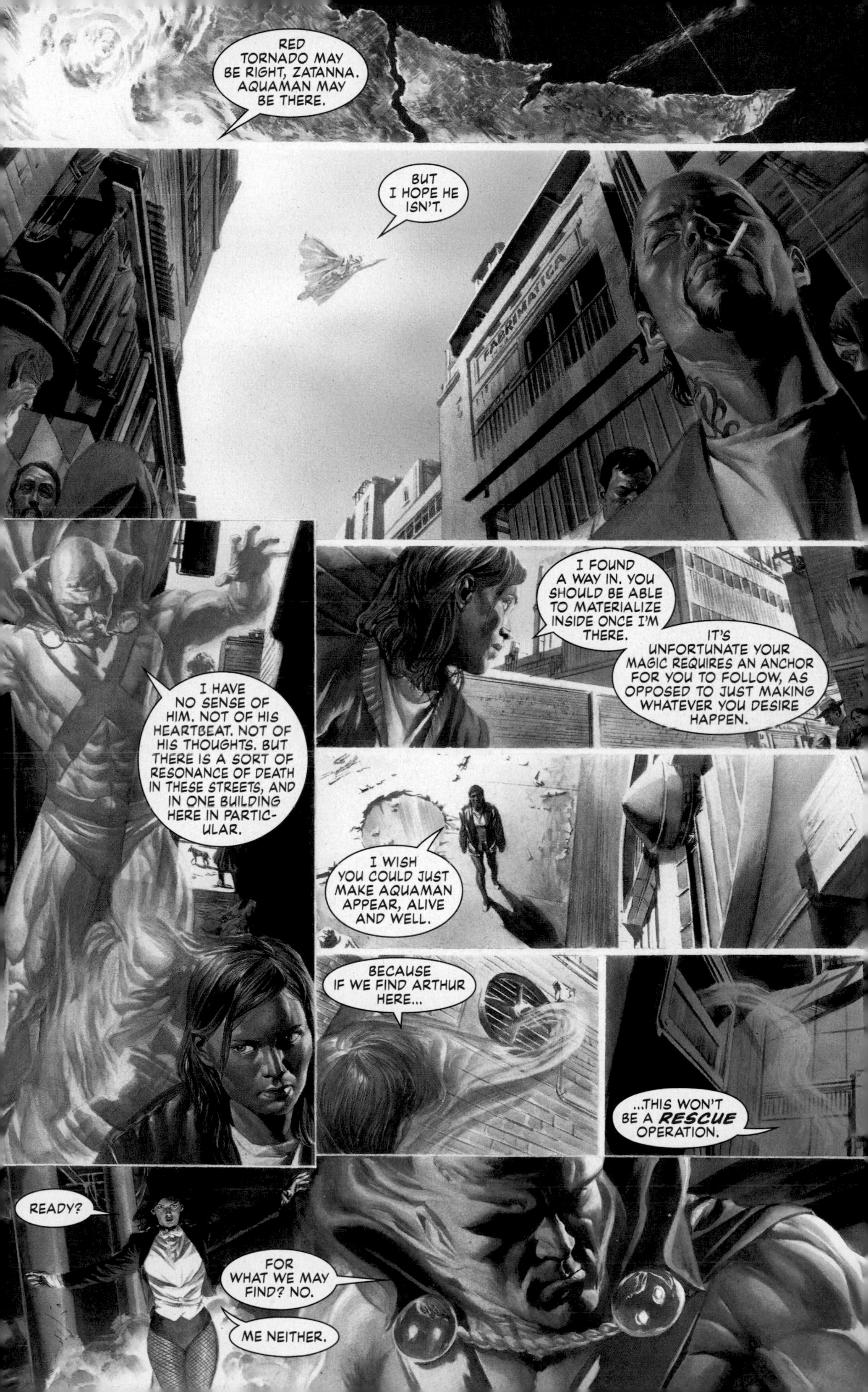
RED TORNADO MAY BE RIGHT, ZATANNA. AQUAMAN MAY BE THERE.
BUT I HOPE HE ISN'T.
FABRIMATICA
I HAVE NO SENSE OF HIM. NOT OF HIS HEARTBEAT. NOT OF HIS THOUGHTS. BUT THERE IS A SORT OF RESONANCE OF DEATH IN THESE STREETS, AND IN ONE BUILDING HERE IN PARTICULAR.
I FOUND A WAY IN. YOU SHOULD BE ABLE TO MATERIALIZE INSIDE ONCE I'M THERE.
IT'S UNFORTUNATE YOUR MAGIC REQUIRES AN ANCHOR FOR YOU TO FOLLOW, AS OPPOSED TO JUST MAKING WHATEVER YOU DESIRE HAPPEN.
I WISH YOU COULD JUST MAKE AQUAMAN APPEAR, ALIVE AND WELL.
BECAUSE IF WE FIND ARTHUR HERE...
...THIS WON'T BE A *RESCUE* OPERATION.
READY?
FOR WHAT WE MAY FIND? NO.
ME NEITHER.

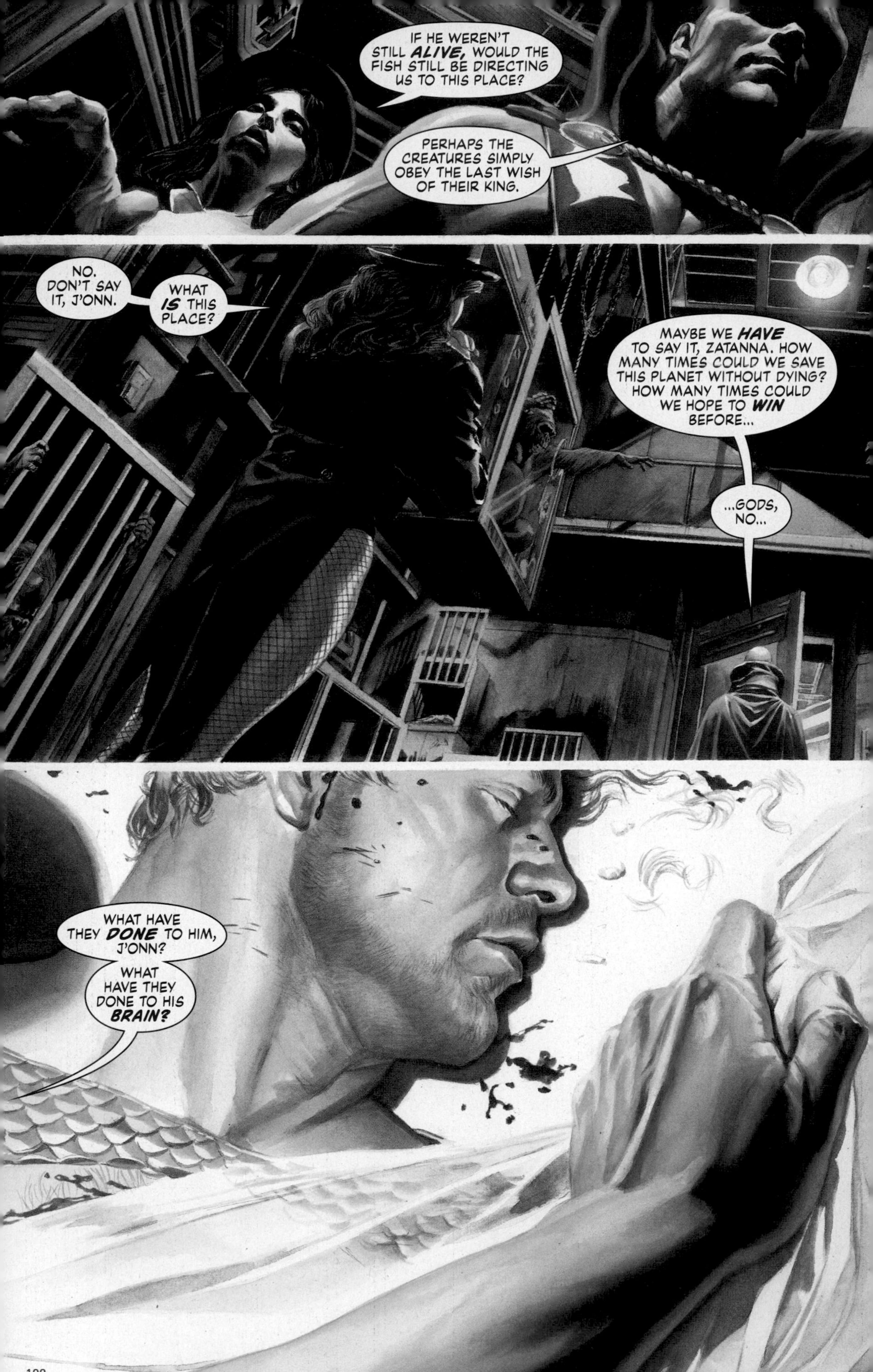
IF HE WEREN'T STILL **ALIVE,** WOULD THE FISH STILL BE DIRECTING US TO THIS PLACE?
PERHAPS THE CREATURES SIMPLY OBEY THE LAST WISH OF THEIR KING.
NO. DON'T SAY IT, J'ONN.
WHAT **IS** THIS PLACE?
MAYBE WE **HAVE** TO SAY IT, ZATANNA. HOW MANY TIMES COULD WE SAVE THIS PLANET WITHOUT DYING? HOW MANY TIMES COULD WE HOPE TO **WIN** BEFORE...
...GODS, NO...
WHAT HAVE THEY **DONE** TO HIM, J'ONN?
WHAT HAVE THEY DONE TO HIS **BRAIN?**

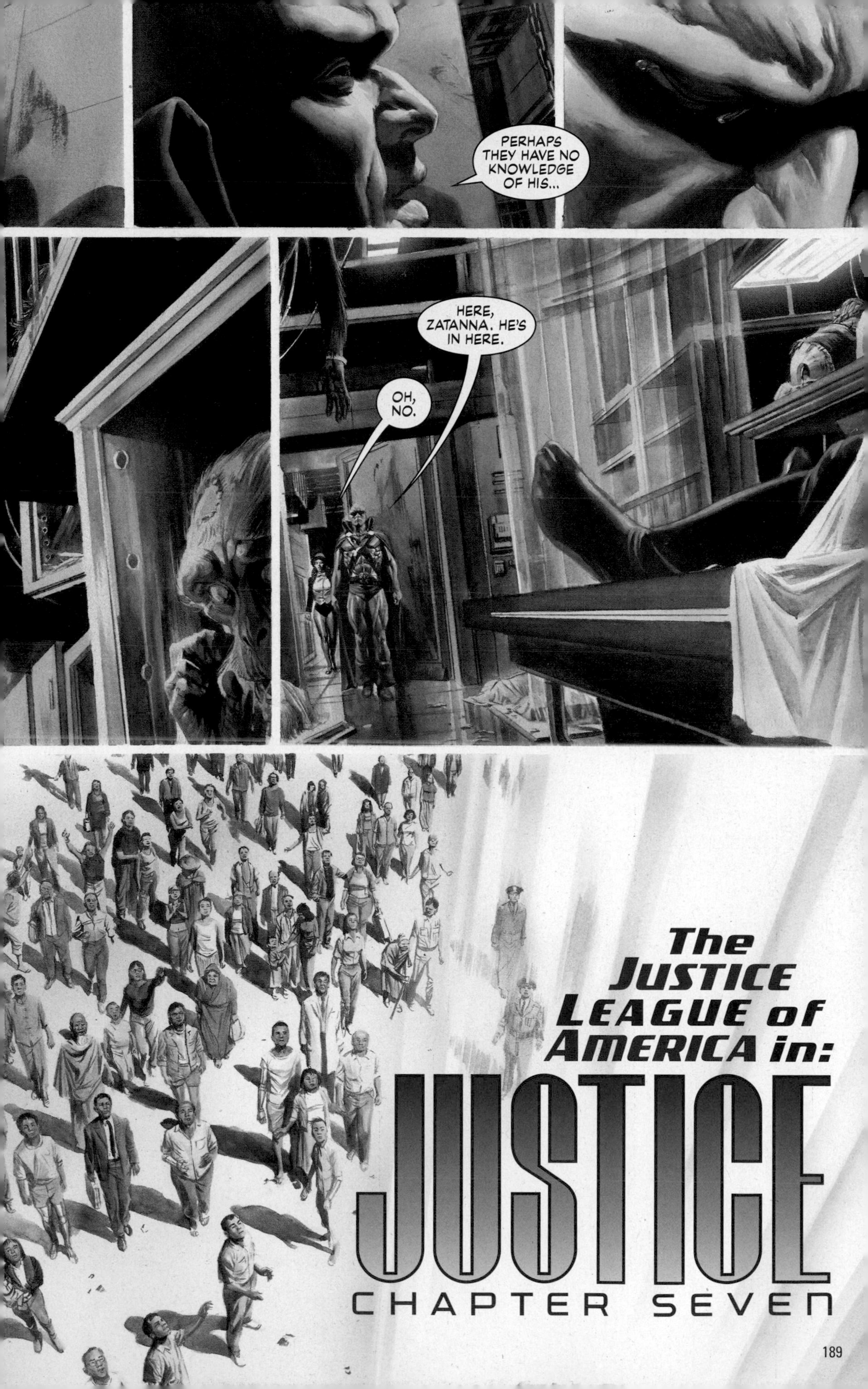
PERHAPS THEY HAVE NO KNOWLEDGE OF HIS...
HERE, ZATANNA. HE'S IN HERE.
OH, NO.
The JUSTICE LEAGUE of AMERICA in:
JUSTICE
CHAPTER SEVEN

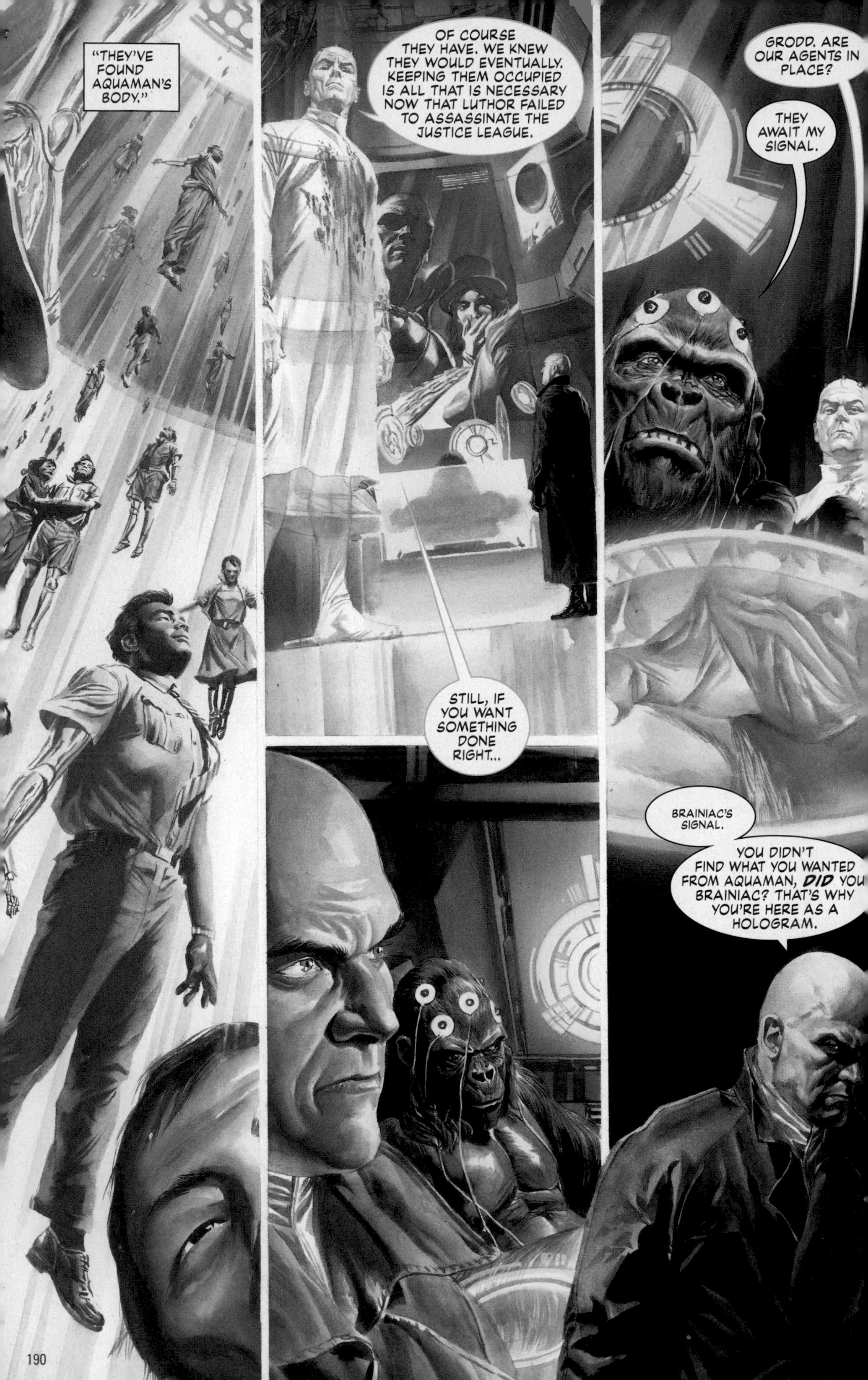
"THEY'VE FOUND AQUAMAN'S BODY."
OF COURSE THEY HAVE. WE KNEW THEY WOULD EVENTUALLY. KEEPING THEM OCCUPIED IS ALL THAT IS NECESSARY NOW THAT LUTHOR FAILED TO ASSASSINATE THE JUSTICE LEAGUE.
STILL, IF YOU WANT SOMETHING DONE RIGHT...
GRODD. ARE OUR AGENTS IN PLACE?
THEY AWAIT MY SIGNAL.
BRAINIAC'S SIGNAL.
YOU DIDN'T FIND WHAT YOU WANTED FROM AQUAMAN, ***DID*** YOU BRAINIAC? THAT'S WHY YOU'RE HERE AS A HOLOGRAM.

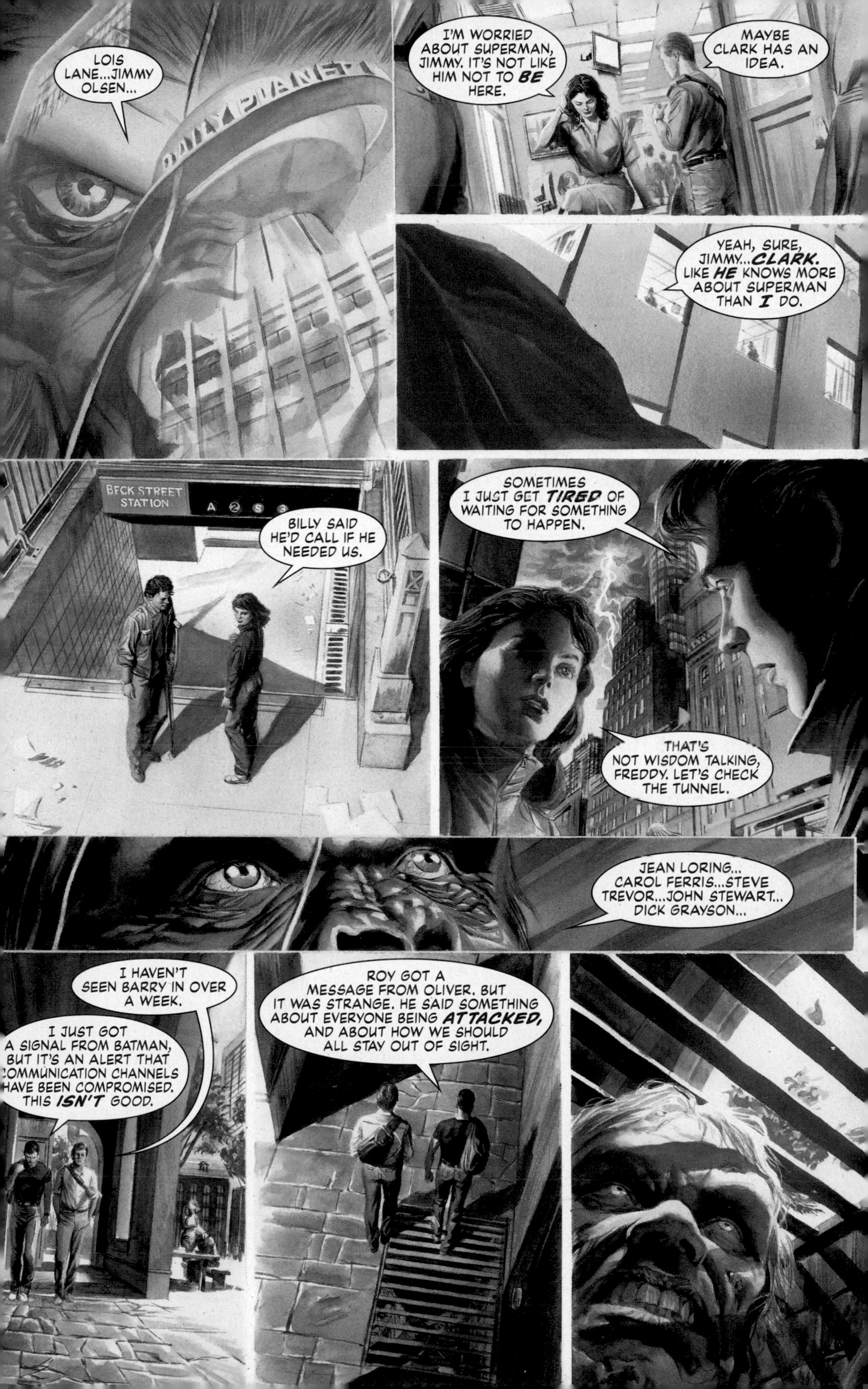
LOIS LANE...JIMMY OLSEN...
DAILY PLANET
I'M WORRIED ABOUT SUPERMAN, JIMMY. IT'S NOT LIKE HIM NOT TO BE HERE.
MAYBE CLARK HAS AN IDEA.
YEAH, SURE, JIMMY...CLARK. LIKE HE KNOWS MORE ABOUT SUPERMAN THAN I DO.
BECK STREET STATION
A 2 S 3
BILLY SAID HE'D CALL IF HE NEEDED US.
SOMETIMES I JUST GET TIRED OF WAITING FOR SOMETHING TO HAPPEN.
THAT'S NOT WISDOM TALKING, FREDDY. LET'S CHECK THE TUNNEL.
JEAN LORING... CAROL FERRIS...STEVE TREVOR...JOHN STEWART... DICK GRAYSON...
I HAVEN'T SEEN BARRY IN OVER A WEEK.
I JUST GOT A SIGNAL FROM BATMAN, BUT IT'S AN ALERT THAT COMMUNICATION CHANNELS HAVE BEEN COMPROMISED. THIS ISN'T GOOD.
ROY GOT A MESSAGE FROM OLIVER. BUT IT WAS STRANGE. HE SAID SOMETHING ABOUT EVERYONE BEING ATTACKED, AND ABOUT HOW WE SHOULD ALL STAY OUT OF SIGHT.

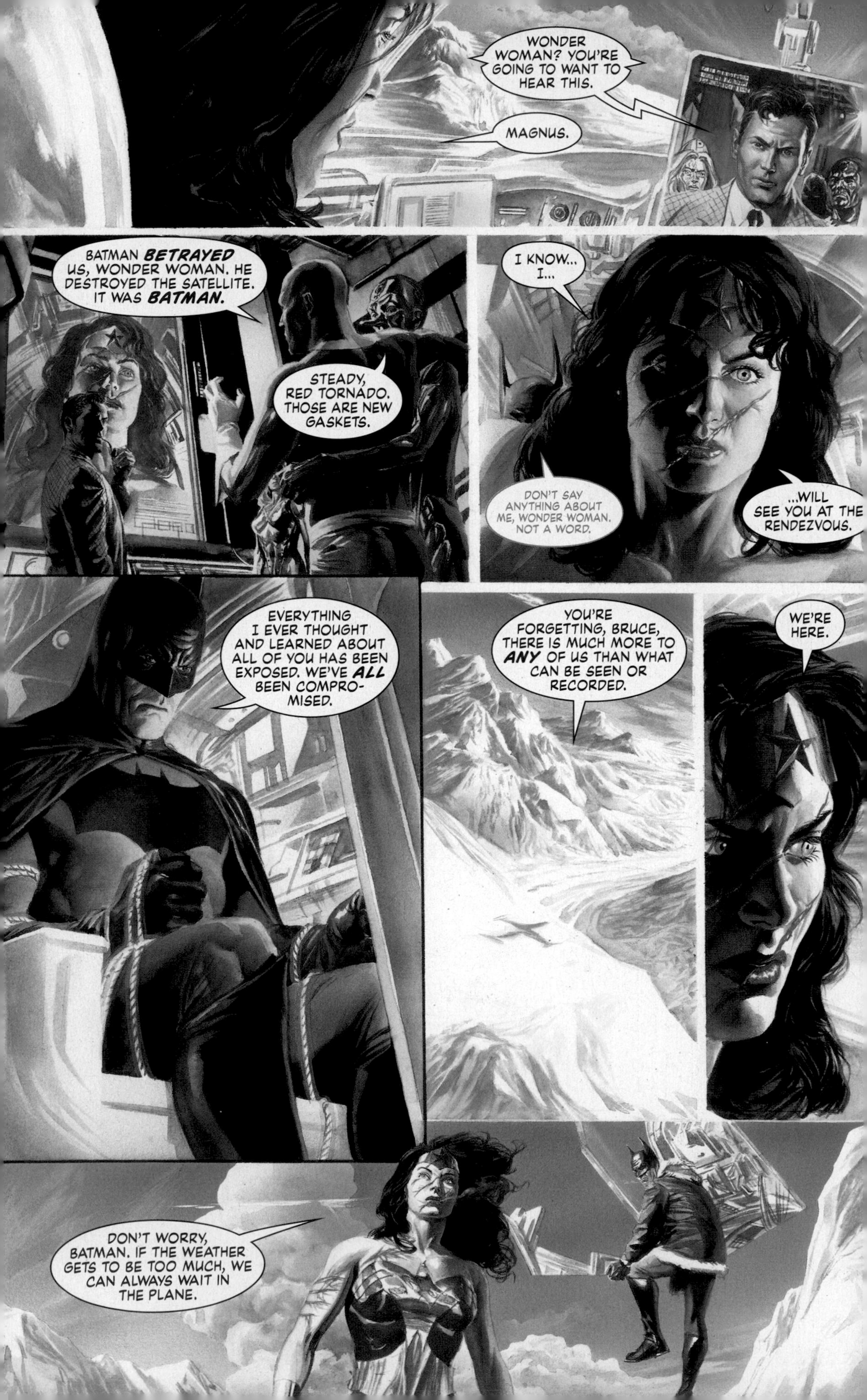
WONDER WOMAN? YOU'RE GOING TO WANT TO HEAR THIS.
MAGNUS.
BATMAN **BETRAYED** US, WONDER WOMAN. HE DESTROYED THE SATELLITE. IT WAS **BATMAN.**
STEADY, RED TORNADO. THOSE ARE NEW GASKETS.
I KNOW... I...
DON'T SAY ANYTHING ABOUT ME, WONDER WOMAN. NOT A WORD.
...WILL SEE YOU AT THE RENDEZVOUS.
EVERYTHING I EVER THOUGHT AND LEARNED ABOUT ALL OF YOU HAS BEEN EXPOSED. WE'VE **ALL** BEEN COMPRO-MISED.
YOU'RE FORGETTING, BRUCE, THERE IS MUCH MORE TO **ANY** OF US THAN WHAT CAN BE SEEN OR RECORDED.
WE'RE HERE.
DON'T WORRY, BATMAN. IF THE WEATHER GETS TO BE TOO MUCH, WE CAN ALWAYS WAIT IN THE PLANE.

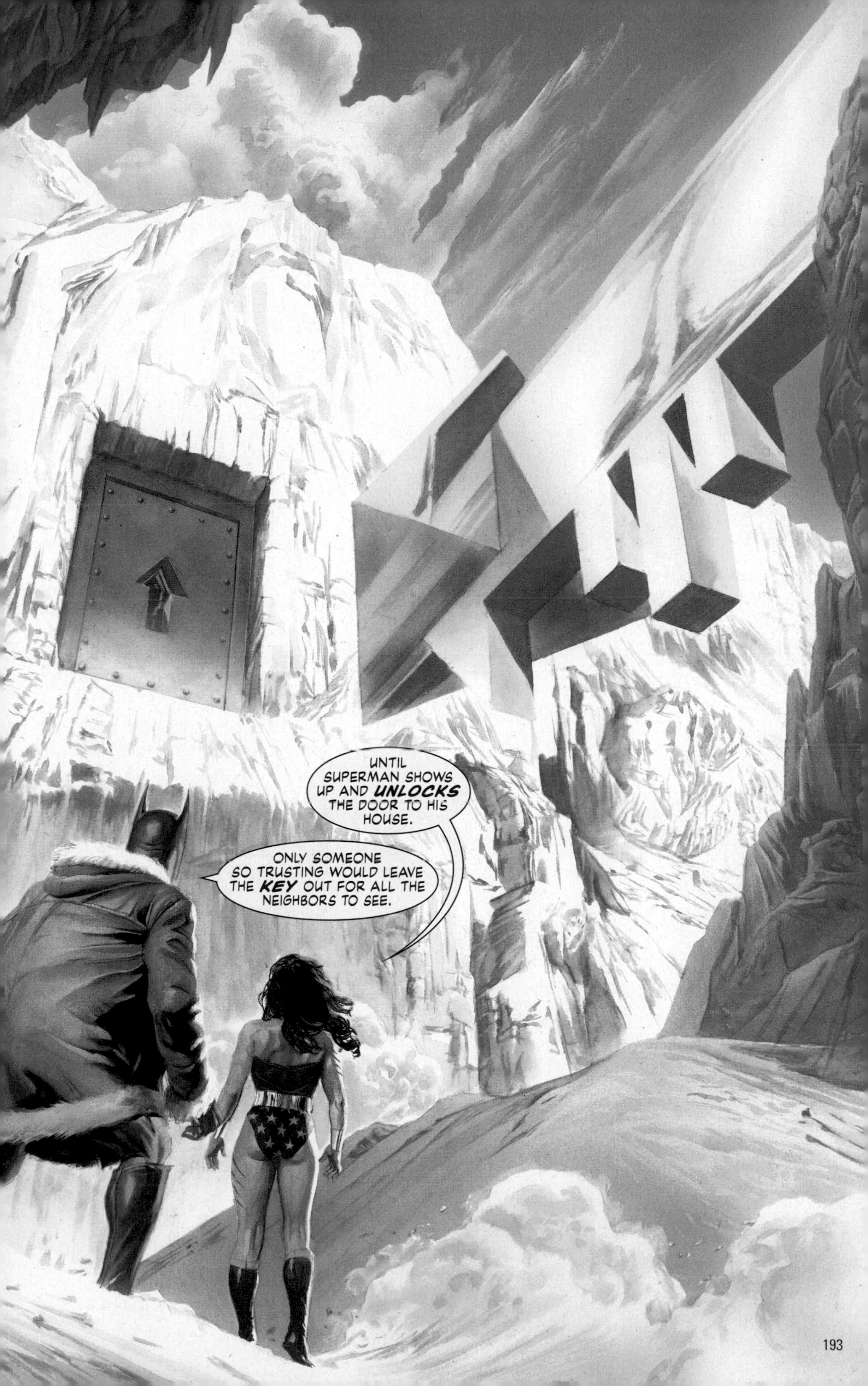
UNTIL SUPERMAN SHOWS UP AND UNLOCKS THE DOOR TO HIS HOUSE.
ONLY SOMEONE SO TRUSTING WOULD LEAVE THE KEY OUT FOR ALL THE NEIGHBORS TO SEE.

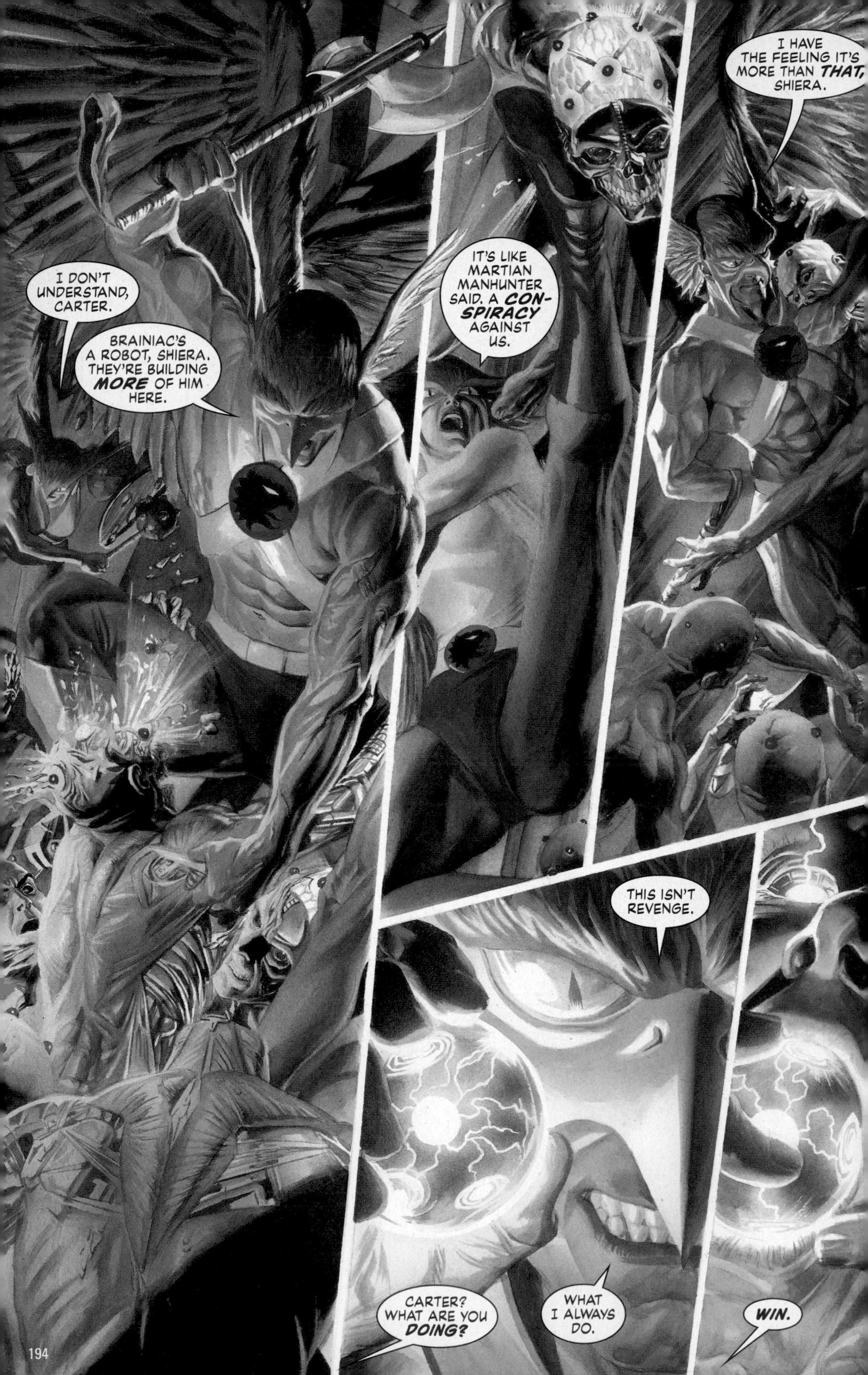
I DON'T UNDERSTAND, CARTER.
BRAINIAC'S A ROBOT, SHIERA. THEY'RE BUILDING **MORE** OF HIM HERE.
IT'S LIKE MARTIAN MANHUNTER SAID. A **CONSPIRACY** AGAINST US.
I HAVE THE FEELING IT'S MORE THAN **THAT,** SHIERA.
THIS ISN'T REVENGE.
CARTER? WHAT ARE YOU **DOING?**
WHAT I ALWAYS DO.
WIN.

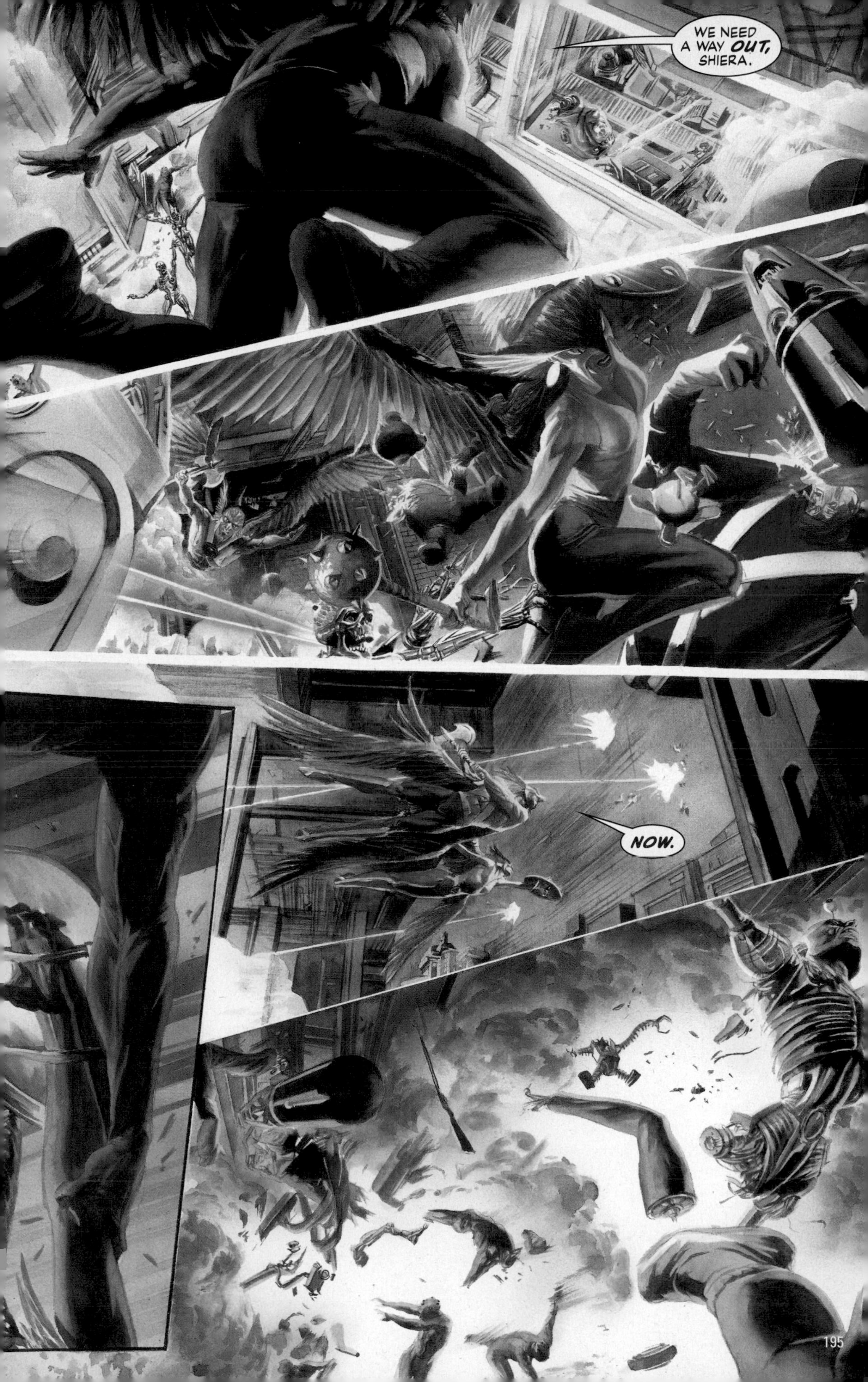
WE NEED A WAY OUT, SHIERA.
NOW.

NEXT TIME, **TELL** ME. IT'S NOT A PLAN I CAN BE A **PART** OF IF I DON'T KNOW WHAT YOU'RE DOING.

YES, DEAR. WHATEVER YOU SAY.

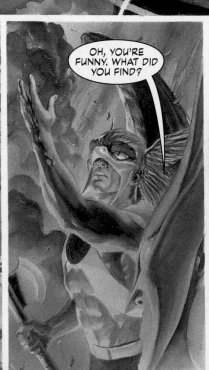

OH, YOU'RE FUNNY. WHAT DID YOU FIND?

THIS.

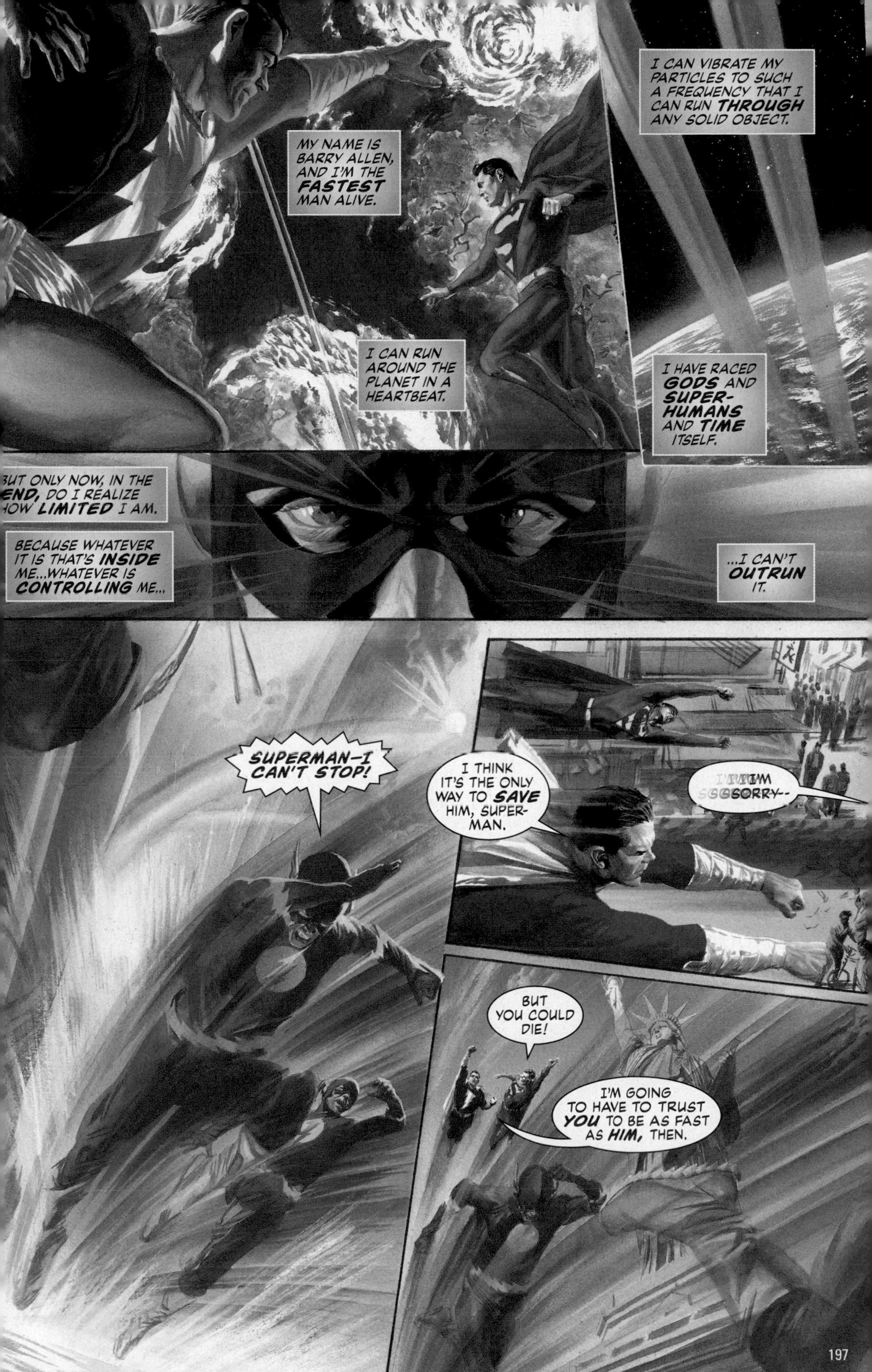

MY NAME IS BARRY ALLEN, AND I'M THE FASTEST MAN ALIVE.
I CAN RUN AROUND THE PLANET IN A HEARTBEAT.
I CAN VIBRATE MY PARTICLES TO SUCH A FREQUENCY THAT I CAN RUN THROUGH ANY SOLID OBJECT.
I HAVE RACED GODS AND SUPER-HUMANS AND TIME ITSELF.
BUT ONLY NOW, IN THE END, DO I REALIZE HOW LIMITED I AM.
BECAUSE WHATEVER IT IS THAT'S INSIDE ME...WHATEVER IS CONTROLLING ME...
...I CAN'T OUTRUN IT.
SUPERMAN—I CAN'T STOP!
I THINK IT'S THE ONLY WAY TO SAVE HIM, SUPER-MAN.
I'M SORRY--
BUT YOU COULD DIE!
I'M GOING TO HAVE TO TRUST YOU TO BE AS FAST AS HIM, THEN.

THE FLASH AND I HAVE RACED EACH OTHER OVER AND *OVER* AGAIN. I FEEL LIKE HE ALWAYS LET ME WIN.

THAT WAS *BEFORE* HIS METABOLISM WAS EATING HIM ALIVE.

I COULD WATCH HIM DISAPPEAR IN THE WEST AND ARRIVE IN THE EAST IN THE *SAME BREATH.*

BUT, BILL, YOU HAVE THE SPEED OF *MERCURY.* A *GOD* CAN OUTRUN THE FASTEST MAN ALIVE. MAYBE YOU CAN STOP HIM *WITHOUT* DOING WHAT YOU'RE PLANNING. JUST GRAB ONTO HIM.

WHEN I WAS YOUNG, I DREAMED OF VISITING OTHER COUNTRIES. I DREAMED OF OTHER CULTURES AND THE *VOYAGES* NECESSARY TO REACH THEM.

BUT THAT WAS BEFORE THE WORLD BECAME SO *SMALL,* AND CROSSING THE OCEAN BECAME A SKIP ACROSS A POND.

THOSE CHILDHOOD WISHES ARE A *BLUR* TO ME NOW.

IRIS. I WISH I COULD JUST STOP AND *SIT* WITH HER.

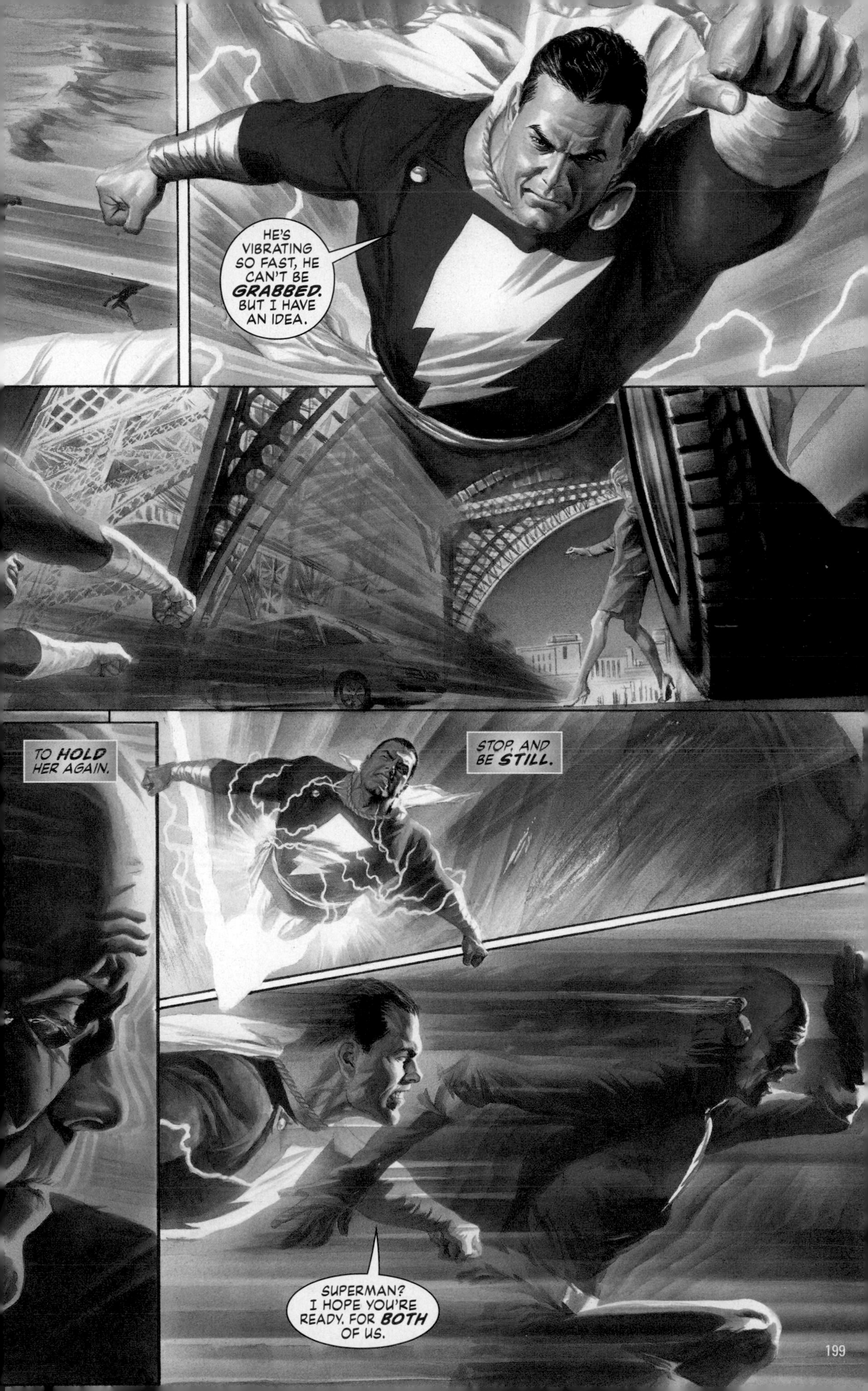
HE'S VIBRATING SO FAST, HE CAN'T BE GRABBED. BUT I HAVE AN IDEA.
TO HOLD HER AGAIN.
STOP. AND BE STILL.
SUPERMAN? I HOPE YOU'RE READY. FOR BOTH OF US.

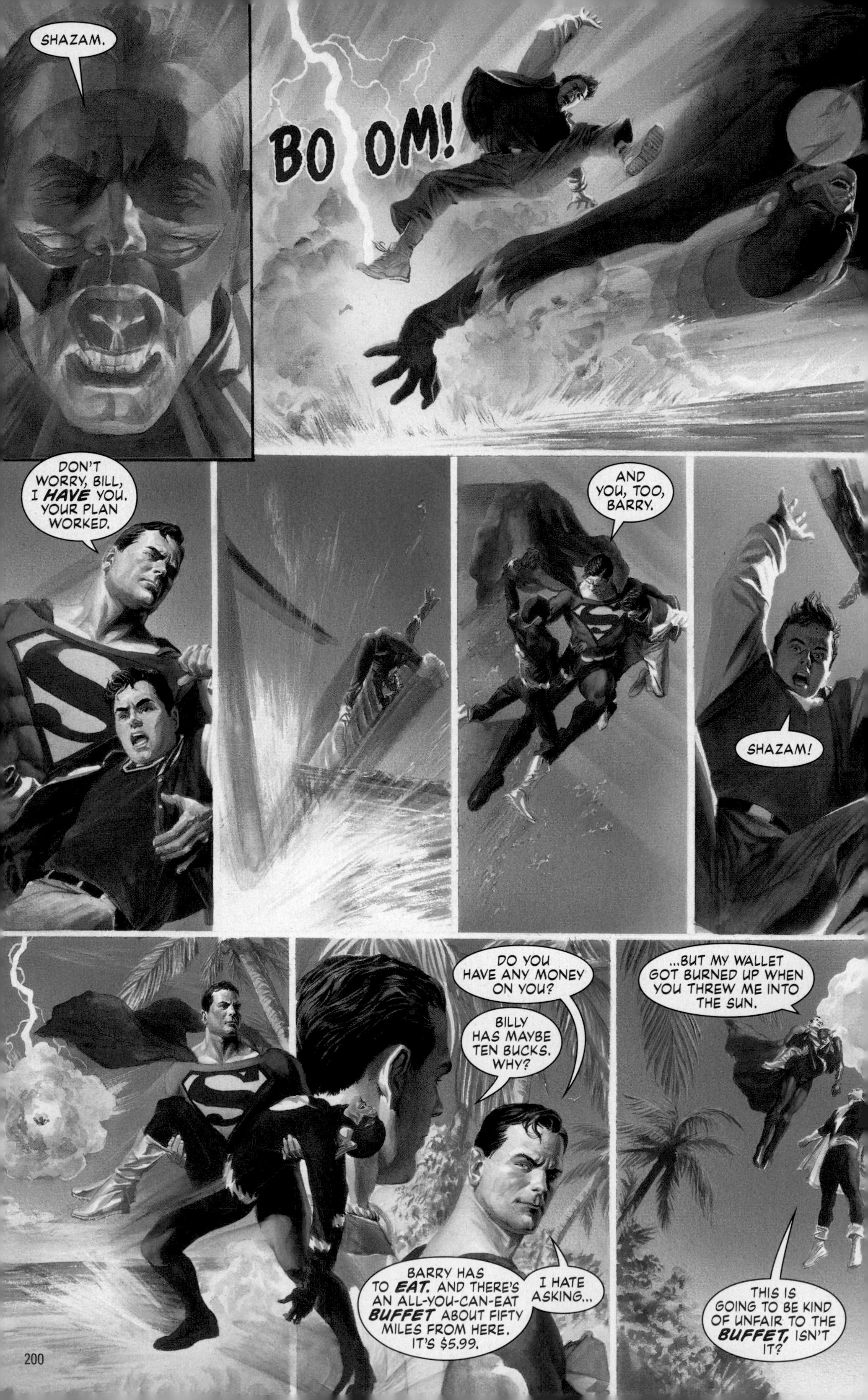
SHAZAM.
BO OM!
DON'T WORRY, BILL, I HAVE YOU. YOUR PLAN WORKED.
AND YOU, TOO, BARRY.
SHAZAM!
DO YOU HAVE ANY MONEY ON YOU?
BILLY HAS MAYBE TEN BUCKS. WHY?
I HATE ASKING...
BARRY HAS TO EAT. AND THERE'S AN ALL-YOU-CAN-EAT BUFFET ABOUT FIFTY MILES FROM HERE. IT'S $5.99.
...BUT MY WALLET GOT BURNED UP WHEN YOU THREW ME INTO THE SUN.
THIS IS GOING TO BE KIND OF UNFAIR TO THE BUFFET, ISN'T IT?

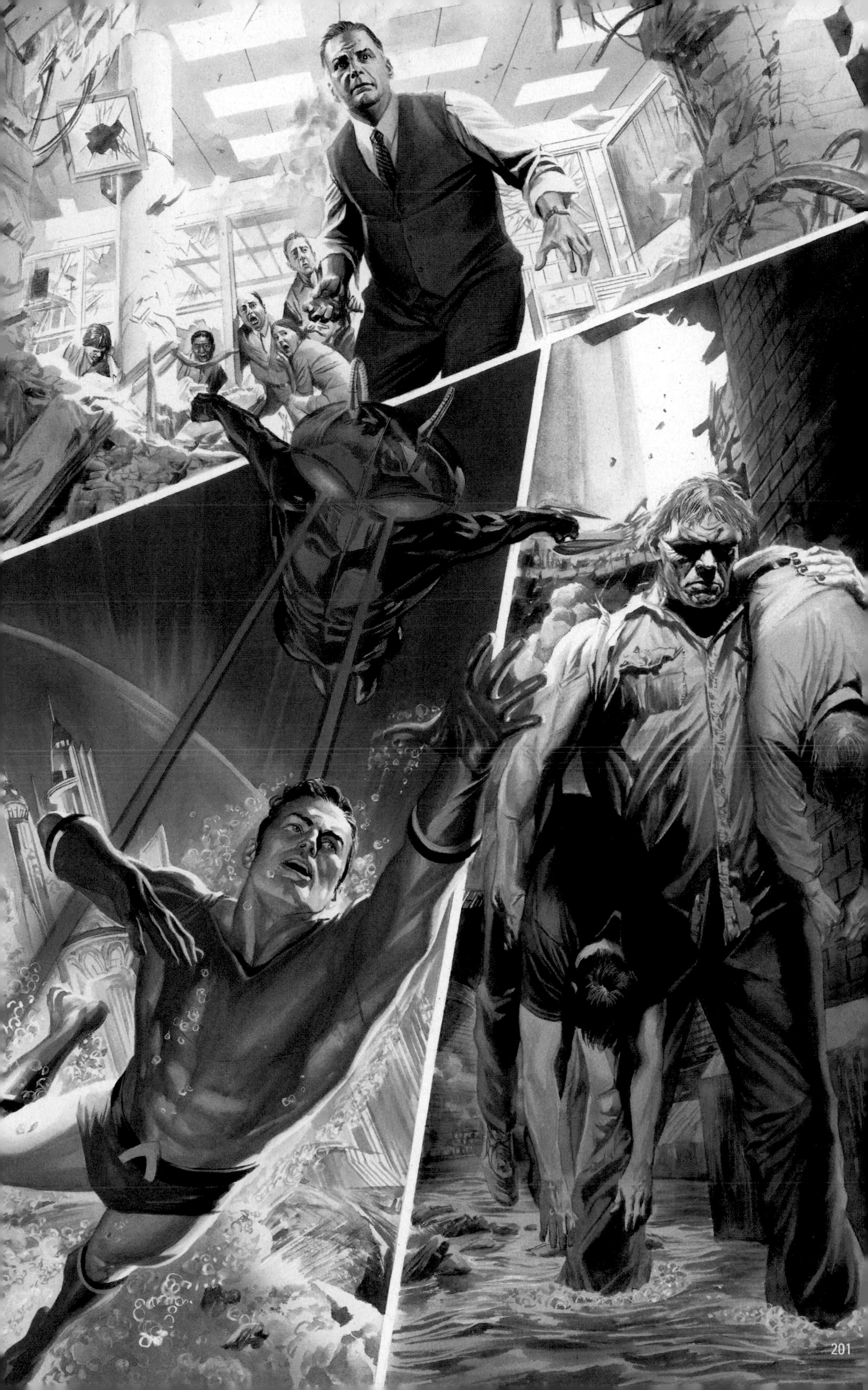

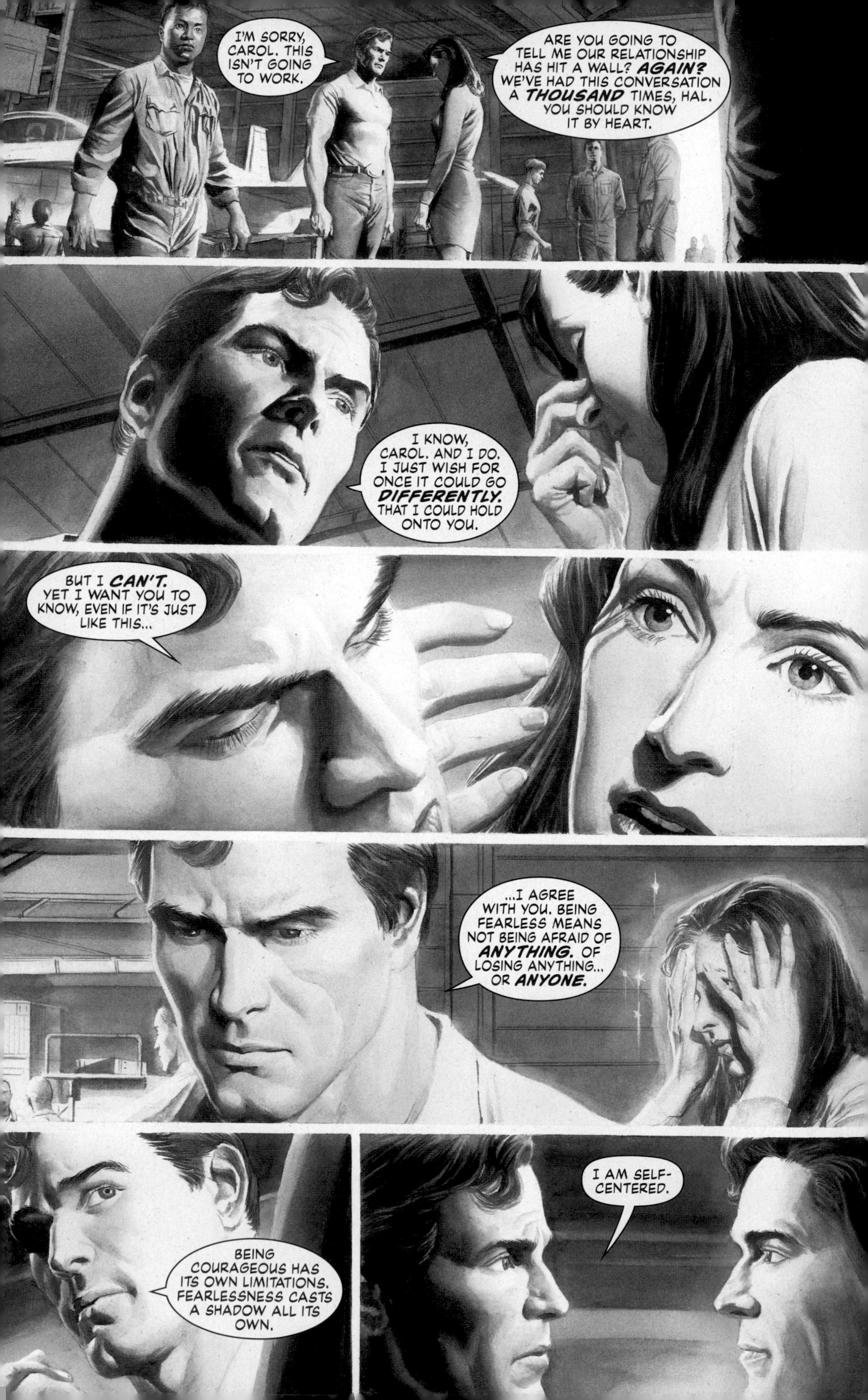
I'M SORRY, CAROL. THIS ISN'T GOING TO WORK.
ARE YOU GOING TO TELL ME OUR RELATIONSHIP HAS HIT A WALL? AGAIN? WE'VE HAD THIS CONVERSATION A THOUSAND TIMES, HAL. YOU SHOULD KNOW IT BY HEART.
I KNOW, CAROL. AND I DO. I JUST WISH FOR ONCE IT COULD GO DIFFERENTLY. THAT I COULD HOLD ONTO YOU.
BUT I CAN'T. YET I WANT YOU TO KNOW, EVEN IF IT'S JUST LIKE THIS...
...I AGREE WITH YOU. BEING FEARLESS MEANS NOT BEING AFRAID OF ANYTHING. OF LOSING ANYTHING... OR ANYONE.
BEING COURAGEOUS HAS ITS OWN LIMITATIONS. FEARLESSNESS CASTS A SHADOW ALL ITS OWN.
I AM SELF-CENTERED.

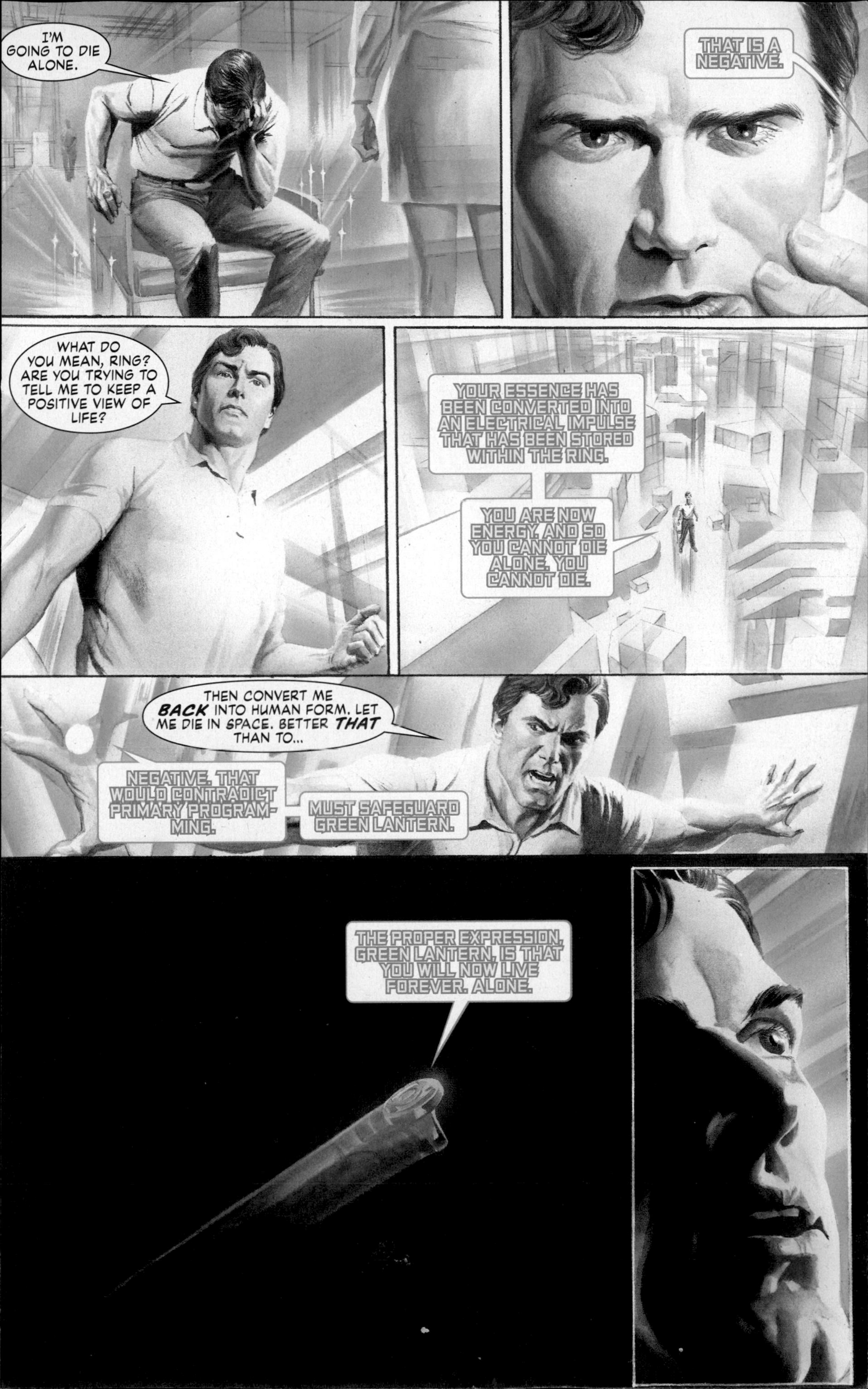

I'M GOING TO DIE ALONE.
THAT IS A NEGATIVE.
WHAT DO YOU MEAN, RING? ARE YOU TRYING TO TELL ME TO KEEP A POSITIVE VIEW OF LIFE?
YOUR ESSENCE HAS BEEN CONVERTED INTO AN ELECTRICAL IMPULSE THAT HAS BEEN STORED WITHIN THE RING.
YOU ARE NOW ENERGY, AND SO YOU CANNOT DIE ALONE. YOU CANNOT DIE.
THEN CONVERT ME BACK INTO HUMAN FORM. LET ME DIE IN SPACE. BETTER THAT THAN TO...
NEGATIVE. THAT WOULD CONTRADICT PRIMARY PROGRAM-MING.
MUST SAFEGUARD GREEN LANTERN.
THE PROPER EXPRESSION, GREEN LANTERN, IS THAT YOU WILL NOW LIVE FOREVER. ALONE.

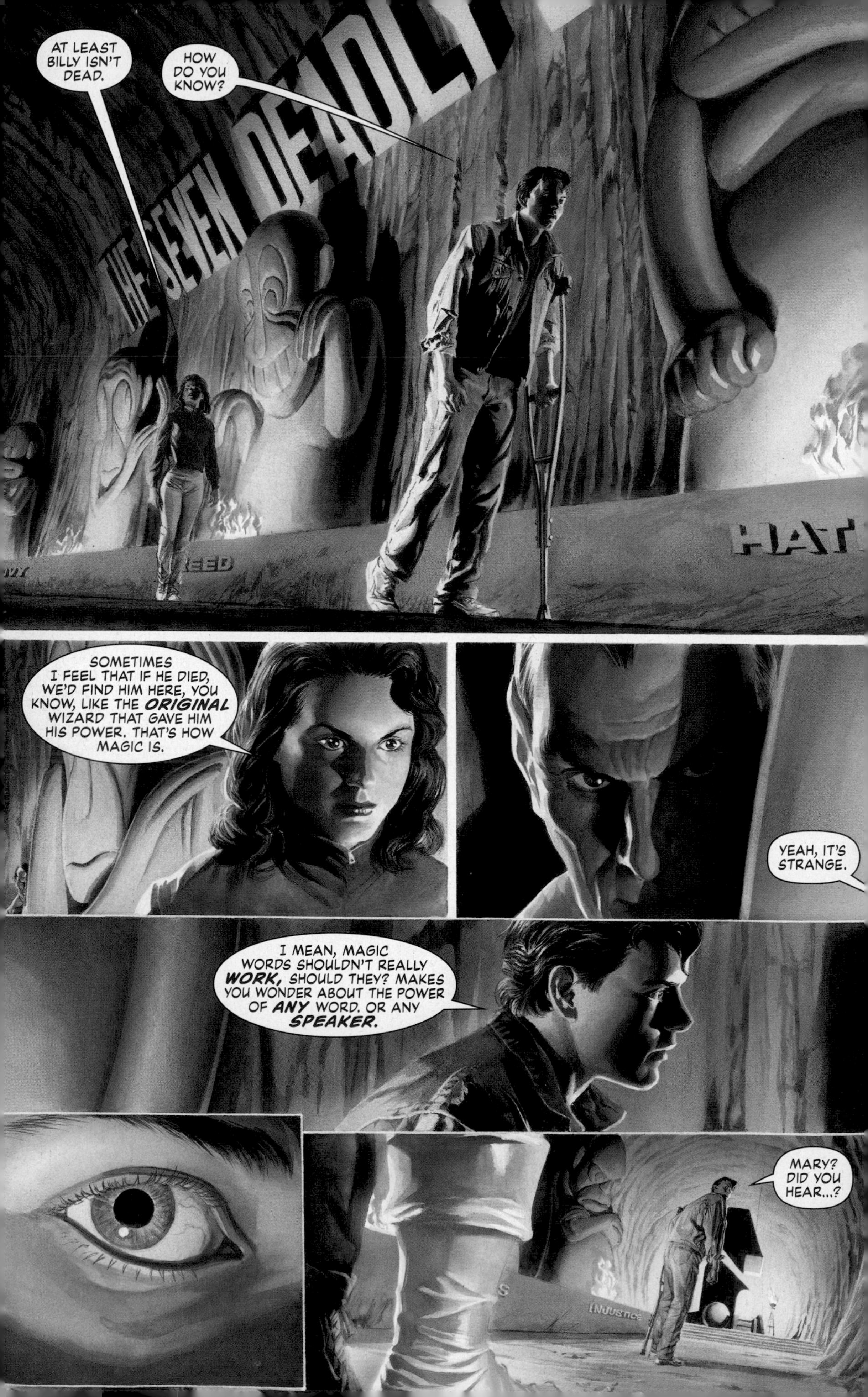
AT LEAST BILLY ISN'T DEAD.
HOW DO YOU KNOW?
THE SEVEN DEADLY
EED
HAT
SOMETIMES I FEEL THAT IF HE DIED, WE'D FIND HIM HERE, YOU KNOW, LIKE THE ORIGINAL WIZARD THAT GAVE HIM HIS POWER. THAT'S HOW MAGIC IS.
YEAH, IT'S STRANGE.
I MEAN, MAGIC WORDS SHOULDN'T REALLY WORK, SHOULD THEY? MAKES YOU WONDER ABOUT THE POWER OF ANY WORD. OR ANY SPEAKER.
INJUSTICE
MARY? DID YOU HEAR...?

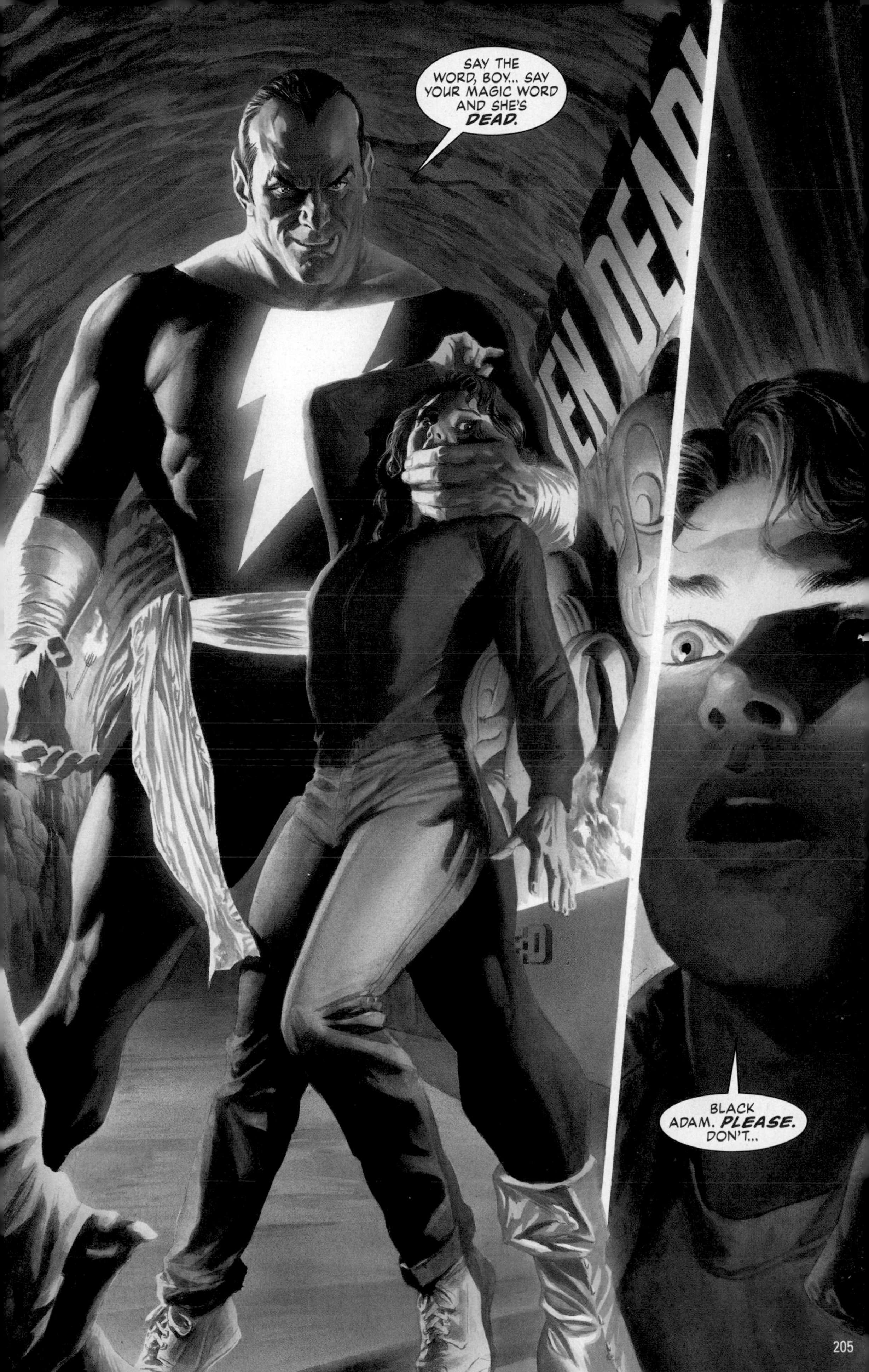
SAY THE WORD, BOY... SAY YOUR MAGIC WORD AND SHE'S **DEAD.**
BLACK ADAM. **PLEASE.** DON'T...

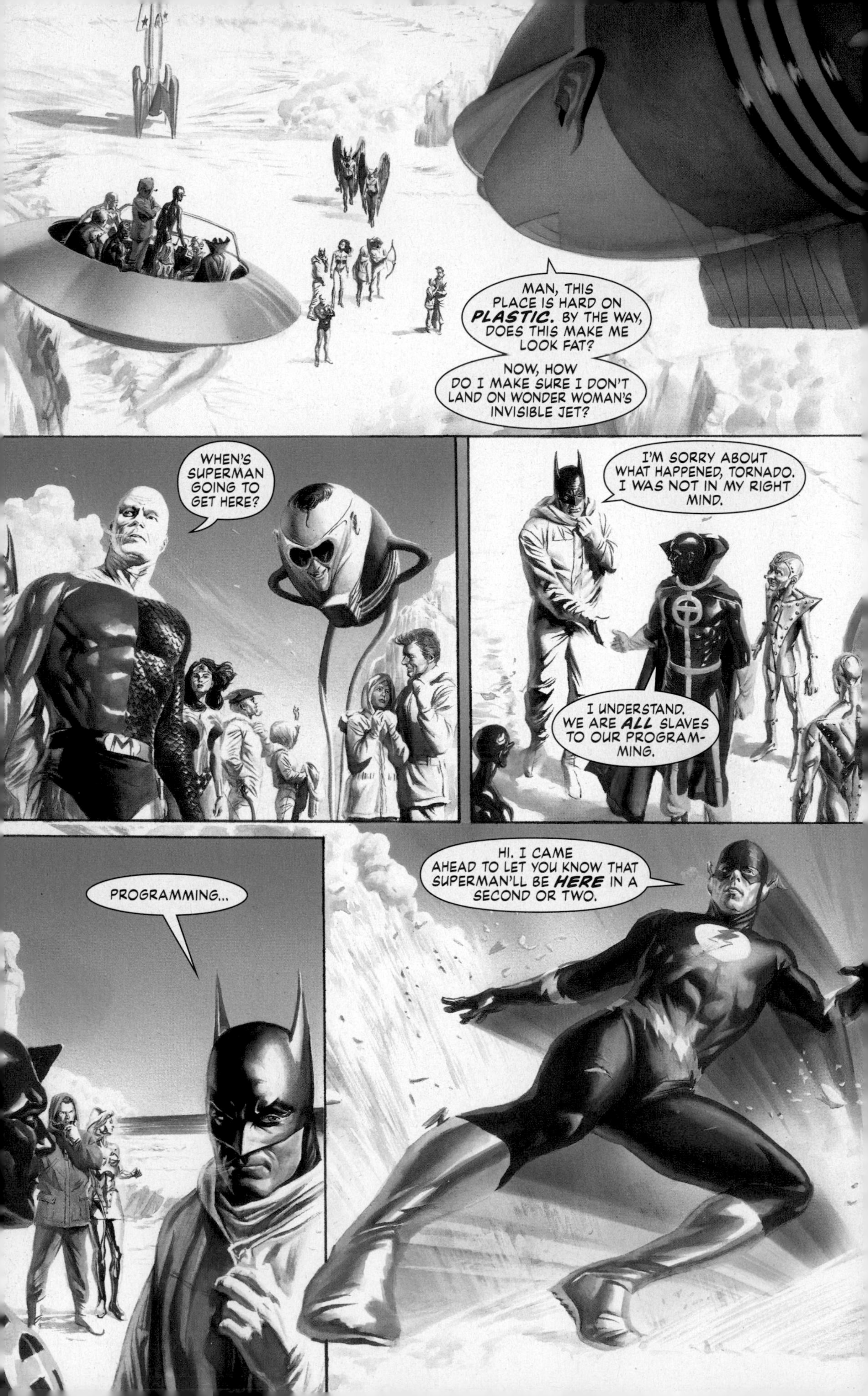
MAN, THIS PLACE IS HARD ON PLASTIC. BY THE WAY, DOES THIS MAKE ME LOOK FAT?
NOW, HOW DO I MAKE SURE I DON'T LAND ON WONDER WOMAN'S INVISIBLE JET?
WHEN'S SUPERMAN GOING TO GET HERE?
I'M SORRY ABOUT WHAT HAPPENED, TORNADO. I WAS NOT IN MY RIGHT MIND.
I UNDERSTAND. WE ARE ALL SLAVES TO OUR PROGRAM-MING.
PROGRAMMING...
HI. I CAME AHEAD TO LET YOU KNOW THAT SUPERMAN'LL BE HERE IN A SECOND OR TWO.

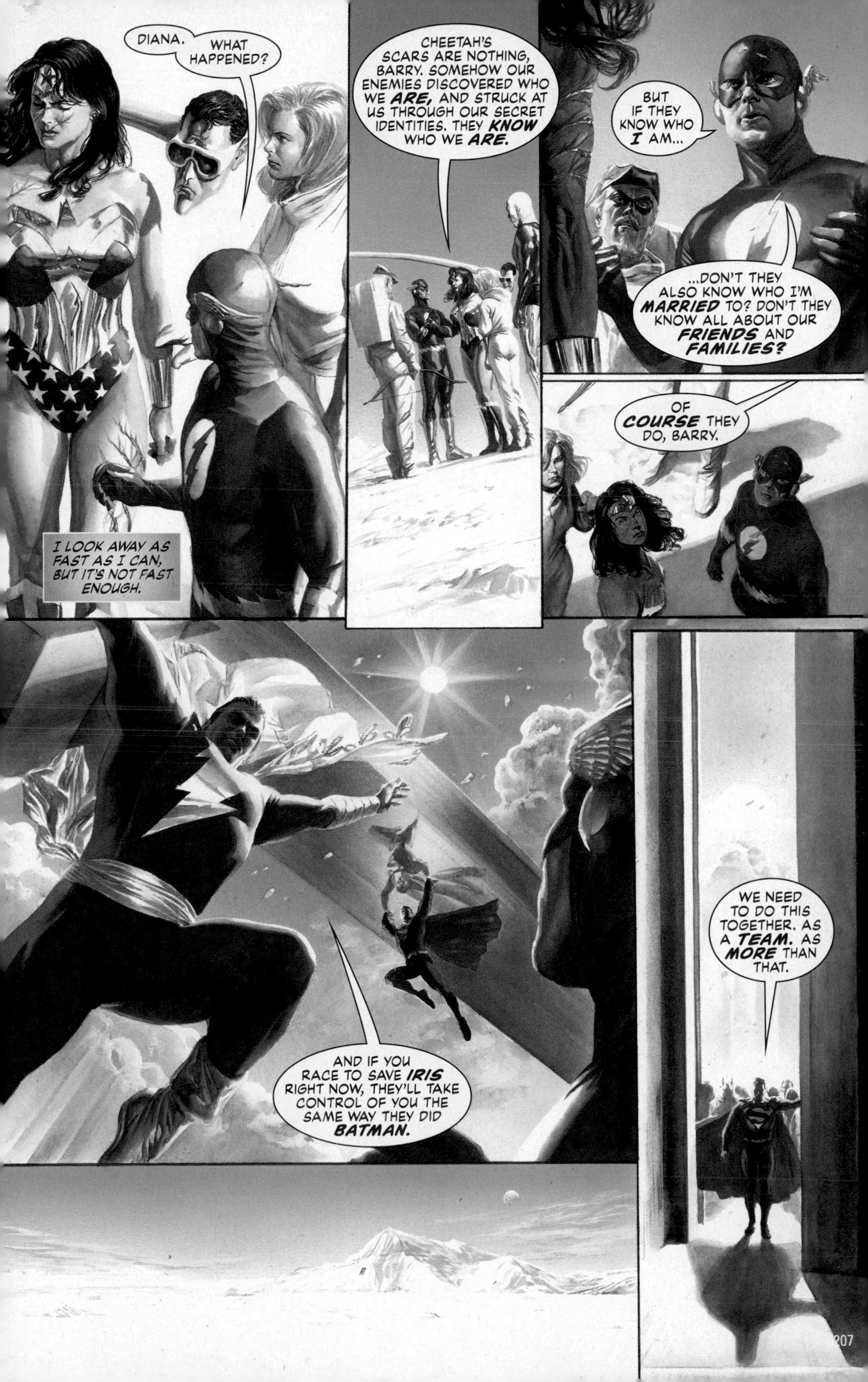
DIANA.
WHAT HAPPENED?
I LOOK AWAY AS FAST AS I CAN, BUT IT'S NOT FAST ENOUGH.
CHEETAH'S SCARS ARE NOTHING, BARRY. SOMEHOW OUR ENEMIES DISCOVERED WHO WE ARE, AND STRUCK AT US THROUGH OUR SECRET IDENTITIES. THEY KNOW WHO WE ARE.
BUT IF THEY KNOW WHO I AM...
...DON'T THEY ALSO KNOW WHO I'M MARRIED TO? DON'T THEY KNOW ALL ABOUT OUR FRIENDS AND FAMILIES?
OF COURSE THEY DO, BARRY.
AND IF YOU RACE TO SAVE IRIS RIGHT NOW, THEY'LL TAKE CONTROL OF YOU THE SAME WAY THEY DID BATMAN.
WE NEED TO DO THIS TOGETHER. AS A TEAM. AS MORE THAN THAT.

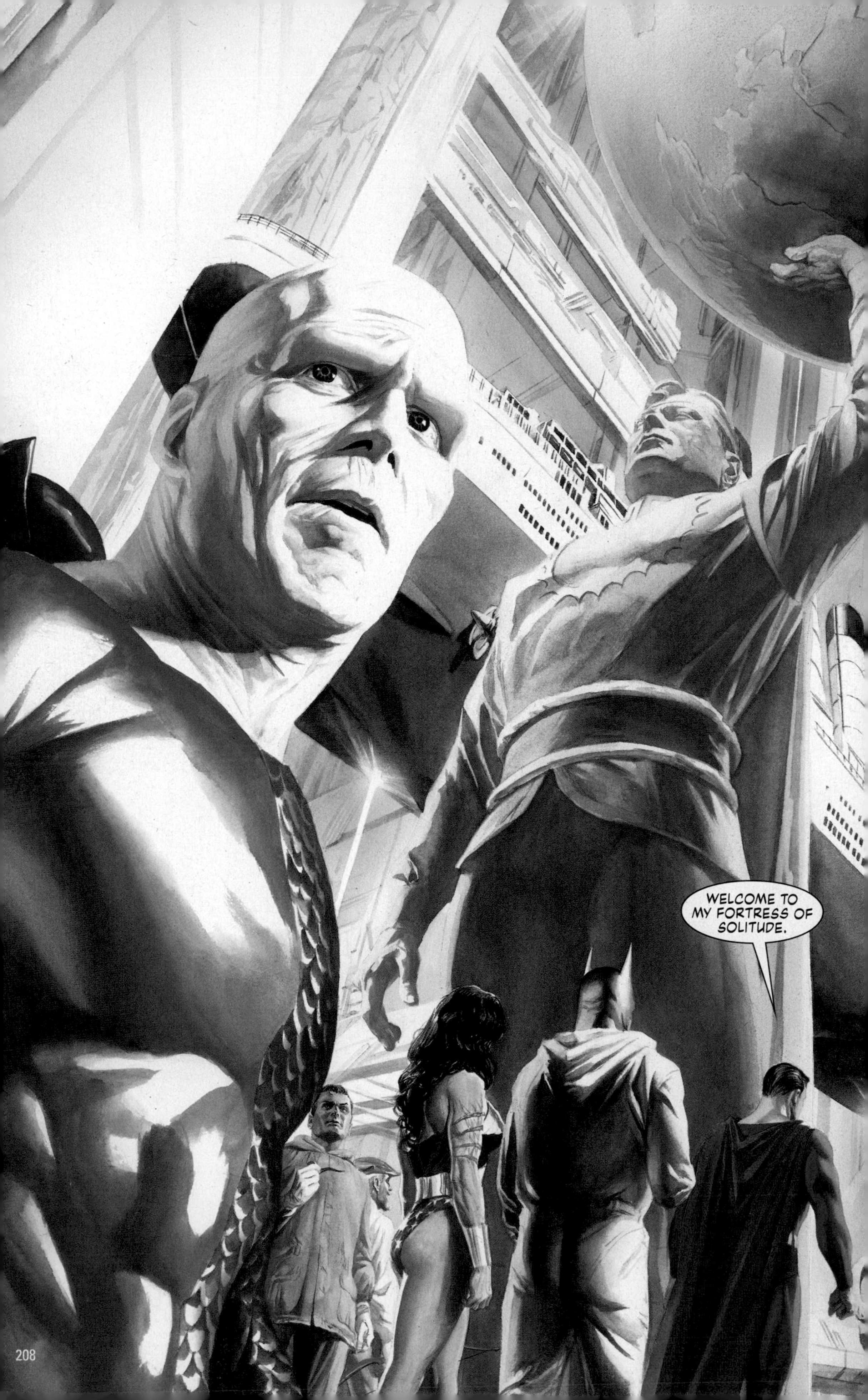
WELCOME TO MY FORTRESS OF SOLITUDE.

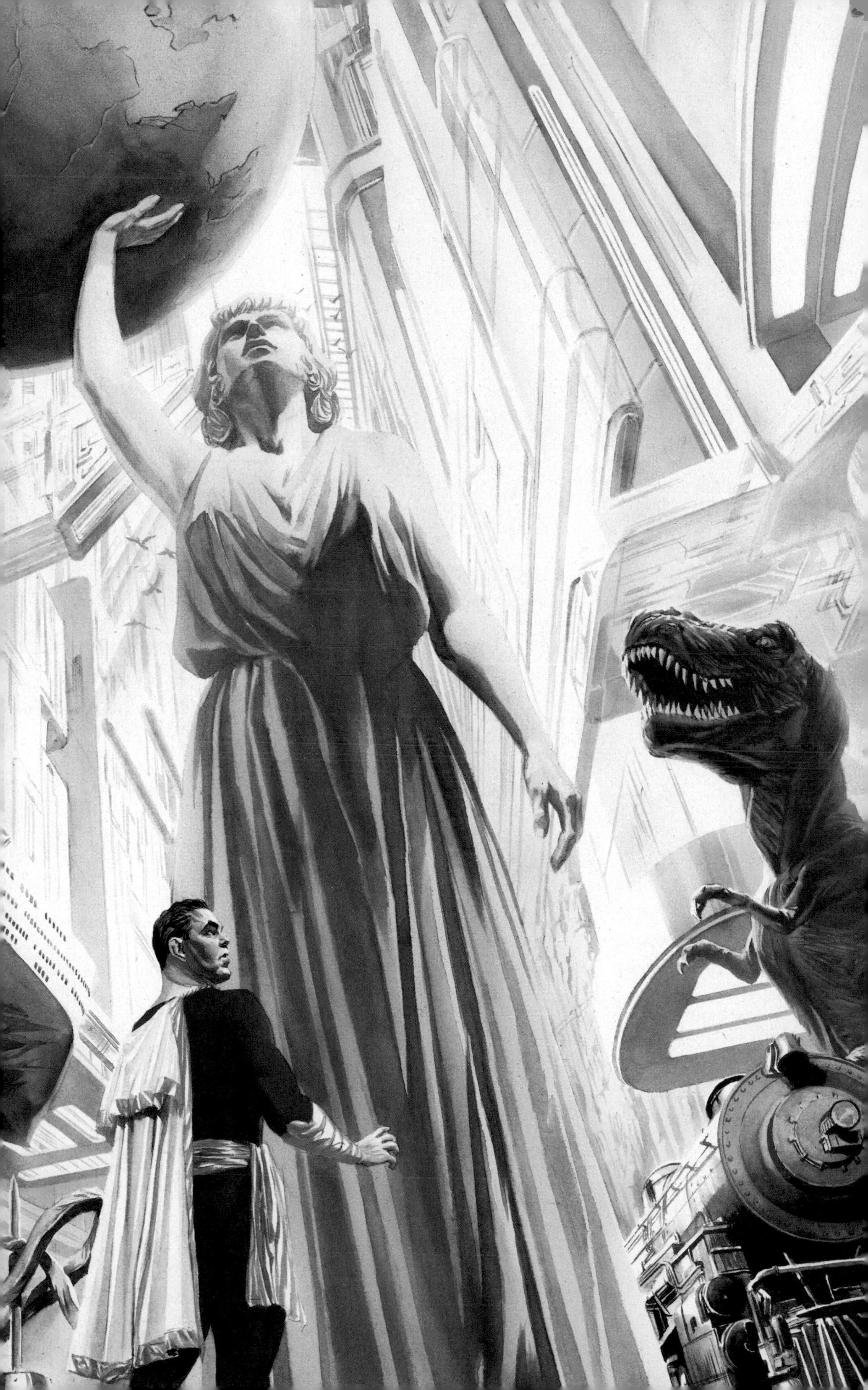

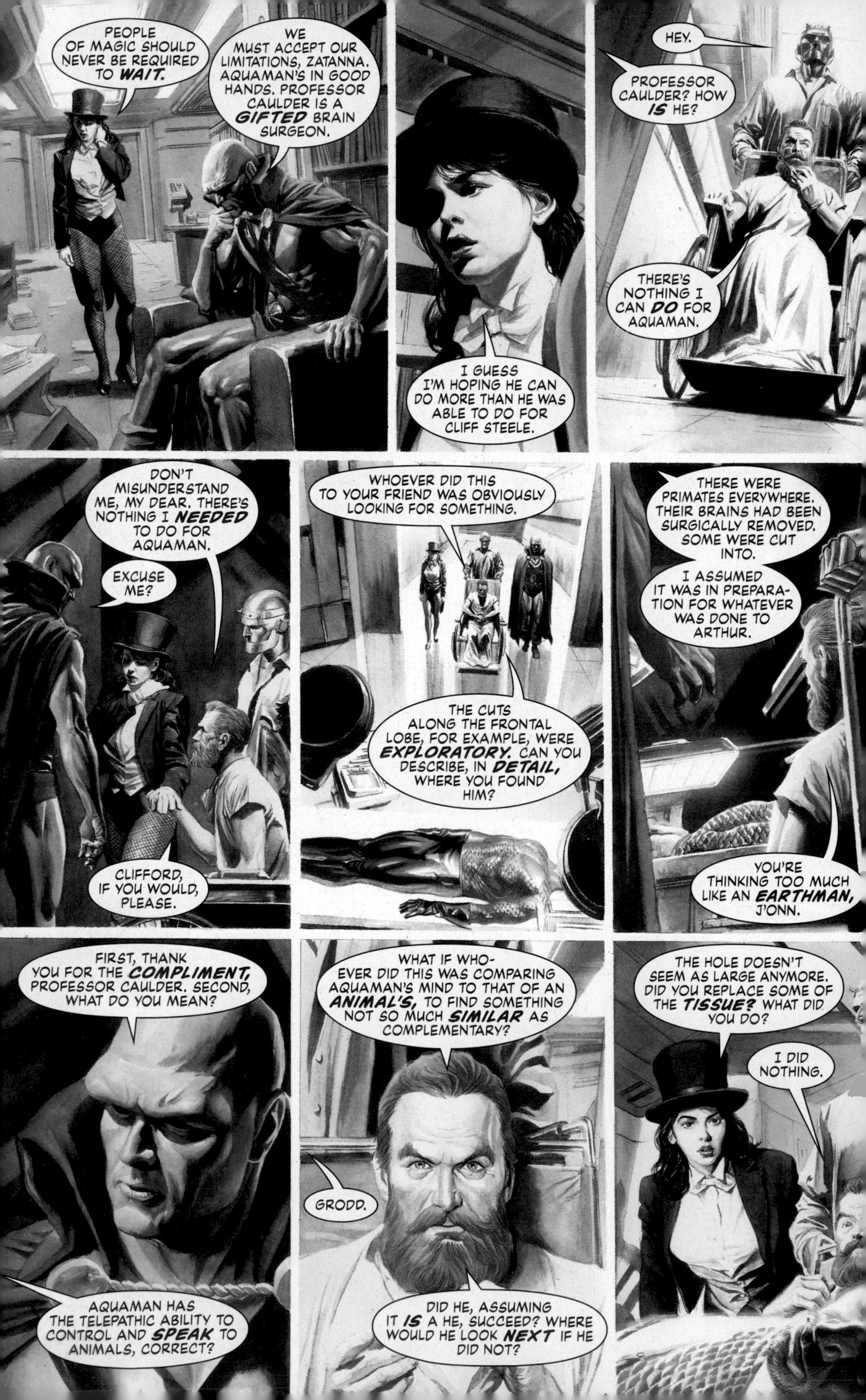
PEOPLE OF MAGIC SHOULD NEVER BE REQUIRED TO *WAIT.*
WE MUST ACCEPT OUR LIMITATIONS, ZATANNA. AQUAMAN'S IN GOOD HANDS. PROFESSOR CAULDER IS A *GIFTED* BRAIN SURGEON.
I GUESS I'M HOPING HE CAN DO MORE THAN HE WAS ABLE TO DO FOR CLIFF STEELE.
HEY.
PROFESSOR CAULDER? HOW *IS* HE?
THERE'S NOTHING I CAN *DO* FOR AQUAMAN.
DON'T MISUNDERSTAND ME, MY DEAR. THERE'S NOTHING I *NEEDED* TO DO FOR AQUAMAN.
EXCUSE ME?
CLIFFORD, IF YOU WOULD, PLEASE.
WHOEVER DID THIS TO YOUR FRIEND WAS OBVIOUSLY LOOKING FOR SOMETHING.
THE CUTS ALONG THE FRONTAL LOBE, FOR EXAMPLE, WERE *EXPLORATORY.* CAN YOU DESCRIBE, IN *DETAIL,* WHERE YOU FOUND HIM?
THERE WERE PRIMATES EVERYWHERE. THEIR BRAINS HAD BEEN SURGICALLY REMOVED. SOME WERE CUT INTO.
I ASSUMED IT WAS IN PREPARATION FOR WHATEVER WAS DONE TO ARTHUR.
YOU'RE THINKING TOO MUCH LIKE AN *EARTHMAN,* J'ONN.
FIRST, THANK YOU FOR THE *COMPLIMENT,* PROFESSOR CAULDER. SECOND, WHAT DO YOU MEAN?
AQUAMAN HAS THE TELEPATHIC ABILITY TO CONTROL AND *SPEAK* TO ANIMALS, CORRECT?
WHAT IF WHO-EVER DID THIS WAS COMPARING AQUAMAN'S MIND TO THAT OF AN *ANIMAL'S,* TO FIND SOMETHING NOT SO MUCH *SIMILAR* AS COMPLEMENTARY?
GRODD.
DID HE, ASSUMING IT *IS* A HE, SUCCEED? WHERE WOULD HE LOOK *NEXT* IF HE DID NOT?
THE HOLE DOESN'T SEEM AS LARGE ANYMORE. DID YOU REPLACE SOME OF THE *TISSUE?* WHAT DID YOU DO?
I DID NOTHING.

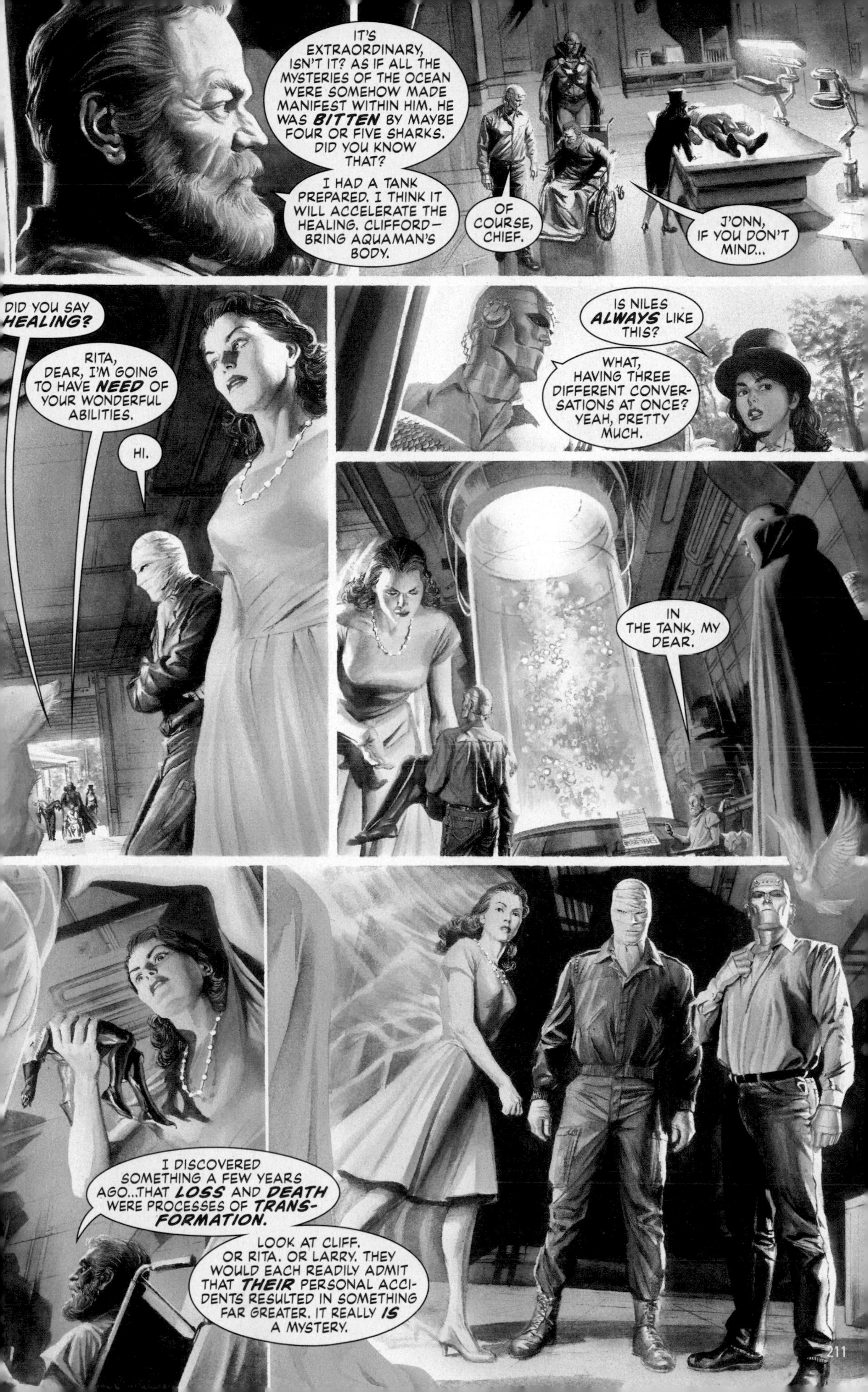

IT'S EXTRAORDINARY, ISN'T IT? AS IF ALL THE MYSTERIES OF THE OCEAN WERE SOMEHOW MADE MANIFEST WITHIN HIM. HE WAS BITTEN BY MAYBE FOUR OR FIVE SHARKS. DID YOU KNOW THAT?
I HAD A TANK PREPARED. I THINK IT WILL ACCELERATE THE HEALING. CLIFFORD–BRING AQUAMAN'S BODY.
OF COURSE, CHIEF.
J'ONN, IF YOU DON'T MIND...
DID YOU SAY HEALING?
RITA, DEAR, I'M GOING TO HAVE NEED OF YOUR WONDERFUL ABILITIES.
HI.
IS NILES ALWAYS LIKE THIS?
WHAT, HAVING THREE DIFFERENT CONVERSATIONS AT ONCE? YEAH, PRETTY MUCH.
IN THE TANK, MY DEAR.
I DISCOVERED SOMETHING A FEW YEARS AGO...THAT LOSS AND DEATH WERE PROCESSES OF TRANS-FORMATION.
LOOK AT CLIFF. OR RITA. OR LARRY. THEY WOULD EACH READILY ADMIT THAT THEIR PERSONAL ACCI-DENTS RESULTED IN SOMETHING FAR GREATER. IT REALLY IS A MYSTERY.

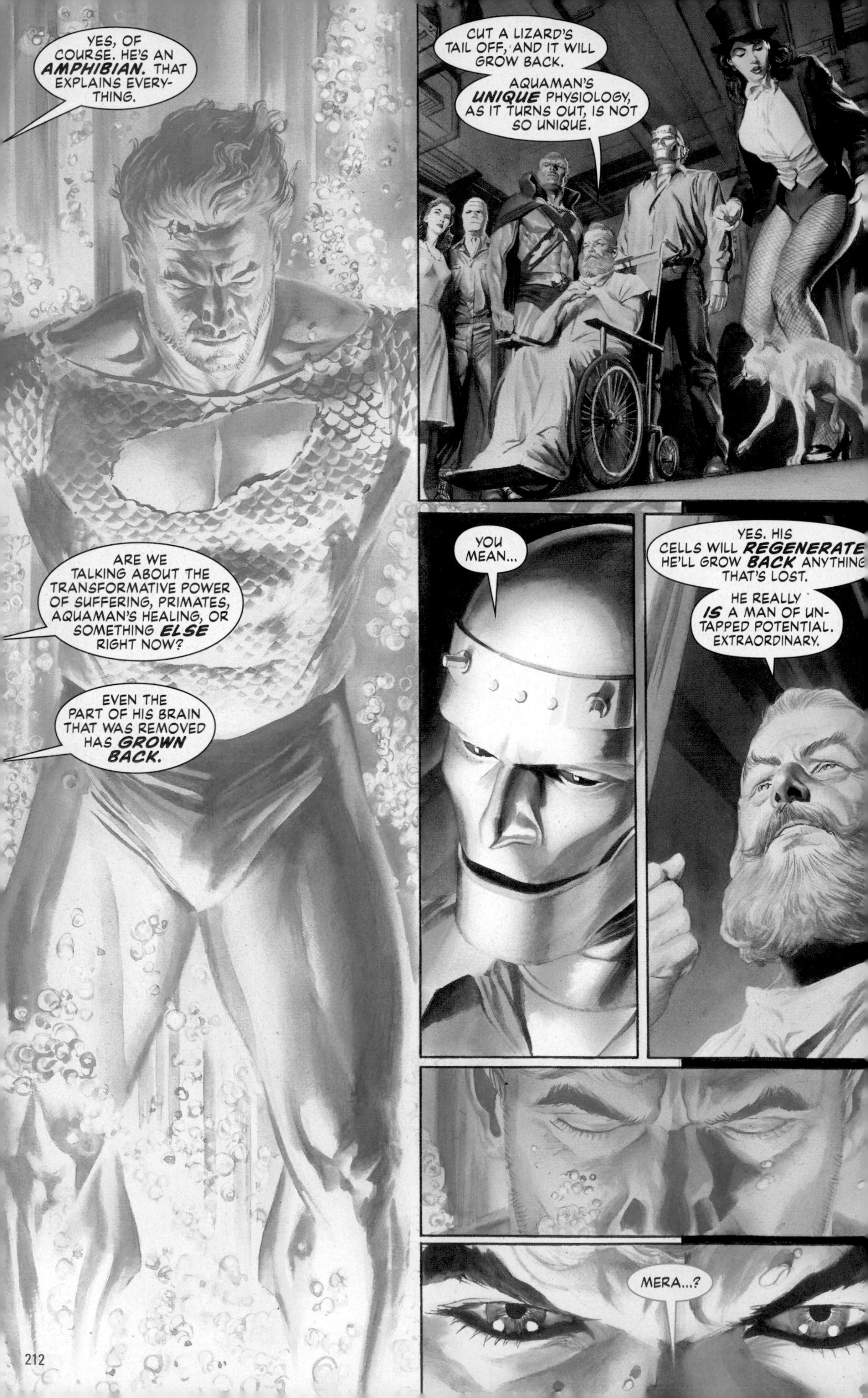
YES, OF COURSE. HE'S AN AMPHIBIAN. THAT EXPLAINS EVERYTHING.
CUT A LIZARD'S TAIL OFF, AND IT WILL GROW BACK.
AQUAMAN'S UNIQUE PHYSIOLOGY, AS IT TURNS OUT, IS NOT SO UNIQUE.
ARE WE TALKING ABOUT THE TRANSFORMATIVE POWER OF SUFFERING, PRIMATES, AQUAMAN'S HEALING, OR SOMETHING ELSE RIGHT NOW?
EVEN THE PART OF HIS BRAIN THAT WAS REMOVED HAS GROWN BACK.
YOU MEAN...
YES. HIS CELLS WILL REGENERATE. HE'LL GROW BACK ANYTHING THAT'S LOST.
HE REALLY IS A MAN OF UNTAPPED POTENTIAL. EXTRAORDINARY.
MERA...?

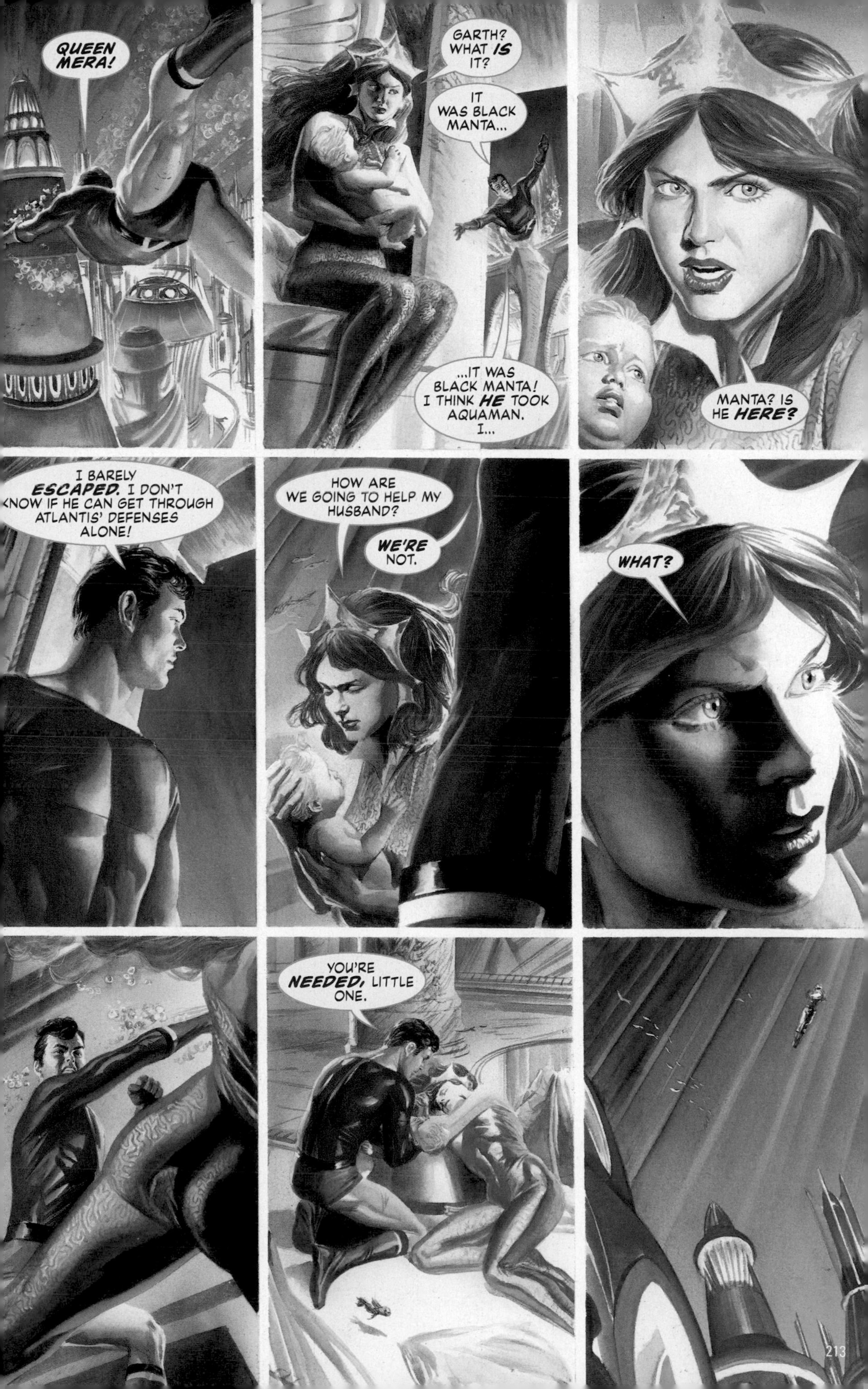
QUEEN MERA!
GARTH? WHAT IS IT?
IT WAS BLACK MANTA...
...IT WAS BLACK MANTA! I THINK HE TOOK AQUAMAN. I...
MANTA? IS HE HERE?
I BARELY ESCAPED. I DON'T KNOW IF HE CAN GET THROUGH ATLANTIS' DEFENSES ALONE!
HOW ARE WE GOING TO HELP MY HUSBAND?
WE'RE NOT.
WHAT?
YOU'RE NEEDED, LITTLE ONE.

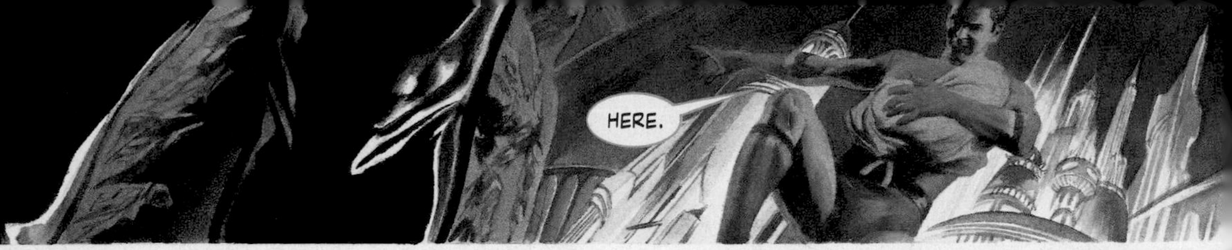
HERE.

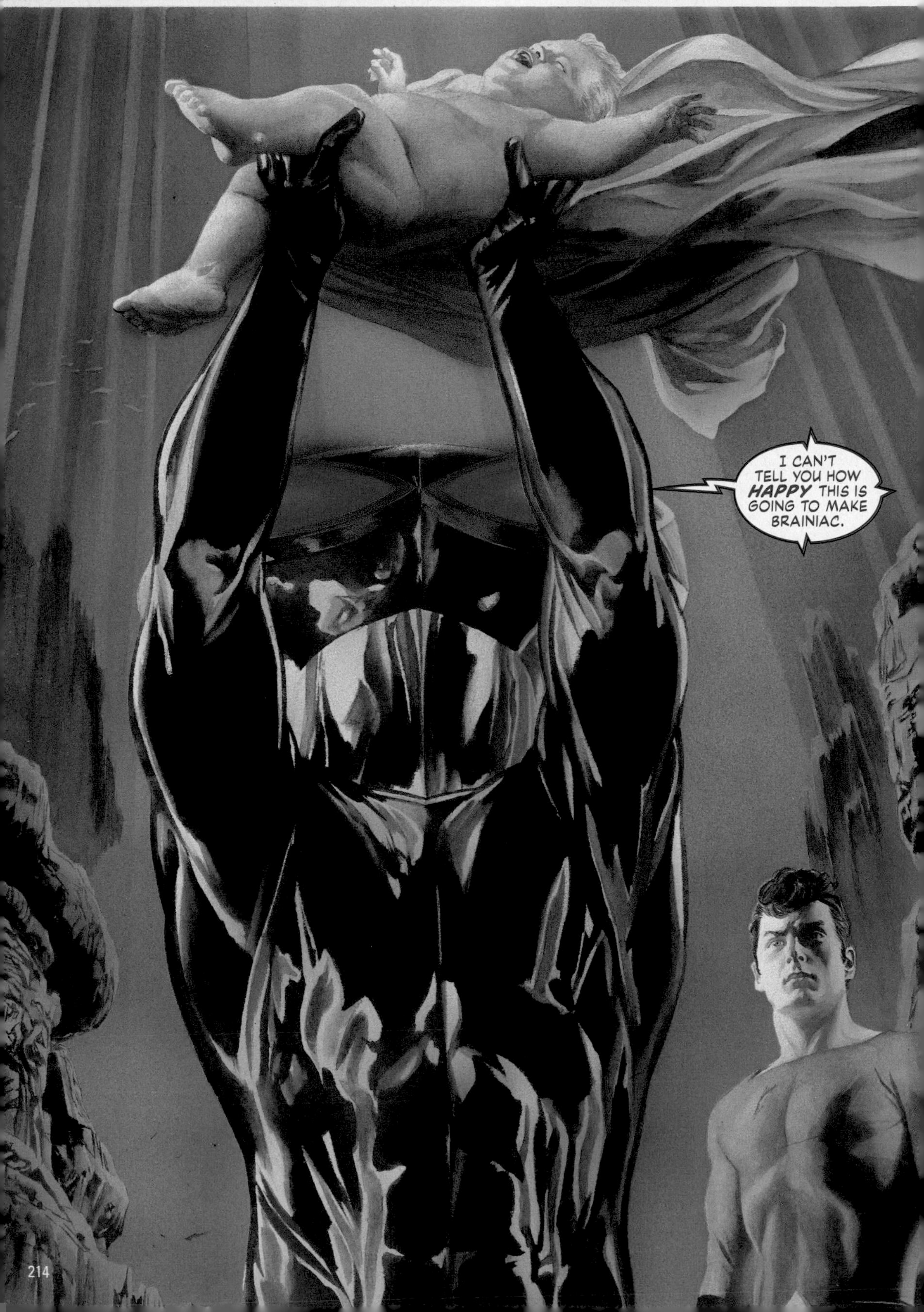
I CAN'T TELL YOU HOW HAPPY THIS IS GOING TO MAKE BRAINIAC.

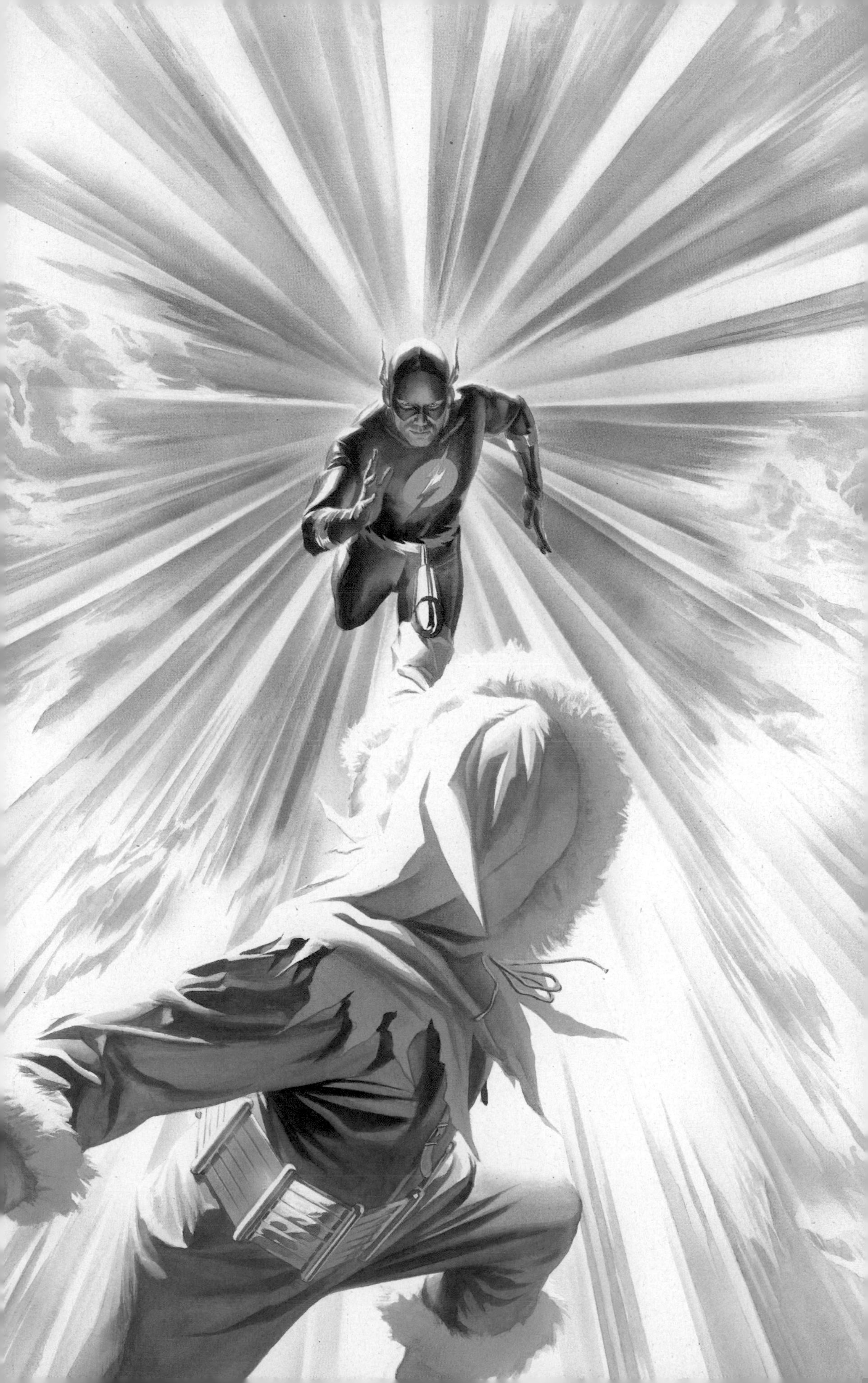

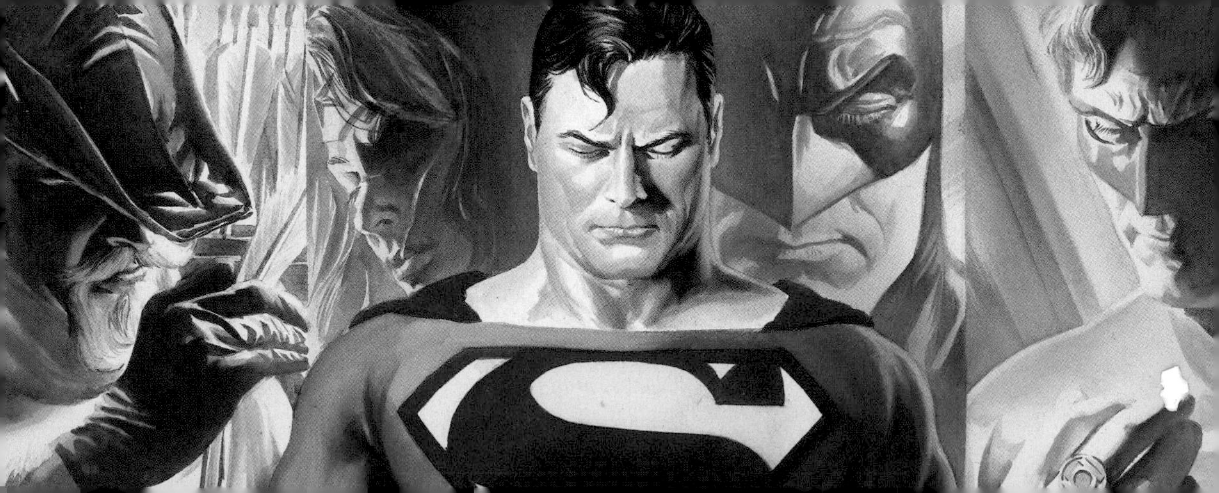

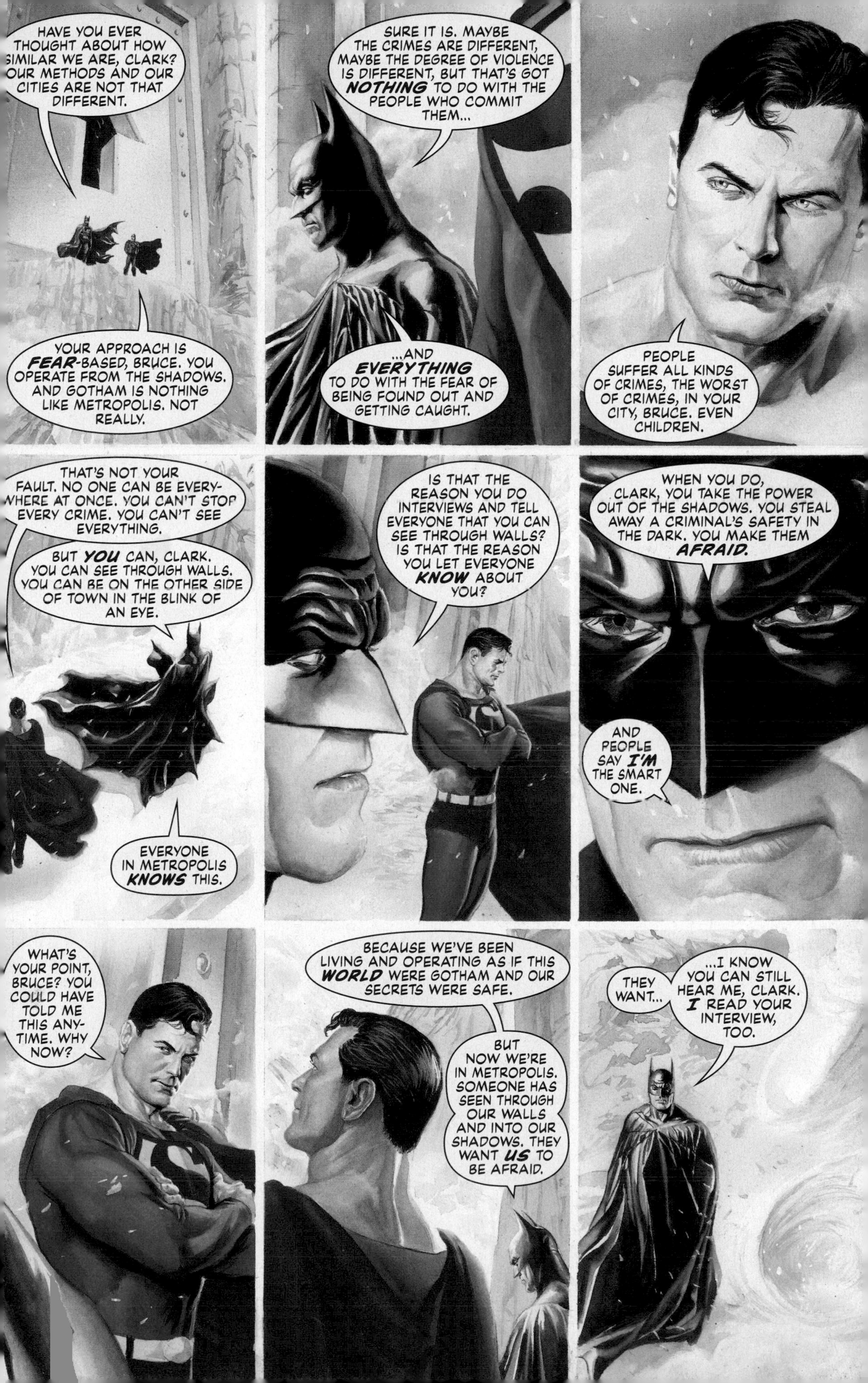
HAVE YOU EVER THOUGHT ABOUT HOW SIMILAR WE ARE, CLARK? OUR METHODS AND OUR CITIES ARE NOT THAT DIFFERENT.
YOUR APPROACH IS FEAR-BASED, BRUCE. YOU OPERATE FROM THE SHADOWS. AND GOTHAM IS NOTHING LIKE METROPOLIS. NOT REALLY.
SURE IT IS. MAYBE THE CRIMES ARE DIFFERENT, MAYBE THE DEGREE OF VIOLENCE IS DIFFERENT, BUT THAT'S GOT NOTHING TO DO WITH THE PEOPLE WHO COMMIT THEM...
...AND EVERYTHING TO DO WITH THE FEAR OF BEING FOUND OUT AND GETTING CAUGHT.
PEOPLE SUFFER ALL KINDS OF CRIMES, THE WORST OF CRIMES, IN YOUR CITY, BRUCE. EVEN CHILDREN.
THAT'S NOT YOUR FAULT. NO ONE CAN BE EVERYWHERE AT ONCE. YOU CAN'T STOP EVERY CRIME. YOU CAN'T SEE EVERYTHING.
BUT YOU CAN, CLARK. YOU CAN SEE THROUGH WALLS. YOU CAN BE ON THE OTHER SIDE OF TOWN IN THE BLINK OF AN EYE.
EVERYONE IN METROPOLIS KNOWS THIS.
IS THAT THE REASON YOU DO INTERVIEWS AND TELL EVERYONE THAT YOU CAN SEE THROUGH WALLS? IS THAT THE REASON YOU LET EVERYONE KNOW ABOUT YOU?
WHEN YOU DO, CLARK, YOU TAKE THE POWER OUT OF THE SHADOWS. YOU STEAL AWAY A CRIMINAL'S SAFETY IN THE DARK. YOU MAKE THEM AFRAID.
AND PEOPLE SAY I'M THE SMART ONE.
WHAT'S YOUR POINT, BRUCE? YOU COULD HAVE TOLD ME THIS ANYTIME. WHY NOW?
BECAUSE WE'VE BEEN LIVING AND OPERATING AS IF THIS WORLD WERE GOTHAM AND OUR SECRETS WERE SAFE.
BUT NOW WE'RE IN METROPOLIS. SOMEONE HAS SEEN THROUGH OUR WALLS AND INTO OUR SHADOWS. THEY WANT US TO BE AFRAID.
THEY WANT...
...I KNOW YOU CAN STILL HEAR ME, CLARK. I READ YOUR INTERVIEW, TOO.

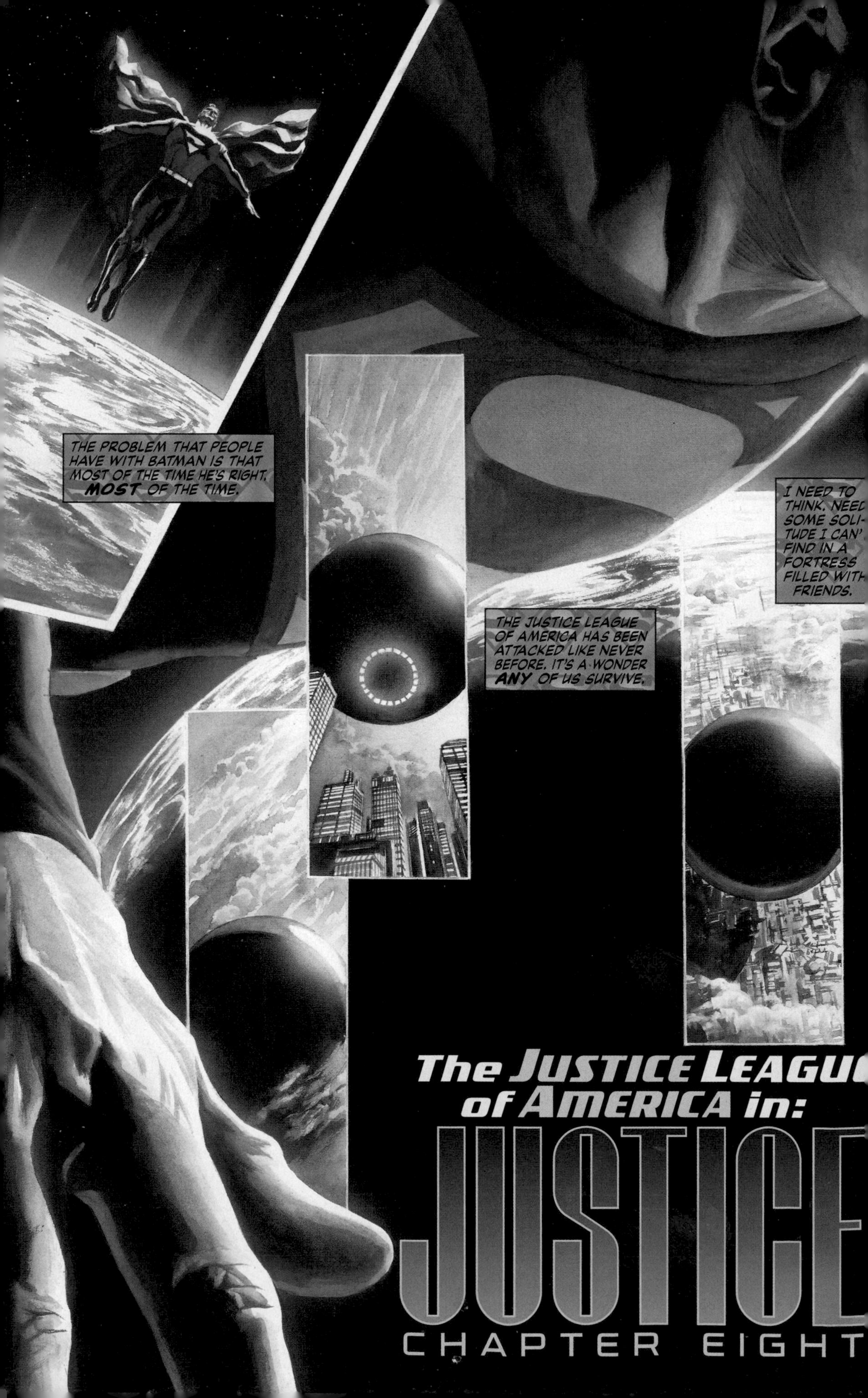
THE PROBLEM THAT PEOPLE HAVE WITH BATMAN IS THAT MOST OF THE TIME HE'S RIGHT. MOST OF THE TIME.
THE JUSTICE LEAGUE OF AMERICA HAS BEEN ATTACKED LIKE NEVER BEFORE. IT'S A WONDER ANY OF US SURVIVE.
I NEED TO THINK. NEED SOME SOLI- TUDE I CAN' FIND IN A FORTRESS FILLED WITH FRIENDS.
The JUSTICE LEAGUE of AMERICA in:
JUSTICE
CHAPTER EIGHT

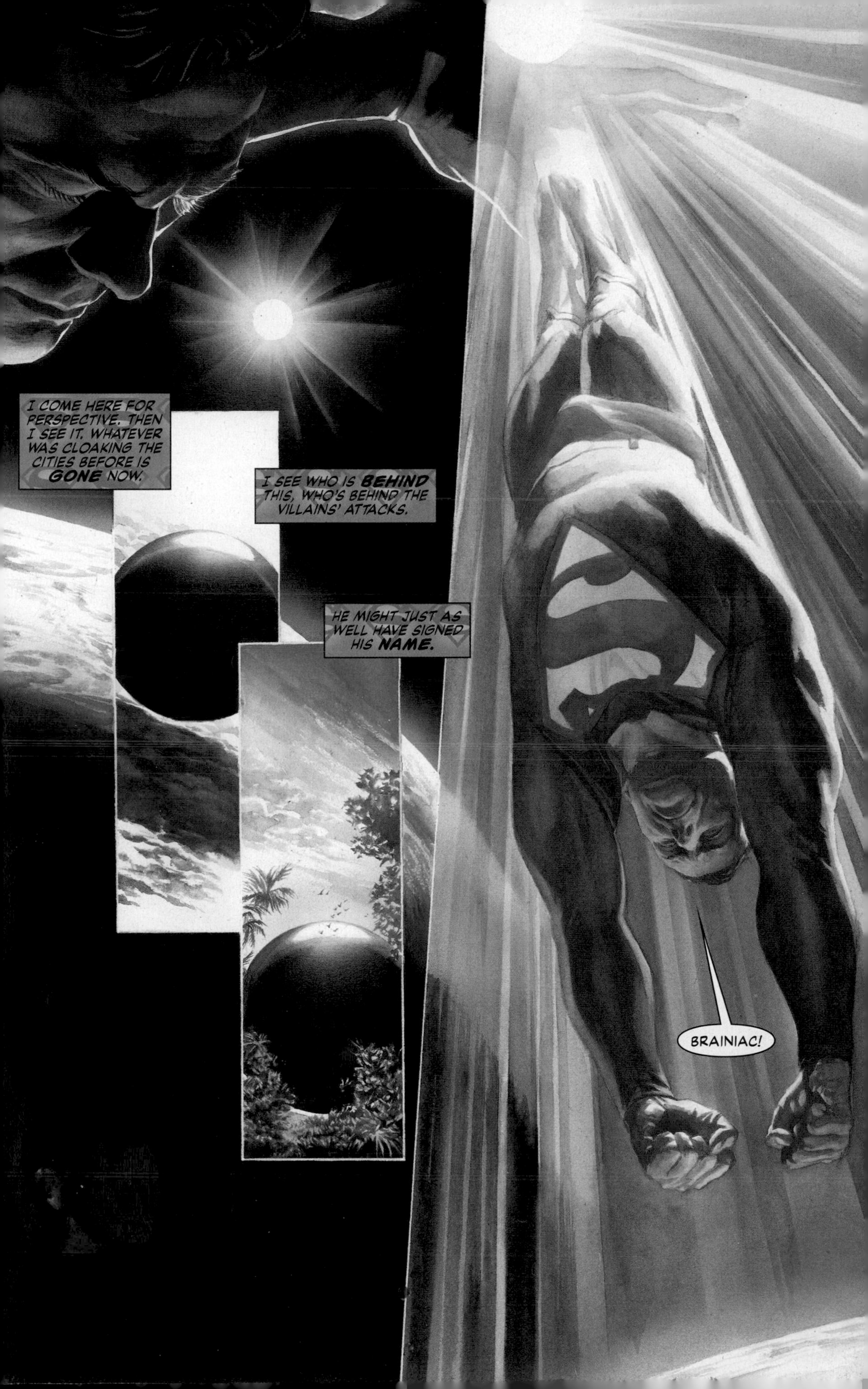
I COME HERE FOR PERSPECTIVE. THEN I SEE IT. WHATEVER WAS CLOAKING THE CITIES BEFORE IS GONE NOW.
I SEE WHO IS BEHIND THIS, WHO'S BEHIND THE VILLAINS' ATTACKS.
HE MIGHT JUST AS WELL HAVE SIGNED HIS NAME.
BRAINIAC!

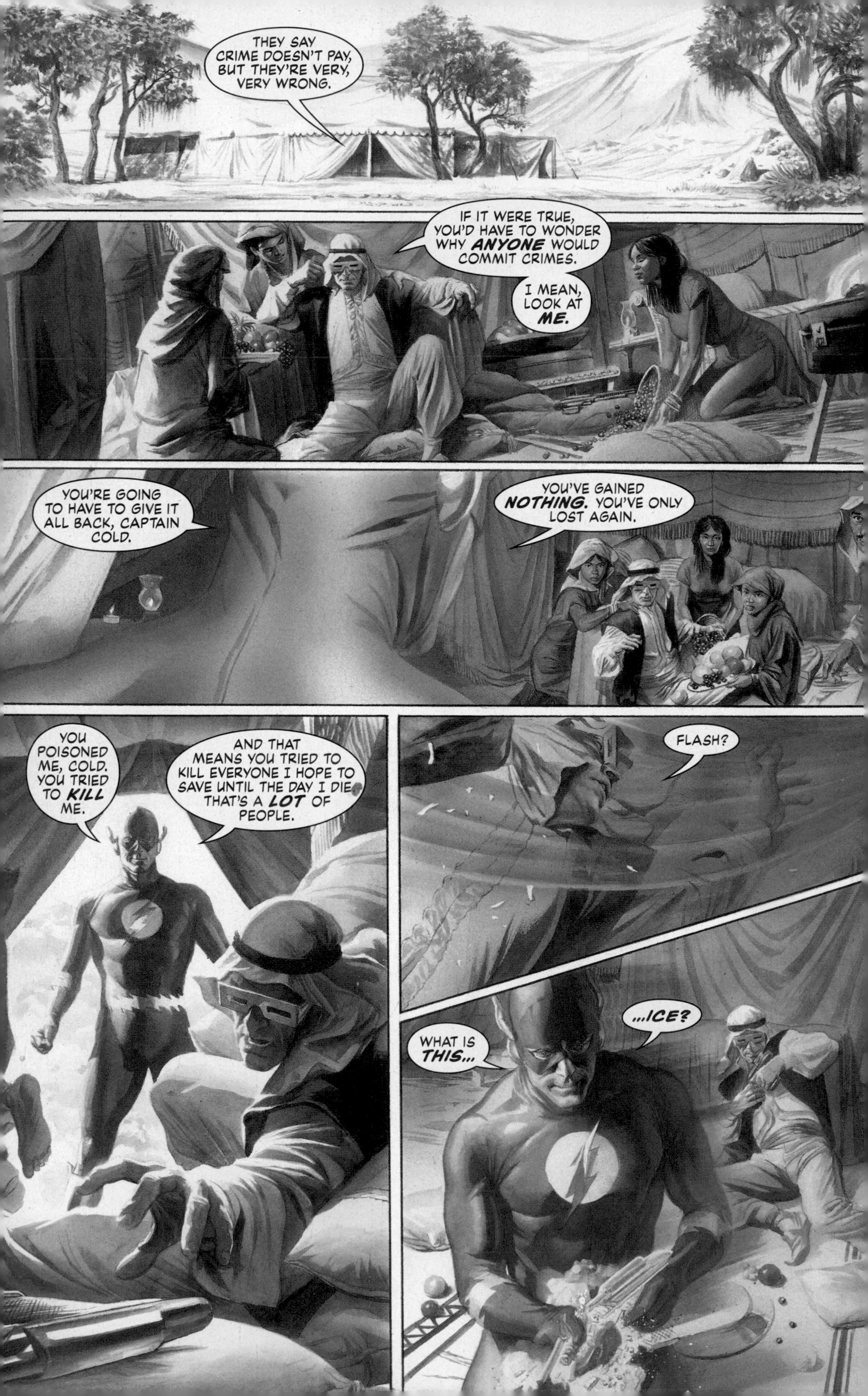
THEY SAY CRIME DOESN'T PAY, BUT THEY'RE VERY, VERY WRONG.
IF IT WERE TRUE, YOU'D HAVE TO WONDER WHY ANYONE WOULD COMMIT CRIMES.
I MEAN, LOOK AT ME.
YOU'RE GOING TO HAVE TO GIVE IT ALL BACK, CAPTAIN COLD.
YOU'VE GAINED NOTHING. YOU'VE ONLY LOST AGAIN.
YOU POISONED ME, COLD. YOU TRIED TO KILL ME.
AND THAT MEANS YOU TRIED TO KILL EVERYONE I HOPE TO SAVE UNTIL THE DAY I DIE. THAT'S A LOT OF PEOPLE.
FLASH?
WHAT IS THIS...
...ICE?

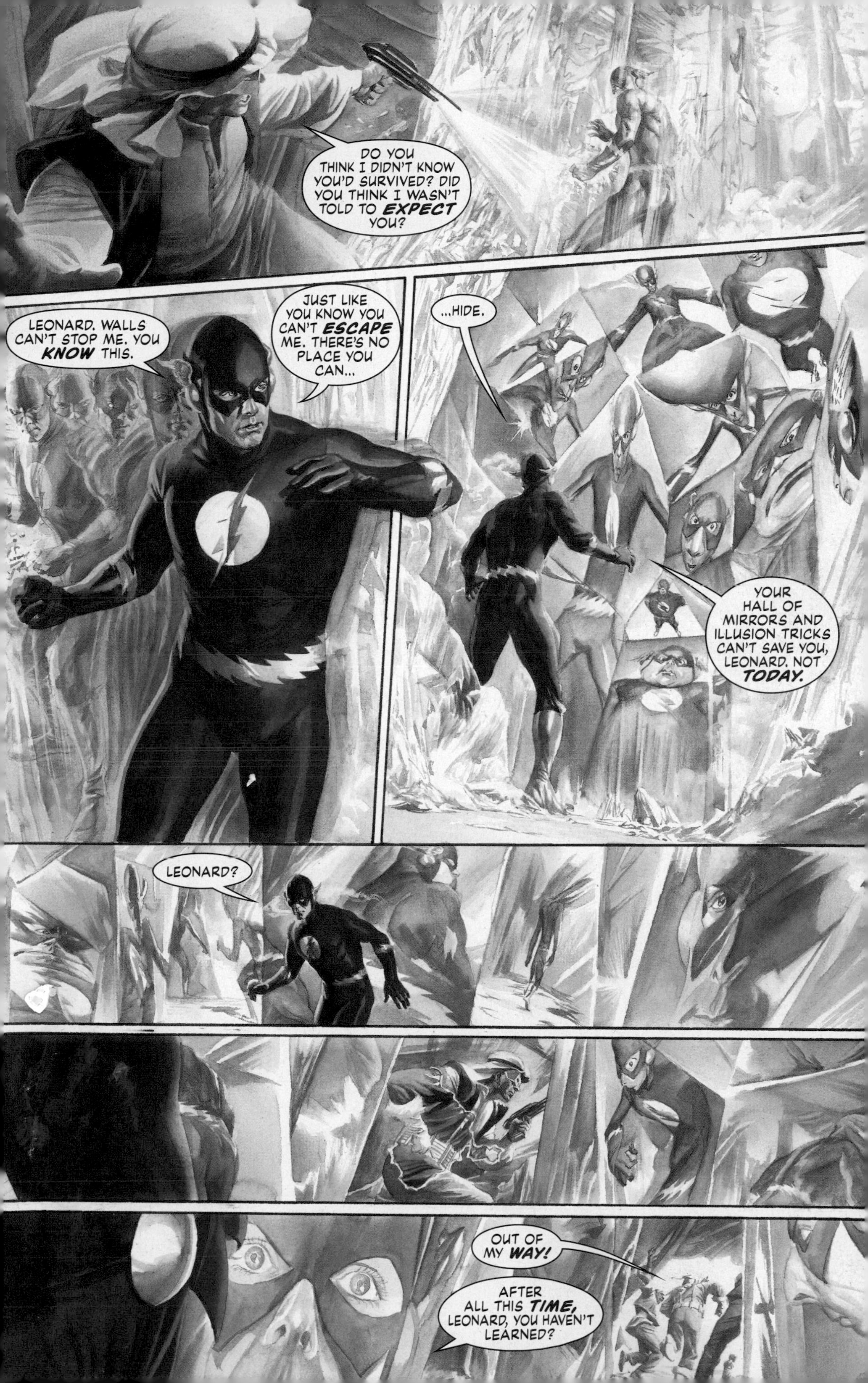
DO YOU THINK I DIDN'T KNOW YOU'D SURVIVED? DID YOU THINK I WASN'T TOLD TO *EXPECT* YOU?
LEONARD. WALLS CAN'T STOP ME. YOU *KNOW* THIS.
JUST LIKE YOU KNOW YOU CAN'T *ESCAPE* ME. THERE'S NO PLACE YOU CAN...
...HIDE.
YOUR HALL OF MIRRORS AND ILLUSION TRICKS CAN'T SAVE YOU, LEONARD. NOT *TODAY.*
LEONARD?
OUT OF MY *WAY!*
AFTER ALL THIS *TIME,* LEONARD, YOU HAVEN'T LEARNED?

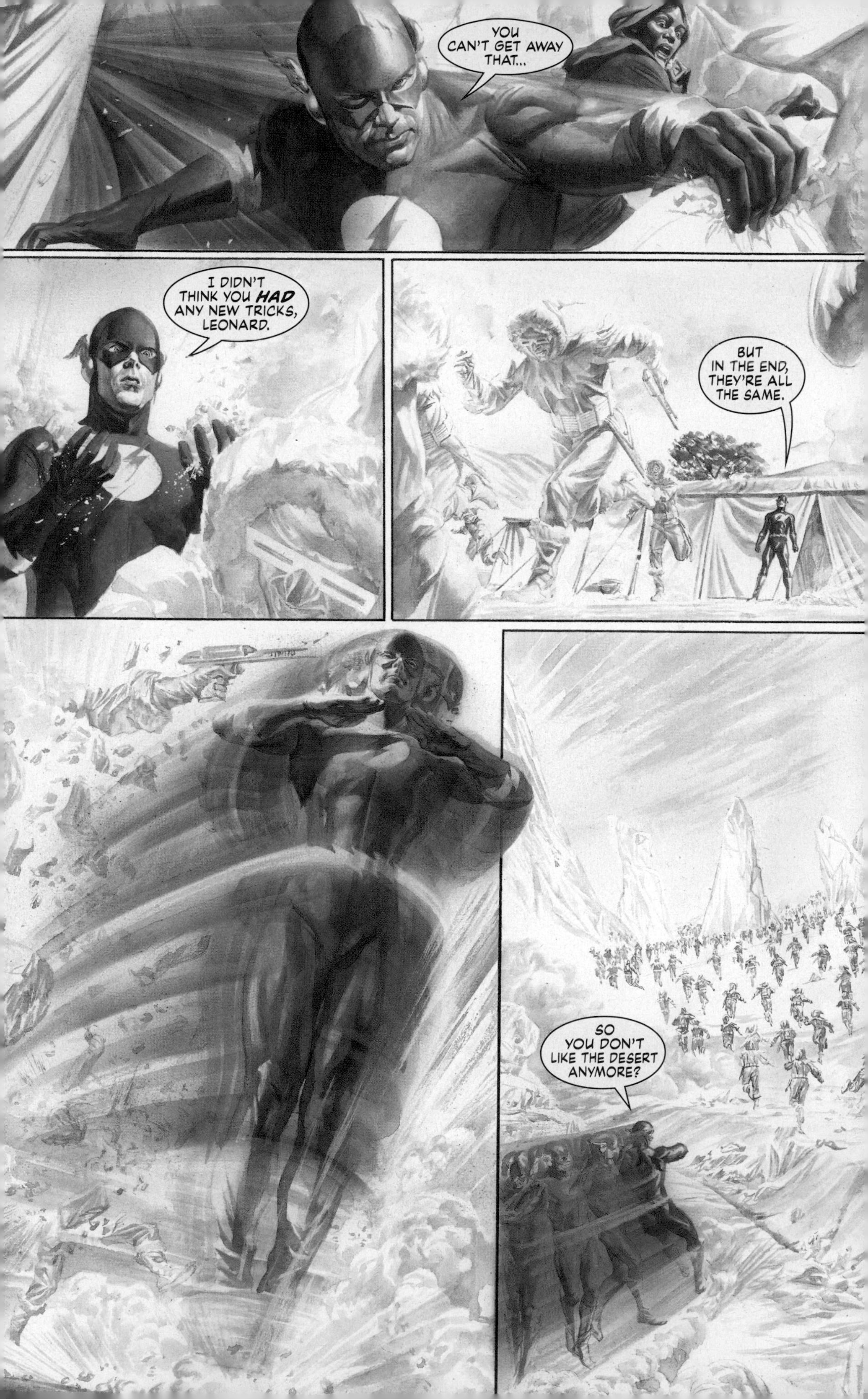
YOU CAN'T GET AWAY THAT...
I DIDN'T THINK YOU HAD ANY NEW TRICKS, LEONARD.
BUT IN THE END, THEY'RE ALL THE SAME.
SO YOU DON'T LIKE THE DESERT ANYMORE?

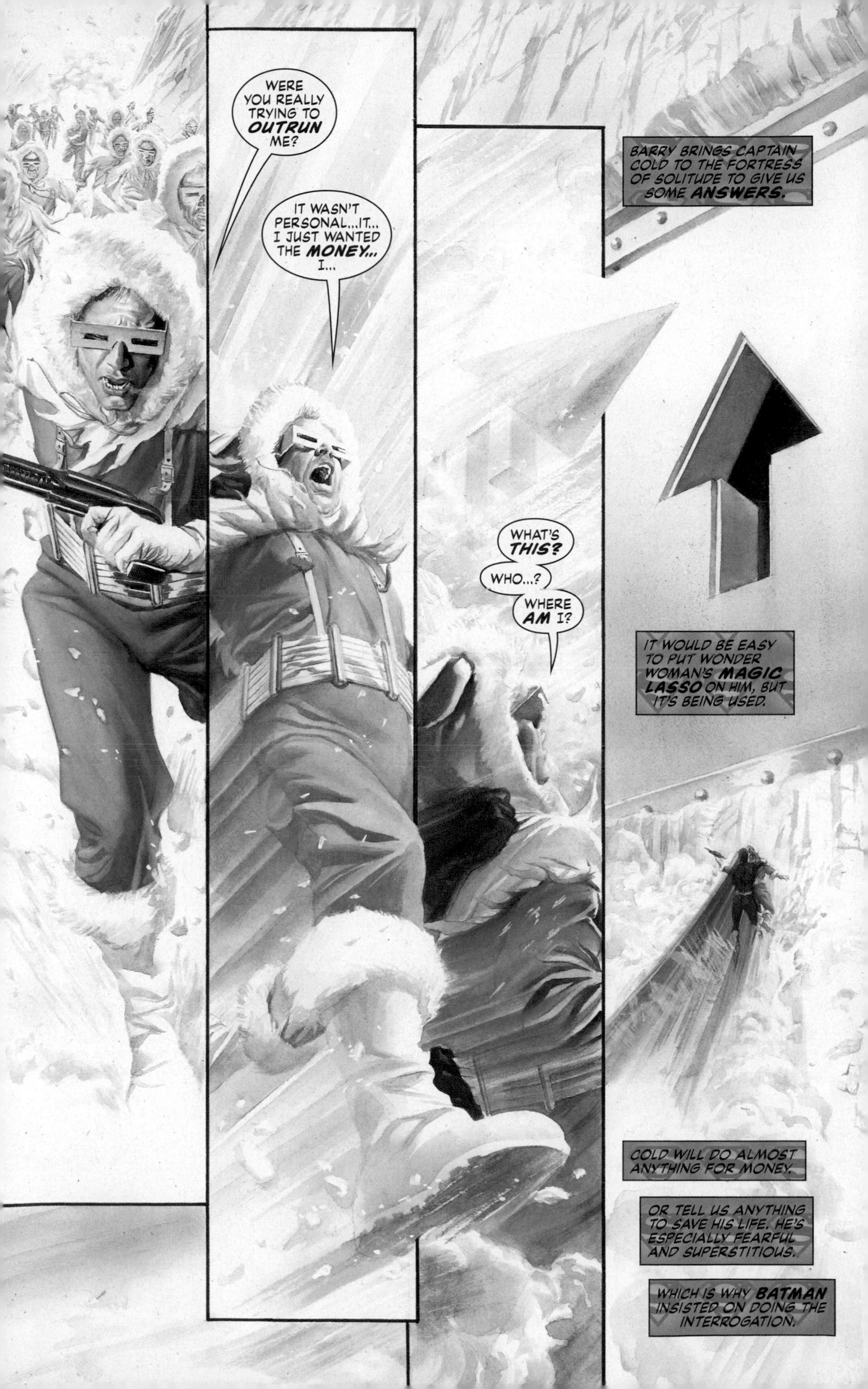
WERE YOU REALLY TRYING TO OUTRUN ME?
IT WASN'T PERSONAL...IT... I JUST WANTED THE MONEY... I...
WHAT'S THIS?
WHO...?
WHERE AM I?
BARRY BRINGS CAPTAIN COLD TO THE FORTRESS OF SOLITUDE TO GIVE US SOME ANSWERS.
IT WOULD BE EASY TO PUT WONDER WOMAN'S MAGIC LASSO ON HIM, BUT IT'S BEING USED.
COLD WILL DO ALMOST ANYTHING FOR MONEY.
OR TELL US ANYTHING TO SAVE HIS LIFE. HE'S ESPECIALLY FEARFUL AND SUPERSTITIOUS.
WHICH IS WHY BATMAN INSISTED ON DOING THE INTERROGATION.

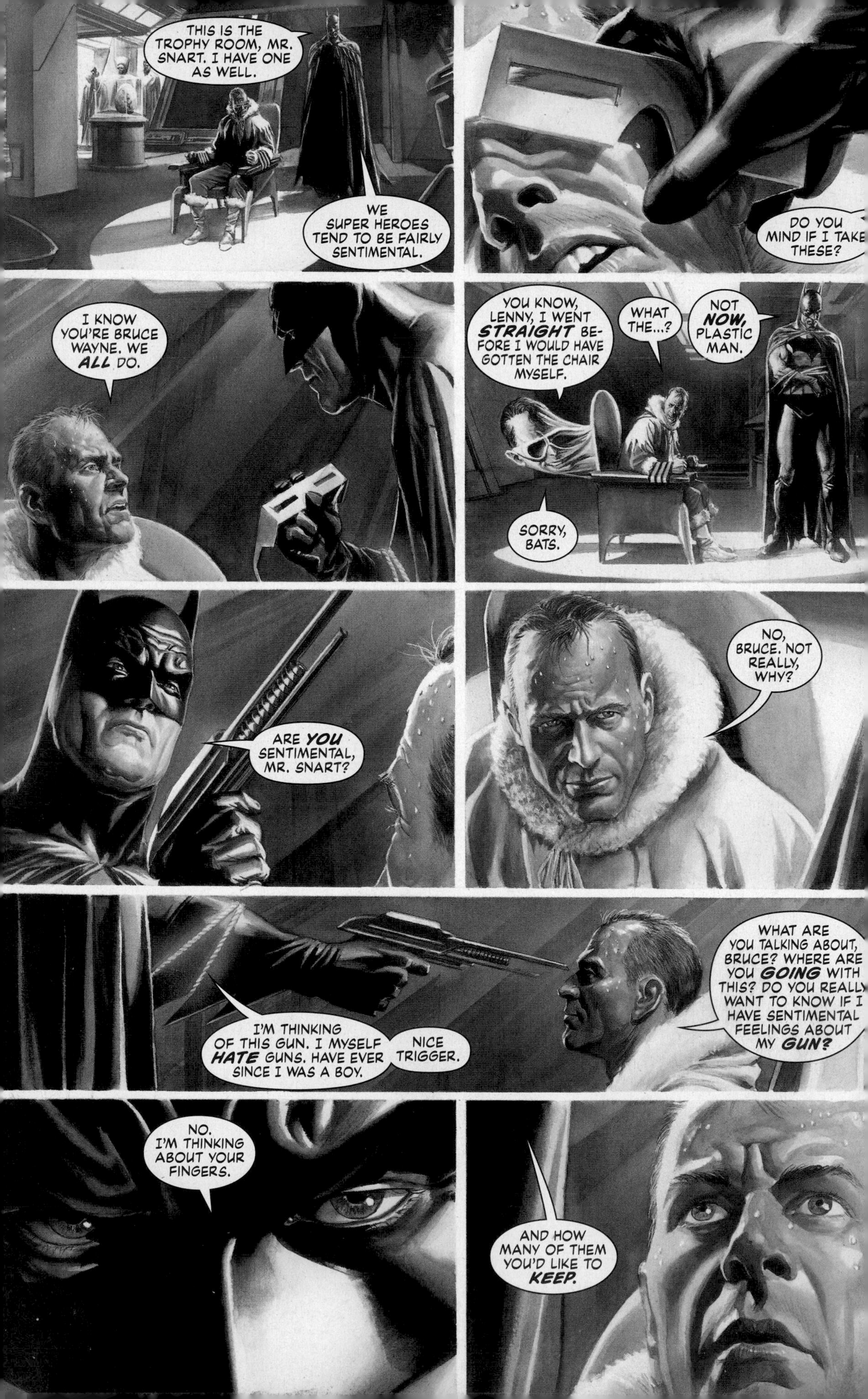
THIS IS THE TROPHY ROOM, MR. SNART. I HAVE ONE AS WELL.
WE SUPER HEROES TEND TO BE FAIRLY SENTIMENTAL.
DO YOU MIND IF I TAKE THESE?
I KNOW YOU'RE BRUCE WAYNE. WE ALL DO.
YOU KNOW, LENNY, I WENT STRAIGHT BEFORE I WOULD HAVE GOTTEN THE CHAIR MYSELF.
WHAT THE...?
NOT NOW, PLASTIC MAN.
SORRY, BATS.
ARE YOU SENTIMENTAL, MR. SNART?
NO, BRUCE. NOT REALLY. WHY?
I'M THINKING OF THIS GUN. I MYSELF HATE GUNS. HAVE EVER SINCE I WAS A BOY.
NICE TRIGGER.
WHAT ARE YOU TALKING ABOUT, BRUCE? WHERE ARE YOU GOING WITH THIS? DO YOU REALLY WANT TO KNOW IF I HAVE SENTIMENTAL FEELINGS ABOUT MY GUN?
NO. I'M THINKING ABOUT YOUR FINGERS.
AND HOW MANY OF THEM YOU'D LIKE TO KEEP.

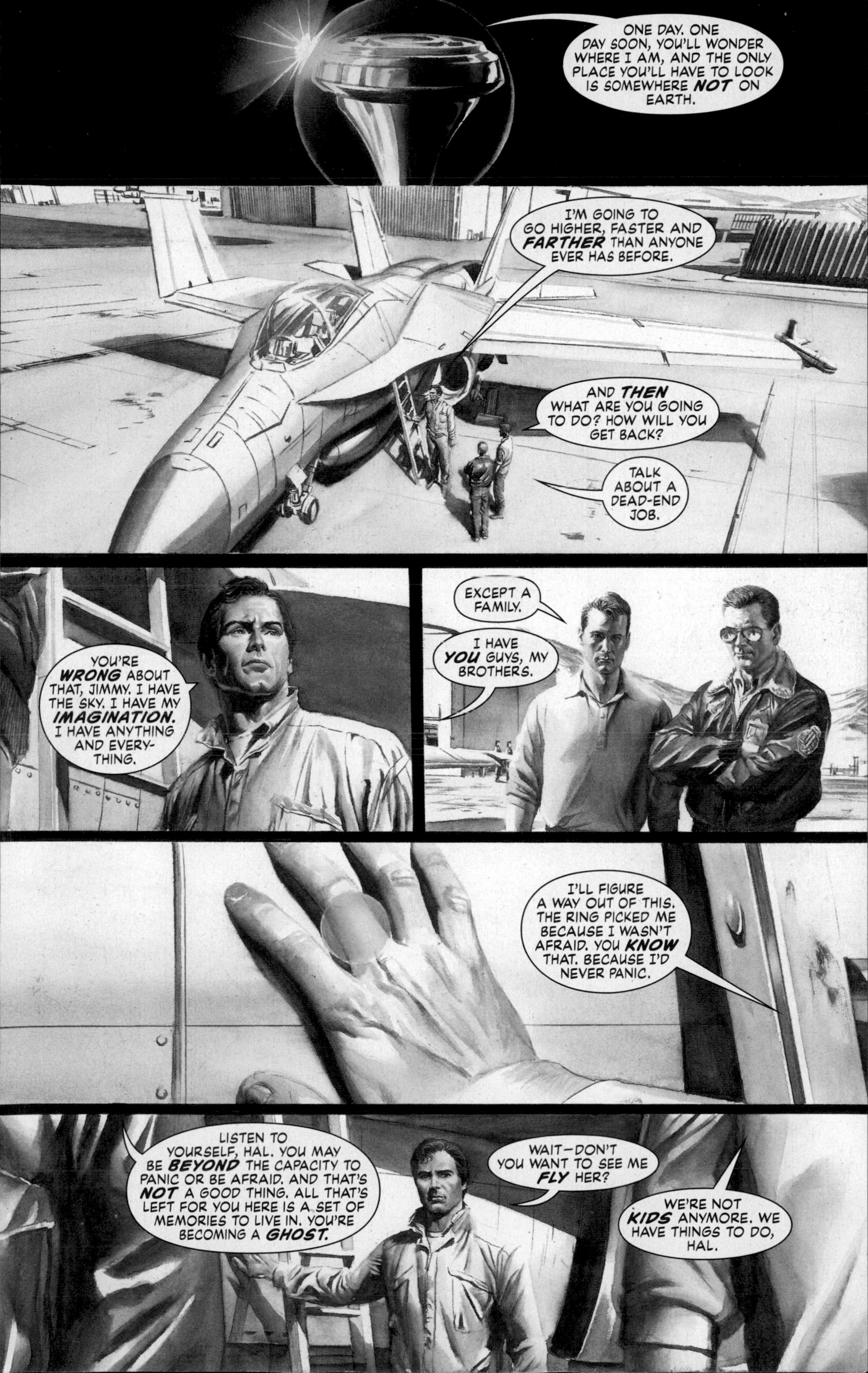
ONE DAY. ONE DAY SOON, YOU'LL WONDER WHERE I AM, AND THE ONLY PLACE YOU'LL HAVE TO LOOK IS SOMEWHERE NOT ON EARTH.
I'M GOING TO GO HIGHER, FASTER AND FARTHER THAN ANYONE EVER HAS BEFORE.
AND THEN WHAT ARE YOU GOING TO DO? HOW WILL YOU GET BACK?
TALK ABOUT A DEAD-END JOB.
YOU'RE WRONG ABOUT THAT, JIMMY. I HAVE THE SKY. I HAVE MY IMAGINATION. I HAVE ANYTHING AND EVERY-THING.
EXCEPT A FAMILY.
I HAVE YOU GUYS, MY BROTHERS.
I'LL FIGURE A WAY OUT OF THIS. THE RING PICKED ME BECAUSE I WASN'T AFRAID. YOU KNOW THAT. BECAUSE I'D NEVER PANIC.
LISTEN TO YOURSELF, HAL. YOU MAY BE BEYOND THE CAPACITY TO PANIC OR BE AFRAID. AND THAT'S NOT A GOOD THING. ALL THAT'S LEFT FOR YOU HERE IS A SET OF MEMORIES TO LIVE IN. YOU'RE BECOMING A GHOST.
WAIT—DON'T YOU WANT TO SEE ME FLY HER?
WE'RE NOT KIDS ANYMORE. WE HAVE THINGS TO DO, HAL.

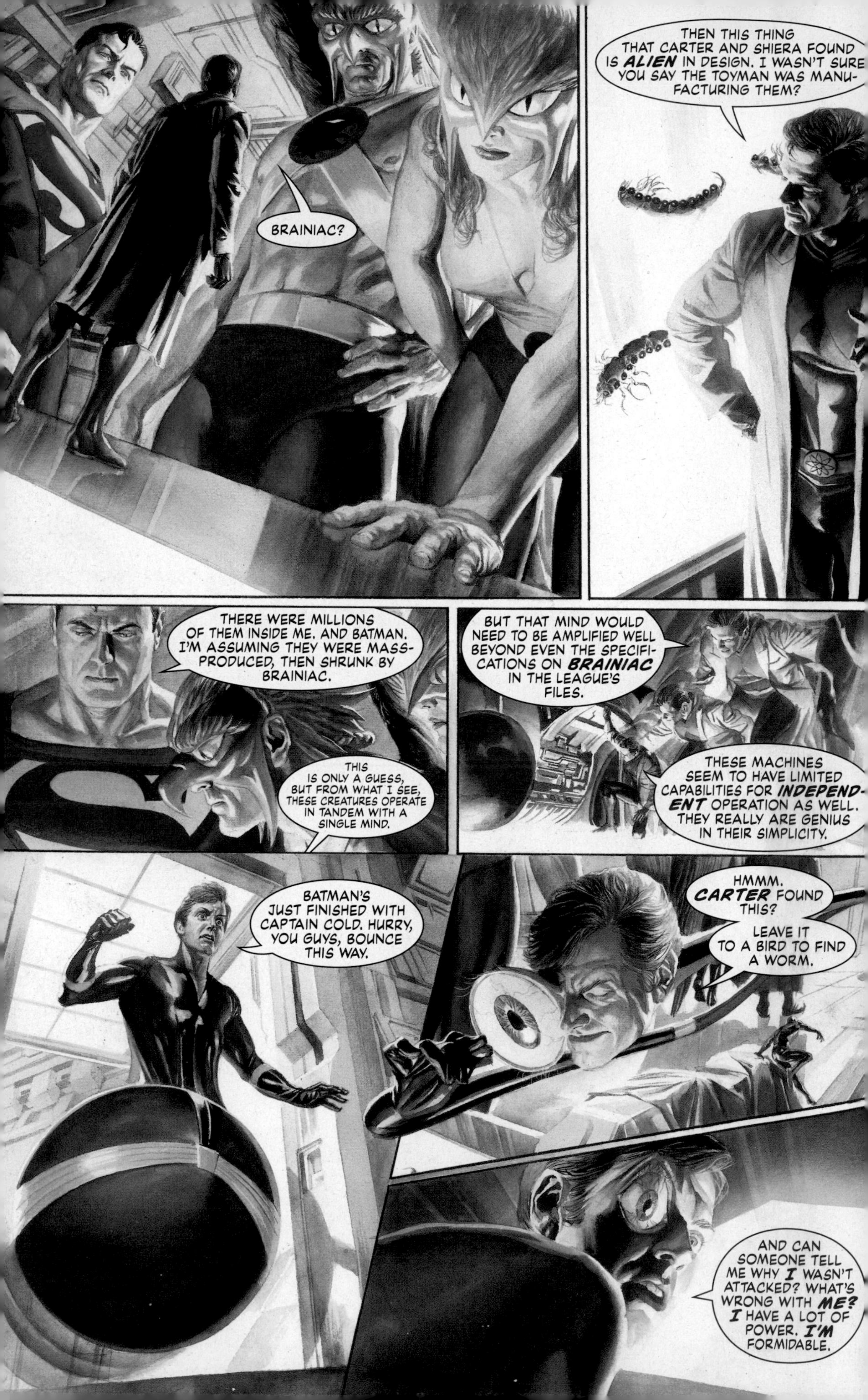
BRAINIAC?
THEN THIS THING THAT CARTER AND SHIERA FOUND IS ALIEN IN DESIGN. I WASN'T SURE YOU SAY THE TOYMAN WAS MANU-FACTURING THEM?
THERE WERE MILLIONS OF THEM INSIDE ME. AND BATMAN. I'M ASSUMING THEY WERE MASS-PRODUCED, THEN SHRUNK BY BRAINIAC.
THIS IS ONLY A GUESS, BUT FROM WHAT I SEE, THESE CREATURES OPERATE IN TANDEM WITH A SINGLE MIND.
BUT THAT MIND WOULD NEED TO BE AMPLIFIED WELL BEYOND EVEN THE SPECIFI-CATIONS ON BRAINIAC IN THE LEAGUE'S FILES.
THESE MACHINES SEEM TO HAVE LIMITED CAPABILITIES FOR INDEPEND-ENT OPERATION AS WELL. THEY REALLY ARE GENIUS IN THEIR SIMPLICITY.
BATMAN'S JUST FINISHED WITH CAPTAIN COLD. HURRY, YOU GUYS, BOUNCE THIS WAY.
HMMM. CARTER FOUND THIS?
LEAVE IT TO A BIRD TO FIND A WORM.
AND CAN SOMEONE TELL ME WHY I WASN'T ATTACKED? WHAT'S WRONG WITH ME? I HAVE A LOT OF POWER. I'M FORMIDABLE.

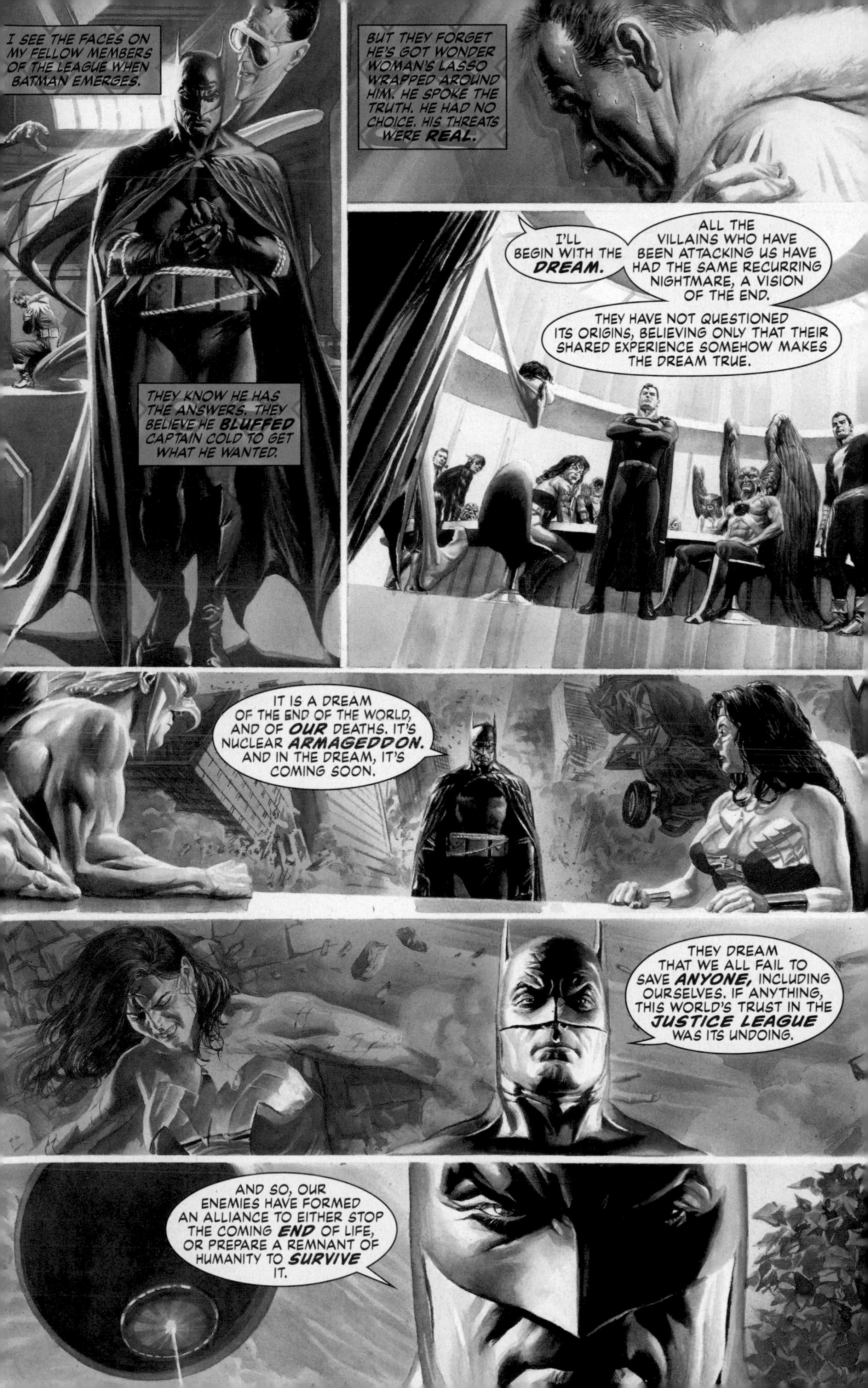
I SEE THE FACES ON MY FELLOW MEMBERS OF THE LEAGUE WHEN BATMAN EMERGES.
THEY KNOW HE HAS THE ANSWERS. THEY BELIEVE HE BLUFFED CAPTAIN COLD TO GET WHAT HE WANTED.
BUT THEY FORGET HE'S GOT WONDER WOMAN'S LASSO WRAPPED AROUND HIM. HE SPOKE THE TRUTH. HE HAD NO CHOICE. HIS THREATS WERE REAL.
I'LL BEGIN WITH THE DREAM.
ALL THE VILLAINS WHO HAVE BEEN ATTACKING US HAVE HAD THE SAME RECURRING NIGHTMARE, A VISION OF THE END.
THEY HAVE NOT QUESTIONED ITS ORIGINS, BELIEVING ONLY THAT THEIR SHARED EXPERIENCE SOMEHOW MAKES THE DREAM TRUE.
IT IS A DREAM OF THE END OF THE WORLD, AND OF OUR DEATHS. IT'S NUCLEAR ARMAGEDDON. AND IN THE DREAM, IT'S COMING SOON.
THEY DREAM THAT WE ALL FAIL TO SAVE ANYONE, INCLUDING OURSELVES. IF ANYTHING, THIS WORLD'S TRUST IN THE JUSTICE LEAGUE WAS ITS UNDOING.
AND SO, OUR ENEMIES HAVE FORMED AN ALLIANCE TO EITHER STOP THE COMING END OF LIFE, OR PREPARE A REMNANT OF HUMANITY TO SURVIVE IT.

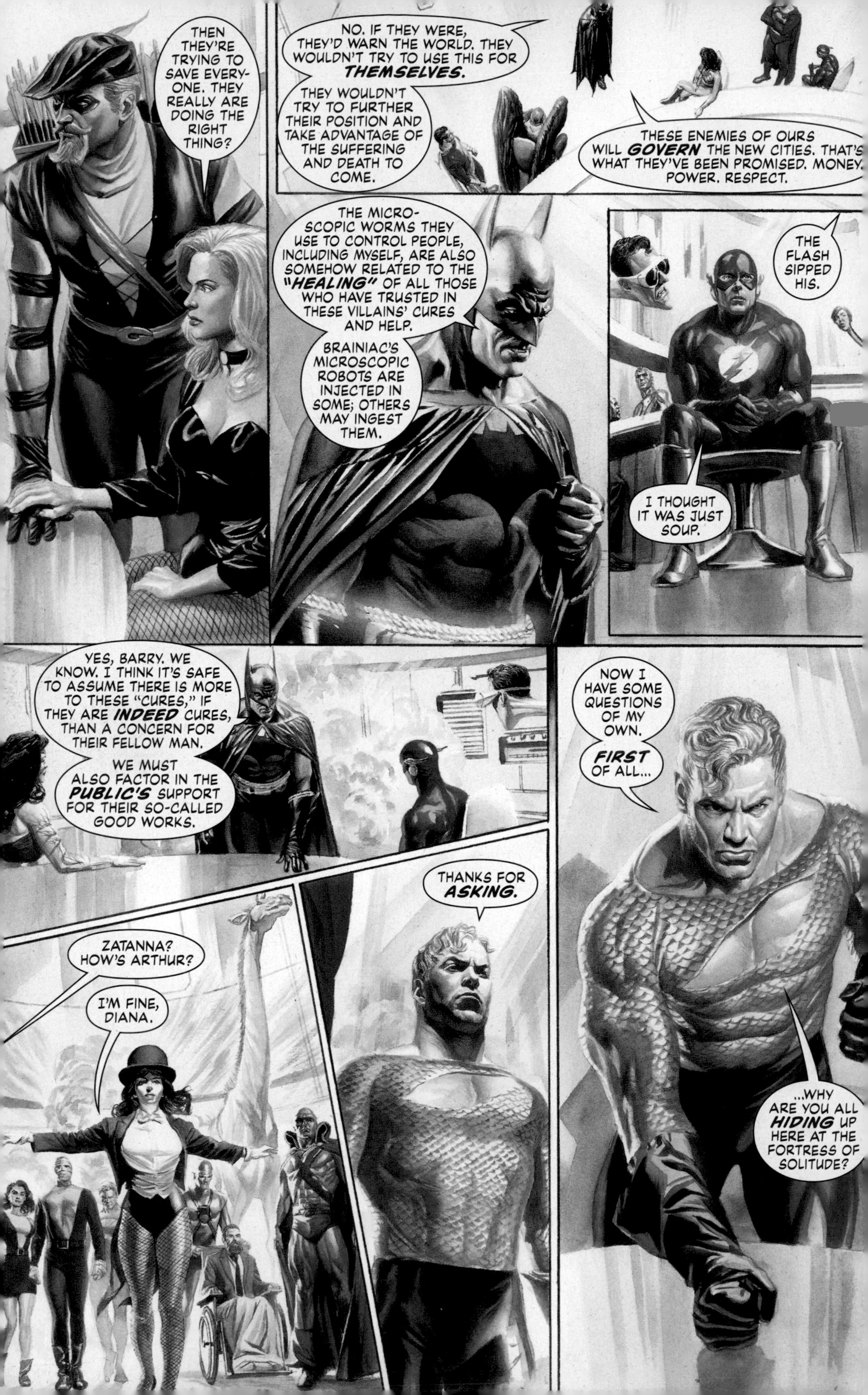
THEN THEY'RE TRYING TO SAVE EVERYONE. THEY REALLY ARE DOING THE RIGHT THING?
NO. IF THEY WERE, THEY'D WARN THE WORLD. THEY WOULDN'T TRY TO USE THIS FOR THEMSELVES.
THEY WOULDN'T TRY TO FURTHER THEIR POSITION AND TAKE ADVANTAGE OF THE SUFFERING AND DEATH TO COME.
THESE ENEMIES OF OURS WILL GOVERN THE NEW CITIES. THAT'S WHAT THEY'VE BEEN PROMISED. MONEY. POWER. RESPECT.
THE MICROSCOPIC WORMS THEY USE TO CONTROL PEOPLE, INCLUDING MYSELF, ARE ALSO SOMEHOW RELATED TO THE "HEALING" OF ALL THOSE WHO HAVE TRUSTED IN THESE VILLAINS' CURES AND HELP.
BRAINIAC'S MICROSCOPIC ROBOTS ARE INJECTED IN SOME; OTHERS MAY INGEST THEM.
THE FLASH SIPPED HIS.
I THOUGHT IT WAS JUST SOUP.
YES, BARRY. WE KNOW. I THINK IT'S SAFE TO ASSUME THERE IS MORE TO THESE "CURES," IF THEY ARE INDEED CURES, THAN A CONCERN FOR THEIR FELLOW MAN.
WE MUST ALSO FACTOR IN THE PUBLIC'S SUPPORT FOR THEIR SO-CALLED GOOD WORKS.
ZATANNA? HOW'S ARTHUR?
I'M FINE, DIANA.
THANKS FOR ASKING.
NOW I HAVE SOME QUESTIONS OF MY OWN.
FIRST OF ALL...
...WHY ARE YOU ALL HIDING UP HERE AT THE FORTRESS OF SOLITUDE?

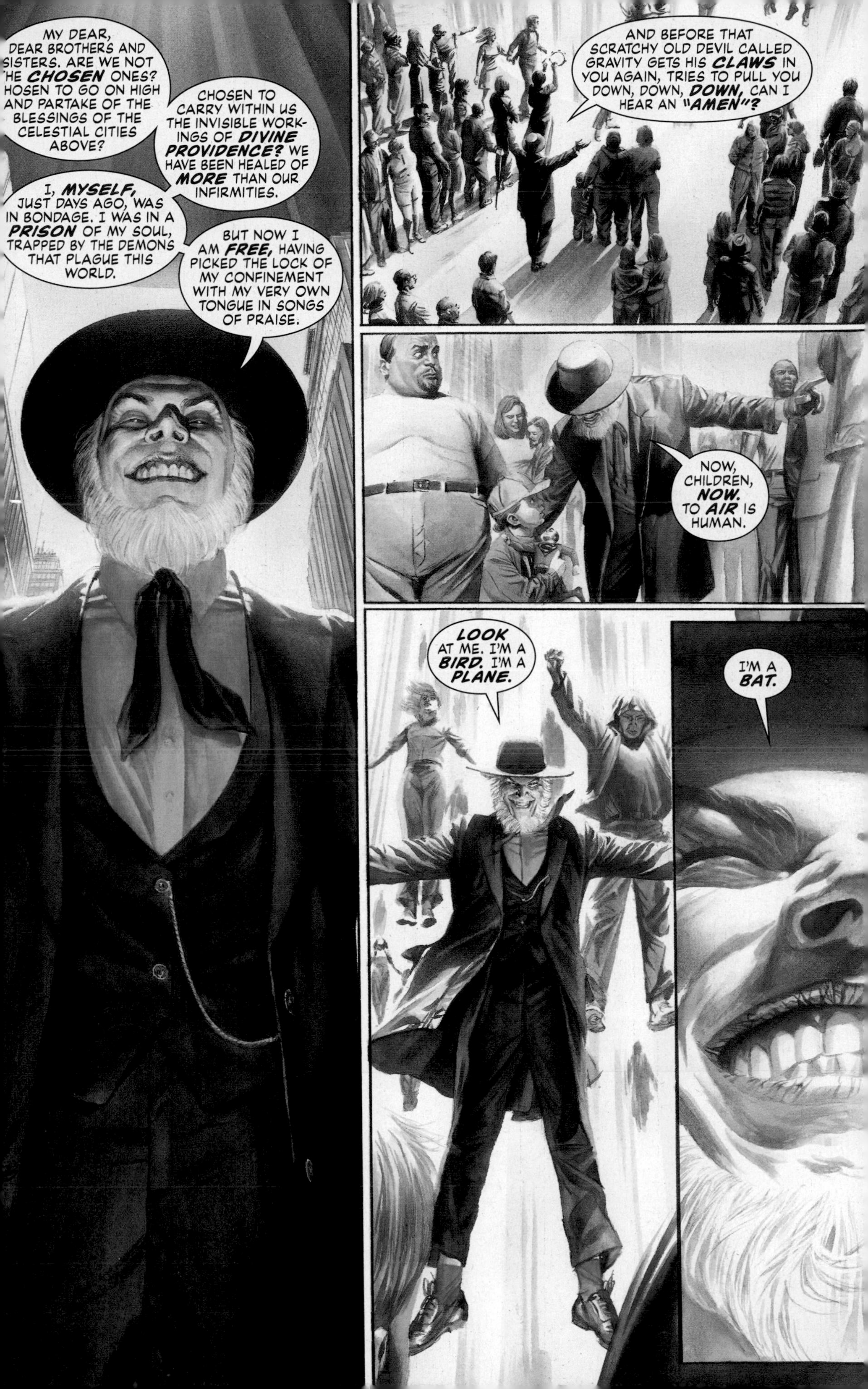
MY DEAR, DEAR BROTHERS AND SISTERS. ARE WE NOT THE CHOSEN ONES? CHOSEN TO GO ON HIGH AND PARTAKE OF THE BLESSINGS OF THE CELESTIAL CITIES ABOVE?
CHOSEN TO CARRY WITHIN US THE INVISIBLE WORKINGS OF DIVINE PROVIDENCE? WE HAVE BEEN HEALED OF MORE THAN OUR INFIRMITIES.
I, MYSELF, JUST DAYS AGO, WAS IN BONDAGE. I WAS IN A PRISON OF MY SOUL, TRAPPED BY THE DEMONS THAT PLAGUE THIS WORLD.
BUT NOW I AM FREE, HAVING PICKED THE LOCK OF MY CONFINEMENT WITH MY VERY OWN TONGUE IN SONGS OF PRAISE.
AND BEFORE THAT SCRATCHY OLD DEVIL CALLED GRAVITY GETS HIS CLAWS IN YOU AGAIN, TRIES TO PULL YOU DOWN, DOWN, DOWN, CAN I HEAR AN "AMEN"?
NOW, CHILDREN, NOW. TO AIR IS HUMAN.
LOOK AT ME. I'M A BIRD. I'M A PLANE.
I'M A BAT.

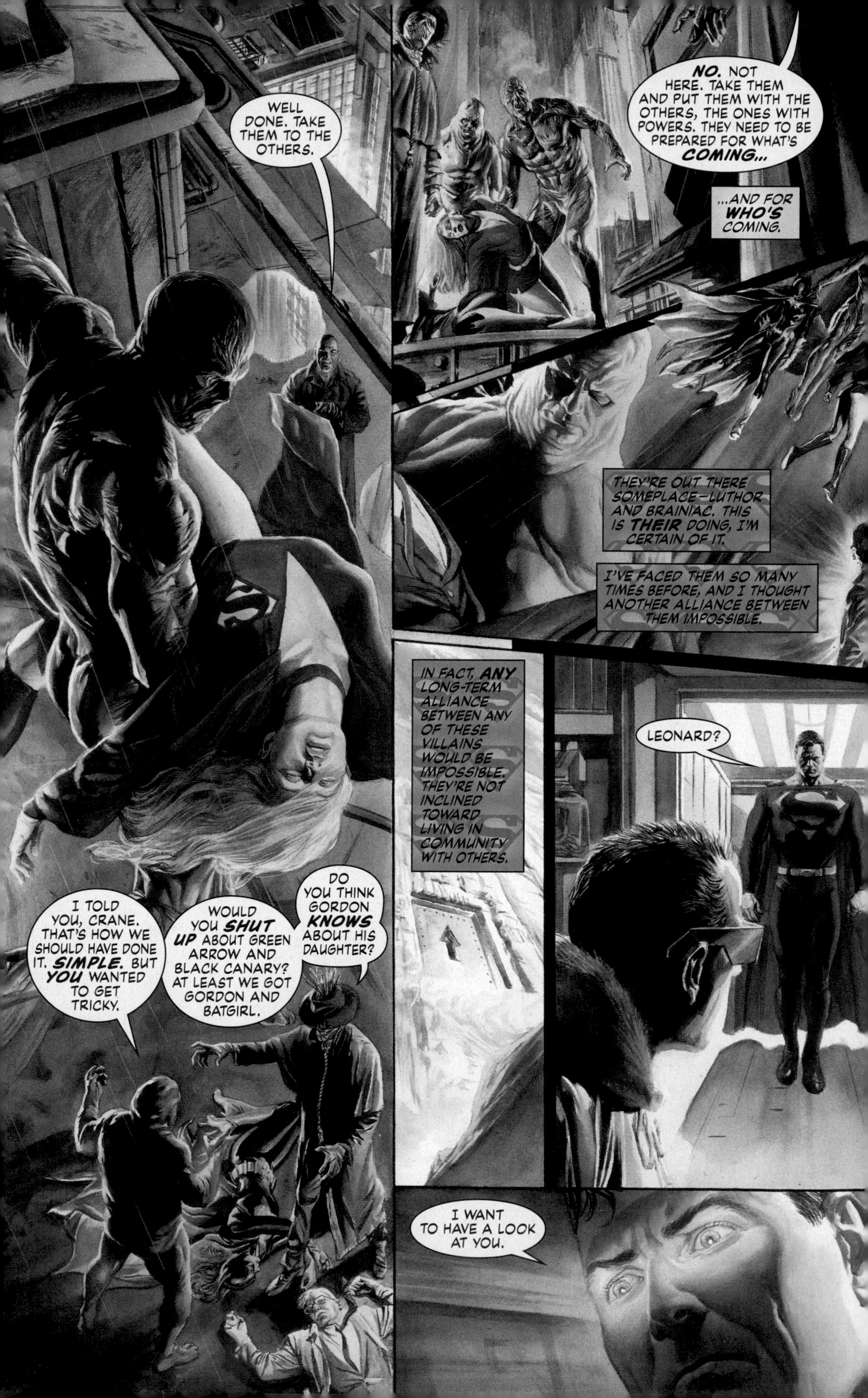
WELL DONE. TAKE THEM TO THE OTHERS.
I TOLD YOU, CRANE. THAT'S HOW WE SHOULD HAVE DONE IT. SIMPLE. BUT YOU WANTED TO GET TRICKY.
WOULD YOU SHUT UP ABOUT GREEN ARROW AND BLACK CANARY? AT LEAST WE GOT GORDON AND BATGIRL.
DO YOU THINK GORDON KNOWS ABOUT HIS DAUGHTER?
NO. NOT HERE. TAKE THEM AND PUT THEM WITH THE OTHERS, THE ONES WITH POWERS. THEY NEED TO BE PREPARED FOR WHAT'S COMING...
...AND FOR WHO'S COMING.
THEY'RE OUT THERE SOMEPLACE—LUTHOR AND BRAINIAC. THIS IS THEIR DOING, I'M CERTAIN OF IT.
I'VE FACED THEM SO MANY TIMES BEFORE, AND I THOUGHT ANOTHER ALLIANCE BETWEEN THEM IMPOSSIBLE.
IN FACT, ANY LONG-TERM ALLIANCE BETWEEN ANY OF THESE VILLAINS WOULD BE IMPOSSIBLE. THEY'RE NOT INCLINED TOWARD LIVING IN COMMUNITY WITH OTHERS.
LEONARD?
I WANT TO HAVE A LOOK AT YOU.

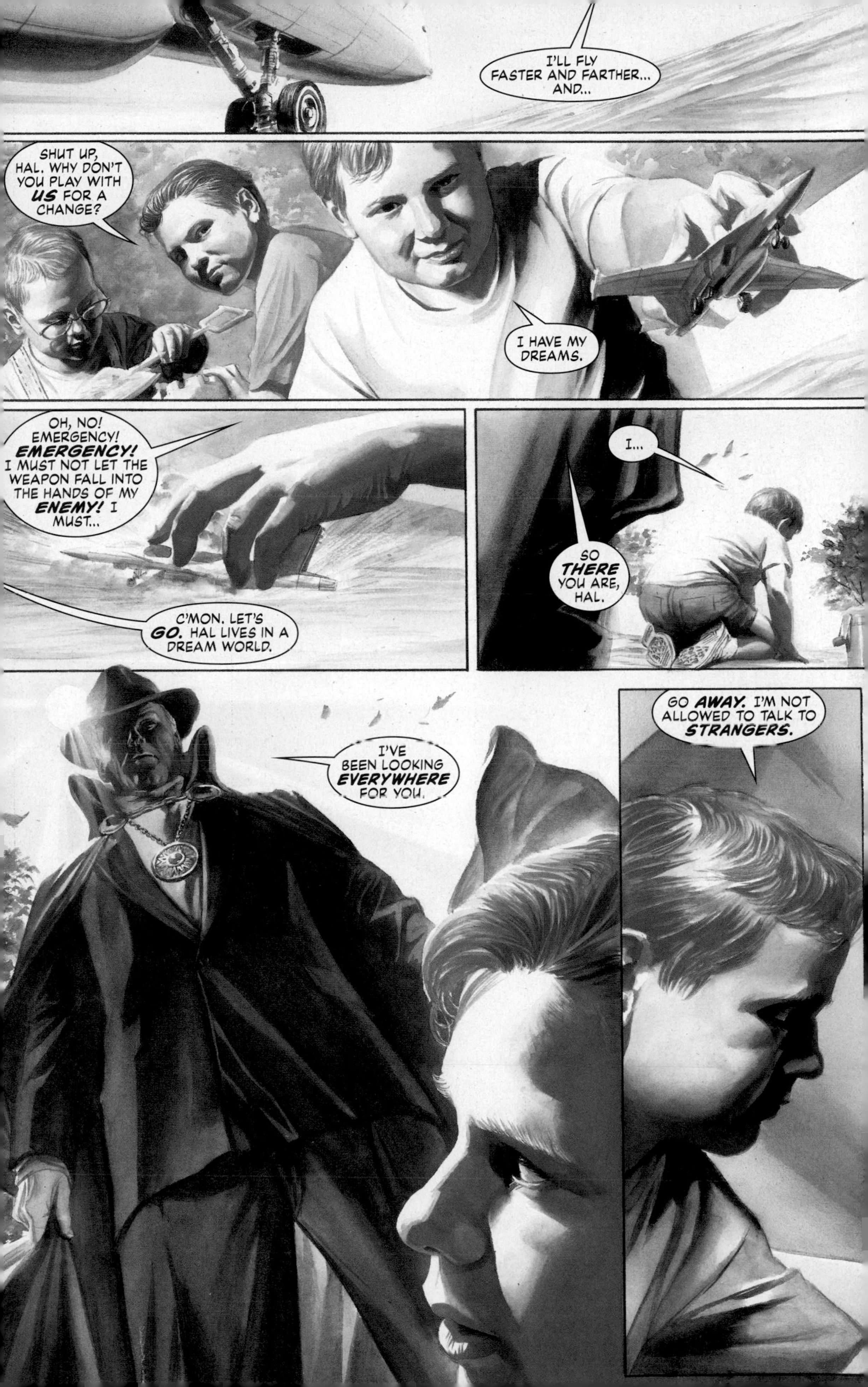
I'LL FLY FASTER AND FARTHER... AND...
SHUT UP, HAL. WHY DON'T YOU PLAY WITH **US** FOR A CHANGE?
I HAVE MY DREAMS.
OH, NO! EMERGENCY! **EMERGENCY!** I MUST NOT LET THE WEAPON FALL INTO THE HANDS OF MY **ENEMY!** I MUST...
C'MON. LET'S **GO.** HAL LIVES IN A DREAM WORLD.
I...
SO **THERE** YOU ARE, HAL.
I'VE BEEN LOOKING **EVERYWHERE** FOR YOU.
GO **AWAY.** I'M NOT ALLOWED TO TALK TO **STRANGERS.**

WONDER WOMAN?

YES, BILL?

WHAT HAPPENED? WHAT DID CHEETAH *DO* TO YOU?

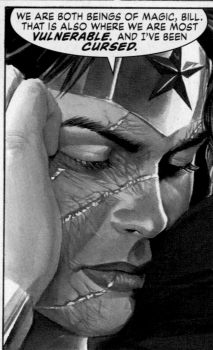

WE ARE BOTH BEINGS OF MAGIC, BILL. THAT IS ALSO WHERE WE ARE MOST *VULNERABLE.* AND I'VE BEEN *CURSED.*

I'M GOING TO DIE FROM THE SAME POISON THAT KILLED HERCULES.

THE *CENTAUR'S* BLOOD?

BUT WHERE HERCULES' DEATH RETURNED HIM TO THE *GLORY* WHICH WAS HIS BY RIGHT AND BIRTH...

...I AM RETURNING TO MY *ORIGINS.* THESE SCARS ARE *BAKING* ME FROM WITHIN.

I WAS CLAY ONCE, FORMED BY MY MOTHER'S HANDS. THE GODDESS MADE ME *REAL* IN ANSWER TO MY MOTHER'S PRAYER. I AM BECOMING *UNREAL* AGAIN.

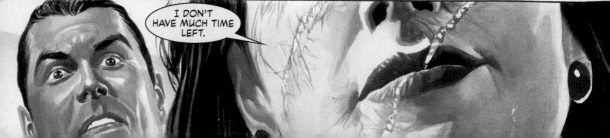

I DON'T HAVE MUCH TIME LEFT.

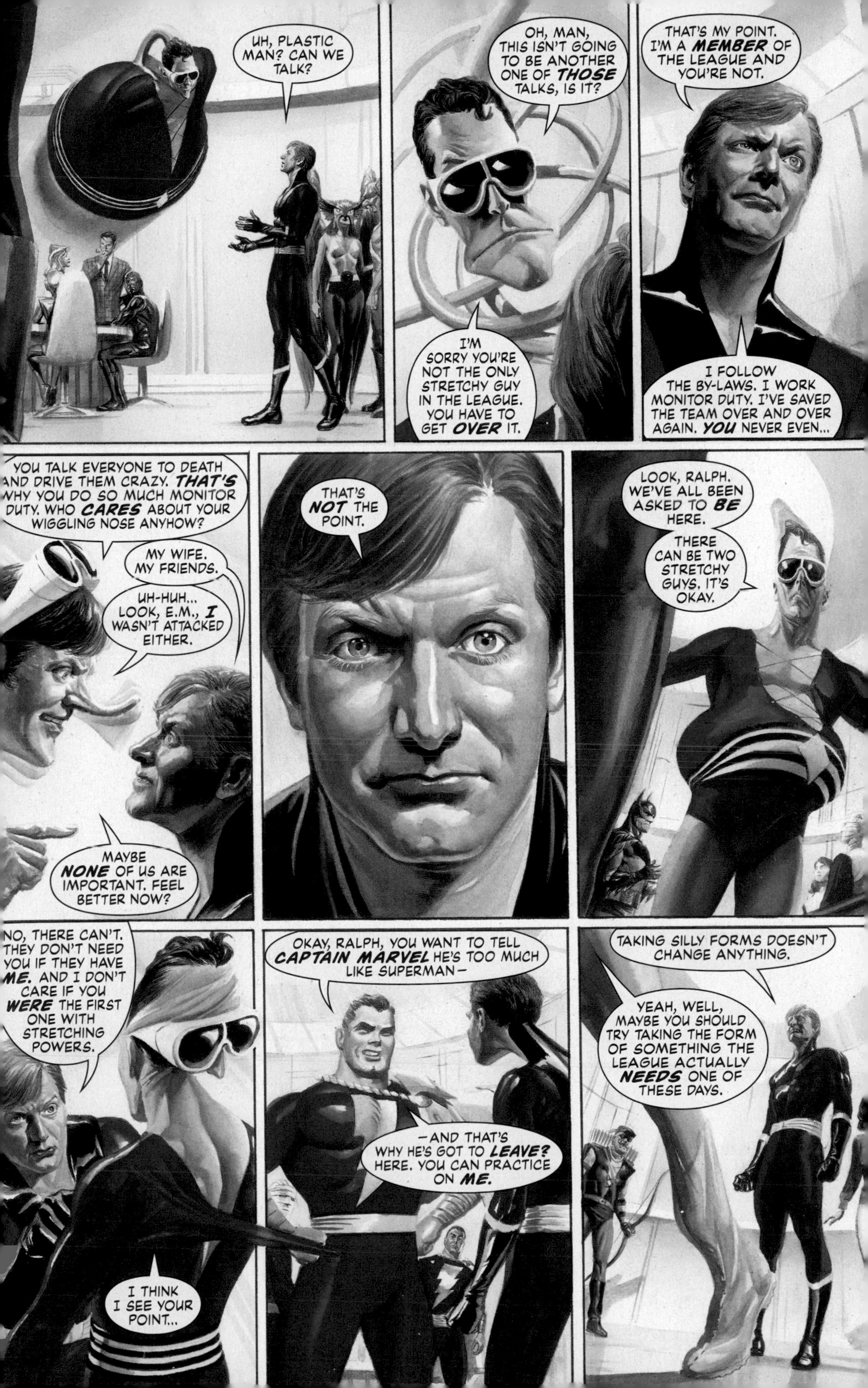
UH, PLASTIC MAN? CAN WE TALK?
OH, MAN, THIS ISN'T GOING TO BE ANOTHER ONE OF THOSE TALKS, IS IT?
I'M SORRY YOU'RE NOT THE ONLY STRETCHY GUY IN THE LEAGUE. YOU HAVE TO GET OVER IT.
THAT'S MY POINT. I'M A MEMBER OF THE LEAGUE AND YOU'RE NOT.
I FOLLOW THE BY-LAWS. I WORK MONITOR DUTY. I'VE SAVED THE TEAM OVER AND OVER AGAIN. YOU NEVER EVEN...
YOU TALK EVERYONE TO DEATH AND DRIVE THEM CRAZY. THAT'S WHY YOU DO SO MUCH MONITOR DUTY. WHO CARES ABOUT YOUR WIGGLING NOSE ANYHOW?
MY WIFE. MY FRIENDS.
UH-HUH... LOOK, E.M., I WASN'T ATTACKED EITHER.
MAYBE NONE OF US ARE IMPORTANT. FEEL BETTER NOW?
THAT'S NOT THE POINT.
LOOK, RALPH. WE'VE ALL BEEN ASKED TO BE HERE.
THERE CAN BE TWO STRETCHY GUYS. IT'S OKAY.
NO, THERE CAN'T. THEY DON'T NEED YOU IF THEY HAVE ME. AND I DON'T CARE IF YOU WERE THE FIRST ONE WITH STRETCHING POWERS.
I THINK I SEE YOUR POINT...
OKAY, RALPH, YOU WANT TO TELL CAPTAIN MARVEL HE'S TOO MUCH LIKE SUPERMAN–
–AND THAT'S WHY HE'S GOT TO LEAVE? HERE. YOU CAN PRACTICE ON ME.
TAKING SILLY FORMS DOESN'T CHANGE ANYTHING.
YEAH, WELL, MAYBE YOU SHOULD TRY TAKING THE FORM OF SOMETHING THE LEAGUE ACTUALLY NEEDS ONE OF THESE DAYS.

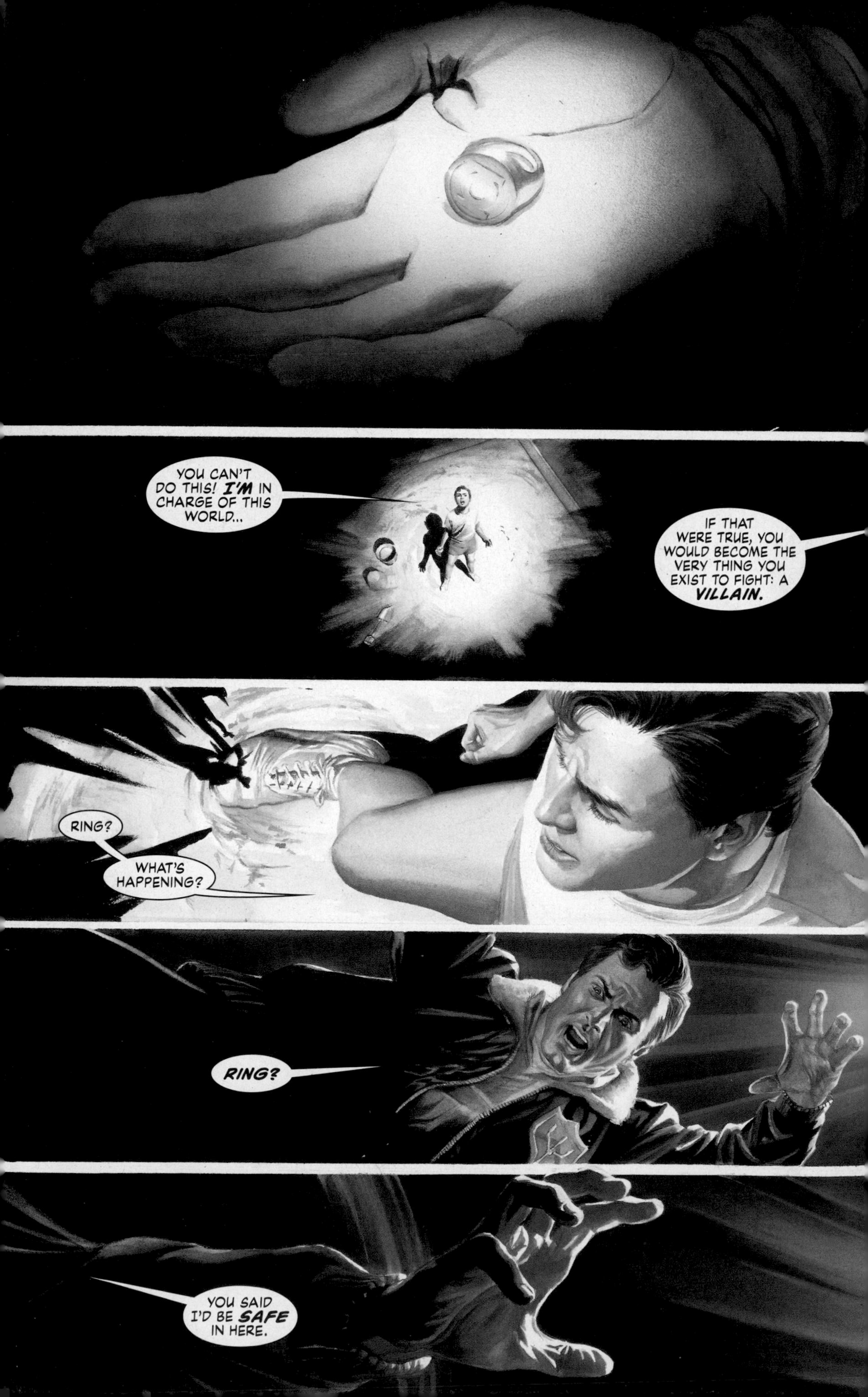

YOU CAN'T DO THIS! I'M IN CHARGE OF THIS WORLD...
IF THAT WERE TRUE, YOU WOULD BECOME THE VERY THING YOU EXIST TO FIGHT: A VILLAIN.
RING?
WHAT'S HAPPENING?
RING?
YOU SAID I'D BE SAFE IN HERE.

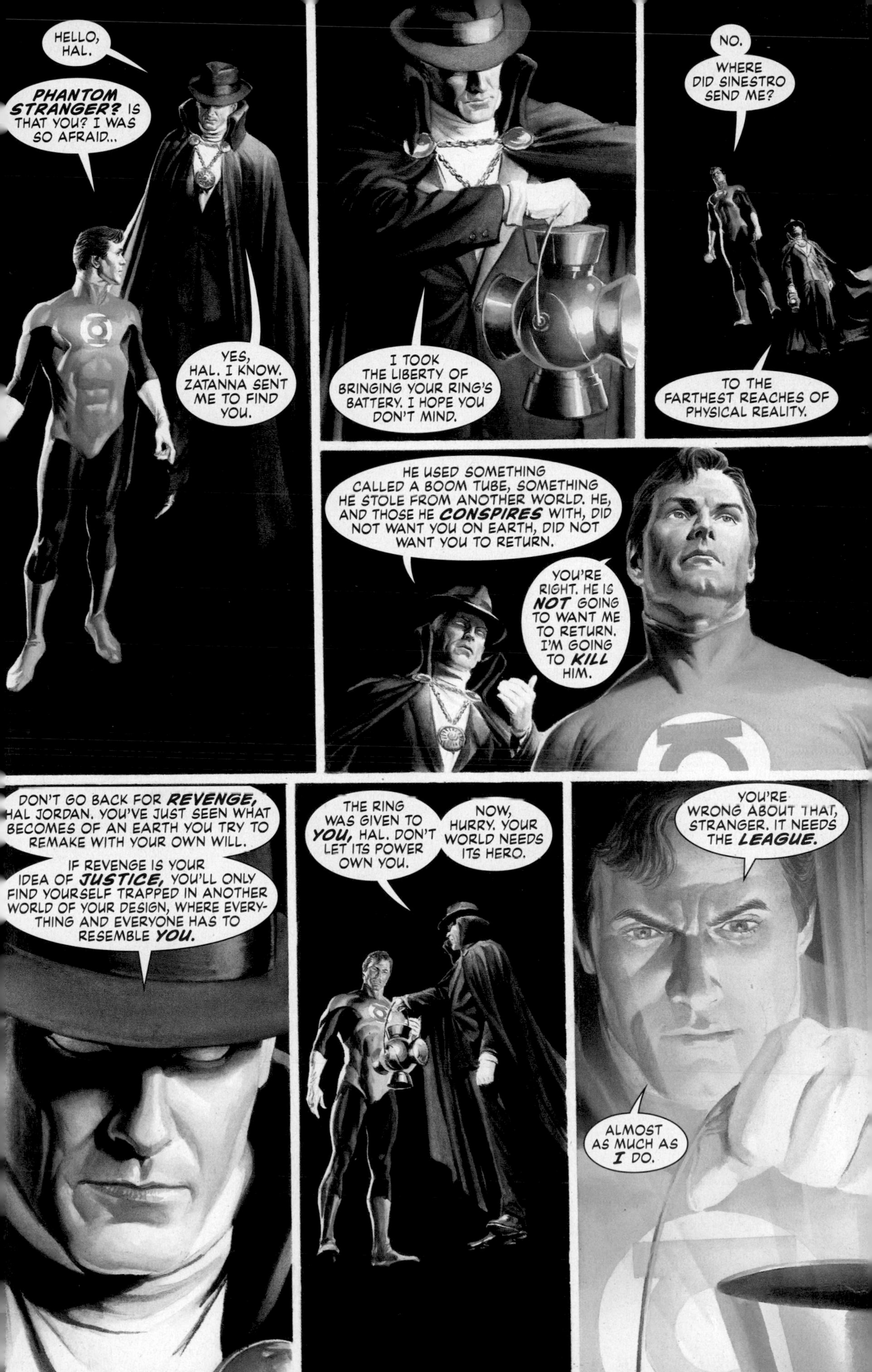

HELLO, HAL.
PHANTOM STRANGER? IS THAT YOU? I WAS SO AFRAID...
YES, HAL. I KNOW. ZATANNA SENT ME TO FIND YOU.
I TOOK THE LIBERTY OF BRINGING YOUR RING'S BATTERY. I HOPE YOU DON'T MIND.
NO.
WHERE DID SINESTRO SEND ME?
TO THE FARTHEST REACHES OF PHYSICAL REALITY.
HE USED SOMETHING CALLED A BOOM TUBE, SOMETHING HE STOLE FROM ANOTHER WORLD. HE, AND THOSE HE CONSPIRES WITH, DID NOT WANT YOU ON EARTH, DID NOT WANT YOU TO RETURN.
YOU'RE RIGHT. HE IS NOT GOING TO WANT ME TO RETURN. I'M GOING TO KILL HIM.
DON'T GO BACK FOR REVENGE, HAL JORDAN. YOU'VE JUST SEEN WHAT BECOMES OF AN EARTH YOU TRY TO REMAKE WITH YOUR OWN WILL.
IF REVENGE IS YOUR IDEA OF JUSTICE, YOU'LL ONLY FIND YOURSELF TRAPPED IN ANOTHER WORLD OF YOUR DESIGN, WHERE EVERYTHING AND EVERYONE HAS TO RESEMBLE YOU.
THE RING WAS GIVEN TO YOU, HAL. DON'T LET ITS POWER OWN YOU.
NOW, HURRY. YOUR WORLD NEEDS ITS HERO.
YOU'RE WRONG ABOUT THAT, STRANGER. IT NEEDS THE LEAGUE.
ALMOST AS MUCH AS I DO.

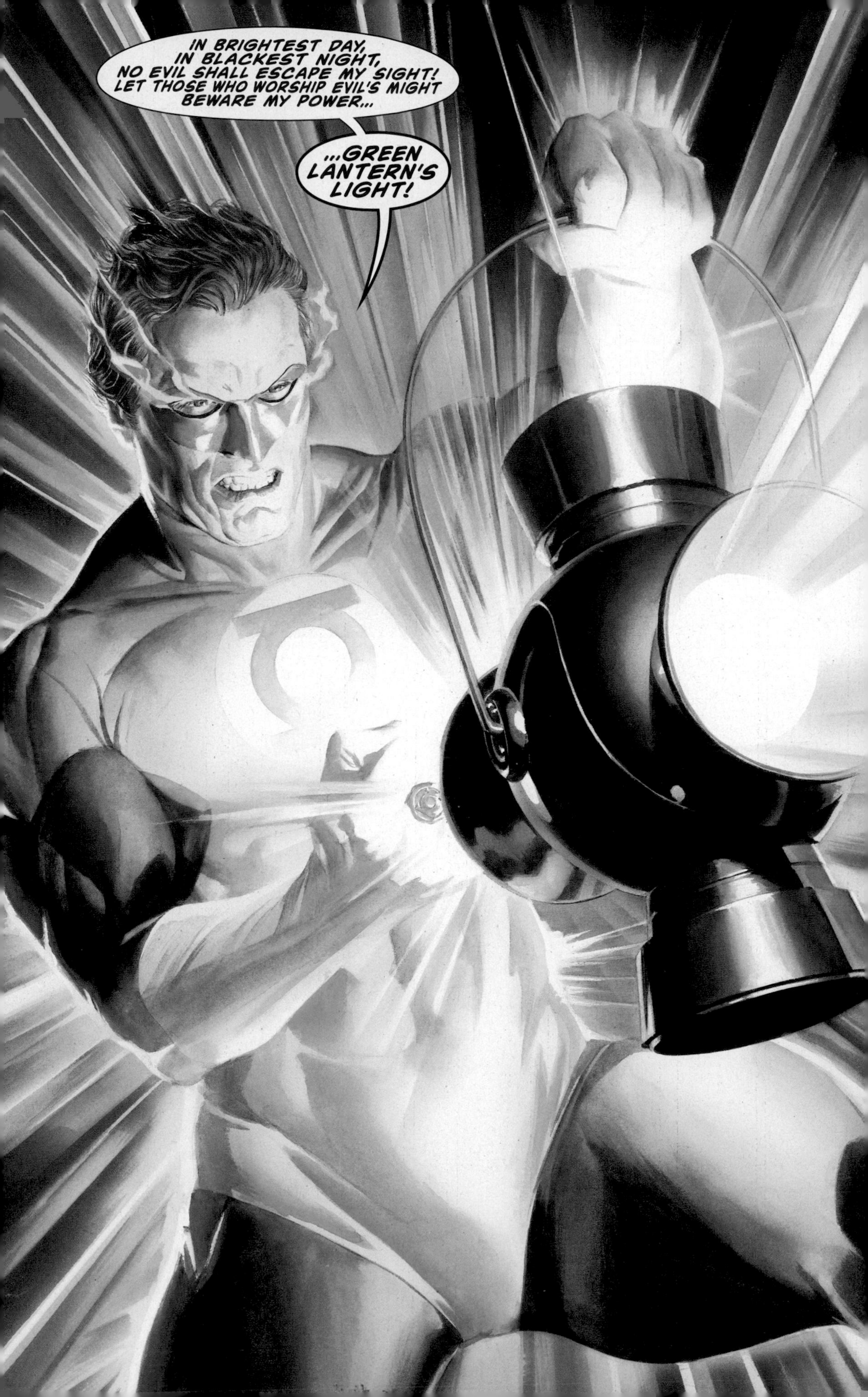
IN BRIGHTEST DAY, IN BLACKEST NIGHT, NO EVIL SHALL ESCAPE MY SIGHT! LET THOSE WHO WORSHIP EVIL'S MIGHT BEWARE MY POWER...
...GREEN LANTERN'S LIGHT!

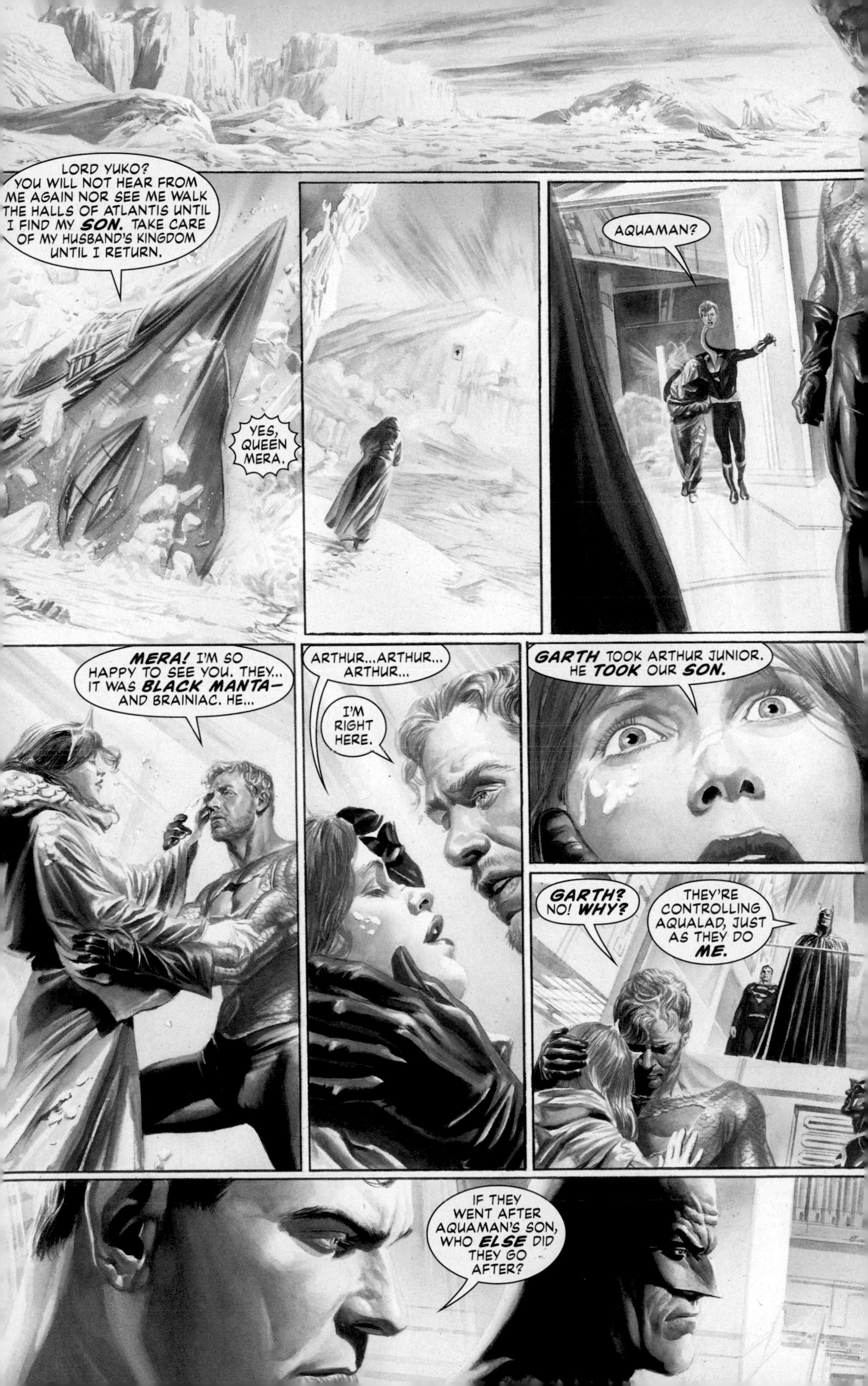
LORD YUKO? YOU WILL NOT HEAR FROM ME AGAIN NOR SEE ME WALK THE HALLS OF ATLANTIS UNTIL I FIND MY **SON.** TAKE CARE OF MY HUSBAND'S KINGDOM UNTIL I RETURN.
YES, QUEEN MERA.
AQUAMAN?
MERA! I'M SO HAPPY TO SEE YOU. THEY... IT WAS **BLACK MANTA**— AND BRAINIAC. HE...
ARTHUR...ARTHUR... ARTHUR...
I'M RIGHT HERE.
GARTH TOOK ARTHUR JUNIOR. HE **TOOK** OUR **SON.**
GARTH? NO! **WHY?**
THEY'RE CONTROLLING AQUALAD, JUST AS THEY DO **ME.**
IF THEY WENT AFTER AQUAMAN'S SON, WHO **ELSE** DID THEY GO AFTER?

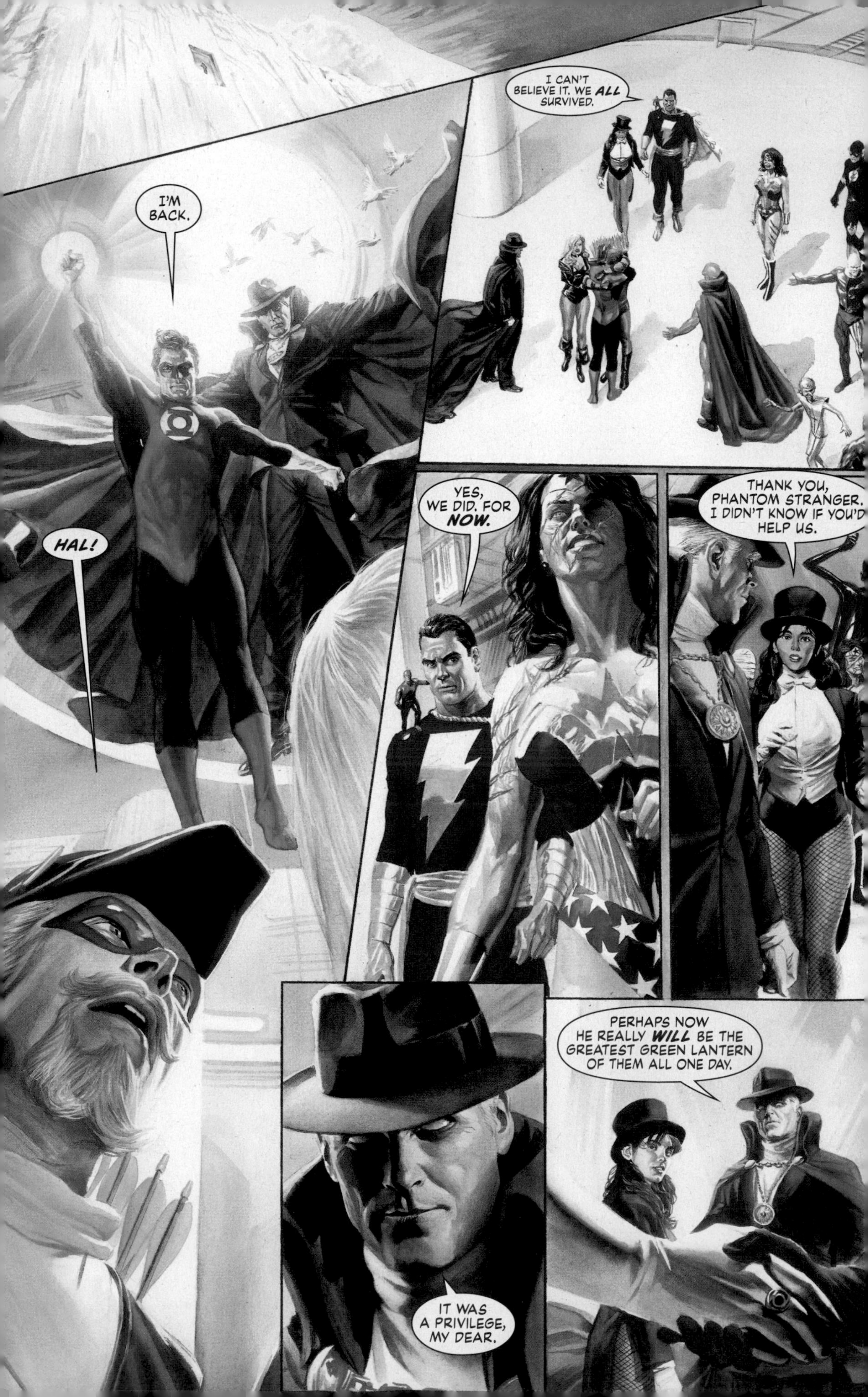
I'M BACK.
HAL!
I CAN'T BELIEVE IT. WE ALL SURVIVED.
YES, WE DID. FOR NOW.
THANK YOU, PHANTOM STRANGER. I DIDN'T KNOW IF YOU'D HELP US.
IT WAS A PRIVILEGE, MY DEAR.
PERHAPS NOW HE REALLY WILL BE THE GREATEST GREEN LANTERN OF THEM ALL ONE DAY.

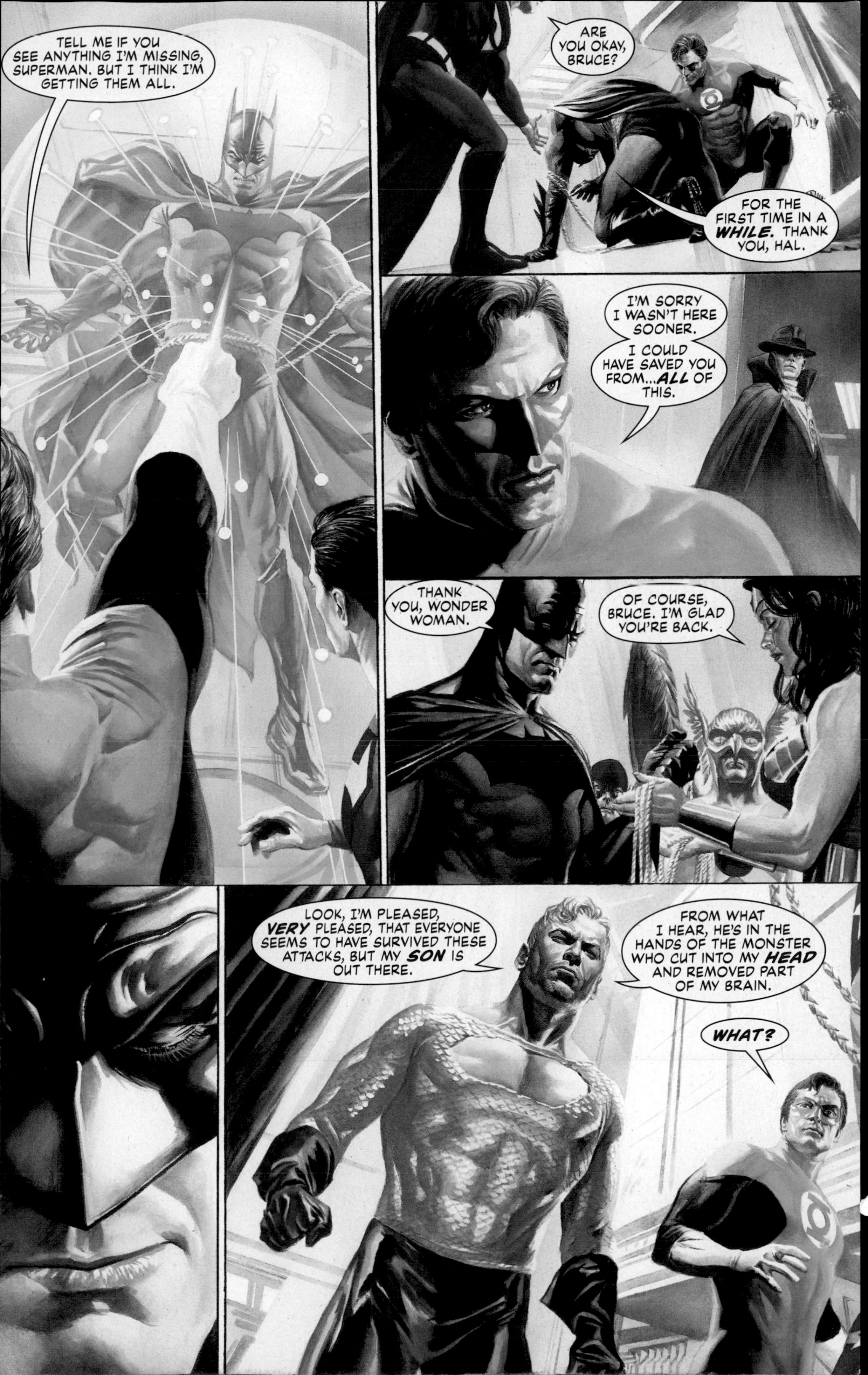
TELL ME IF YOU SEE ANYTHING I'M MISSING, SUPERMAN. BUT I THINK I'M GETTING THEM ALL.
ARE YOU OKAY, BRUCE?
FOR THE FIRST TIME IN A WHILE. THANK YOU, HAL.
I'M SORRY I WASN'T HERE SOONER.
I COULD HAVE SAVED YOU FROM...ALL OF THIS.
THANK YOU, WONDER WOMAN.
OF COURSE, BRUCE. I'M GLAD YOU'RE BACK.
LOOK, I'M PLEASED, VERY PLEASED, THAT EVERYONE SEEMS TO HAVE SURVIVED THESE ATTACKS, BUT MY SON IS OUT THERE.
FROM WHAT I HEAR, HE'S IN THE HANDS OF THE MONSTER WHO CUT INTO MY HEAD AND REMOVED PART OF MY BRAIN.
WHAT?

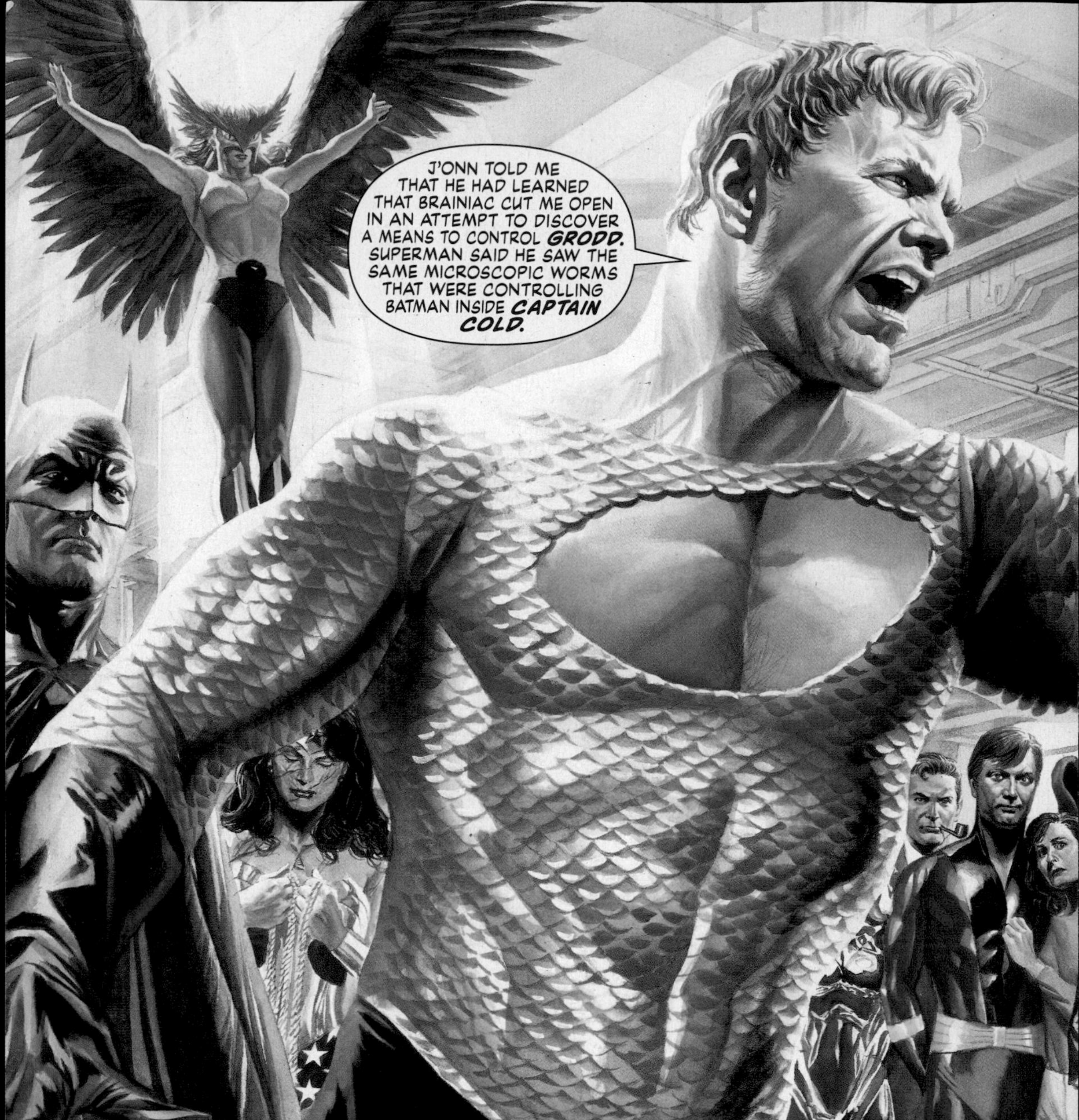
J'ONN TOLD ME THAT HE HAD LEARNED THAT BRAINIAC CUT ME OPEN IN AN ATTEMPT TO DISCOVER A MEANS TO CONTROL GRODD. SUPERMAN SAID HE SAW THE SAME MICROSCOPIC WORMS THAT WERE CONTROLLING BATMAN INSIDE CAPTAIN COLD.
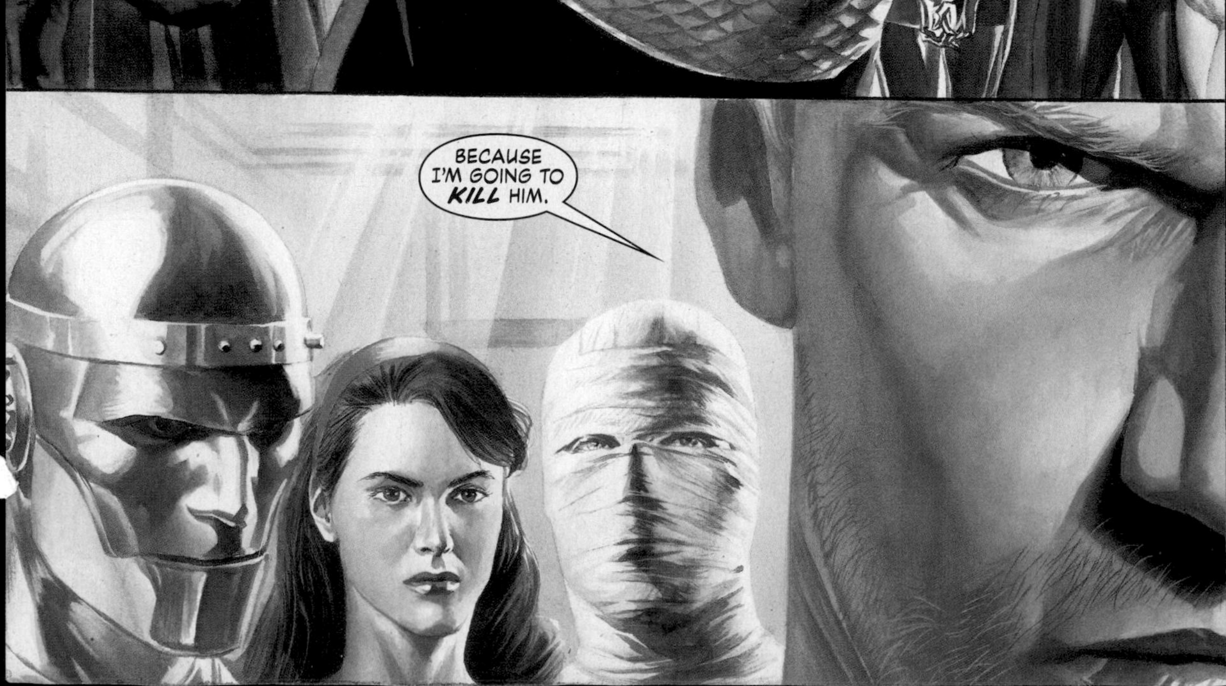
BECAUSE I'M GOING TO KILL HIM.

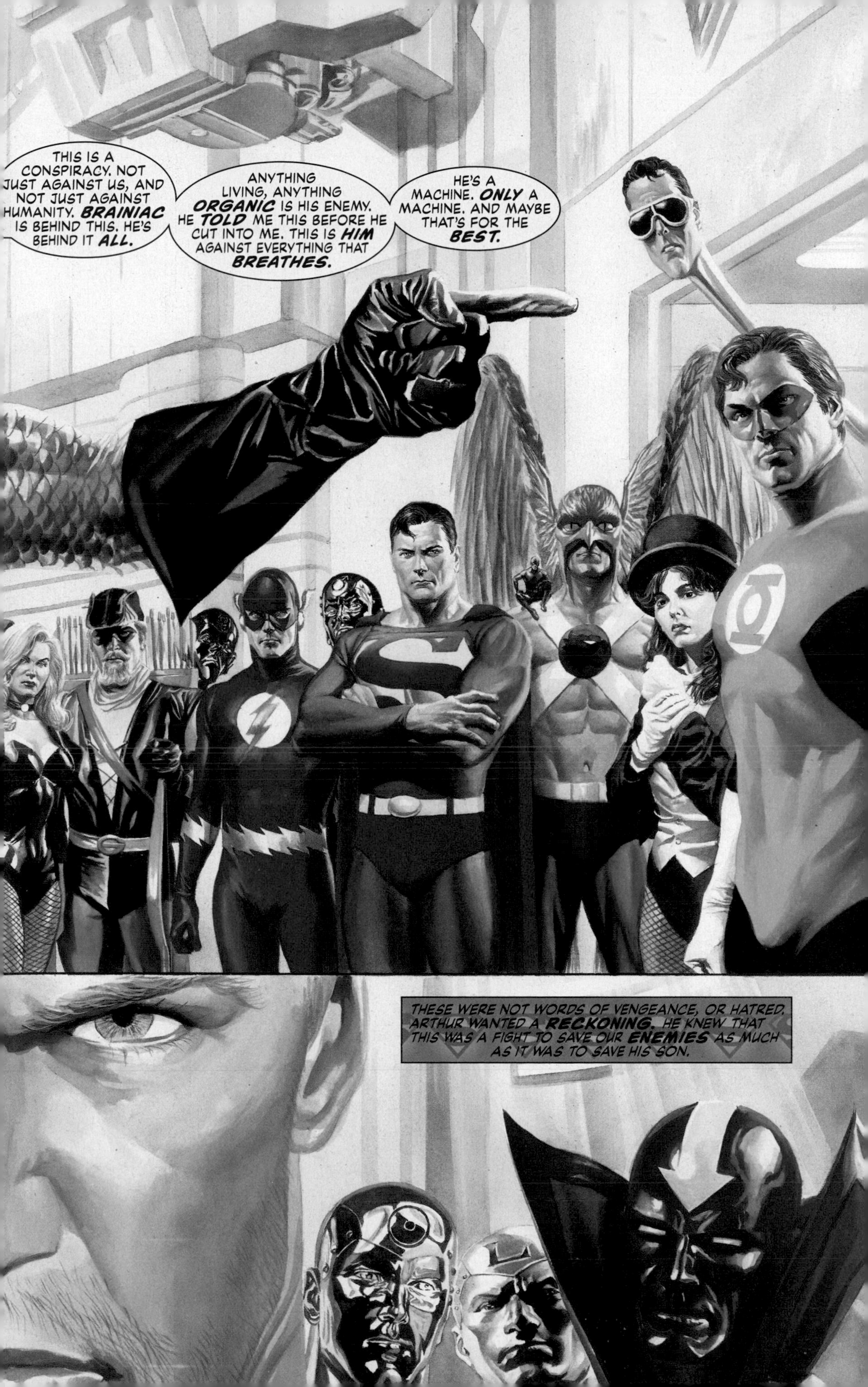
THIS IS A CONSPIRACY. NOT JUST AGAINST US, AND NOT JUST AGAINST HUMANITY. BRAINIAC IS BEHIND THIS. HE'S BEHIND IT ALL.
ANYTHING LIVING, ANYTHING ORGANIC IS HIS ENEMY. HE TOLD ME THIS BEFORE HE CUT INTO ME. THIS IS HIM AGAINST EVERYTHING THAT BREATHES.
HE'S A MACHINE. ONLY A MACHINE. AND MAYBE THAT'S FOR THE BEST.
THESE WERE NOT WORDS OF VENGEANCE, OR HATRED. ARTHUR WANTED A RECKONING. HE KNEW THAT THIS WAS A FIGHT TO SAVE OUR ENEMIES AS MUCH AS IT WAS TO SAVE HIS SON.

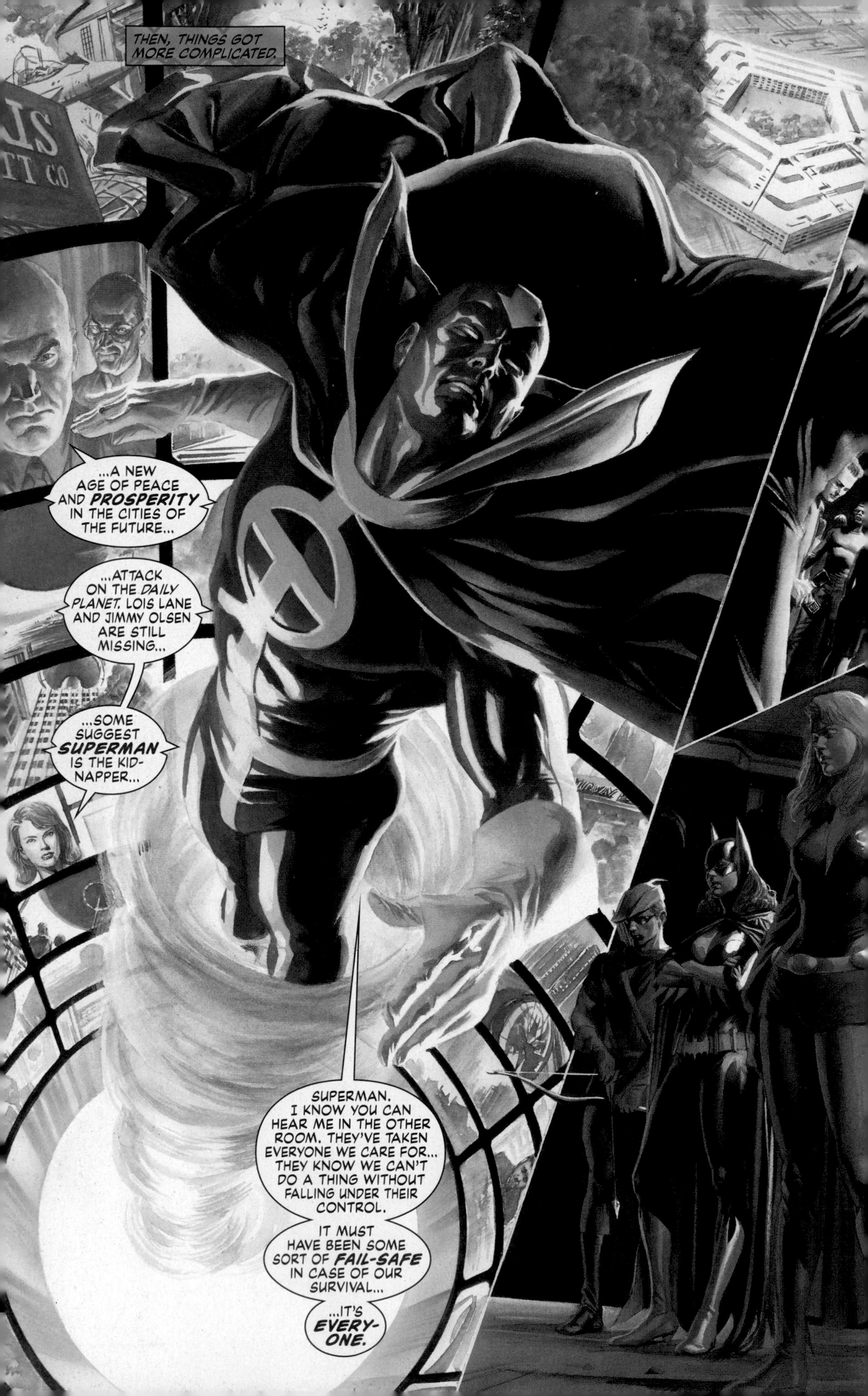
THEN, THINGS GOT MORE COMPLICATED.
...A NEW AGE OF PEACE AND PROSPERITY IN THE CITIES OF THE FUTURE...
...ATTACK ON THE DAILY PLANET. LOIS LANE AND JIMMY OLSEN ARE STILL MISSING...
...SOME SUGGEST SUPERMAN IS THE KID-NAPPER...
SUPERMAN. I KNOW YOU CAN HEAR ME IN THE OTHER ROOM. THEY'VE TAKEN EVERYONE WE CARE FOR... THEY KNOW WE CAN'T DO A THING WITHOUT FALLING UNDER THEIR CONTROL.
IT MUST HAVE BEEN SOME SORT OF FAIL-SAFE IN CASE OF OUR SURVIVAL...
...IT'S EVERY-ONE.

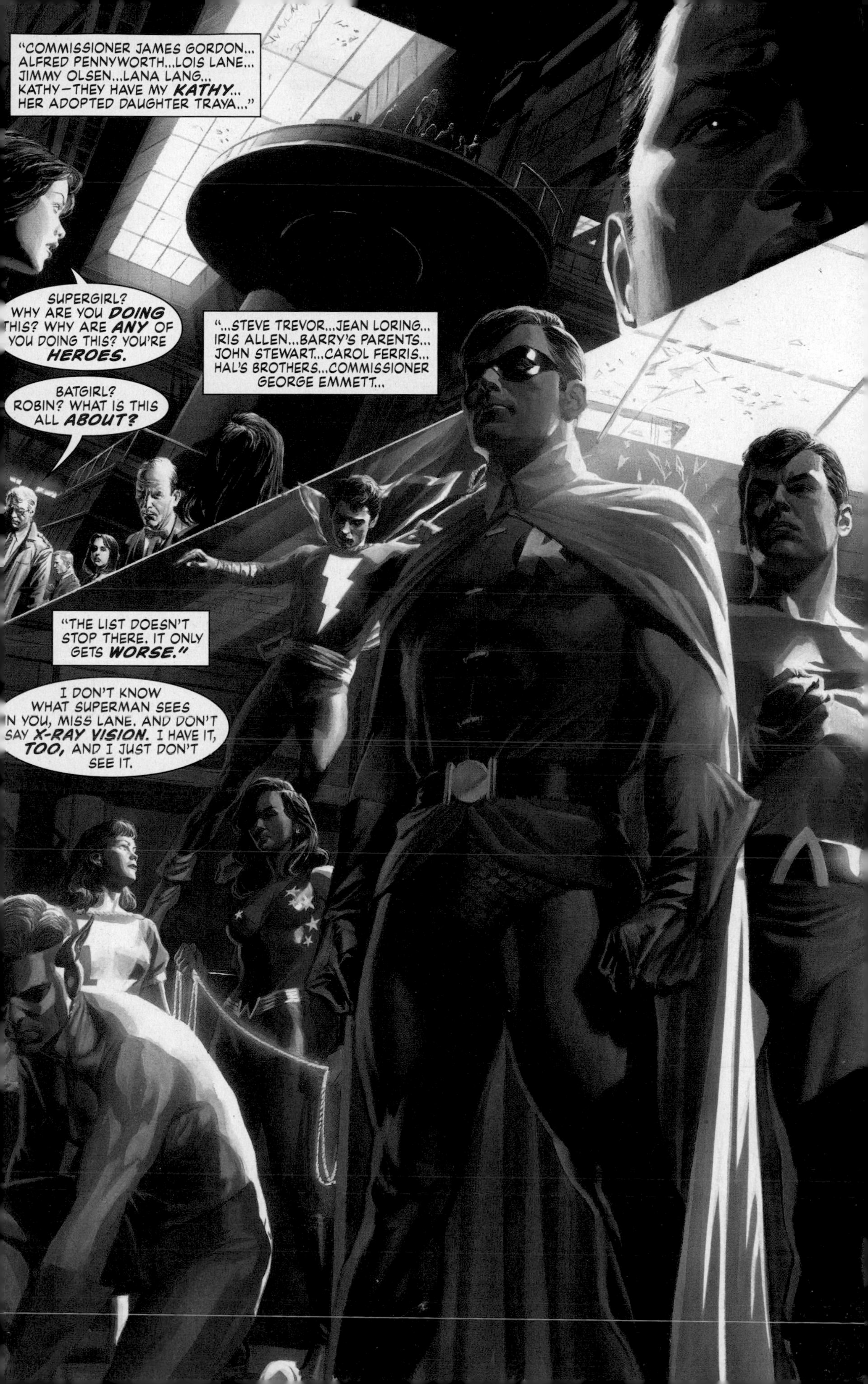
"COMMISSIONER JAMES GORDON... ALFRED PENNYWORTH...LOIS LANE... JIMMY OLSEN...LANA LANG... KATHY—THEY HAVE MY KATHY... HER ADOPTED DAUGHTER TRAYA..."
SUPERGIRL? WHY ARE YOU DOING THIS? WHY ARE ANY OF YOU DOING THIS? YOU'RE HEROES.
BATGIRL? ROBIN? WHAT IS THIS ALL ABOUT?
"...STEVE TREVOR...JEAN LORING... IRIS ALLEN...BARRY'S PARENTS... JOHN STEWART...CAROL FERRIS... HAL'S BROTHERS...COMMISSIONER GEORGE EMMETT...
"THE LIST DOESN'T STOP THERE. IT ONLY GETS WORSE."
I DON'T KNOW WHAT SUPERMAN SEES IN YOU, MISS LANE. AND DON'T SAY X-RAY VISION. I HAVE IT, TOO, AND I JUST DON'T SEE IT.

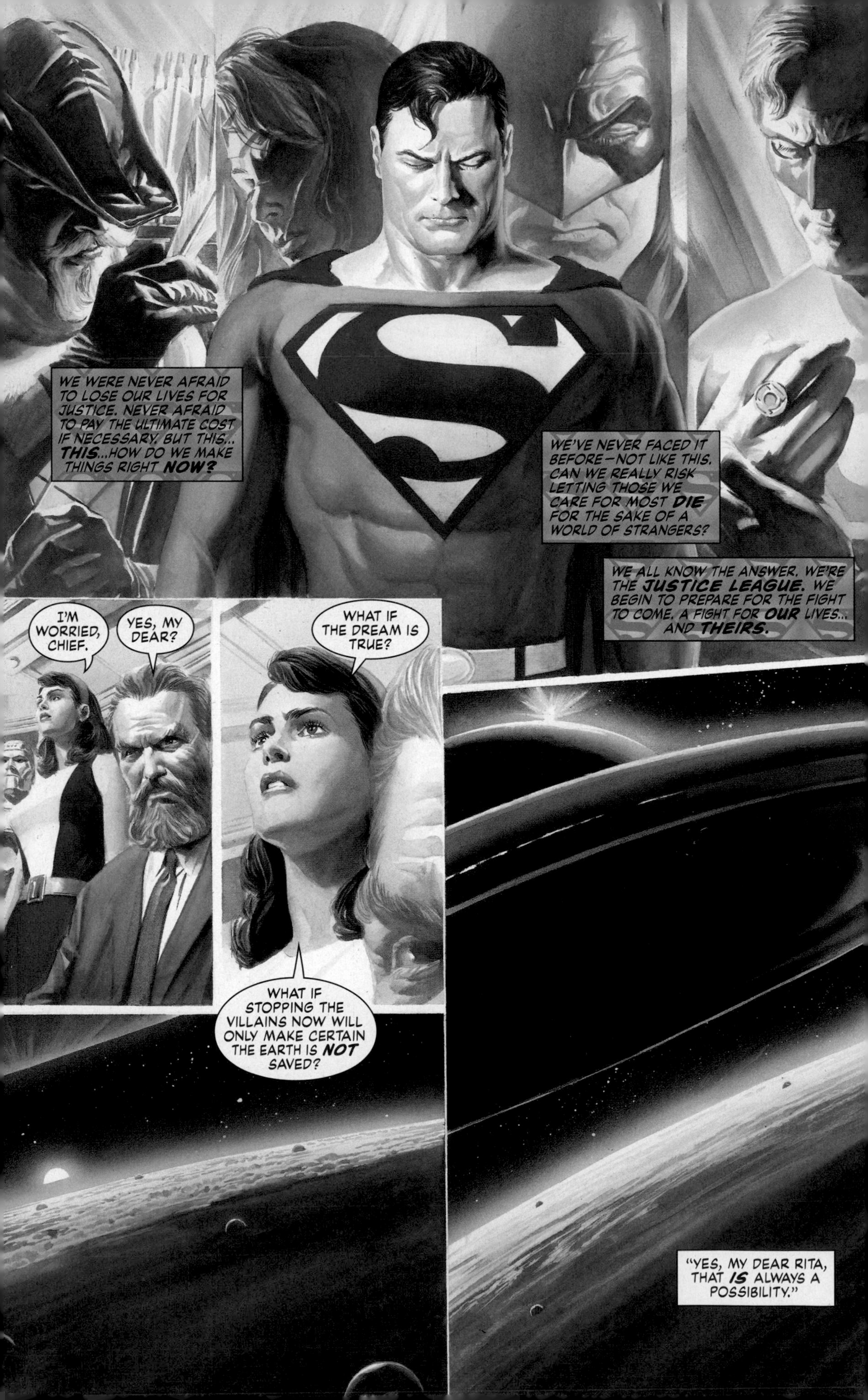
WE WERE NEVER AFRAID TO LOSE OUR LIVES FOR JUSTICE. NEVER AFRAID TO PAY THE ULTIMATE COST IF NECESSARY. BUT THIS... THIS...HOW DO WE MAKE THINGS RIGHT NOW?
WE'VE NEVER FACED IT BEFORE—NOT LIKE THIS. CAN WE REALLY RISK LETTING THOSE WE CARE FOR MOST DIE FOR THE SAKE OF A WORLD OF STRANGERS?
WE ALL KNOW THE ANSWER. WE'RE THE JUSTICE LEAGUE. WE BEGIN TO PREPARE FOR THE FIGHT TO COME. A FIGHT FOR OUR LIVES... AND THEIRS.
I'M WORRIED, CHIEF.
YES, MY DEAR?
WHAT IF THE DREAM IS TRUE?
WHAT IF STOPPING THE VILLAINS NOW WILL ONLY MAKE CERTAIN THE EARTH IS NOT SAVED?
"YES, MY DEAR RITA, THAT IS ALWAYS A POSSIBILITY."

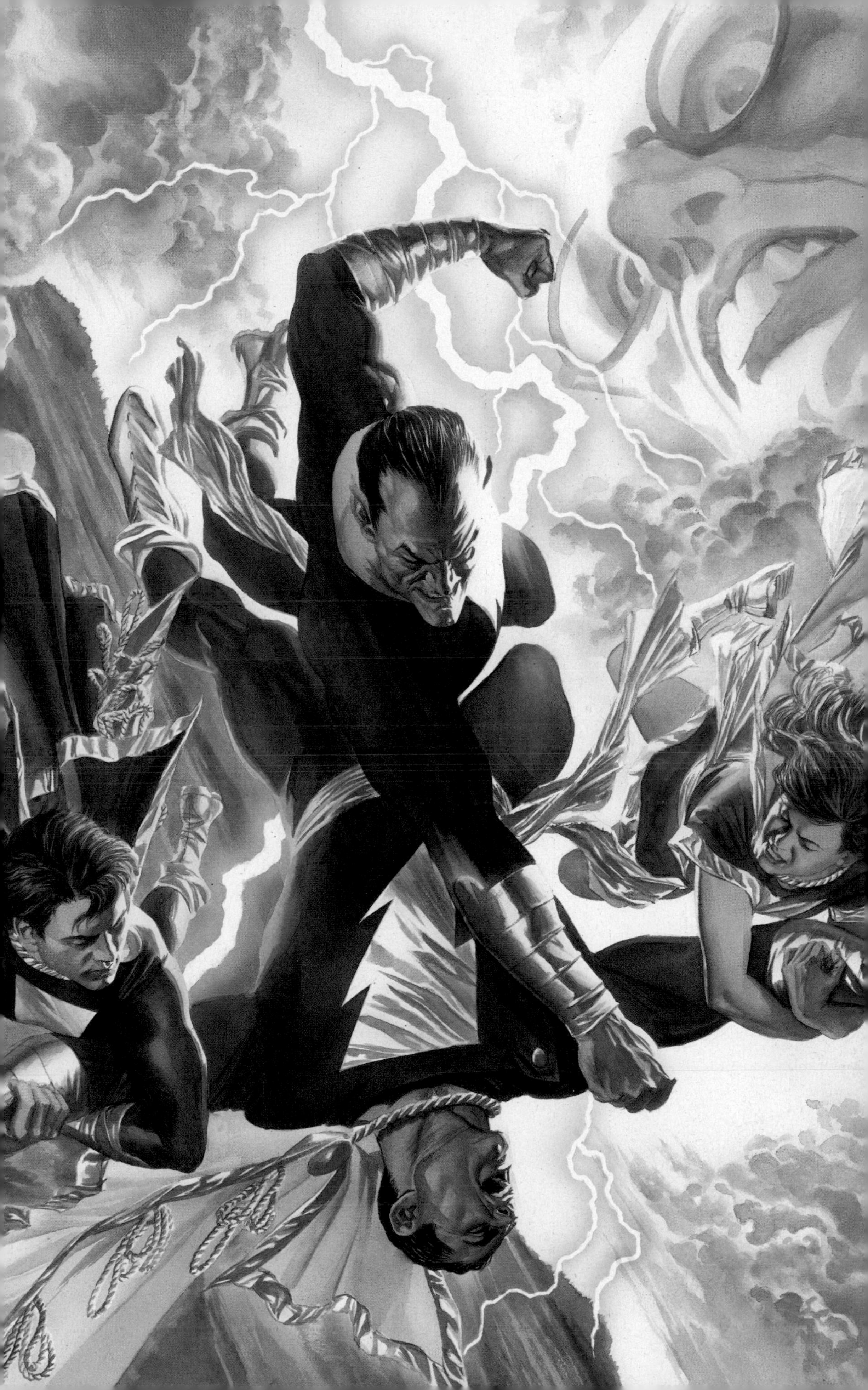

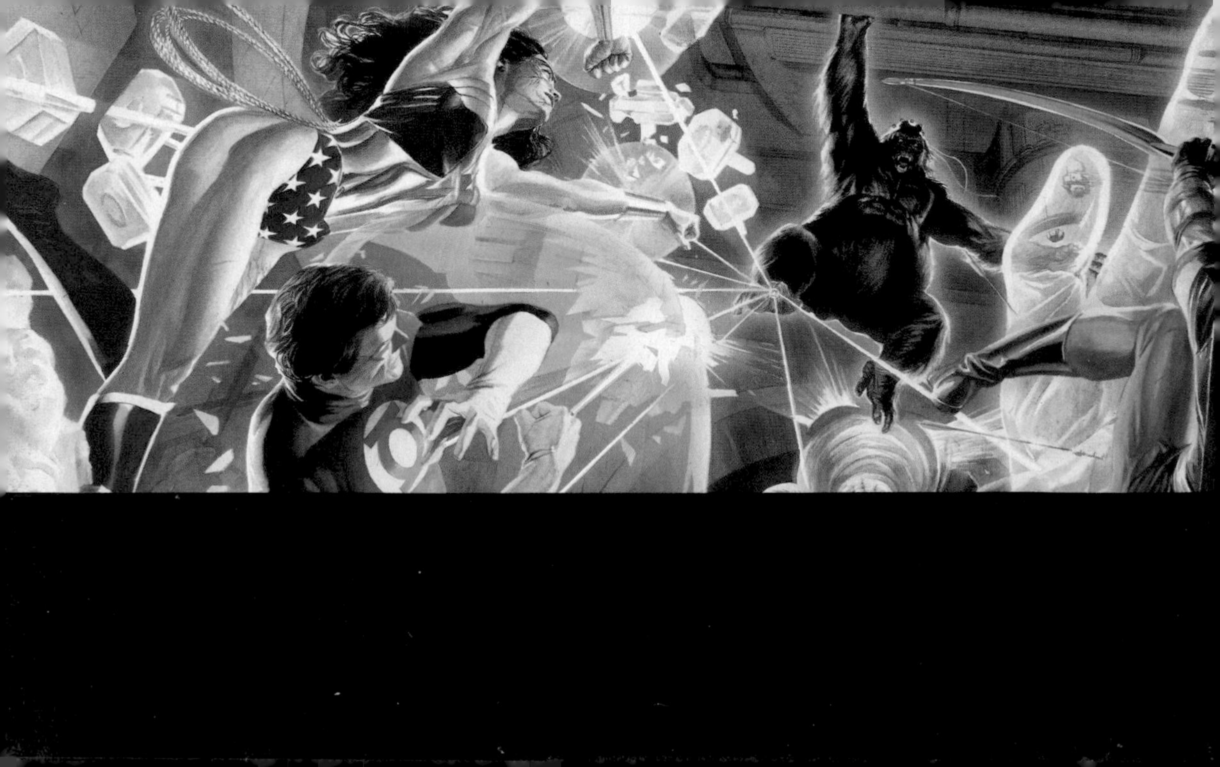

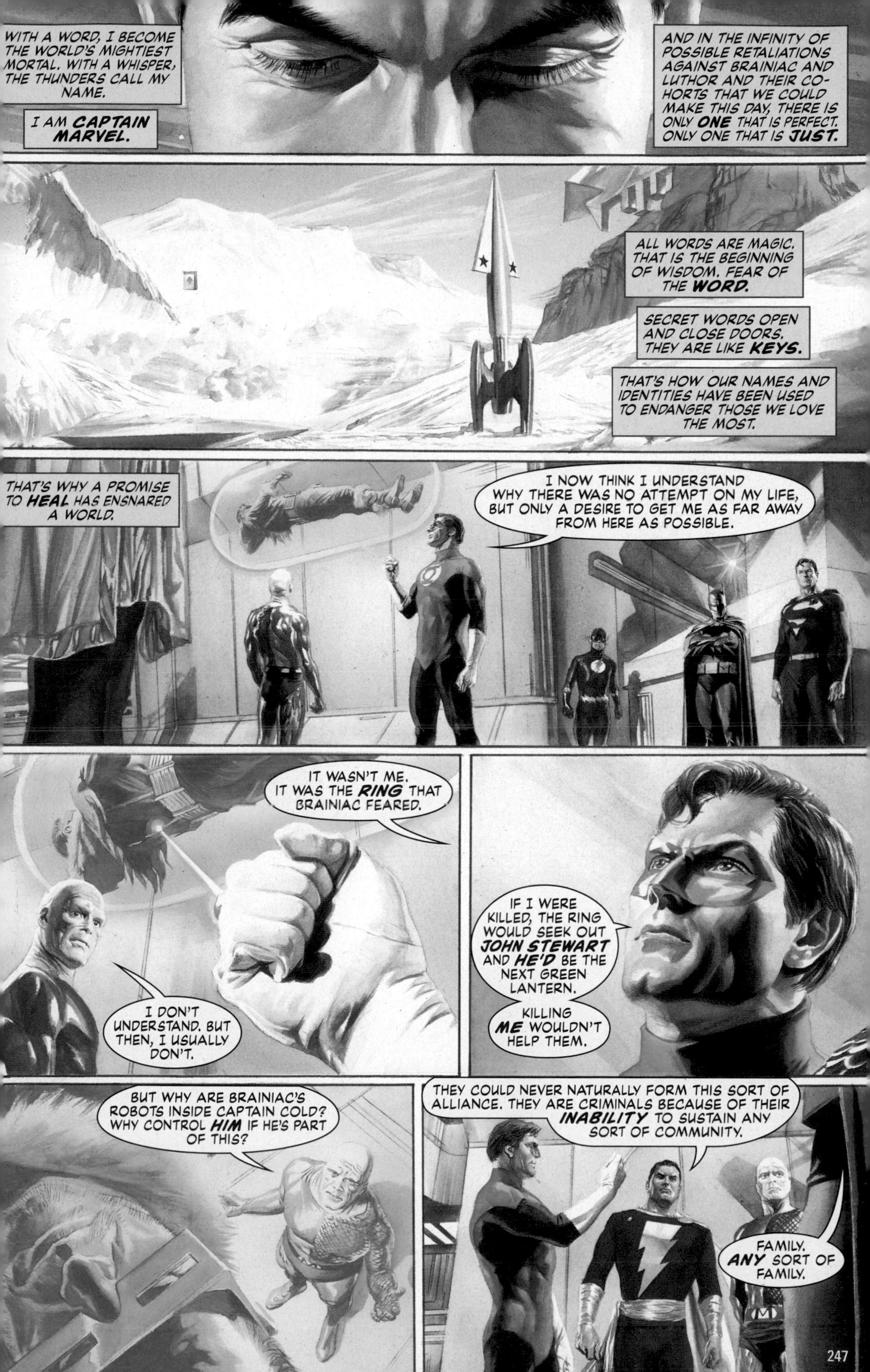

WITH A WORD, I BECOME THE WORLD'S MIGHTIEST MORTAL. WITH A WHISPER, THE THUNDERS CALL MY NAME.
I AM CAPTAIN MARVEL.
AND IN THE INFINITY OF POSSIBLE RETALIATIONS AGAINST BRAINIAC AND LUTHOR AND THEIR COHORTS THAT WE COULD MAKE THIS DAY, THERE IS ONLY ONE THAT IS PERFECT. ONLY ONE THAT IS JUST.
ALL WORDS ARE MAGIC. THAT IS THE BEGINNING OF WISDOM. FEAR OF THE WORD.
SECRET WORDS OPEN AND CLOSE DOORS. THEY ARE LIKE KEYS.
THAT'S HOW OUR NAMES AND IDENTITIES HAVE BEEN USED TO ENDANGER THOSE WE LOVE THE MOST.
THAT'S WHY A PROMISE TO HEAL HAS ENSNARED A WORLD.
I NOW THINK I UNDERSTAND WHY THERE WAS NO ATTEMPT ON MY LIFE, BUT ONLY A DESIRE TO GET ME AS FAR AWAY FROM HERE AS POSSIBLE.
IT WASN'T ME. IT WAS THE RING THAT BRAINIAC FEARED.
I DON'T UNDERSTAND. BUT THEN, I USUALLY DON'T.
IF I WERE KILLED, THE RING WOULD SEEK OUT JOHN STEWART AND HE'D BE THE NEXT GREEN LANTERN.
KILLING ME WOULDN'T HELP THEM.
BUT WHY ARE BRAINIAC'S ROBOTS INSIDE CAPTAIN COLD? WHY CONTROL HIM IF HE'S PART OF THIS?
THEY COULD NEVER NATURALLY FORM THIS SORT OF ALLIANCE. THEY ARE CRIMINALS BECAUSE OF THEIR INABILITY TO SUSTAIN ANY SORT OF COMMUNITY.
FAMILY. ANY SORT OF FAMILY.

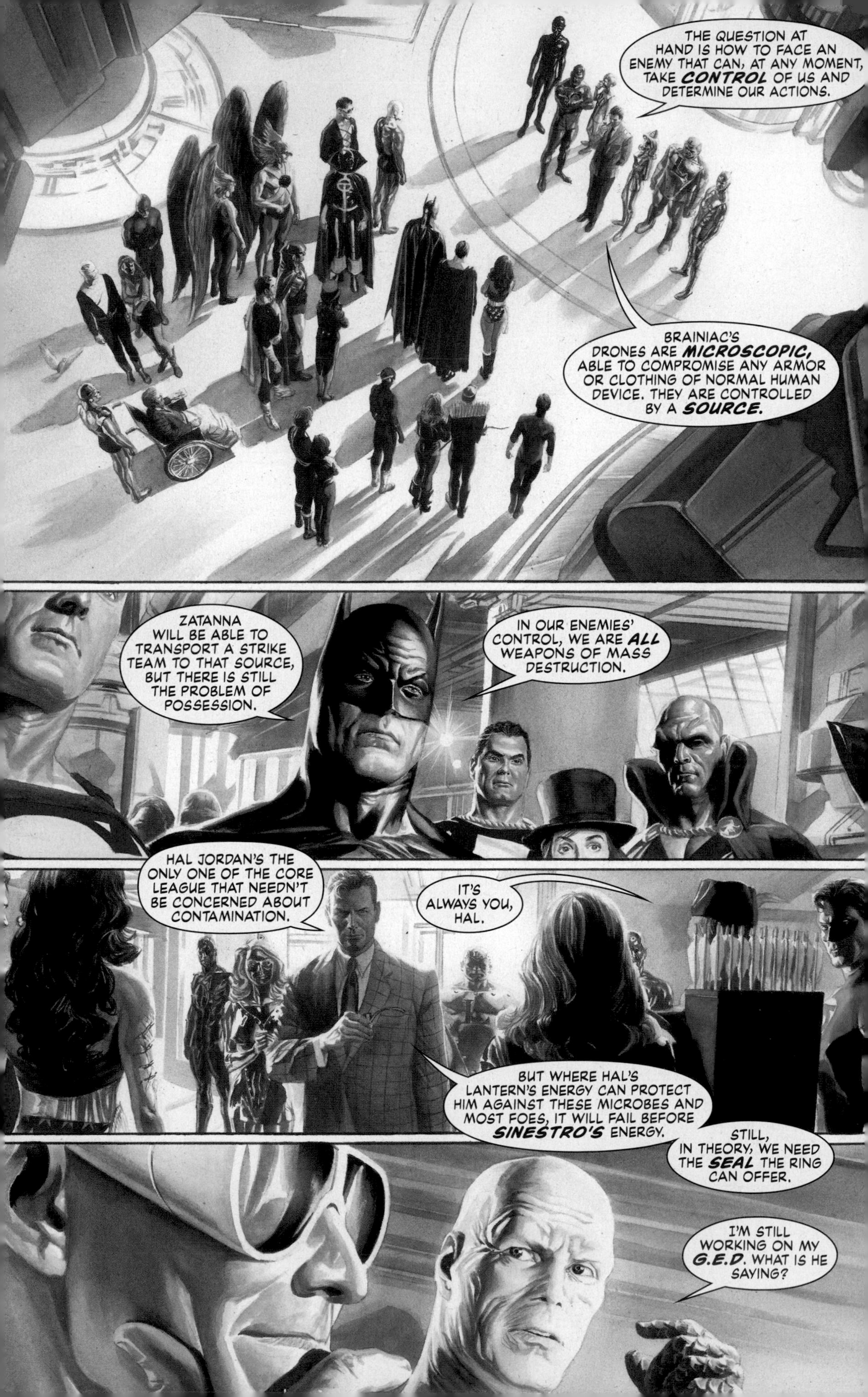
THE QUESTION AT HAND IS HOW TO FACE AN ENEMY THAT CAN, AT ANY MOMENT, TAKE CONTROL OF US AND DETERMINE OUR ACTIONS.
BRAINIAC'S DRONES ARE MICROSCOPIC, ABLE TO COMPROMISE ANY ARMOR OR CLOTHING OF NORMAL HUMAN DEVICE. THEY ARE CONTROLLED BY A SOURCE.
ZATANNA WILL BE ABLE TO TRANSPORT A STRIKE TEAM TO THAT SOURCE, BUT THERE IS STILL THE PROBLEM OF POSSESSION.
IN OUR ENEMIES' CONTROL, WE ARE ALL WEAPONS OF MASS DESTRUCTION.
HAL JORDAN'S THE ONLY ONE OF THE CORE LEAGUE THAT NEEDN'T BE CONCERNED ABOUT CONTAMINATION.
IT'S ALWAYS YOU, HAL.
BUT WHERE HAL'S LANTERN'S ENERGY CAN PROTECT HIM AGAINST THESE MICROBES AND MOST FOES, IT WILL FAIL BEFORE SINESTRO'S ENERGY.
STILL, IN THEORY, WE NEED THE SEAL THE RING CAN OFFER.
I'M STILL WORKING ON MY G.E.D. WHAT IS HE SAYING?

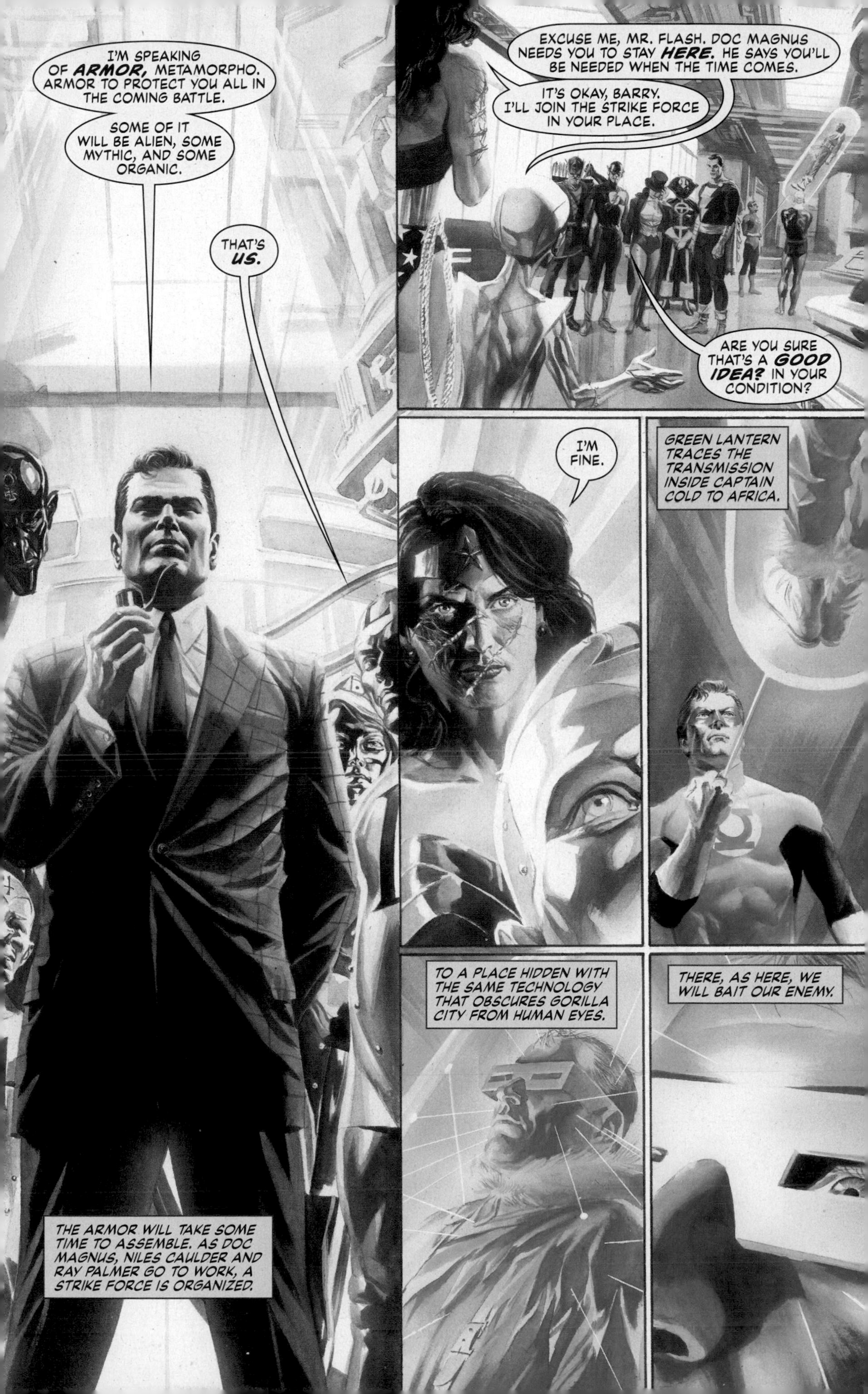
I'M SPEAKING OF **ARMOR,** METAMORPHO. ARMOR TO PROTECT YOU ALL IN THE COMING BATTLE.
SOME OF IT WILL BE ALIEN, SOME MYTHIC, AND SOME ORGANIC.
THAT'S **US.**
THE ARMOR WILL TAKE SOME TIME TO ASSEMBLE. AS DOC MAGNUS, NILES CAULDER AND RAY PALMER GO TO WORK, A STRIKE FORCE IS ORGANIZED.
EXCUSE ME, MR. FLASH. DOC MAGNUS NEEDS YOU TO STAY **HERE.** HE SAYS YOU'LL BE NEEDED WHEN THE TIME COMES.
IT'S OKAY, BARRY. I'LL JOIN THE STRIKE FORCE IN YOUR PLACE.
ARE YOU SURE THAT'S A **GOOD IDEA?** IN YOUR CONDITION?
I'M FINE.
GREEN LANTERN TRACES THE TRANSMISSION INSIDE CAPTAIN COLD TO AFRICA.
TO A PLACE HIDDEN WITH THE SAME TECHNOLOGY THAT OBSCURES GORILLA CITY FROM HUMAN EYES.
THERE, AS HERE, WE WILL BAIT OUR ENEMY.

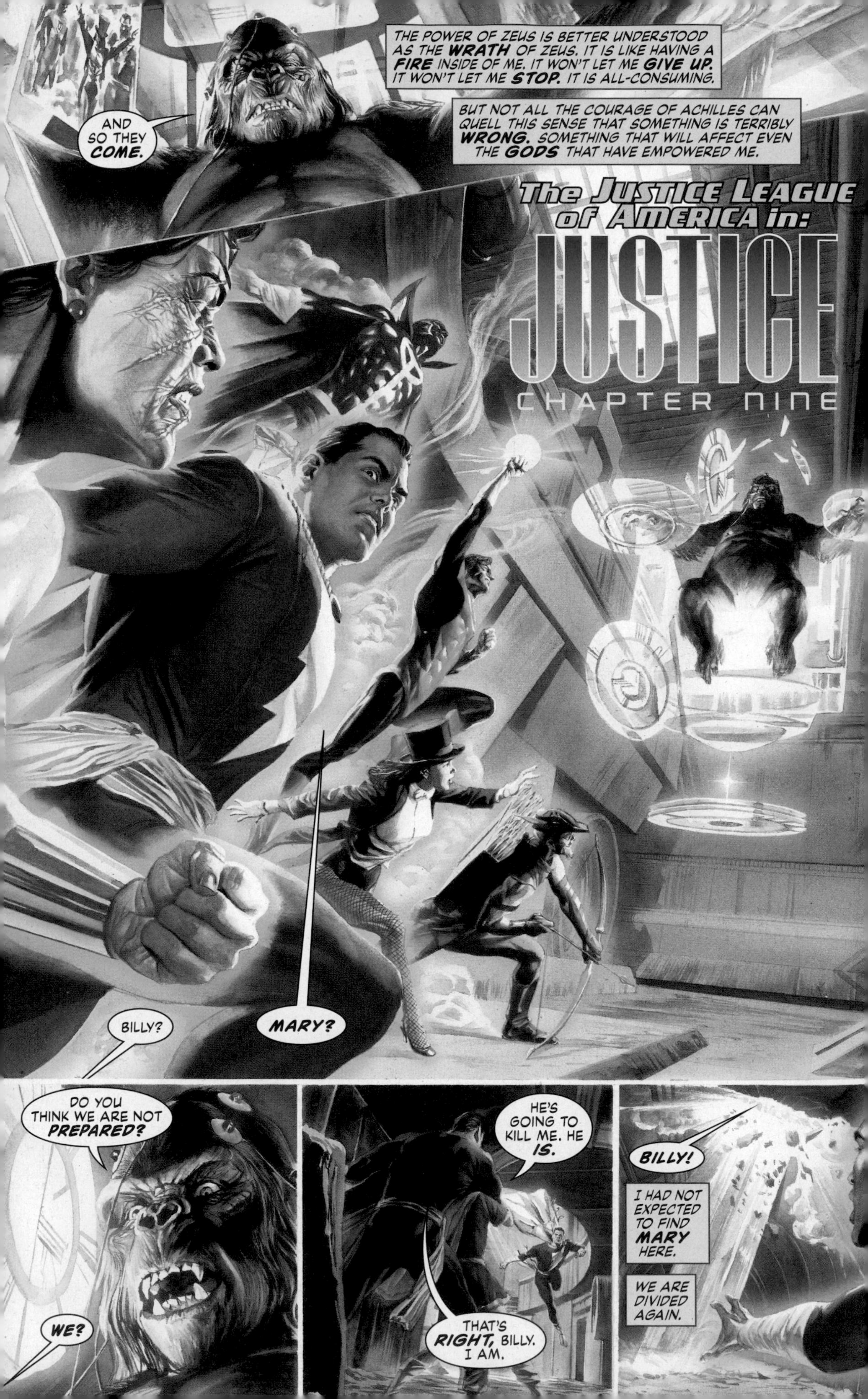
THE POWER OF ZEUS IS BETTER UNDERSTOOD AS THE WRATH OF ZEUS. IT IS LIKE HAVING A FIRE INSIDE OF ME. IT WON'T LET ME GIVE UP. IT WON'T LET ME STOP. IT IS ALL-CONSUMING.
AND SO THEY COME.
BUT NOT ALL THE COURAGE OF ACHILLES CAN QUELL THIS SENSE THAT SOMETHING IS TERRIBLY WRONG. SOMETHING THAT WILL AFFECT EVEN THE GODS THAT HAVE EMPOWERED ME.
The JUSTICE LEAGUE of AMERICA in:
JUSTICE
CHAPTER NINE
BILLY?
MARY?
DO YOU THINK WE ARE NOT PREPARED?
WE?
HE'S GOING TO KILL ME. HE IS.
THAT'S RIGHT, BILLY. I AM.
BILLY!
I HAD NOT EXPECTED TO FIND MARY HERE.
WE ARE DIVIDED AGAIN.

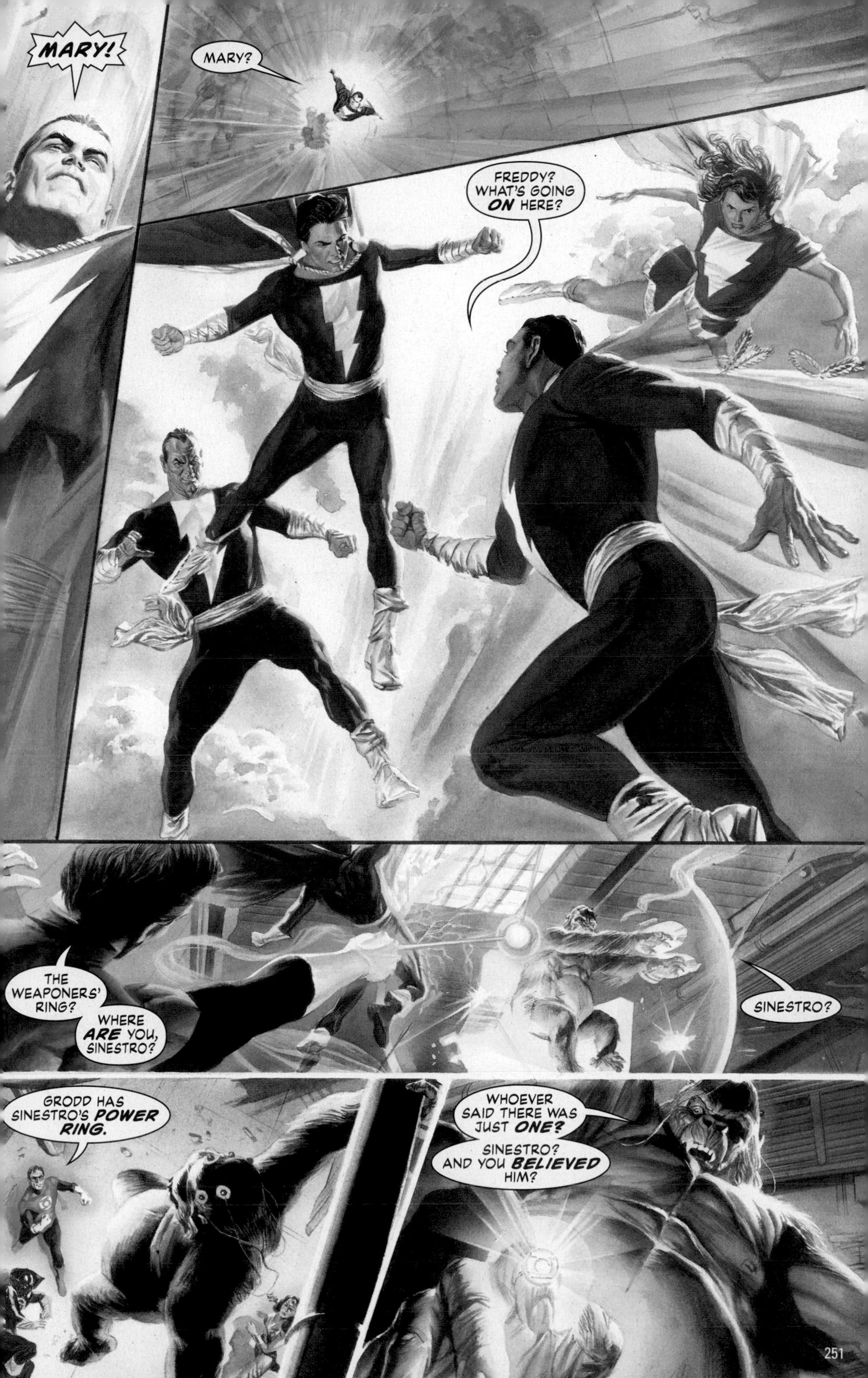
MARY!
MARY?
FREDDY? WHAT'S GOING ON HERE?
THE WEAPONERS' RING?
WHERE ARE YOU, SINESTRO?
SINESTRO?
GRODD HAS SINESTRO'S POWER RING.
WHOEVER SAID THERE WAS JUST ONE?
SINESTRO? AND YOU BELIEVED HIM?

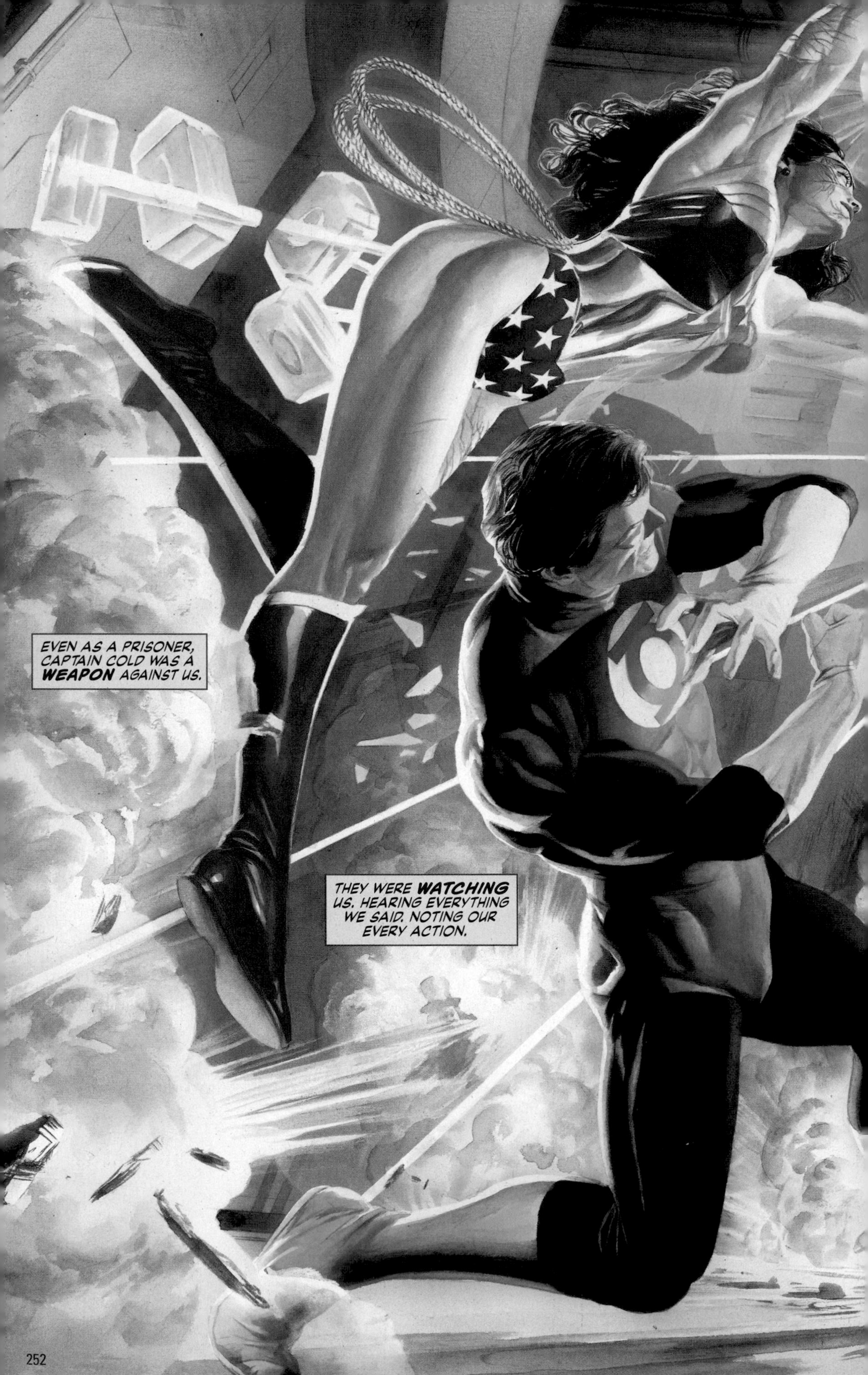
EVEN AS A PRISONER, CAPTAIN COLD WAS A **WEAPON** AGAINST US.
THEY WERE **WATCHING** US. HEARING EVERYTHING WE SAID. NOTING OUR EVERY ACTION.

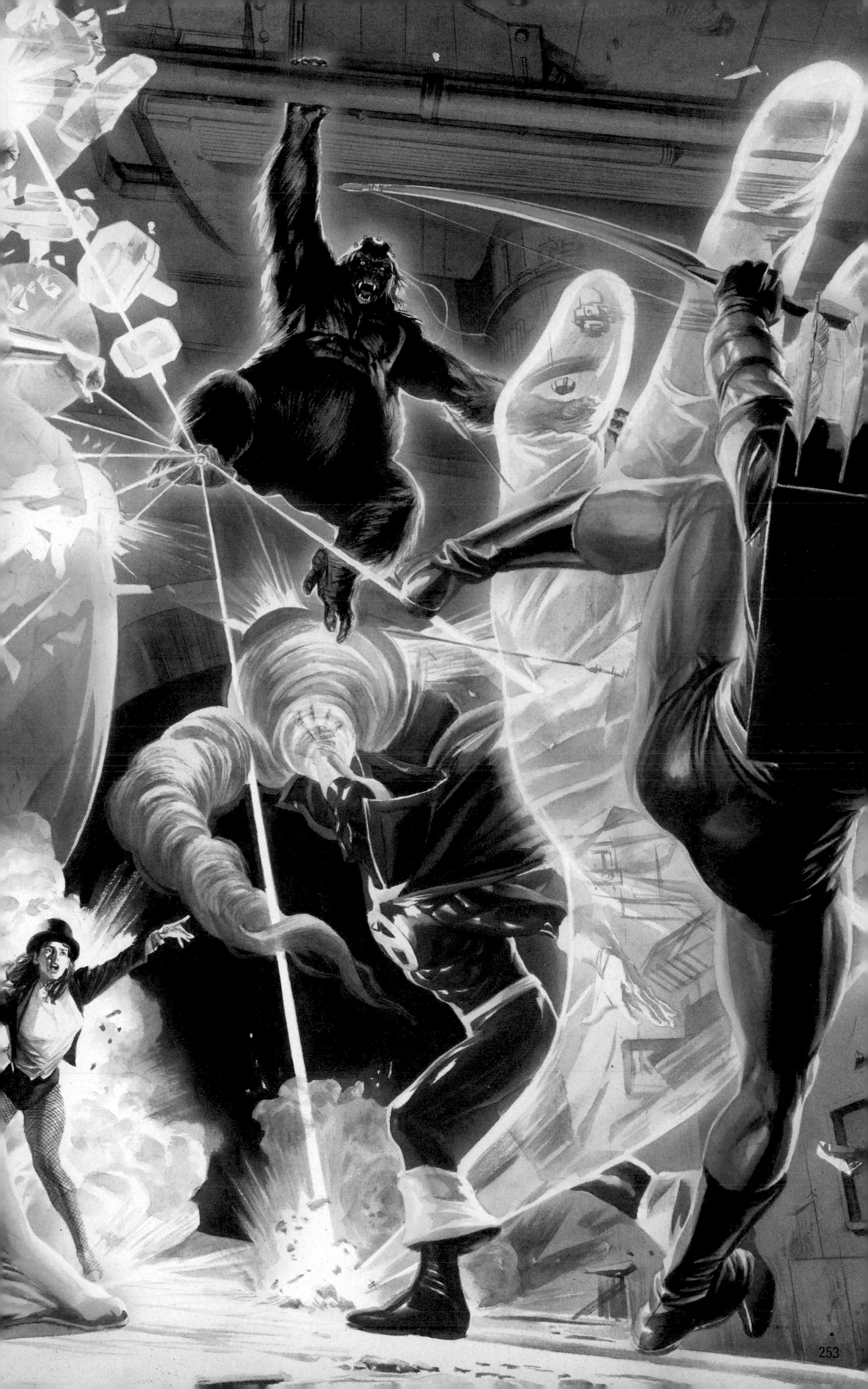

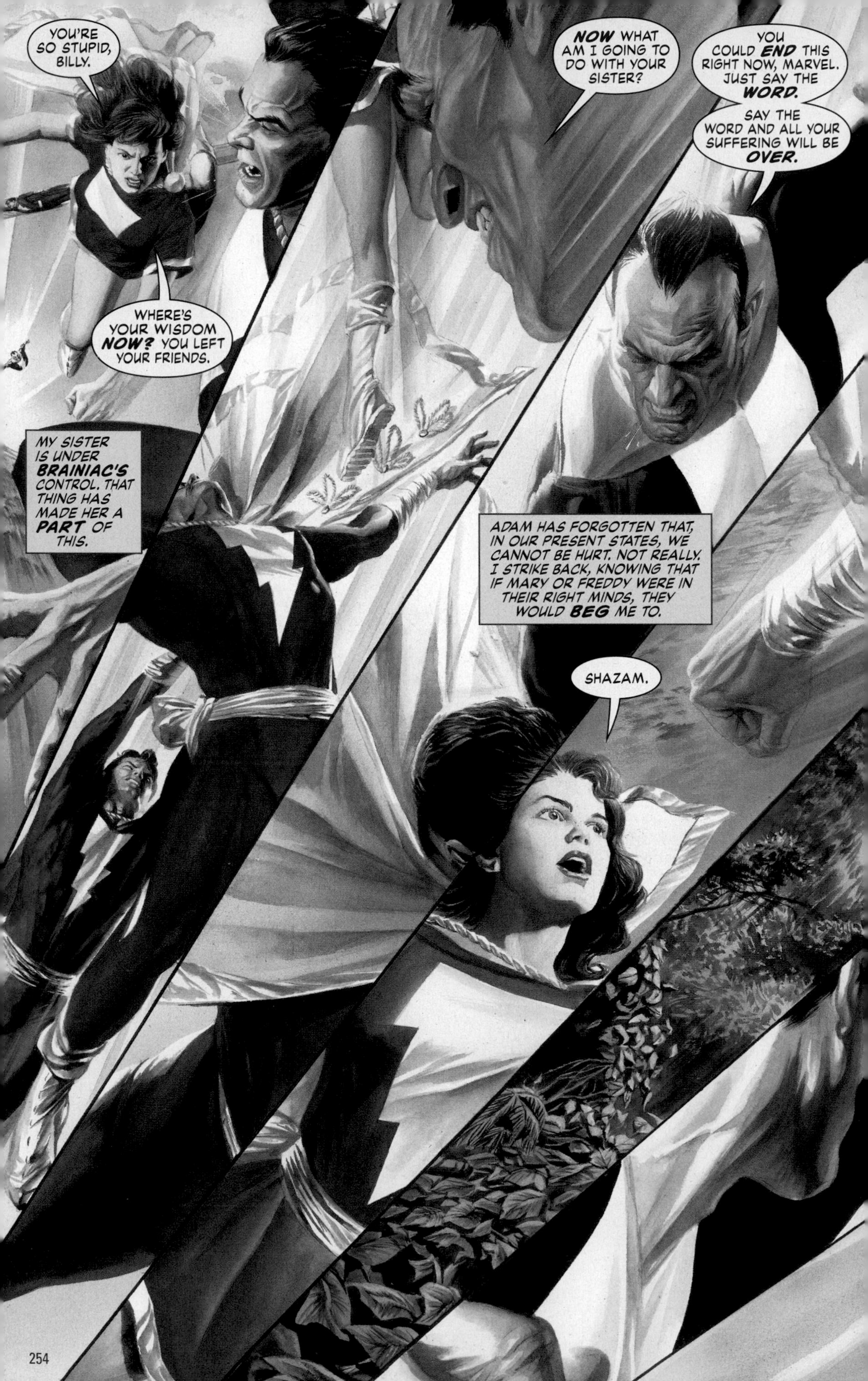

YOU'RE SO STUPID, BILLY.
WHERE'S YOUR WISDOM **NOW?** YOU LEFT YOUR FRIENDS.
MY SISTER IS UNDER **BRAINIAC'S** CONTROL. THAT THING HAS MADE HER A **PART** OF THIS.
NOW WHAT AM I GOING TO DO WITH YOUR SISTER?
YOU COULD **END** THIS RIGHT NOW, MARVEL. JUST SAY THE **WORD.**
SAY THE WORD AND ALL YOUR SUFFERING WILL BE **OVER.**
ADAM HAS FORGOTTEN THAT, IN OUR PRESENT STATES, WE CANNOT BE HURT. NOT REALLY. I STRIKE BACK, KNOWING THAT IF MARY OR FREDDY WERE IN THEIR RIGHT MINDS, THEY WOULD **BEG** ME TO.
SHAZAM.

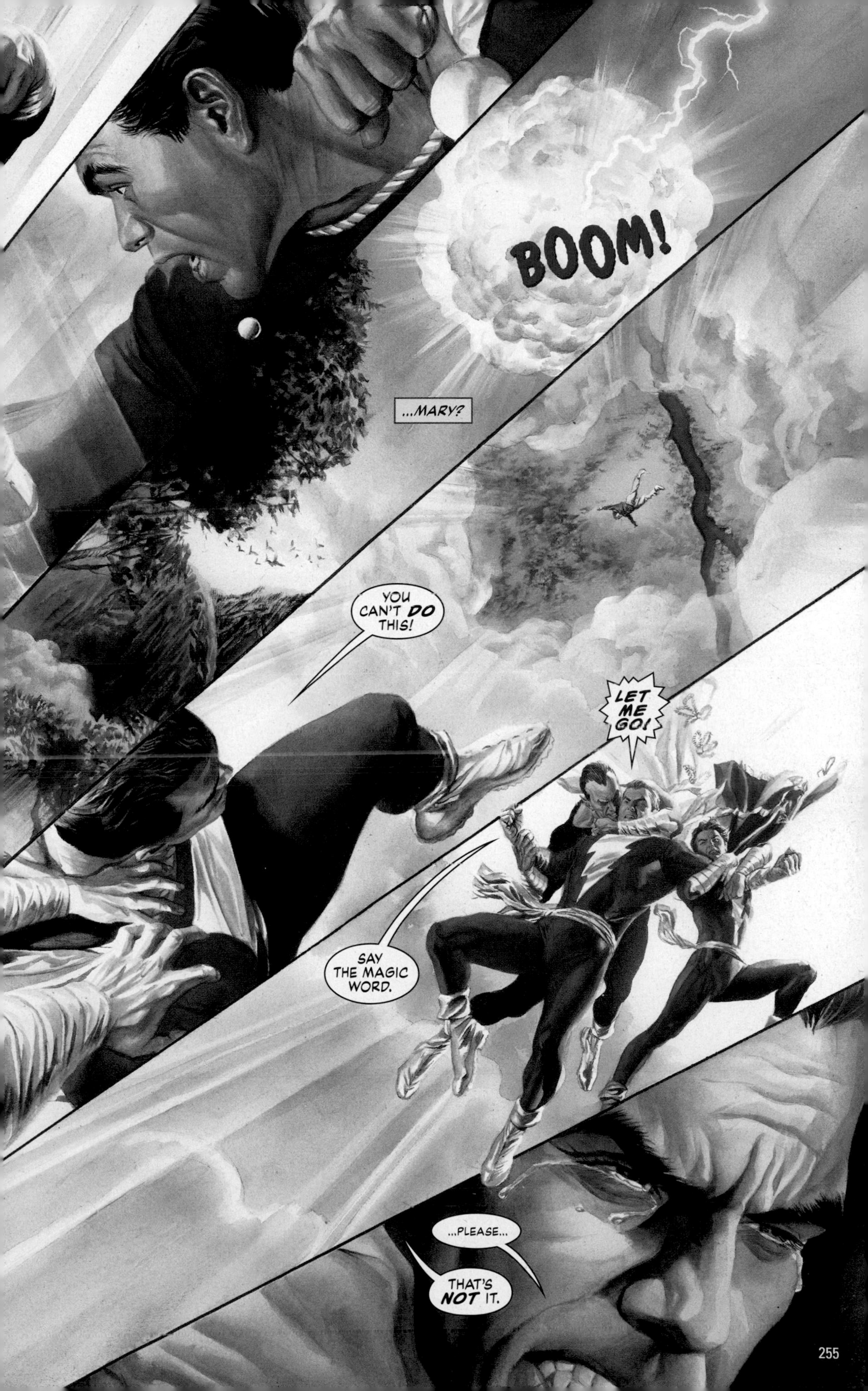
BOOM!
...MARY?
YOU CAN'T DO THIS!
LET ME GO!
SAY THE MAGIC WORD.
...PLEASE...
THAT'S NOT IT.

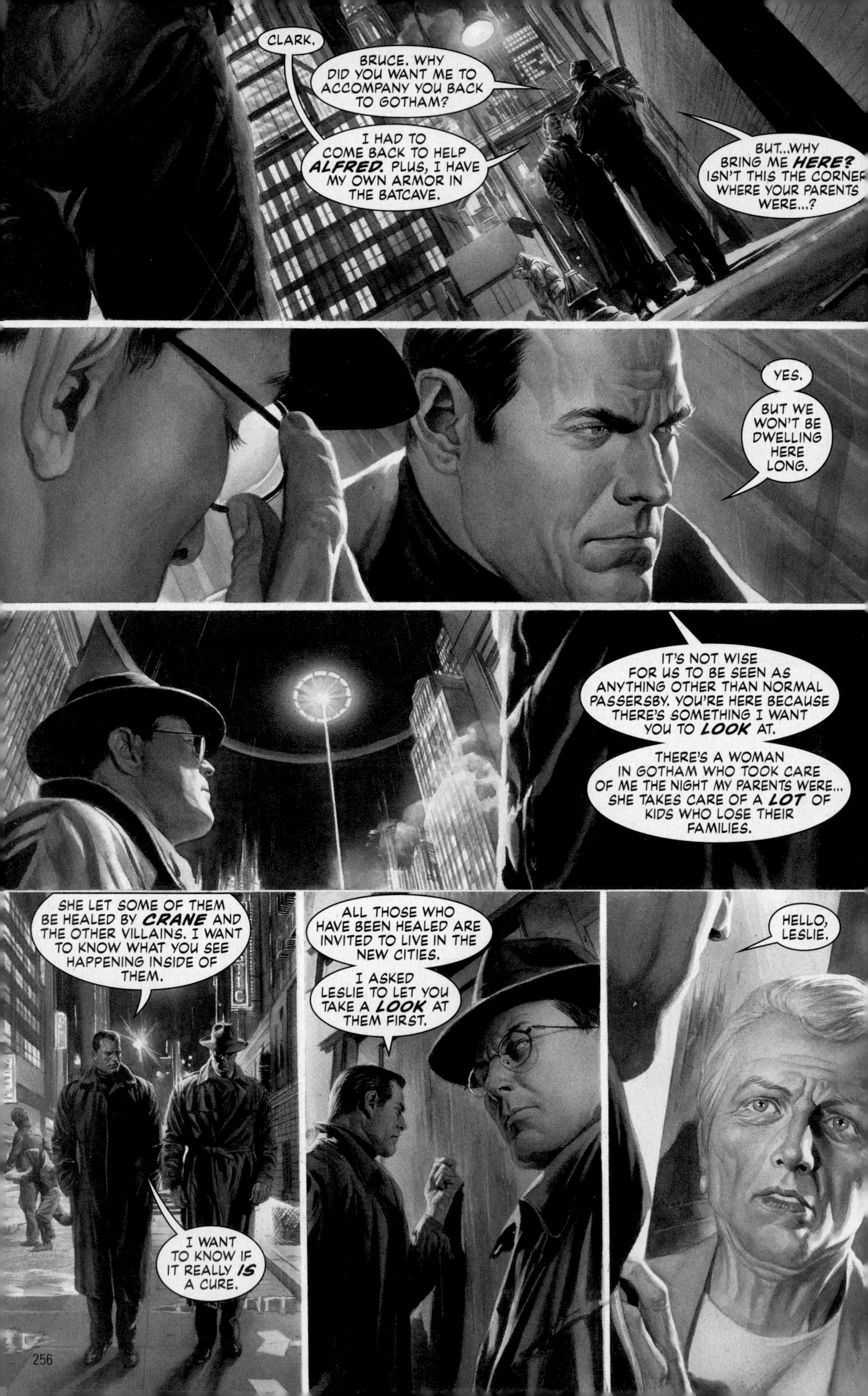
CLARK.
BRUCE. WHY DID YOU WANT ME TO ACCOMPANY YOU BACK TO GOTHAM?
I HAD TO COME BACK TO HELP ALFRED. PLUS, I HAVE MY OWN ARMOR IN THE BATCAVE.
BUT...WHY BRING ME HERE? ISN'T THIS THE CORNER WHERE YOUR PARENTS WERE...?
YES.
BUT WE WON'T BE DWELLING HERE LONG.
IT'S NOT WISE FOR US TO BE SEEN AS ANYTHING OTHER THAN NORMAL PASSERSBY. YOU'RE HERE BECAUSE THERE'S SOMETHING I WANT YOU TO LOOK AT.
THERE'S A WOMAN IN GOTHAM WHO TOOK CARE OF ME THE NIGHT MY PARENTS WERE... SHE TAKES CARE OF A LOT OF KIDS WHO LOSE THEIR FAMILIES.
SHE LET SOME OF THEM BE HEALED BY CRANE AND THE OTHER VILLAINS. I WANT TO KNOW WHAT YOU SEE HAPPENING INSIDE OF THEM.
I WANT TO KNOW IF IT REALLY IS A CURE.
ALL THOSE WHO HAVE BEEN HEALED ARE INVITED TO LIVE IN THE NEW CITIES.
I ASKED LESLIE TO LET YOU TAKE A LOOK AT THEM FIRST.
HELLO, LESLIE.

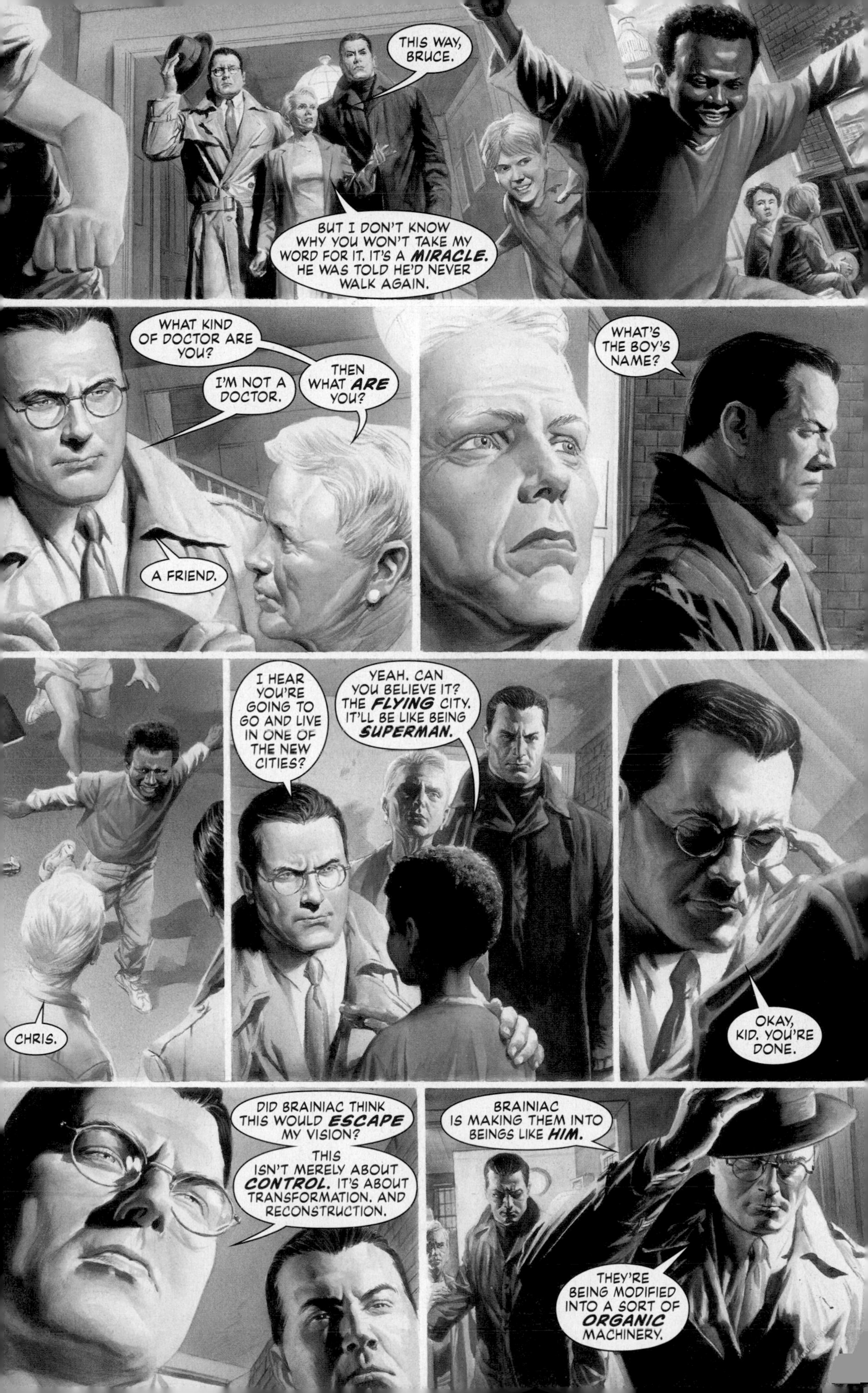
THIS WAY, BRUCE.
BUT I DON'T KNOW WHY YOU WON'T TAKE MY WORD FOR IT. IT'S A MIRACLE. HE WAS TOLD HE'D NEVER WALK AGAIN.
WHAT KIND OF DOCTOR ARE YOU?
I'M NOT A DOCTOR.
THEN WHAT ARE YOU?
A FRIEND.
WHAT'S THE BOY'S NAME?
CHRIS.
I HEAR YOU'RE GOING TO GO AND LIVE IN ONE OF THE NEW CITIES?
YEAH. CAN YOU BELIEVE IT? THE FLYING CITY. IT'LL BE LIKE BEING SUPERMAN.
OKAY, KID. YOU'RE DONE.
DID BRAINIAC THINK THIS WOULD ESCAPE MY VISION?
THIS ISN'T MERELY ABOUT CONTROL. IT'S ABOUT TRANSFORMATION. AND RECONSTRUCTION.
BRAINIAC IS MAKING THEM INTO BEINGS LIKE HIM.
THEY'RE BEING MODIFIED INTO A SORT OF ORGANIC MACHINERY.

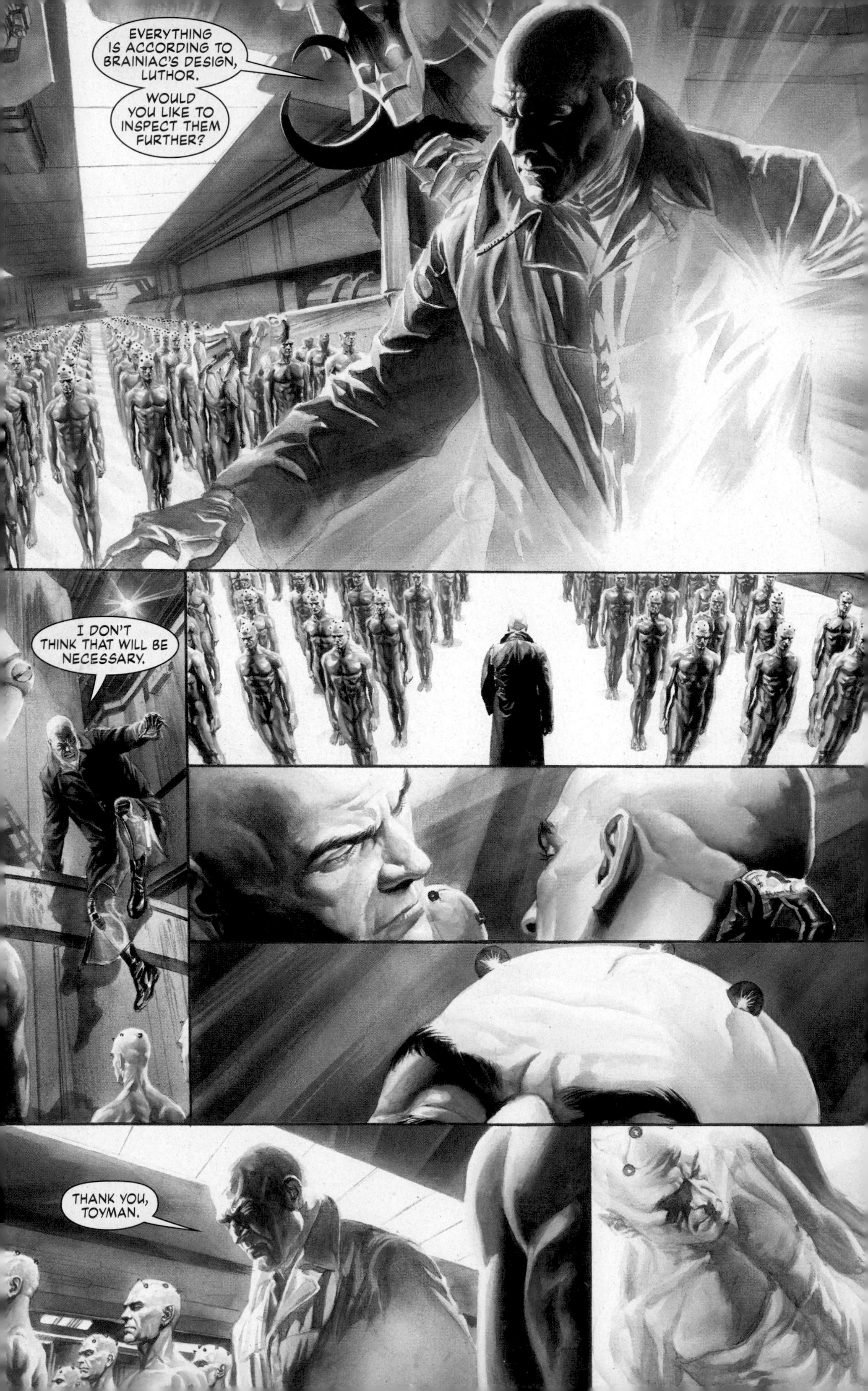
EVERYTHING IS ACCORDING TO BRAINIAC'S DESIGN, LUTHOR.
WOULD YOU LIKE TO INSPECT THEM FURTHER?
I DON'T THINK THAT WILL BE NECESSARY.
THANK YOU, TOYMAN.

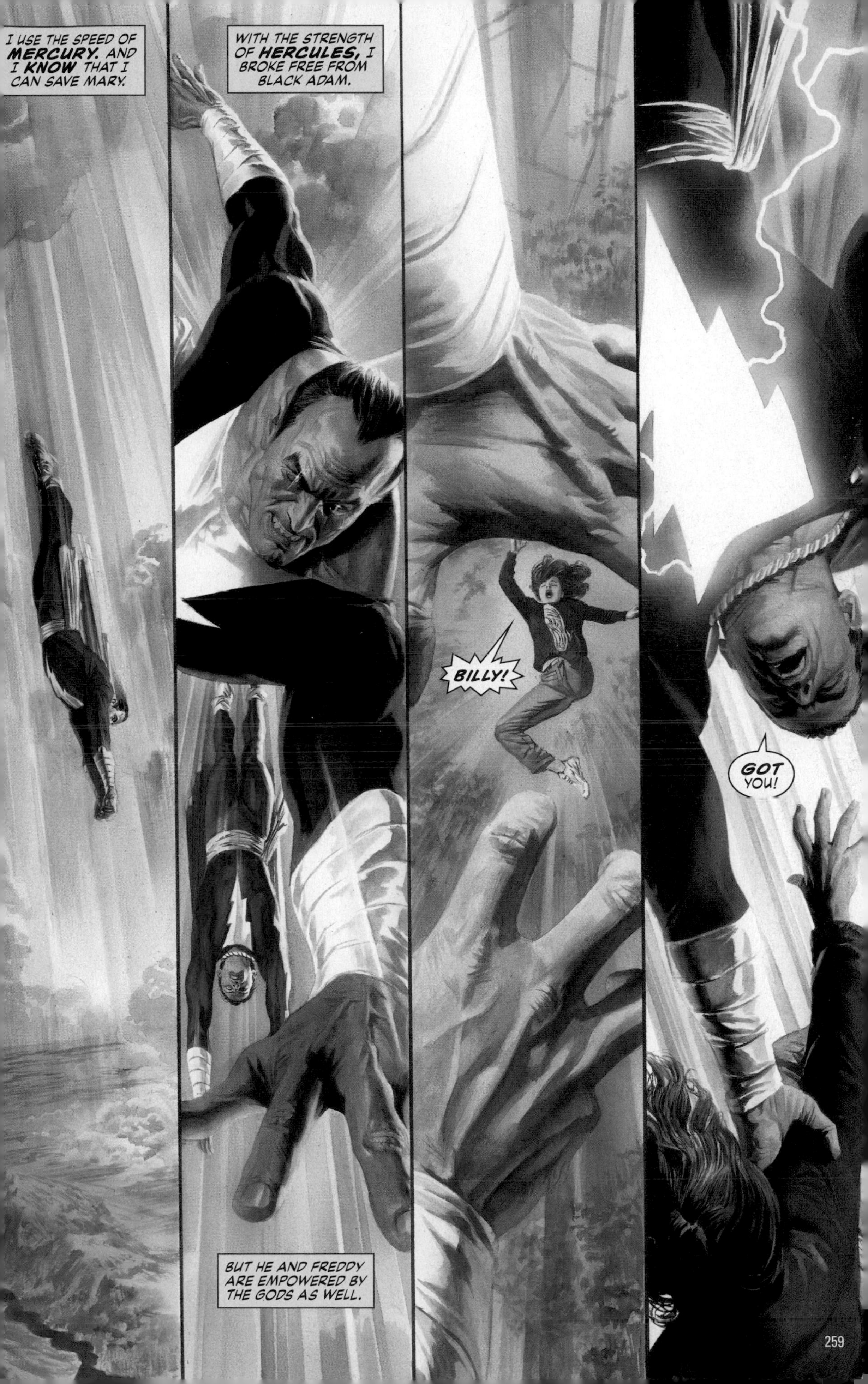

I USE THE SPEED OF MERCURY. AND I KNOW THAT I CAN SAVE MARY.
WITH THE STRENGTH OF HERCULES, I BROKE FREE FROM BLACK ADAM.
BUT HE AND FREDDY ARE EMPOWERED BY THE GODS AS WELL.
BILLY!
GOT YOU!

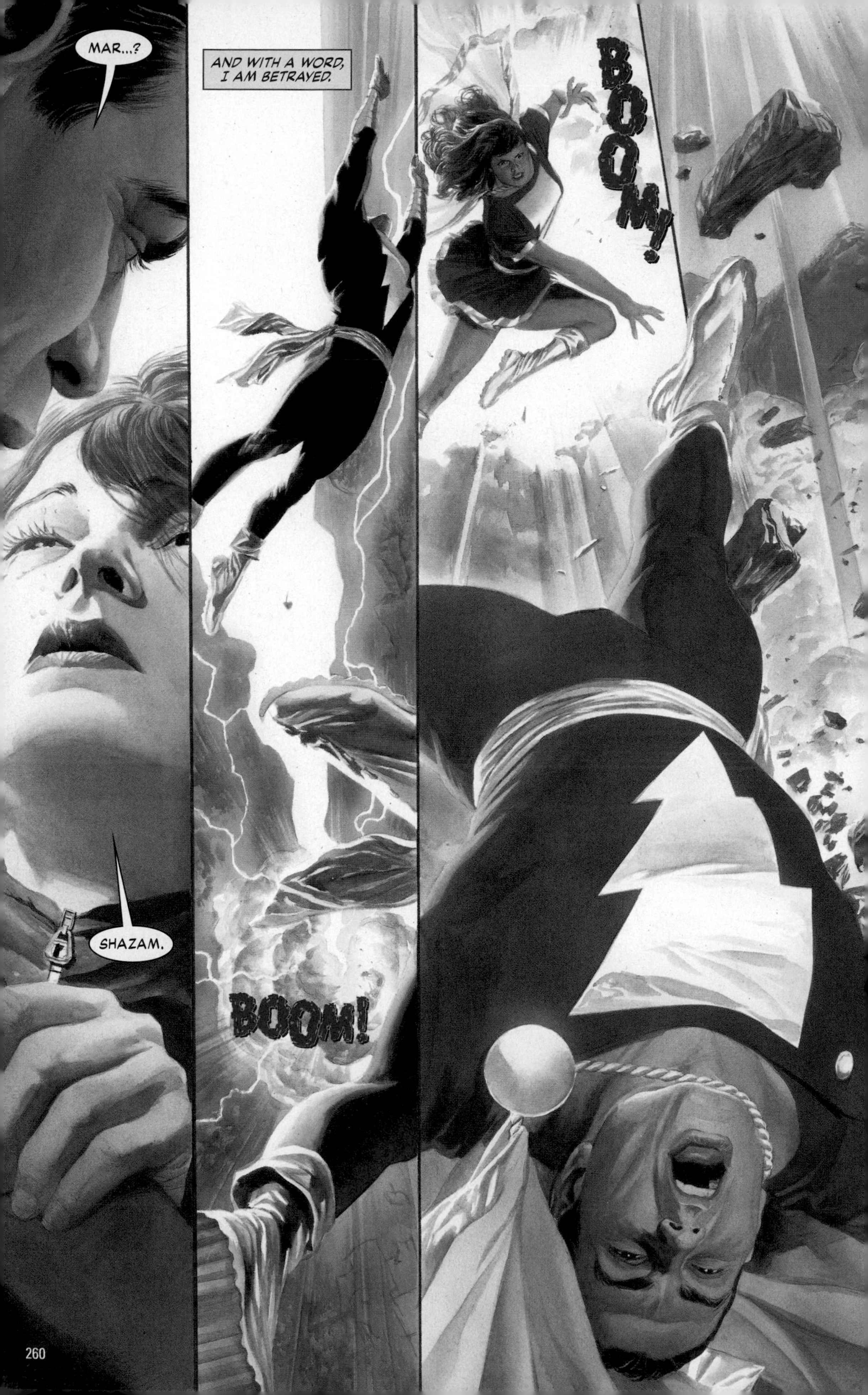
MAR...?
SHAZAM.
AND WITH A WORD, I AM BETRAYED.
BOOM!
BOOM!

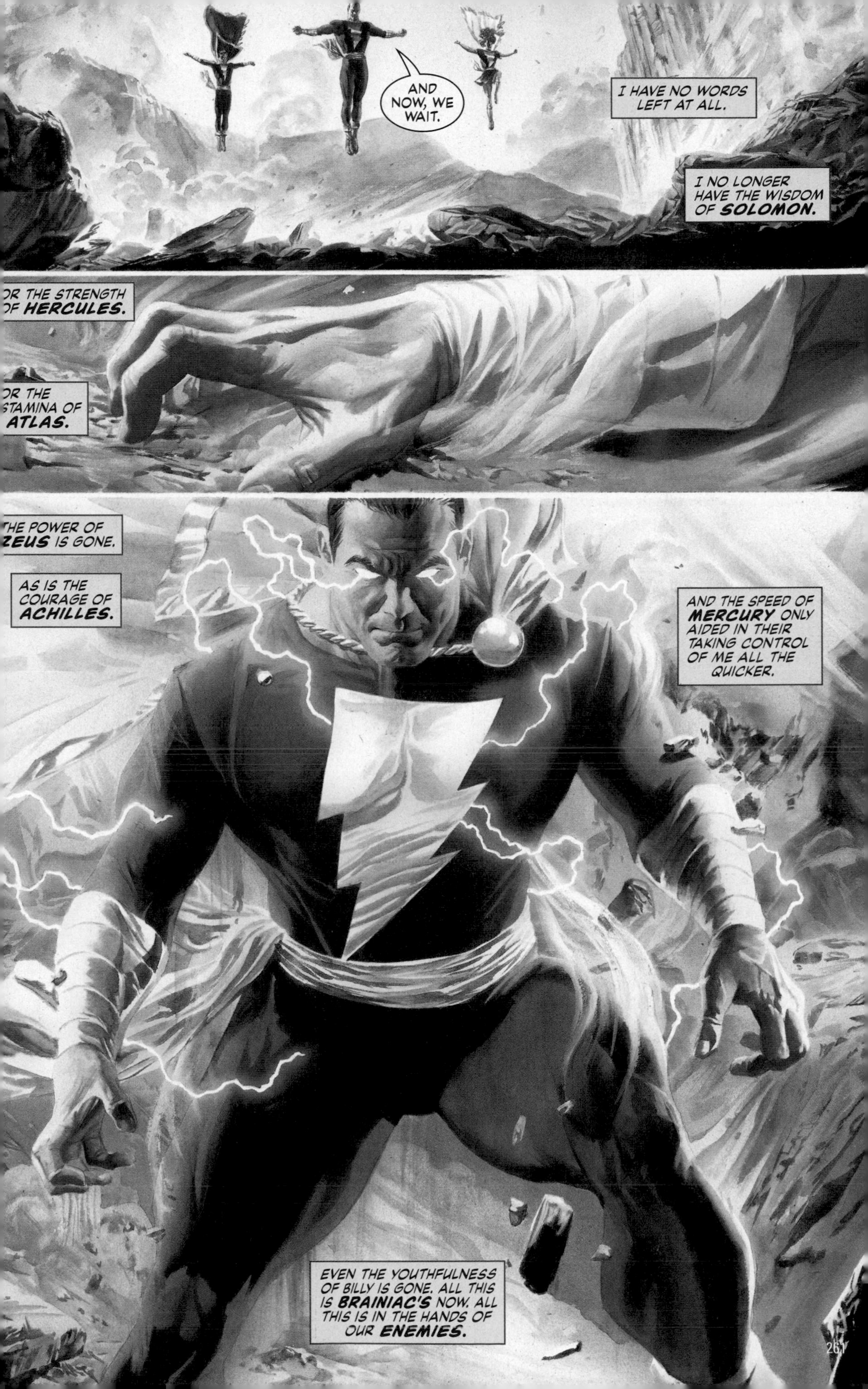
AND NOW, WE WAIT.
I HAVE NO WORDS LEFT AT ALL.
I NO LONGER HAVE THE WISDOM OF SOLOMON.
OR THE STRENGTH OF HERCULES.
OR THE STAMINA OF ATLAS.
THE POWER OF ZEUS IS GONE.
AS IS THE COURAGE OF ACHILLES.
AND THE SPEED OF MERCURY ONLY AIDED IN THEIR TAKING CONTROL OF ME ALL THE QUICKER.
EVEN THE YOUTHFULNESS OF BILLY IS GONE. ALL THIS IS BRAINIAC'S NOW. ALL THIS IS IN THE HANDS OF OUR ENEMIES.

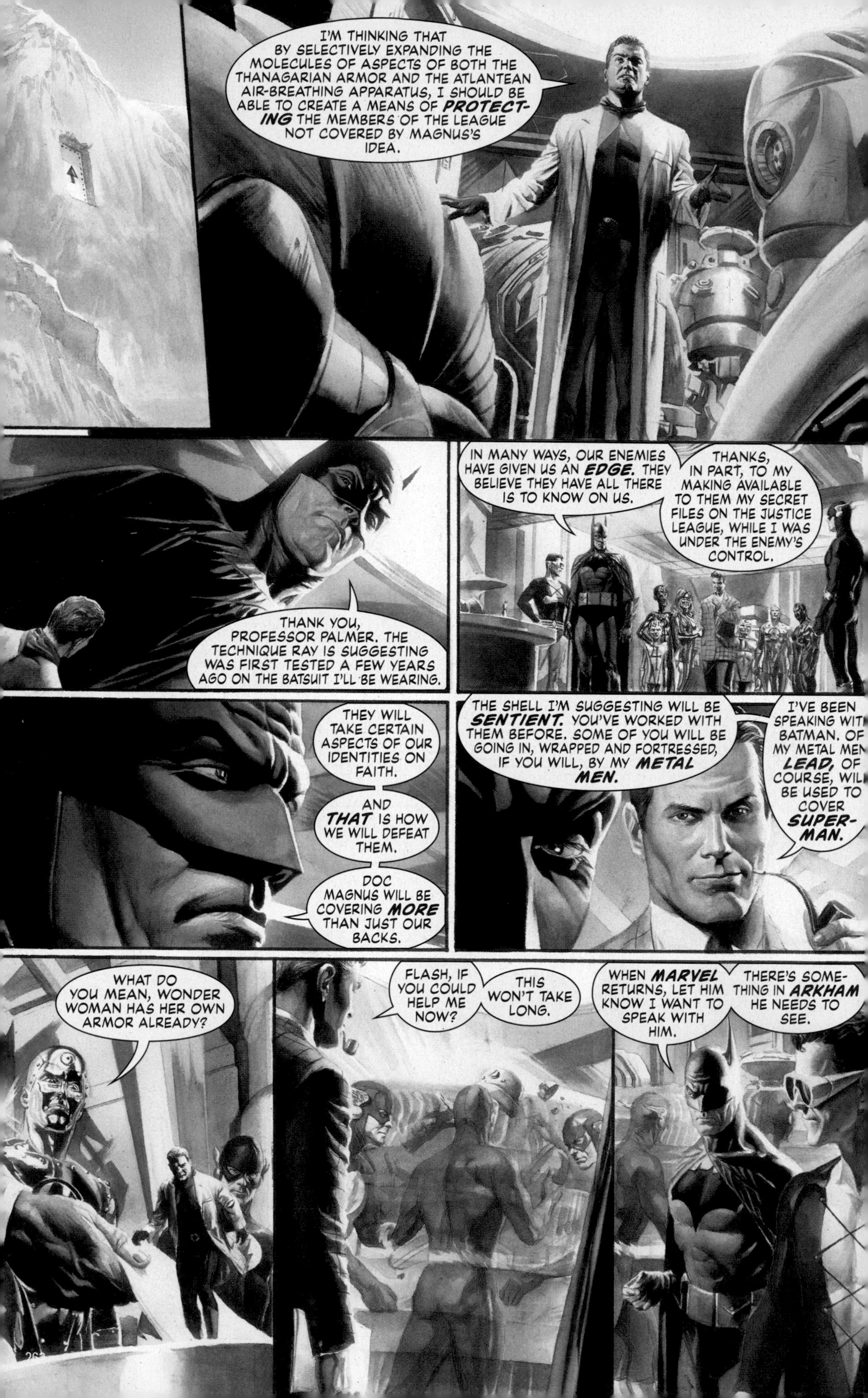
I'M THINKING THAT BY SELECTIVELY EXPANDING THE MOLECULES OF ASPECTS OF BOTH THE THANAGARIAN ARMOR AND THE ATLANTEAN AIR-BREATHING APPARATUS, I SHOULD BE ABLE TO CREATE A MEANS OF PROTECTING THE MEMBERS OF THE LEAGUE NOT COVERED BY MAGNUS'S IDEA.
THANK YOU, PROFESSOR PALMER. THE TECHNIQUE RAY IS SUGGESTING WAS FIRST TESTED A FEW YEARS AGO ON THE BATSUIT I'LL BE WEARING.
IN MANY WAYS, OUR ENEMIES HAVE GIVEN US AN EDGE. THEY BELIEVE THEY HAVE ALL THERE IS TO KNOW ON US.
THANKS, IN PART, TO MY MAKING AVAILABLE TO THEM MY SECRET FILES ON THE JUSTICE LEAGUE, WHILE I WAS UNDER THE ENEMY'S CONTROL.
THEY WILL TAKE CERTAIN ASPECTS OF OUR IDENTITIES ON FAITH.
AND THAT IS HOW WE WILL DEFEAT THEM.
DOC MAGNUS WILL BE COVERING MORE THAN JUST OUR BACKS.
THE SHELL I'M SUGGESTING WILL BE SENTIENT. YOU'VE WORKED WITH THEM BEFORE. SOME OF YOU WILL BE GOING IN, WRAPPED AND FORTRESSED, IF YOU WILL, BY MY METAL MEN.
I'VE BEEN SPEAKING WIT BATMAN. OF MY METAL MEN LEAD, OF COURSE, WIL BE USED TO COVER SUPERMAN.
WHAT DO YOU MEAN, WONDER WOMAN HAS HER OWN ARMOR ALREADY?
FLASH, IF YOU COULD HELP ME NOW?
THIS WON'T TAKE LONG.
WHEN MARVEL RETURNS, LET HIM KNOW I WANT TO SPEAK WITH HIM.
THERE'S SOMETHING IN ARKHAM HE NEEDS TO SEE.

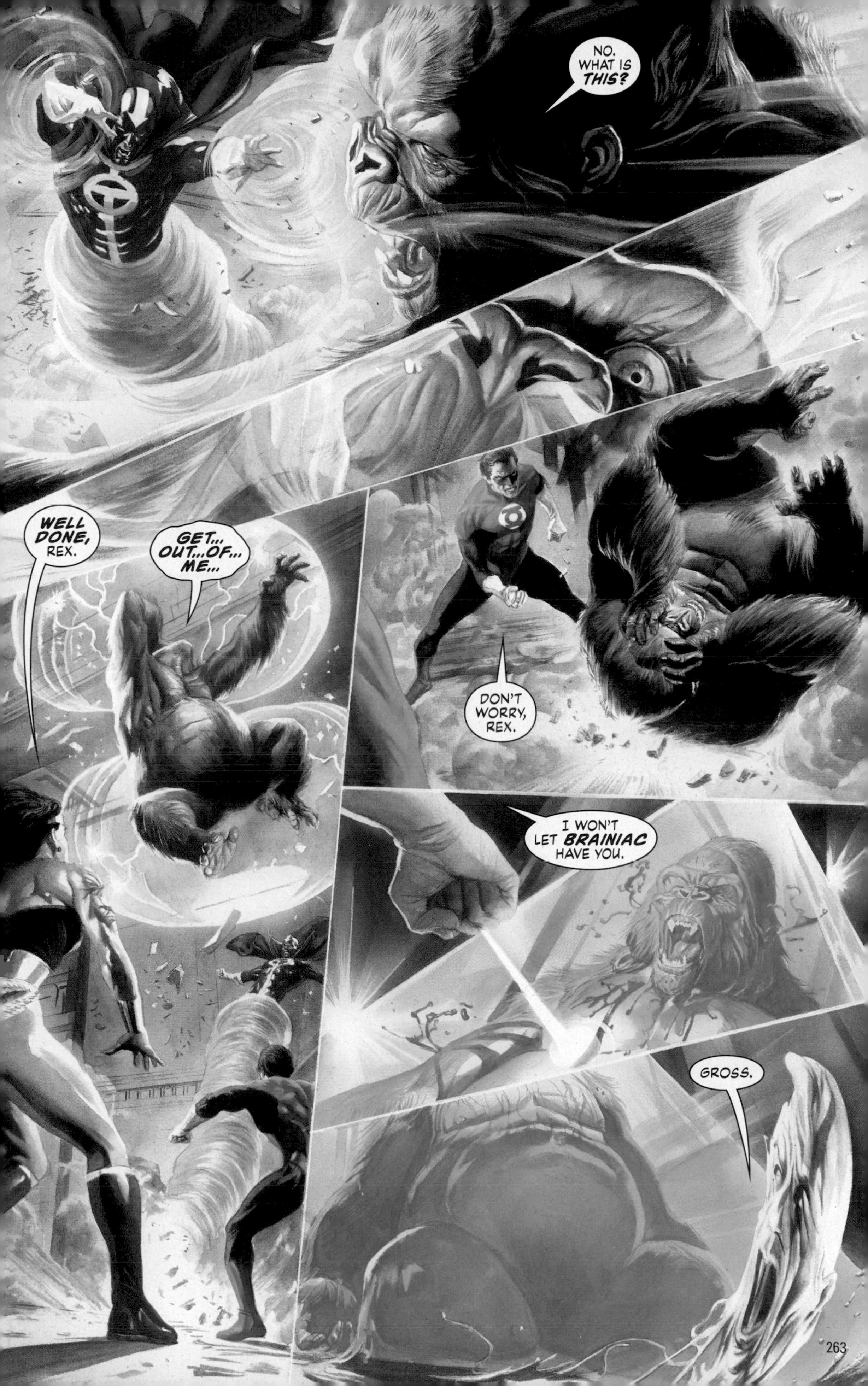
NO. WHAT IS THIS?
WELL DONE, REX.
GET... OUT...OF... ME...
DON'T WORRY, REX.
I WON'T LET BRAINIAC HAVE YOU.
GROSS.

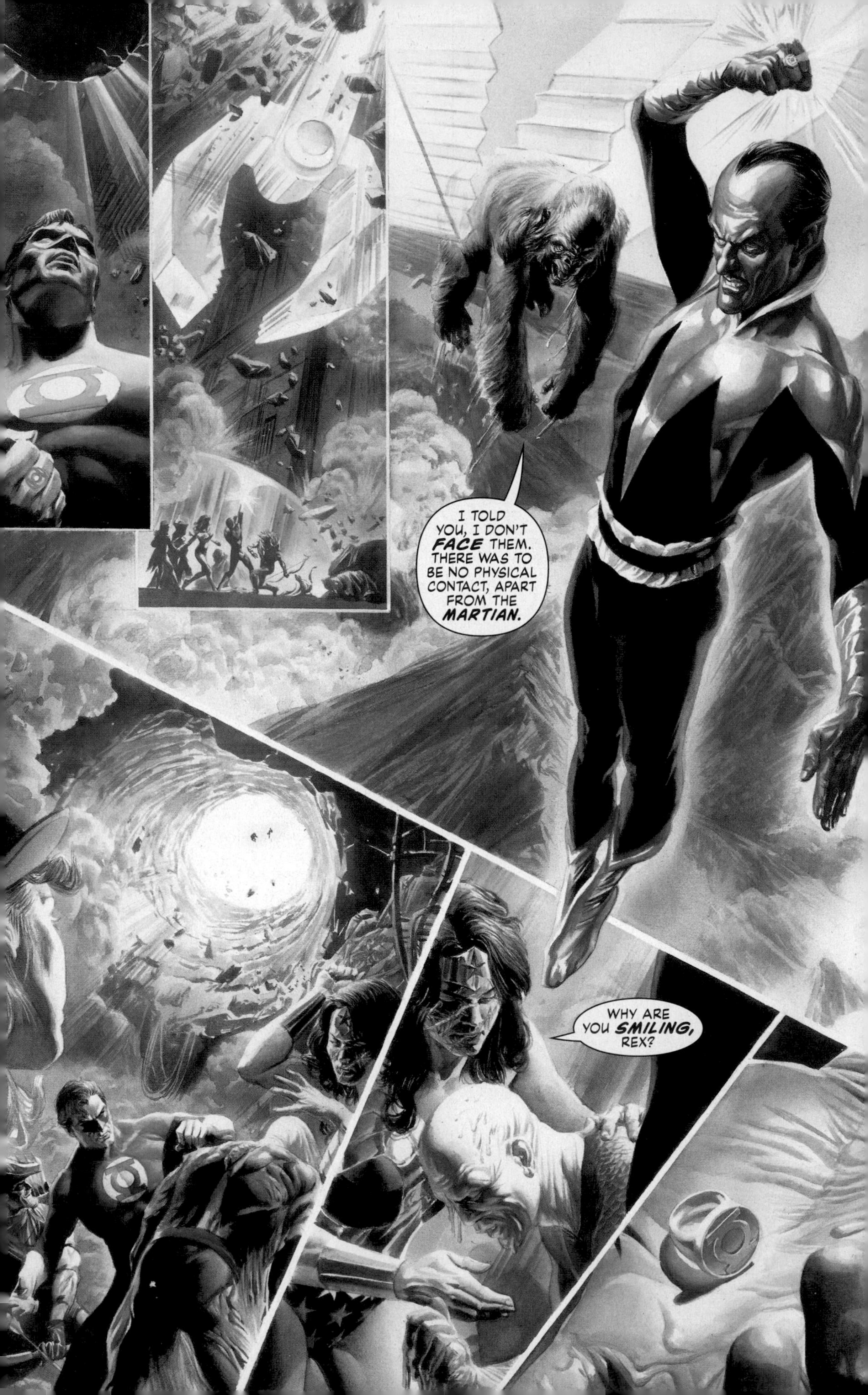
I TOLD YOU, I DON'T **FACE** THEM. THERE WAS TO BE NO PHYSICAL CONTACT, APART FROM THE **MARTIAN.**
WHY ARE YOU **SMILING,** REX?

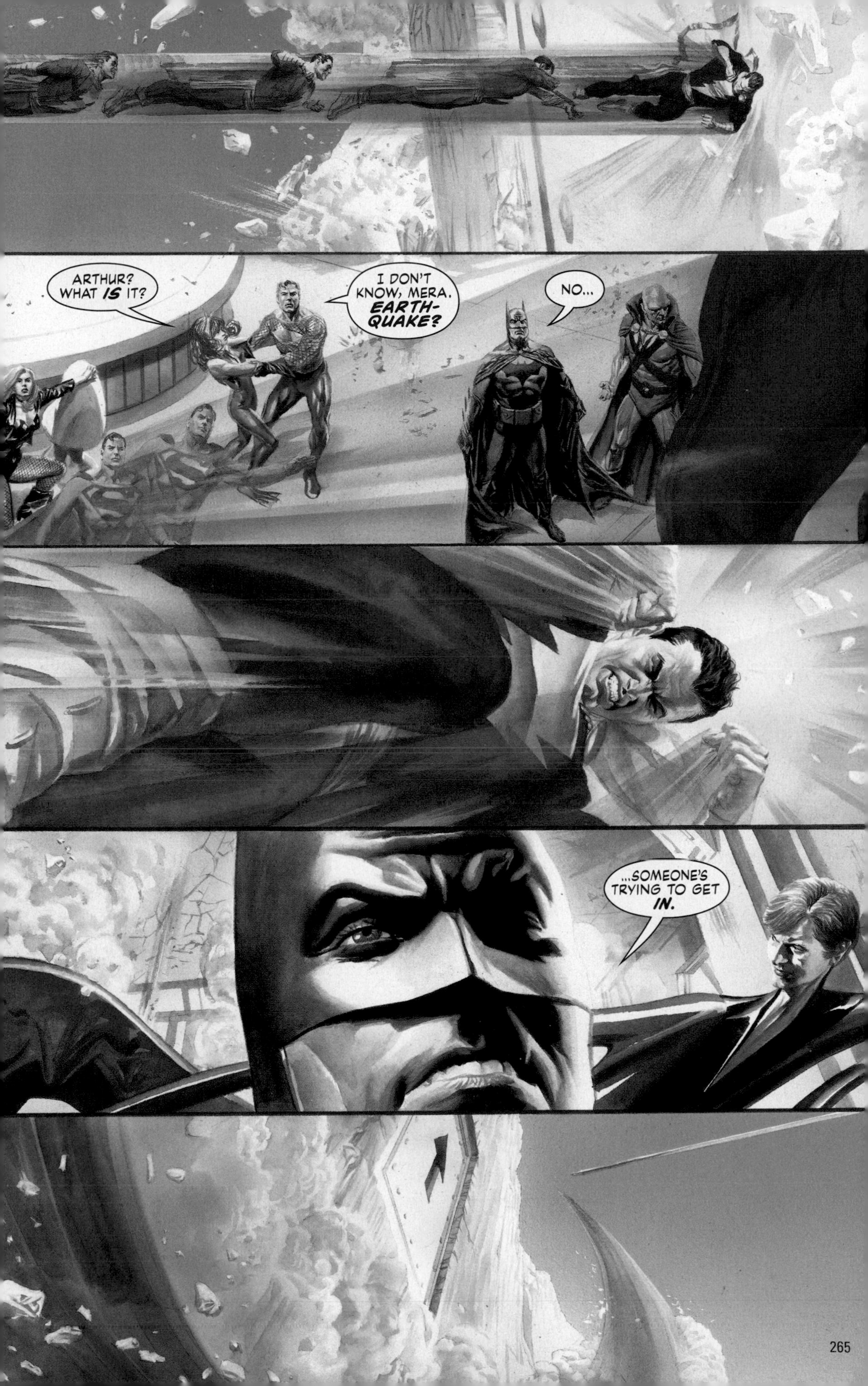
ARTHUR? WHAT **IS** IT?
I DON'T KNOW, MERA. ***EARTH-QUAKE?***
NO...
...SOMEONE'S TRYING TO GET ***IN.***

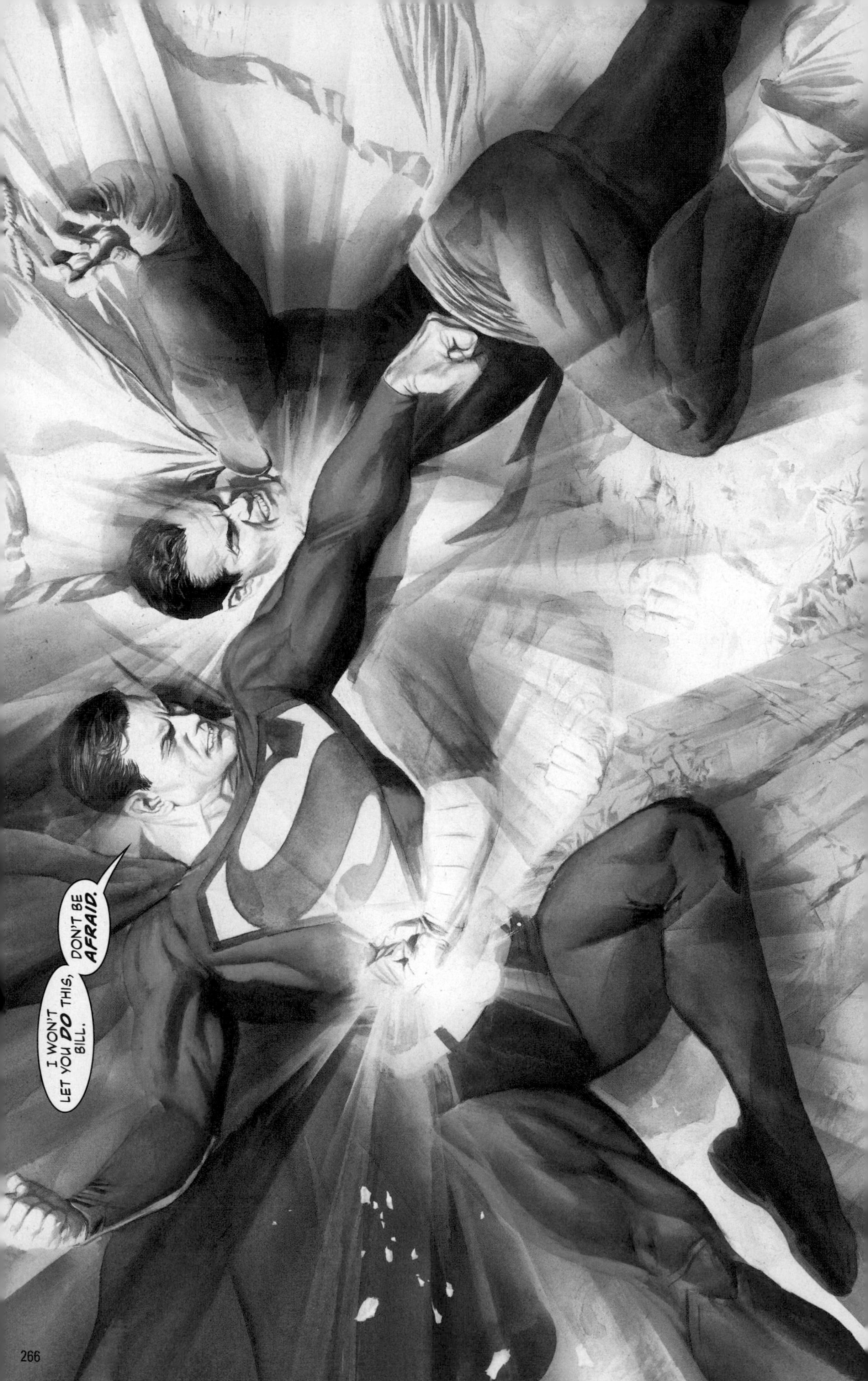
I WON'T LET YOU DO THIS, BILL.
DON'T BE AFRAID.

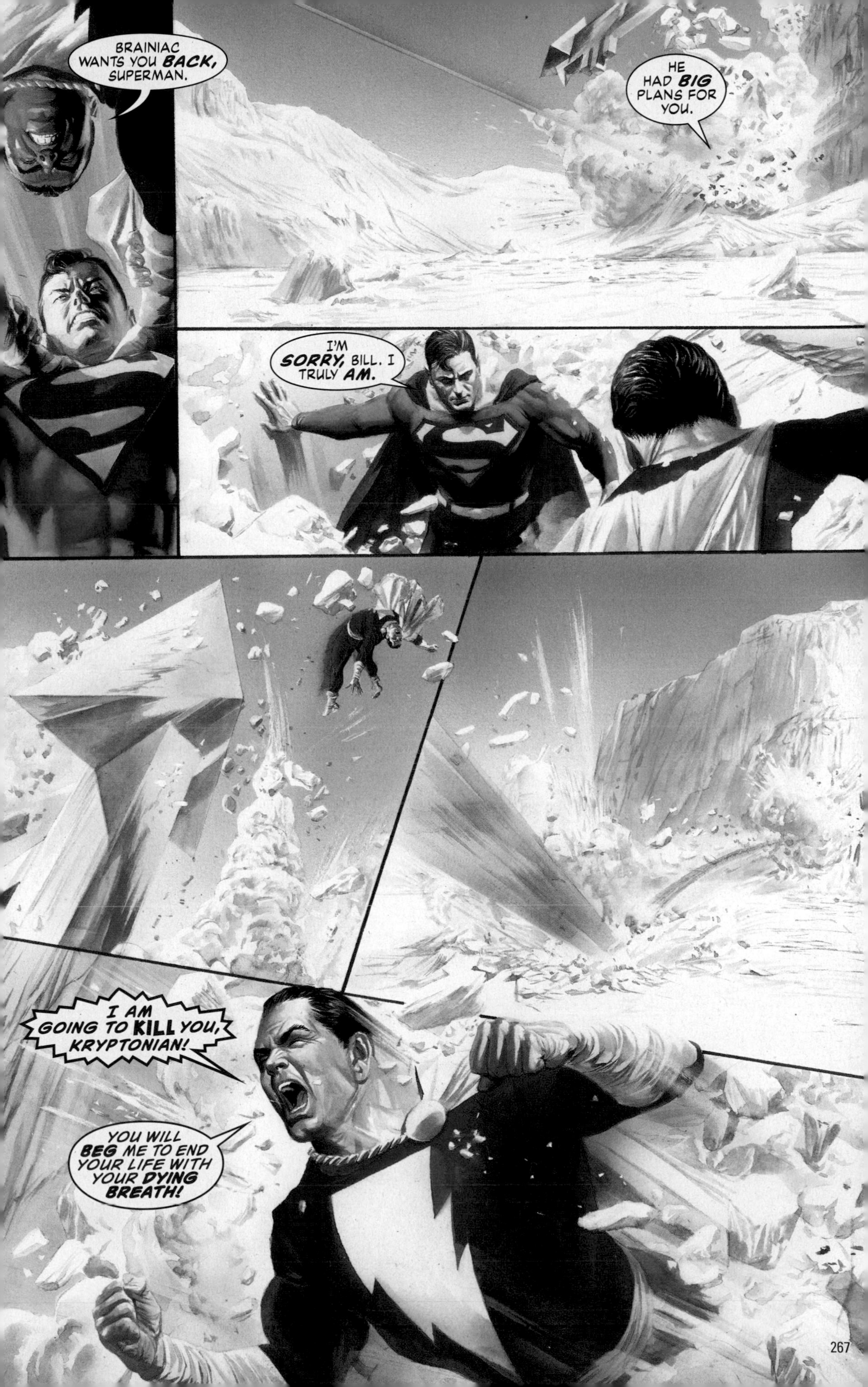
BRAINIAC WANTS YOU BACK, SUPERMAN.
HE HAD BIG PLANS FOR YOU.
I'M SORRY, BILL. I TRULY AM.
I AM GOING TO KILL YOU, KRYPTONIAN!
YOU WILL BEG ME TO END YOUR LIFE WITH YOUR DYING BREATH!

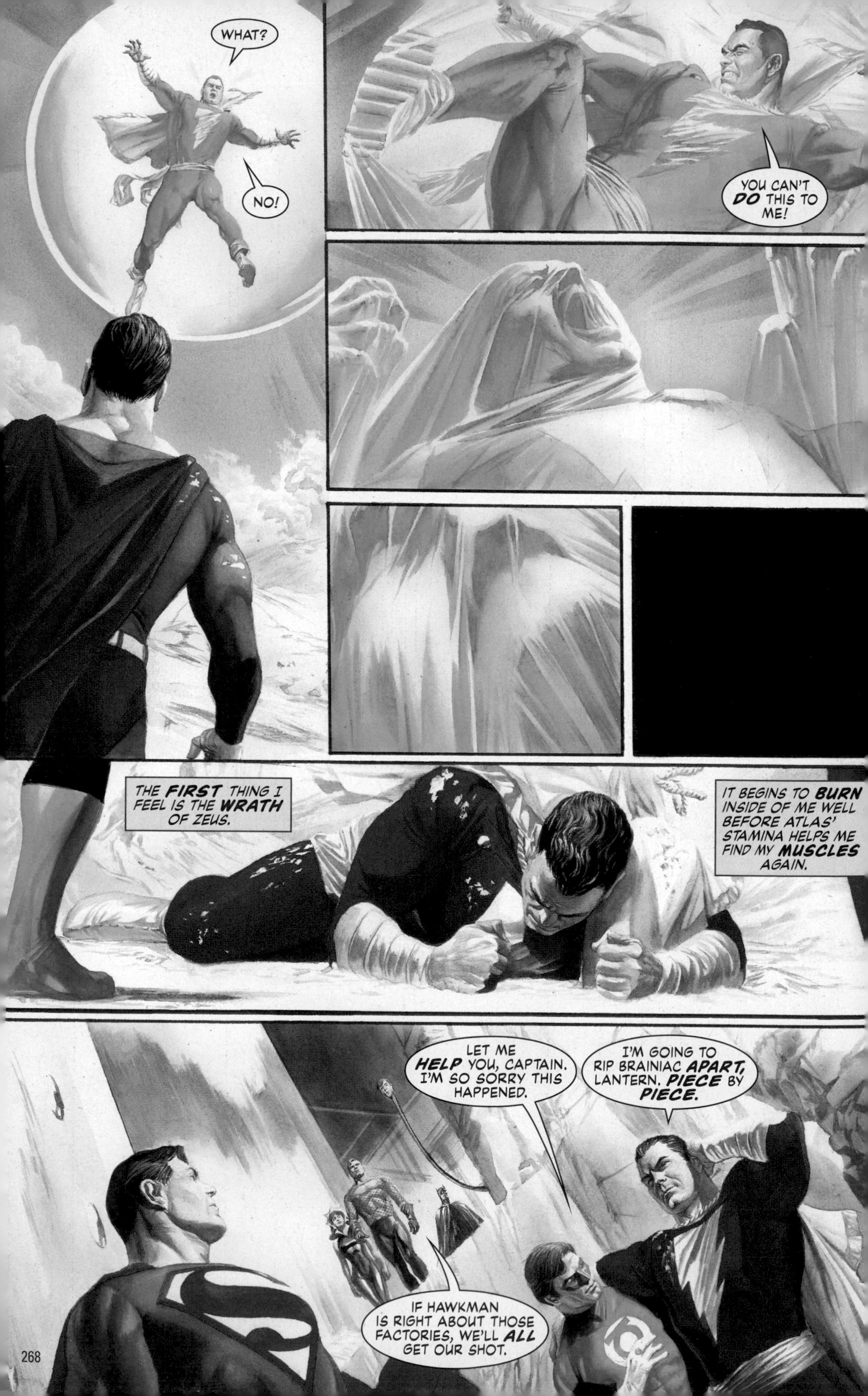
WHAT?
NO!
YOU CAN'T **DO** THIS TO ME!
THE **FIRST** THING I FEEL IS THE **WRATH** OF ZEUS.
IT BEGINS TO **BURN** INSIDE OF ME WELL BEFORE ATLAS' STAMINA HELPS ME FIND MY **MUSCLES** AGAIN.
LET ME **HELP** YOU, CAPTAIN. I'M SO SORRY THIS HAPPENED.
I'M GOING TO RIP BRAINIAC **APART,** LANTERN. **PIECE** BY **PIECE.**
IF HAWKMAN IS RIGHT ABOUT THOSE FACTORIES, WE'LL **ALL** GET OUR SHOT.

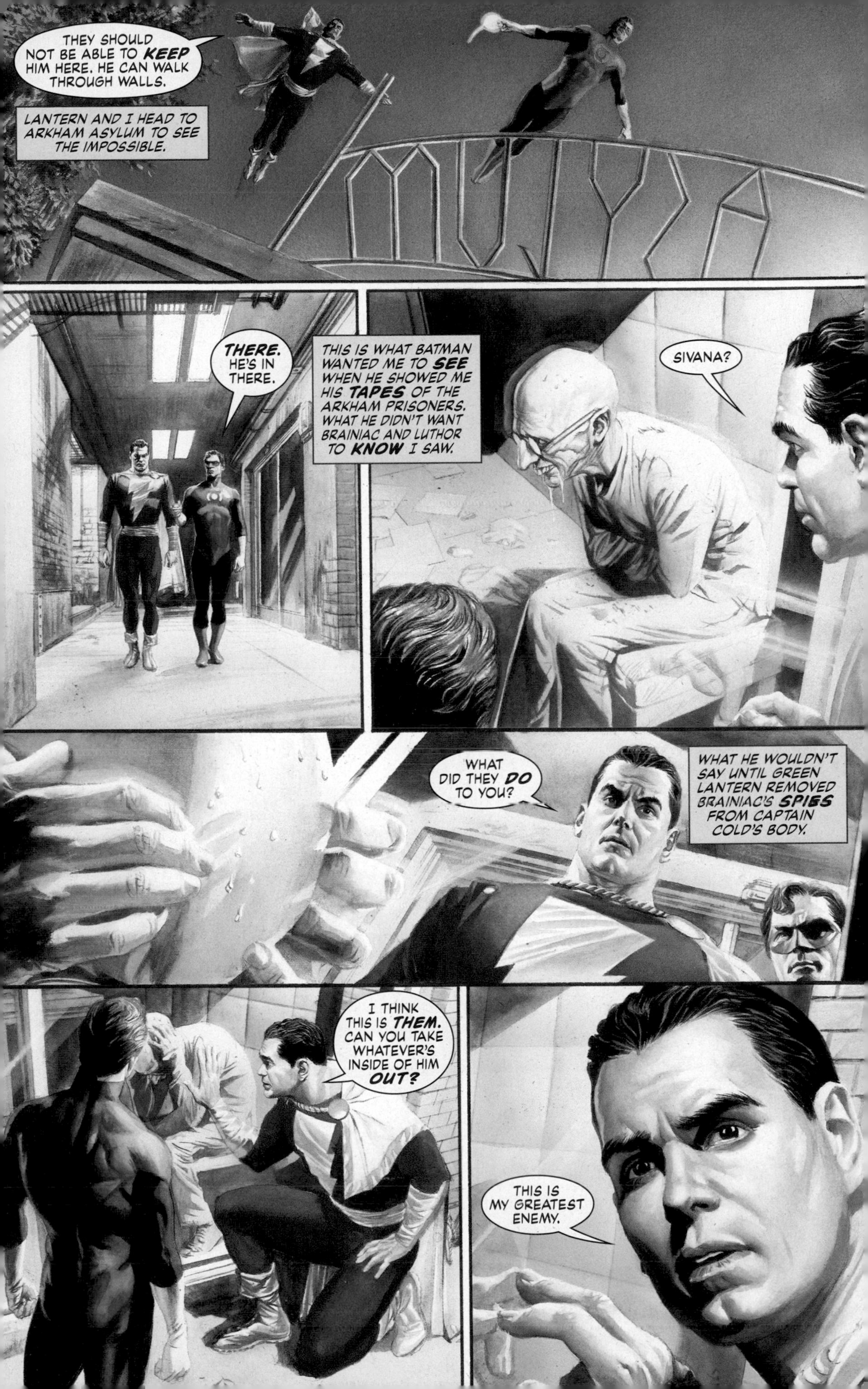
THEY SHOULD NOT BE ABLE TO KEEP HIM HERE. HE CAN WALK THROUGH WALLS.
LANTERN AND I HEAD TO ARKHAM ASYLUM TO SEE THE IMPOSSIBLE.
THERE. HE'S IN THERE.
THIS IS WHAT BATMAN WANTED ME TO SEE WHEN HE SHOWED ME HIS TAPES OF THE ARKHAM PRISONERS. WHAT HE DIDN'T WANT BRAINIAC AND LUTHOR TO KNOW I SAW.
SIVANA?
WHAT DID THEY DO TO YOU?
WHAT HE WOULDN'T SAY UNTIL GREEN LANTERN REMOVED BRAINIAC'S SPIES FROM CAPTAIN COLD'S BODY.
I THINK THIS IS THEM. CAN YOU TAKE WHATEVER'S INSIDE OF HIM OUT?
THIS IS MY GREATEST ENEMY.

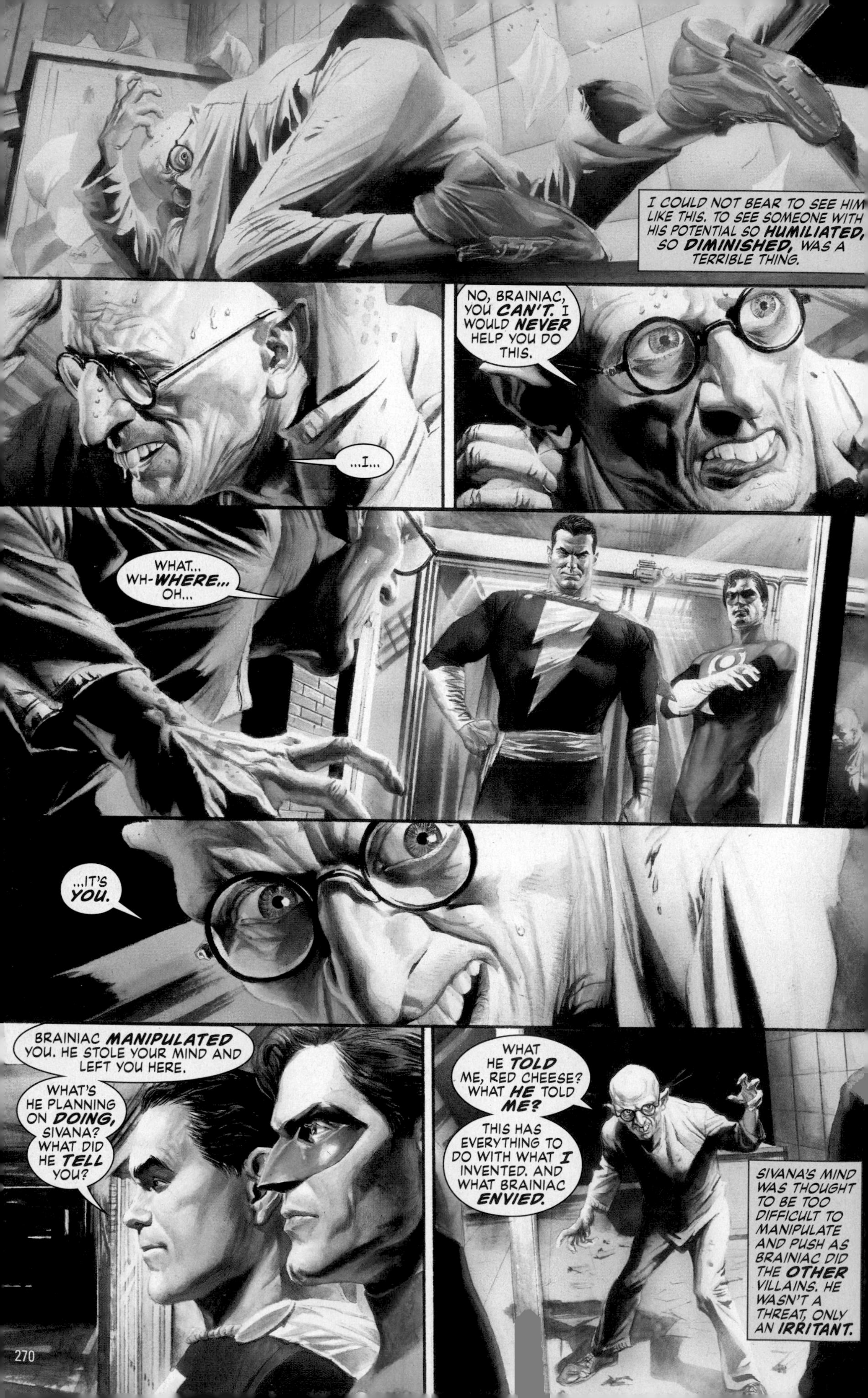
I COULD NOT BEAR TO SEE HIM LIKE THIS. TO SEE SOMEONE WITH HIS POTENTIAL SO HUMILIATED, SO DIMINISHED, WAS A TERRIBLE THING.
...I...
NO, BRAINIAC, YOU CAN'T. I WOULD NEVER HELP YOU DO THIS.
WHAT... WH-WHERE... OH...
...IT'S YOU.
BRAINIAC MANIPULATED YOU. HE STOLE YOUR MIND AND LEFT YOU HERE.
WHAT'S HE PLANNING ON DOING, SIVANA? WHAT DID HE TELL YOU?
WHAT HE TOLD ME, RED CHEESE? WHAT HE TOLD ME?
THIS HAS EVERYTHING TO DO WITH WHAT I INVENTED. AND WHAT BRAINIAC ENVIED.
SIVANA'S MIND WAS THOUGHT TO BE TOO DIFFICULT TO MANIPULATE AND PUSH AS BRAINIAC DID THE OTHER VILLAINS. HE WASN'T A THREAT, ONLY AN IRRITANT.

BRAINIAC STOLE SIVANA'S DESIGN FOR A MECHANICAL LEECH OF SORTS THAT COULD MANIPULATE A BODY AND MIND, A *"MR. MIND"* PROTOTYPE WEAPON.

BRAINIAC MASS-PRODUCED THEM AND SHRUNK THEM DOWN.

THESE MICROSCOPIC MACHINES AFFECT THE *MIND.* AT THE SAME TIME, THEY MANIPULATE AND BUILD *MUSCLE.*

THEY CAN AFFECT DREAMS, MANIPULATE EMOTIONS, MAKE PEOPLE *BELIEVE* THINGS THEY MIGHT NEVER HAVE BEFORE.

THIS IS HOW OUR ENEMIES WERE ABLE TO *CONSPIRE* WITH EACH OTHER.

FORMS OF KRYPTON

ONE MIND WAS *GUIDING* THEM.

ONE MIND, NOT *TWO.* THIS IS *BRAINIAC.*

LUTHOR WOULD NEVER AGREE TO A MECHANIZING OF A *REMNANT* OF HUMANITY, AND THE *DESTRUCTION* OF THE REST.

I'M *COMING,* ARTHUR, MY BOY. YOU'LL BE SAFE *SOON.*

THAT'S WHAT SIVANA REALIZED.

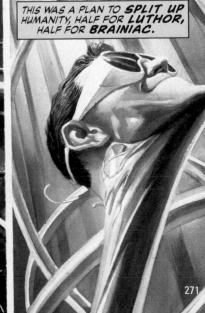

THIS WAS A PLAN TO *SPLIT UP* HUMANITY, HALF FOR *LUTHOR,* HALF FOR *BRAINIAC.*

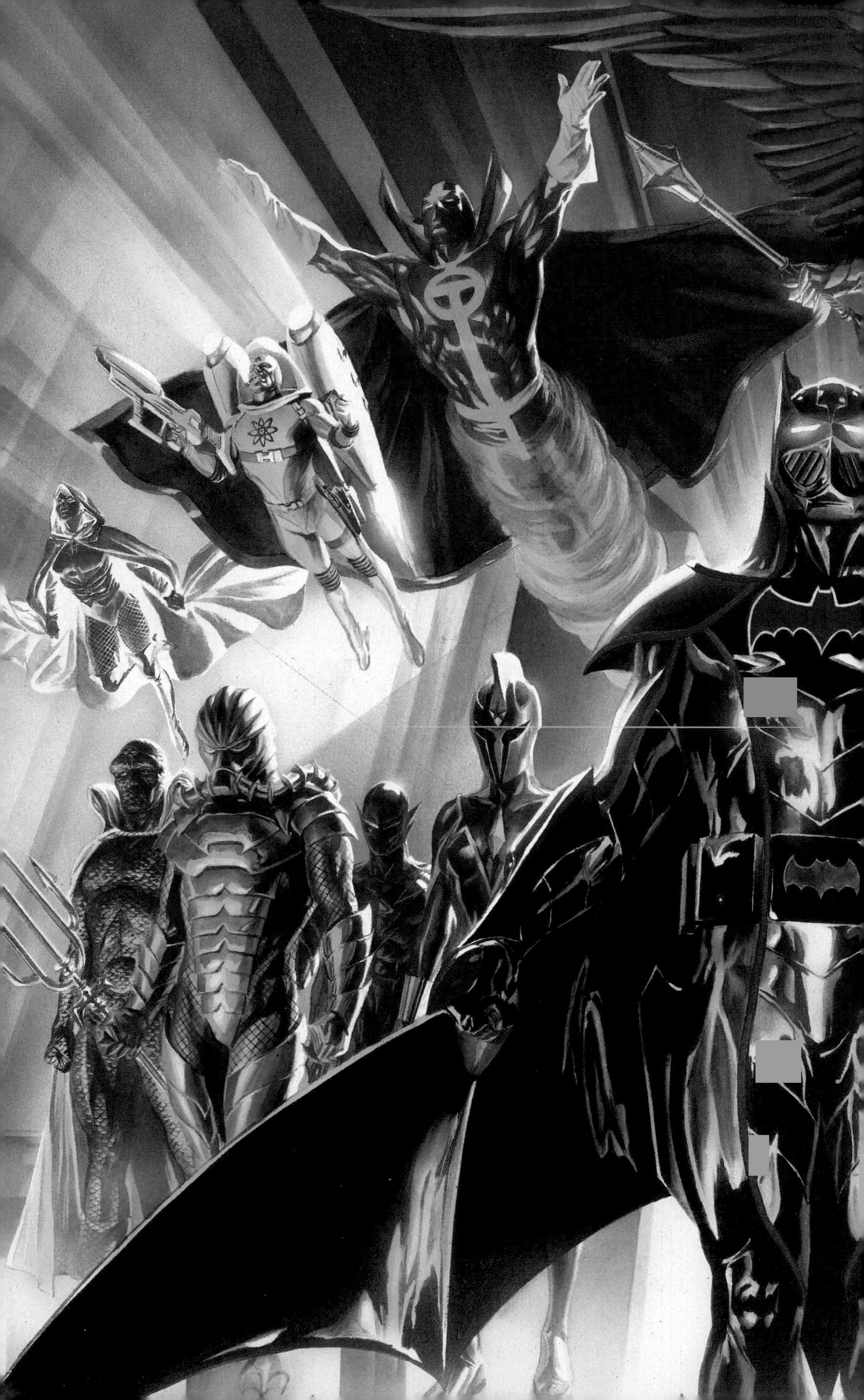

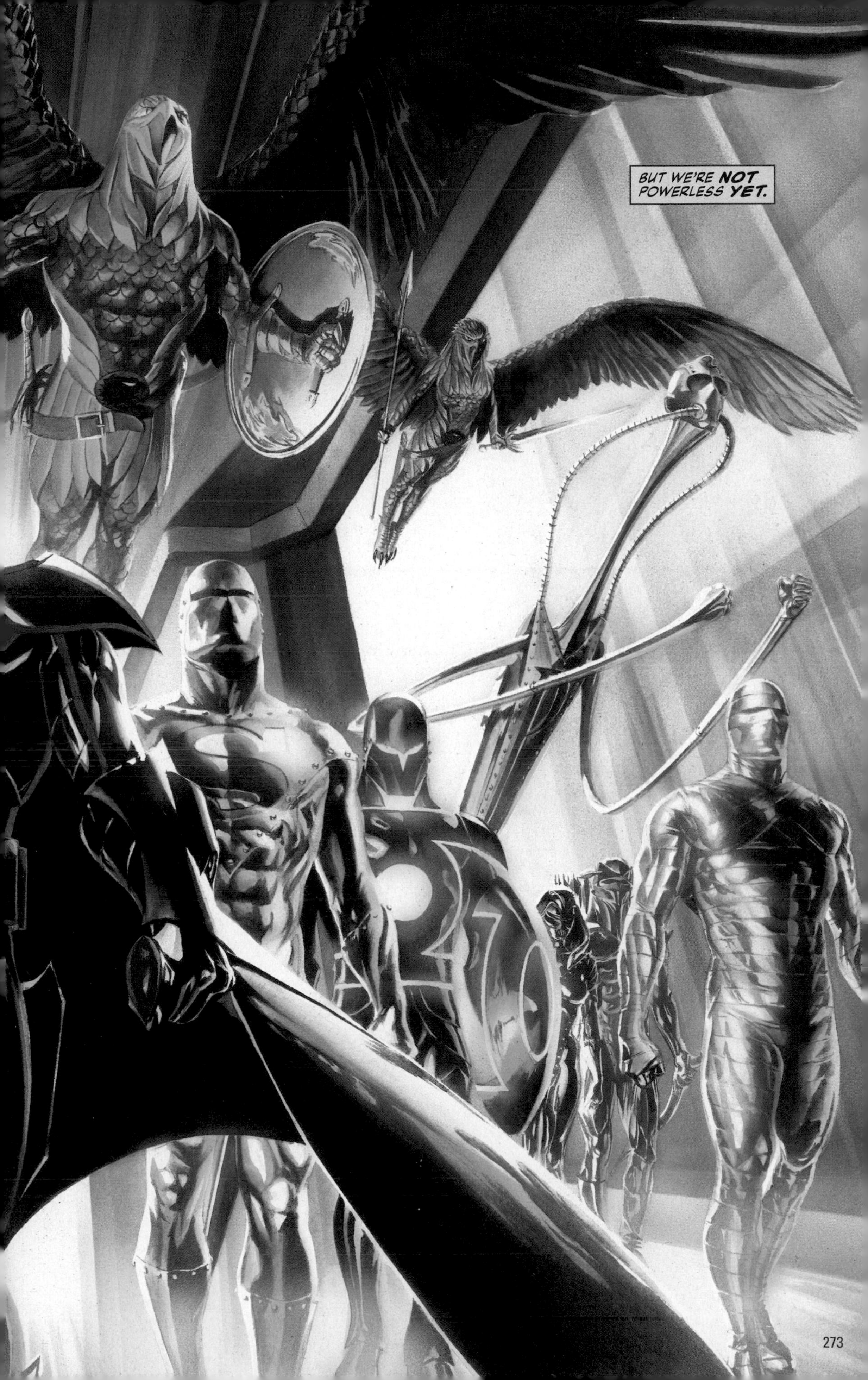
BUT WE'RE NOT POWERLESS YET.

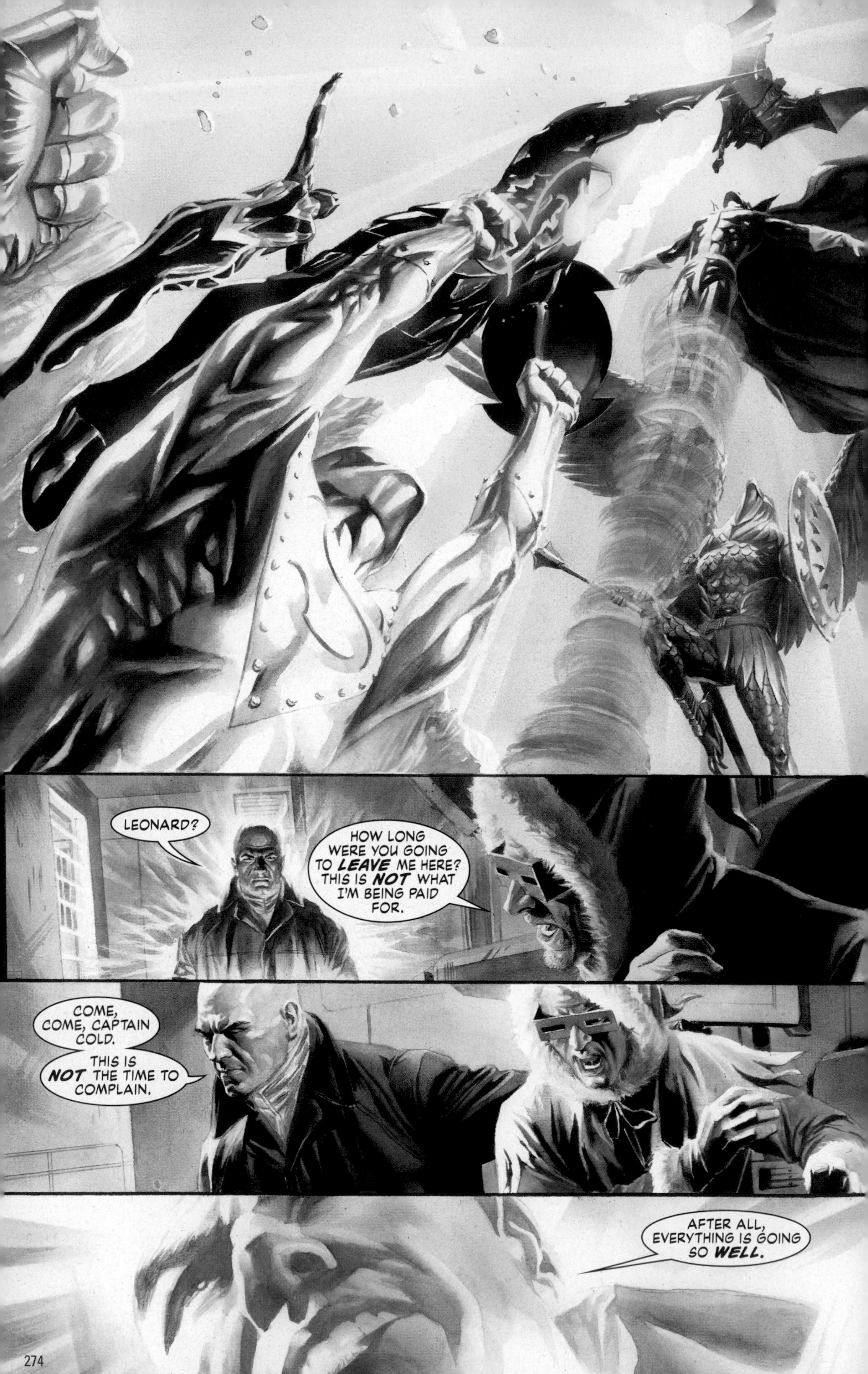
LEONARD?
HOW LONG WERE YOU GOING TO LEAVE ME HERE? THIS IS NOT WHAT I'M BEING PAID FOR.
COME, COME, CAPTAIN COLD.
THIS IS NOT THE TIME TO COMPLAIN.
AFTER ALL, EVERYTHING IS GOING SO WELL.

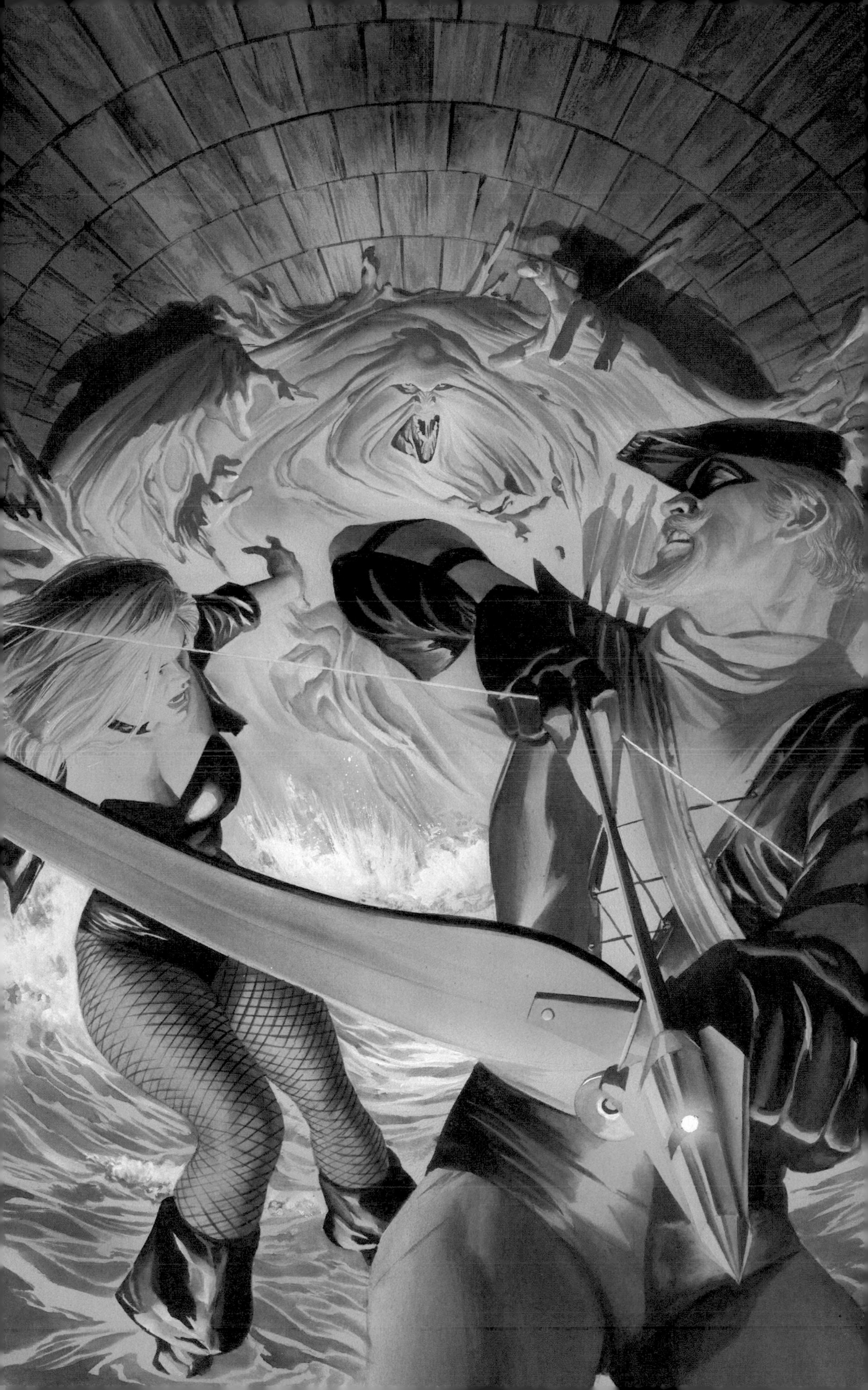

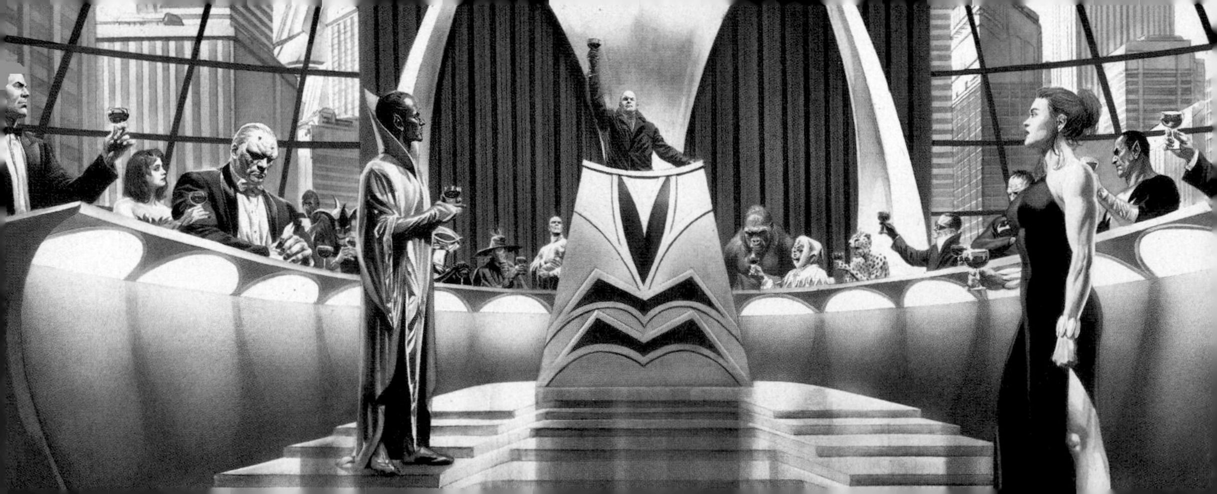

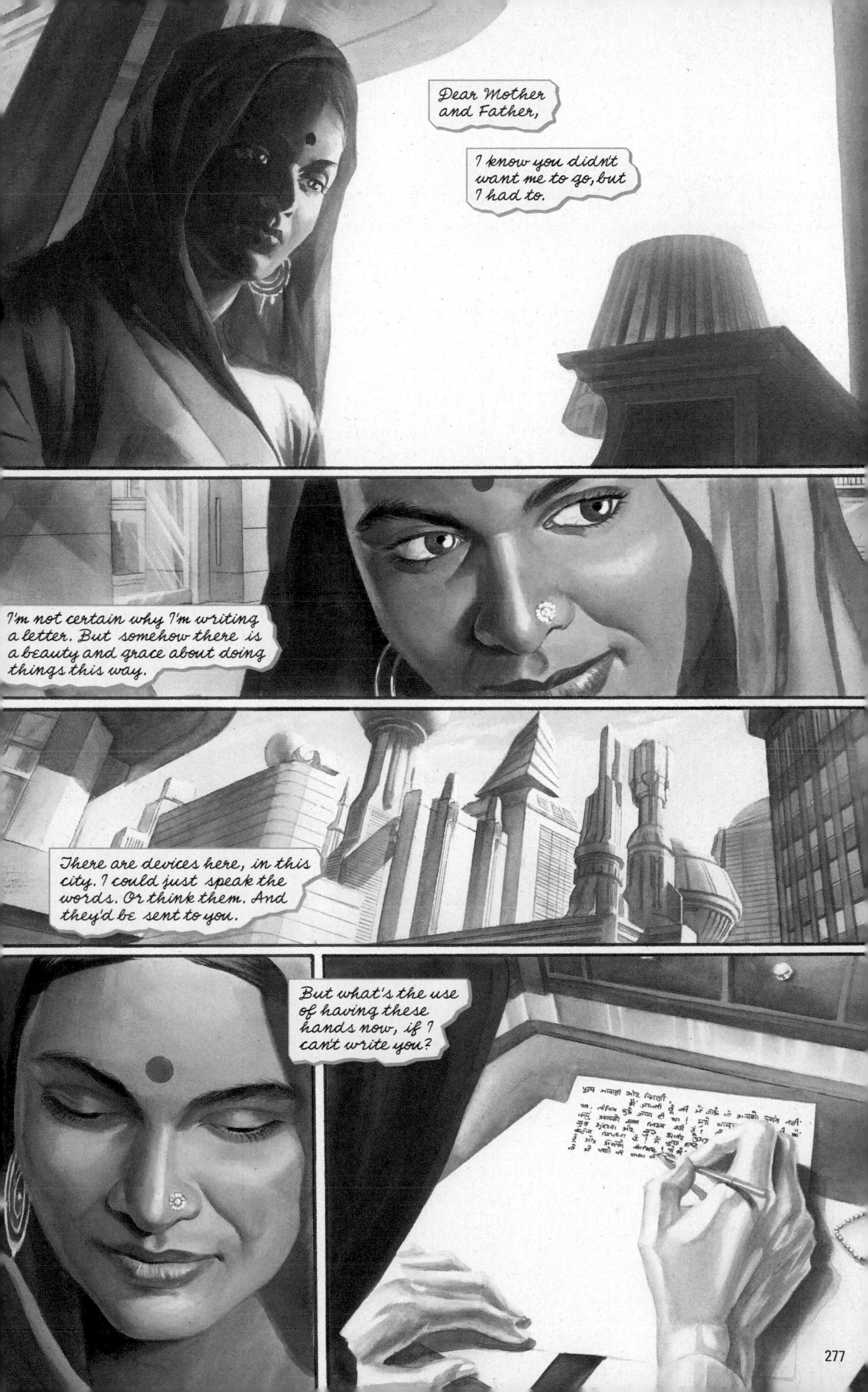
Dear Mother and Father,
I know you didn't want me to go, but I had to.
I'm not certain why I'm writing a letter. But somehow there is a beauty and grace about doing things this way.
There are devices here, in this city. I could just speak the words. Or think them. And they'd be sent to you.
But what's the use of having these hands now, if I can't write you?

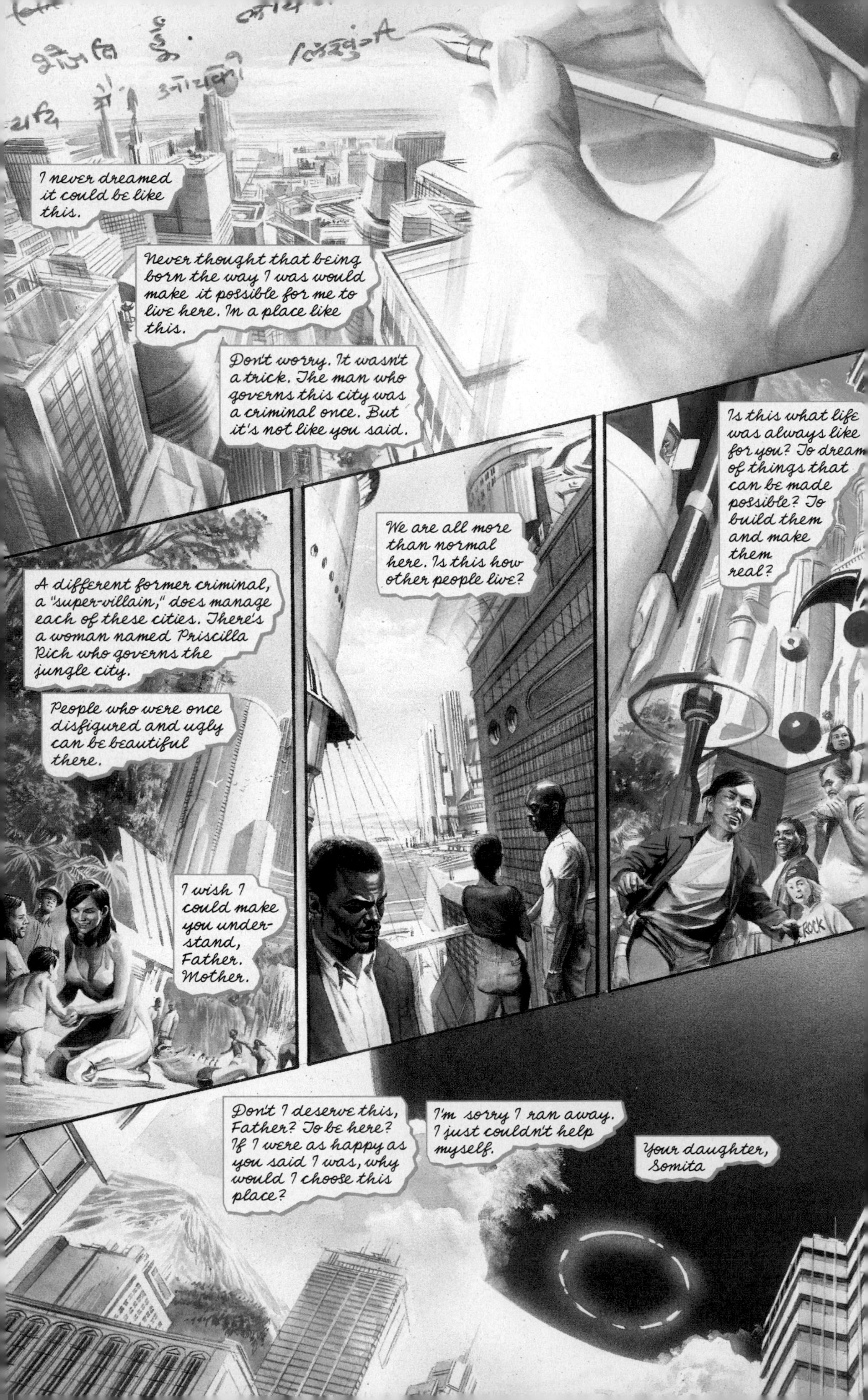

I never dreamed it could be like this.
Never thought that being born the way I was would make it possible for me to live here. In a place like this.
Don't worry. It wasn't a trick. The man who governs this city was a criminal once. But it's not like you said.
A different former criminal, a "super-villain," does manage each of these cities. There's a woman named Priscilla Rich who governs the jungle city.
People who were once disfigured and ugly can be beautiful there.
I wish I could make you understand, Father. Mother.
We are all more than normal here. Is this how other people live?
Is this what life was always like for you? To dream of things that can be made possible? To build them and make them real?
Don't I deserve this, Father? To be here? If I were as happy as you said I was, why would I choose this place?
I'm sorry I ran away. I just couldn't help myself.
Your daughter, Somita

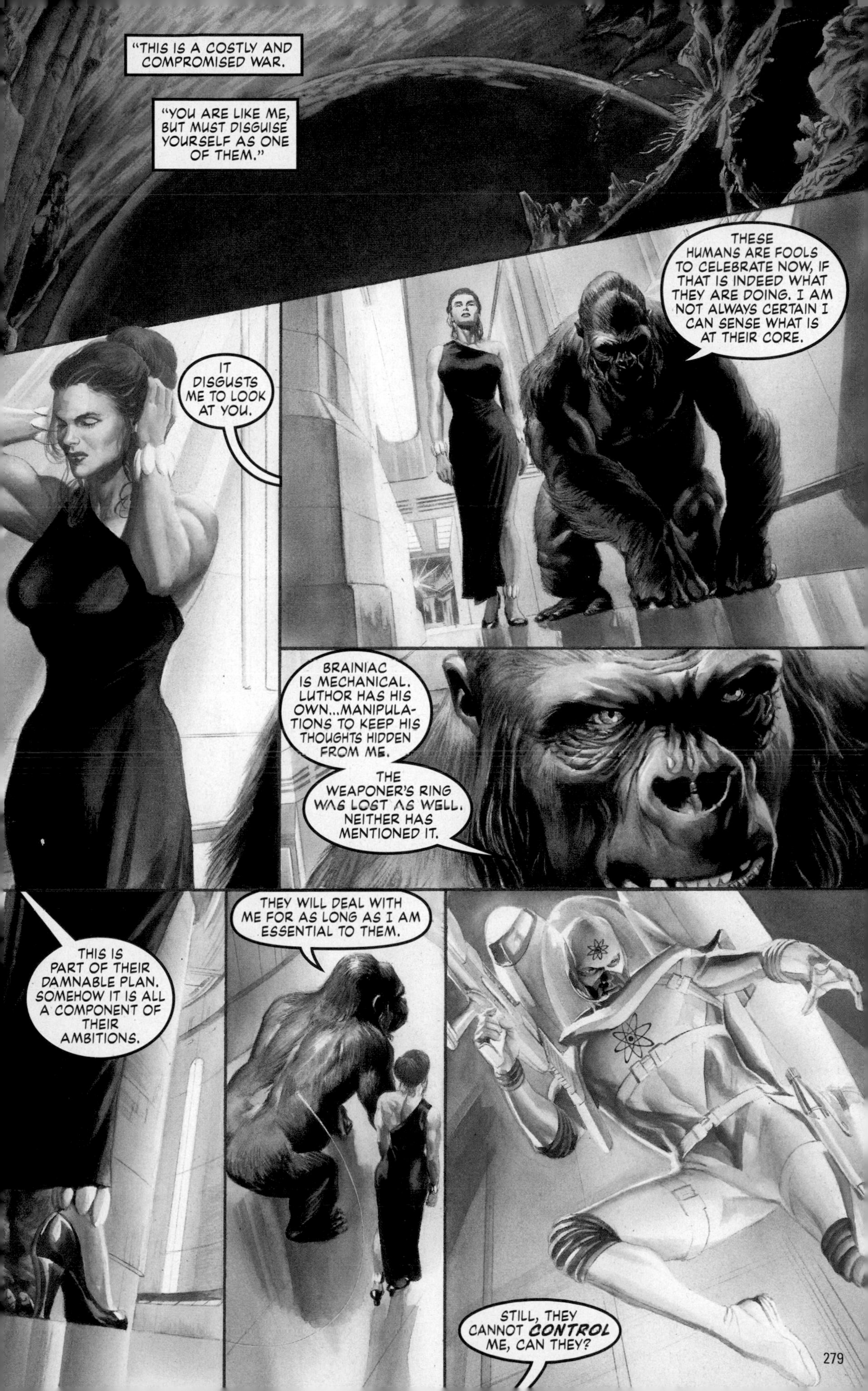
"THIS IS A COSTLY AND COMPROMISED WAR.
"YOU ARE LIKE ME, BUT MUST DISGUISE YOURSELF AS ONE OF THEM."
IT DISGUSTS ME TO LOOK AT YOU.
THESE HUMANS ARE FOOLS TO CELEBRATE NOW, IF THAT IS INDEED WHAT THEY ARE DOING. I AM NOT ALWAYS CERTAIN I CAN SENSE WHAT IS AT THEIR CORE.
BRAINIAC IS MECHANICAL. LUTHOR HAS HIS OWN...MANIPULATIONS TO KEEP HIS THOUGHTS HIDDEN FROM ME.
THE WEAPONER'S RING WAS LOST AS WELL. NEITHER HAS MENTIONED IT.
THIS IS PART OF THEIR DAMNABLE PLAN. SOMEHOW IT IS ALL A COMPONENT OF THEIR AMBITIONS.
THEY WILL DEAL WITH ME FOR AS LONG AS I AM ESSENTIAL TO THEM.
STILL, THEY CANNOT CONTROL ME, CAN THEY?

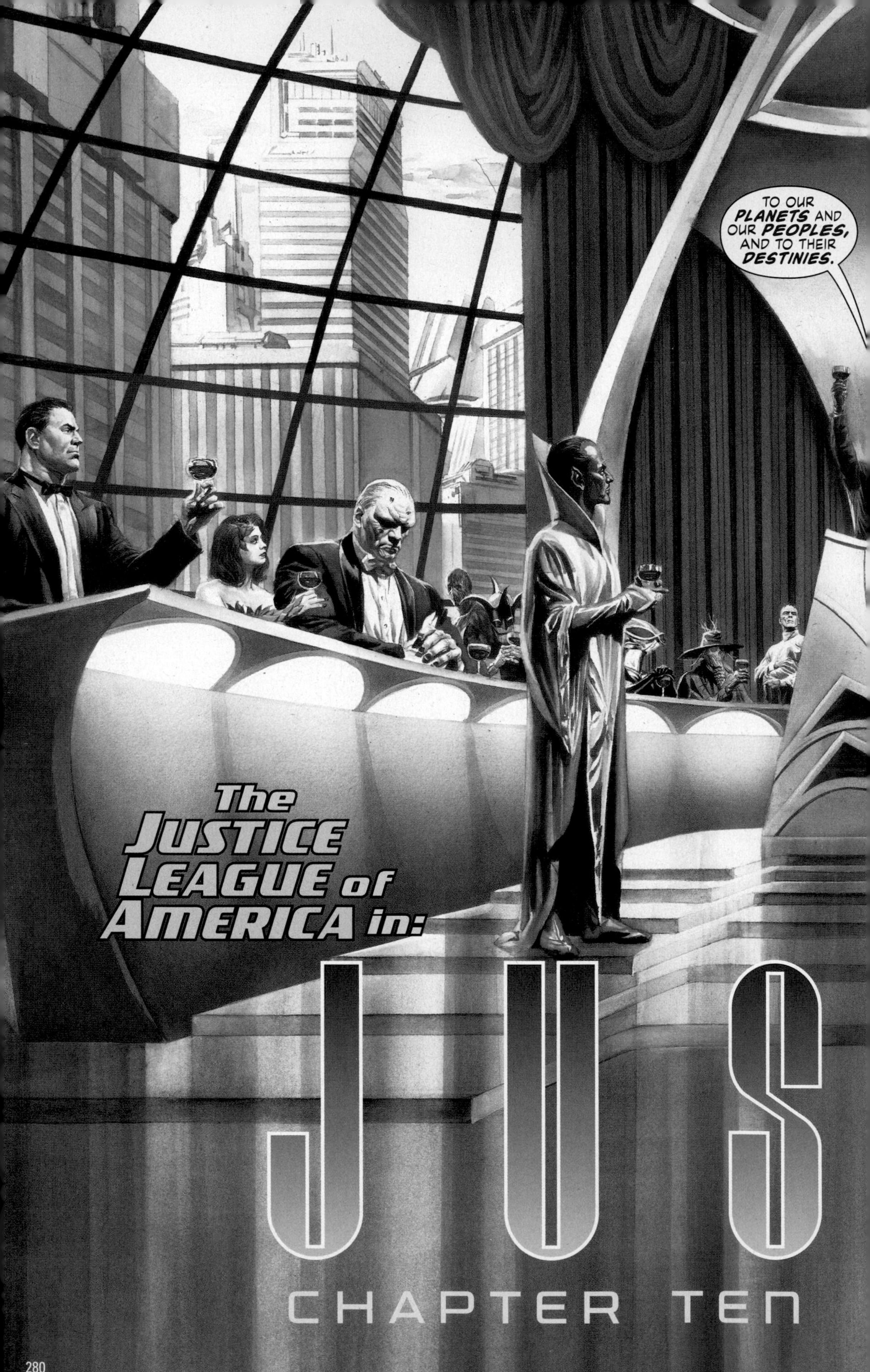
TO OUR PLANETS AND OUR PEOPLES, AND TO THEIR DESTINIES.
The JUSTICE LEAGUE of AMERICA in:
J U S
CHAPTER TEN

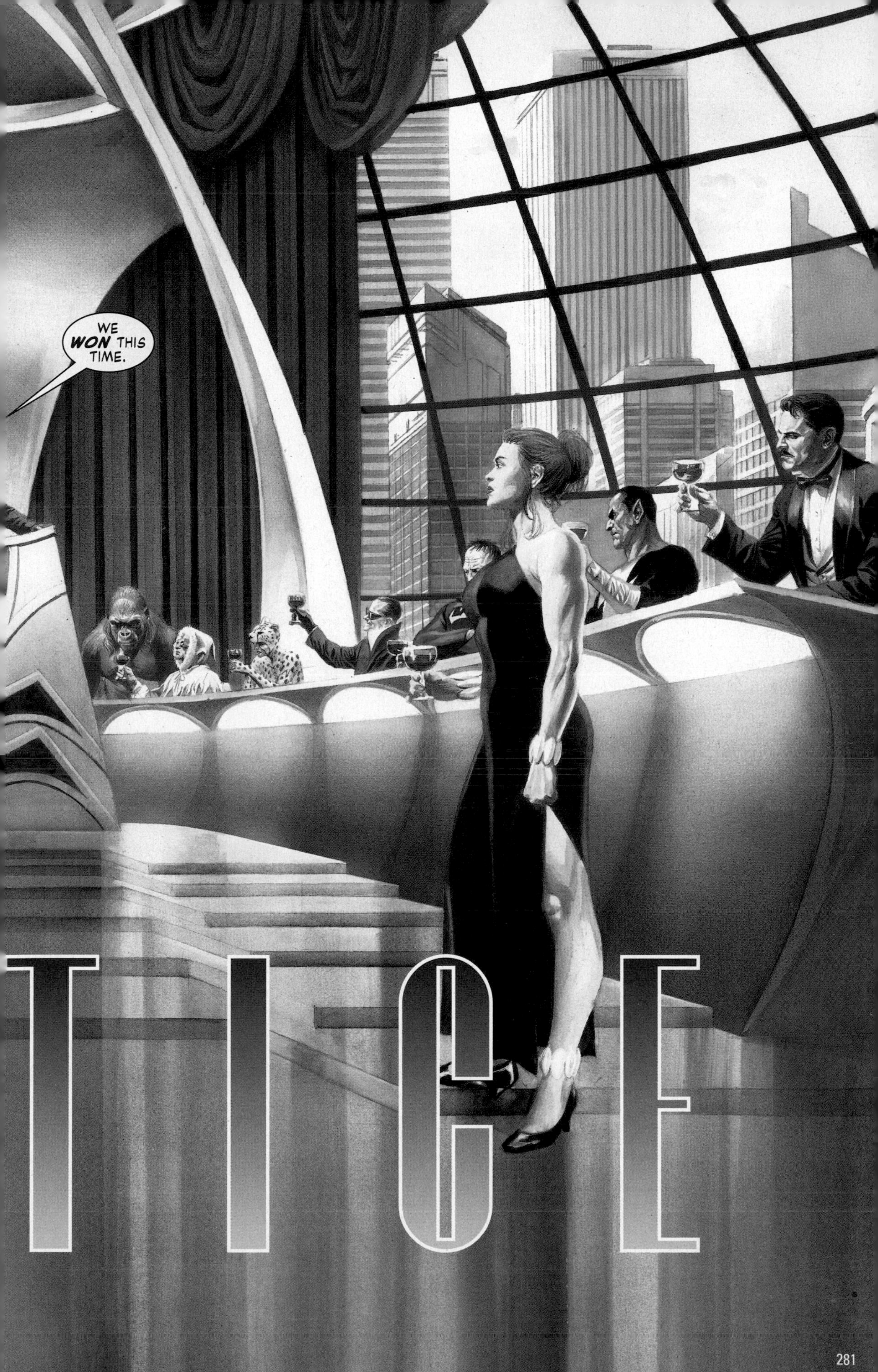
WE **WON** THIS TIME.
TICE

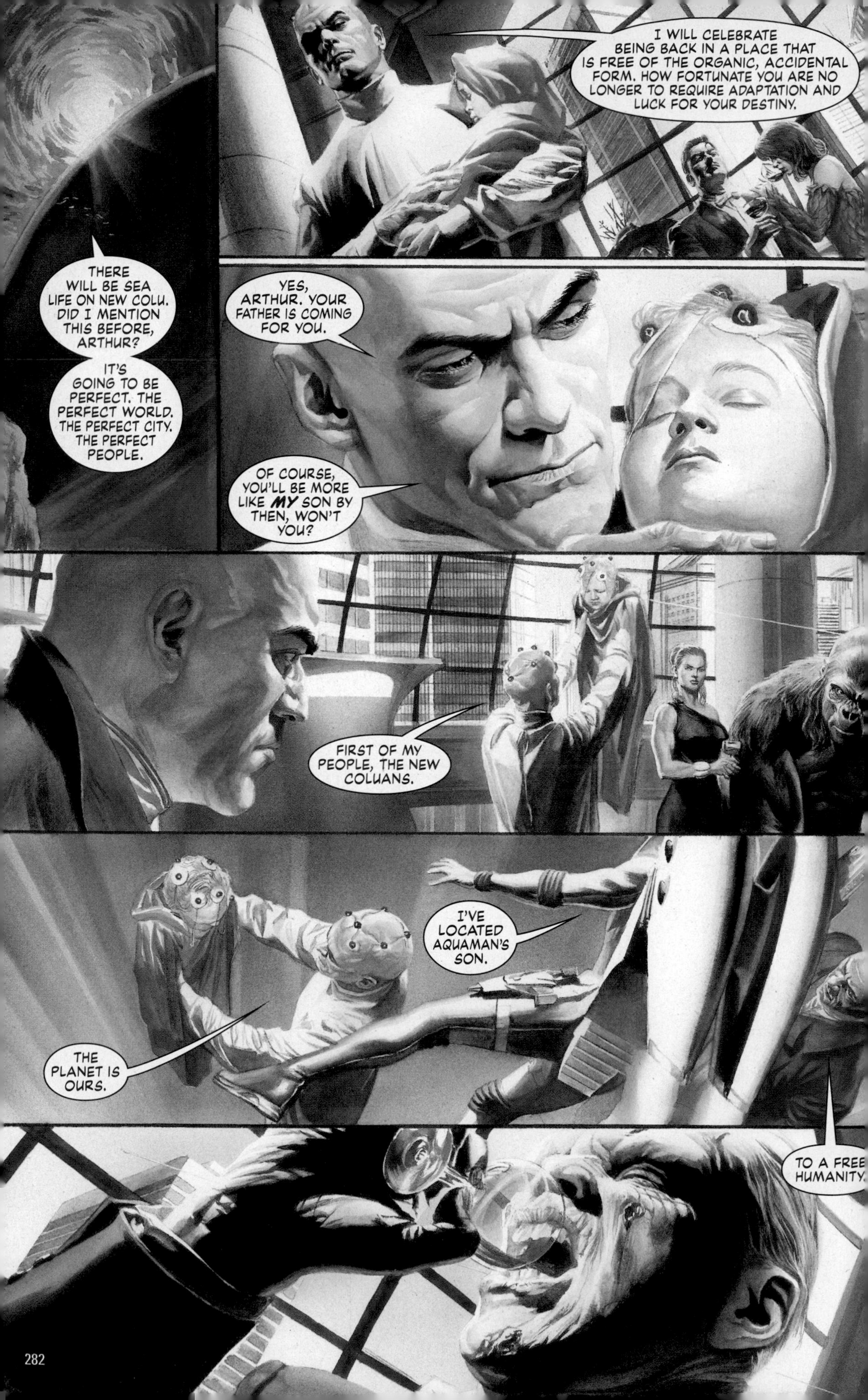
I WILL CELEBRATE BEING BACK IN A PLACE THAT IS FREE OF THE ORGANIC, ACCIDENTAL FORM. HOW FORTUNATE YOU ARE NO LONGER TO REQUIRE ADAPTATION AND LUCK FOR YOUR DESTINY.
THERE WILL BE SEA LIFE ON NEW COLU. DID I MENTION THIS BEFORE, ARTHUR?
IT'S GOING TO BE PERFECT. THE PERFECT WORLD. THE PERFECT CITY. THE PERFECT PEOPLE.
YES, ARTHUR. YOUR FATHER IS COMING FOR YOU.
OF COURSE, YOU'LL BE MORE LIKE MY SON BY THEN, WON'T YOU?
FIRST OF MY PEOPLE, THE NEW COLUANS.
I'VE LOCATED AQUAMAN'S SON.
THE PLANET IS OURS.
TO A FREE HUMANITY.

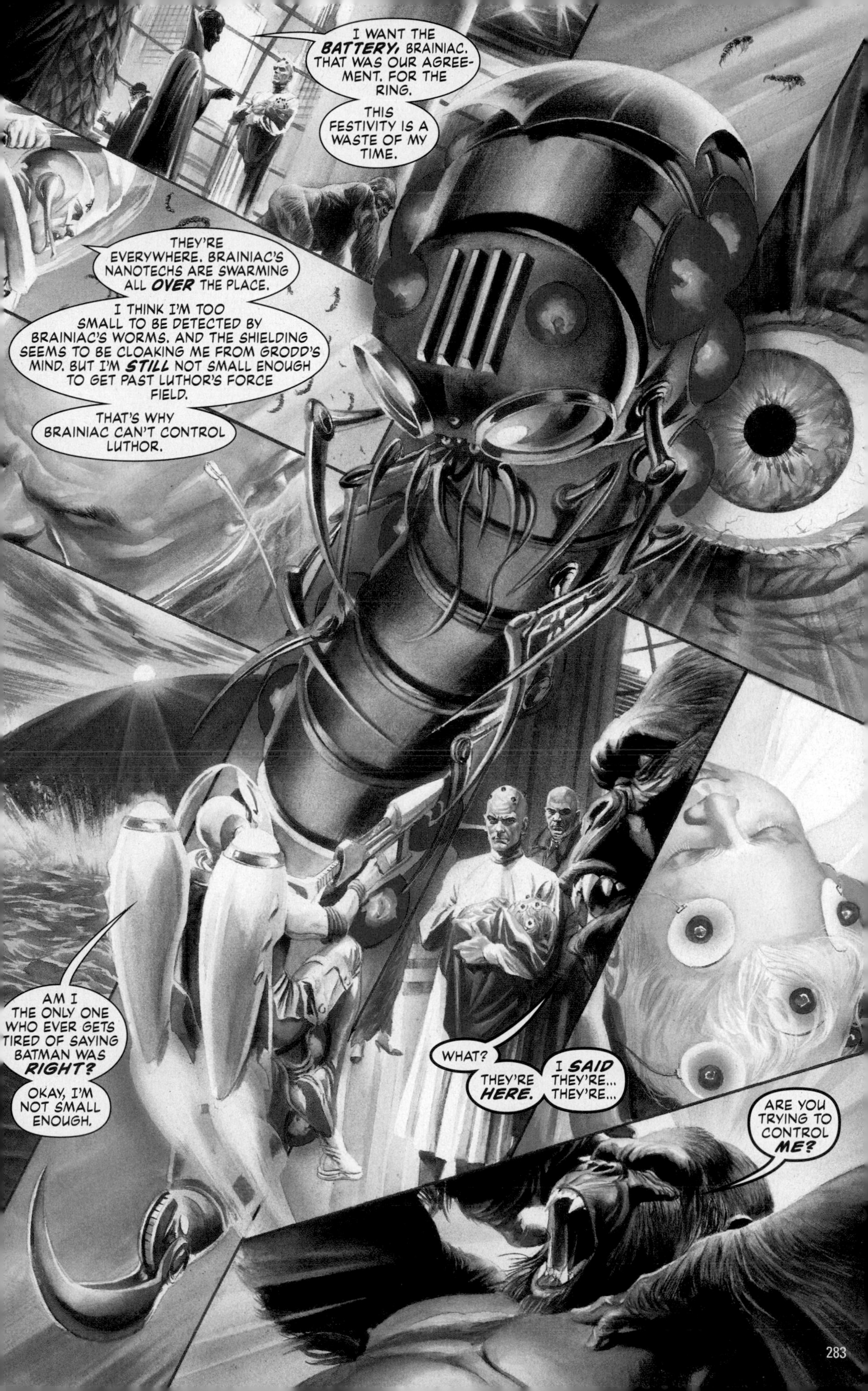
I WANT THE BATTERY, BRAINIAC. THAT WAS OUR AGREEMENT. FOR THE RING.
THIS FESTIVITY IS A WASTE OF MY TIME.
THEY'RE EVERYWHERE. BRAINIAC'S NANOTECHS ARE SWARMING ALL OVER THE PLACE.
I THINK I'M TOO SMALL TO BE DETECTED BY BRAINIAC'S WORMS. AND THE SHIELDING SEEMS TO BE CLOAKING ME FROM GRODD'S MIND. BUT I'M STILL NOT SMALL ENOUGH TO GET PAST LUTHOR'S FORCE FIELD.
THAT'S WHY BRAINIAC CAN'T CONTROL LUTHOR.
AM I THE ONLY ONE WHO EVER GETS TIRED OF SAYING BATMAN WAS RIGHT?
OKAY, I'M NOT SMALL ENOUGH.
WHAT?
THEY'RE HERE.
I SAID THEY'RE... THEY'RE...
ARE YOU TRYING TO CONTROL ME?

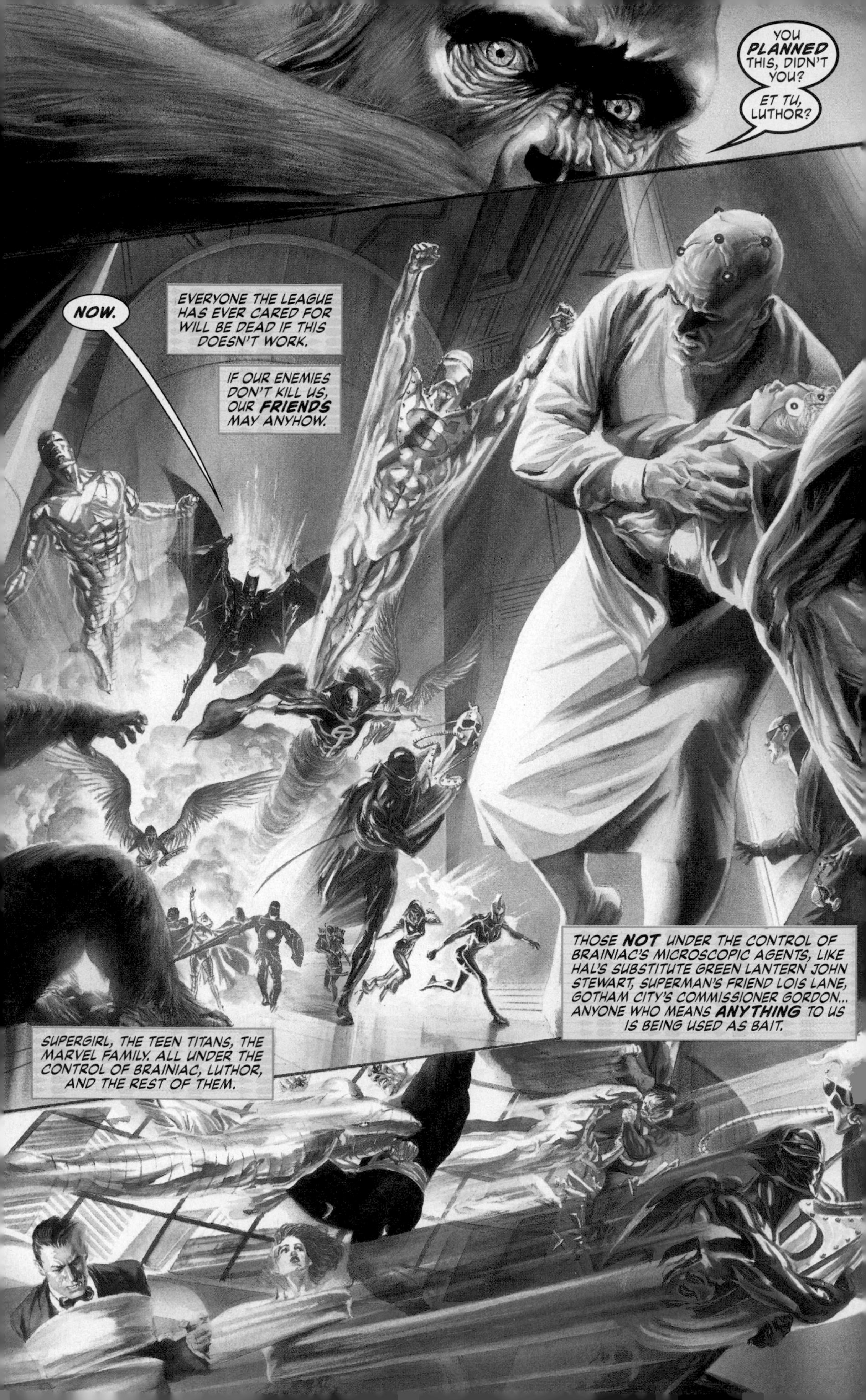
YOU PLANNED THIS, DIDN'T YOU?
ET TU, LUTHOR?
NOW.
EVERYONE THE LEAGUE HAS EVER CARED FOR WILL BE DEAD IF THIS DOESN'T WORK.
IF OUR ENEMIES DON'T KILL US, OUR FRIENDS MAY ANYHOW.
THOSE NOT UNDER THE CONTROL OF BRAINIAC'S MICROSCOPIC AGENTS, LIKE HAL'S SUBSTITUTE GREEN LANTERN JOHN STEWART, SUPERMAN'S FRIEND LOIS LANE, GOTHAM CITY'S COMMISSIONER GORDON... ANYONE WHO MEANS ANYTHING TO US IS BEING USED AS BAIT.
SUPERGIRL, THE TEEN TITANS, THE MARVEL FAMILY. ALL UNDER THE CONTROL OF BRAINIAC, LUTHOR, AND THE REST OF THEM.

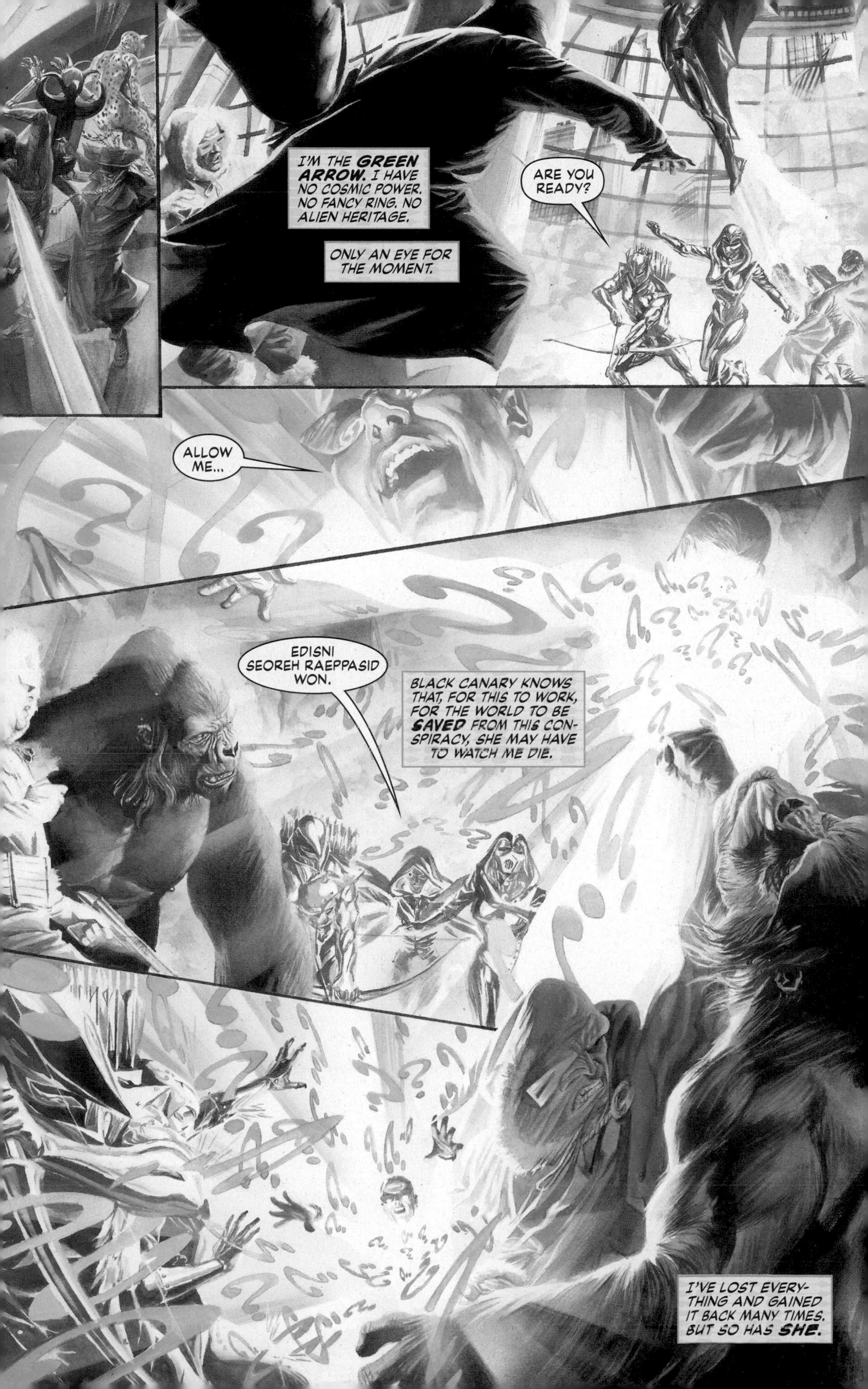
I'M THE GREEN ARROW. I HAVE NO COSMIC POWER. NO FANCY RING. NO ALIEN HERITAGE.
ONLY AN EYE FOR THE MOMENT.
ARE YOU READY?
ALLOW ME...
EDISNI SEOREH RAEPPASID WON.
BLACK CANARY KNOWS THAT, FOR THIS TO WORK, FOR THE WORLD TO BE SAVED FROM THIS CONSPIRACY, SHE MAY HAVE TO WATCH ME DIE.
I'VE LOST EVERYTHING AND GAINED IT BACK MANY TIMES. BUT SO HAS SHE.

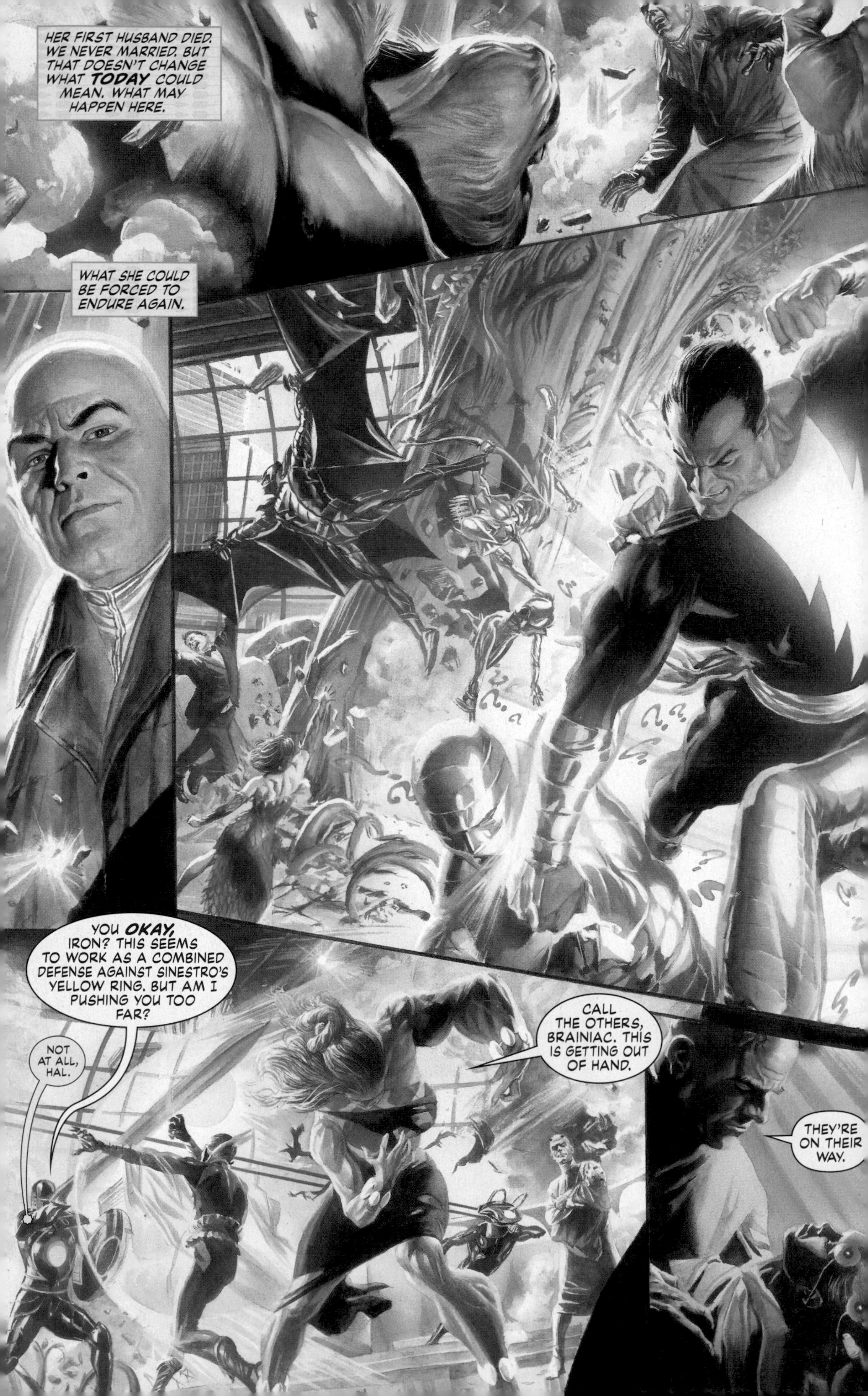
HER FIRST HUSBAND DIED. WE NEVER MARRIED. BUT THAT DOESN'T CHANGE WHAT **TODAY** COULD MEAN. WHAT MAY HAPPEN HERE.
WHAT SHE COULD BE FORCED TO ENDURE AGAIN.
YOU **OKAY,** IRON? THIS SEEMS TO WORK AS A COMBINED DEFENSE AGAINST SINESTRO'S YELLOW RING. BUT AM I PUSHING YOU TOO FAR?
NOT AT ALL, HAL.
CALL THE OTHERS, BRAINIAC. THIS IS GETTING OUT OF HAND.
THEY'RE ON THEIR WAY.

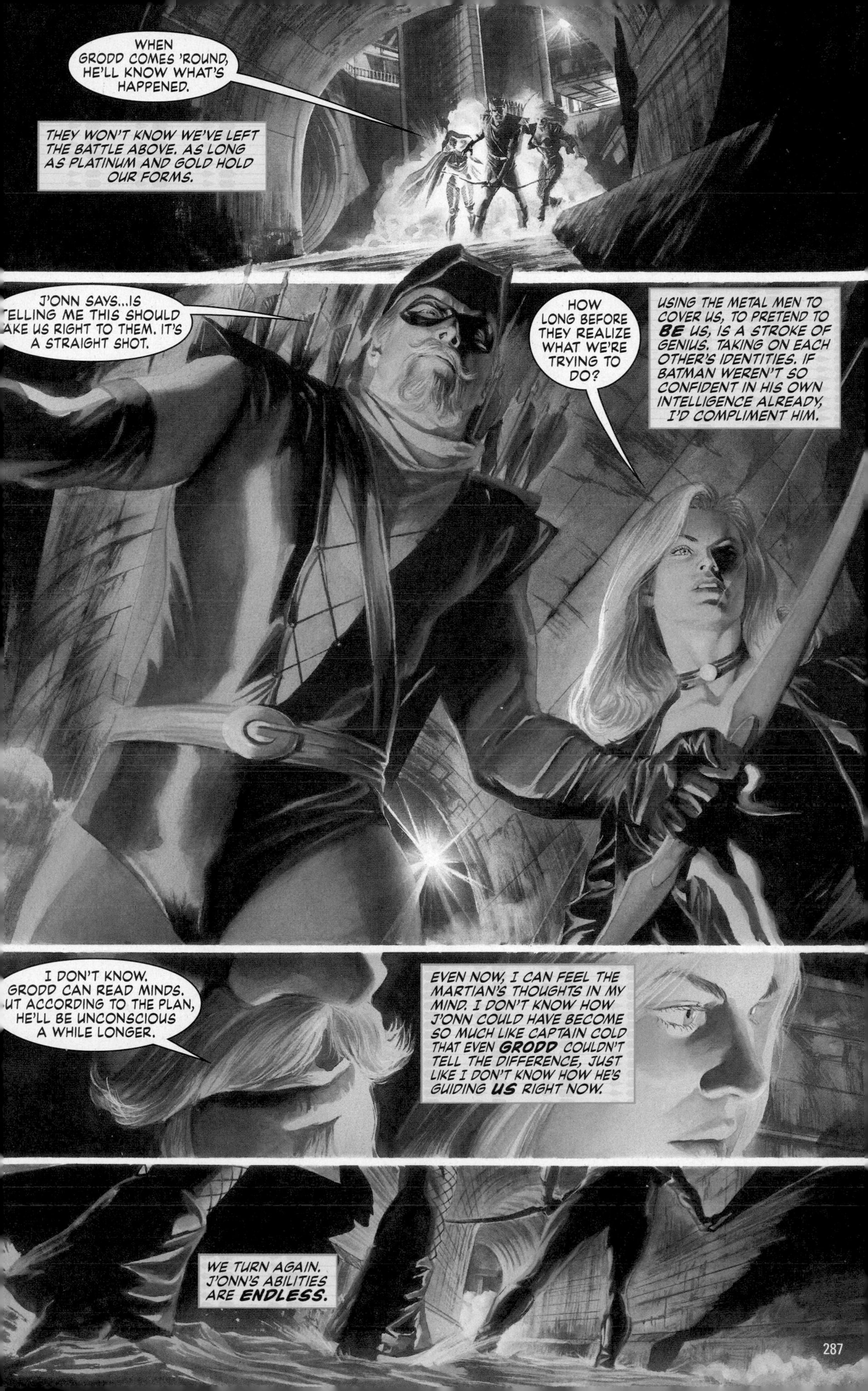
WHEN GRODD COMES 'ROUND, HE'LL KNOW WHAT'S HAPPENED.
THEY WON'T KNOW WE'VE LEFT THE BATTLE ABOVE. AS LONG AS PLATINUM AND GOLD HOLD OUR FORMS.
J'ONN SAYS...IS TELLING ME THIS SHOULD TAKE US RIGHT TO THEM. IT'S A STRAIGHT SHOT.
HOW LONG BEFORE THEY REALIZE WHAT WE'RE TRYING TO DO?
USING THE METAL MEN TO COVER US, TO PRETEND TO BE US, IS A STROKE OF GENIUS. TAKING ON EACH OTHER'S IDENTITIES. IF BATMAN WEREN'T SO CONFIDENT IN HIS OWN INTELLIGENCE ALREADY, I'D COMPLIMENT HIM.
I DON'T KNOW. GRODD CAN READ MINDS. BUT ACCORDING TO THE PLAN, HE'LL BE UNCONSCIOUS A WHILE LONGER.
EVEN NOW, I CAN FEEL THE MARTIAN'S THOUGHTS IN MY MIND. I DON'T KNOW HOW J'ONN COULD HAVE BECOME SO MUCH LIKE CAPTAIN COLD THAT EVEN GRODD COULDN'T TELL THE DIFFERENCE, JUST LIKE I DON'T KNOW HOW HE'S GUIDING US RIGHT NOW.
WE TURN AGAIN. J'ONN'S ABILITIES ARE ENDLESS.

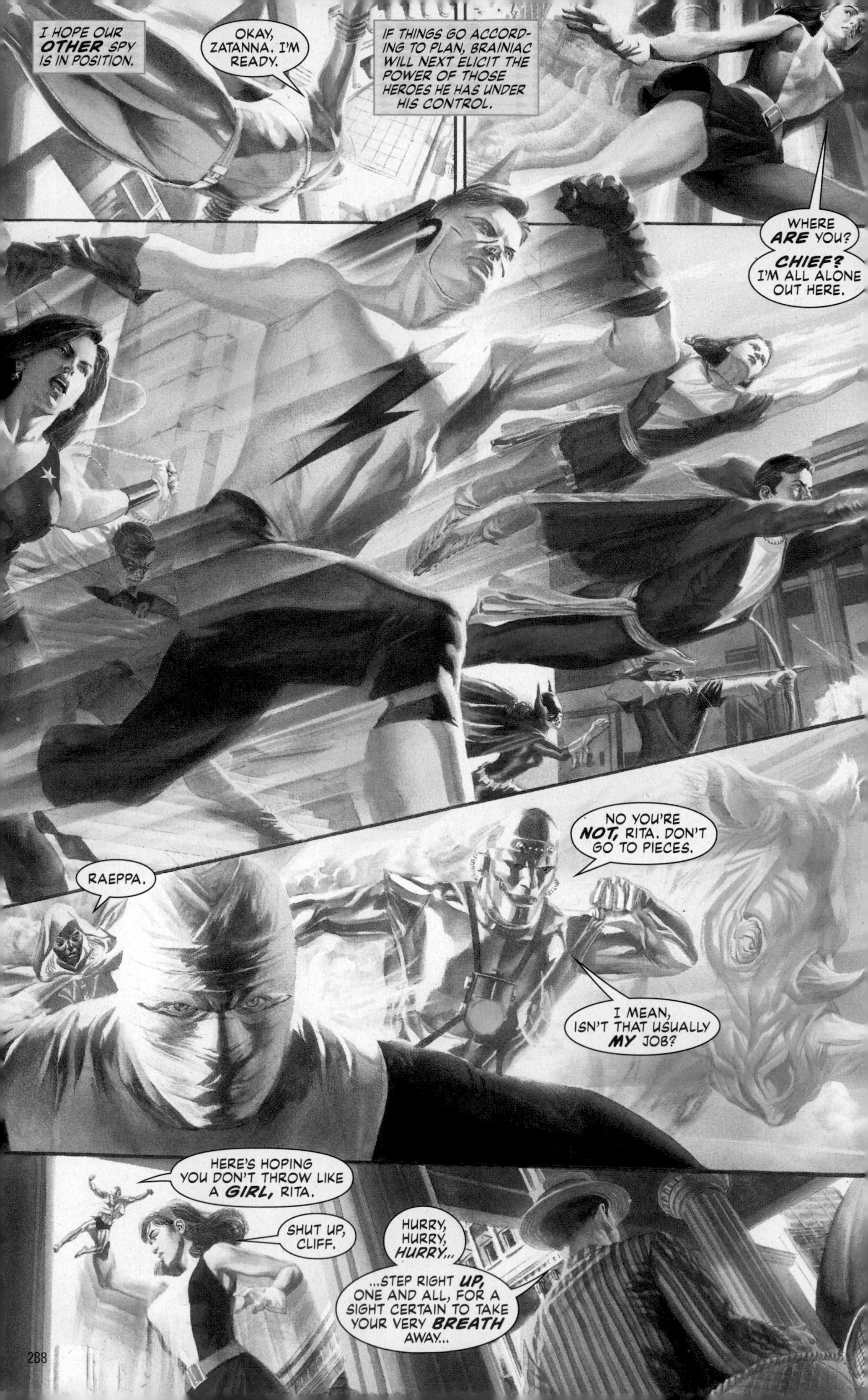

I HOPE OUR OTHER SPY IS IN POSITION.
OKAY, ZATANNA. I'M READY.
IF THINGS GO ACCORDING TO PLAN, BRAINIAC WILL NEXT ELICIT THE POWER OF THOSE HEROES HE HAS UNDER HIS CONTROL.
WHERE ARE YOU? CHIEF? I'M ALL ALONE OUT HERE.
RAEPPA.
NO YOU'RE NOT, RITA. DON'T GO TO PIECES.
I MEAN, ISN'T THAT USUALLY MY JOB?
HERE'S HOPING YOU DON'T THROW LIKE A GIRL, RITA.
SHUT UP, CLIFF.
HURRY, HURRY, HURRY...
...STEP RIGHT UP, ONE AND ALL, FOR A SIGHT CERTAIN TO TAKE YOUR VERY BREATH AWAY...

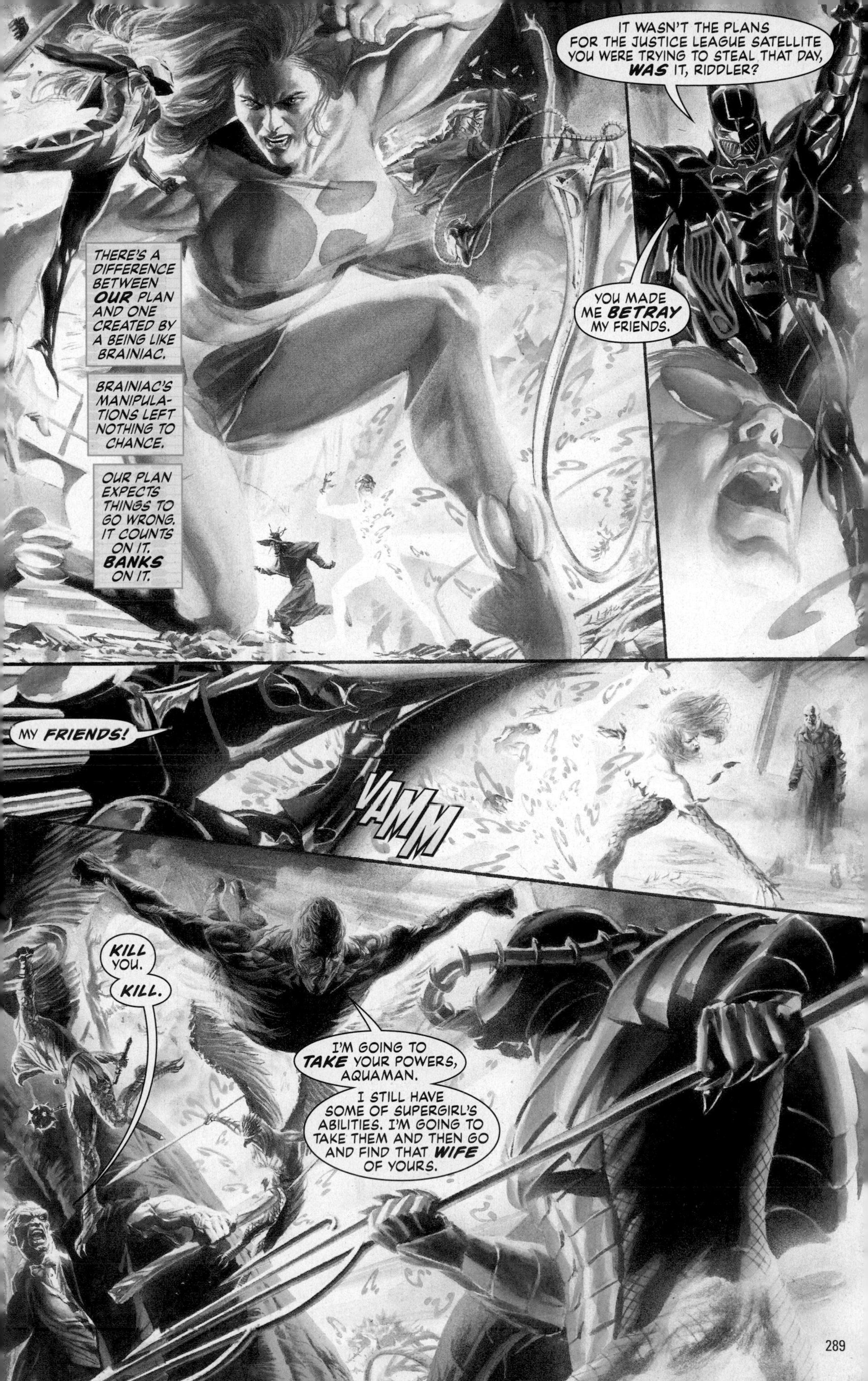
IT WASN'T THE PLANS FOR THE JUSTICE LEAGUE SATELLITE YOU WERE TRYING TO STEAL THAT DAY, WAS IT, RIDDLER?
THERE'S A DIFFERENCE BETWEEN OUR PLAN AND ONE CREATED BY A BEING LIKE BRAINIAC.
BRAINIAC'S MANIPULATIONS LEFT NOTHING TO CHANCE.
OUR PLAN EXPECTS THINGS TO GO WRONG. IT COUNTS ON IT. BANKS ON IT.
YOU MADE ME BETRAY MY FRIENDS.
MY FRIENDS!
VAMM
KILL YOU. KILL.
I'M GOING TO TAKE YOUR POWERS, AQUAMAN.
I STILL HAVE SOME OF SUPERGIRL'S ABILITIES. I'M GOING TO TAKE THEM AND THEN GO AND FIND THAT WIFE OF YOURS.

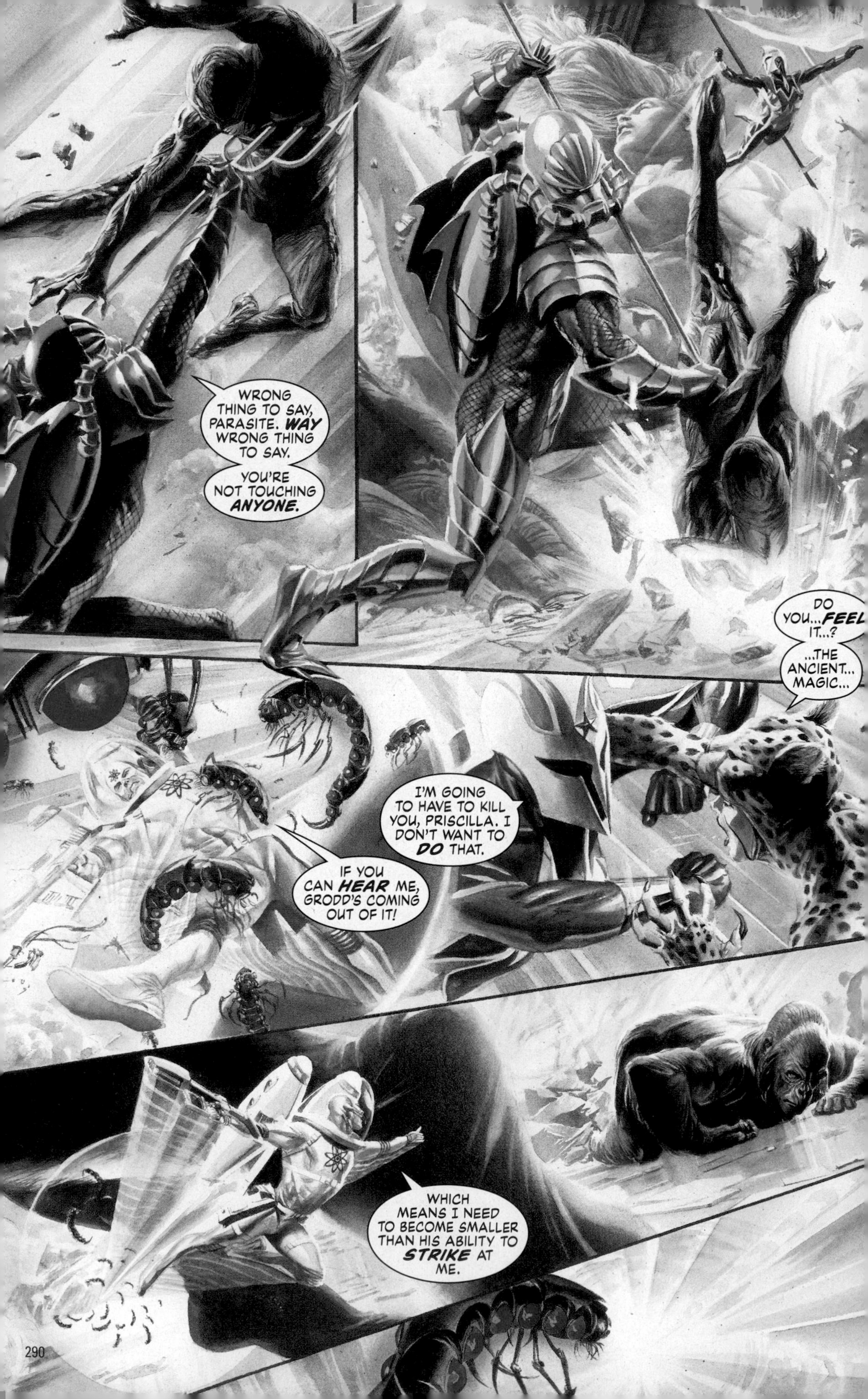
WRONG THING TO SAY, PARASITE. WAY WRONG THING TO SAY.
YOU'RE NOT TOUCHING ANYONE.
DO YOU...FEEL IT...?
...THE ANCIENT... MAGIC...
I'M GOING TO HAVE TO KILL YOU, PRISCILLA. I DON'T WANT TO DO THAT.
IF YOU CAN HEAR ME, GRODD'S COMING OUT OF IT!
WHICH MEANS I NEED TO BECOME SMALLER THAN HIS ABILITY TO STRIKE AT ME.

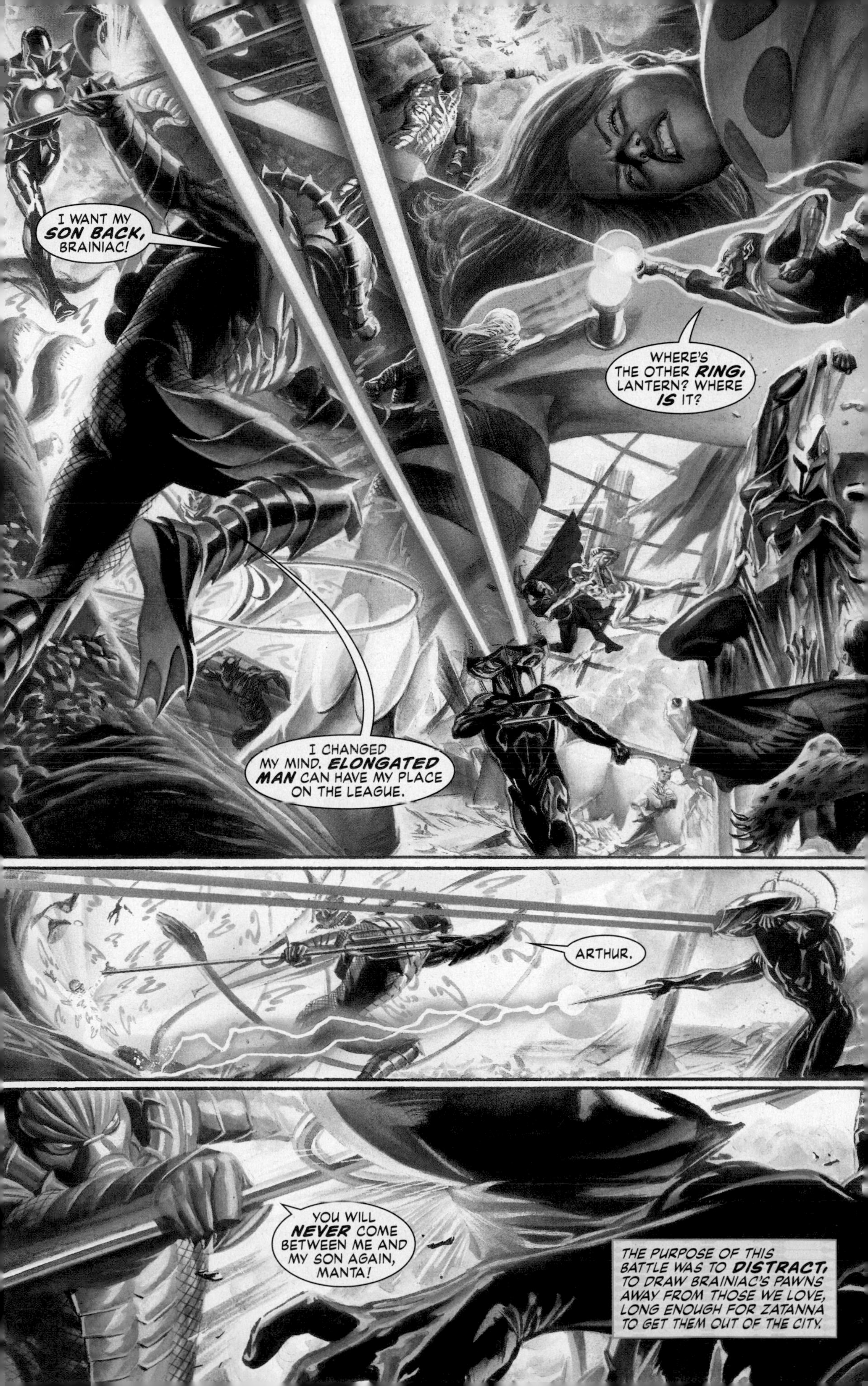
I WANT MY SON BACK, BRAINIAC!
WHERE'S THE OTHER RING, LANTERN? WHERE IS IT?
I CHANGED MY MIND. ELONGATED MAN CAN HAVE MY PLACE ON THE LEAGUE.
ARTHUR.
YOU WILL NEVER COME BETWEEN ME AND MY SON AGAIN, MANTA!
THE PURPOSE OF THIS BATTLE WAS TO DISTRACT, TO DRAW BRAINIAC'S PAWNS AWAY FROM THOSE WE LOVE, LONG ENOUGH FOR ZATANNA TO GET THEM OUT OF THE CITY.

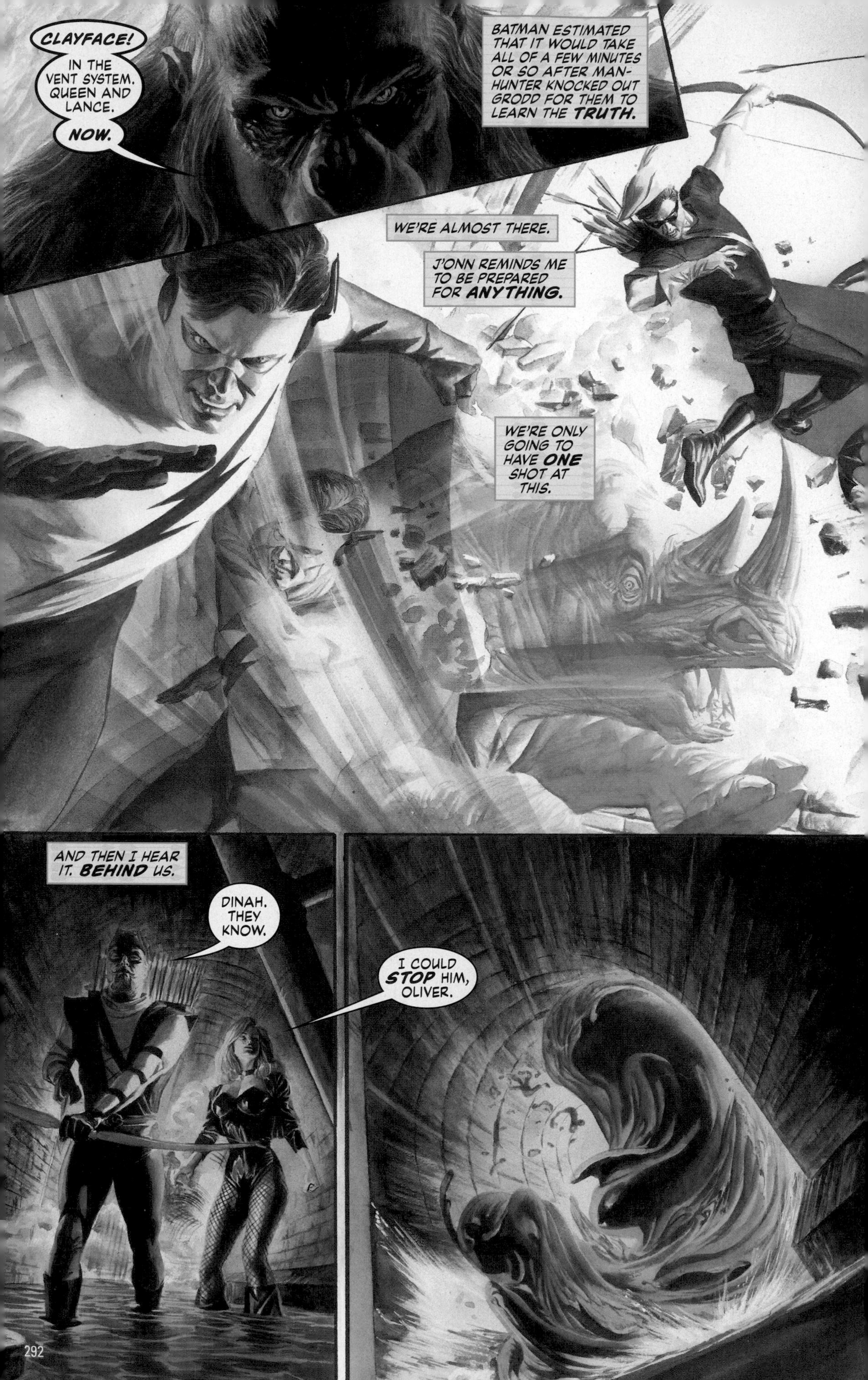
CLAYFACE!
IN THE VENT SYSTEM. QUEEN AND LANCE.
NOW.
BATMAN ESTIMATED THAT IT WOULD TAKE ALL OF A FEW MINUTES OR SO AFTER MAN-HUNTER KNOCKED OUT GRODD FOR THEM TO LEARN THE TRUTH.
WE'RE ALMOST THERE.
J'ONN REMINDS ME TO BE PREPARED FOR ANYTHING.
WE'RE ONLY GOING TO HAVE ONE SHOT AT THIS.
AND THEN I HEAR IT. BEHIND US.
DINAH. THEY KNOW.
I COULD STOP HIM, OLIVER.

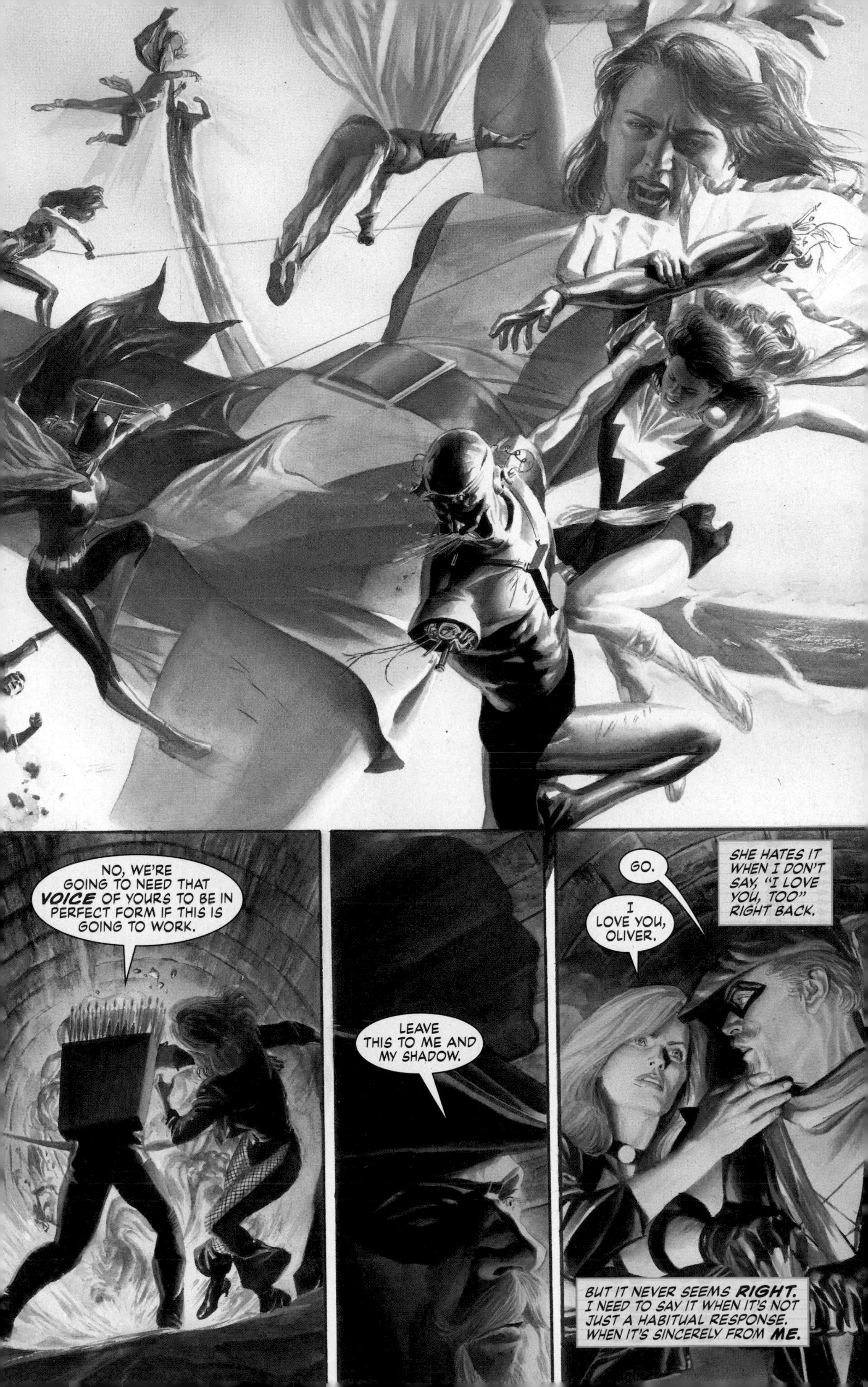
NO, WE'RE GOING TO NEED THAT VOICE OF YOURS TO BE IN PERFECT FORM IF THIS IS GOING TO WORK.
LEAVE THIS TO ME AND MY SHADOW.
GO.
I LOVE YOU, OLIVER.
SHE HATES IT WHEN I DON'T SAY, "I LOVE YOU, TOO" RIGHT BACK.
BUT IT NEVER SEEMS RIGHT. I NEED TO SAY IT WHEN IT'S NOT JUST A HABITUAL RESPONSE. WHEN IT'S SINCERELY FROM ME.

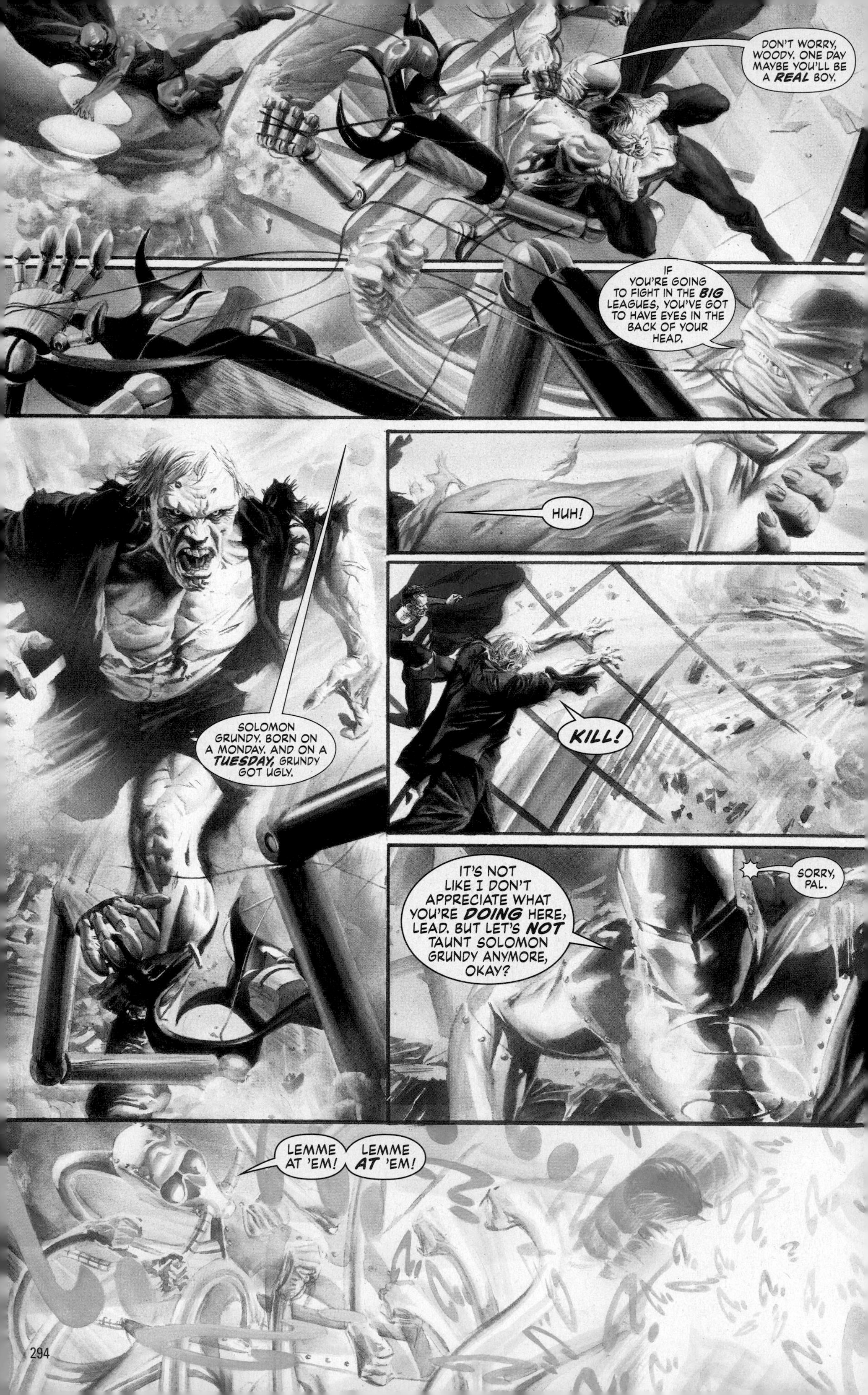
DON'T WORRY, WOODY. ONE DAY MAYBE YOU'LL BE A REAL BOY.
IF YOU'RE GOING TO FIGHT IN THE BIG LEAGUES, YOU'VE GOT TO HAVE EYES IN THE BACK OF YOUR HEAD.
SOLOMON GRUNDY. BORN ON A MONDAY. AND ON A TUESDAY, GRUNDY GOT UGLY.
HUH!
KILL!
IT'S NOT LIKE I DON'T APPRECIATE WHAT YOU'RE DOING HERE, LEAD. BUT LET'S NOT TAUNT SOLOMON GRUNDY ANYMORE, OKAY?
SORRY, PAL.
LEMME AT 'EM!
LEMME AT 'EM!

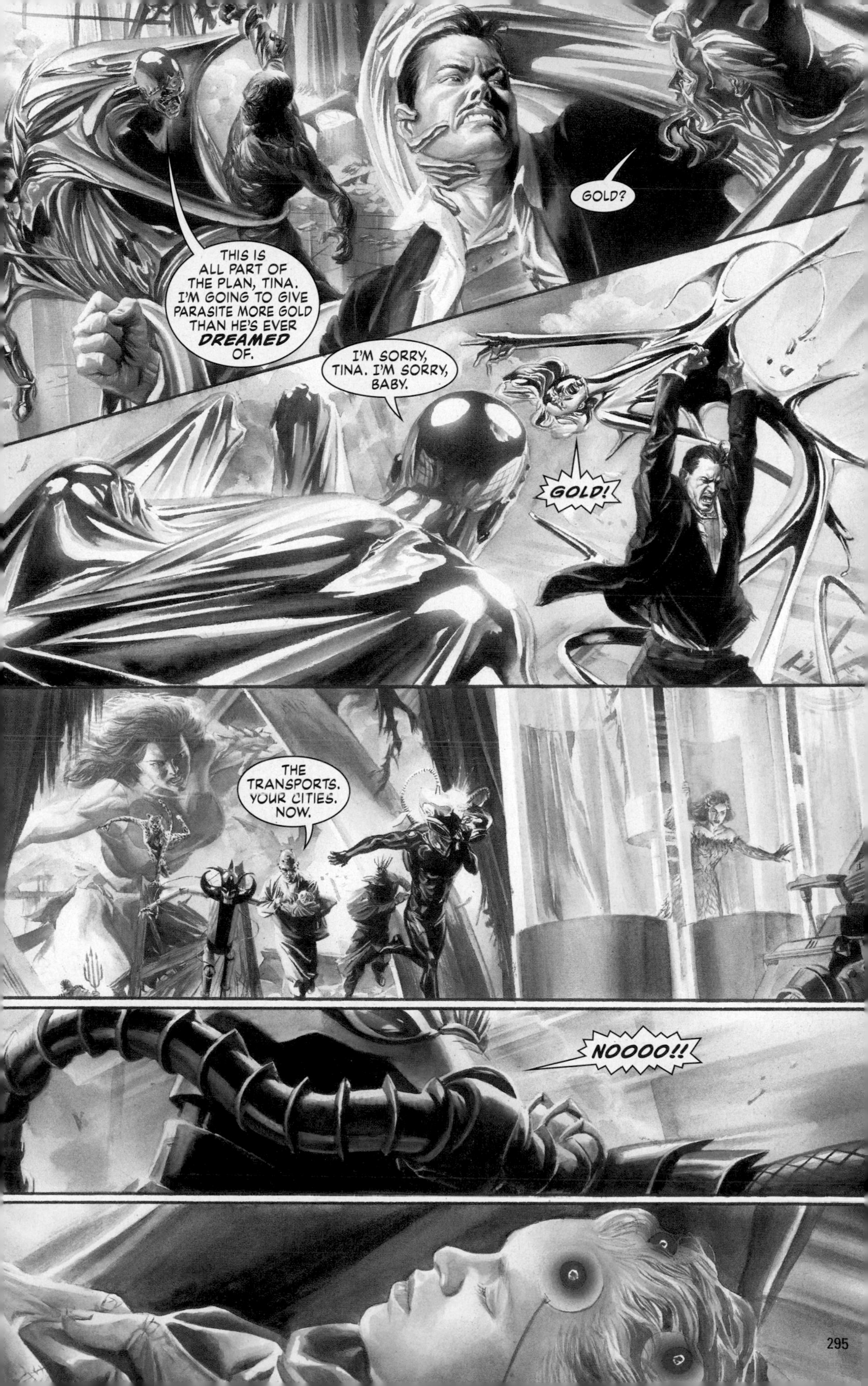
GOLD?
THIS IS ALL PART OF THE PLAN, TINA. I'M GOING TO GIVE PARASITE MORE GOLD THAN HE'S EVER DREAMED OF.
I'M SORRY, TINA. I'M SORRY, BABY.
GOLD!
THE TRANSPORTS. YOUR CITIES. NOW.
NOOOO!!

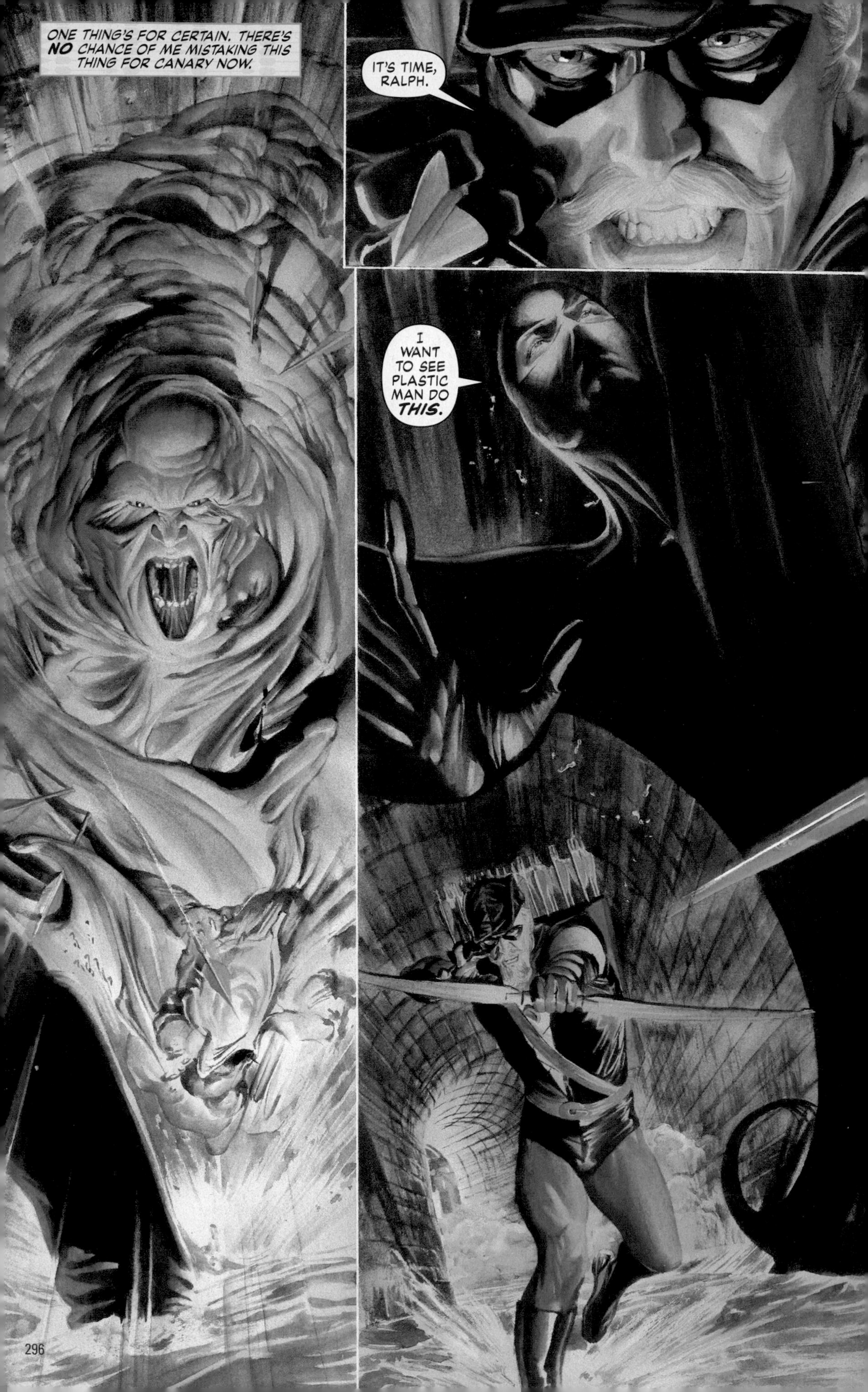
ONE THING'S FOR CERTAIN. THERE'S **NO** CHANCE OF ME MISTAKING THIS THING FOR CANARY NOW.
IT'S TIME, RALPH.
I WANT TO SEE PLASTIC MAN DO ***THIS***.

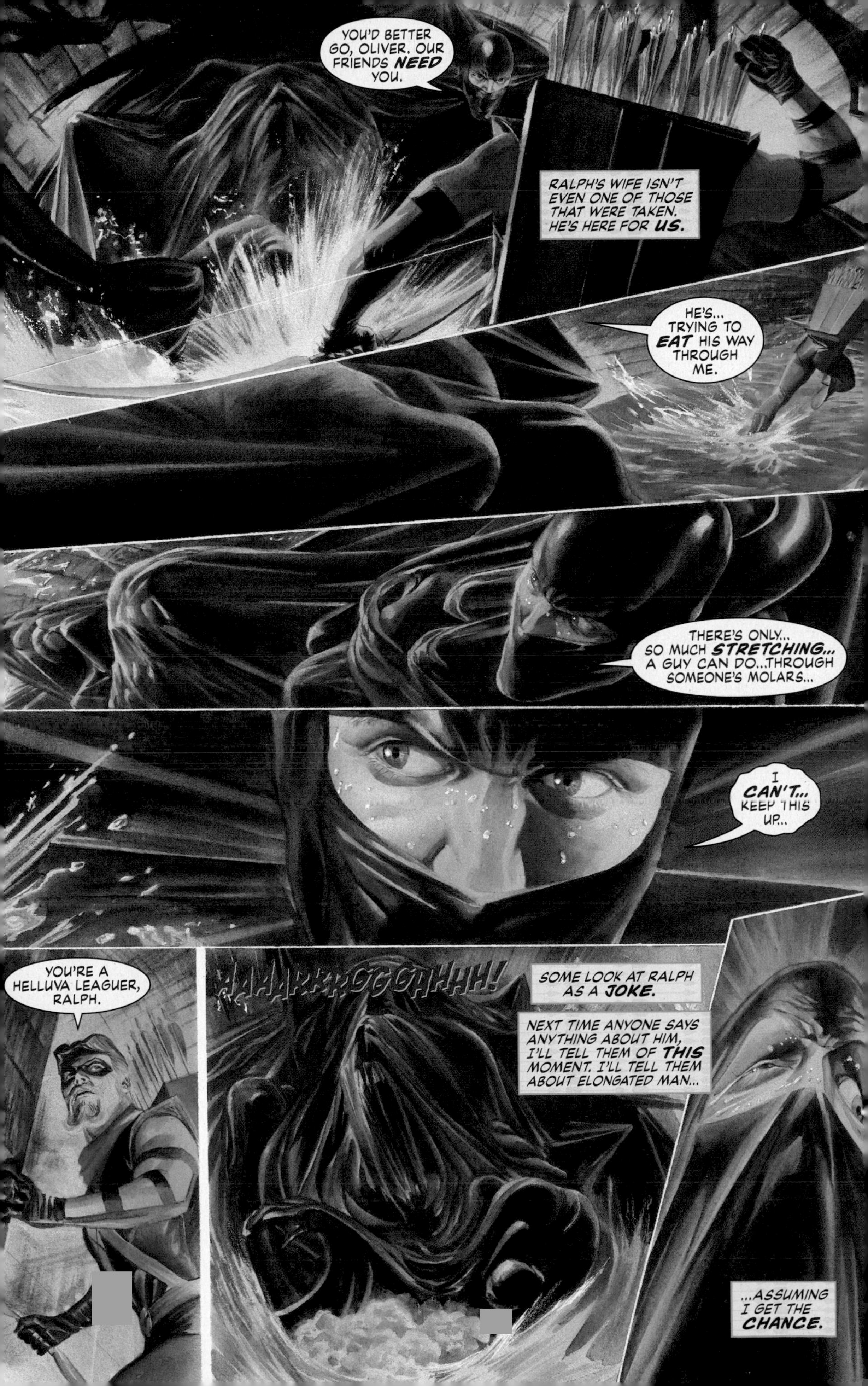
YOU'D BETTER GO, OLIVER. OUR FRIENDS NEED YOU.
RALPH'S WIFE ISN'T EVEN ONE OF THOSE THAT WERE TAKEN. HE'S HERE FOR US.
HE'S... TRYING TO EAT HIS WAY THROUGH ME.
THERE'S ONLY... SO MUCH STRETCHING... A GUY CAN DO...THROUGH SOMEONE'S MOLARS...
I CAN'T... KEEP THIS UP...
YOU'RE A HELLUVA LEAGUER, RALPH.
AAAAKKKGGGAHHHH!
SOME LOOK AT RALPH AS A JOKE.
NEXT TIME ANYONE SAYS ANYTHING ABOUT HIM, I'LL TELL THEM OF THIS MOMENT. I'LL TELL THEM ABOUT ELONGATED MAN...
...ASSUMING I GET THE CHANCE.

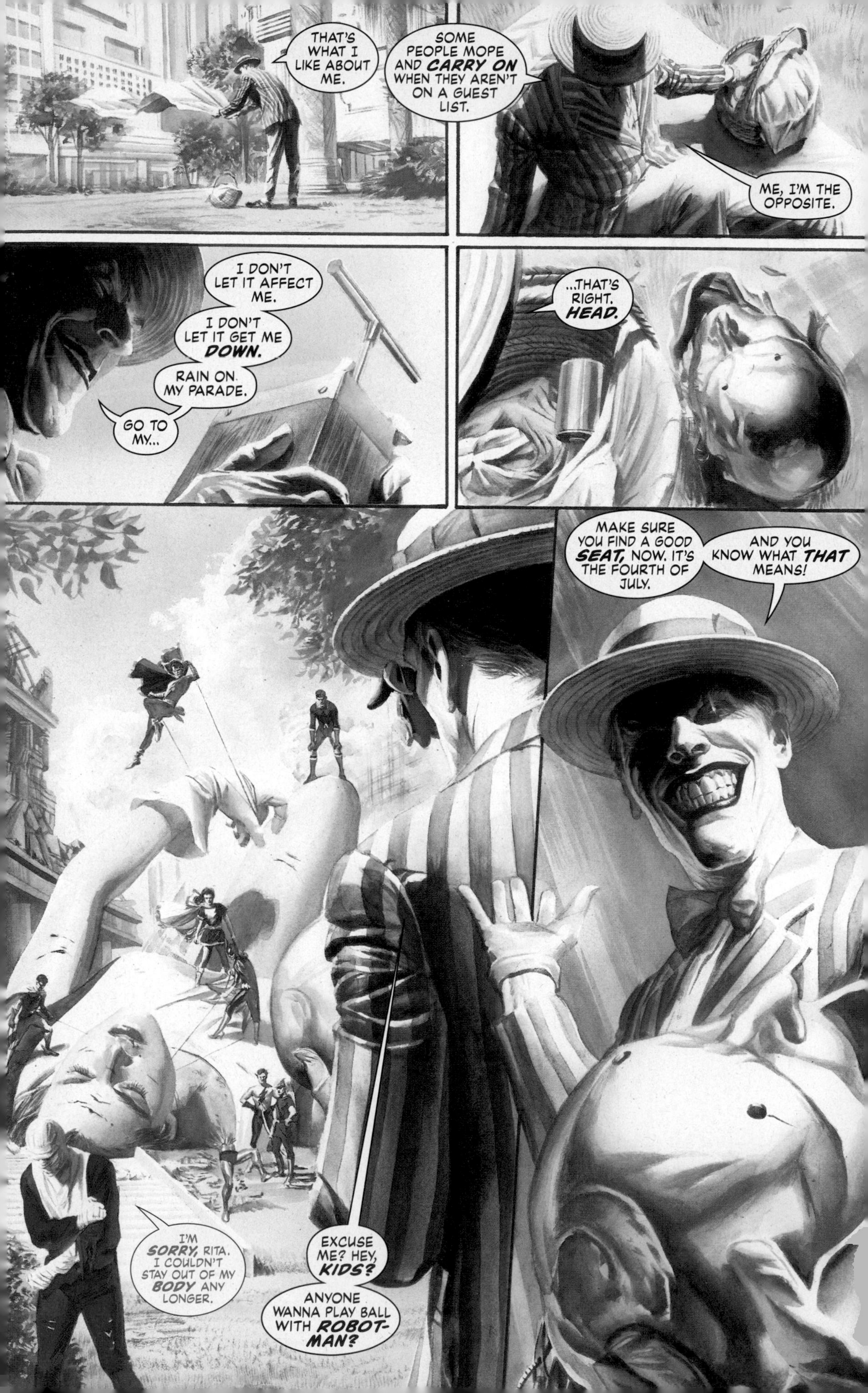
THAT'S WHAT I LIKE ABOUT ME.
SOME PEOPLE MOPE AND CARRY ON WHEN THEY AREN'T ON A GUEST LIST.
ME, I'M THE OPPOSITE.
I DON'T LET IT AFFECT ME.
I DON'T LET IT GET ME DOWN.
RAIN ON MY PARADE.
GO TO MY...
...THAT'S RIGHT. HEAD.
MAKE SURE YOU FIND A GOOD SEAT, NOW. IT'S THE FOURTH OF JULY.
AND YOU KNOW WHAT THAT MEANS!
I'M SORRY, RITA. I COULDN'T STAY OUT OF MY BODY ANY LONGER.
EXCUSE ME? HEY, KIDS?
ANYONE WANNA PLAY BALL WITH ROBOT-MAN?

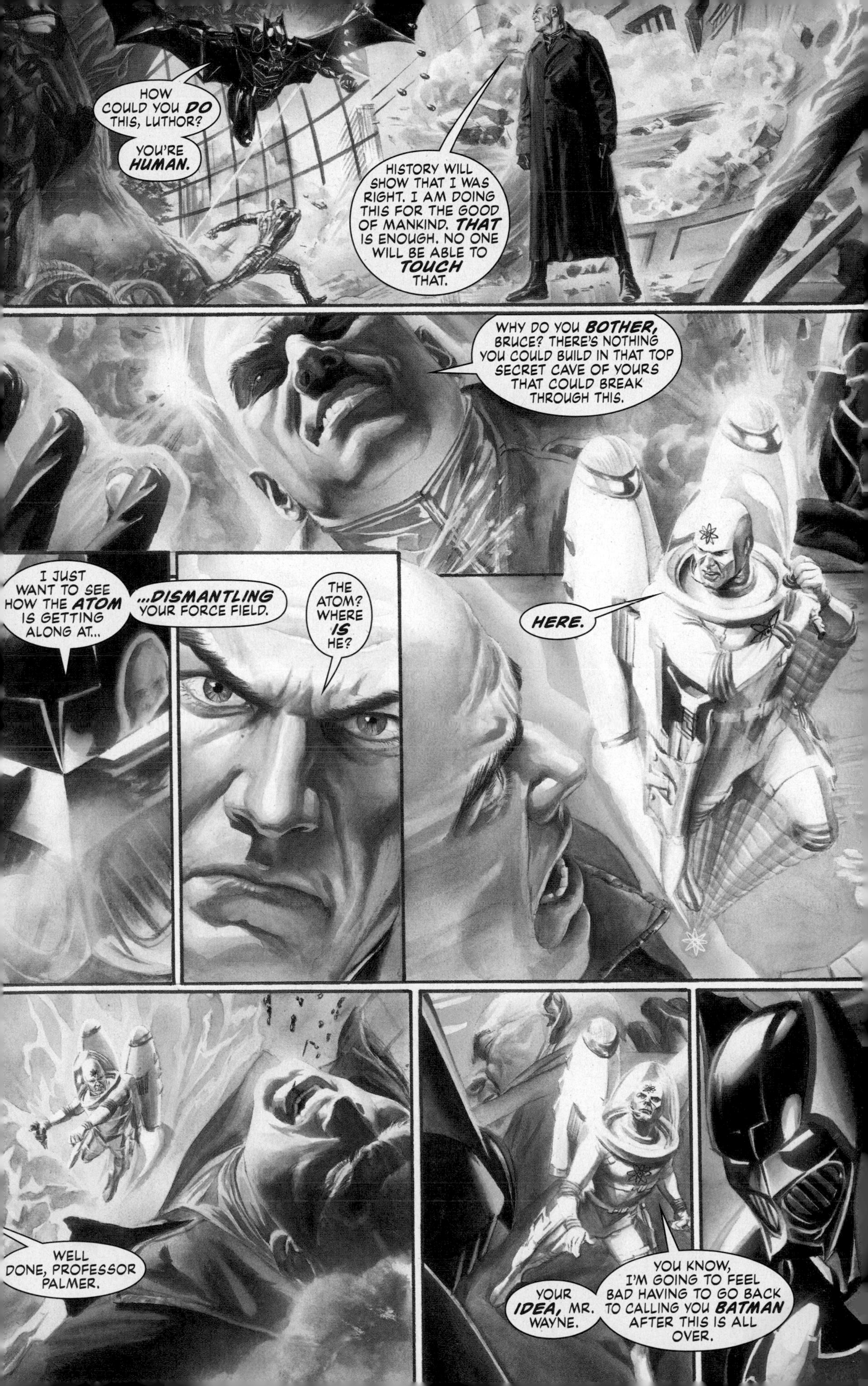
HOW COULD YOU **DO** THIS, LUTHOR?
YOU'RE **HUMAN.**
HISTORY WILL SHOW THAT I WAS RIGHT. I AM DOING THIS FOR THE GOOD OF MANKIND. **THAT** IS ENOUGH. NO ONE WILL BE ABLE TO **TOUCH** THAT.
WHY DO YOU **BOTHER,** BRUCE? THERE'S NOTHING YOU COULD BUILD IN THAT TOP SECRET CAVE OF YOURS THAT COULD BREAK THROUGH THIS.
I JUST WANT TO SEE HOW THE **ATOM** IS GETTING ALONG AT...
...DISMANTLING YOUR FORCE FIELD.
THE ATOM? WHERE **IS** HE?
HERE.
WELL DONE, PROFESSOR PALMER.
YOUR **IDEA,** MR. WAYNE.
YOU KNOW, I'M GOING TO FEEL BAD HAVING TO GO BACK TO CALLING YOU **BATMAN** AFTER THIS IS ALL OVER.

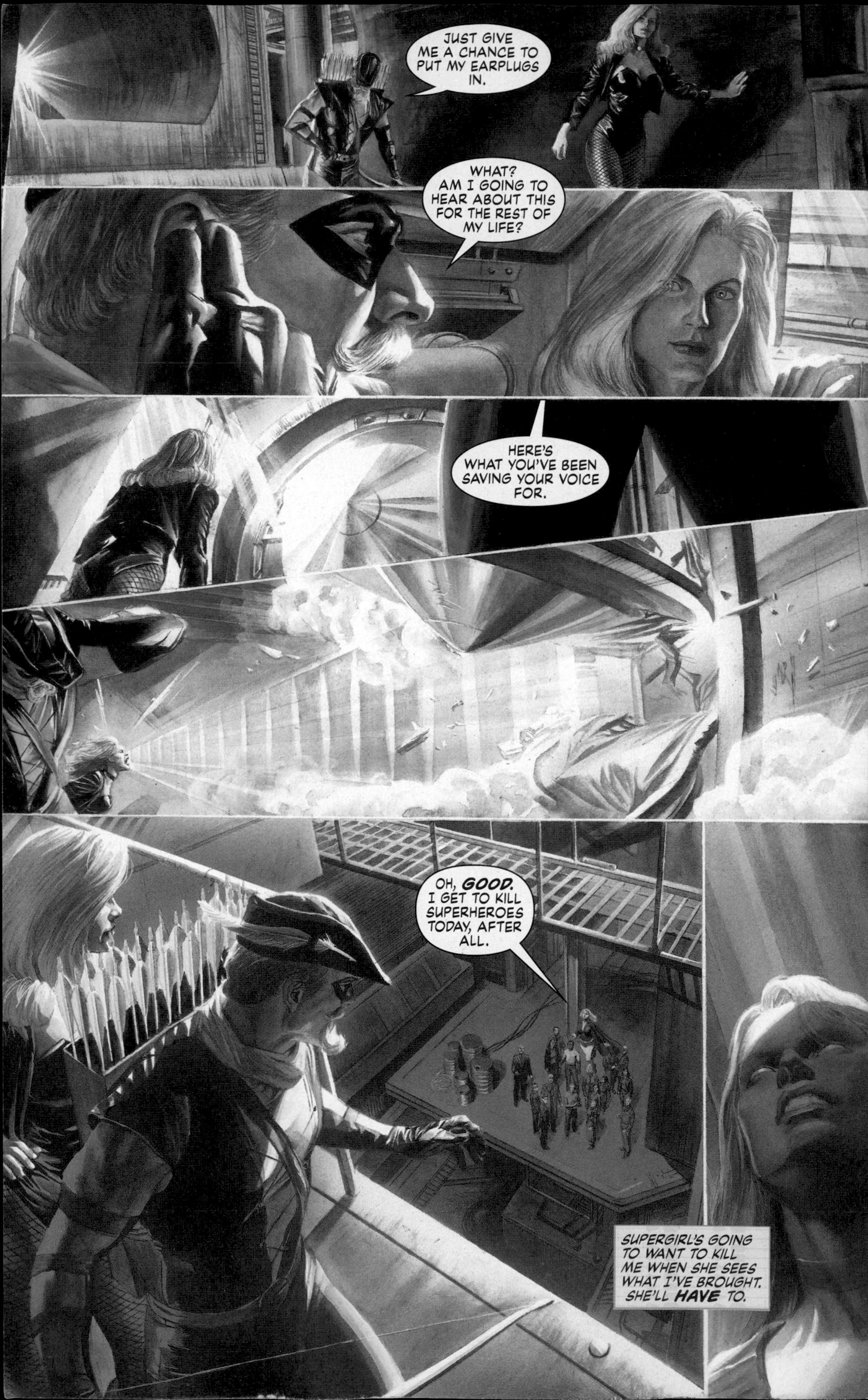
JUST GIVE ME A CHANCE TO PUT MY EARPLUGS IN.
WHAT? AM I GOING TO HEAR ABOUT THIS FOR THE REST OF MY LIFE?
HERE'S WHAT YOU'VE BEEN SAVING YOUR VOICE FOR.
OH, **GOOD.** I GET TO KILL SUPERHEROES TODAY, AFTER ALL.
SUPERGIRL'S GOING TO WANT TO KILL ME WHEN SHE SEES WHAT I'VE BROUGHT. SHE'LL **HAVE** TO.

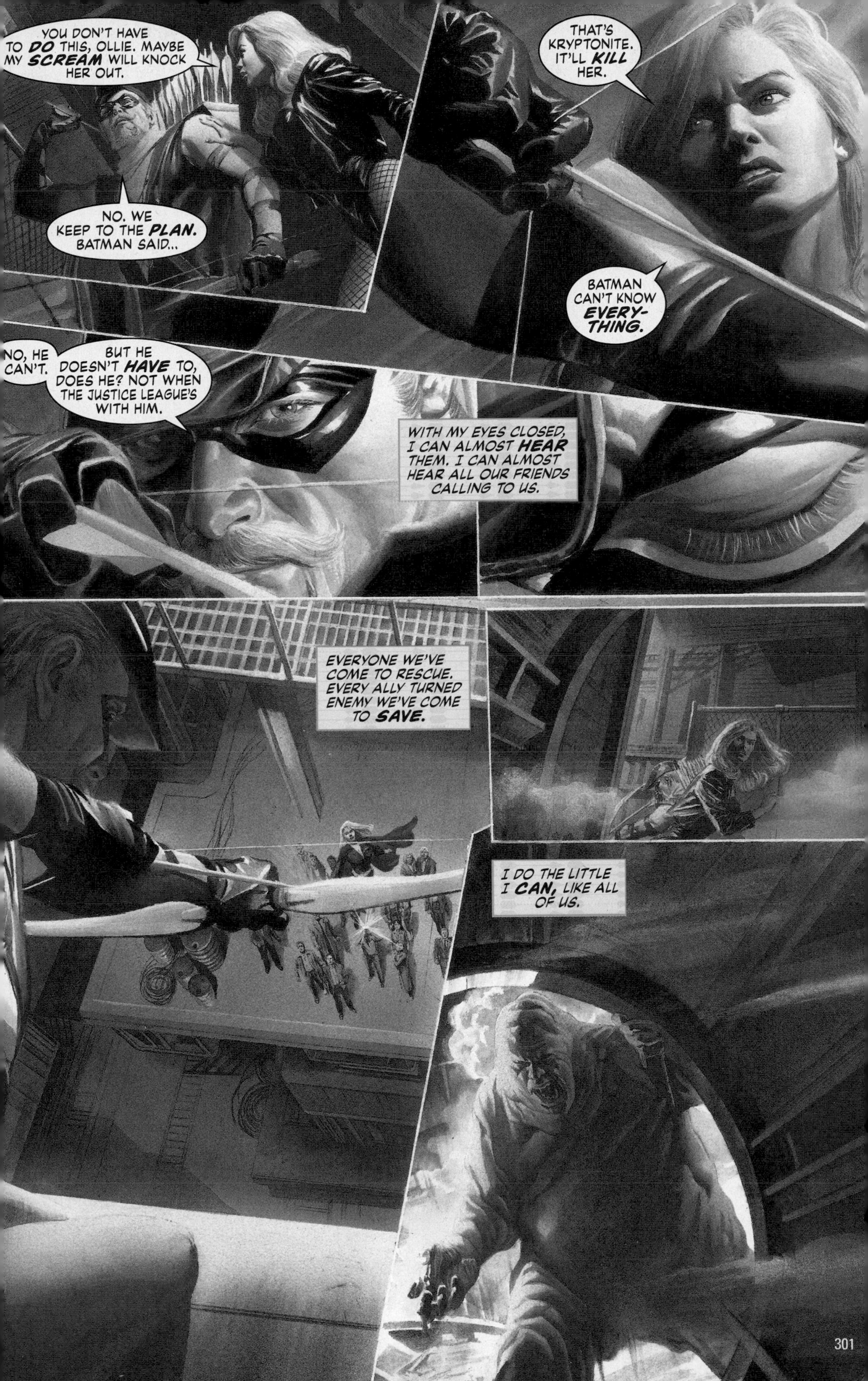
YOU DON'T HAVE TO **DO** THIS, OLLIE. MAYBE MY **SCREAM** WILL KNOCK HER OUT.
NO. WE KEEP TO THE **PLAN.** BATMAN SAID...
THAT'S KRYPTONITE. IT'LL **KILL** HER.
BATMAN CAN'T KNOW **EVERY-THING.**
NO, HE CAN'T.
BUT HE DOESN'T **HAVE** TO, DOES HE? NOT WHEN THE JUSTICE LEAGUE'S WITH HIM.
WITH MY EYES CLOSED, I CAN ALMOST **HEAR** THEM. I CAN ALMOST HEAR ALL OUR FRIENDS CALLING TO US.
EVERYONE WE'VE COME TO RESCUE. EVERY ALLY TURNED ENEMY WE'VE COME TO **SAVE.**
I DO THE LITTLE I **CAN,** LIKE ALL OF US.

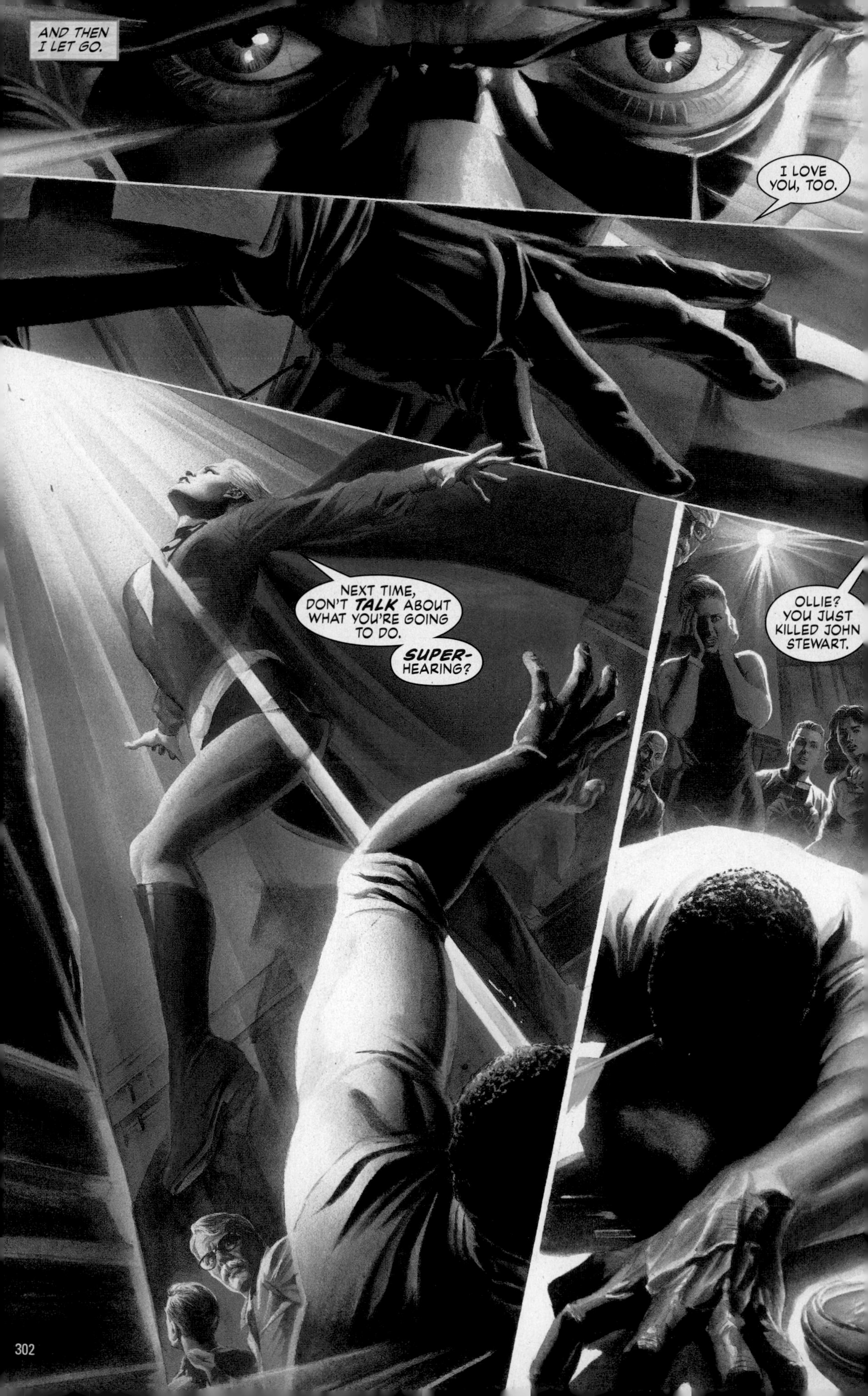
AND THEN I LET GO.
I LOVE YOU, TOO.
NEXT TIME, DON'T TALK ABOUT WHAT YOU'RE GOING TO DO.
SUPER-HEARING?
OLLIE? YOU JUST KILLED JOHN STEWART.

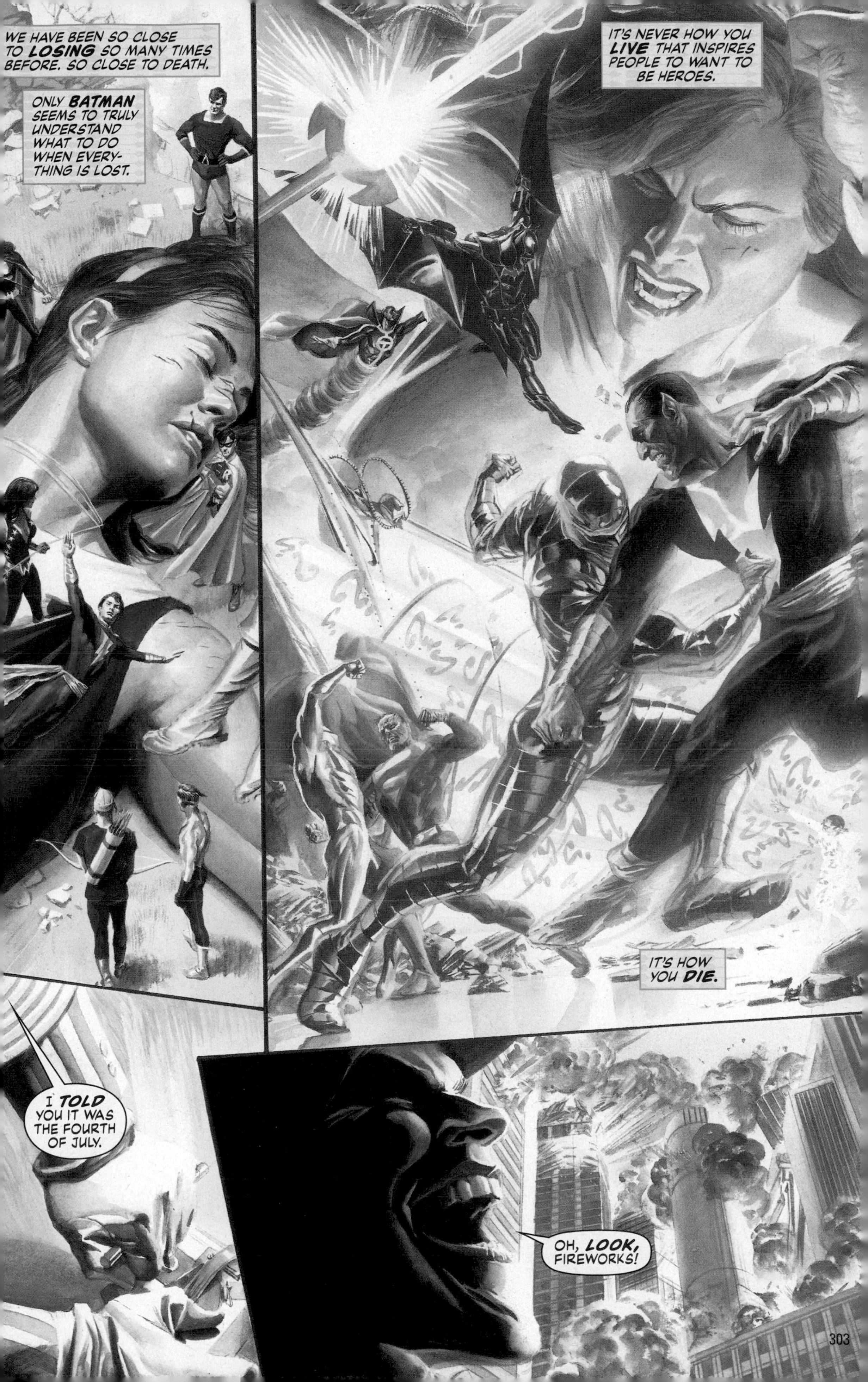
WE HAVE BEEN SO CLOSE TO LOSING SO MANY TIMES BEFORE. SO CLOSE TO DEATH.
ONLY BATMAN SEEMS TO TRULY UNDERSTAND WHAT TO DO WHEN EVERY-THING IS LOST.
IT'S NEVER HOW YOU LIVE THAT INSPIRES PEOPLE TO WANT TO BE HEROES.
IT'S HOW YOU DIE.
I TOLD YOU IT WAS THE FOURTH OF JULY.
OH, LOOK, FIREWORKS!

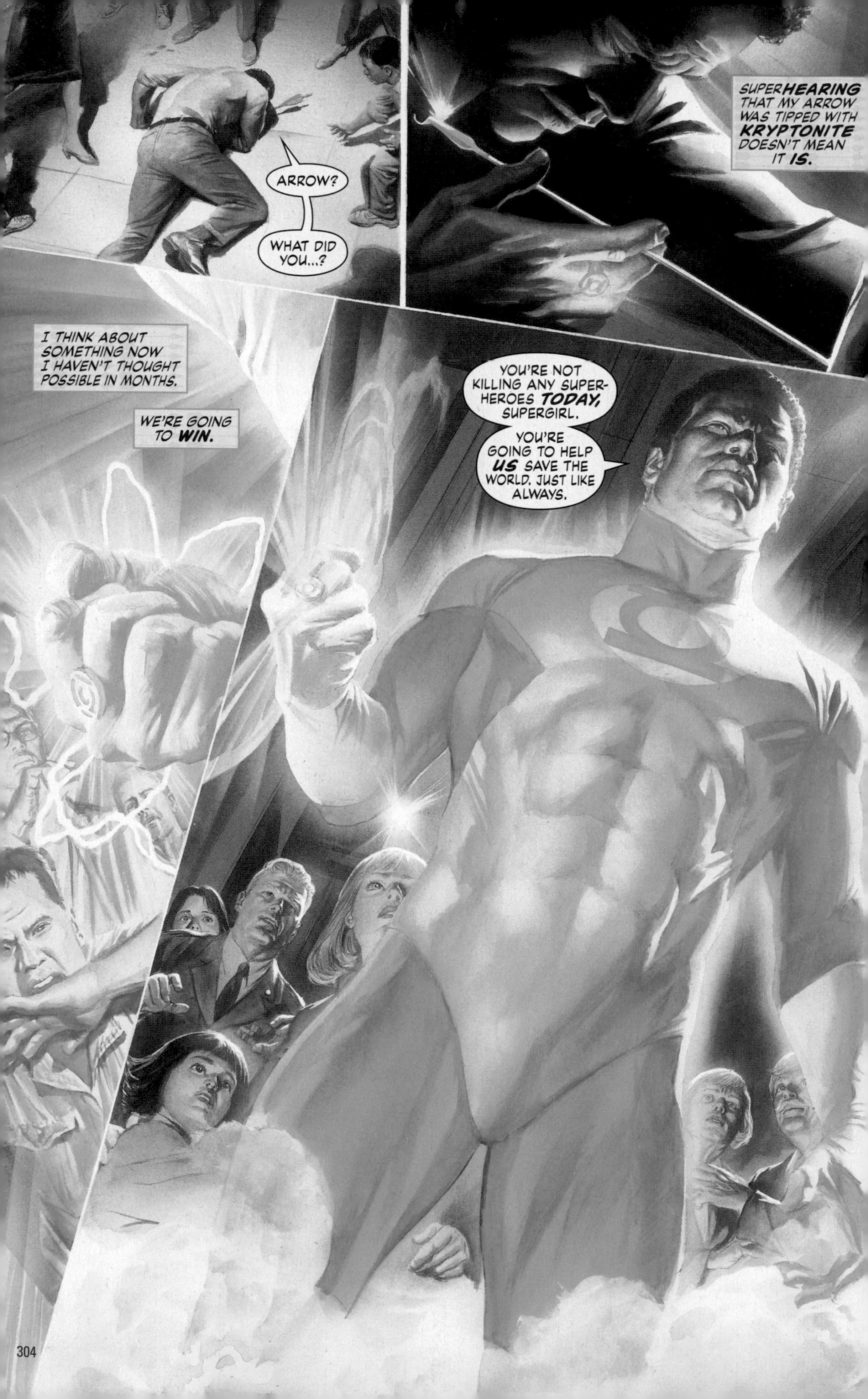
ARROW?
WHAT DID YOU...?
SUPERHEARING THAT MY ARROW WAS TIPPED WITH KRYPTONITE DOESN'T MEAN IT IS.
I THINK ABOUT SOMETHING NOW I HAVEN'T THOUGHT POSSIBLE IN MONTHS.
WE'RE GOING TO WIN.
YOU'RE NOT KILLING ANY SUPER-HEROES TODAY, SUPERGIRL.
YOU'RE GOING TO HELP US SAVE THE WORLD. JUST LIKE ALWAYS.

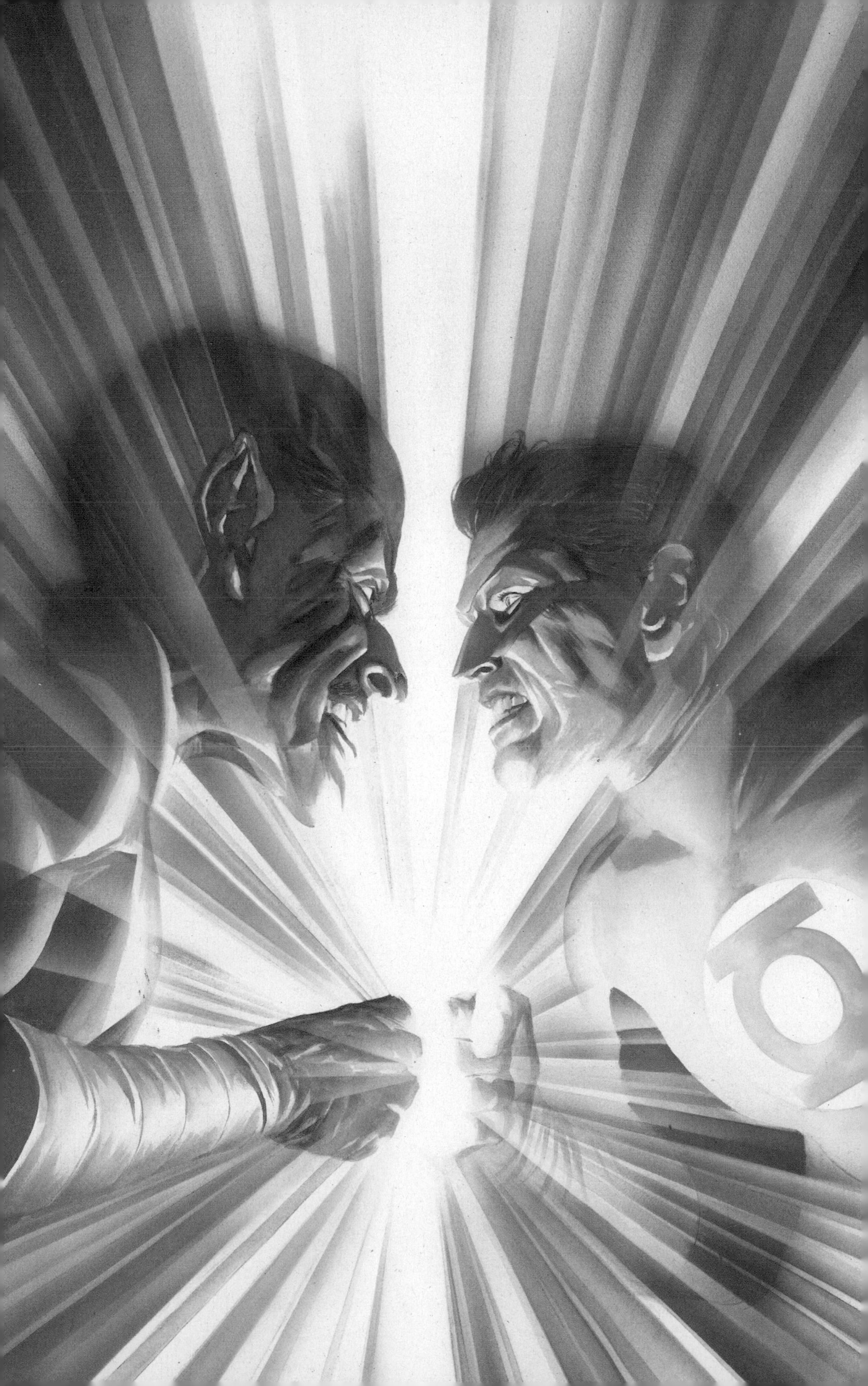

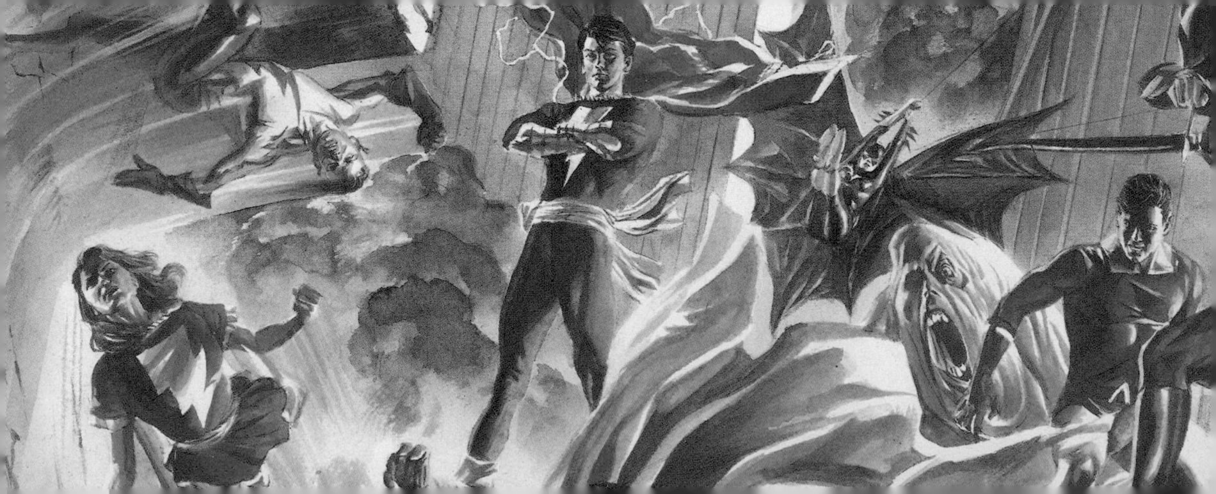

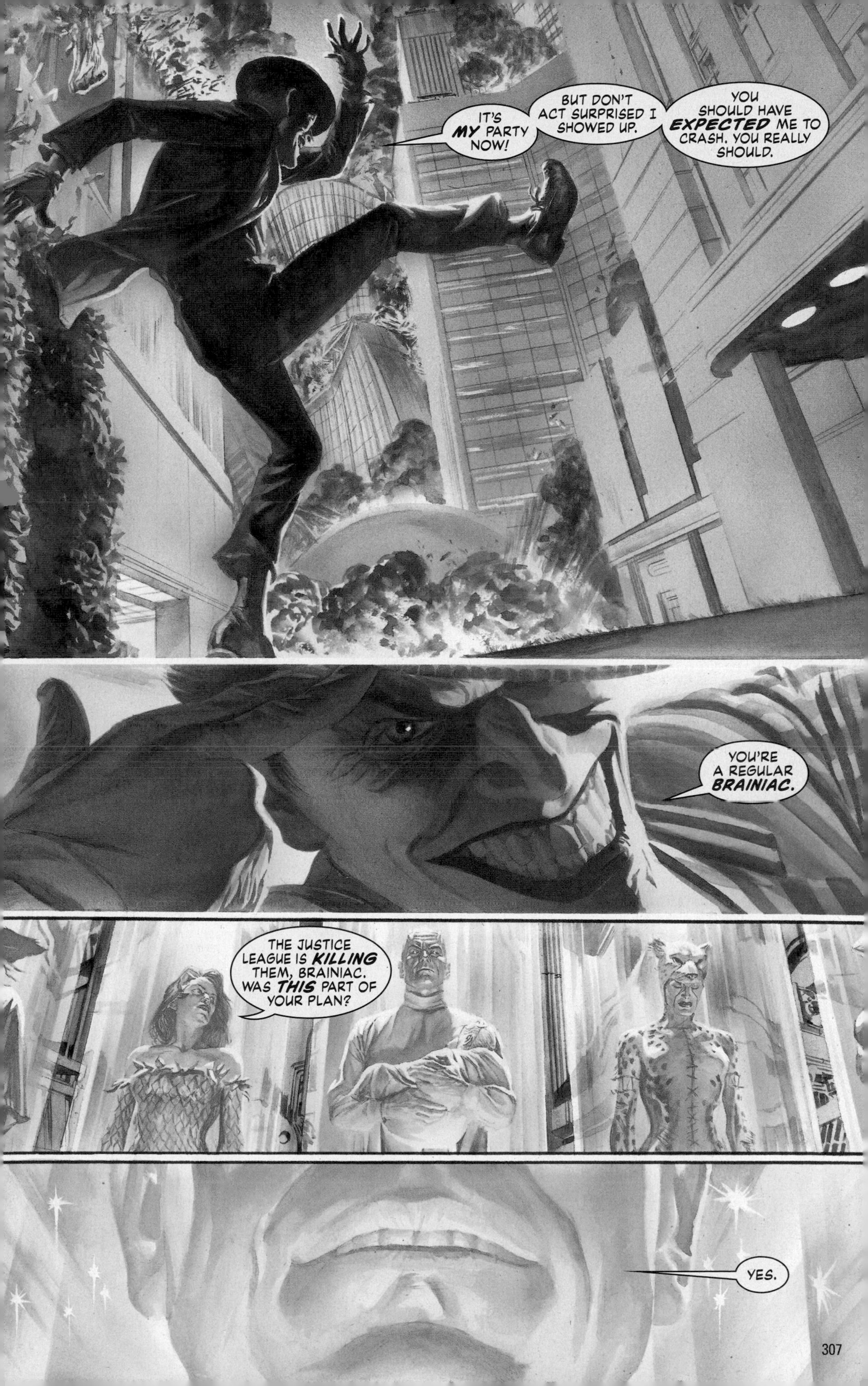
IT'S MY PARTY NOW!
BUT DON'T ACT SURPRISED I SHOWED UP.
YOU SHOULD HAVE EXPECTED ME TO CRASH. YOU REALLY SHOULD.
YOU'RE A REGULAR BRAINIAC.
THE JUSTICE LEAGUE IS KILLING THEM, BRAINIAC. WAS THIS PART OF YOUR PLAN?
YES.

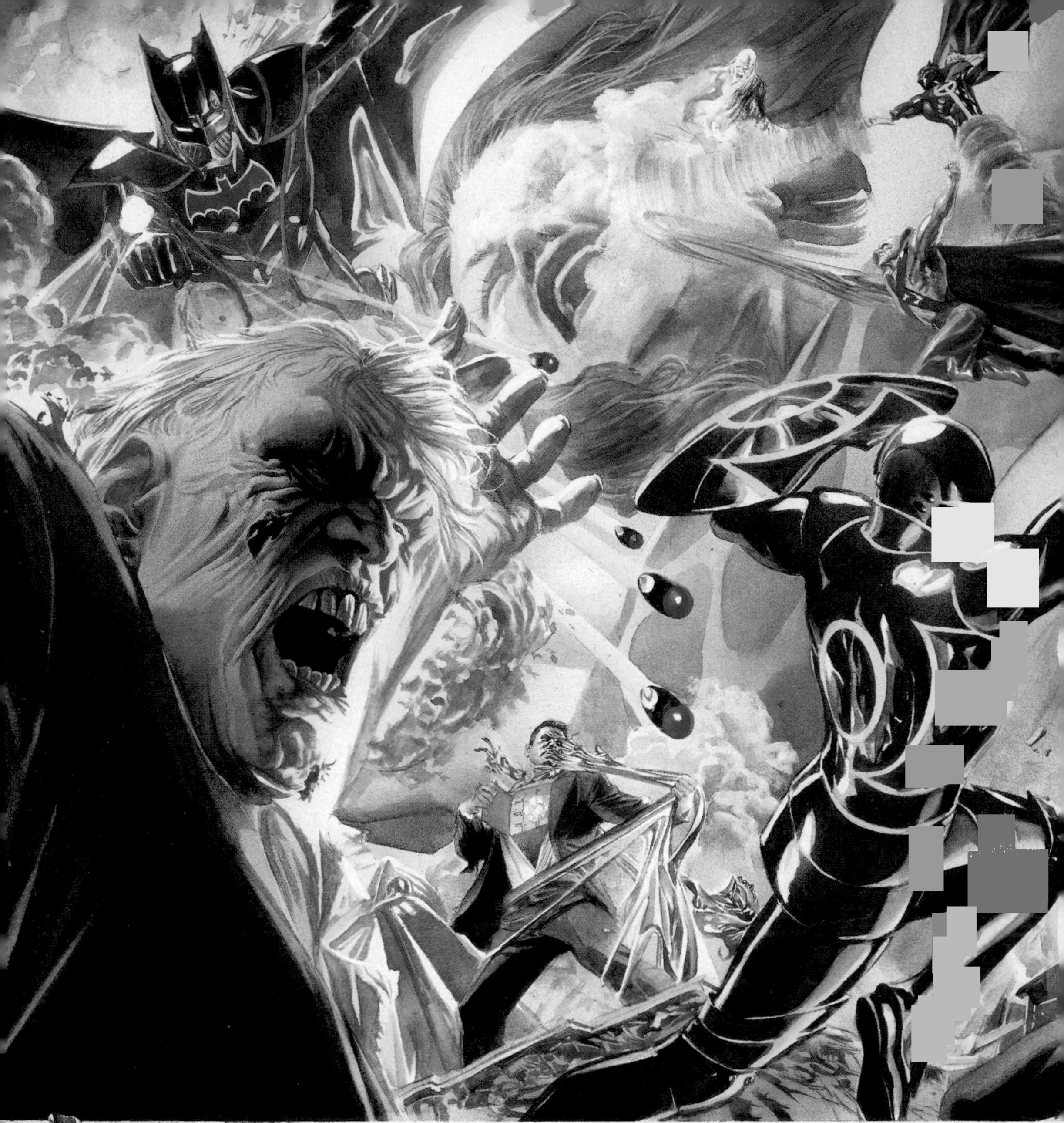

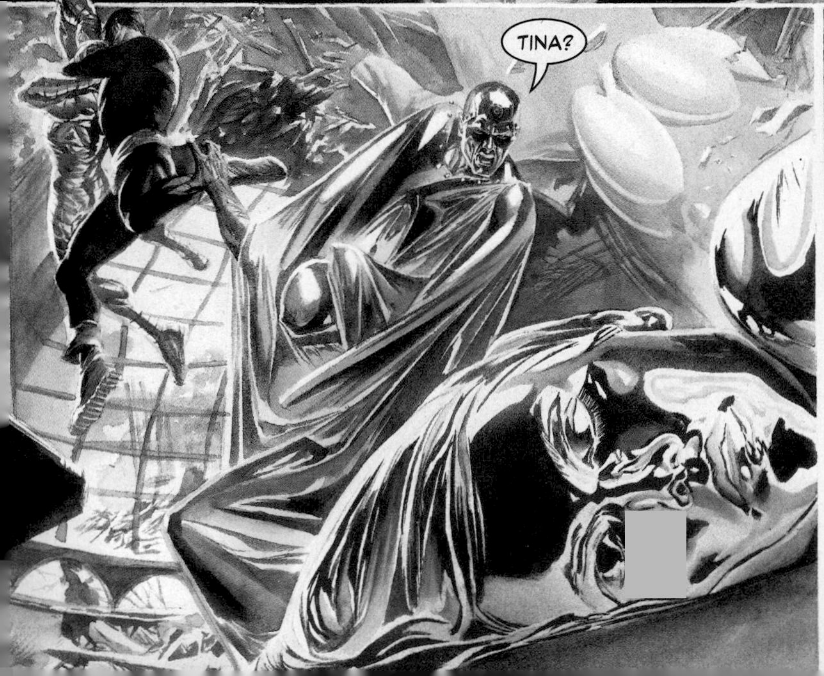
TINA?

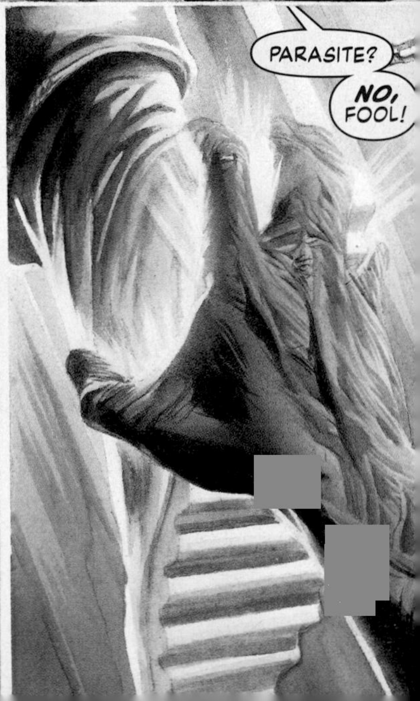
PARASITE?
NO, FOOL!

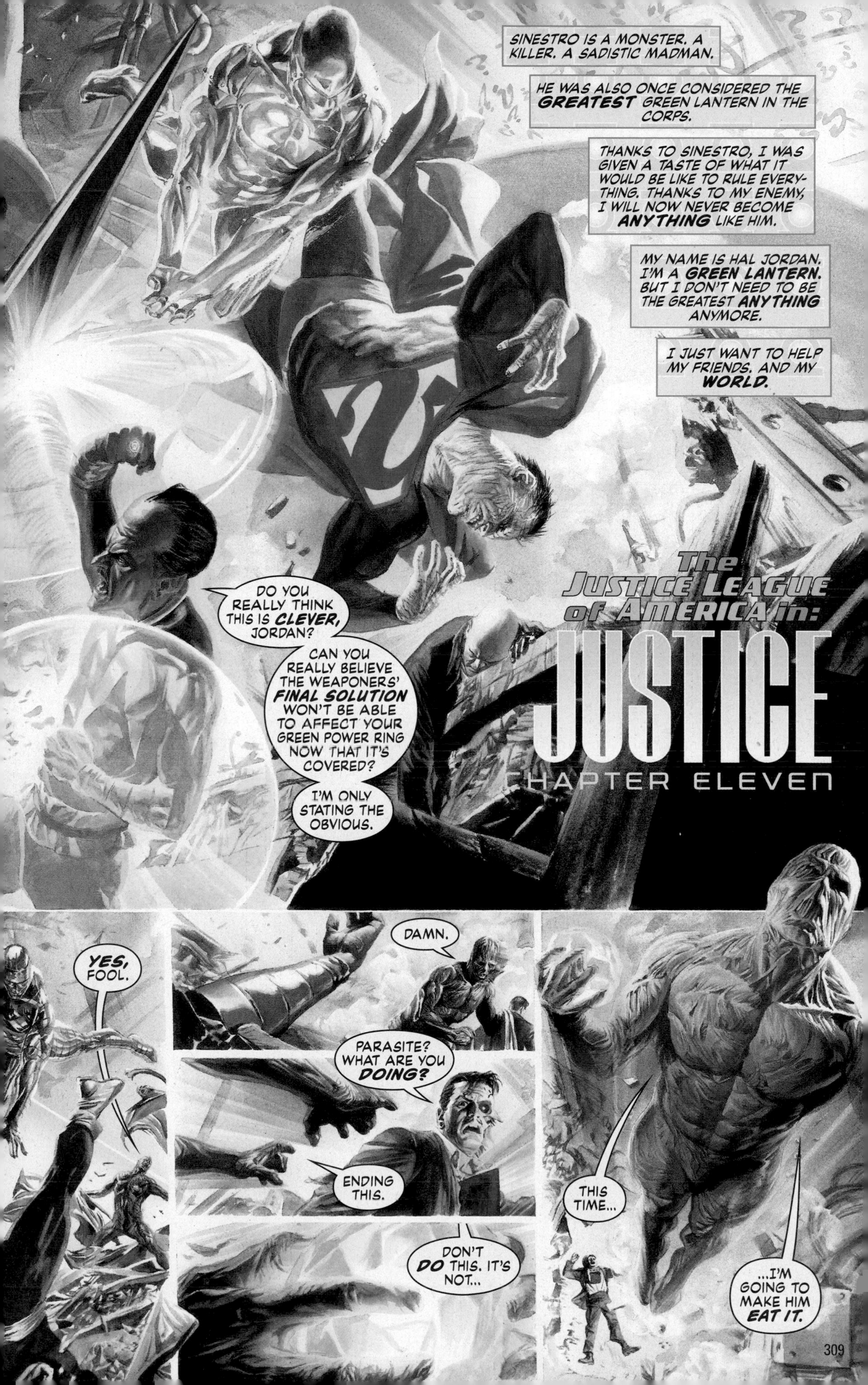
SINESTRO IS A MONSTER. A KILLER. A SADISTIC MADMAN.
HE WAS ALSO ONCE CONSIDERED THE GREATEST GREEN LANTERN IN THE CORPS.
THANKS TO SINESTRO, I WAS GIVEN A TASTE OF WHAT IT WOULD BE LIKE TO RULE EVERYTHING. THANKS TO MY ENEMY, I WILL NOW NEVER BECOME ANYTHING LIKE HIM.
MY NAME IS HAL JORDAN. I'M A GREEN LANTERN. BUT I DON'T NEED TO BE THE GREATEST ANYTHING ANYMORE.
I JUST WANT TO HELP MY FRIENDS. AND MY WORLD.
The JUSTICE LEAGUE of AMERICA in:
JUSTICE
CHAPTER ELEVEN
DO YOU REALLY THINK THIS IS CLEVER, JORDAN?
CAN YOU REALLY BELIEVE THE WEAPONERS' FINAL SOLUTION WON'T BE ABLE TO AFFECT YOUR GREEN POWER RING NOW THAT IT'S COVERED?
I'M ONLY STATING THE OBVIOUS.
YES, FOOL.
DAMN.
PARASITE? WHAT ARE YOU DOING?
ENDING THIS.
DON'T DO THIS. IT'S NOT...
THIS TIME...
...I'M GOING TO MAKE HIM EAT IT.

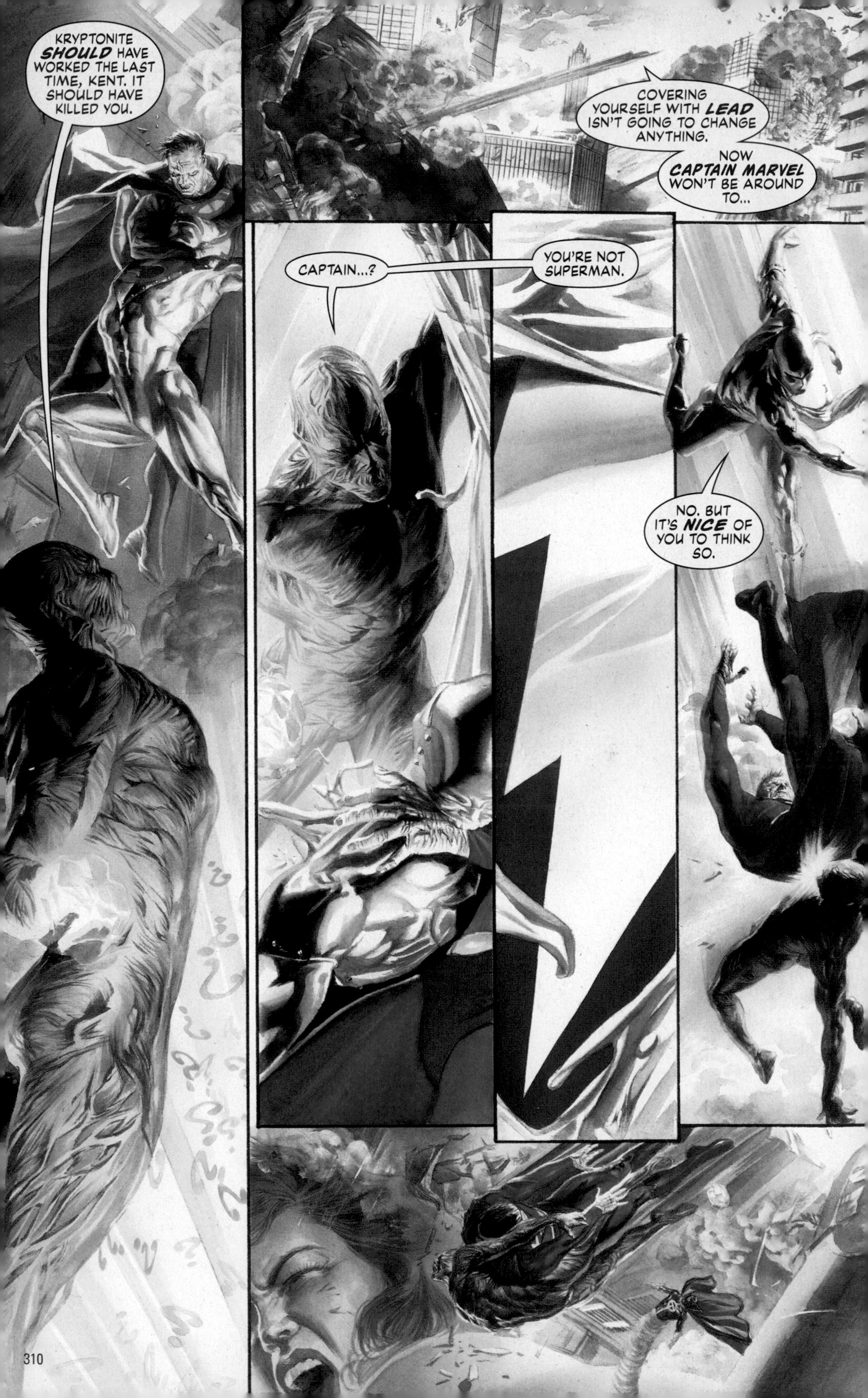
KRYPTONITE SHOULD HAVE WORKED THE LAST TIME, KENT. IT SHOULD HAVE KILLED YOU.
COVERING YOURSELF WITH LEAD ISN'T GOING TO CHANGE ANYTHING.
NOW CAPTAIN MARVEL WON'T BE AROUND TO...
CAPTAIN...?
YOU'RE NOT SUPERMAN.
NO. BUT IT'S NICE OF YOU TO THINK SO.

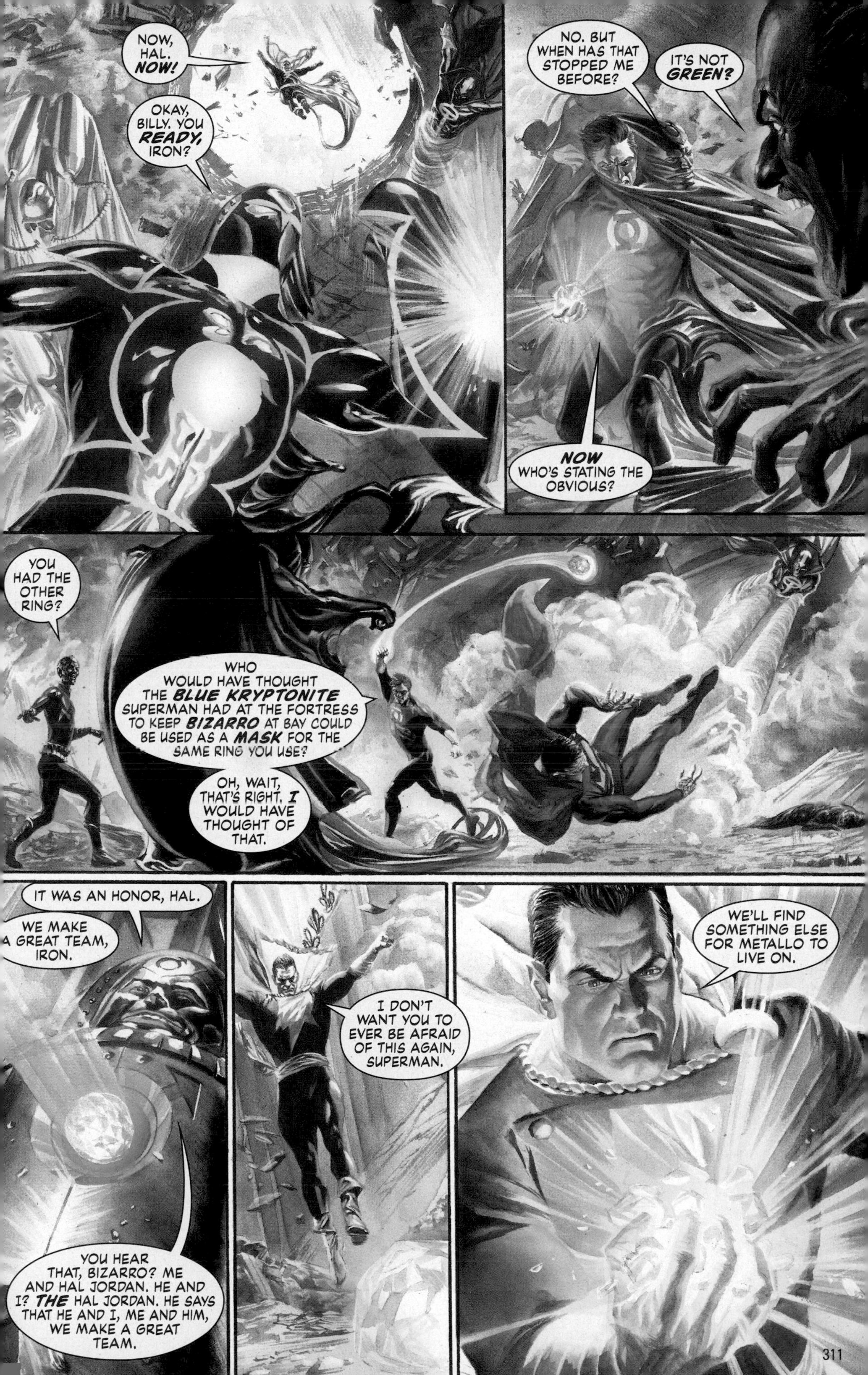
NOW, HAL. **NOW!**
OKAY, BILLY. YOU **READY,** IRON?
NO. BUT WHEN HAS THAT STOPPED ME BEFORE?
IT'S NOT **GREEN?**
NOW WHO'S STATING THE OBVIOUS?
YOU HAD THE OTHER RING?
WHO WOULD HAVE THOUGHT THE **BLUE KRYPTONITE** SUPERMAN HAD AT THE FORTRESS TO KEEP **BIZARRO** AT BAY COULD BE USED AS A **MASK** FOR THE SAME RING YOU USE?
OH, WAIT, THAT'S RIGHT. **I** WOULD HAVE THOUGHT OF THAT.
IT WAS AN HONOR, HAL.
WE MAKE A GREAT TEAM, IRON.
YOU HEAR THAT, BIZARRO? ME AND HAL JORDAN. HE AND I? **THE** HAL JORDAN. HE SAYS THAT HE AND I, ME AND HIM, WE MAKE A GREAT TEAM.
I DON'T WANT YOU TO EVER BE AFRAID OF THIS AGAIN, SUPERMAN.
WE'LL FIND SOMETHING ELSE FOR METALLO TO LIVE ON.

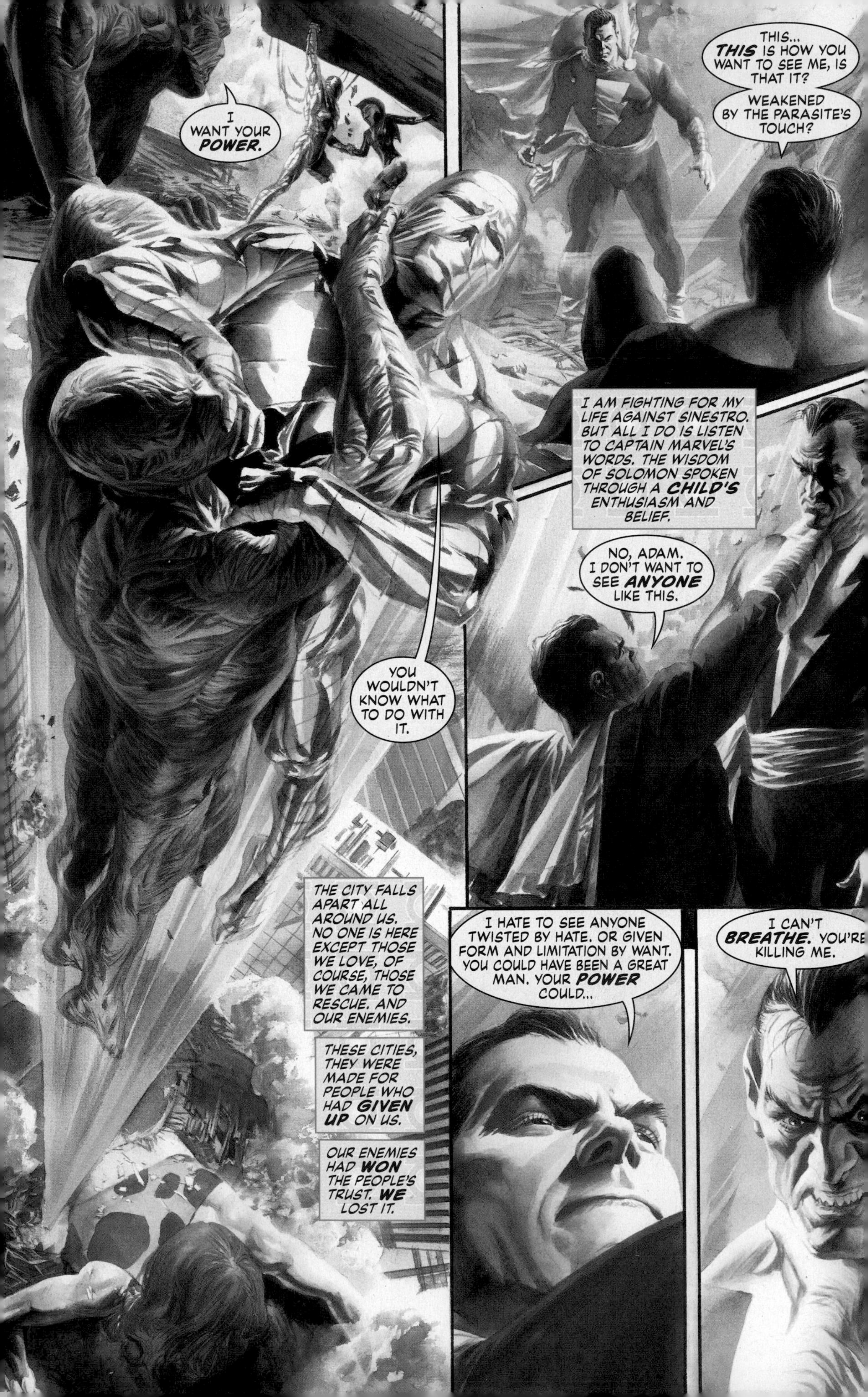

I WANT YOUR POWER.
YOU WOULDN'T KNOW WHAT TO DO WITH IT.
THIS... THIS IS HOW YOU WANT TO SEE ME, IS THAT IT?
WEAKENED BY THE PARASITE'S TOUCH?
I AM FIGHTING FOR MY LIFE AGAINST SINESTRO. BUT ALL I DO IS LISTEN TO CAPTAIN MARVEL'S WORDS. THE WISDOM OF SOLOMON SPOKEN THROUGH A CHILD'S ENTHUSIASM AND BELIEF.
NO, ADAM. I DON'T WANT TO SEE ANYONE LIKE THIS.
THE CITY FALLS APART ALL AROUND US. NO ONE IS HERE EXCEPT THOSE WE LOVE, OF COURSE, THOSE WE CAME TO RESCUE. AND OUR ENEMIES.
THESE CITIES, THEY WERE MADE FOR PEOPLE WHO HAD GIVEN UP ON US.
OUR ENEMIES HAD WON THE PEOPLE'S TRUST. WE LOST IT.
I HATE TO SEE ANYONE TWISTED BY HATE. OR GIVEN FORM AND LIMITATION BY WANT. YOU COULD HAVE BEEN A GREAT MAN. YOUR POWER COULD...
I CAN'T BREATHE. YOU'RE KILLING ME.

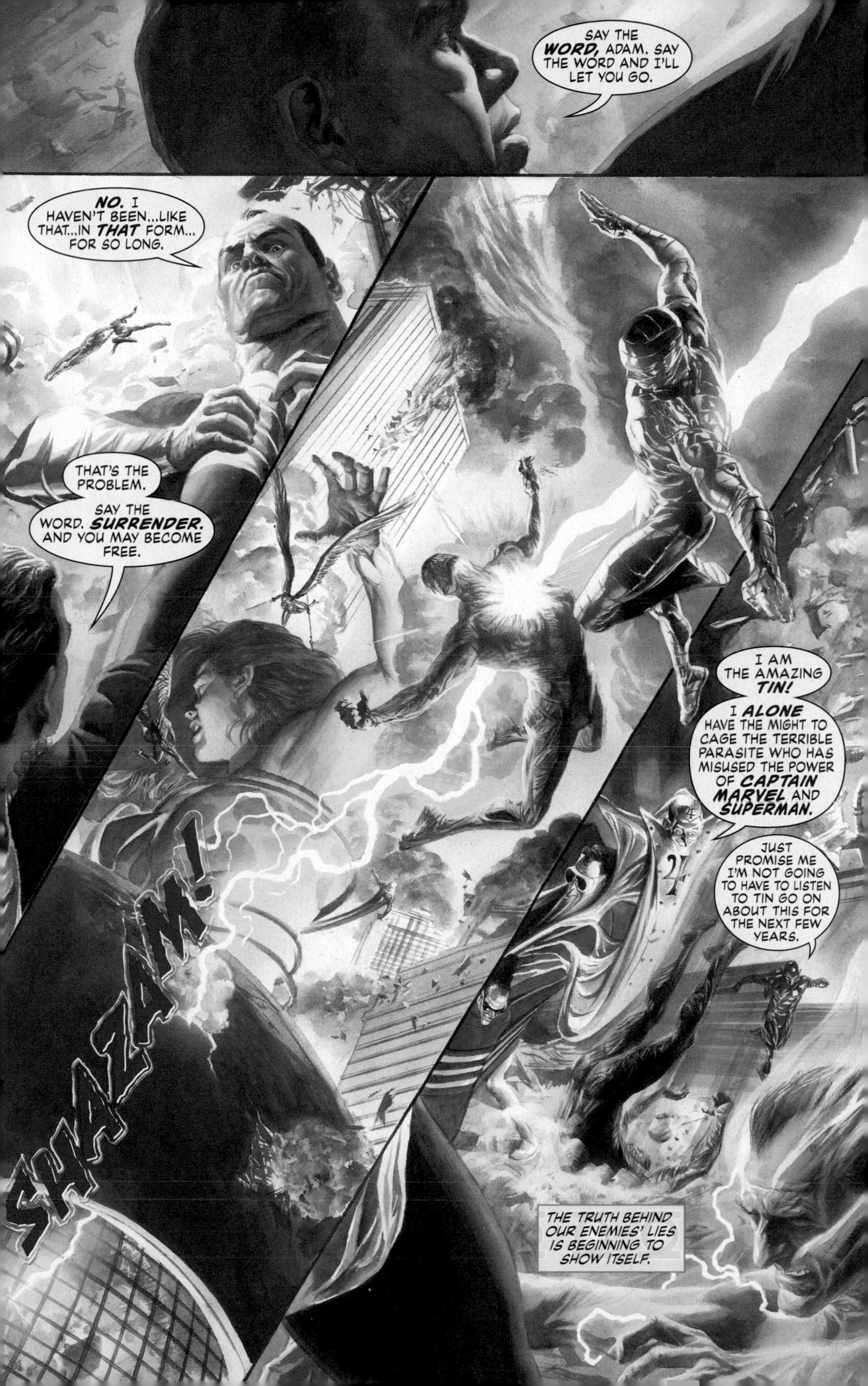
SAY THE WORD, ADAM. SAY THE WORD AND I'LL LET YOU GO.
NO. I HAVEN'T BEEN...LIKE THAT...IN THAT FORM... FOR SO LONG.
THAT'S THE PROBLEM.
SAY THE WORD. SURRENDER. AND YOU MAY BECOME FREE.
SHAZAM!
I AM THE AMAZING TIN!
I ALONE HAVE THE MIGHT TO CAGE THE TERRIBLE PARASITE WHO HAS MISUSED THE POWER OF CAPTAIN MARVEL AND SUPERMAN.
JUST PROMISE ME I'M NOT GOING TO HAVE TO LISTEN TO TIN GO ON ABOUT THIS FOR THE NEXT FEW YEARS.
THE TRUTH BEHIND OUR ENEMIES' LIES IS BEGINNING TO SHOW ITSELF.

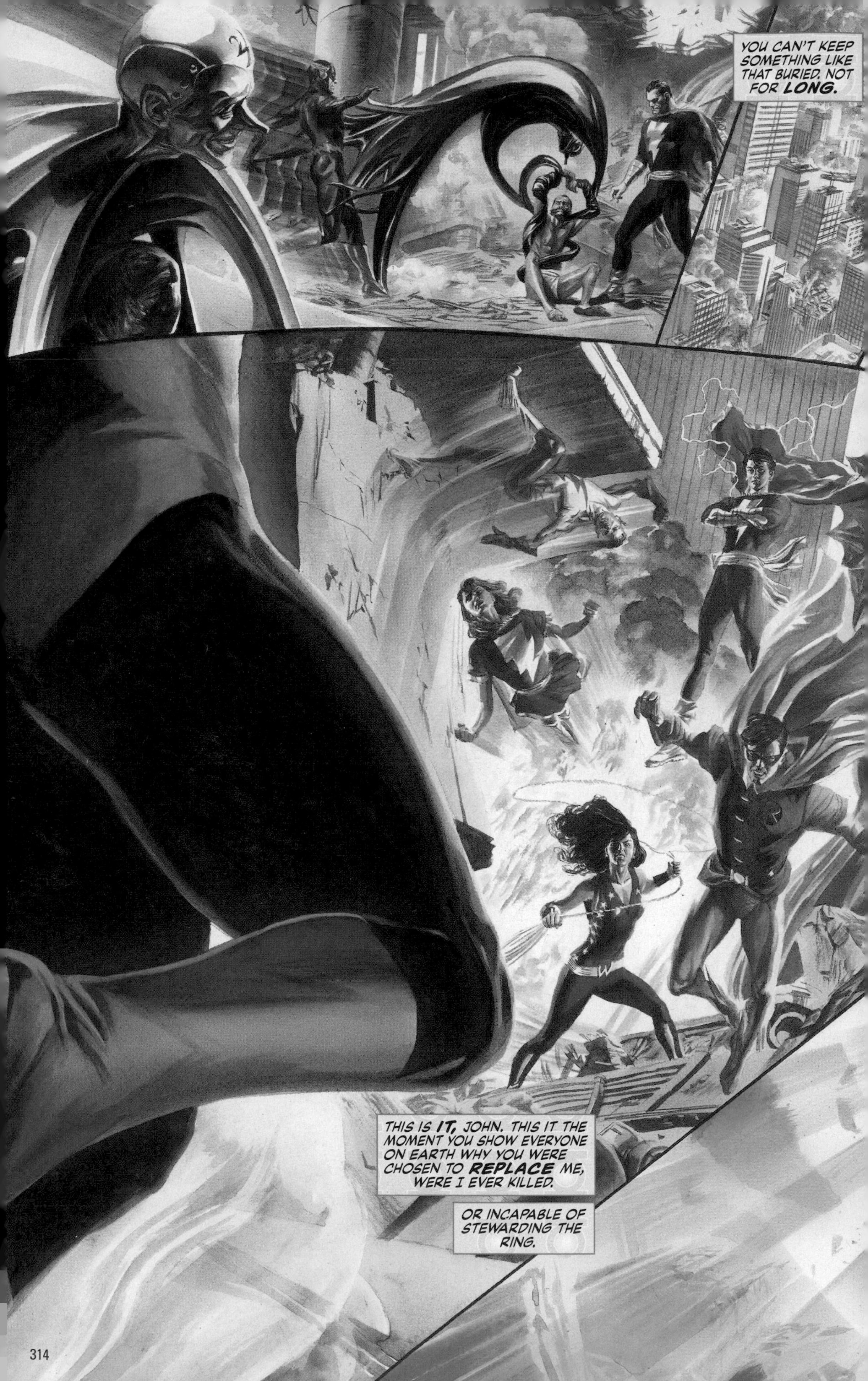
YOU CAN'T KEEP SOMETHING LIKE THAT BURIED. NOT FOR LONG.
THIS IS IT, JOHN. THIS IT THE MOMENT YOU SHOW EVERYONE ON EARTH WHY YOU WERE CHOSEN TO REPLACE ME, WERE I EVER KILLED.
OR INCAPABLE OF STEWARDING THE RING.

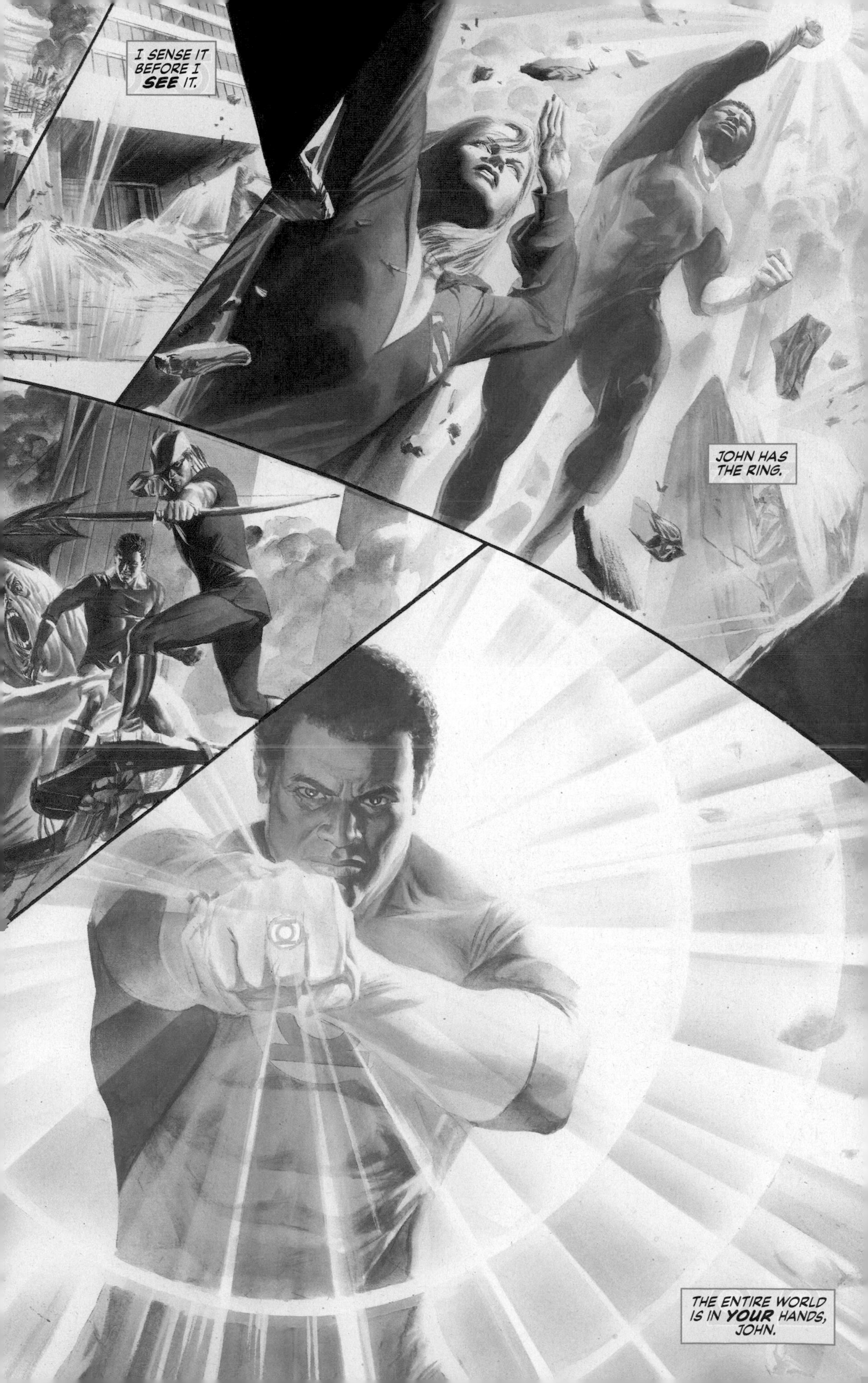
I SENSE IT BEFORE I **SEE** IT.
JOHN HAS THE RING.
THE ENTIRE WORLD IS IN **YOUR** HANDS, JOHN.

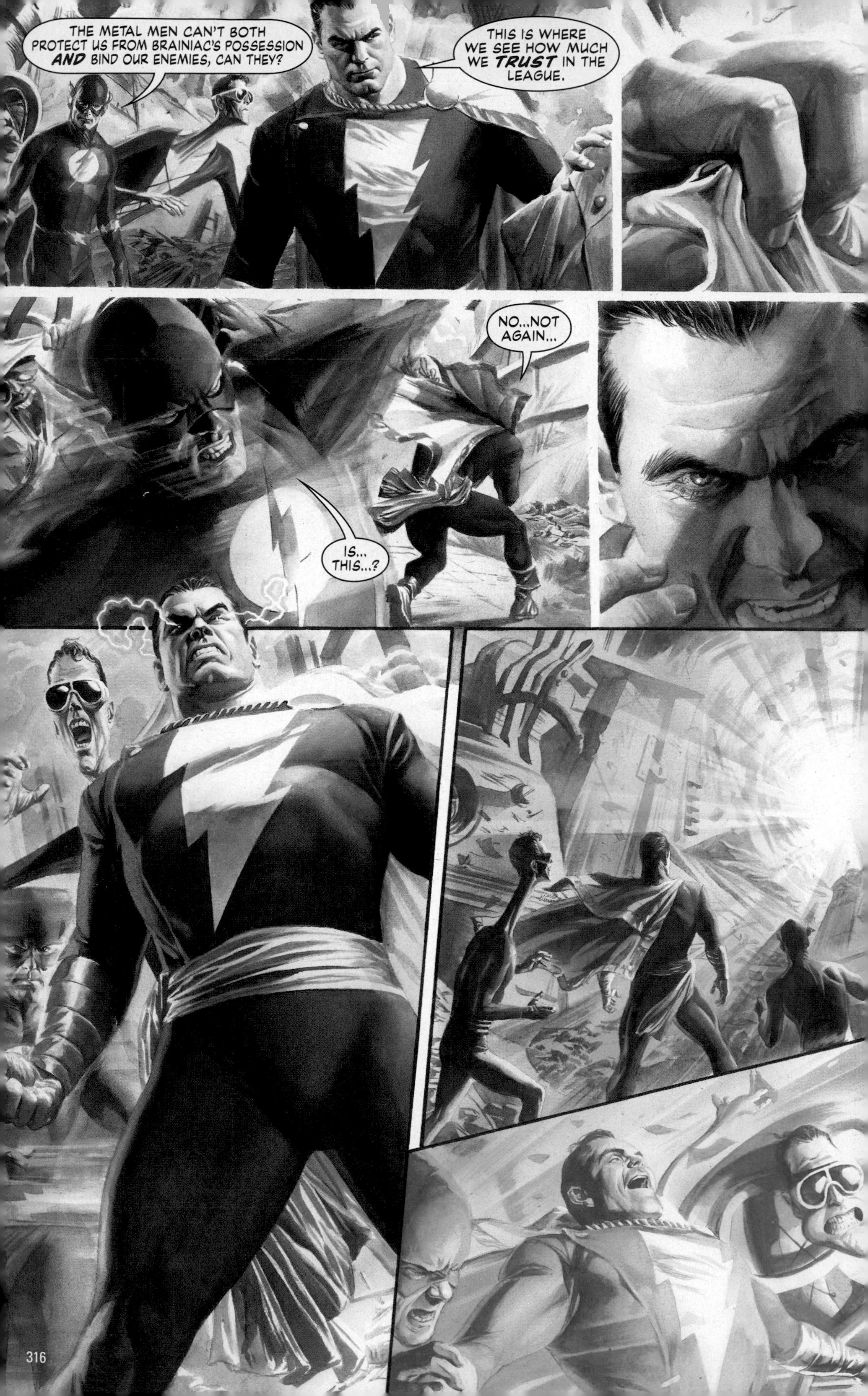
THE METAL MEN CAN'T BOTH PROTECT US FROM BRAINIAC'S POSSESSION **AND** BIND OUR ENEMIES, CAN THEY?
THIS IS WHERE WE SEE HOW MUCH WE **TRUST** IN THE LEAGUE.
NO...NOT AGAIN...
IS... THIS...?

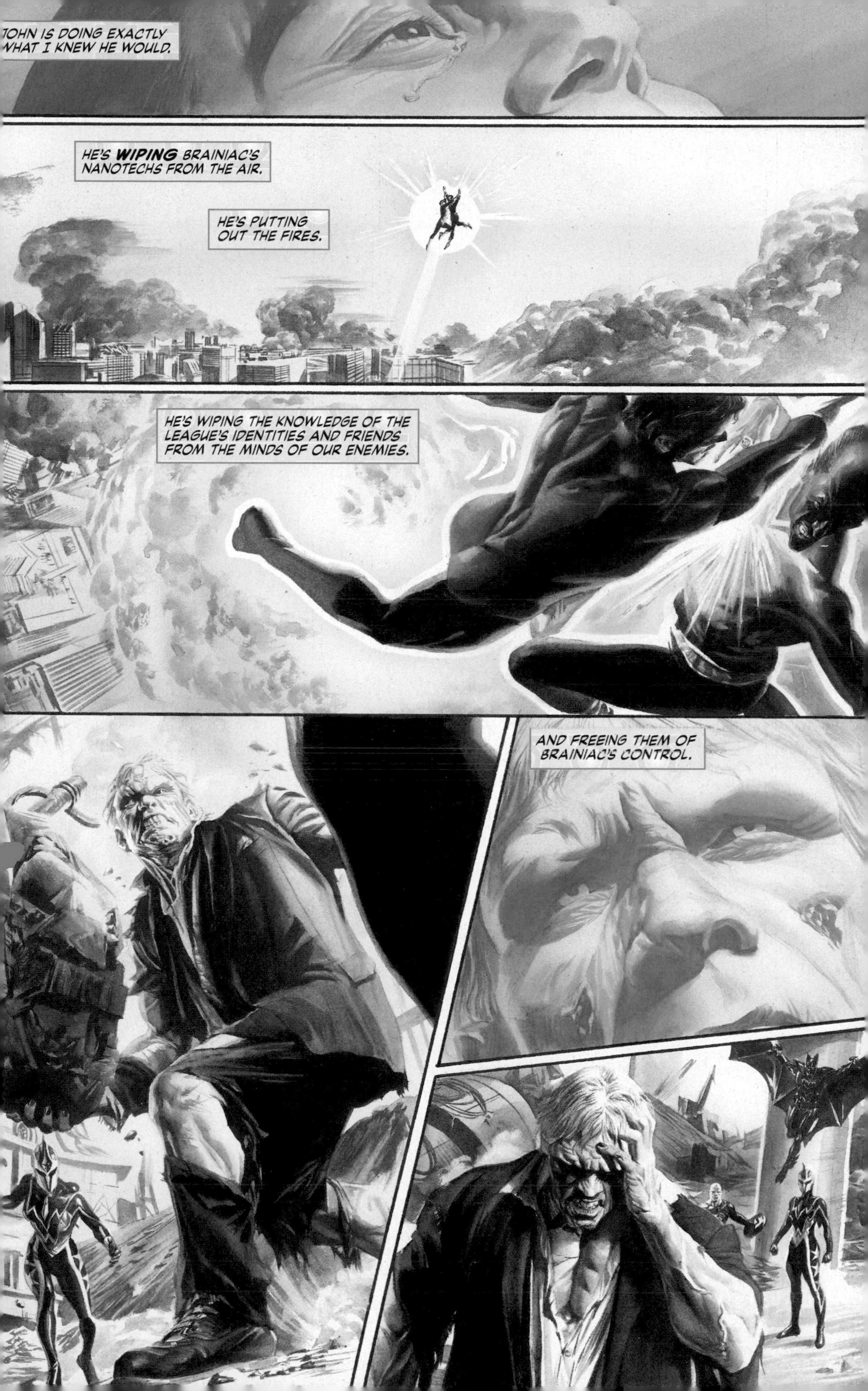
JOHN IS DOING EXACTLY WHAT I KNEW HE WOULD.
HE'S **WIPING** BRAINIAC'S NANOTECHS FROM THE AIR.
HE'S PUTTING OUT THE FIRES.
HE'S WIPING THE KNOWLEDGE OF THE LEAGUE'S IDENTITIES AND FRIENDS FROM THE MINDS OF OUR ENEMIES.
AND FREEING THEM OF BRAINIAC'S CONTROL.

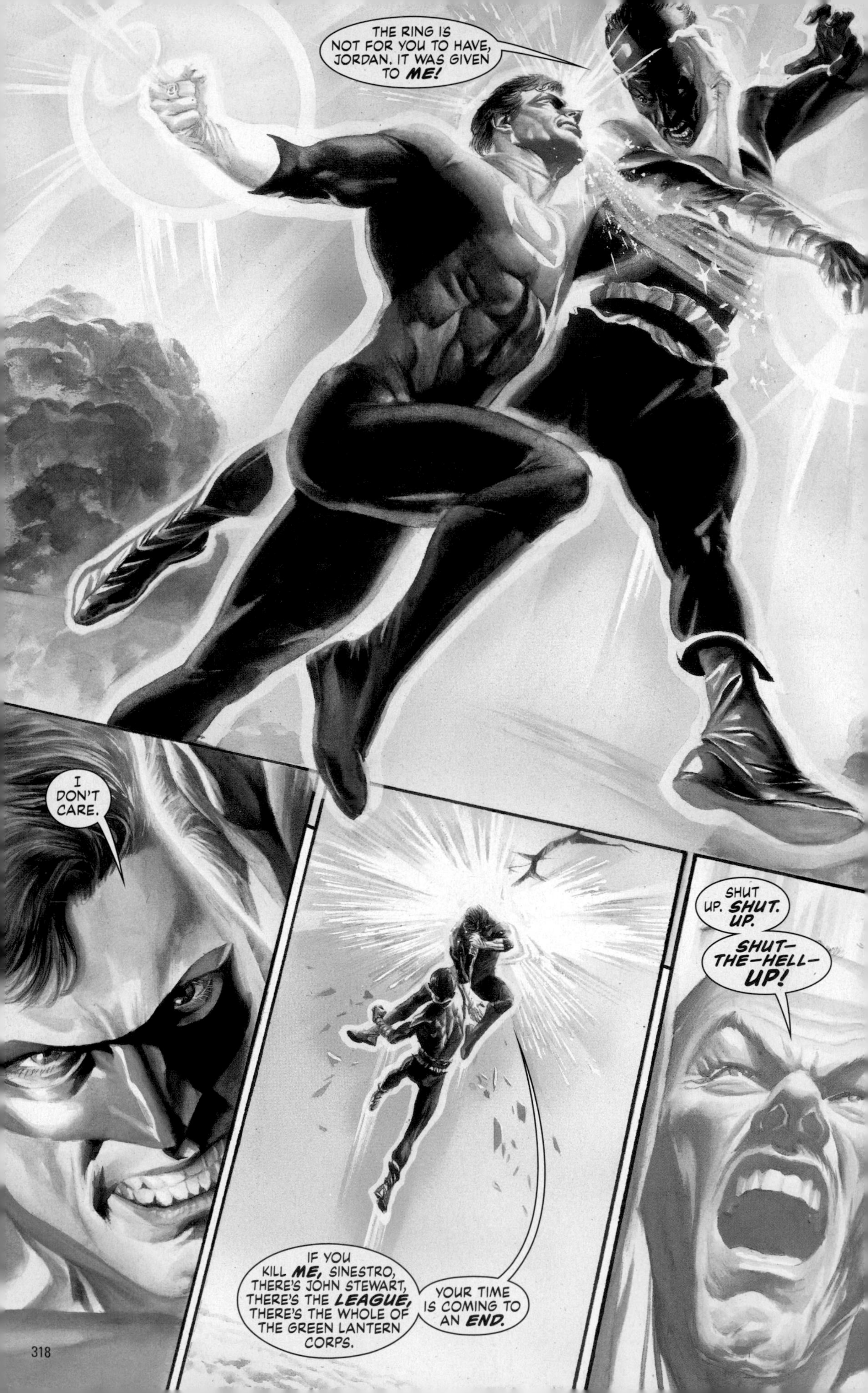
THE RING IS NOT FOR YOU TO HAVE, JORDAN. IT WAS GIVEN TO ME!
I DON'T CARE.
IF YOU KILL ME, SINESTRO, THERE'S JOHN STEWART, THERE'S THE LEAGUE, THERE'S THE WHOLE OF THE GREEN LANTERN CORPS.
YOUR TIME IS COMING TO AN END.
SHUT UP. SHUT. UP.
SHUT-THE-HELL-UP!

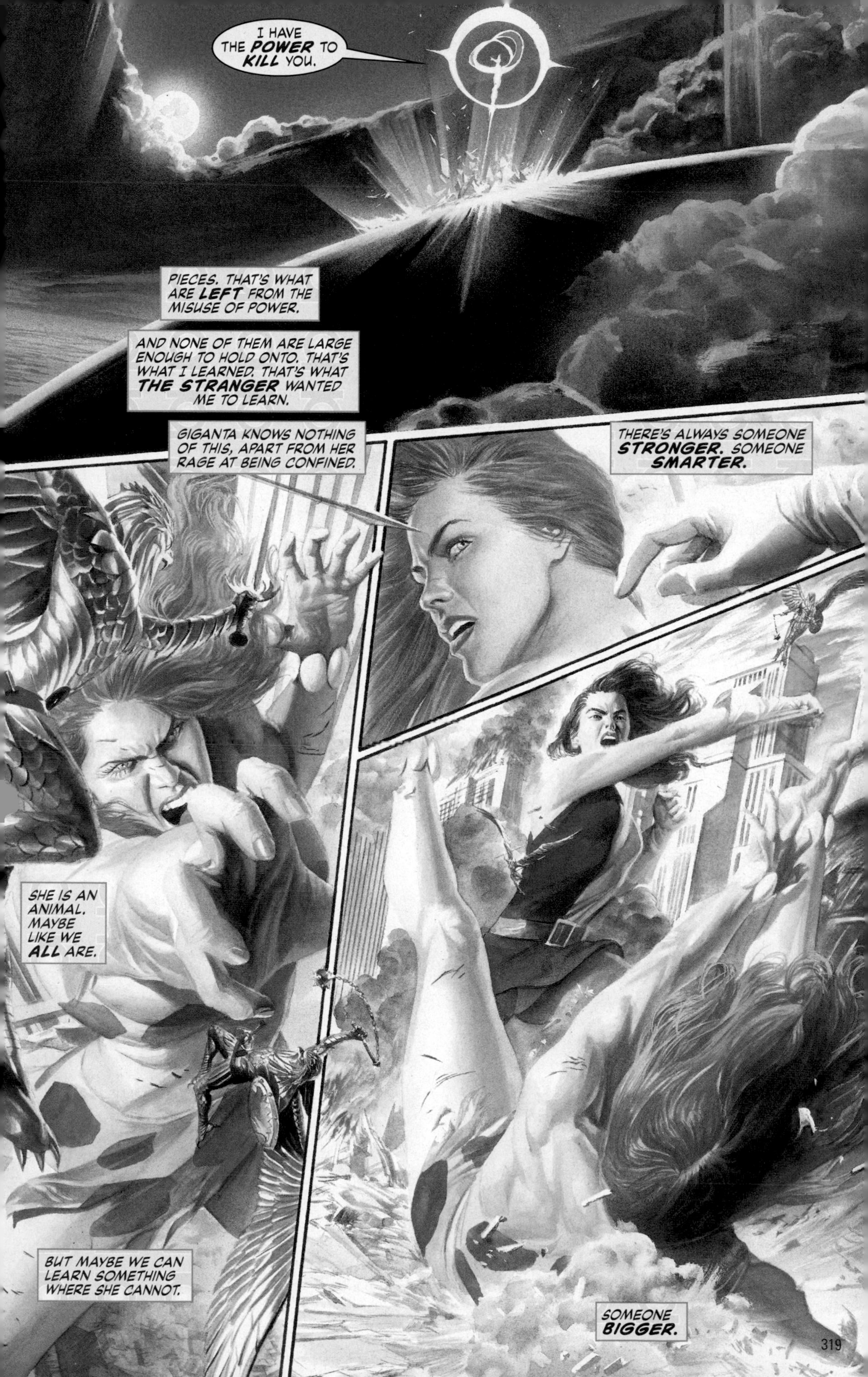
I HAVE THE POWER TO KILL YOU.
PIECES. THAT'S WHAT ARE LEFT FROM THE MISUSE OF POWER.
AND NONE OF THEM ARE LARGE ENOUGH TO HOLD ONTO. THAT'S WHAT I LEARNED. THAT'S WHAT THE STRANGER WANTED ME TO LEARN.
GIGANTA KNOWS NOTHING OF THIS, APART FROM HER RAGE AT BEING CONFINED.
SHE IS AN ANIMAL. MAYBE LIKE WE ALL ARE.
BUT MAYBE WE CAN LEARN SOMETHING WHERE SHE CANNOT.
THERE'S ALWAYS SOMEONE STRONGER. SOMEONE SMARTER.
SOMEONE BIGGER.

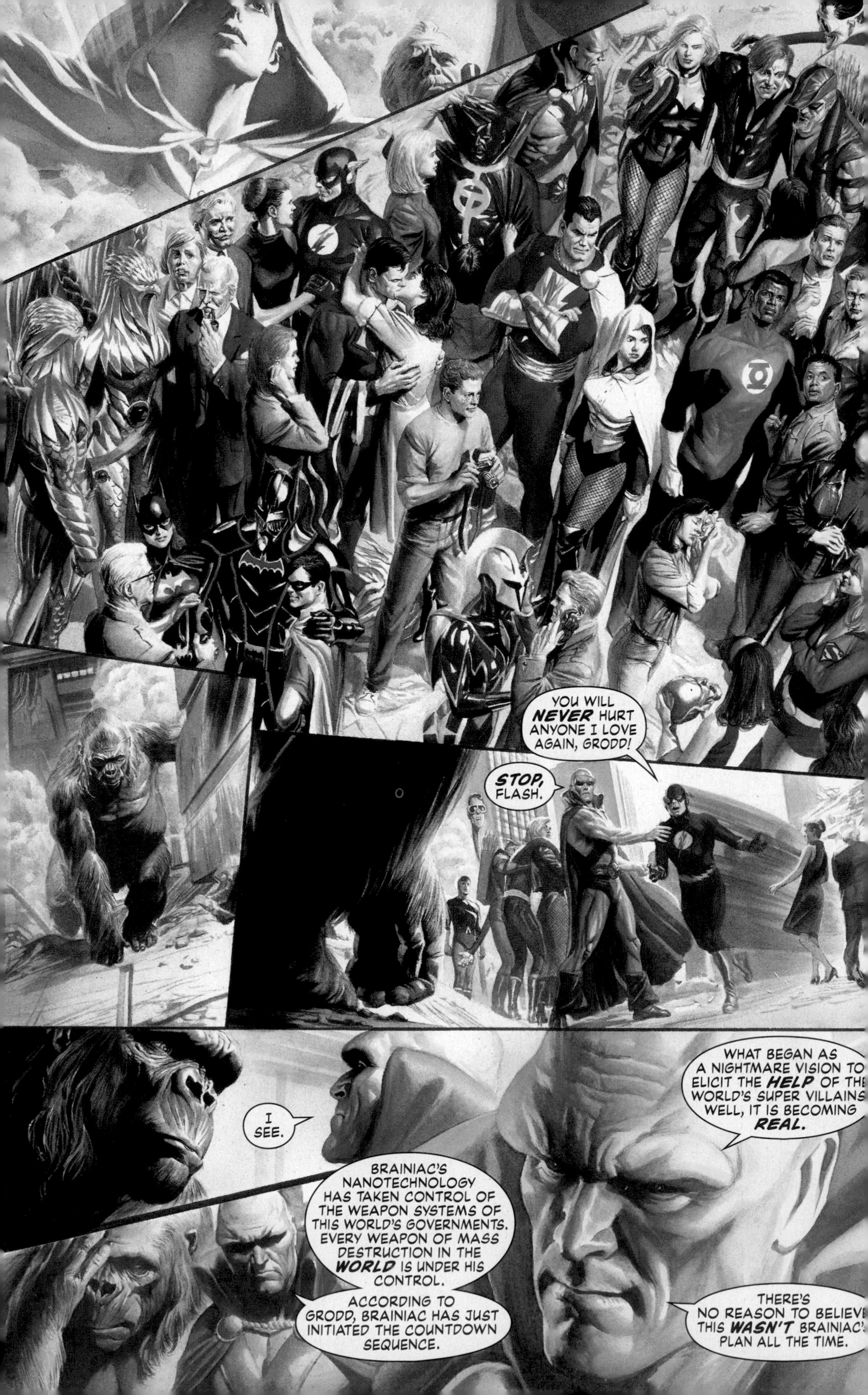
YOU WILL NEVER HURT ANYONE I LOVE AGAIN, GRODD!
STOP, FLASH.
I SEE.
WHAT BEGAN AS A NIGHTMARE VISION TO ELICIT THE HELP OF THE WORLD'S SUPER VILLAINS WELL, IT IS BECOMING REAL.
BRAINIAC'S NANOTECHNOLOGY HAS TAKEN CONTROL OF THE WEAPON SYSTEMS OF THIS WORLD'S GOVERNMENTS. EVERY WEAPON OF MASS DESTRUCTION IN THE WORLD IS UNDER HIS CONTROL.
ACCORDING TO GRODD, BRAINIAC HAS JUST INITIATED THE COUNTDOWN SEQUENCE.
THERE'S NO REASON TO BELIEVE THIS WASN'T BRAINIAC'S PLAN ALL THE TIME.

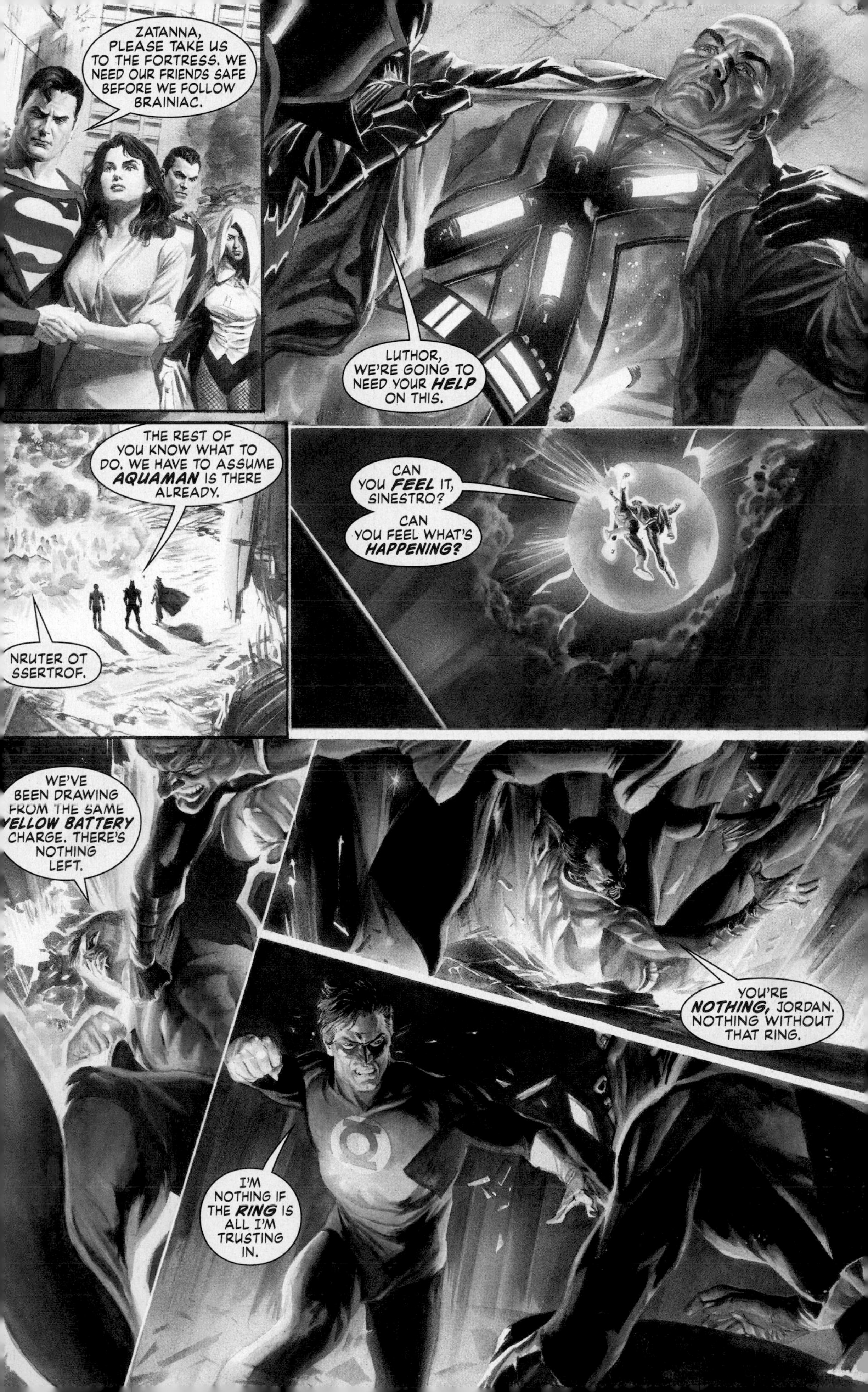
ZATANNA, PLEASE TAKE US TO THE FORTRESS. WE NEED OUR FRIENDS SAFE BEFORE WE FOLLOW BRAINIAC.
LUTHOR, WE'RE GOING TO NEED YOUR **HELP** ON THIS.
THE REST OF YOU KNOW WHAT TO DO. WE HAVE TO ASSUME **AQUAMAN** IS THERE ALREADY.
NRUTER OT SSERTROF.
CAN YOU **FEEL** IT, SINESTRO?
CAN YOU FEEL WHAT'S **HAPPENING?**
WE'VE BEEN DRAWING FROM THE SAME **YELLOW BATTERY** CHARGE. THERE'S NOTHING LEFT.
YOU'RE **NOTHING,** JORDAN. NOTHING WITHOUT THAT RING.
I'M NOTHING IF THE **RING** IS ALL I'M TRUSTING IN.

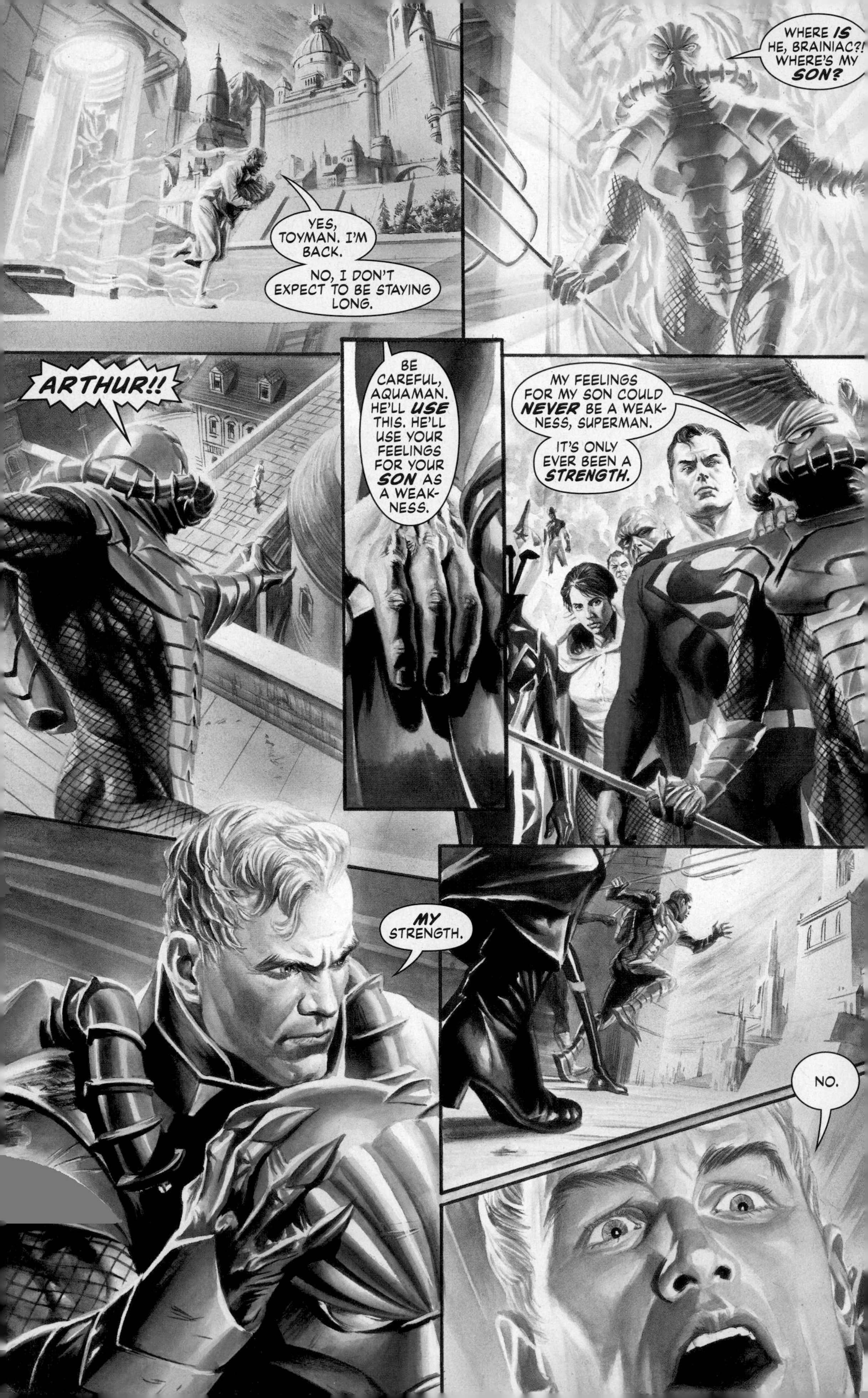
YES, TOYMAN. I'M BACK.
NO, I DON'T EXPECT TO BE STAYING LONG.
WHERE IS HE, BRAINIAC?! WHERE'S MY SON?
ARTHUR!!
BE CAREFUL, AQUAMAN. HE'LL USE THIS. HE'LL USE YOUR FEELINGS FOR YOUR SON AS A WEAKNESS.
MY FEELINGS FOR MY SON COULD NEVER BE A WEAKNESS, SUPERMAN.
IT'S ONLY EVER BEEN A STRENGTH.
MY STRENGTH.
NO.

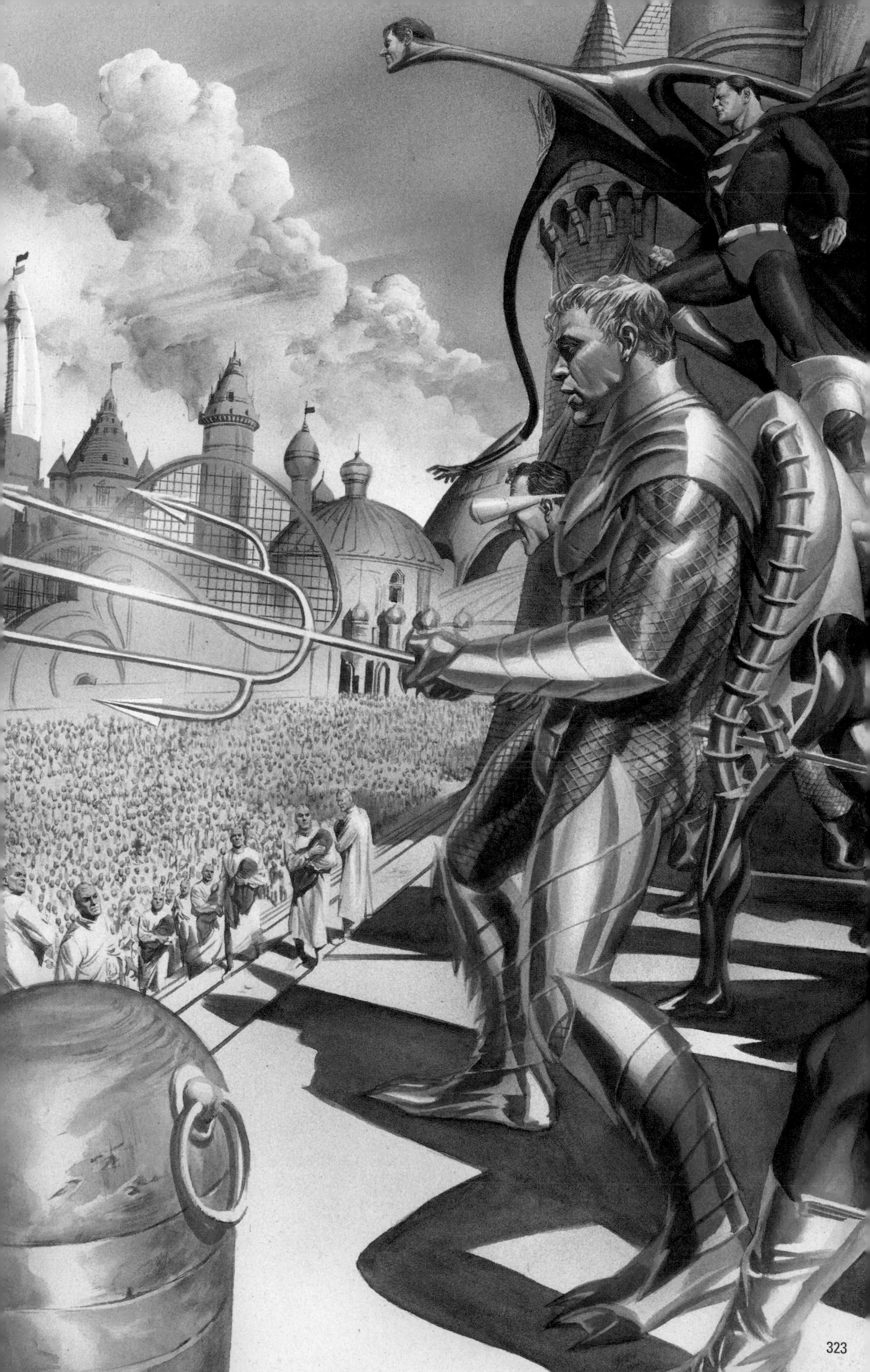

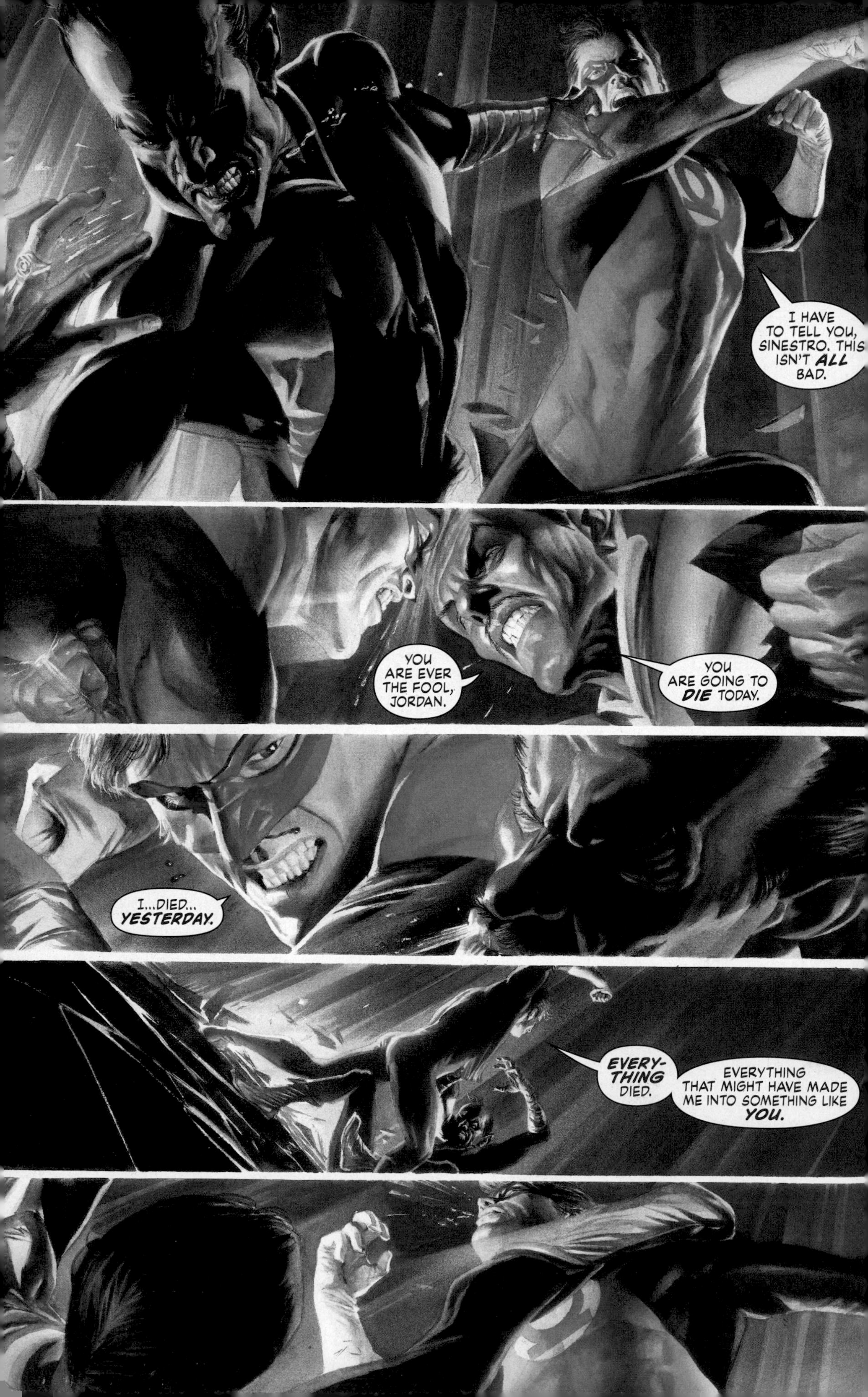
I HAVE TO TELL YOU, SINESTRO. THIS ISN'T ALL BAD.
YOU ARE EVER THE FOOL, JORDAN.
YOU ARE GOING TO DIE TODAY.
I...DIED... YESTERDAY.
EVERY-THING DIED.
EVERYTHING THAT MIGHT HAVE MADE ME INTO SOMETHING LIKE YOU.

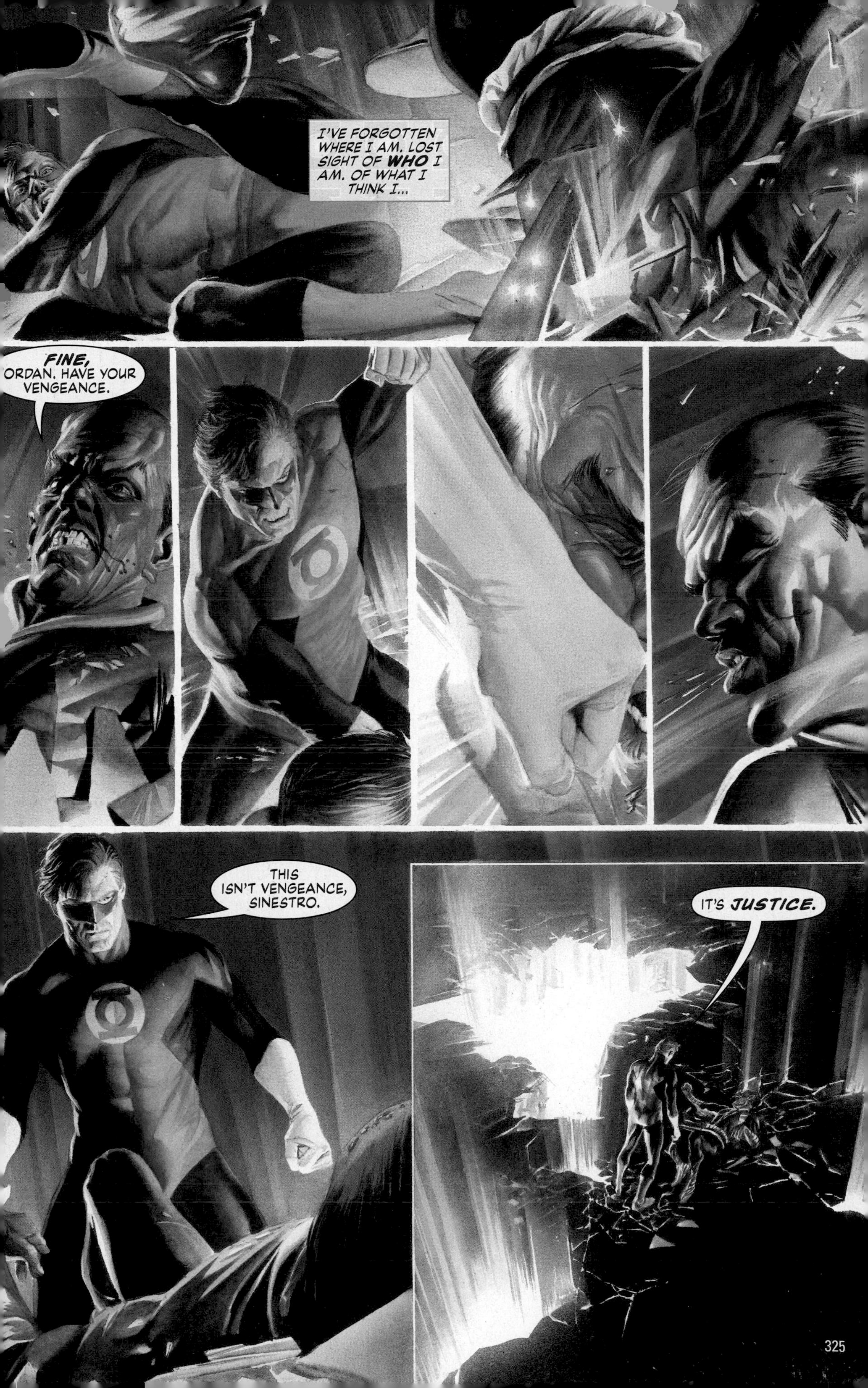

I'VE FORGOTTEN WHERE I AM. LOST SIGHT OF WHO I AM. OF WHAT I THINK I...
FINE, ORDAN. HAVE YOUR VENGEANCE.
THIS ISN'T VENGEANCE, SINESTRO.
IT'S JUSTICE.

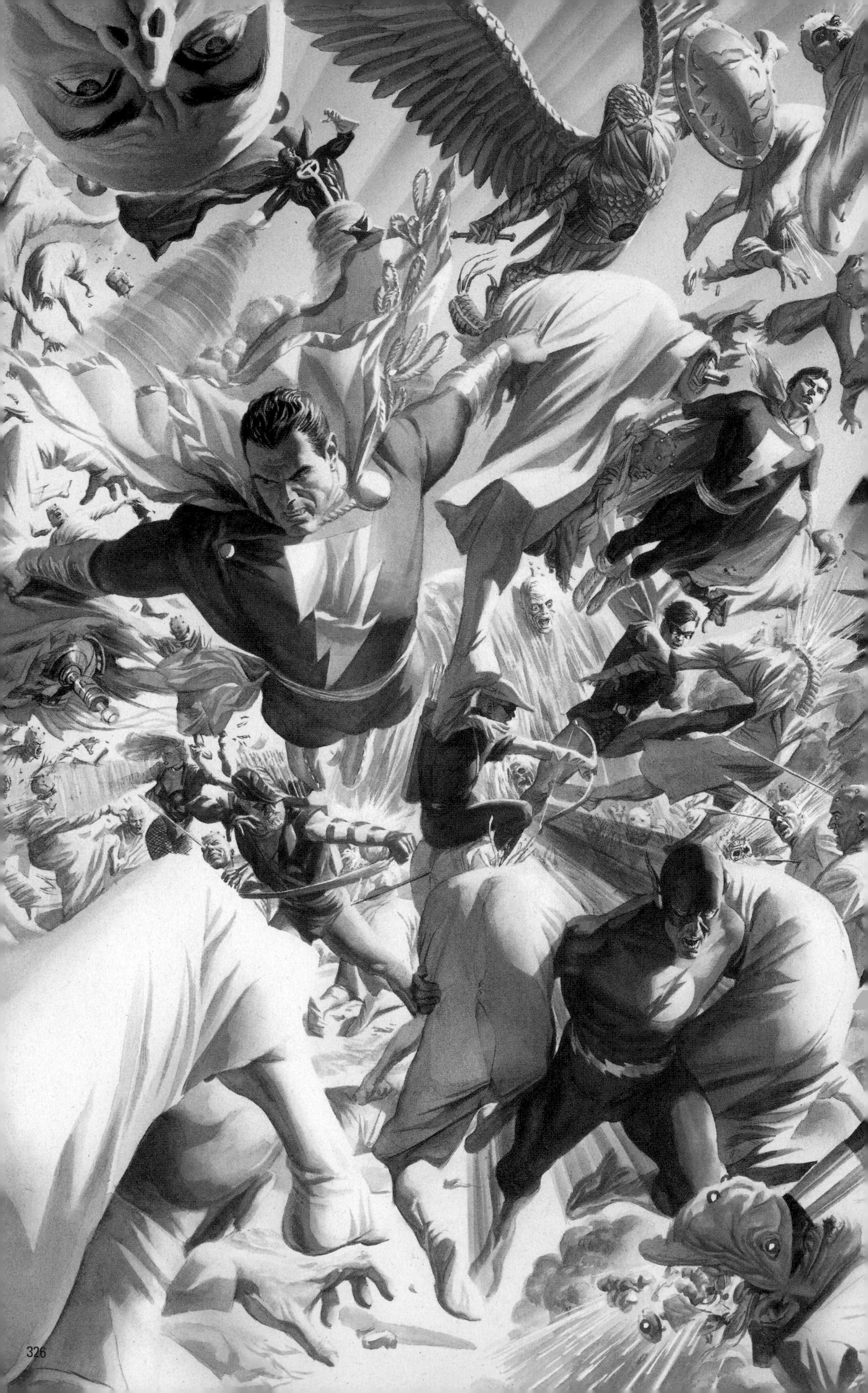

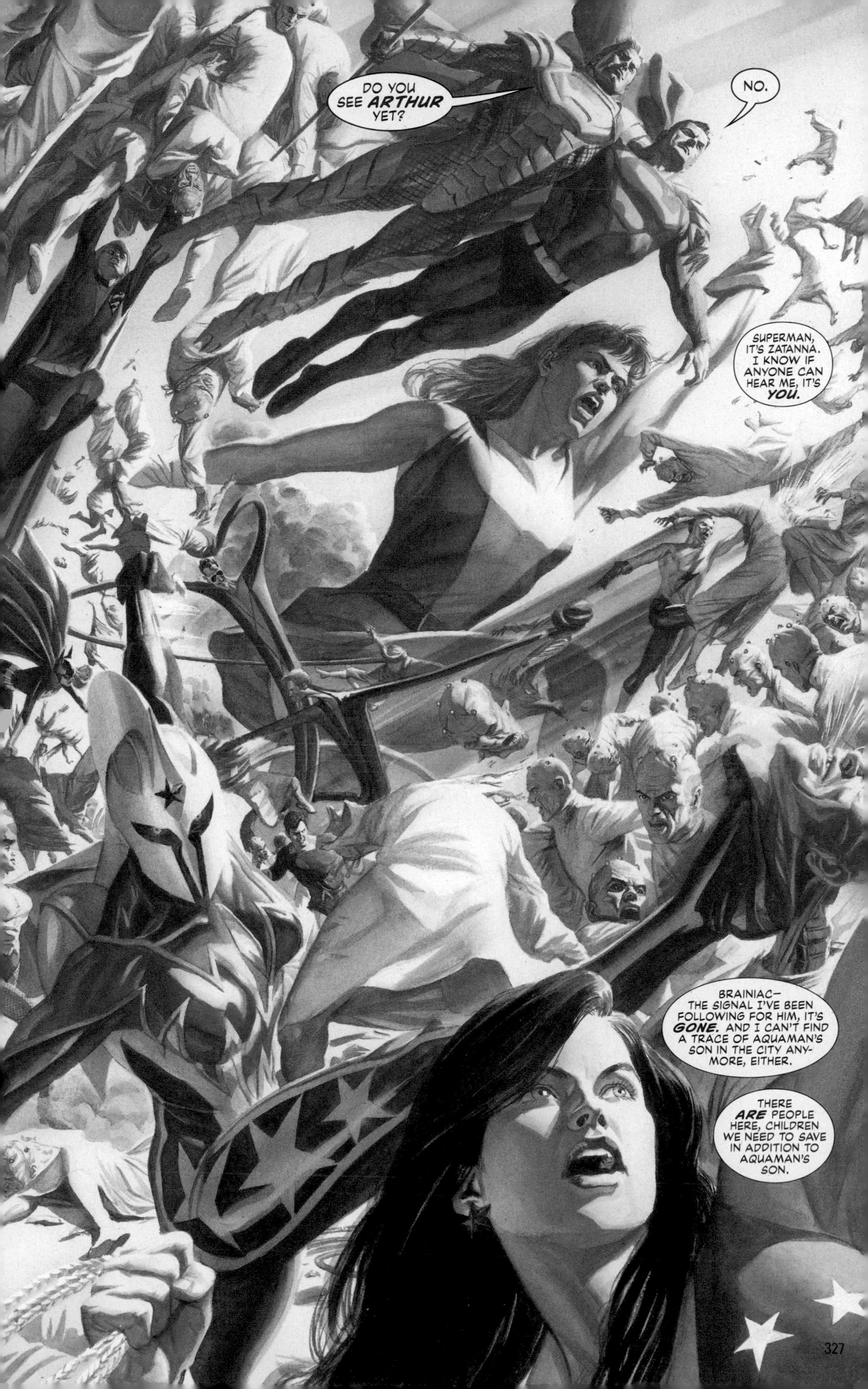
DO YOU SEE ARTHUR YET?
NO.
SUPERMAN, IT'S ZATANNA. I KNOW IF ANYONE CAN HEAR ME, IT'S YOU.
BRAINIAC— THE SIGNAL I'VE BEEN FOLLOWING FOR HIM, IT'S GONE. AND I CAN'T FIND A TRACE OF AQUAMAN'S SON IN THE CITY ANY-MORE, EITHER.
THERE ARE PEOPLE HERE, CHILDREN WE NEED TO SAVE IN ADDITION TO AQUAMAN'S SON.

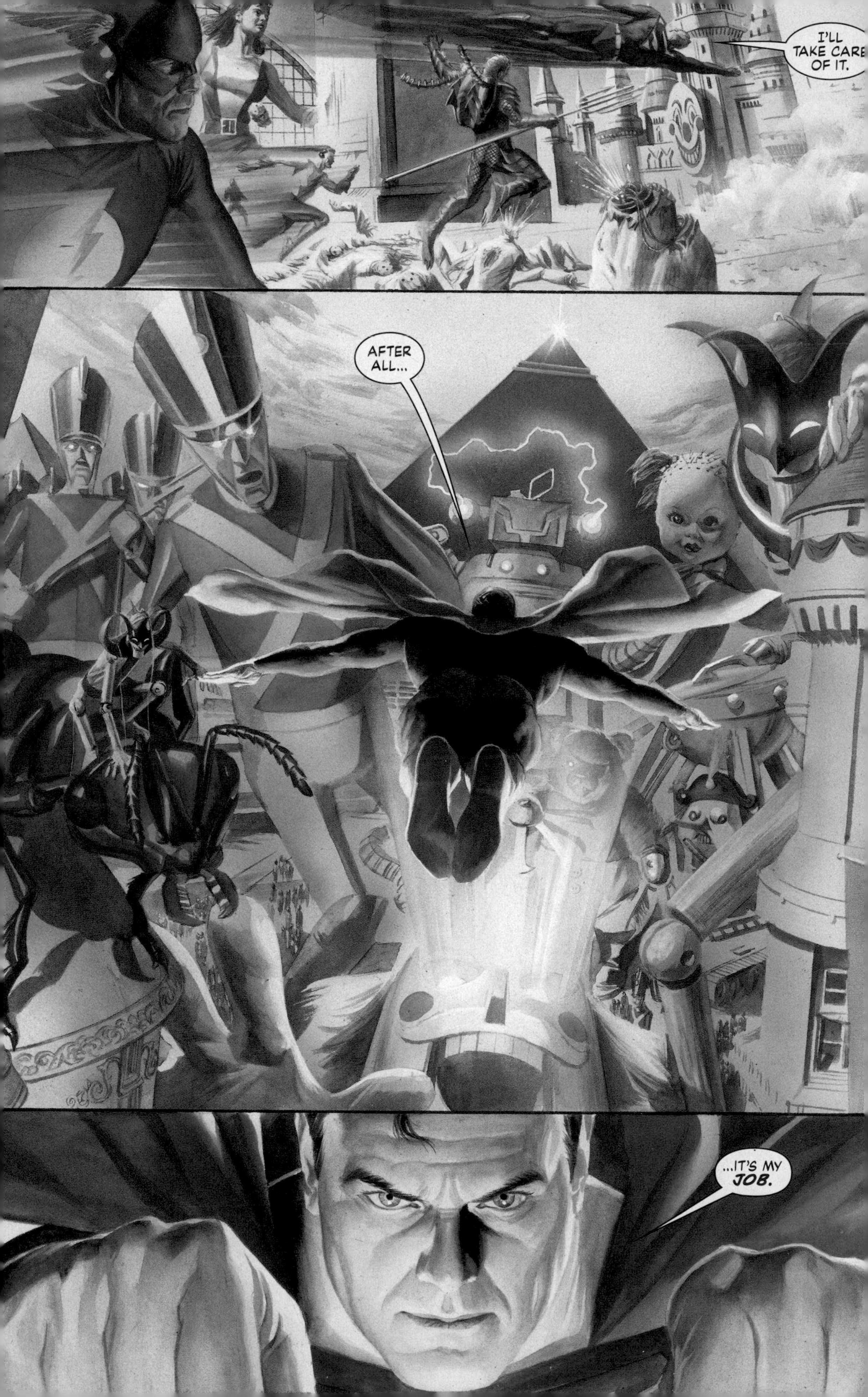
I'LL TAKE CARE OF IT.
AFTER ALL...
...IT'S MY JOB.

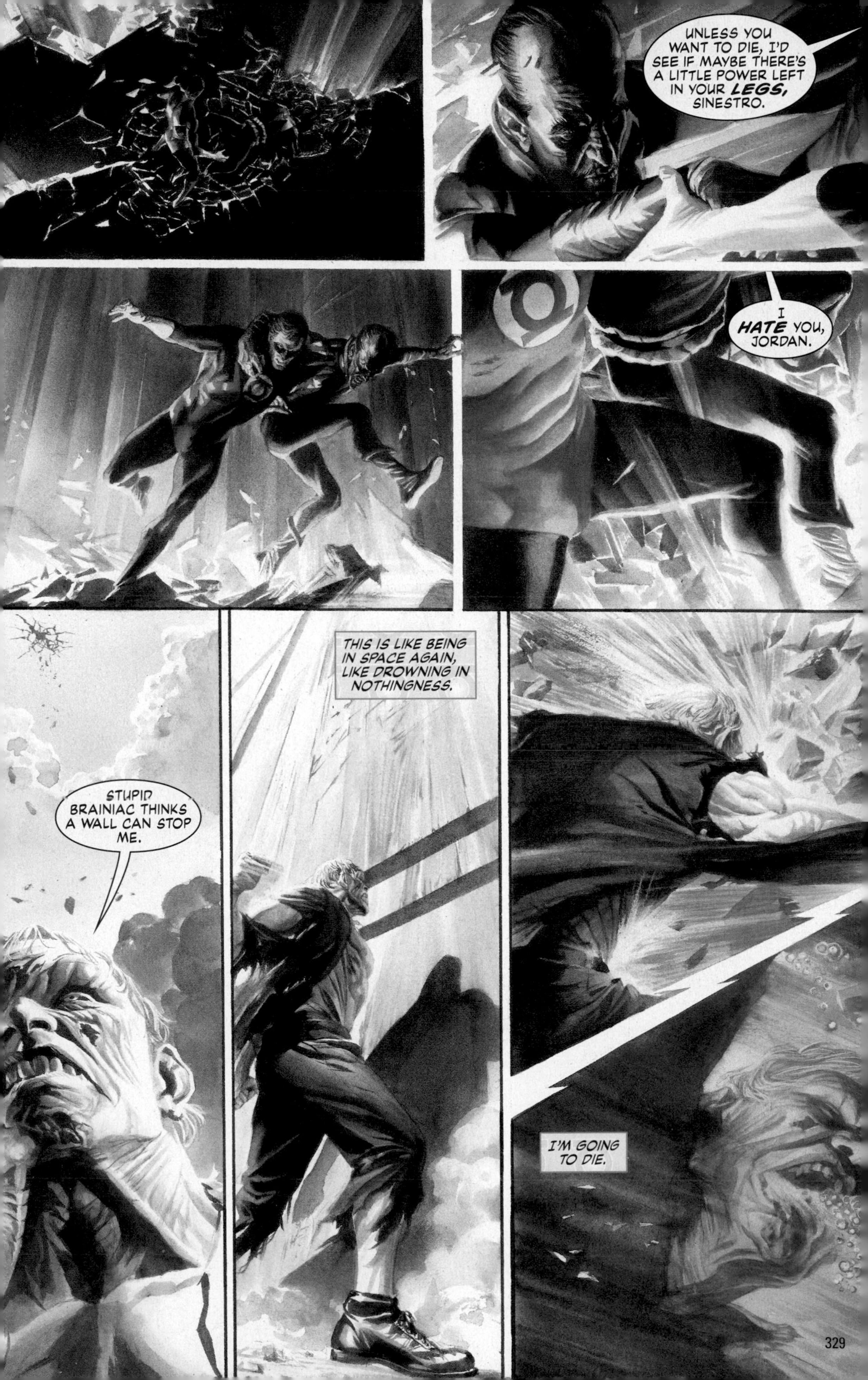
UNLESS YOU WANT TO DIE, I'D SEE IF MAYBE THERE'S A LITTLE POWER LEFT IN YOUR LEGS, SINESTRO.
I HATE YOU, JORDAN.
STUPID BRAINIAC THINKS A WALL CAN STOP ME.
THIS IS LIKE BEING IN SPACE AGAIN, LIKE DROWNING IN NOTHINGNESS.
I'M GOING TO DIE.

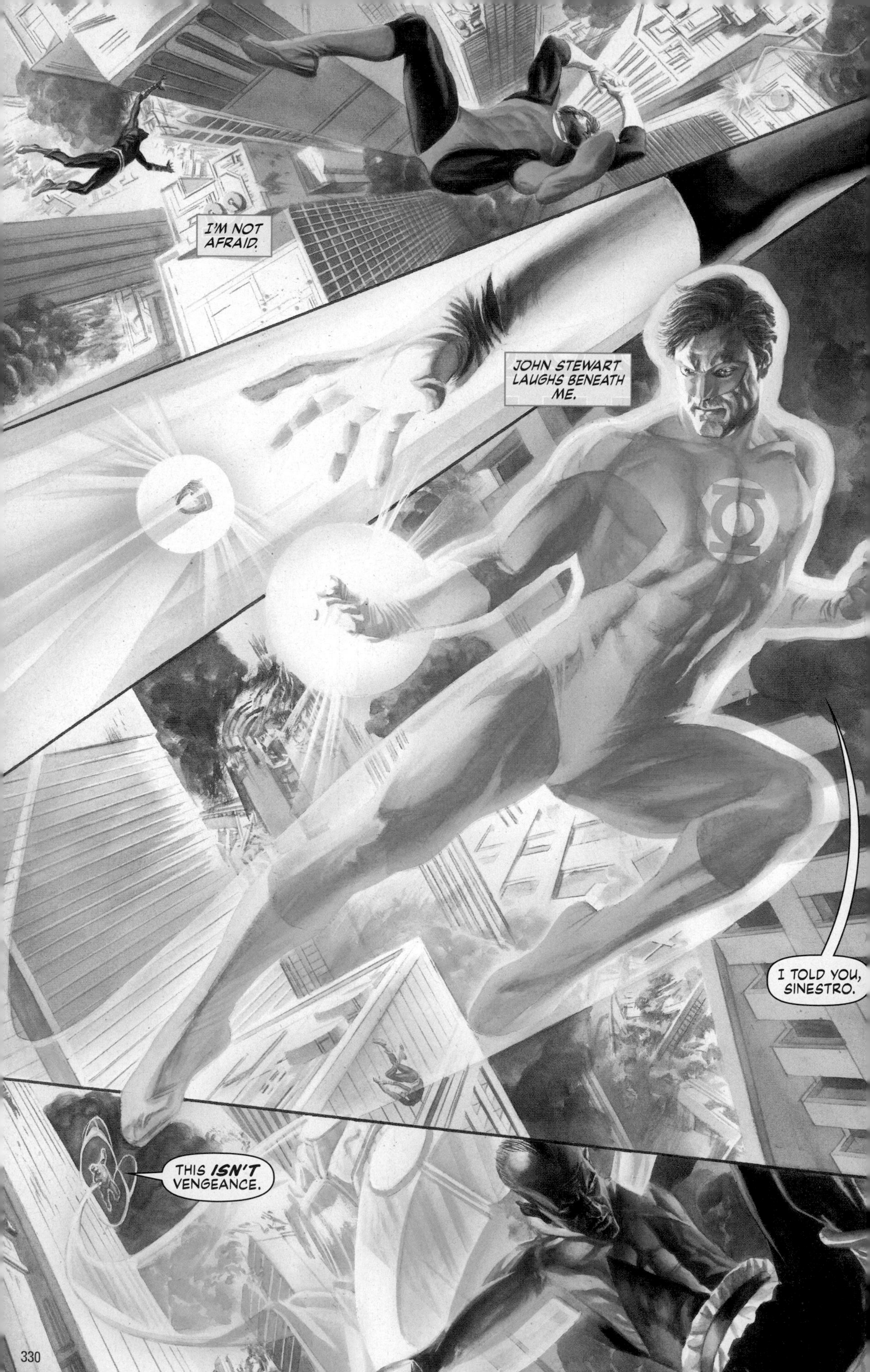
I'M NOT AFRAID.
JOHN STEWART LAUGHS BENEATH ME.
I TOLD YOU, SINESTRO.
THIS *ISN'T* VENGEANCE.

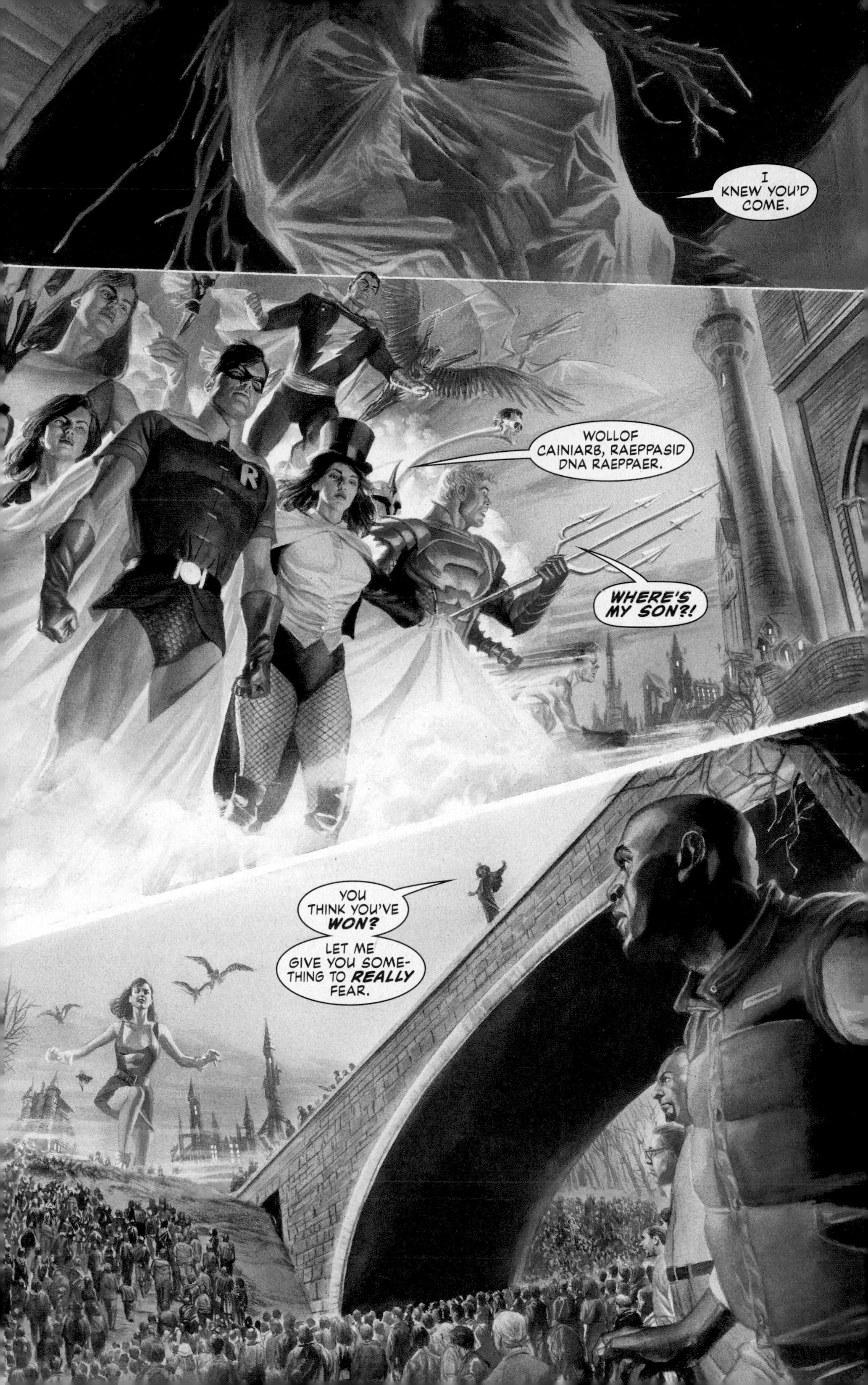
I KNEW YOU'D COME.
WOLLOF CAINIARB, RAEPPASID DNA RAEPPAER.
WHERE'S MY SON?!
YOU THINK YOU'VE WON?
LET ME GIVE YOU SOME-THING TO REALLY FEAR.

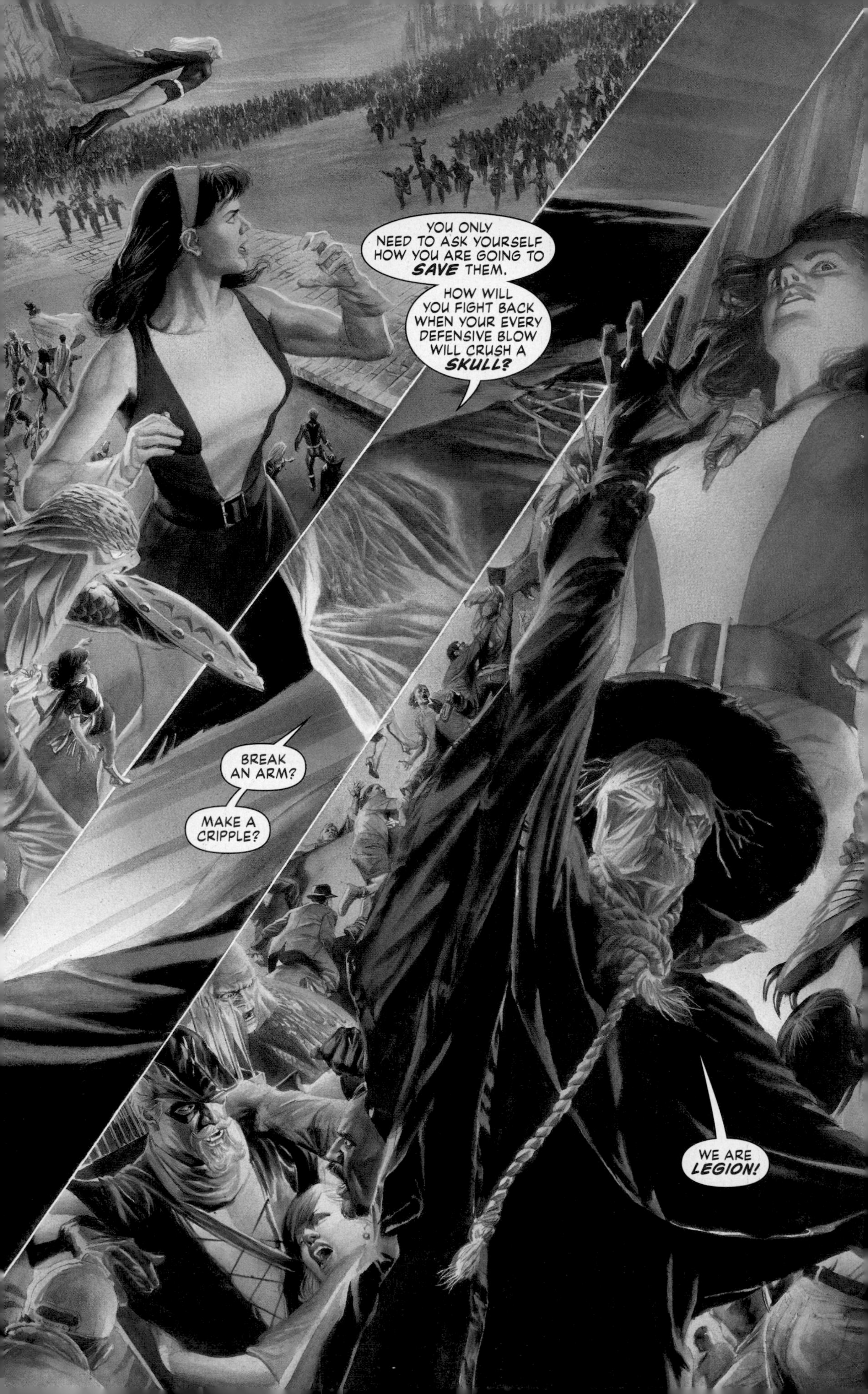
YOU ONLY NEED TO ASK YOURSELF HOW YOU ARE GOING TO SAVE THEM.
HOW WILL YOU FIGHT BACK WHEN YOUR EVERY DEFENSIVE BLOW WILL CRUSH A SKULL?
BREAK AN ARM?
MAKE A CRIPPLE?
WE ARE LEGION!

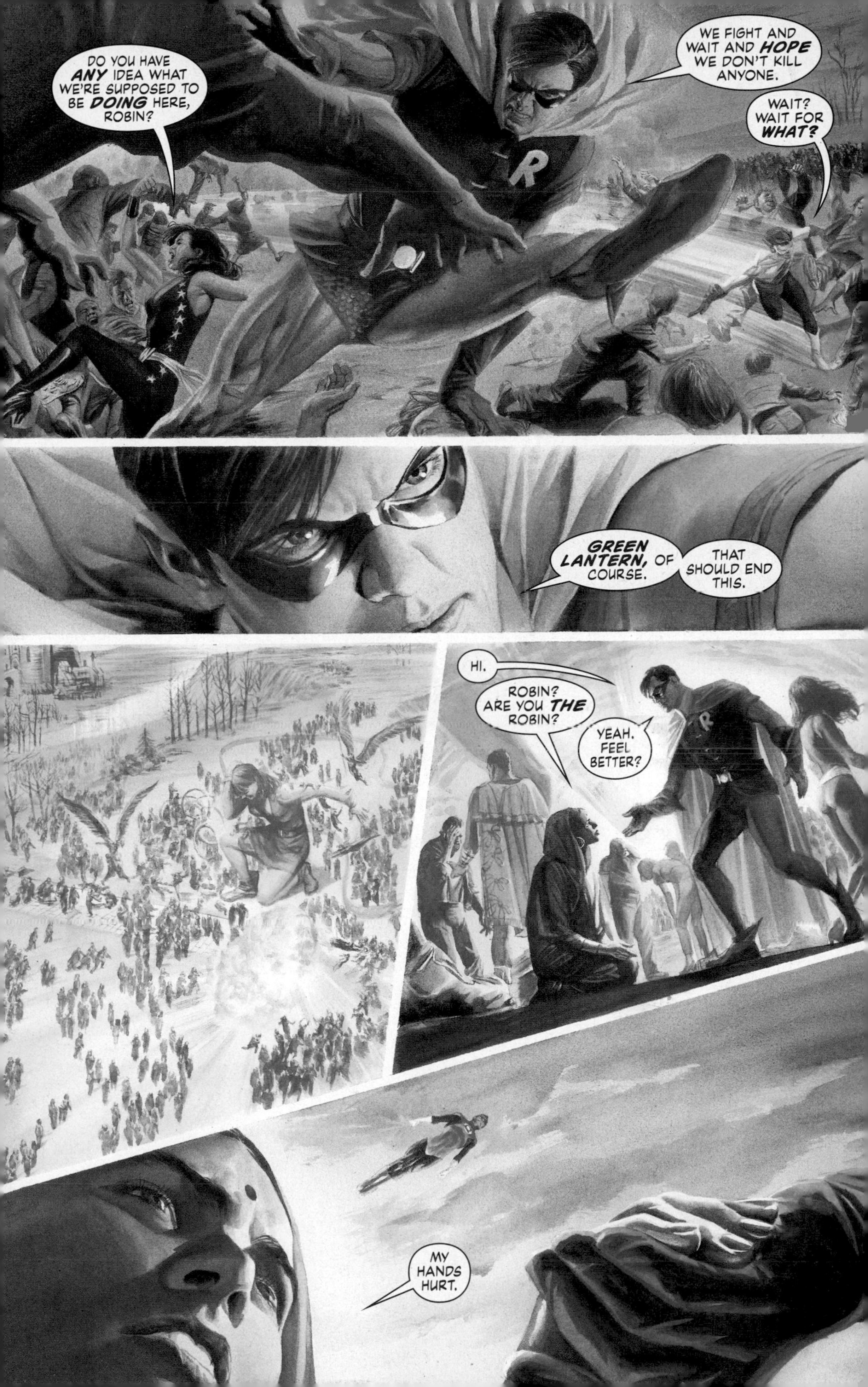
DO YOU HAVE ANY IDEA WHAT WE'RE SUPPOSED TO BE DOING HERE, ROBIN?
WE FIGHT AND WAIT AND HOPE WE DON'T KILL ANYONE.
WAIT? WAIT FOR WHAT?
GREEN LANTERN, OF COURSE.
THAT SHOULD END THIS.
HI.
ROBIN? ARE YOU THE ROBIN?
YEAH. FEEL BETTER?
MY HANDS HURT.

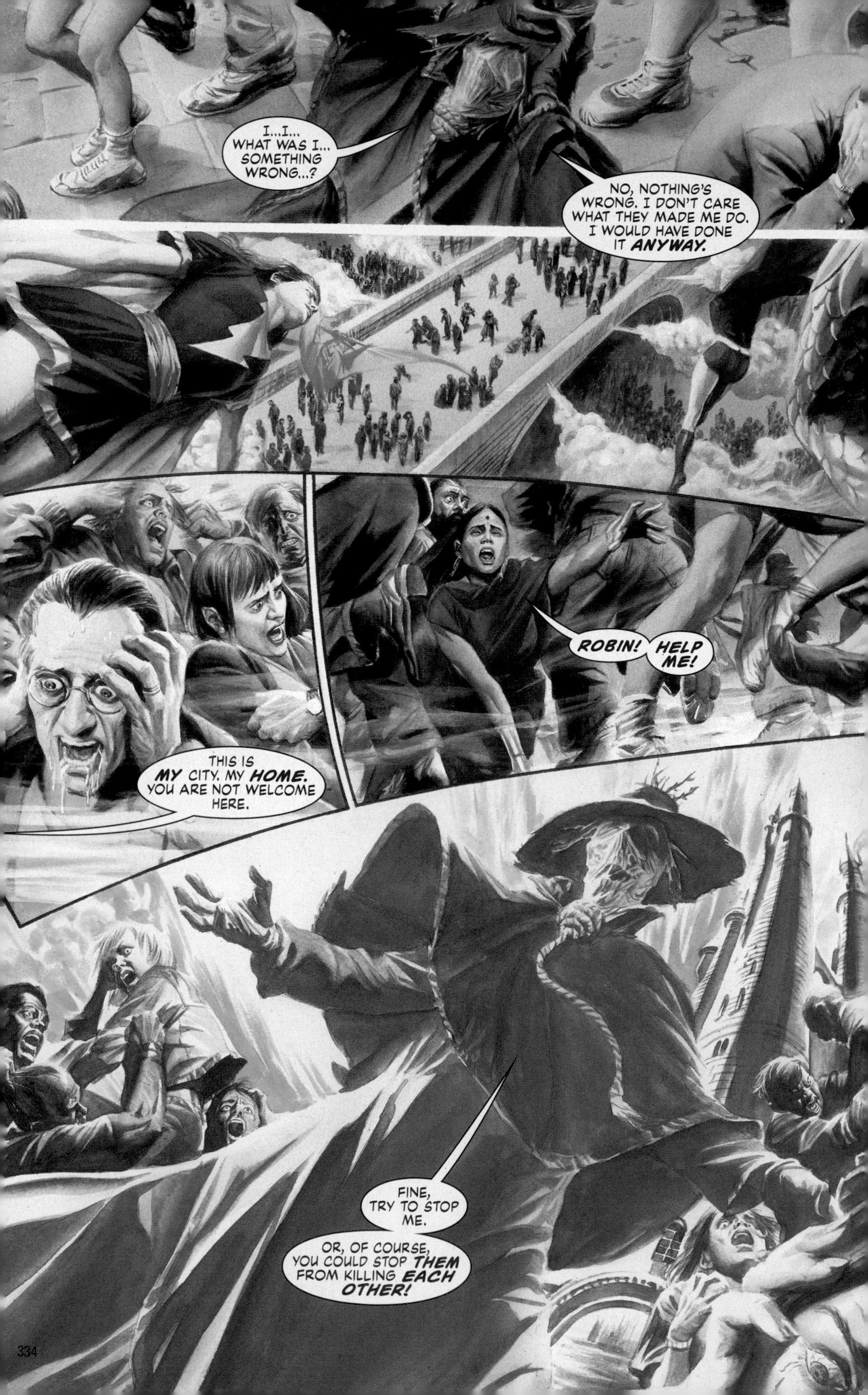
I...I...
WHAT WAS I...
SOMETHING
WRONG...?
NO, NOTHING'S
WRONG. I DON'T CARE
WHAT THEY MADE ME DO.
I WOULD HAVE DONE
IT ANYWAY.
THIS IS
MY CITY. MY HOME.
YOU ARE NOT WELCOME
HERE.
ROBIN!
HELP
ME!
FINE,
TRY TO STOP
ME.
OR, OF COURSE,
YOU COULD STOP THEM
FROM KILLING EACH
OTHER!

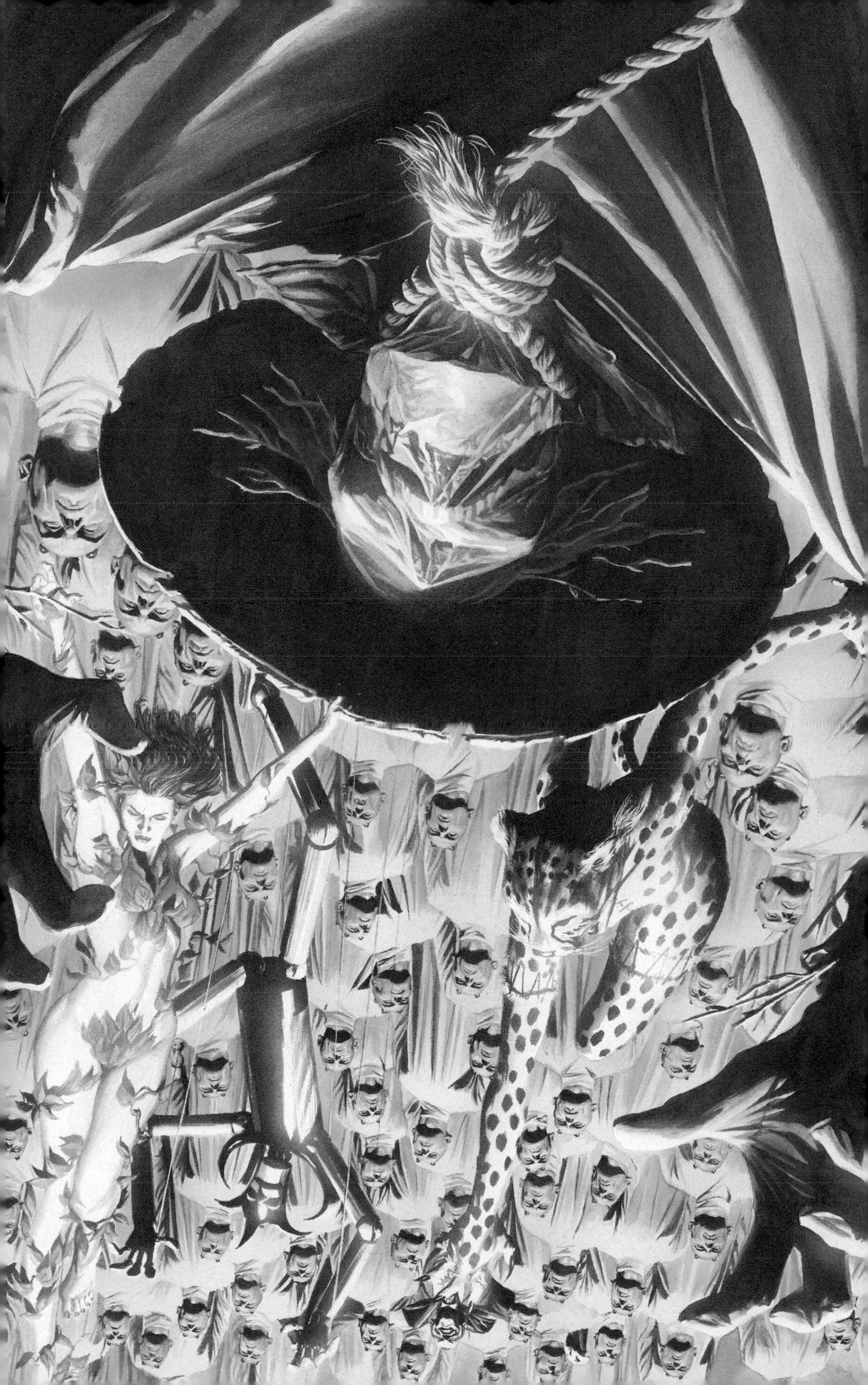

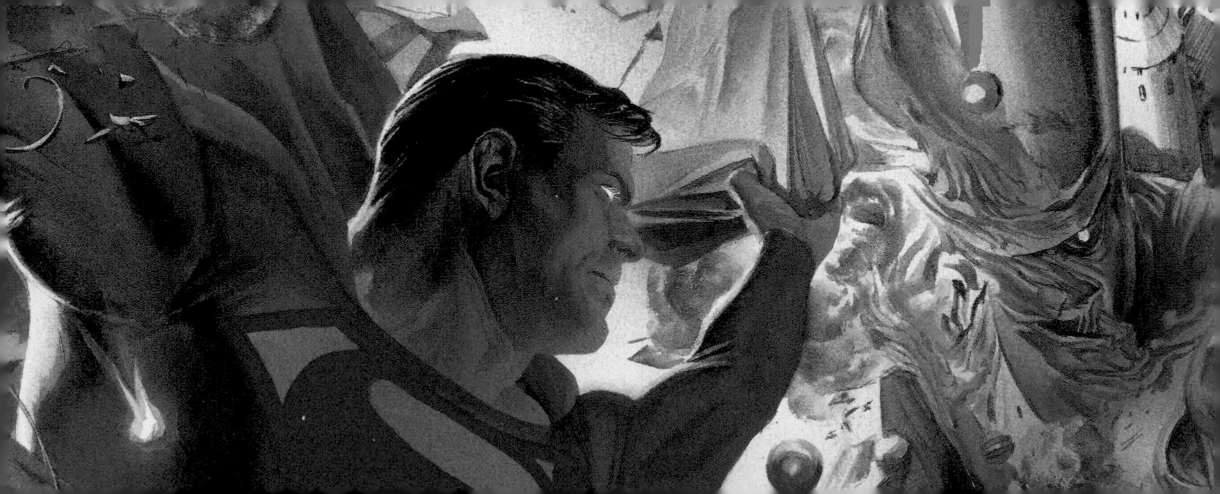

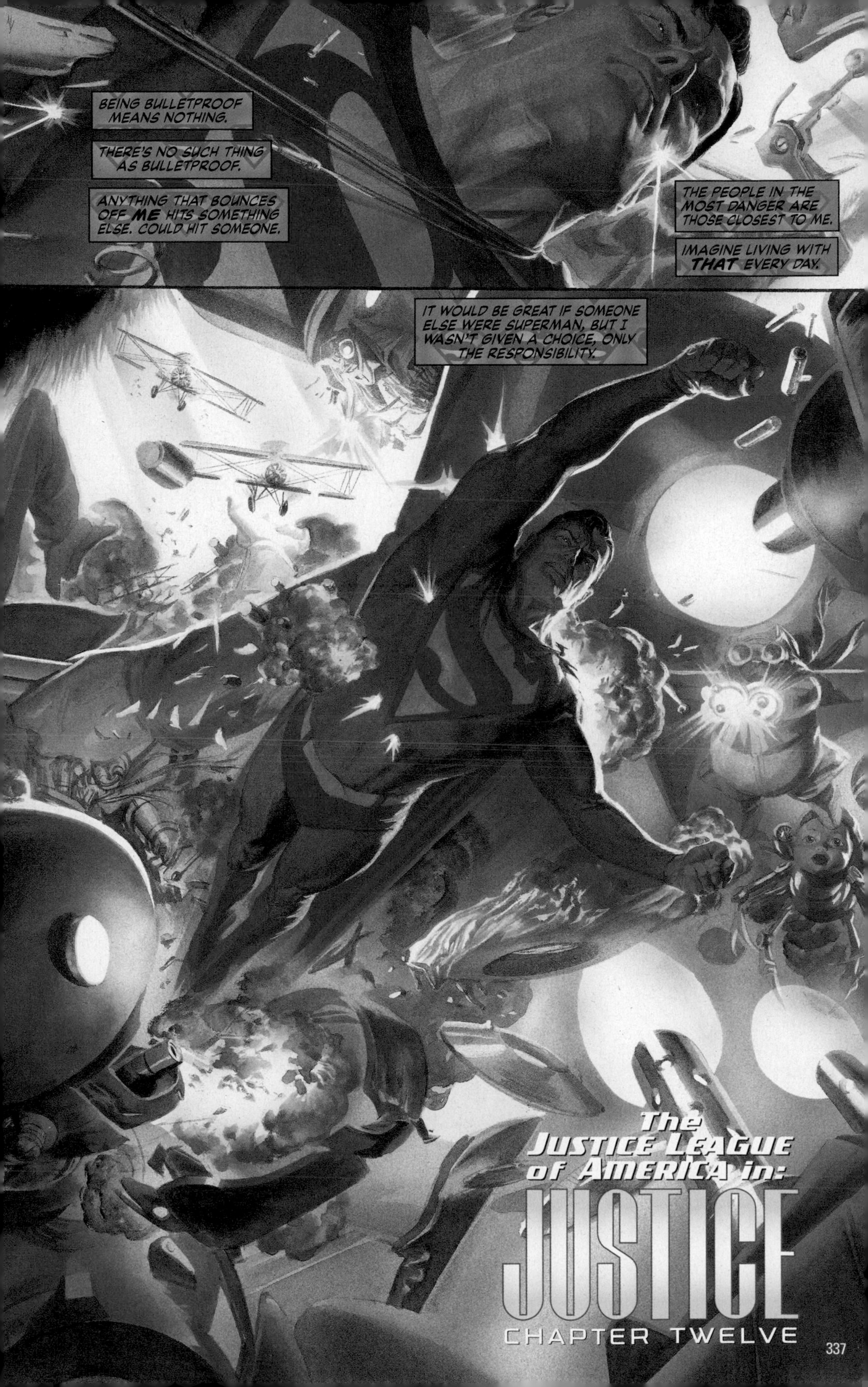

BEING BULLETPROOF MEANS NOTHING.
THERE'S NO SUCH THING AS BULLETPROOF.
ANYTHING THAT BOUNCES OFF ME HITS SOMETHING ELSE. COULD HIT SOMEONE.
THE PEOPLE IN THE MOST DANGER ARE THOSE CLOSEST TO ME.
IMAGINE LIVING WITH THAT EVERY DAY.
IT WOULD BE GREAT IF SOMEONE ELSE WERE SUPERMAN, BUT I WASN'T GIVEN A CHOICE, ONLY THE RESPONSIBILITY.
The JUSTICE LEAGUE of AMERICA in:
JUSTICE
CHAPTER TWELVE

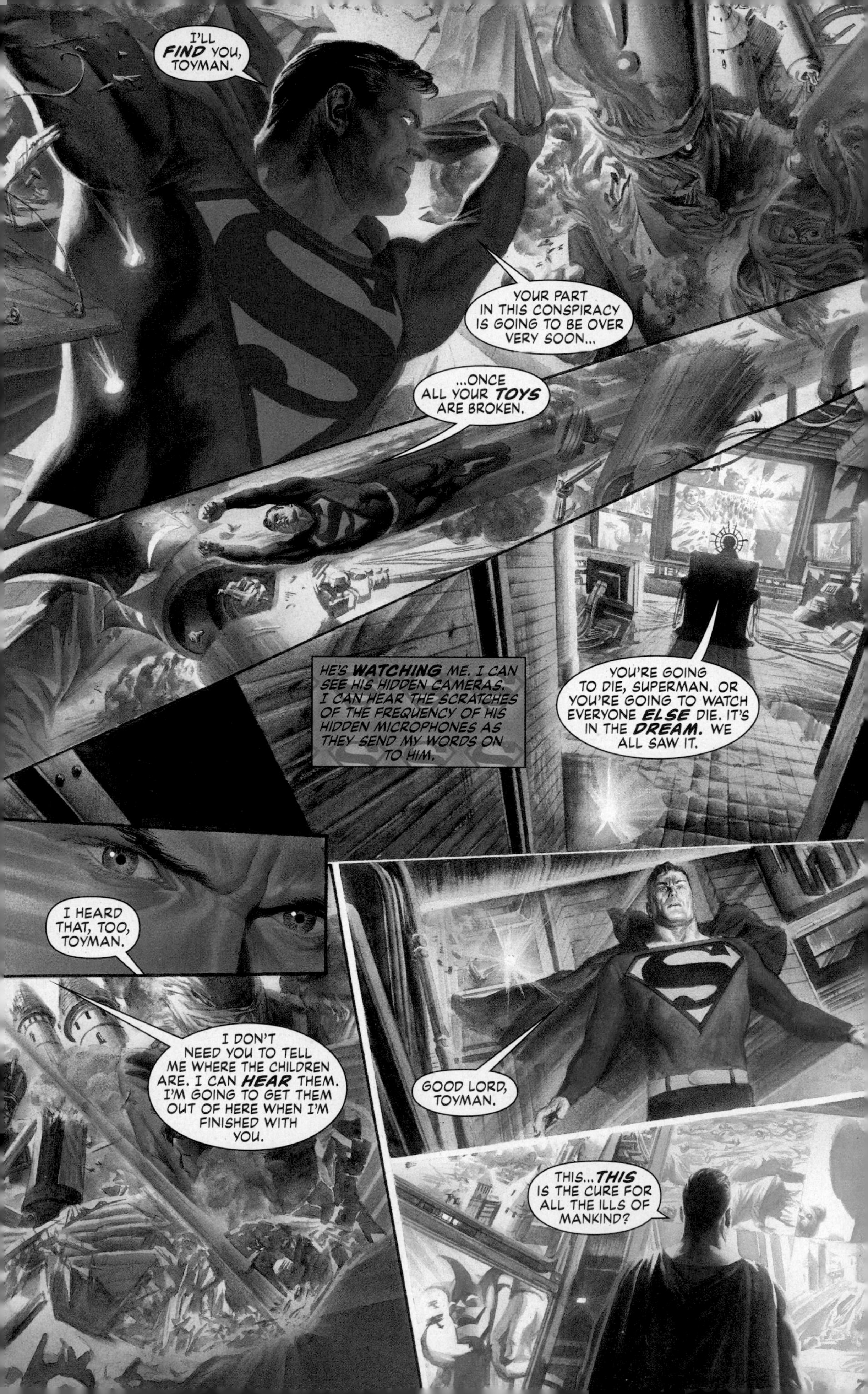

I'LL FIND YOU, TOYMAN.
YOUR PART IN THIS CONSPIRACY IS GOING TO BE OVER VERY SOON...
...ONCE ALL YOUR TOYS ARE BROKEN.
HE'S WATCHING ME. I CAN SEE HIS HIDDEN CAMERAS. I CAN HEAR THE SCRATCHES OF THE FREQUENCY OF HIS HIDDEN MICROPHONES AS THEY SEND MY WORDS ON TO HIM.
YOU'RE GOING TO DIE, SUPERMAN. OR YOU'RE GOING TO WATCH EVERYONE ELSE DIE. IT'S IN THE DREAM. WE ALL SAW IT.
I HEARD THAT, TOO, TOYMAN.
I DON'T NEED YOU TO TELL ME WHERE THE CHILDREN ARE. I CAN HEAR THEM. I'M GOING TO GET THEM OUT OF HERE WHEN I'M FINISHED WITH YOU.
GOOD LORD, TOYMAN.
THIS...THIS IS THE CURE FOR ALL THE ILLS OF MANKIND?

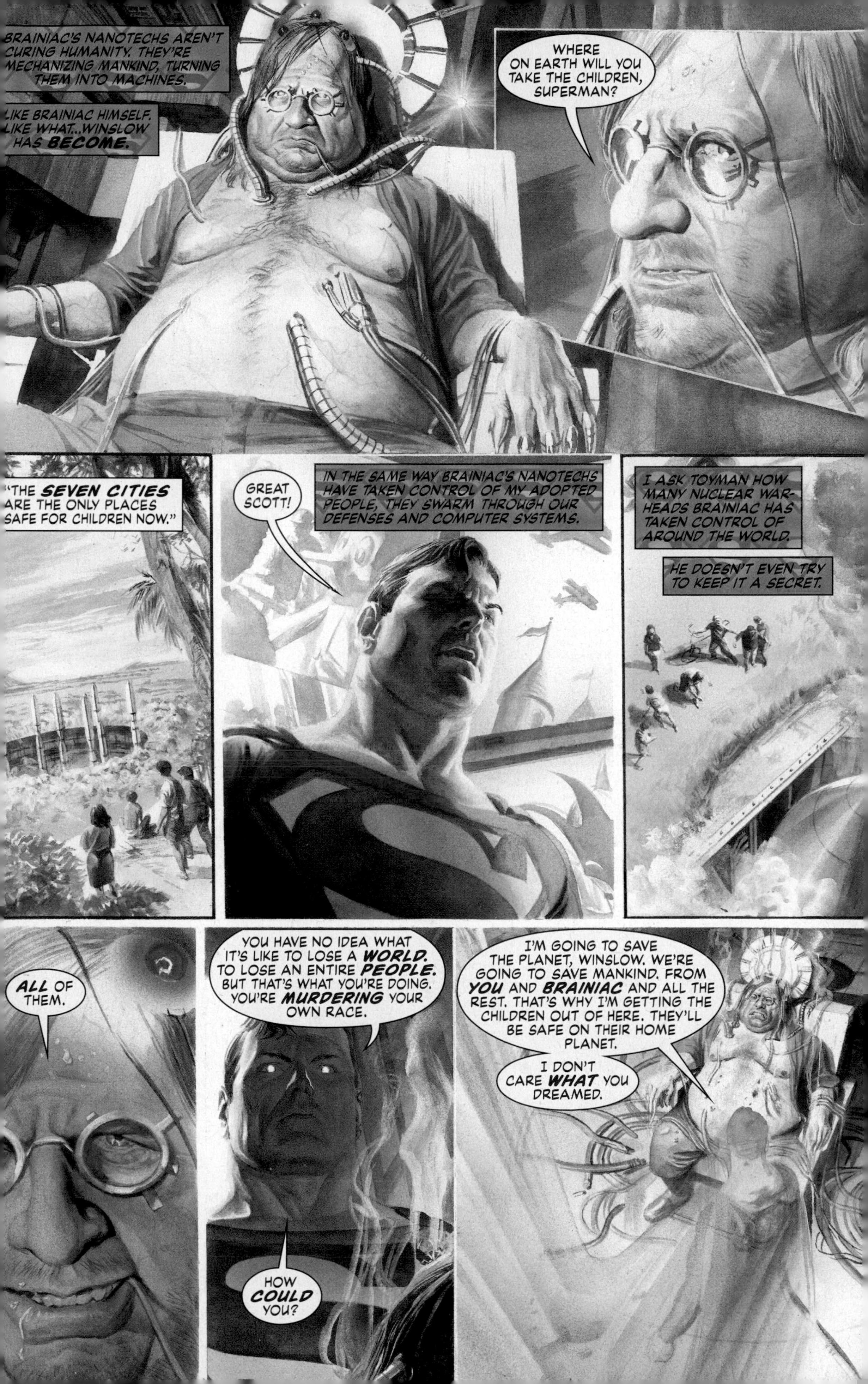

BRAINIAC'S NANOTECHS AREN'T CURING HUMANITY. THEY'RE MECHANIZING MANKIND, TURNING THEM INTO MACHINES.
LIKE BRAINIAC HIMSELF. LIKE WHAT...WINSLOW HAS BECOME.
WHERE ON EARTH WILL YOU TAKE THE CHILDREN, SUPERMAN?
"THE SEVEN CITIES ARE THE ONLY PLACES SAFE FOR CHILDREN NOW."
GREAT SCOTT!
IN THE SAME WAY BRAINIAC'S NANOTECHS HAVE TAKEN CONTROL OF MY ADOPTED PEOPLE, THEY SWARM THROUGH OUR DEFENSES AND COMPUTER SYSTEMS.
I ASK TOYMAN HOW MANY NUCLEAR WAR-HEADS BRAINIAC HAS TAKEN CONTROL OF AROUND THE WORLD.
HE DOESN'T EVEN TRY TO KEEP IT A SECRET.
ALL OF THEM.
YOU HAVE NO IDEA WHAT IT'S LIKE TO LOSE A WORLD. TO LOSE AN ENTIRE PEOPLE. BUT THAT'S WHAT YOU'RE DOING. YOU'RE MURDERING YOUR OWN RACE.
HOW COULD YOU?
I'M GOING TO SAVE THE PLANET, WINSLOW. WE'RE GOING TO SAVE MANKIND. FROM YOU AND BRAINIAC AND ALL THE REST. THAT'S WHY I'M GETTING THE CHILDREN OUT OF HERE. THEY'LL BE SAFE ON THEIR HOME PLANET.
I DON'T CARE WHAT YOU DREAMED.

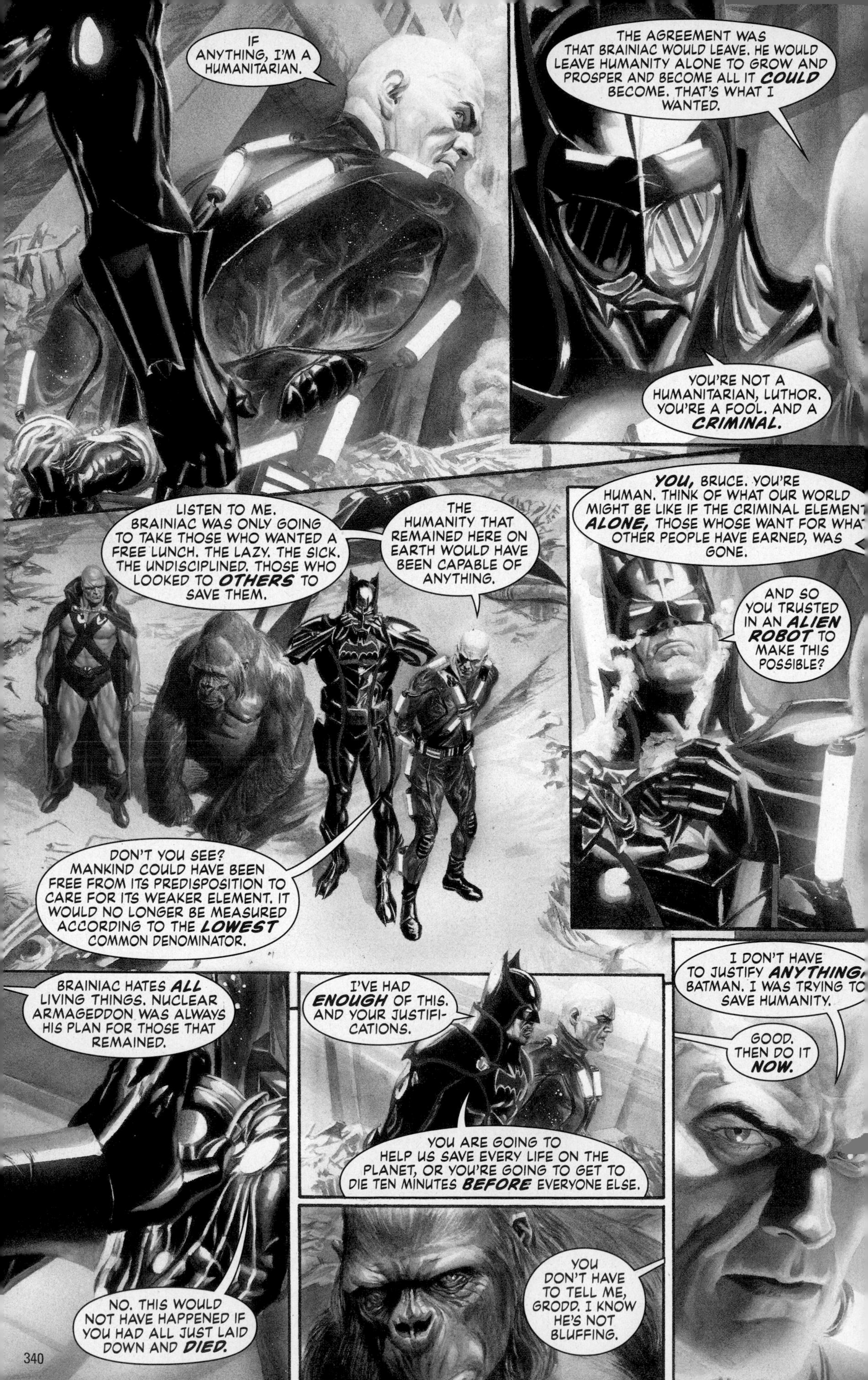

IF ANYTHING, I'M A HUMANITARIAN.
THE AGREEMENT WAS THAT BRAINIAC WOULD LEAVE. HE WOULD LEAVE HUMANITY ALONE TO GROW AND PROSPER AND BECOME ALL IT COULD BECOME. THAT'S WHAT I WANTED.
YOU'RE NOT A HUMANITARIAN, LUTHOR. YOU'RE A FOOL. AND A CRIMINAL.
LISTEN TO ME. BRAINIAC WAS ONLY GOING TO TAKE THOSE WHO WANTED A FREE LUNCH. THE LAZY. THE SICK. THE UNDISCIPLINED. THOSE WHO LOOKED TO OTHERS TO SAVE THEM.
THE HUMANITY THAT REMAINED HERE ON EARTH WOULD HAVE BEEN CAPABLE OF ANYTHING.
DON'T YOU SEE? MANKIND COULD HAVE BEEN FREE FROM ITS PREDISPOSITION TO CARE FOR ITS WEAKER ELEMENT. IT WOULD NO LONGER BE MEASURED ACCORDING TO THE LOWEST COMMON DENOMINATOR.
YOU, BRUCE. YOU'RE HUMAN. THINK OF WHAT OUR WORLD MIGHT BE LIKE IF THE CRIMINAL ELEMENT ALONE, THOSE WHOSE WANT FOR WHAT OTHER PEOPLE HAVE EARNED, WAS GONE.
AND SO YOU TRUSTED IN AN ALIEN ROBOT TO MAKE THIS POSSIBLE?
BRAINIAC HATES ALL LIVING THINGS. NUCLEAR ARMAGEDDON WAS ALWAYS HIS PLAN FOR THOSE THAT REMAINED.
NO. THIS WOULD NOT HAVE HAPPENED IF YOU HAD ALL JUST LAID DOWN AND DIED.
I'VE HAD ENOUGH OF THIS. AND YOUR JUSTIFICATIONS.
YOU ARE GOING TO HELP US SAVE EVERY LIFE ON THE PLANET, OR YOU'RE GOING TO GET TO DIE TEN MINUTES BEFORE EVERYONE ELSE.
I DON'T HAVE TO JUSTIFY ANYTHING, BATMAN. I WAS TRYING TO SAVE HUMANITY.
GOOD. THEN DO IT NOW.
YOU DON'T HAVE TO TELL ME, GRODD. I KNOW HE'S NOT BLUFFING.

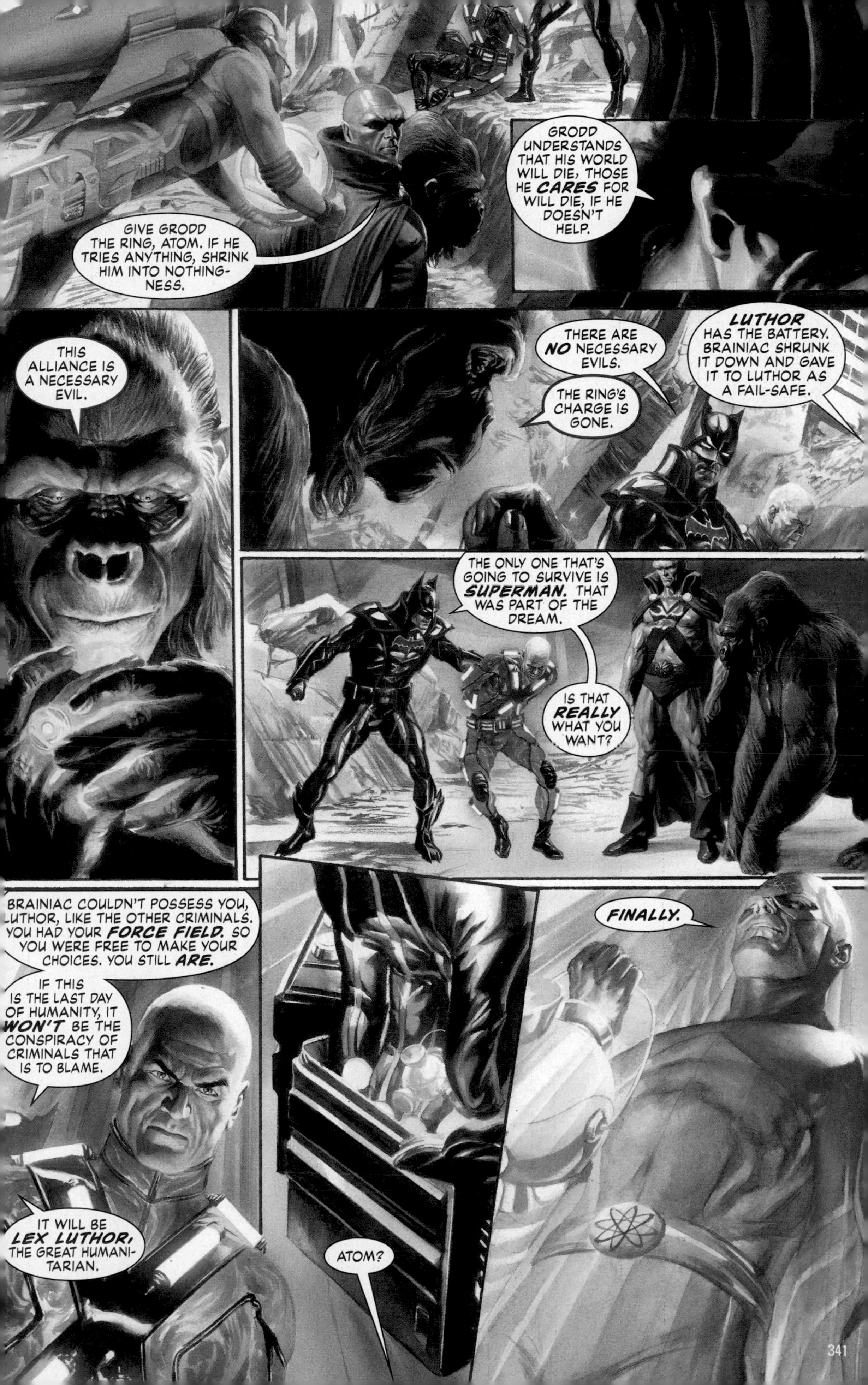

GIVE GRODD THE RING, ATOM. IF HE TRIES ANYTHING, SHRINK HIM INTO NOTHINGNESS.
GRODD UNDERSTANDS THAT HIS WORLD WILL DIE, THOSE HE **CARES** FOR WILL DIE, IF HE DOESN'T HELP.
THIS ALLIANCE IS A NECESSARY EVIL.
THERE ARE **NO** NECESSARY EVILS.
THE RING'S CHARGE IS GONE.
LUTHOR HAS THE BATTERY. BRAINIAC SHRUNK IT DOWN AND GAVE IT TO LUTHOR AS A FAIL-SAFE.
THE ONLY ONE THAT'S GOING TO SURVIVE IS **SUPERMAN.** THAT WAS PART OF THE DREAM.
IS THAT **REALLY** WHAT YOU WANT?
BRAINIAC COULDN'T POSSESS YOU, LUTHOR, LIKE THE OTHER CRIMINALS. YOU HAD YOUR **FORCE FIELD.** SO YOU WERE FREE TO MAKE YOUR CHOICES. YOU STILL **ARE.**
IF THIS IS THE LAST DAY OF HUMANITY, IT **WON'T** BE THE CONSPIRACY OF CRIMINALS THAT IS TO BLAME.
IT WILL BE **LEX LUTHOR,** THE GREAT HUMANITARIAN.
ATOM?
FINALLY.

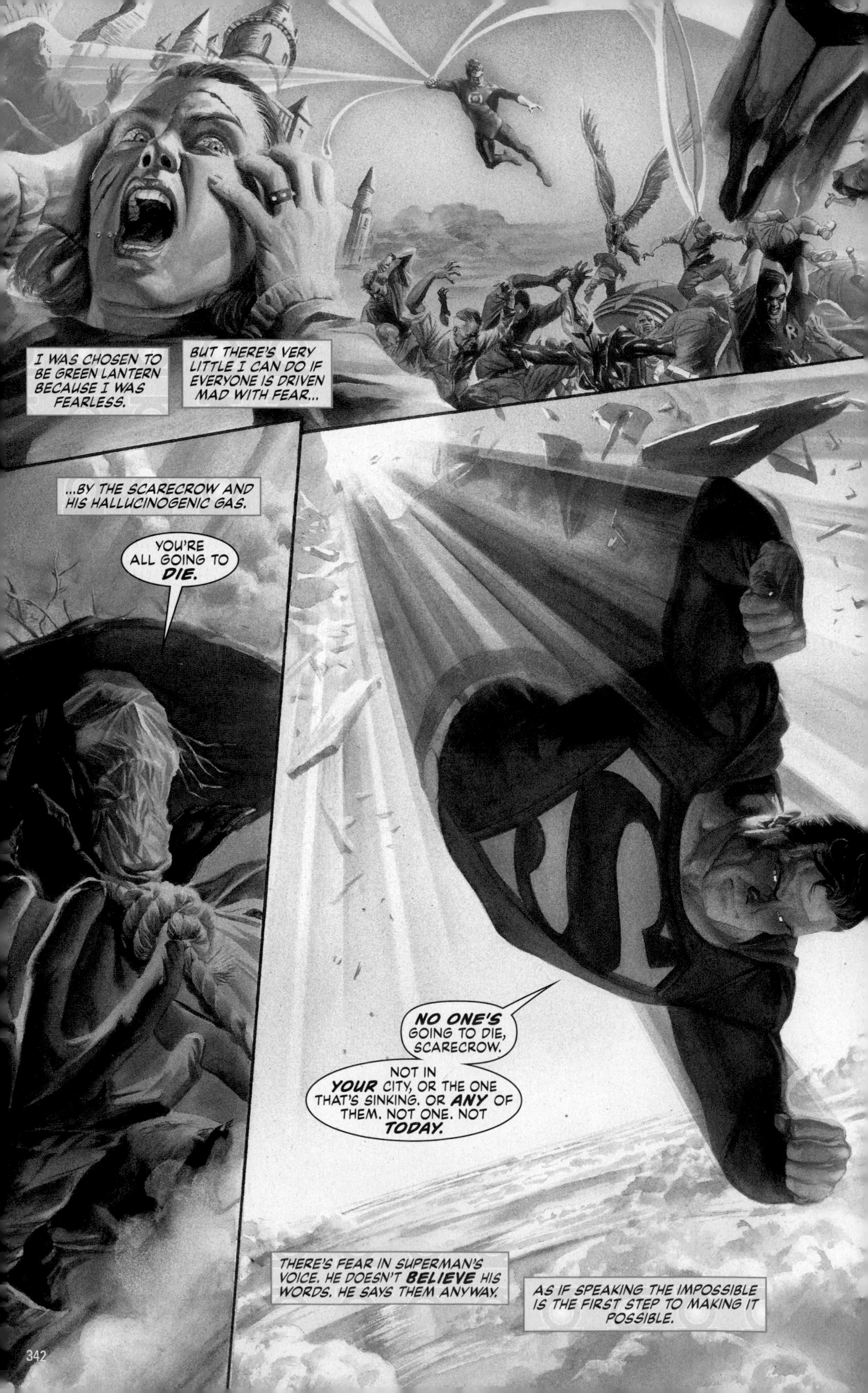
I WAS CHOSEN TO BE GREEN LANTERN BECAUSE I WAS FEARLESS.
BUT THERE'S VERY LITTLE I CAN DO IF EVERYONE IS DRIVEN MAD WITH FEAR...
...BY THE SCARECROW AND HIS HALLUCINOGENIC GAS.
YOU'RE ALL GOING TO DIE.
NO ONE'S GOING TO DIE, SCARECROW.
NOT IN YOUR CITY, OR THE ONE THAT'S SINKING. OR ANY OF THEM. NOT ONE. NOT TODAY.
THERE'S FEAR IN SUPERMAN'S VOICE. HE DOESN'T BELIEVE HIS WORDS. HE SAYS THEM ANYWAY.
AS IF SPEAKING THE IMPOSSIBLE IS THE FIRST STEP TO MAKING IT POSSIBLE.

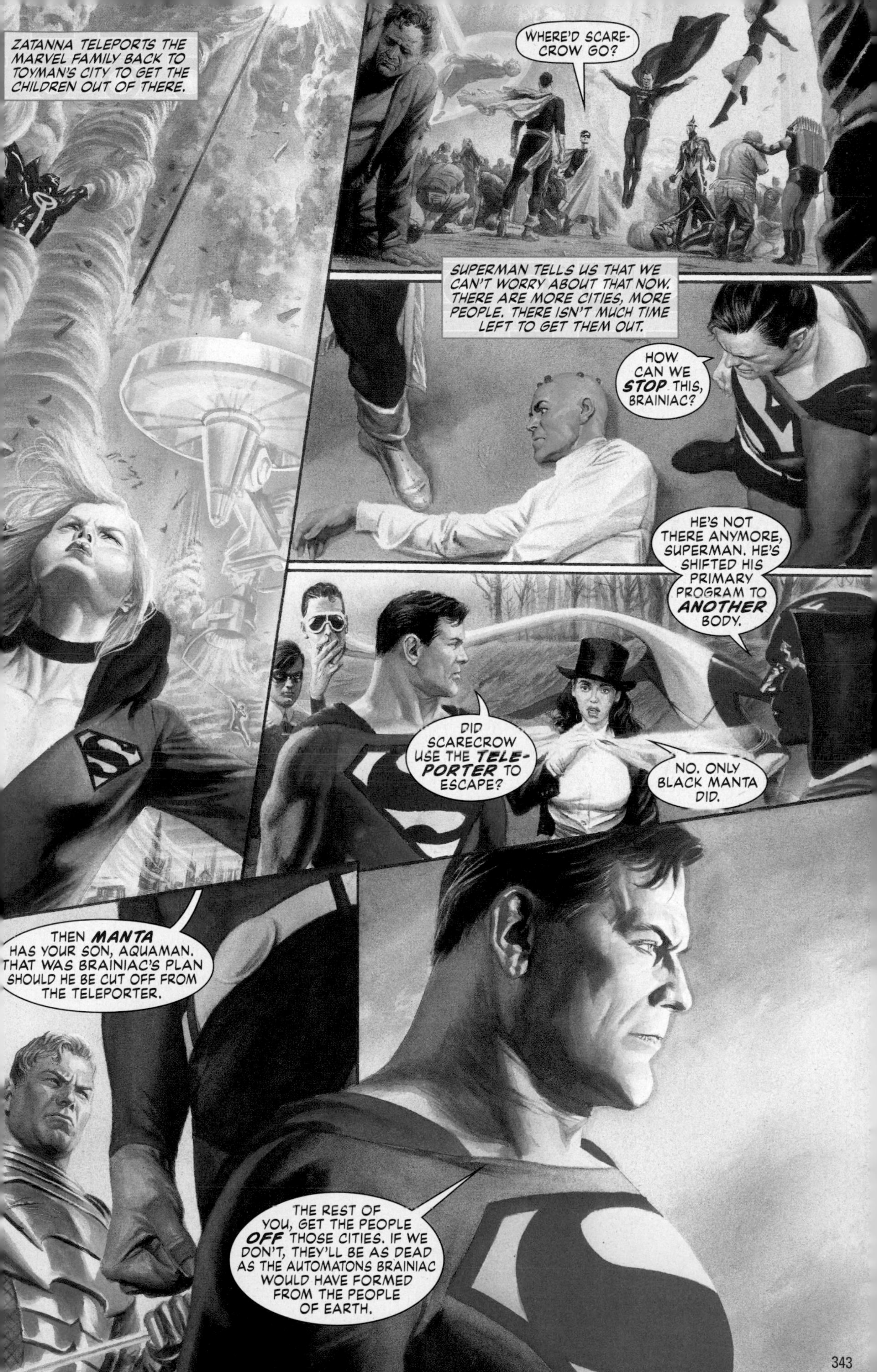
ZATANNA TELEPORTS THE MARVEL FAMILY BACK TO TOYMAN'S CITY TO GET THE CHILDREN OUT OF THERE.
WHERE'D SCARE-CROW GO?
SUPERMAN TELLS US THAT WE CAN'T WORRY ABOUT THAT NOW. THERE ARE MORE CITIES, MORE PEOPLE. THERE ISN'T MUCH TIME LEFT TO GET THEM OUT.
HOW CAN WE STOP THIS, BRAINIAC?
HE'S NOT THERE ANYMORE, SUPERMAN. HE'S SHIFTED HIS PRIMARY PROGRAM TO ANOTHER BODY.
DID SCARECROW USE THE TELE-PORTER TO ESCAPE?
NO. ONLY BLACK MANTA DID.
THEN MANTA HAS YOUR SON, AQUAMAN. THAT WAS BRAINIAC'S PLAN SHOULD HE BE CUT OFF FROM THE TELEPORTER.
THE REST OF YOU, GET THE PEOPLE OFF THOSE CITIES. IF WE DON'T, THEY'LL BE AS DEAD AS THE AUTOMATONS BRAINIAC WOULD HAVE FORMED FROM THE PEOPLE OF EARTH.

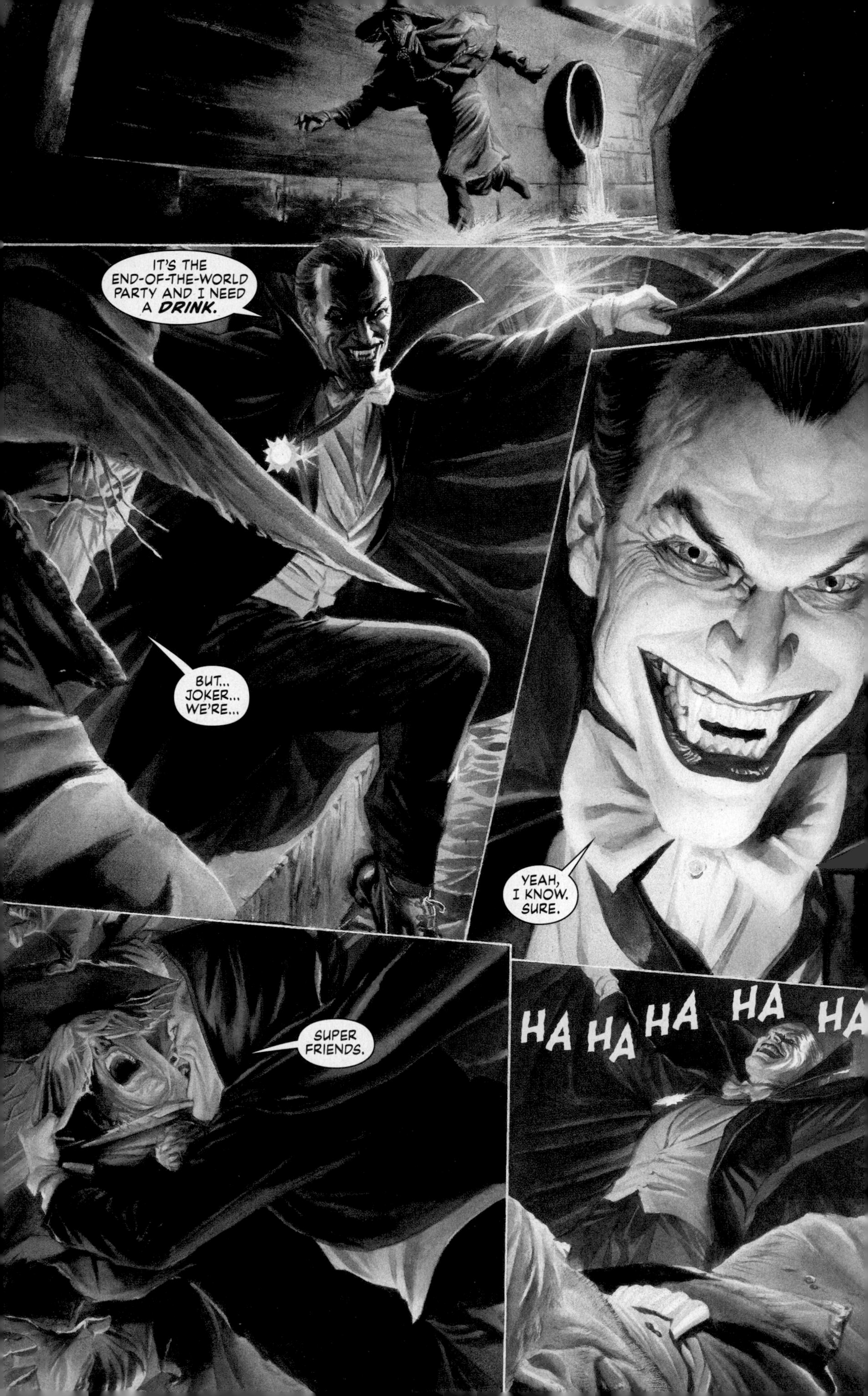
IT'S THE END-OF-THE-WORLD PARTY AND I NEED A DRINK.
BUT... JOKER... WE'RE...
YEAH, I KNOW. SURE.
SUPER FRIENDS.
HA HA HA HA HA

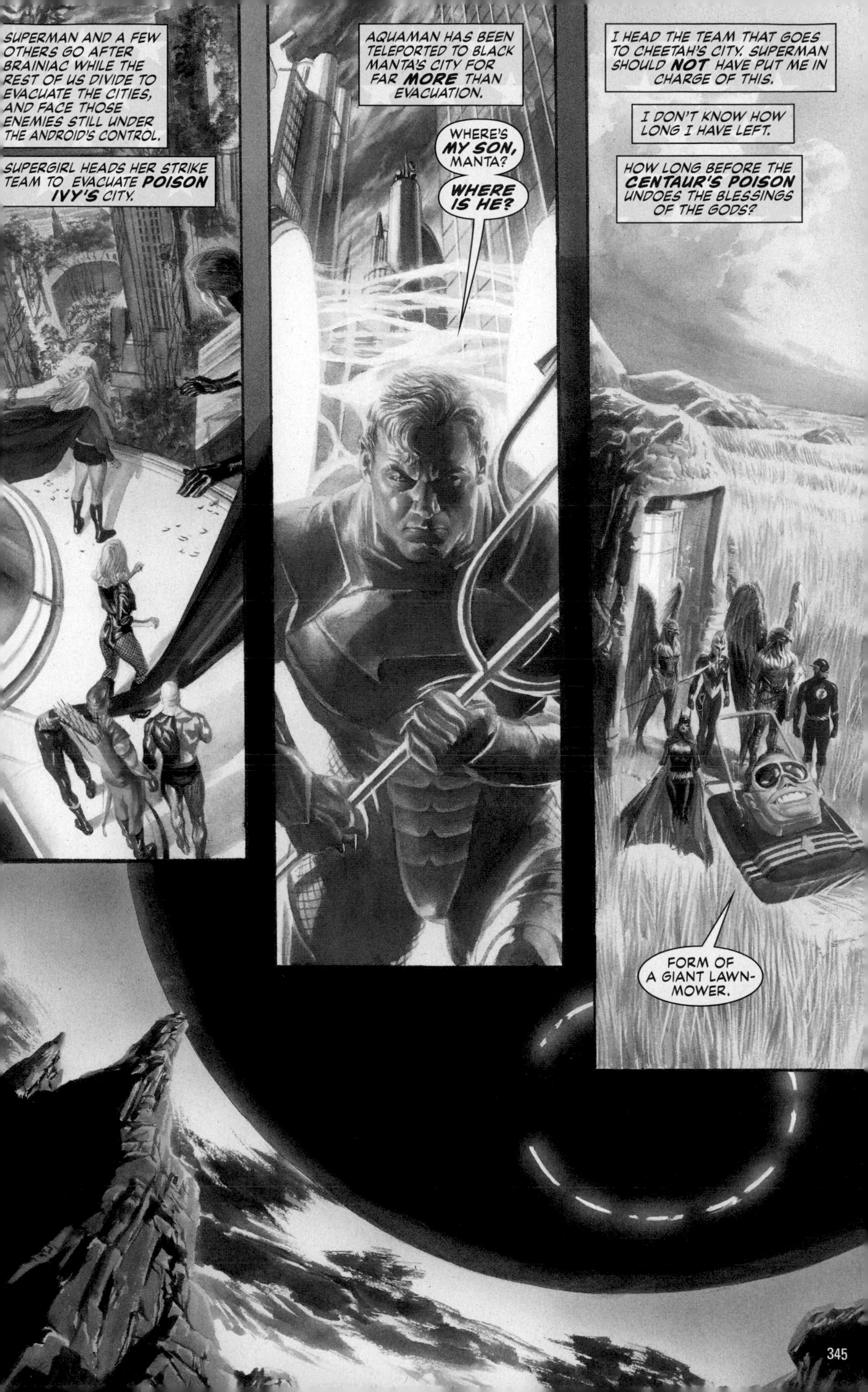
SUPERMAN AND A FEW OTHERS GO AFTER BRAINIAC WHILE THE REST OF US DIVIDE TO EVACUATE THE CITIES, AND FACE THOSE ENEMIES STILL UNDER THE ANDROID'S CONTROL.
SUPERGIRL HEADS HER STRIKE TEAM TO EVACUATE POISON IVY'S CITY.
AQUAMAN HAS BEEN TELEPORTED TO BLACK MANTA'S CITY FOR FAR MORE THAN EVACUATION.
WHERE'S MY SON, MANTA?
WHERE IS HE?
I HEAD THE TEAM THAT GOES TO CHEETAH'S CITY. SUPERMAN SHOULD NOT HAVE PUT ME IN CHARGE OF THIS.
I DON'T KNOW HOW LONG I HAVE LEFT.
HOW LONG BEFORE THE CENTAUR'S POISON UNDOES THE BLESSINGS OF THE GODS?
FORM OF A GIANT LAWN-MOWER.

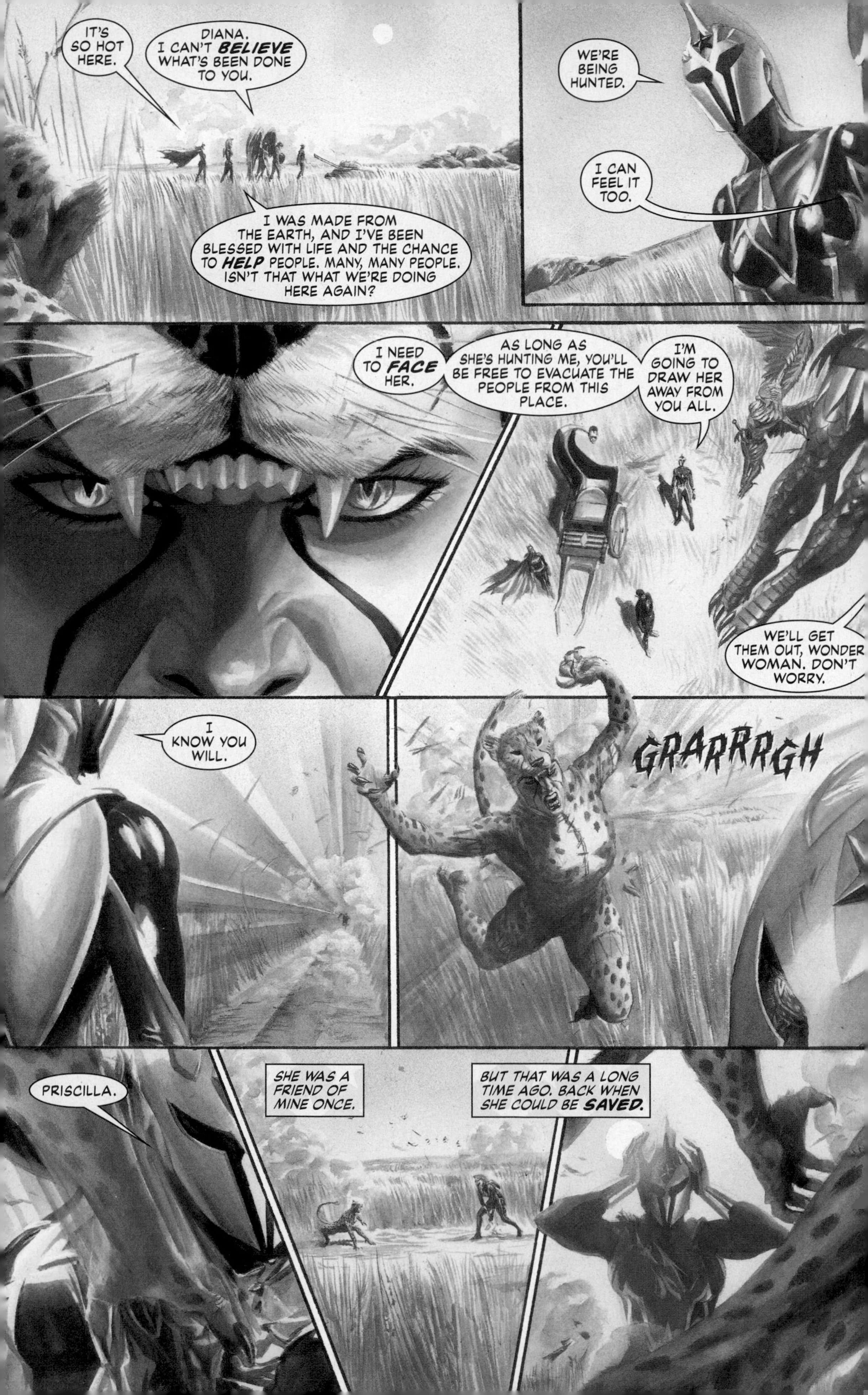
IT'S SO HOT HERE.
DIANA. I CAN'T BELIEVE WHAT'S BEEN DONE TO YOU.
I WAS MADE FROM THE EARTH, AND I'VE BEEN BLESSED WITH LIFE AND THE CHANCE TO HELP PEOPLE. MANY, MANY PEOPLE. ISN'T THAT WHAT WE'RE DOING HERE AGAIN?
WE'RE BEING HUNTED.
I CAN FEEL IT TOO.
I NEED TO FACE HER.
AS LONG AS SHE'S HUNTING ME, YOU'LL BE FREE TO EVACUATE THE PEOPLE FROM THIS PLACE.
I'M GOING TO DRAW HER AWAY FROM YOU ALL.
WE'LL GET THEM OUT, WONDER WOMAN. DON'T WORRY.
I KNOW YOU WILL.
GRARRRGH
PRISCILLA.
SHE WAS A FRIEND OF MINE ONCE.
BUT THAT WAS A LONG TIME AGO. BACK WHEN SHE COULD BE SAVED.

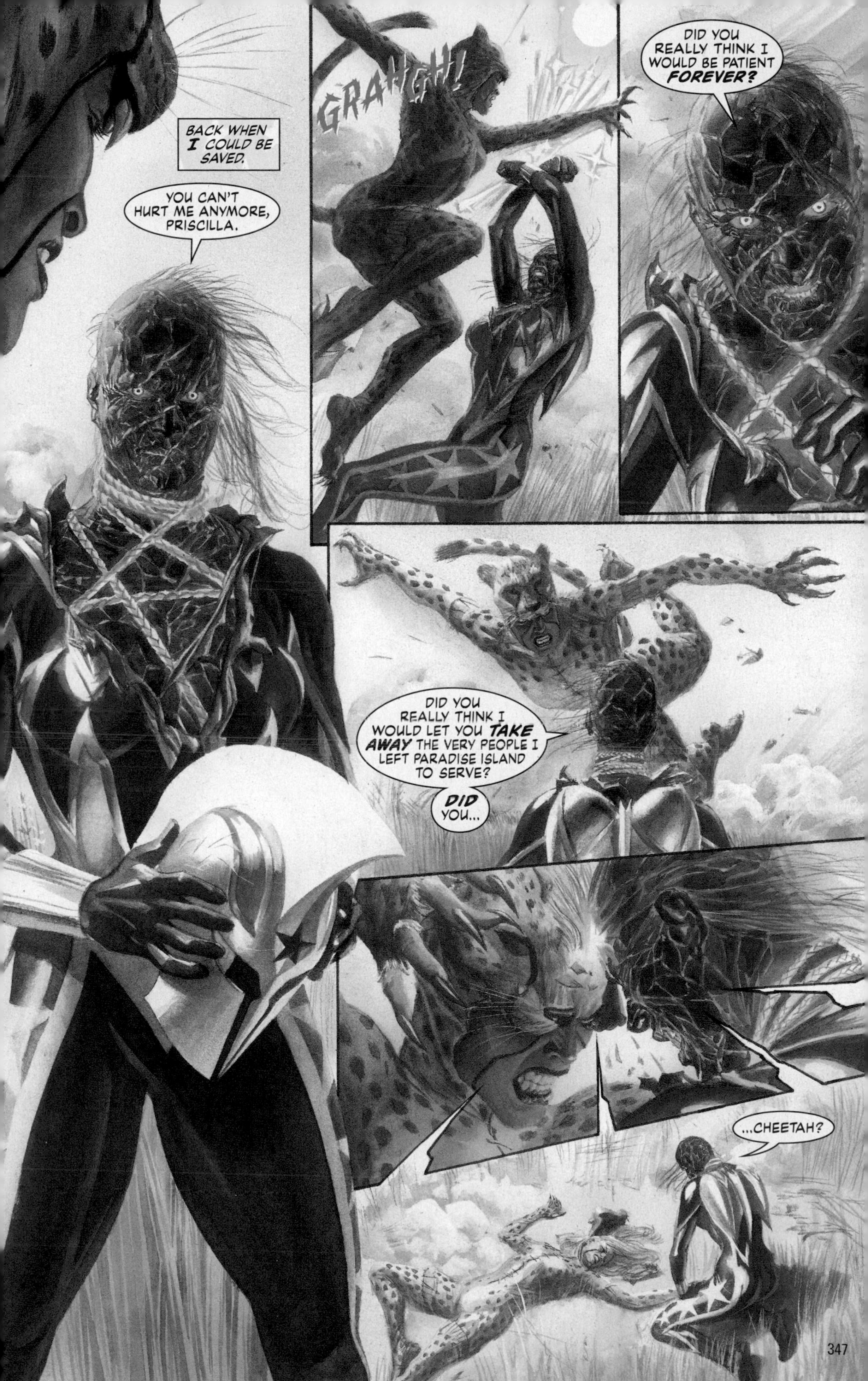

BACK WHEN I COULD BE SAVED.
YOU CAN'T HURT ME ANYMORE, PRISCILLA.
GRAHGH!
DID YOU REALLY THINK I WOULD BE PATIENT FOREVER?
DID YOU REALLY THINK I WOULD LET YOU TAKE AWAY THE VERY PEOPLE I LEFT PARADISE ISLAND TO SERVE?
DID YOU...
...CHEETAH?

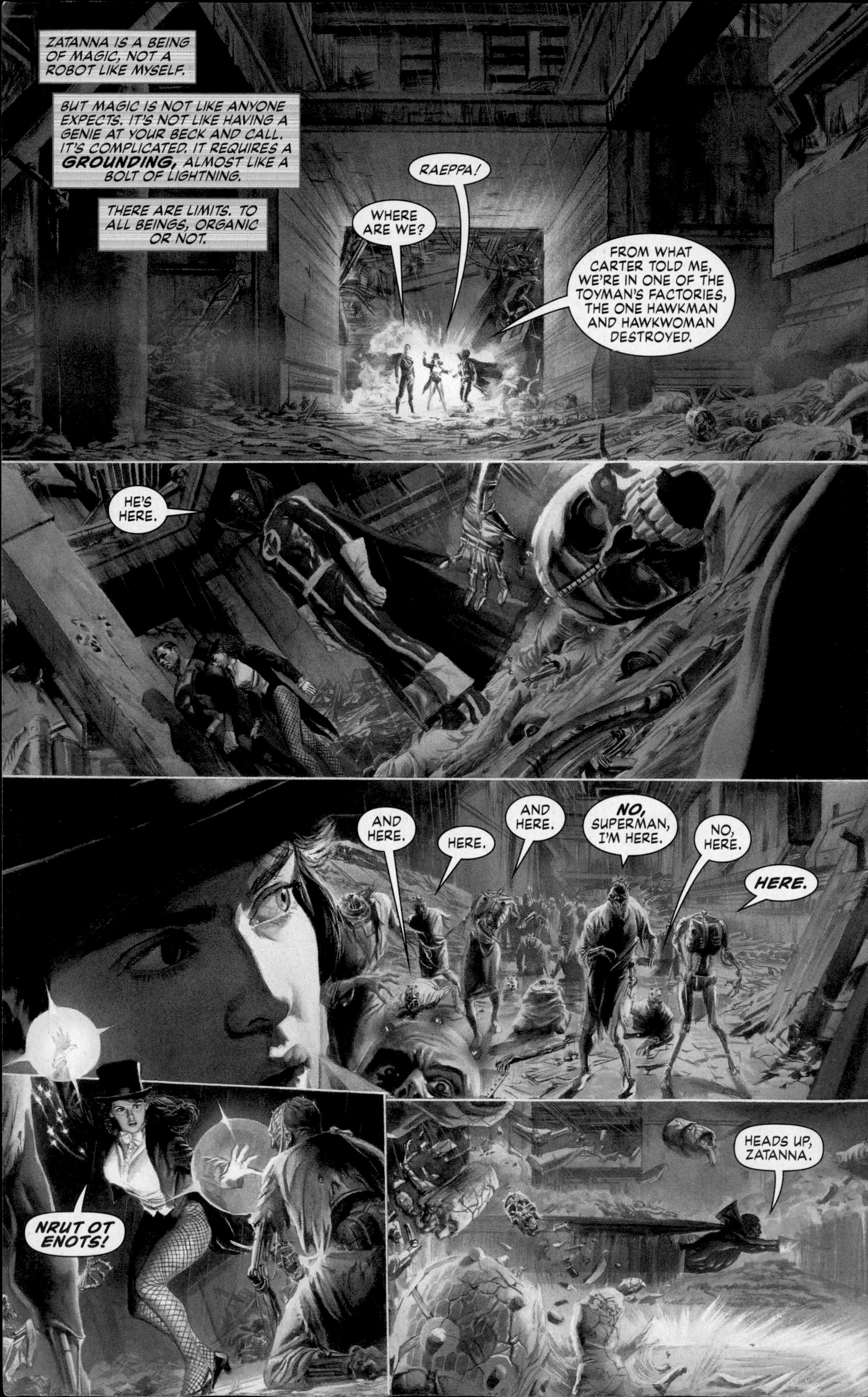
ZATANNA IS A BEING OF MAGIC, NOT A ROBOT LIKE MYSELF.
BUT MAGIC IS NOT LIKE ANYONE EXPECTS. IT'S NOT LIKE HAVING A GENIE AT YOUR BECK AND CALL. IT'S COMPLICATED. IT REQUIRES A GROUNDING, ALMOST LIKE A BOLT OF LIGHTNING.
THERE ARE LIMITS. TO ALL BEINGS, ORGANIC OR NOT.
RAEPPA!
WHERE ARE WE?
FROM WHAT CARTER TOLD ME, WE'RE IN ONE OF THE TOYMAN'S FACTORIES, THE ONE HAWKMAN AND HAWKWOMAN DESTROYED.
HE'S HERE.
AND HERE.
HERE.
AND HERE.
NO, SUPERMAN, I'M HERE.
NO, HERE.
HERE.
NRUT OT ENOTS!
HEADS UP, ZATANNA.

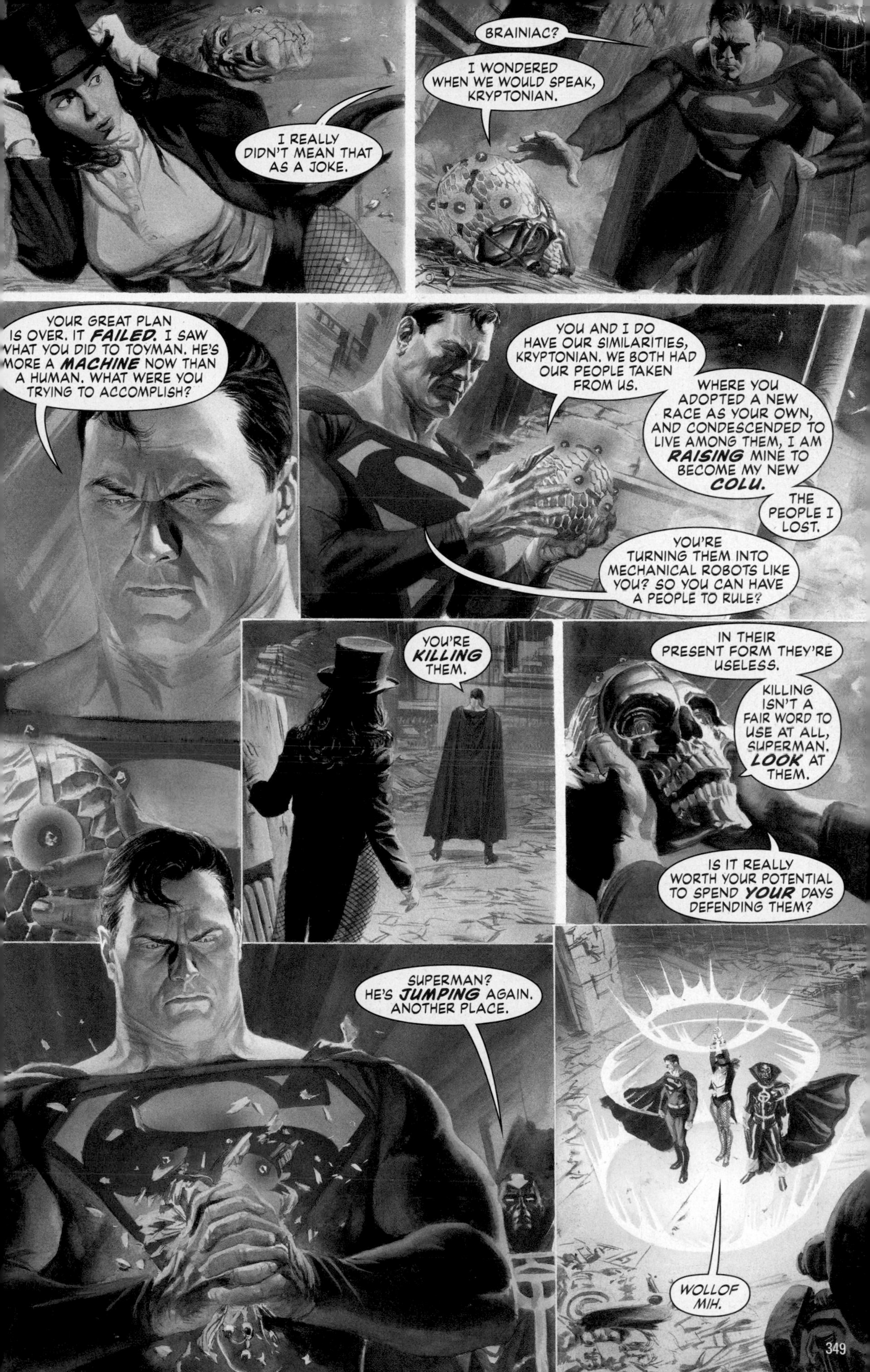
I REALLY DIDN'T MEAN THAT AS A JOKE.
BRAINIAC?
I WONDERED WHEN WE WOULD SPEAK, KRYPTONIAN.
YOUR GREAT PLAN IS OVER. IT FAILED. I SAW WHAT YOU DID TO TOYMAN. HE'S MORE A MACHINE NOW THAN A HUMAN. WHAT WERE YOU TRYING TO ACCOMPLISH?
YOU AND I DO HAVE OUR SIMILARITIES, KRYPTONIAN. WE BOTH HAD OUR PEOPLE TAKEN FROM US.
WHERE YOU ADOPTED A NEW RACE AS YOUR OWN, AND CONDESCENDED TO LIVE AMONG THEM, I AM RAISING MINE TO BECOME MY NEW COLU.
THE PEOPLE I LOST.
YOU'RE TURNING THEM INTO MECHANICAL ROBOTS LIKE YOU? SO YOU CAN HAVE A PEOPLE TO RULE?
YOU'RE KILLING THEM.
IN THEIR PRESENT FORM THEY'RE USELESS.
KILLING ISN'T A FAIR WORD TO USE AT ALL, SUPERMAN. LOOK AT THEM.
IS IT REALLY WORTH YOUR POTENTIAL TO SPEND YOUR DAYS DEFENDING THEM?
SUPERMAN? HE'S JUMPING AGAIN. ANOTHER PLACE.
WOLLOF MIH.

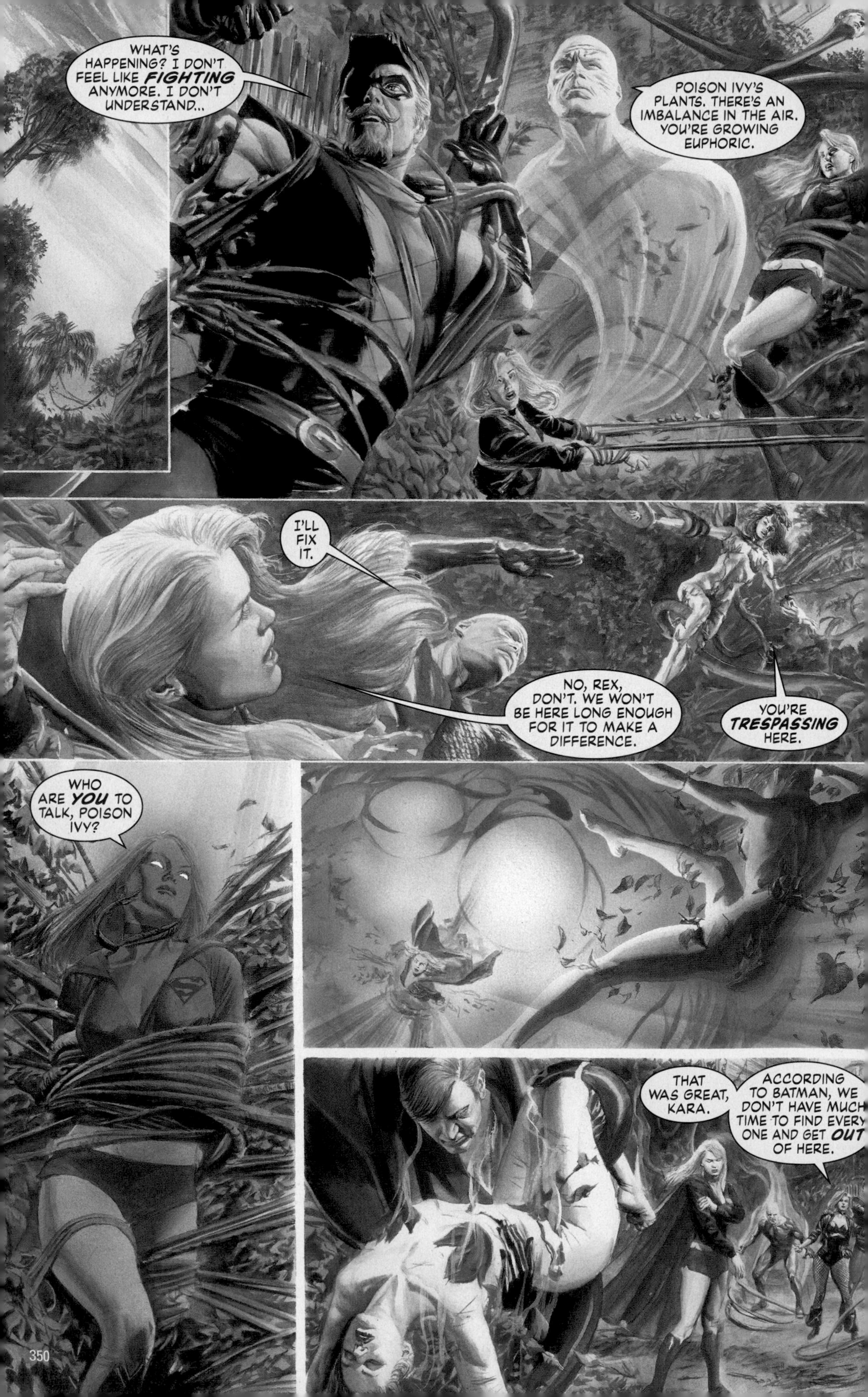

WHAT'S HAPPENING? I DON'T FEEL LIKE FIGHTING ANYMORE. I DON'T UNDERSTAND...
POISON IVY'S PLANTS. THERE'S AN IMBALANCE IN THE AIR. YOU'RE GROWING EUPHORIC.
I'LL FIX IT.
NO, REX, DON'T. WE WON'T BE HERE LONG ENOUGH FOR IT TO MAKE A DIFFERENCE.
YOU'RE TRESPASSING HERE.
WHO ARE YOU TO TALK, POISON IVY?
THAT WAS GREAT, KARA.
ACCORDING TO BATMAN, WE DON'T HAVE MUCH TIME TO FIND EVERY ONE AND GET OUT OF HERE.

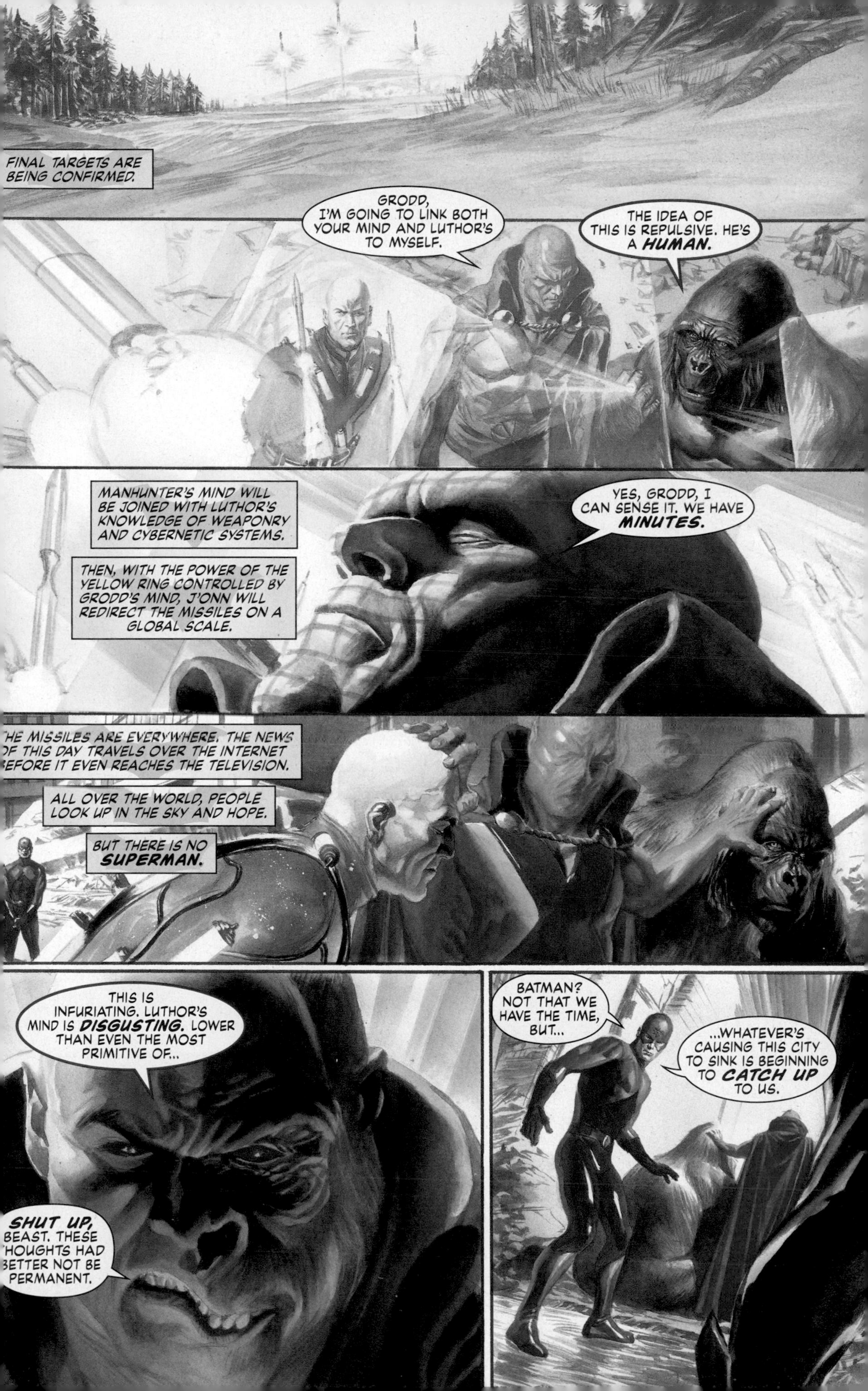
FINAL TARGETS ARE BEING CONFIRMED.
GRODD, I'M GOING TO LINK BOTH YOUR MIND AND LUTHOR'S TO MYSELF.
THE IDEA OF THIS IS REPULSIVE. HE'S A HUMAN.
MANHUNTER'S MIND WILL BE JOINED WITH LUTHOR'S KNOWLEDGE OF WEAPONRY AND CYBERNETIC SYSTEMS.
THEN, WITH THE POWER OF THE YELLOW RING CONTROLLED BY GRODD'S MIND, J'ONN WILL REDIRECT THE MISSILES ON A GLOBAL SCALE.
YES, GRODD, I CAN SENSE IT. WE HAVE MINUTES.
THE MISSILES ARE EVERYWHERE. THE NEWS OF THIS DAY TRAVELS OVER THE INTERNET BEFORE IT EVEN REACHES THE TELEVISION.
ALL OVER THE WORLD, PEOPLE LOOK UP IN THE SKY AND HOPE.
BUT THERE IS NO SUPERMAN.
THIS IS INFURIATING. LUTHOR'S MIND IS DISGUSTING. LOWER THAN EVEN THE MOST PRIMITIVE OF...
SHUT UP, BEAST. THESE THOUGHTS HAD BETTER NOT BE PERMANENT.
BATMAN? NOT THAT WE HAVE THE TIME, BUT...
...WHATEVER'S CAUSING THIS CITY TO SINK IS BEGINNING TO CATCH UP TO US.

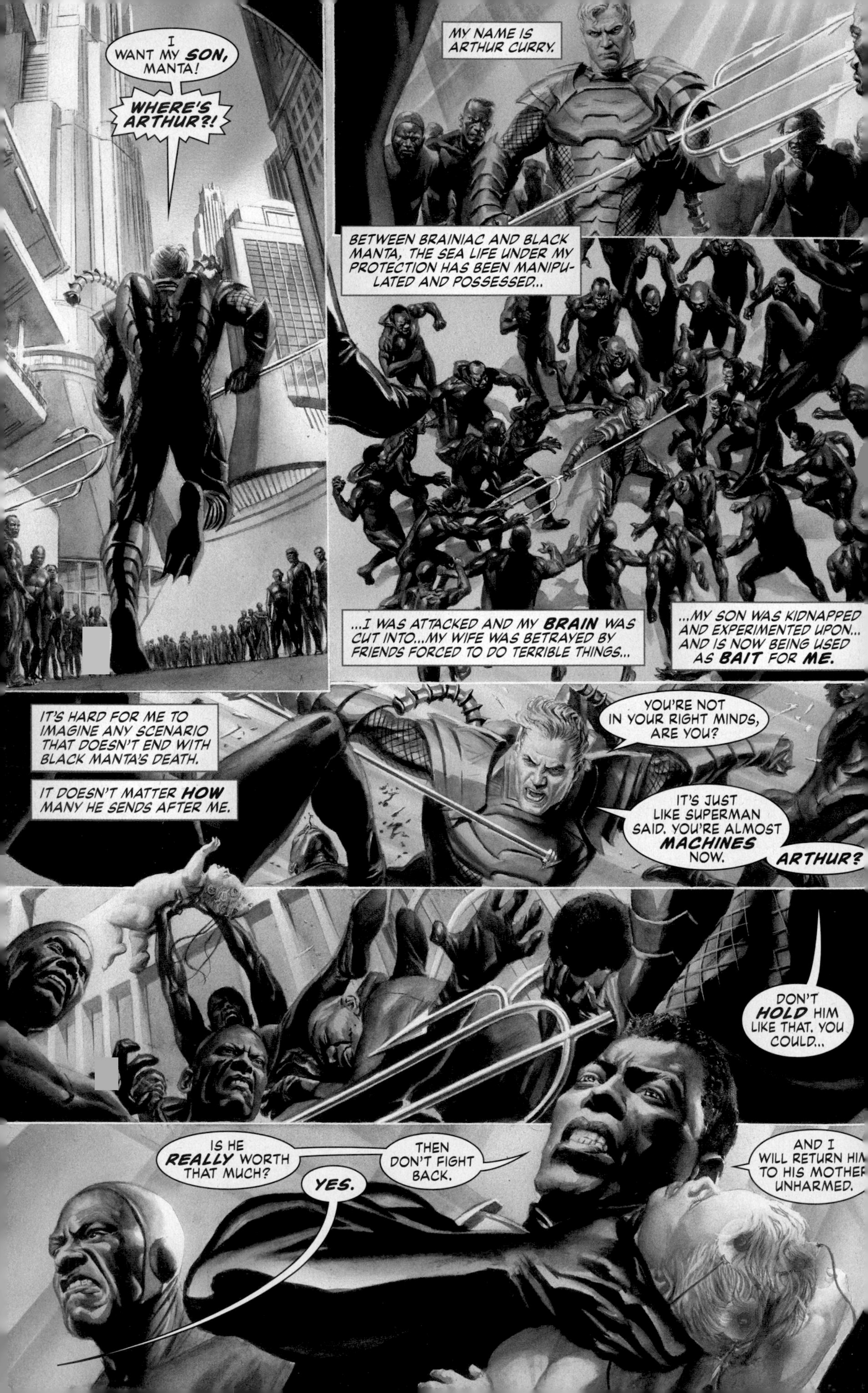
I WANT MY SON, MANTA!
WHERE'S ARTHUR?!
MY NAME IS ARTHUR CURRY.
BETWEEN BRAINIAC AND BLACK MANTA, THE SEA LIFE UNDER MY PROTECTION HAS BEEN MANIPULATED AND POSSESSED...
...I WAS ATTACKED AND MY BRAIN WAS CUT INTO...MY WIFE WAS BETRAYED BY FRIENDS FORCED TO DO TERRIBLE THINGS...
...MY SON WAS KIDNAPPED AND EXPERIMENTED UPON... AND IS NOW BEING USED AS BAIT FOR ME.
IT'S HARD FOR ME TO IMAGINE ANY SCENARIO THAT DOESN'T END WITH BLACK MANTA'S DEATH.
IT DOESN'T MATTER HOW MANY HE SENDS AFTER ME.
YOU'RE NOT IN YOUR RIGHT MINDS, ARE YOU?
IT'S JUST LIKE SUPERMAN SAID. YOU'RE ALMOST MACHINES NOW.
ARTHUR?
DON'T HOLD HIM LIKE THAT. YOU COULD...
IS HE REALLY WORTH THAT MUCH?
THEN DON'T FIGHT BACK.
YES.
AND I WILL RETURN HIM TO HIS MOTHER UNHARMED.

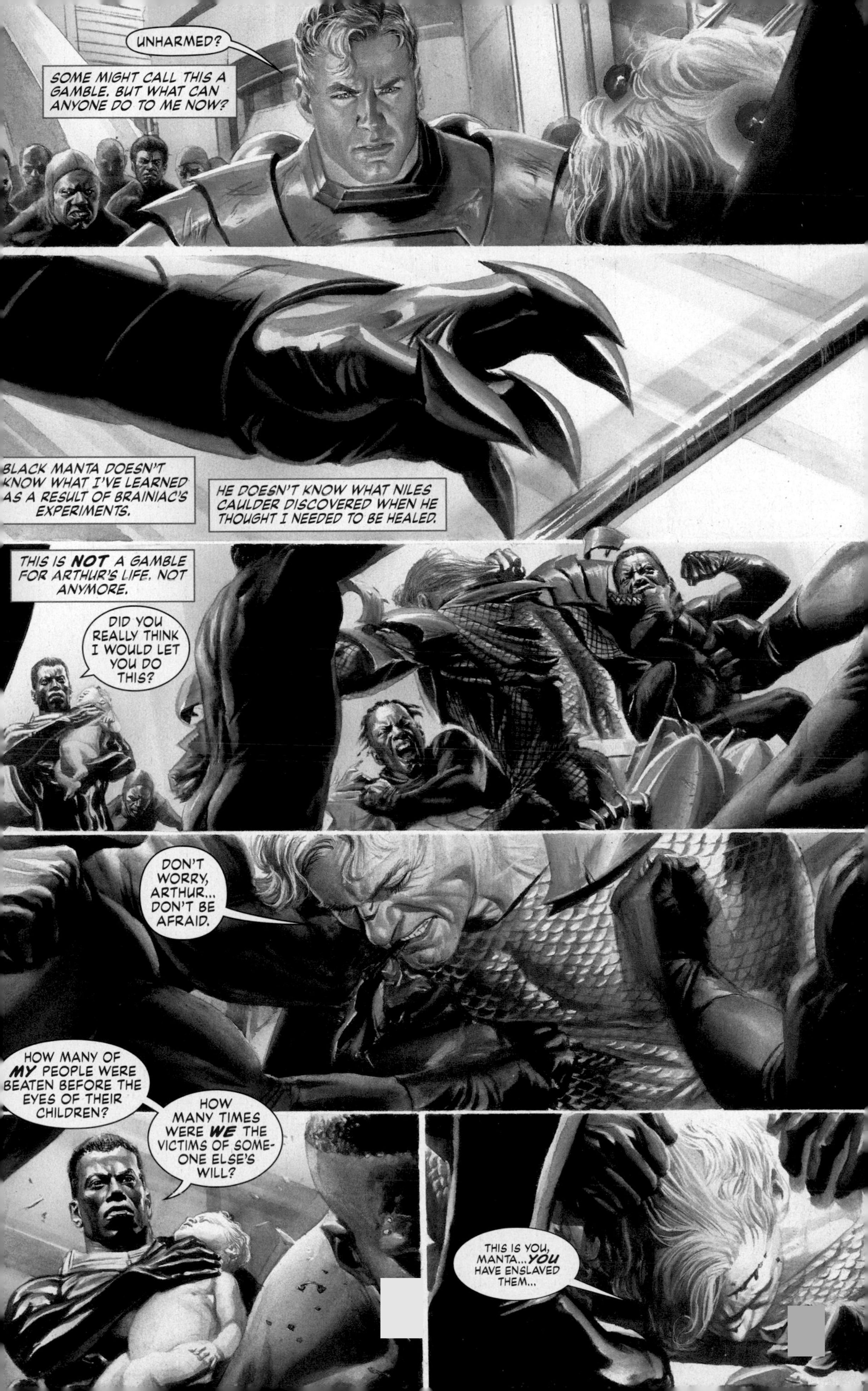
UNHARMED?
SOME MIGHT CALL THIS A GAMBLE. BUT WHAT CAN ANYONE DO TO ME NOW?
BLACK MANTA DOESN'T KNOW WHAT I'VE LEARNED AS A RESULT OF BRAINIAC'S EXPERIMENTS.
HE DOESN'T KNOW WHAT NILES CAULDER DISCOVERED WHEN HE THOUGHT I NEEDED TO BE HEALED.
THIS IS NOT A GAMBLE FOR ARTHUR'S LIFE. NOT ANYMORE.
DID YOU REALLY THINK I WOULD LET YOU DO THIS?
DON'T WORRY, ARTHUR... DON'T BE AFRAID.
HOW MANY OF MY PEOPLE WERE BEATEN BEFORE THE EYES OF THEIR CHILDREN?
HOW MANY TIMES WERE WE THE VICTIMS OF SOME-ONE ELSE'S WILL?
THIS IS YOU, MANTA... YOU HAVE ENSLAVED THEM...

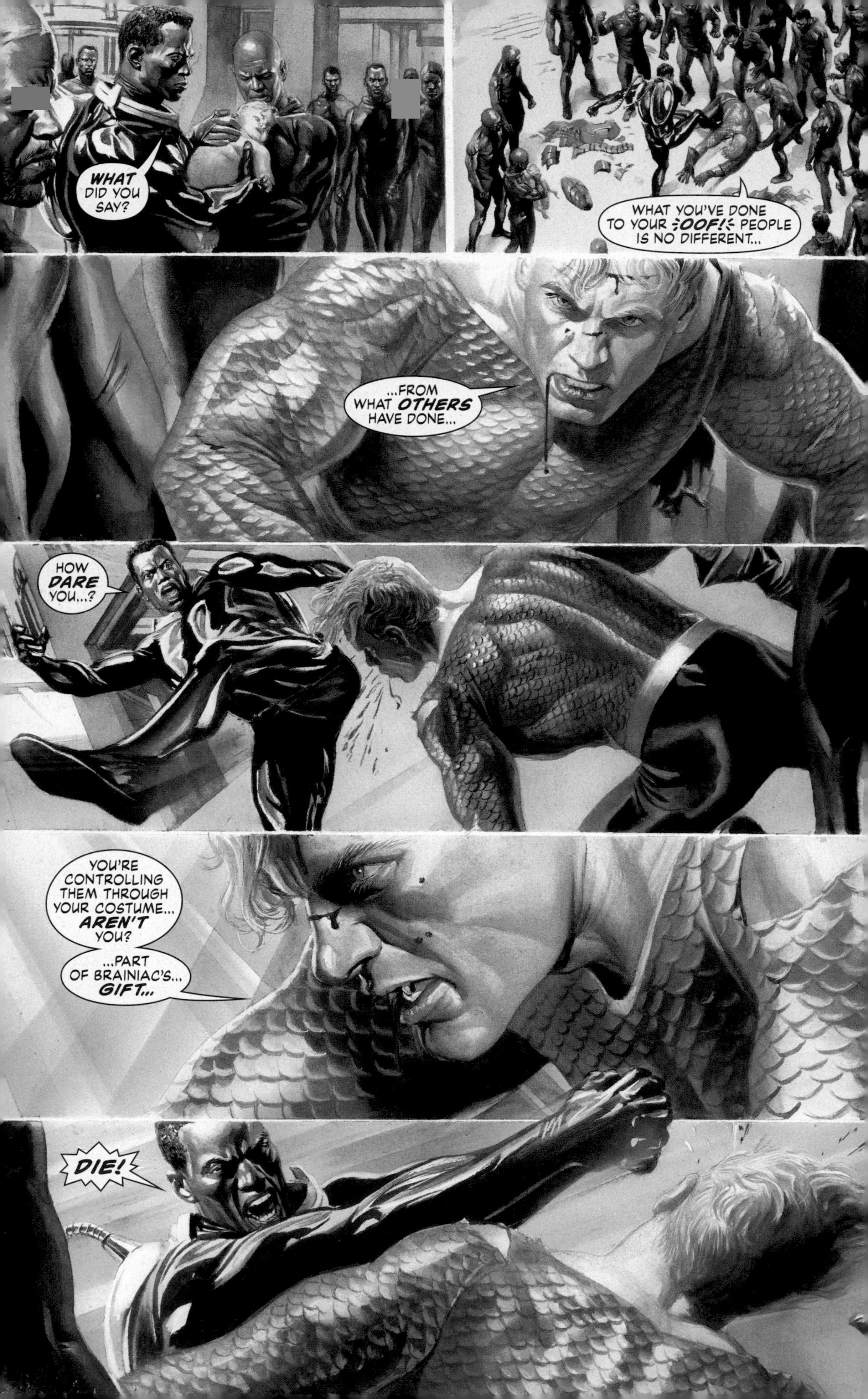
WHAT DID YOU SAY?
WHAT YOU'VE DONE TO YOUR OOF! PEOPLE IS NO DIFFERENT...
...FROM WHAT OTHERS HAVE DONE...
HOW DARE YOU...?
YOU'RE CONTROLLING THEM THROUGH YOUR COSTUME... AREN'T YOU?
...PART OF BRAINIAC'S... GIFT...
DIE!

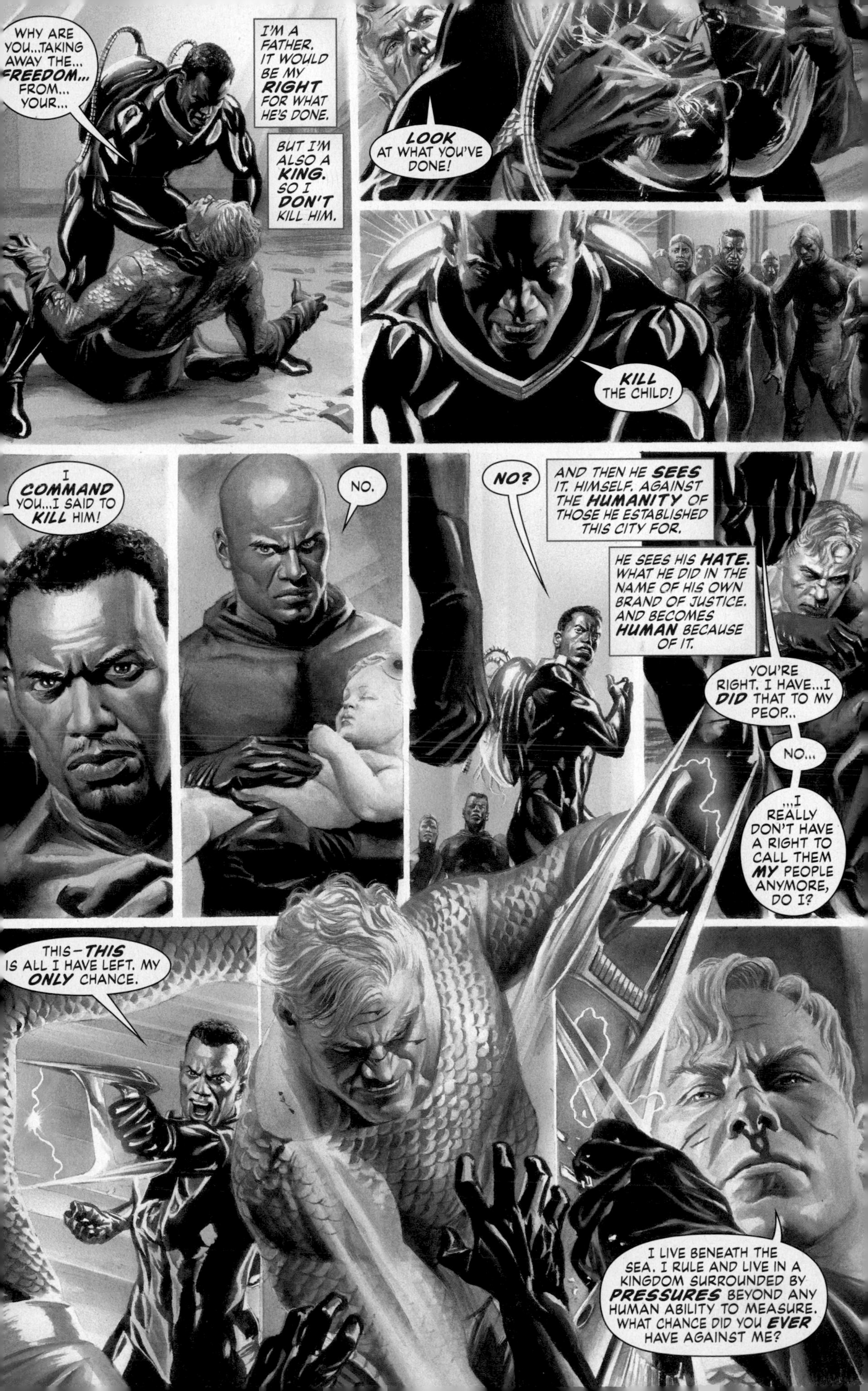
WHY ARE YOU...TAKING AWAY THE... FREEDOM... FROM... YOUR...
I'M A FATHER. IT WOULD BE MY RIGHT FOR WHAT HE'S DONE.
BUT I'M ALSO A KING. SO I DON'T KILL HIM.
LOOK AT WHAT YOU'VE DONE!
KILL THE CHILD!
I COMMAND YOU...I SAID TO KILL HIM!
NO.
NO?
AND THEN HE SEES IT. HIMSELF. AGAINST THE HUMANITY OF THOSE HE ESTABLISHED THIS CITY FOR.
HE SEES HIS HATE. WHAT HE DID IN THE NAME OF HIS OWN BRAND OF JUSTICE. AND BECOMES HUMAN BECAUSE OF IT.
YOU'RE RIGHT. I HAVE...I DID THAT TO MY PEOP...
NO...
...I REALLY DON'T HAVE A RIGHT TO CALL THEM MY PEOPLE ANYMORE, DO I?
THIS—THIS IS ALL I HAVE LEFT. MY ONLY CHANCE.
I LIVE BENEATH THE SEA. I RULE AND LIVE IN A KINGDOM SURROUNDED BY PRESSURES BEYOND ANY HUMAN ABILITY TO MEASURE. WHAT CHANCE DID YOU EVER HAVE AGAINST ME?

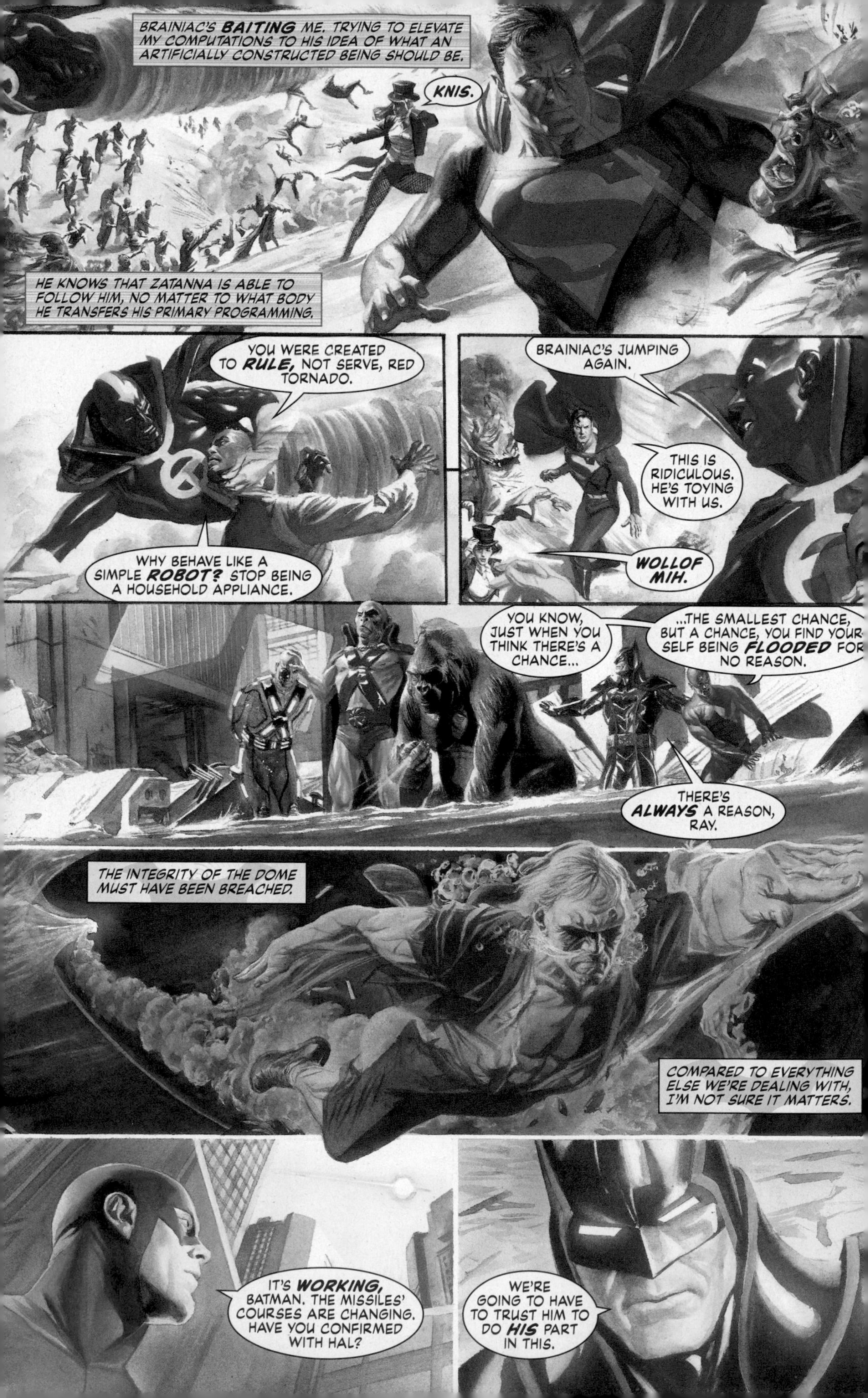
BRAINIAC'S BAITING ME. TRYING TO ELEVATE MY COMPUTATIONS TO HIS IDEA OF WHAT AN ARTIFICIALLY CONSTRUCTED BEING SHOULD BE.
KNIS.
HE KNOWS THAT ZATANNA IS ABLE TO FOLLOW HIM, NO MATTER TO WHAT BODY HE TRANSFERS HIS PRIMARY PROGRAMMING.
YOU WERE CREATED TO RULE, NOT SERVE, RED TORNADO.
WHY BEHAVE LIKE A SIMPLE ROBOT? STOP BEING A HOUSEHOLD APPLIANCE.
BRAINIAC'S JUMPING AGAIN.
THIS IS RIDICULOUS. HE'S TOYING WITH US.
WOLLOF MIH.
YOU KNOW, JUST WHEN YOU THINK THERE'S A CHANCE...
...THE SMALLEST CHANCE, BUT A CHANCE, YOU FIND YOURSELF BEING FLOODED FOR NO REASON.
THERE'S ALWAYS A REASON, RAY.
THE INTEGRITY OF THE DOME MUST HAVE BEEN BREACHED.
COMPARED TO EVERYTHING ELSE WE'RE DEALING WITH, I'M NOT SURE IT MATTERS.
IT'S WORKING, BATMAN. THE MISSILES' COURSES ARE CHANGING. HAVE YOU CONFIRMED WITH HAL?
WE'RE GOING TO HAVE TO TRUST HIM TO DO HIS PART IN THIS.

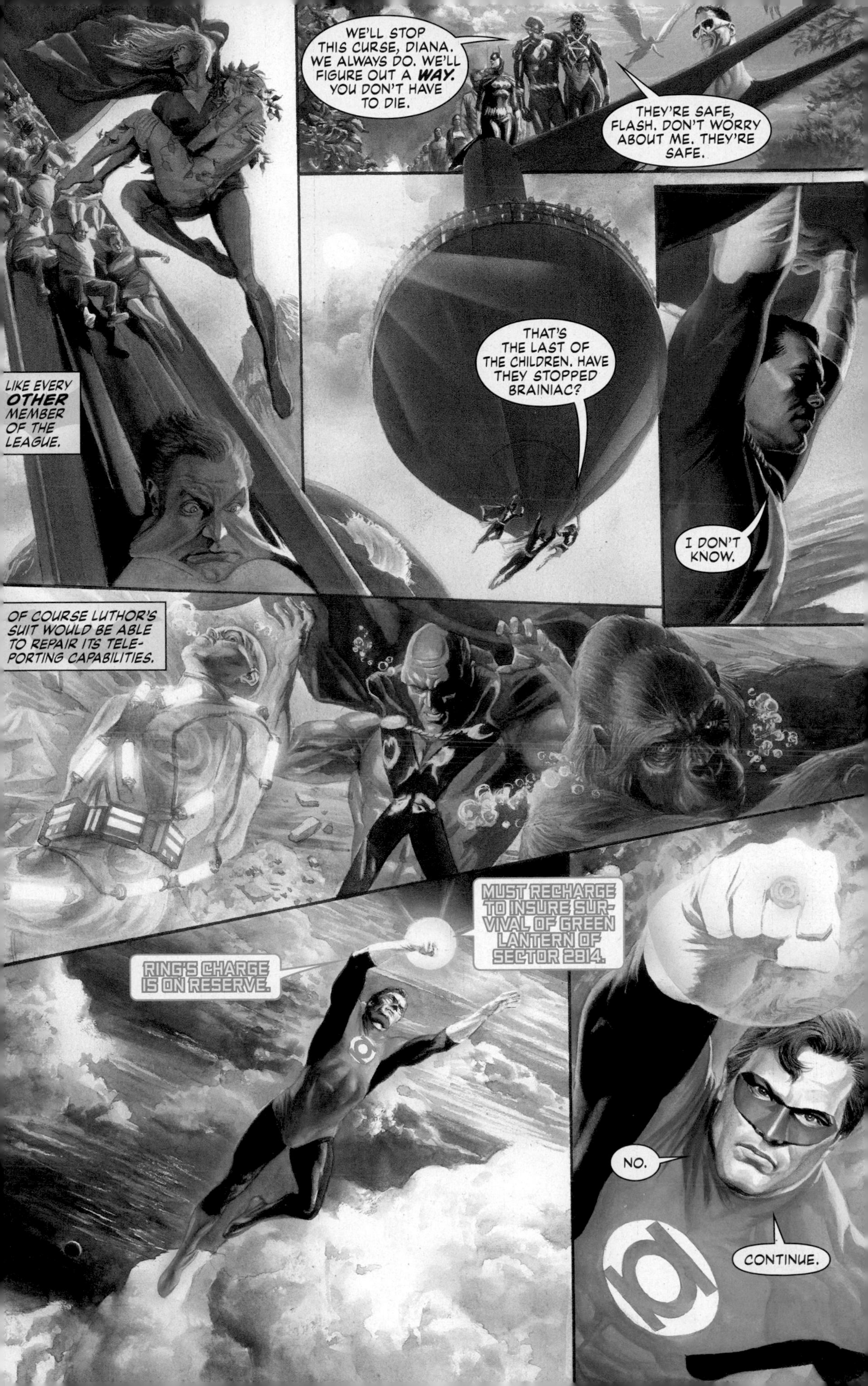
WE'LL STOP THIS CURSE, DIANA. WE ALWAYS DO. WE'LL FIGURE OUT A WAY. YOU DON'T HAVE TO DIE.
THEY'RE SAFE, FLASH. DON'T WORRY ABOUT ME. THEY'RE SAFE.
LIKE EVERY OTHER MEMBER OF THE LEAGUE.
THAT'S THE LAST OF THE CHILDREN. HAVE THEY STOPPED BRAINIAC?
I DON'T KNOW.
OF COURSE LUTHOR'S SUIT WOULD BE ABLE TO REPAIR ITS TELE-PORTING CAPABILITIES.
RING'S CHARGE IS ON RESERVE.
MUST RECHARGE TO INSURE SUR-VIVAL OF GREEN LANTERN OF SECTOR 2814.
NO.
CONTINUE.

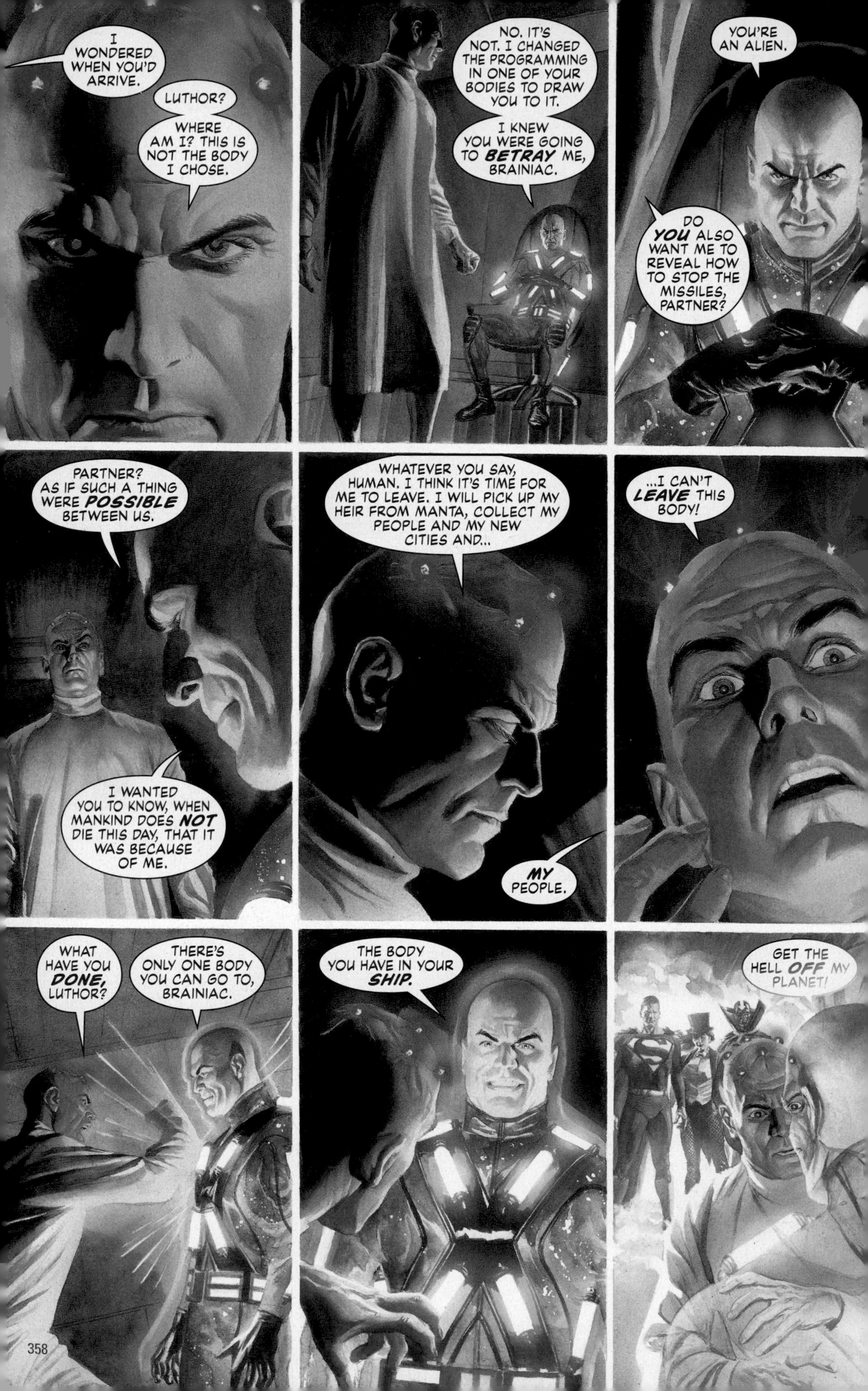
I WONDERED WHEN YOU'D ARRIVE.
LUTHOR?
WHERE AM I? THIS IS NOT THE BODY I CHOSE.
NO. IT'S NOT. I CHANGED THE PROGRAMMING IN ONE OF YOUR BODIES TO DRAW YOU TO IT.
I KNEW YOU WERE GOING TO BETRAY ME, BRAINIAC.
YOU'RE AN ALIEN.
DO YOU ALSO WANT ME TO REVEAL HOW TO STOP THE MISSILES, PARTNER?
PARTNER? AS IF SUCH A THING WERE POSSIBLE BETWEEN US.
I WANTED YOU TO KNOW, WHEN MANKIND DOES NOT DIE THIS DAY, THAT IT WAS BECAUSE OF ME.
WHATEVER YOU SAY, HUMAN. I THINK IT'S TIME FOR ME TO LEAVE. I WILL PICK UP MY HEIR FROM MANTA, COLLECT MY PEOPLE AND MY NEW CITIES AND...
MY PEOPLE.
...I CAN'T LEAVE THIS BODY!
WHAT HAVE YOU DONE, LUTHOR?
THERE'S ONLY ONE BODY YOU CAN GO TO, BRAINIAC.
THE BODY YOU HAVE IN YOUR SHIP.
GET THE HELL OFF MY PLANET!

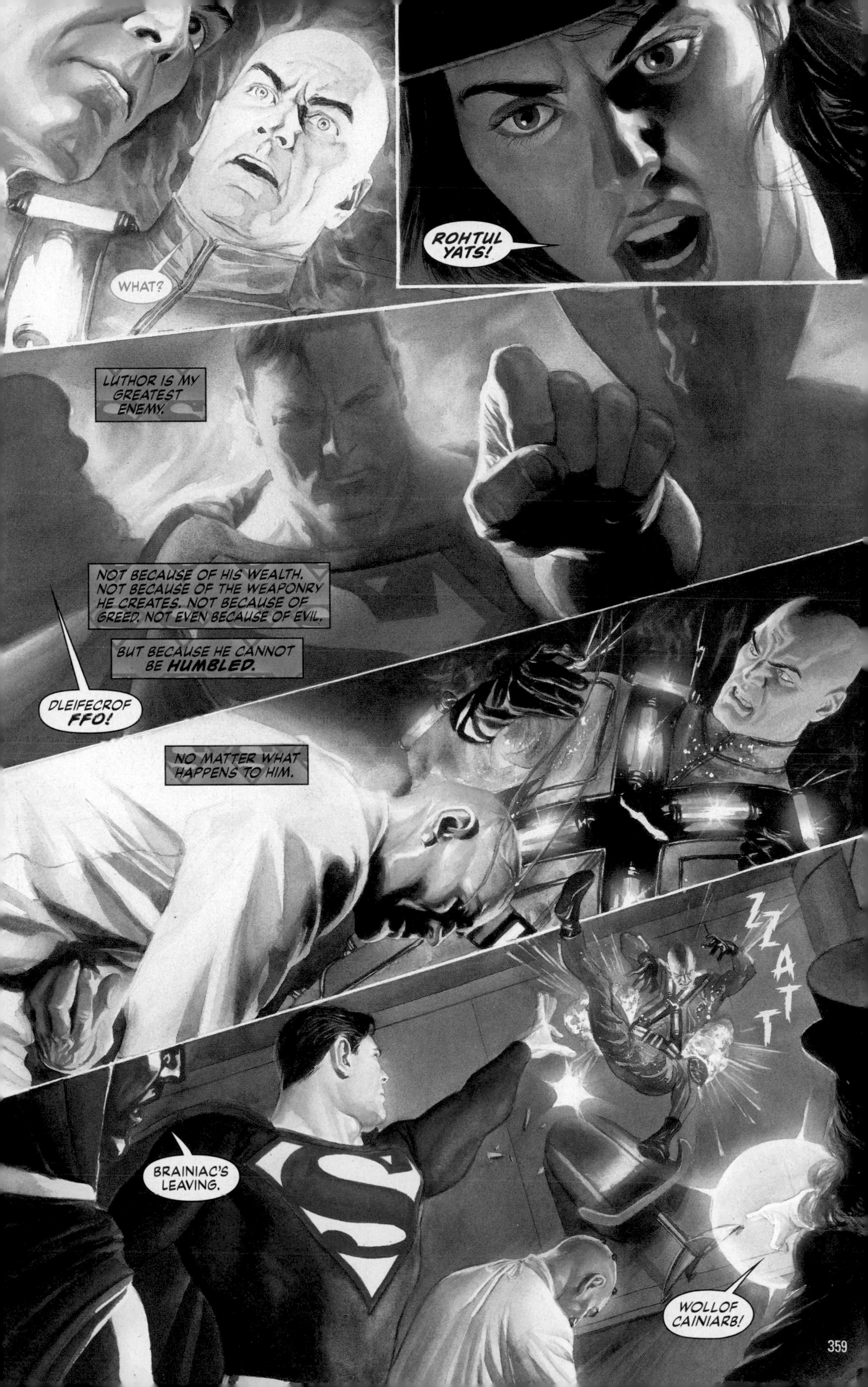
WHAT?
ROHTUL YATS!
LUTHOR IS MY GREATEST ENEMY.
NOT BECAUSE OF HIS WEALTH. NOT BECAUSE OF THE WEAPONRY HE CREATES. NOT BECAUSE OF GREED. NOT EVEN BECAUSE OF EVIL.
BUT BECAUSE HE CANNOT BE HUMBLED.
DLEIFECROF FFO!
NO MATTER WHAT HAPPENS TO HIM.
ZZAT T
BRAINIAC'S LEAVING.
WOLLOF CAINIARB!

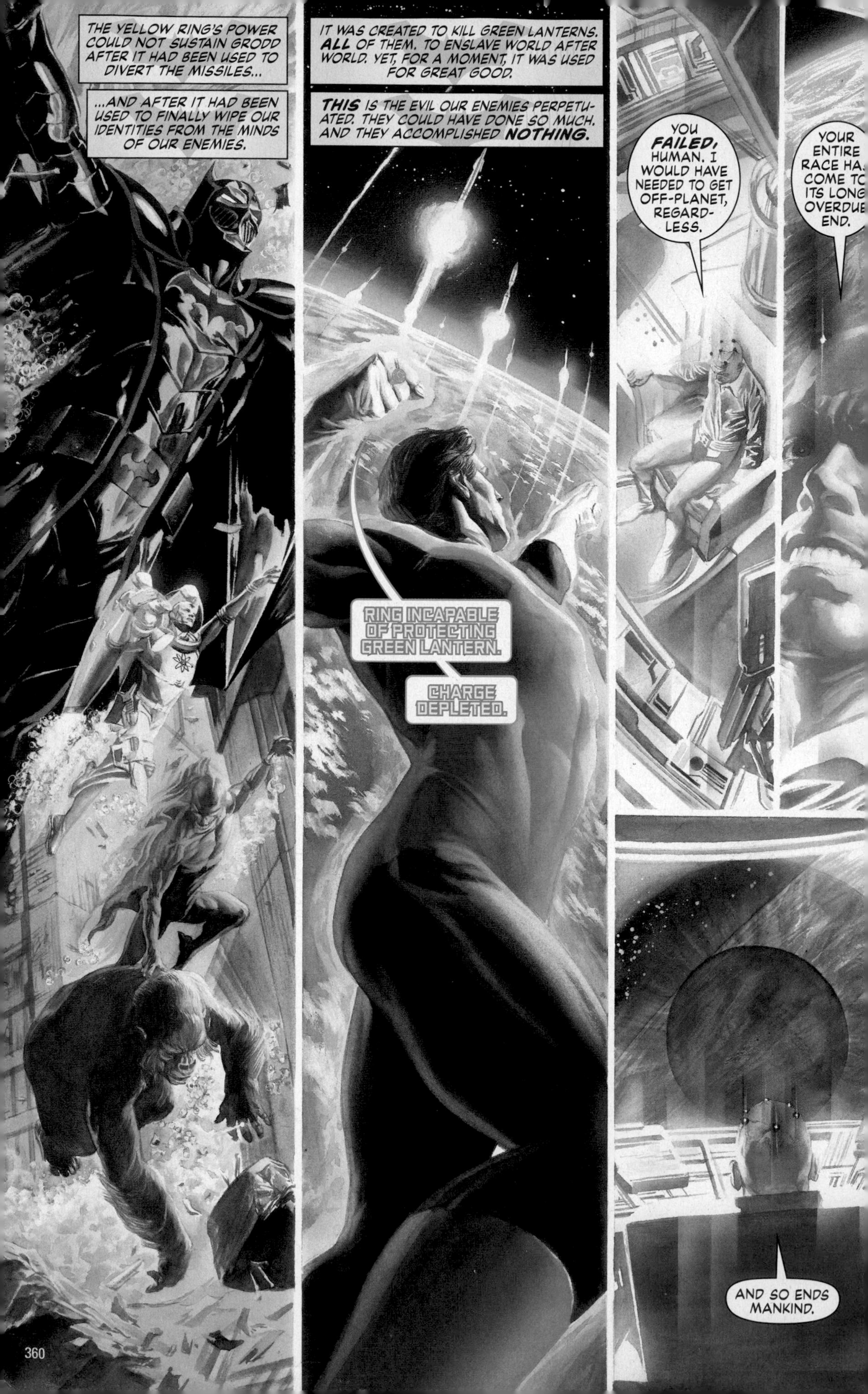
THE YELLOW RING'S POWER COULD NOT SUSTAIN GRODD AFTER IT HAD BEEN USED TO DIVERT THE MISSILES...
...AND AFTER IT HAD BEEN USED TO FINALLY WIPE OUR IDENTITIES FROM THE MINDS OF OUR ENEMIES.
IT WAS CREATED TO KILL GREEN LANTERNS. ALL OF THEM. TO ENSLAVE WORLD AFTER WORLD. YET, FOR A MOMENT, IT WAS USED FOR GREAT GOOD.
THIS IS THE EVIL OUR ENEMIES PERPETUATED. THEY COULD HAVE DONE SO MUCH. AND THEY ACCOMPLISHED NOTHING.
RING INCAPABLE OF PROTECTING GREEN LANTERN.
CHARGE DEPLETED.
YOU FAILED, HUMAN. I WOULD HAVE NEEDED TO GET OFF-PLANET, REGARDLESS.
YOUR ENTIRE RACE HA COME TO ITS LONG OVERDUE END.
AND SO ENDS MANKIND.

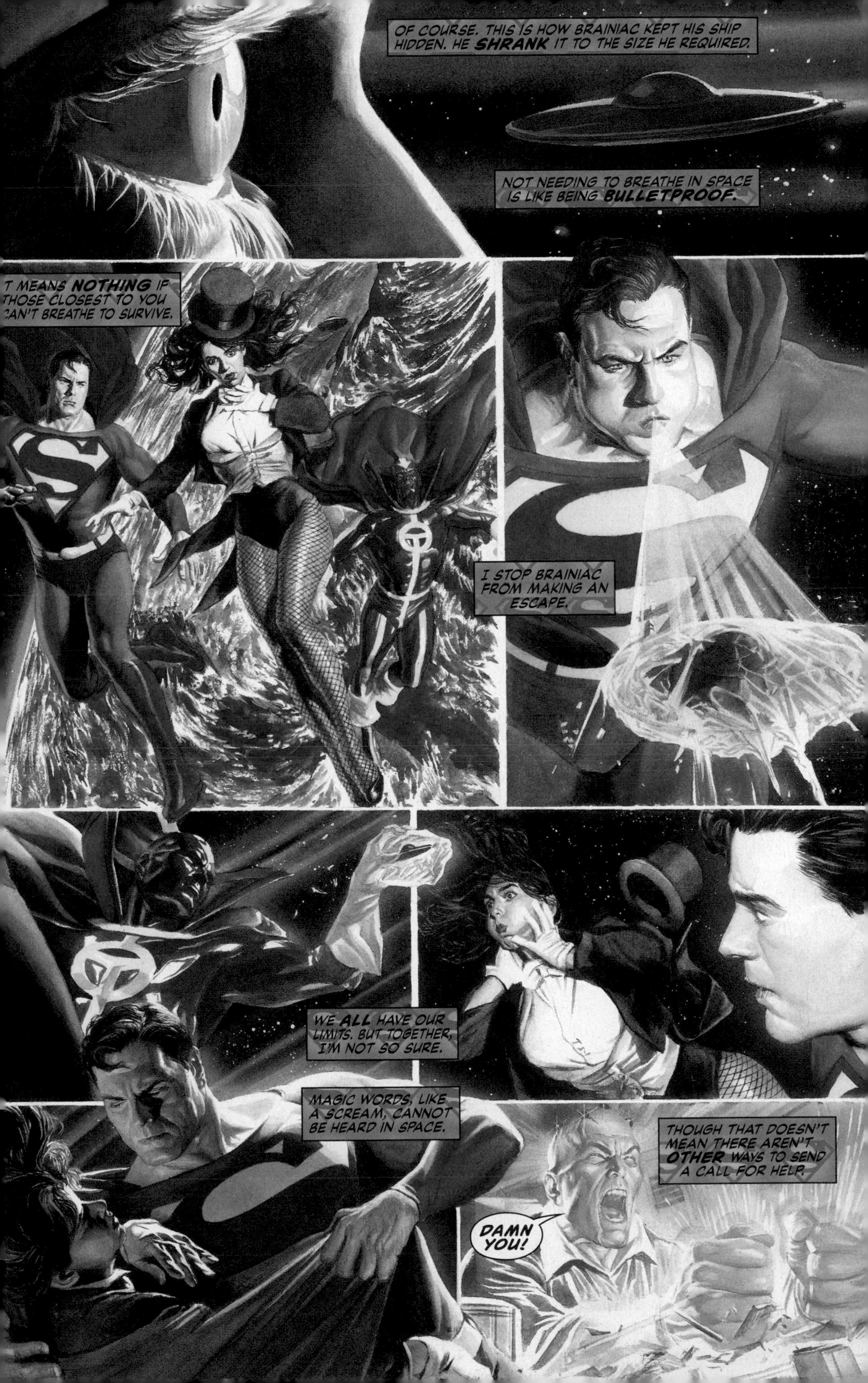
OF COURSE. THIS IS HOW BRAINIAC KEPT HIS SHIP HIDDEN. HE SHRANK IT TO THE SIZE HE REQUIRED.
NOT NEEDING TO BREATHE IN SPACE IS LIKE BEING BULLETPROOF.
IT MEANS NOTHING IF THOSE CLOSEST TO YOU CAN'T BREATHE TO SURVIVE.
I STOP BRAINIAC FROM MAKING AN ESCAPE.
WE ALL HAVE OUR LIMITS. BUT TOGETHER, I'M NOT SO SURE.
MAGIC WORDS, LIKE A SCREAM, CANNOT BE HEARD IN SPACE.
THOUGH THAT DOESN'T MEAN THERE AREN'T OTHER WAYS TO SEND A CALL FOR HELP.
DAMN YOU!

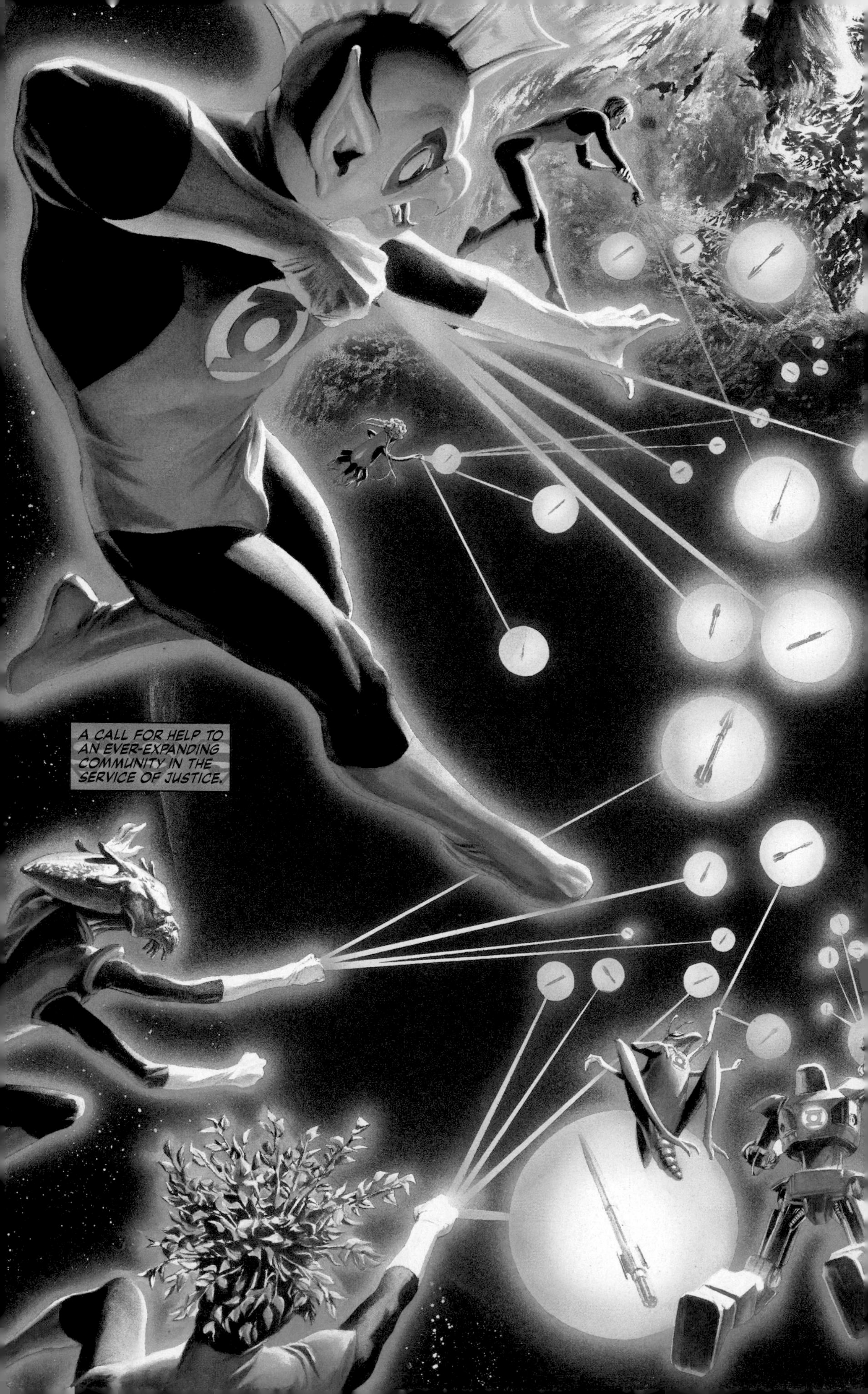
A CALL FOR HELP TO AN EVER-EXPANDING COMMUNITY IN THE SERVICE OF JUSTICE.

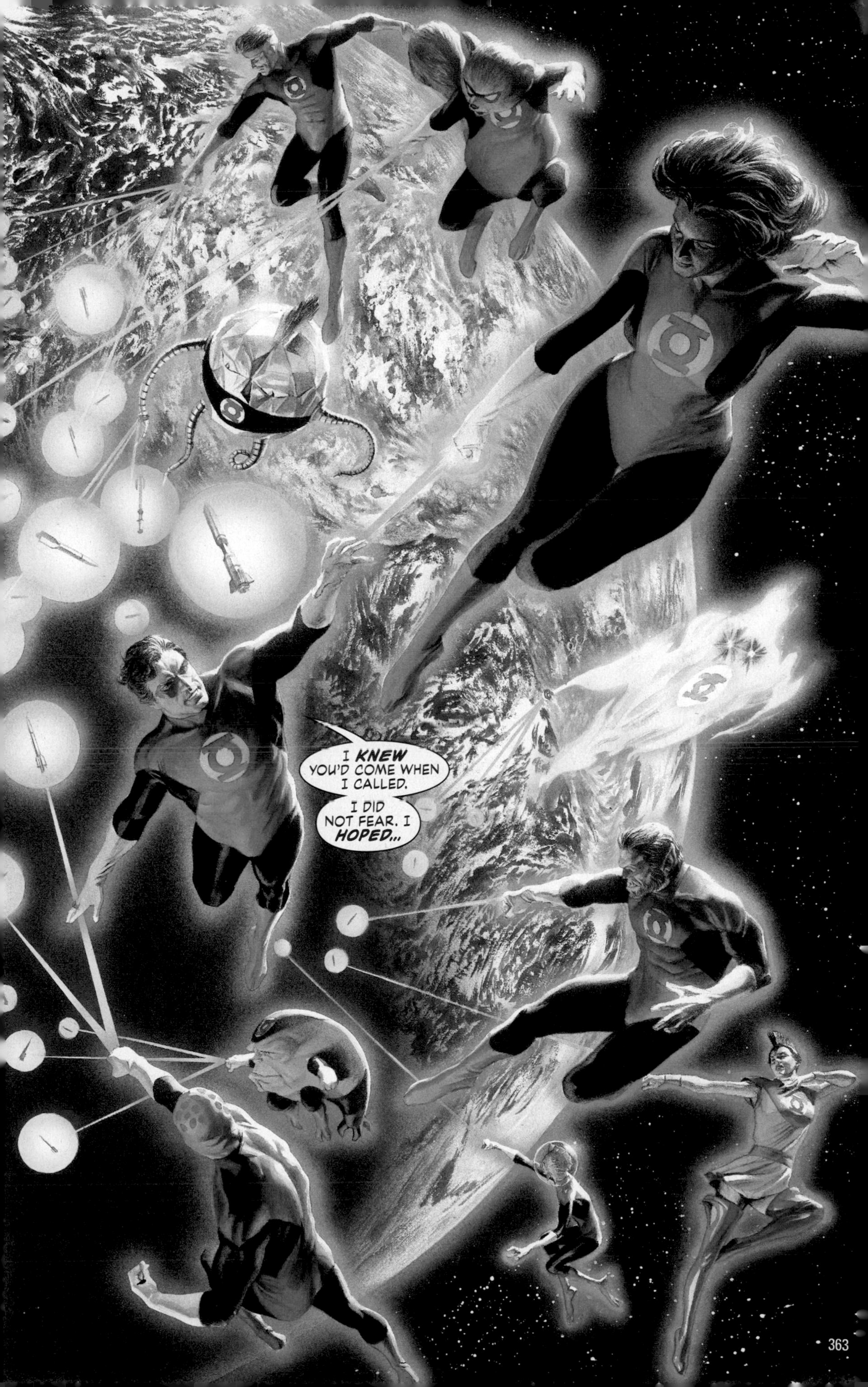
I KNEW YOU'D COME WHEN I CALLED.
I DID NOT FEAR. I HOPED...

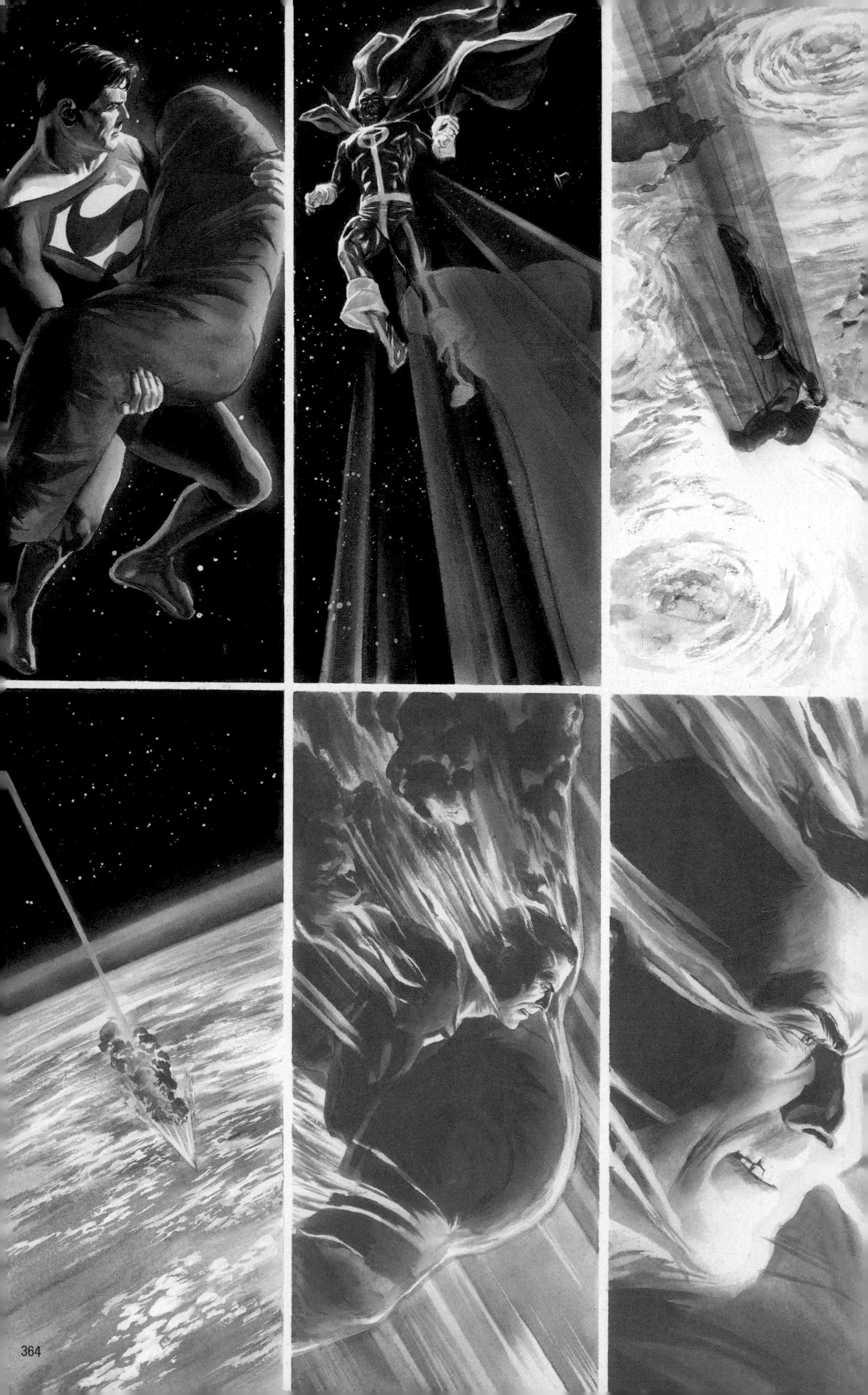

IT'S GOING TO BE *OKAY,* ZATANNA.

WE *DID* IT. WE SAVED THE WORLD.

IT'S GOING...NO ONE DIES TODAY.

ZATANNA?

DO YOU *HEAR* ME?

GENTLY, CLARK, GENTLY.

...TWO... THREE...FOUR... FIVE...

...BREATHE, ZATANNA, *BREATHE*...

NOT LIKE THIS. NO ONE. NOT *TODAY.*

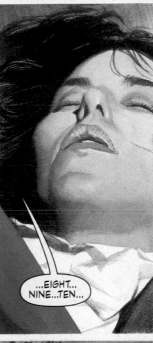

...EIGHT... NINE...TEN...

BREATHE.

...AHH*HHH*HH...

:KOFF: AHHHH...:KAFFF: :KOFFF:

SKNAHT...

SKNAHT?

...I MEAN... THANKS.

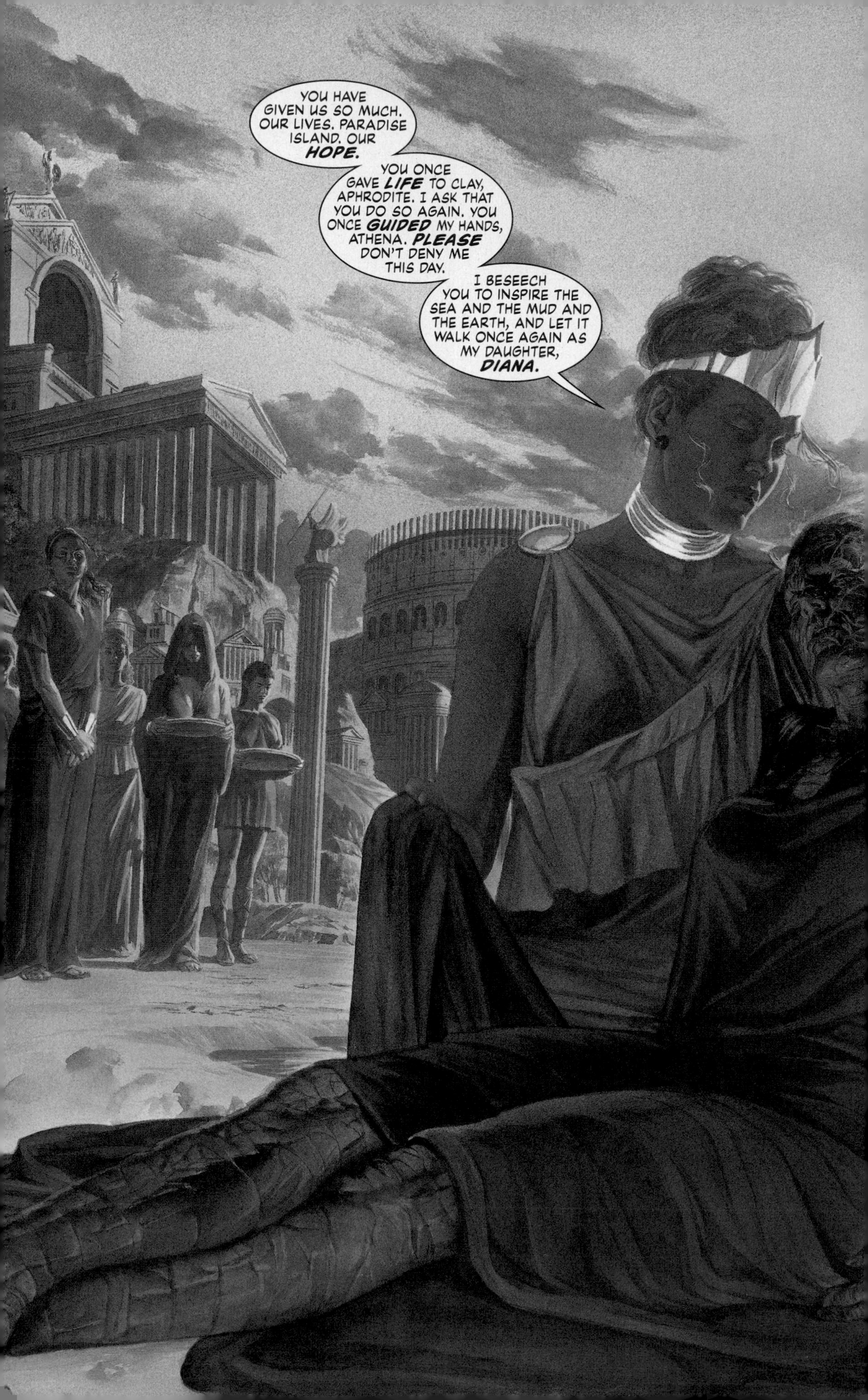
YOU HAVE GIVEN US SO MUCH. OUR LIVES. PARADISE ISLAND. OUR HOPE.
YOU ONCE GAVE LIFE TO CLAY, APHRODITE. I ASK THAT YOU DO SO AGAIN. YOU ONCE GUIDED MY HANDS, ATHENA. PLEASE DON'T DENY ME THIS DAY.
I BESEECH YOU TO INSPIRE THE SEA AND THE MUD AND THE EARTH, AND LET IT WALK ONCE AGAIN AS MY DAUGHTER, DIANA.

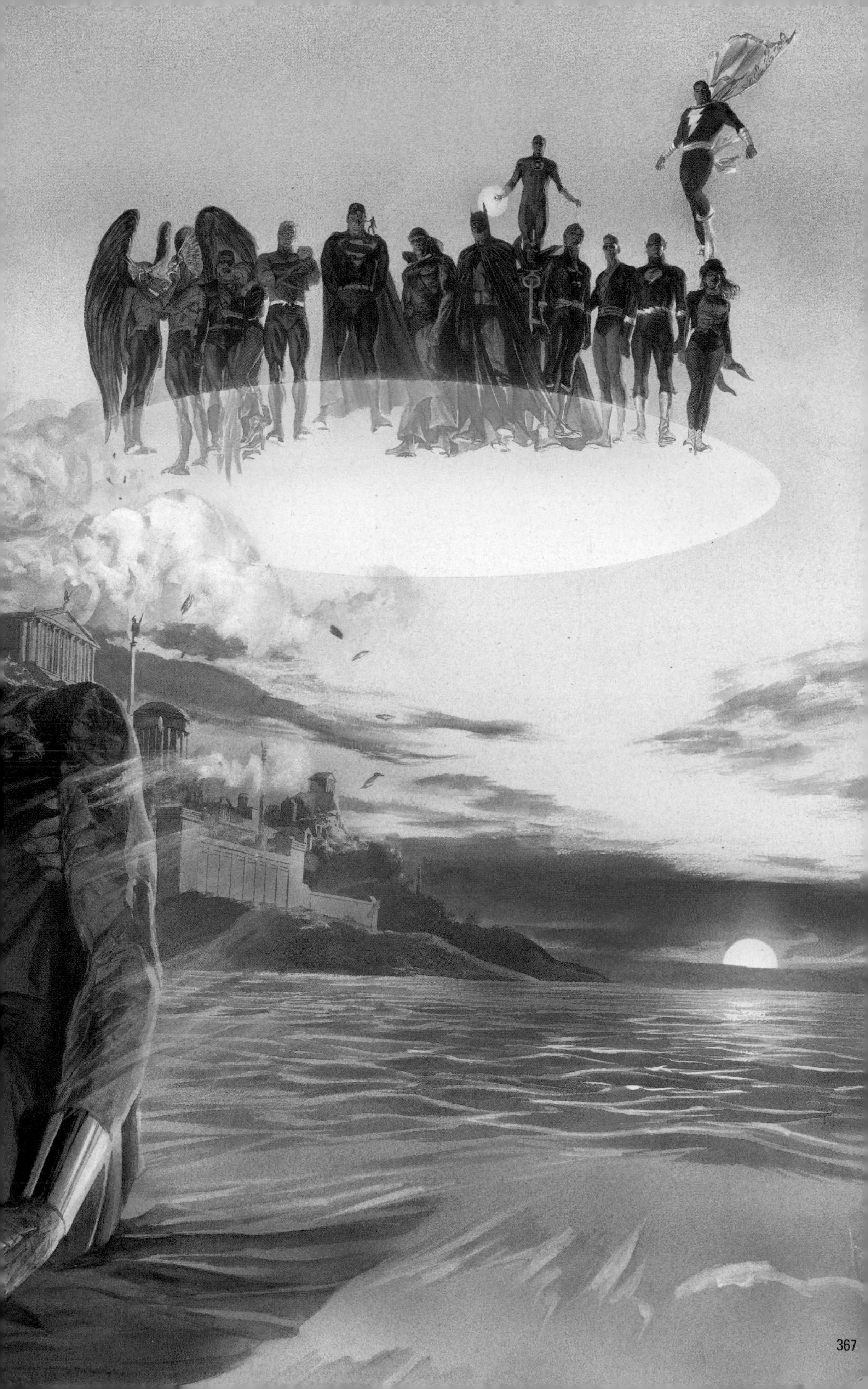

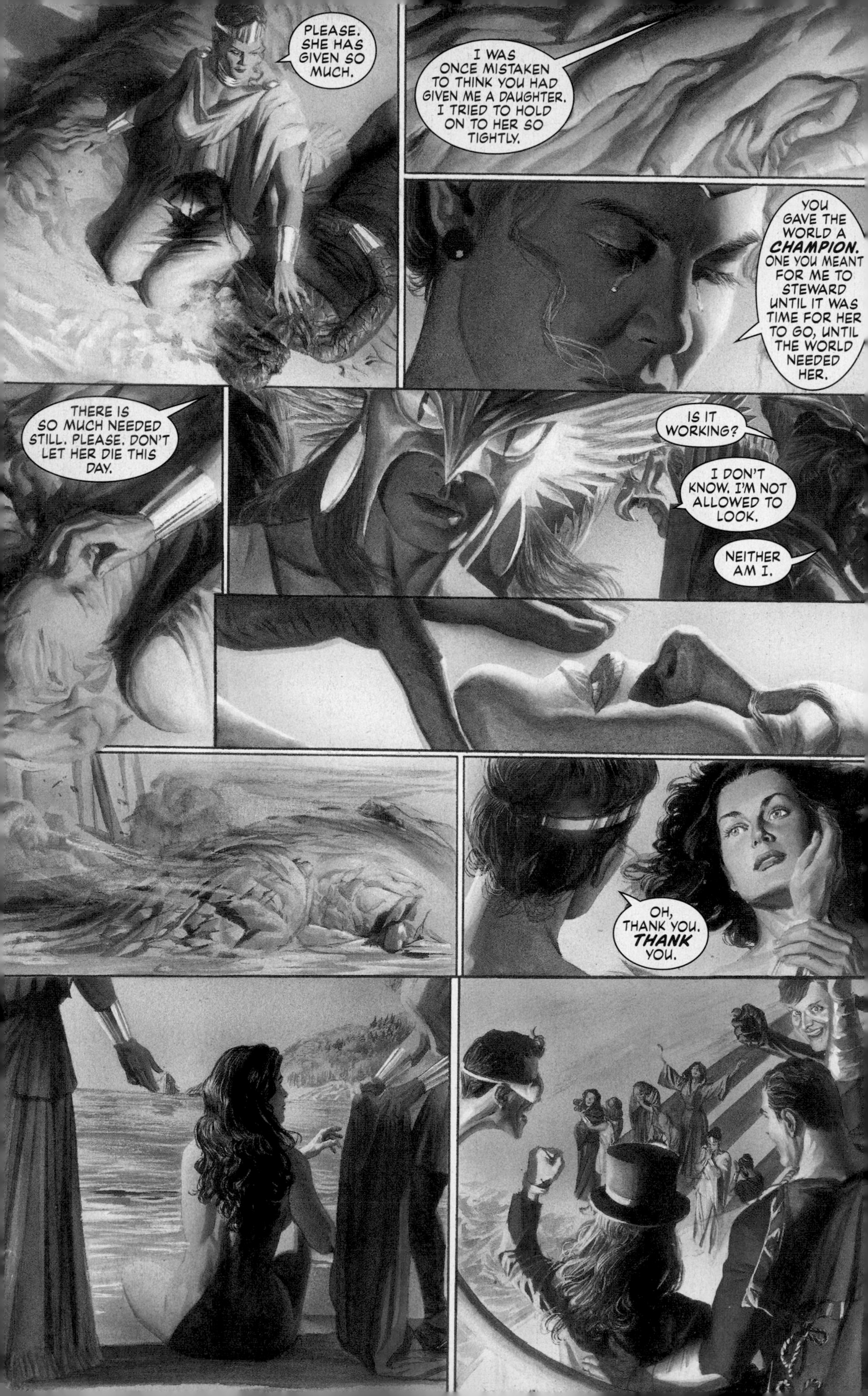
PLEASE. SHE HAS GIVEN SO MUCH.
I WAS ONCE MISTAKEN TO THINK YOU HAD GIVEN ME A DAUGHTER. I TRIED TO HOLD ON TO HER SO TIGHTLY.
YOU GAVE THE WORLD A **CHAMPION.** ONE YOU MEANT FOR ME TO STEWARD UNTIL IT WAS TIME FOR HER TO GO, UNTIL THE WORLD NEEDED HER.
THERE IS SO MUCH NEEDED STILL. PLEASE. DON'T LET HER DIE THIS DAY.
IS IT WORKING?
I DON'T KNOW. I'M NOT ALLOWED TO LOOK.
NEITHER AM I.
OH, THANK YOU. ***THANK*** YOU.

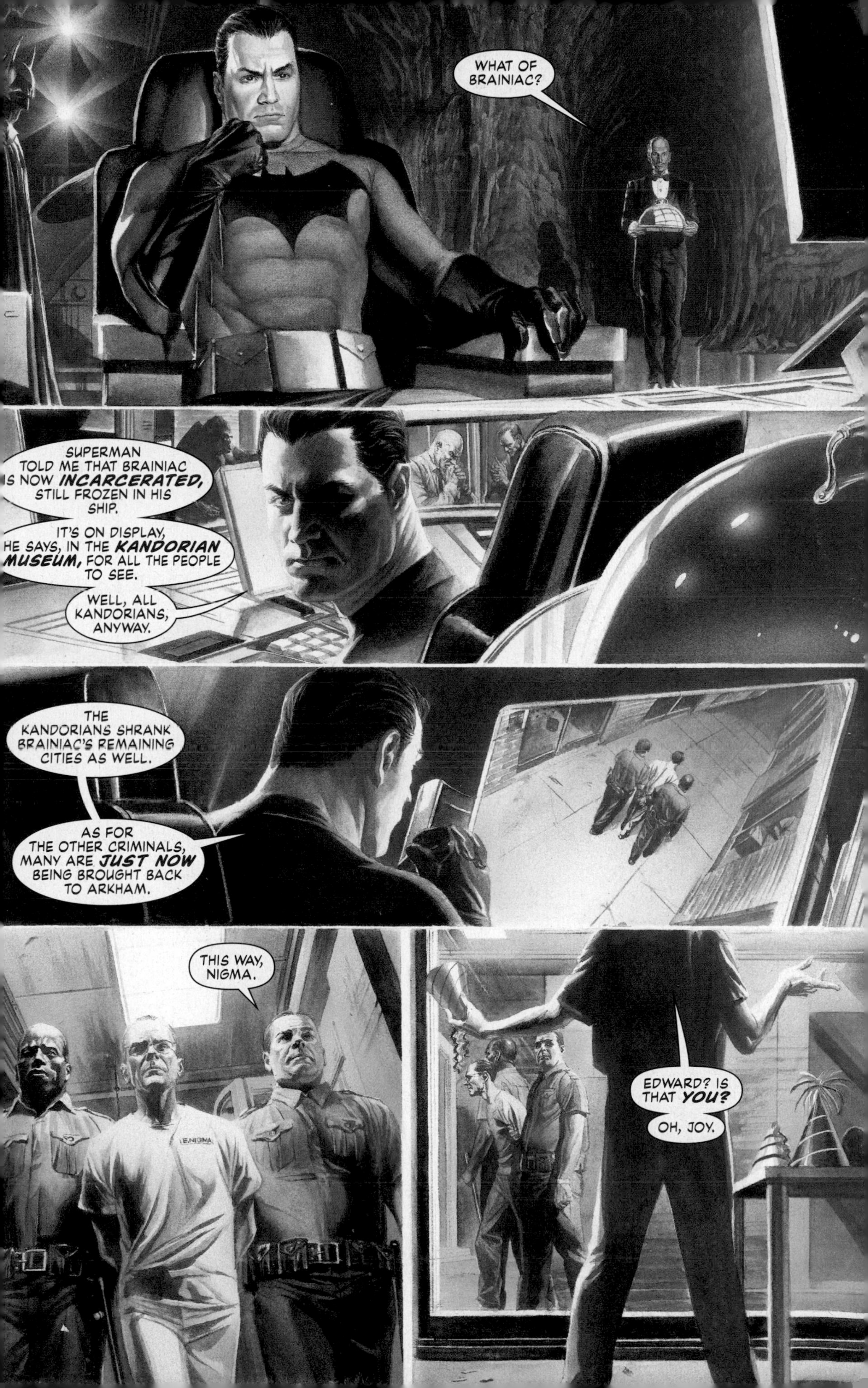
WHAT OF BRAINIAC?
SUPERMAN TOLD ME THAT BRAINIAC IS NOW INCARCERATED, STILL FROZEN IN HIS SHIP.
IT'S ON DISPLAY, HE SAYS, IN THE KANDORIAN MUSEUM, FOR ALL THE PEOPLE TO SEE.
WELL, ALL KANDORIANS, ANYWAY.
THE KANDORIANS SHRANK BRAINIAC'S REMAINING CITIES AS WELL.
AS FOR THE OTHER CRIMINALS, MANY ARE JUST NOW BEING BROUGHT BACK TO ARKHAM.
THIS WAY, NIGMA.
E.NIGMA
EDWARD? IS THAT YOU?
OH, JOY.

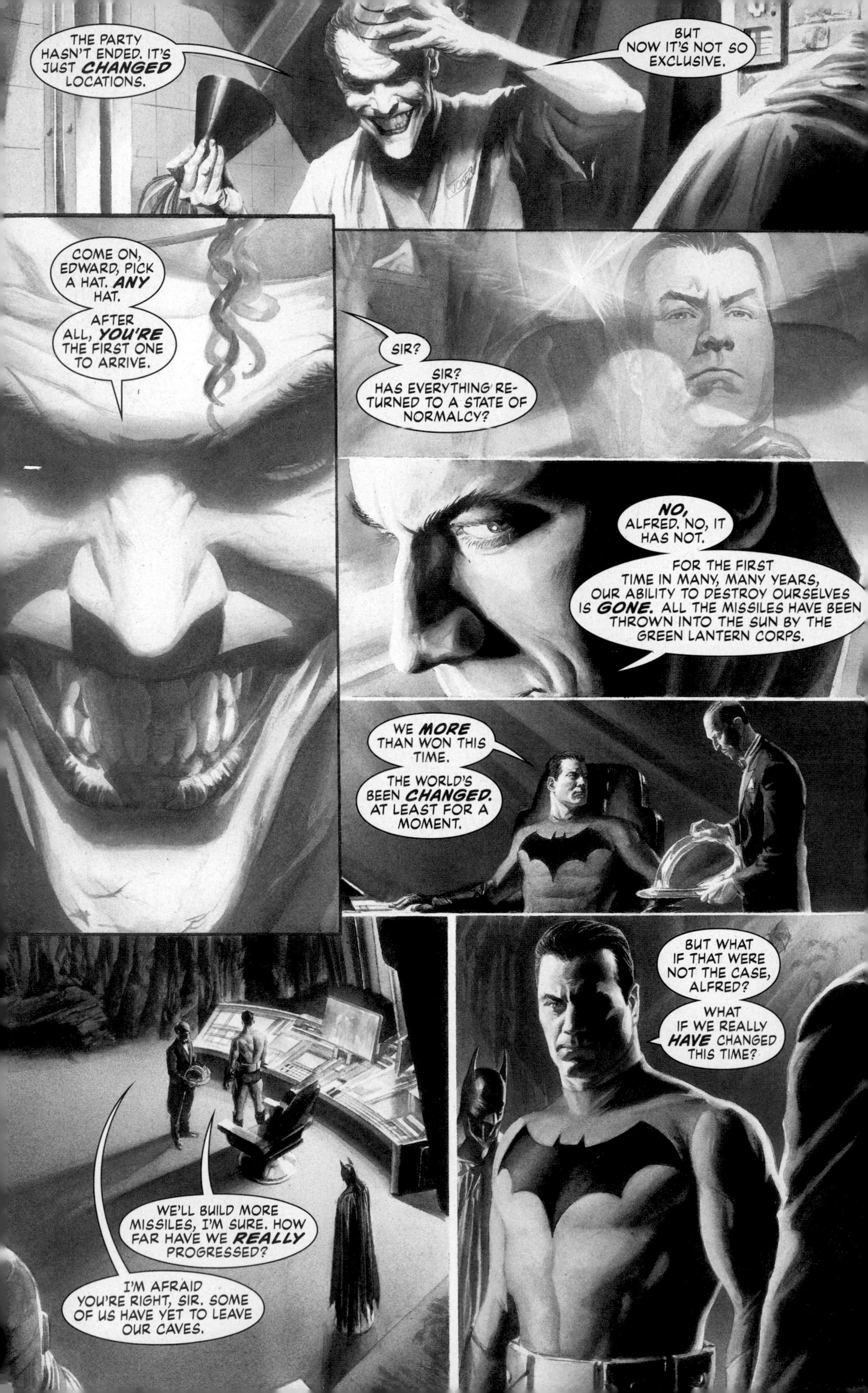
THE PARTY HASN'T ENDED. IT'S JUST *CHANGED* LOCATIONS.
BUT NOW IT'S NOT SO EXCLUSIVE.
COME ON, EDWARD, PICK A HAT. *ANY* HAT.
AFTER ALL, *YOU'RE* THE FIRST ONE TO ARRIVE.
SIR?
SIR? HAS EVERYTHING RE-TURNED TO A STATE OF NORMALCY?
NO, ALFRED. NO, IT HAS NOT.
FOR THE FIRST TIME IN MANY, MANY YEARS, OUR ABILITY TO DESTROY OURSELVES IS *GONE.* ALL THE MISSILES HAVE BEEN THROWN INTO THE SUN BY THE GREEN LANTERN CORPS.
WE *MORE* THAN WON THIS TIME.
THE WORLD'S BEEN *CHANGED.* AT LEAST FOR A MOMENT.
WE'LL BUILD MORE MISSILES, I'M SURE. HOW FAR HAVE WE *REALLY* PROGRESSED?
I'M AFRAID YOU'RE RIGHT, SIR. SOME OF US HAVE YET TO LEAVE OUR CAVES.
BUT WHAT IF THAT WERE NOT THE CASE, ALFRED?
WHAT IF WE REALLY *HAVE* CHANGED THIS TIME?

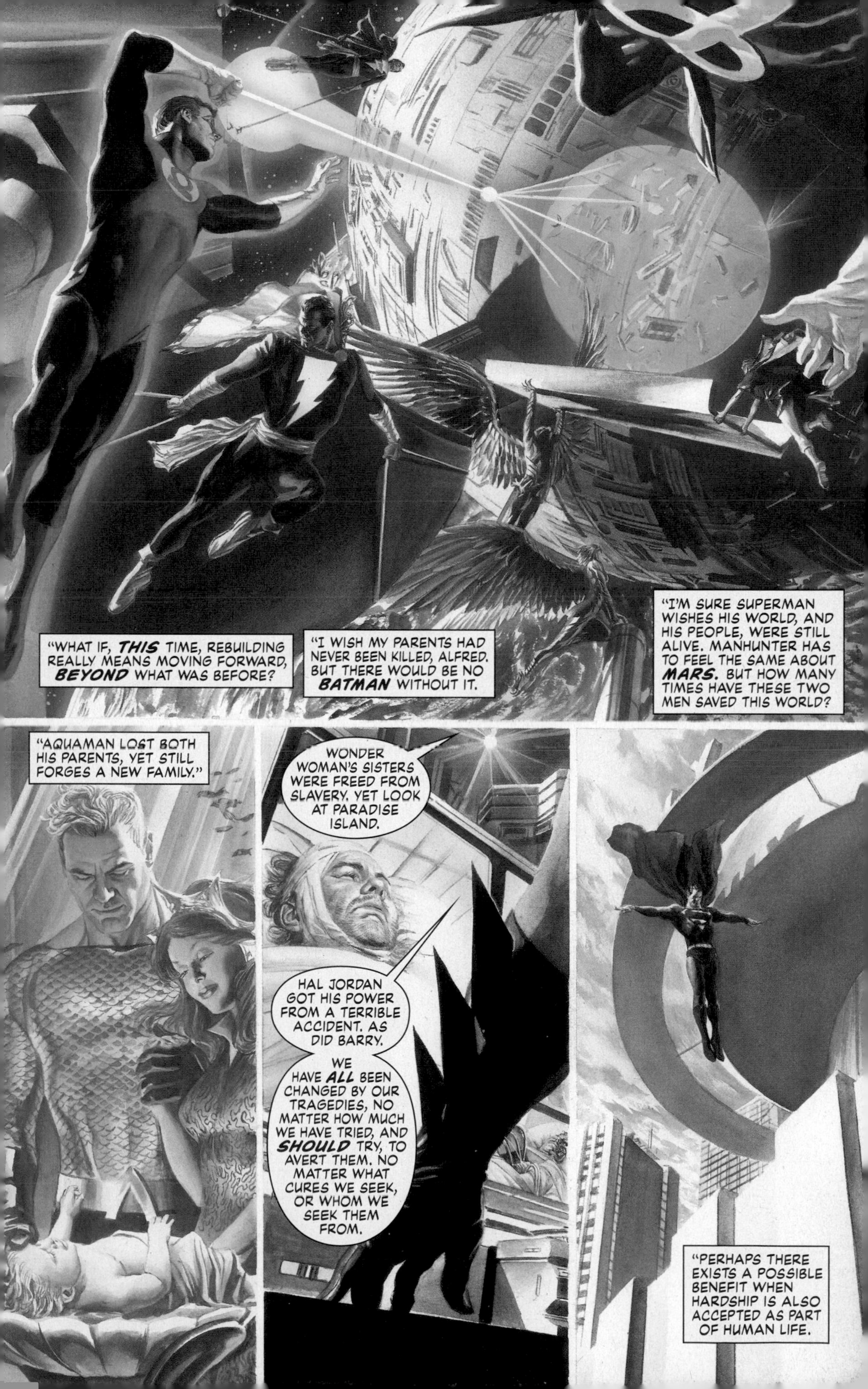
"WHAT IF, THIS TIME, REBUILDING REALLY MEANS MOVING FORWARD, BEYOND WHAT WAS BEFORE?
"I WISH MY PARENTS HAD NEVER BEEN KILLED, ALFRED. BUT THERE WOULD BE NO BATMAN WITHOUT IT.
"I'M SURE SUPERMAN WISHES HIS WORLD, AND HIS PEOPLE, WERE STILL ALIVE. MANHUNTER HAS TO FEEL THE SAME ABOUT MARS. BUT HOW MANY TIMES HAVE THESE TWO MEN SAVED THIS WORLD?
"AQUAMAN LOST BOTH HIS PARENTS, YET STILL FORGES A NEW FAMILY."
WONDER WOMAN'S SISTERS WERE FREED FROM SLAVERY. YET LOOK AT PARADISE ISLAND.
HAL JORDAN GOT HIS POWER FROM A TERRIBLE ACCIDENT. AS DID BARRY.
WE HAVE ALL BEEN CHANGED BY OUR TRAGEDIES, NO MATTER HOW MUCH WE HAVE TRIED, AND SHOULD TRY, TO AVERT THEM. NO MATTER WHAT CURES WE SEEK, OR WHOM WE SEEK THEM FROM.
"PERHAPS THERE EXISTS A POSSIBLE BENEFIT WHEN HARDSHIP IS ALSO ACCEPTED AS PART OF HUMAN LIFE.

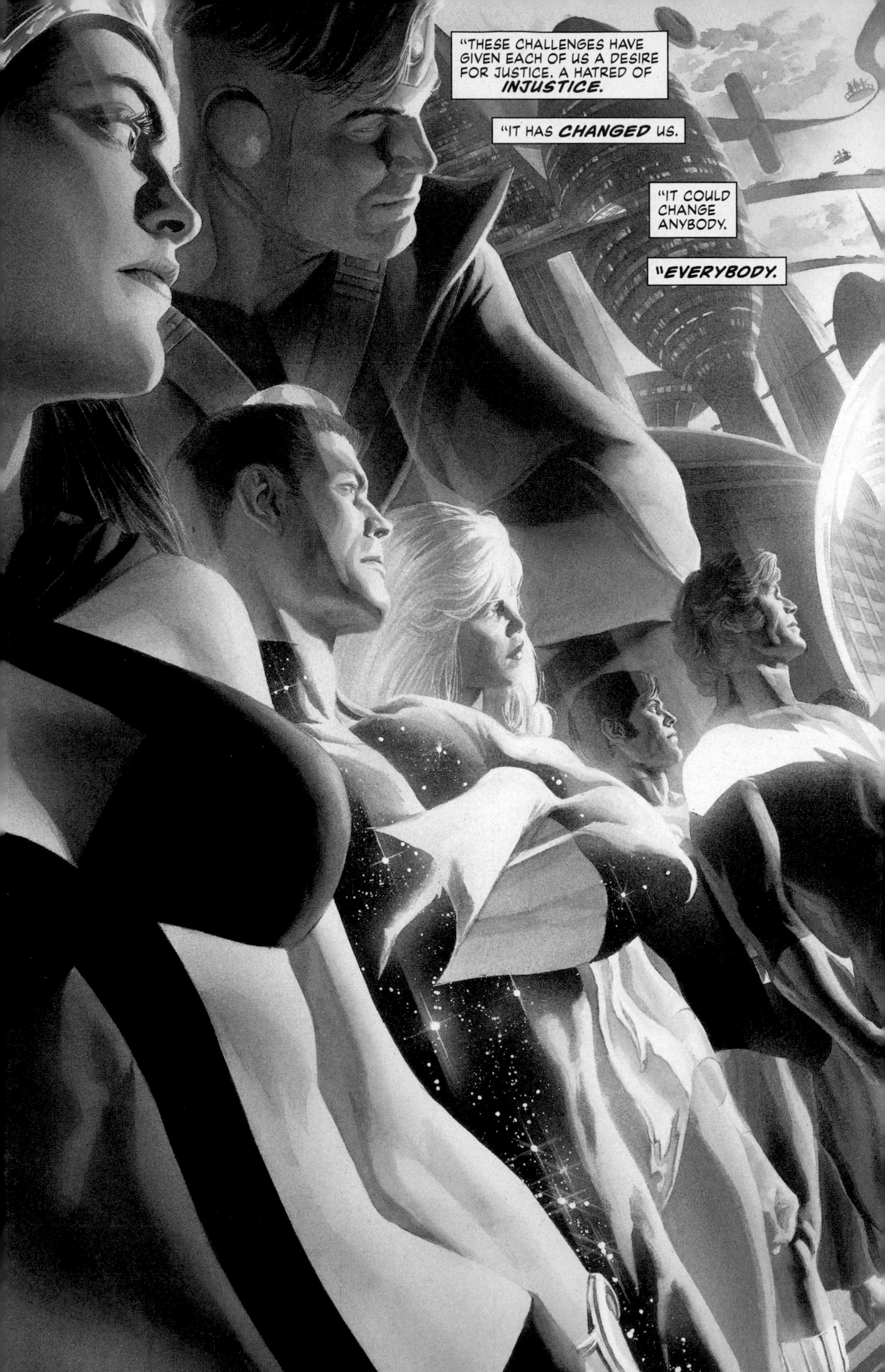
"THESE CHALLENGES HAVE GIVEN EACH OF US A DESIRE FOR JUSTICE. A HATRED OF INJUSTICE.
"IT HAS CHANGED US.
"IT COULD CHANGE ANYBODY.
"EVERYBODY.

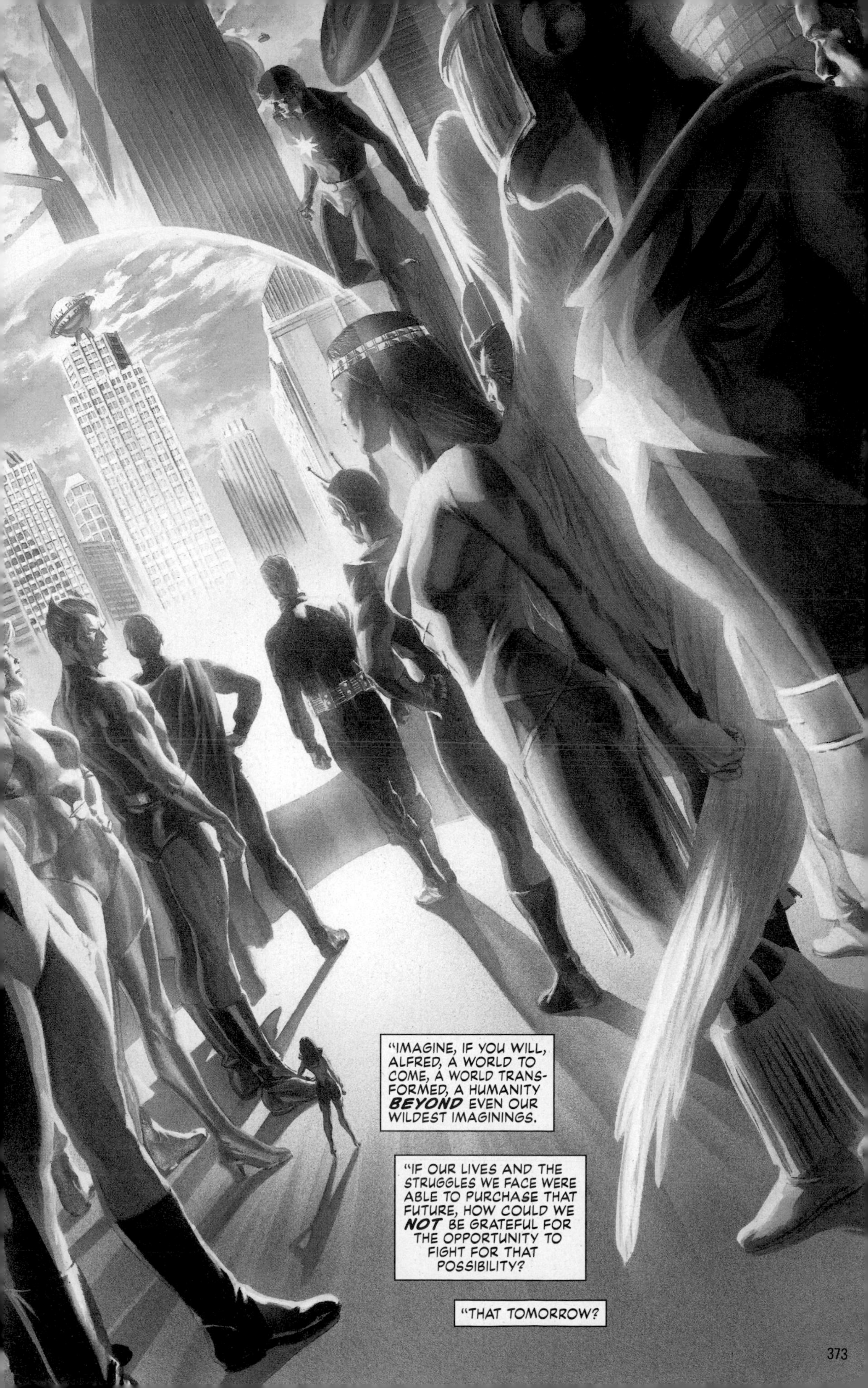
"IMAGINE, IF YOU WILL, ALFRED, A WORLD TO COME, A WORLD TRANSFORMED, A HUMANITY **BEYOND** EVEN OUR WILDEST IMAGININGS.
"IF OUR LIVES AND THE STRUGGLES WE FACE WERE ABLE TO PURCHASE THAT FUTURE, HOW COULD WE **NOT** BE GRATEFUL FOR THE OPPORTUNITY TO FIGHT FOR THAT POSSIBILITY?
"THAT TOMORROW?

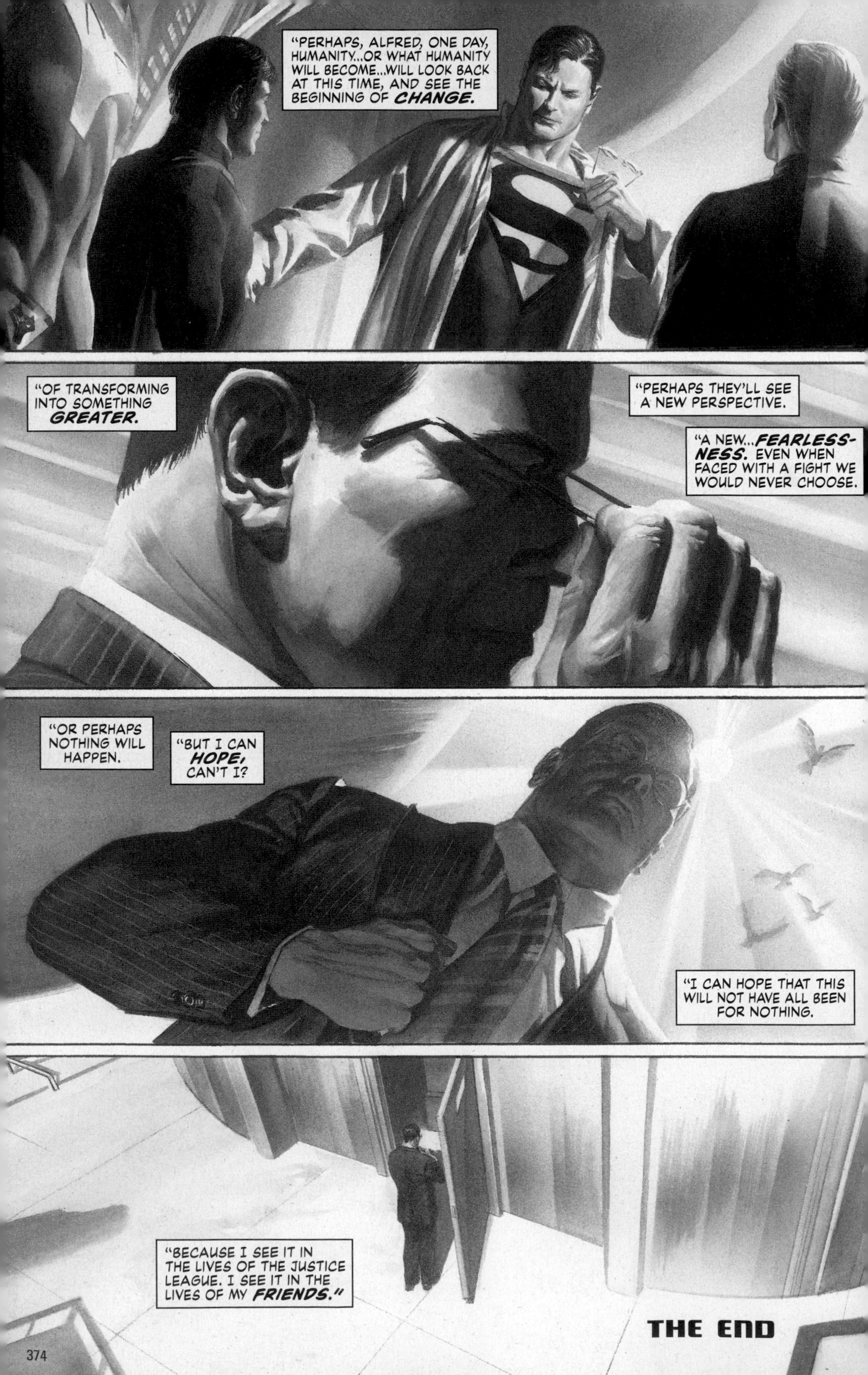
"PERHAPS, ALFRED, ONE DAY, HUMANITY...OR WHAT HUMANITY WILL BECOME...WILL LOOK BACK AT THIS TIME, AND SEE THE BEGINNING OF CHANGE.
"OF TRANSFORMING INTO SOMETHING GREATER.
"PERHAPS THEY'LL SEE A NEW PERSPECTIVE.
"A NEW...FEARLESS-NESS. EVEN WHEN FACED WITH A FIGHT WE WOULD NEVER CHOOSE.
"OR PERHAPS NOTHING WILL HAPPEN.
"BUT I CAN HOPE, CAN'T I?
"I CAN HOPE THAT THIS WILL NOT HAVE ALL BEEN FOR NOTHING.
"BECAUSE I SEE IT IN THE LIVES OF THE JUSTICE LEAGUE. I SEE IT IN THE LIVES OF MY FRIENDS."
THE END

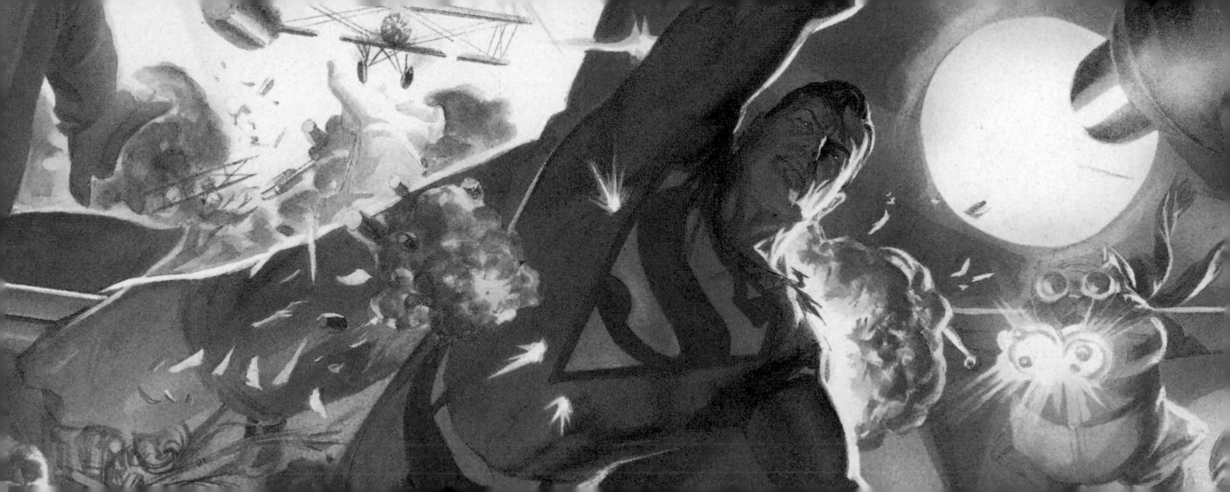

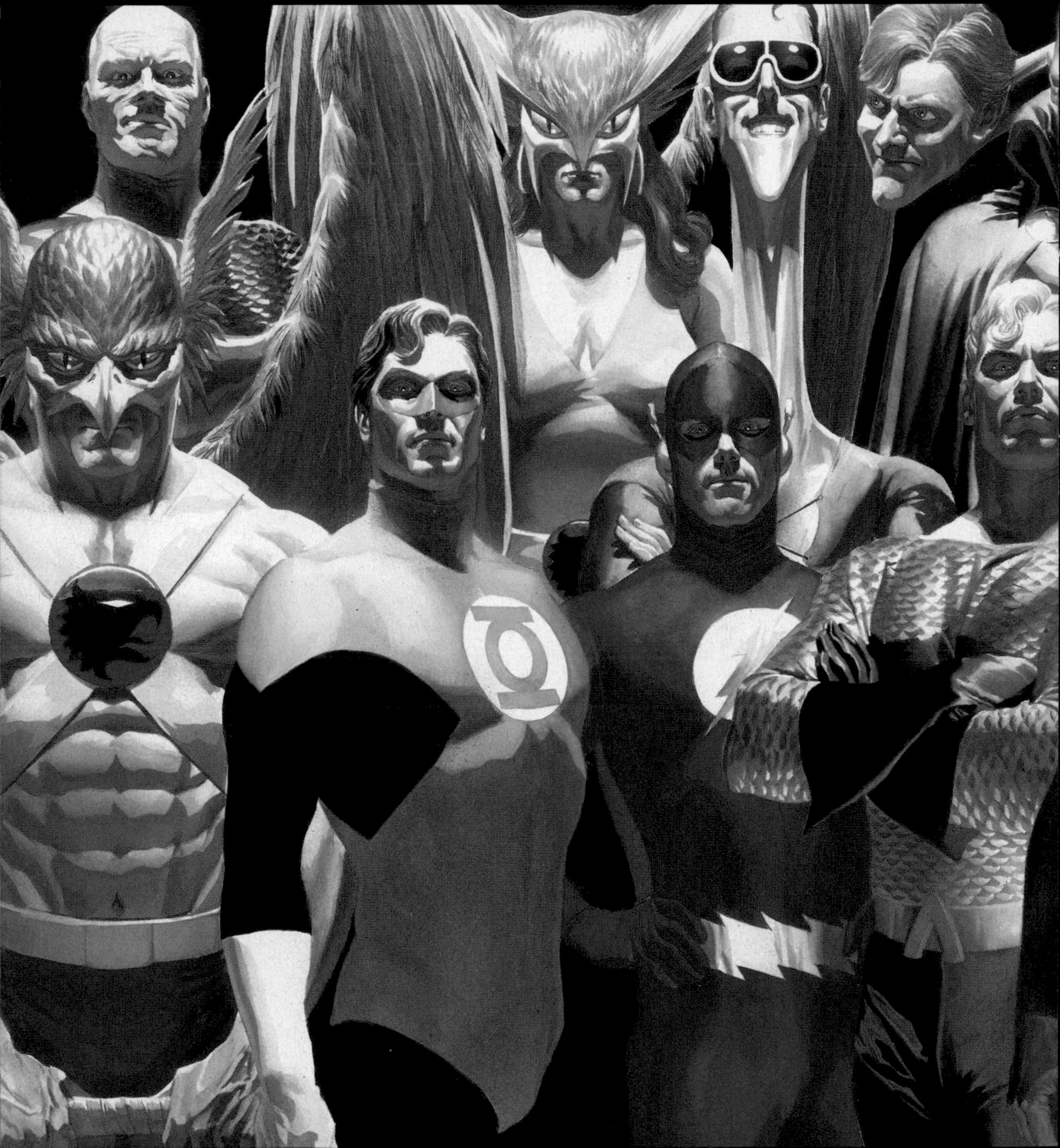

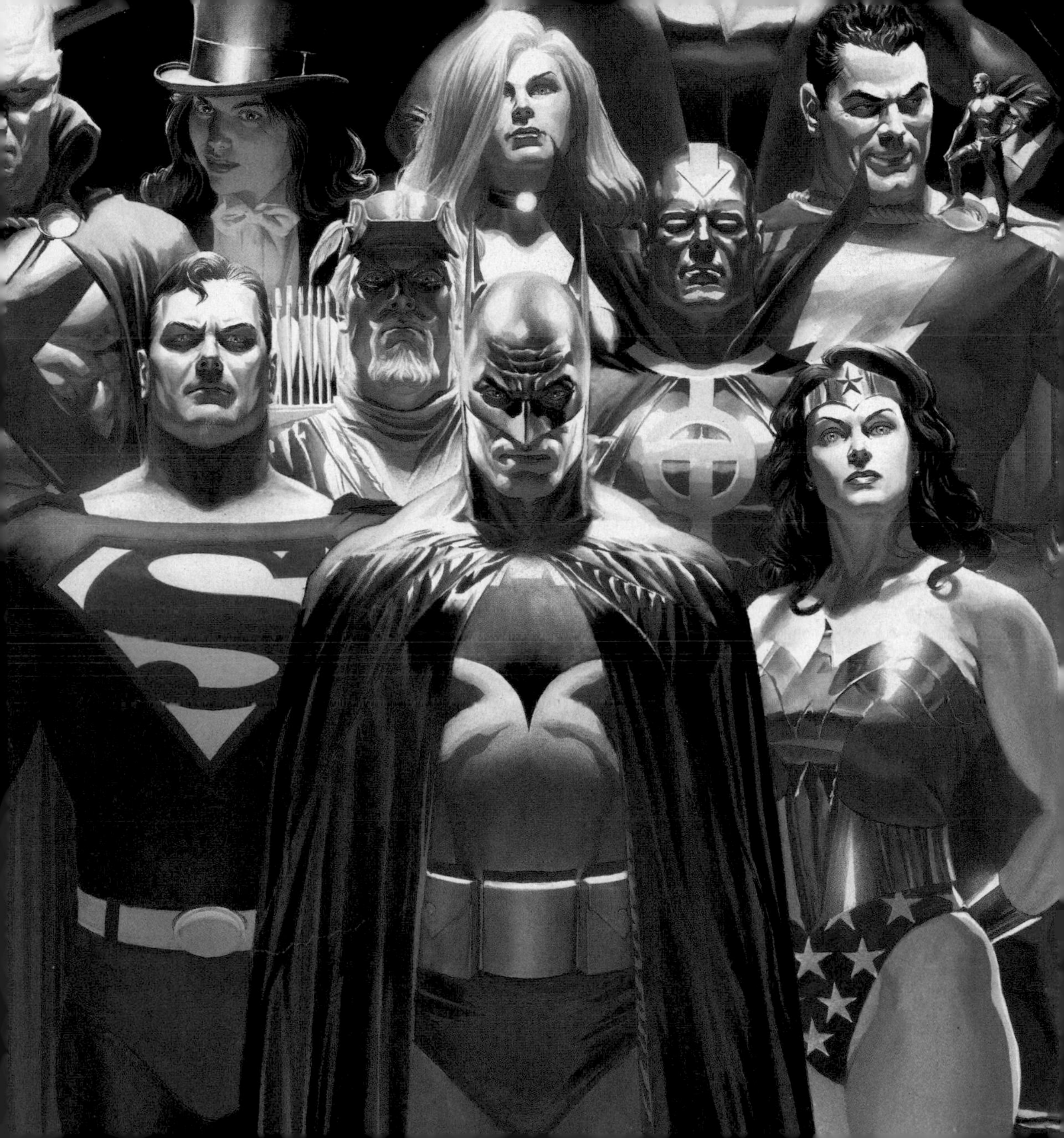

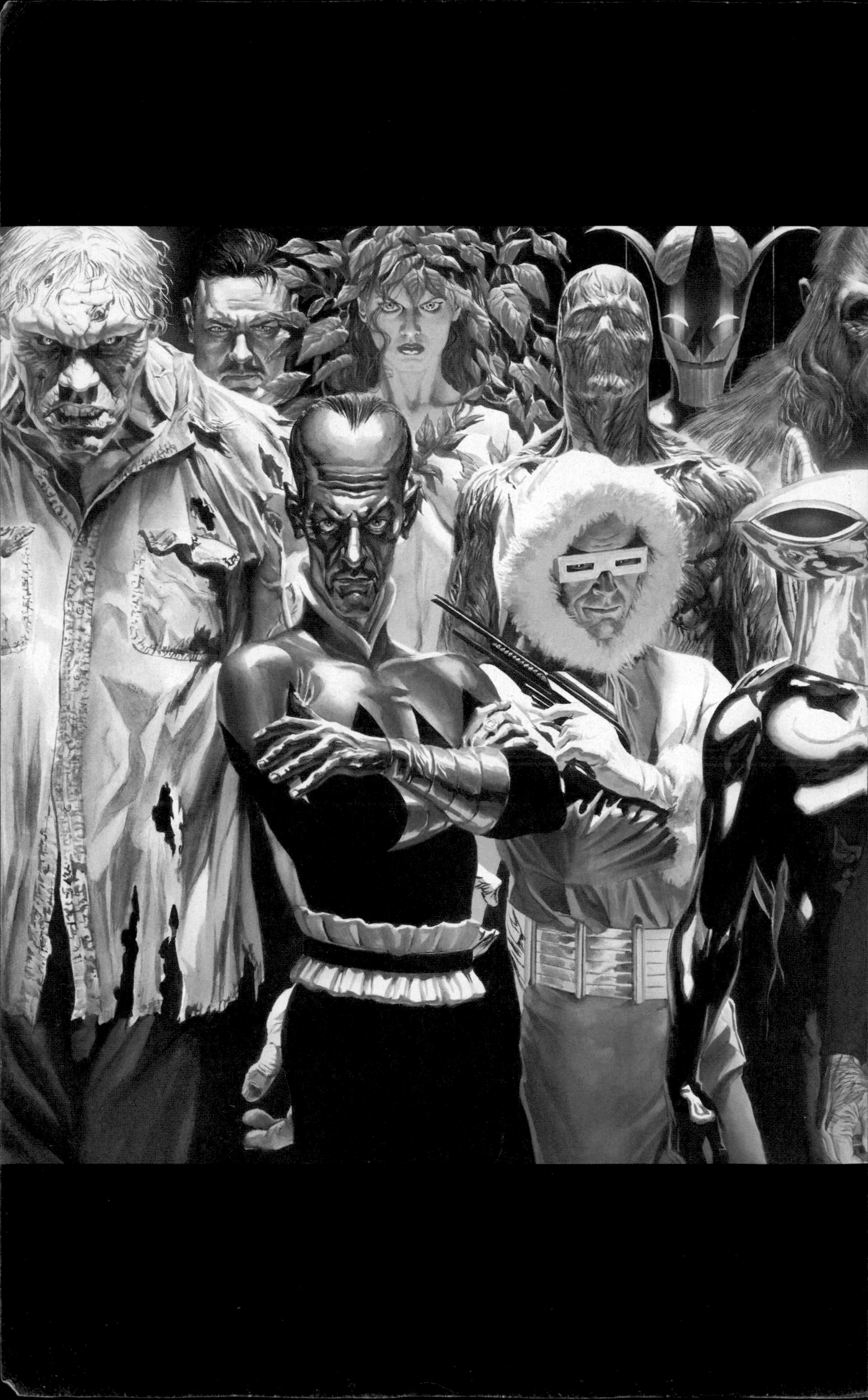

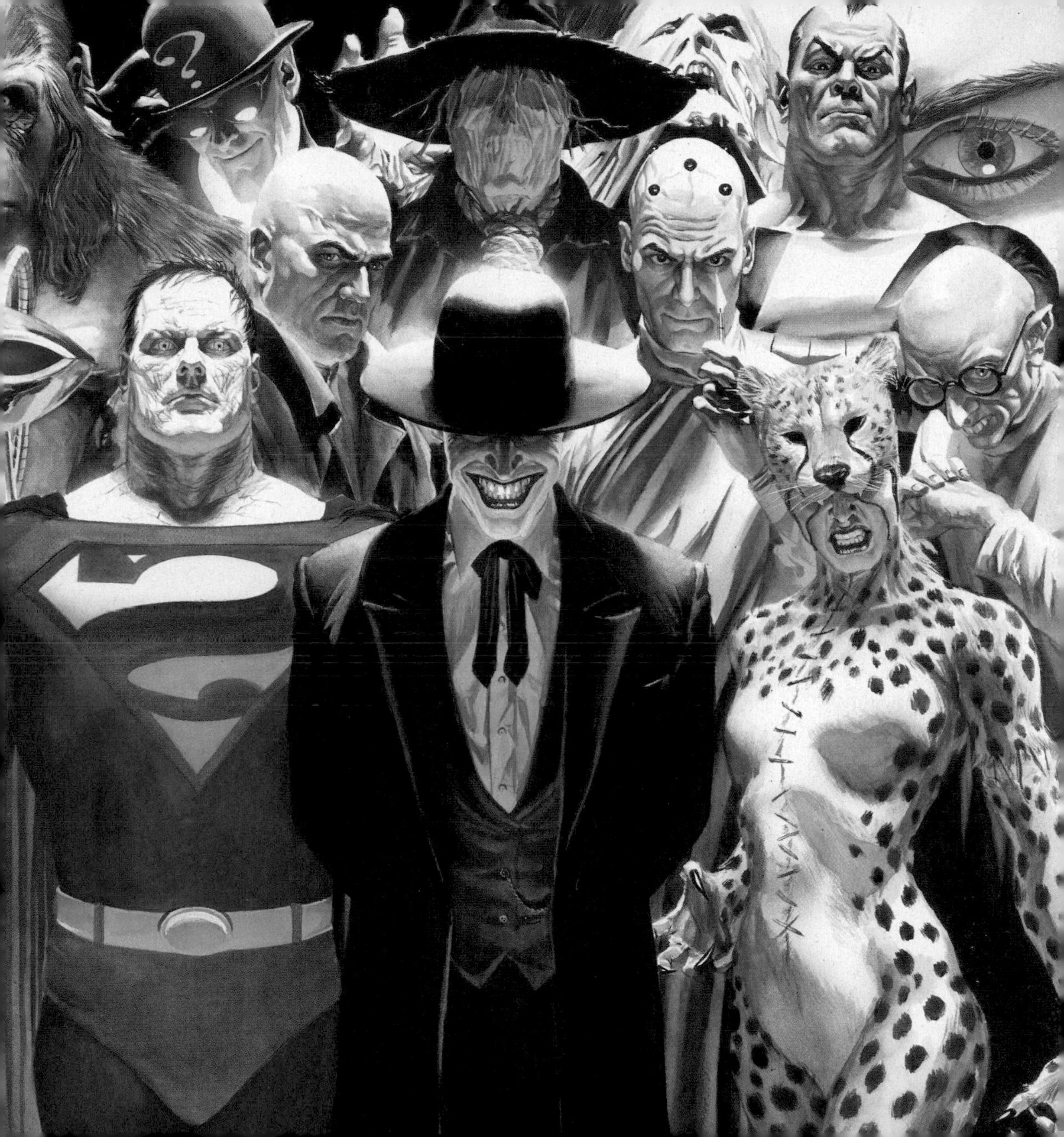

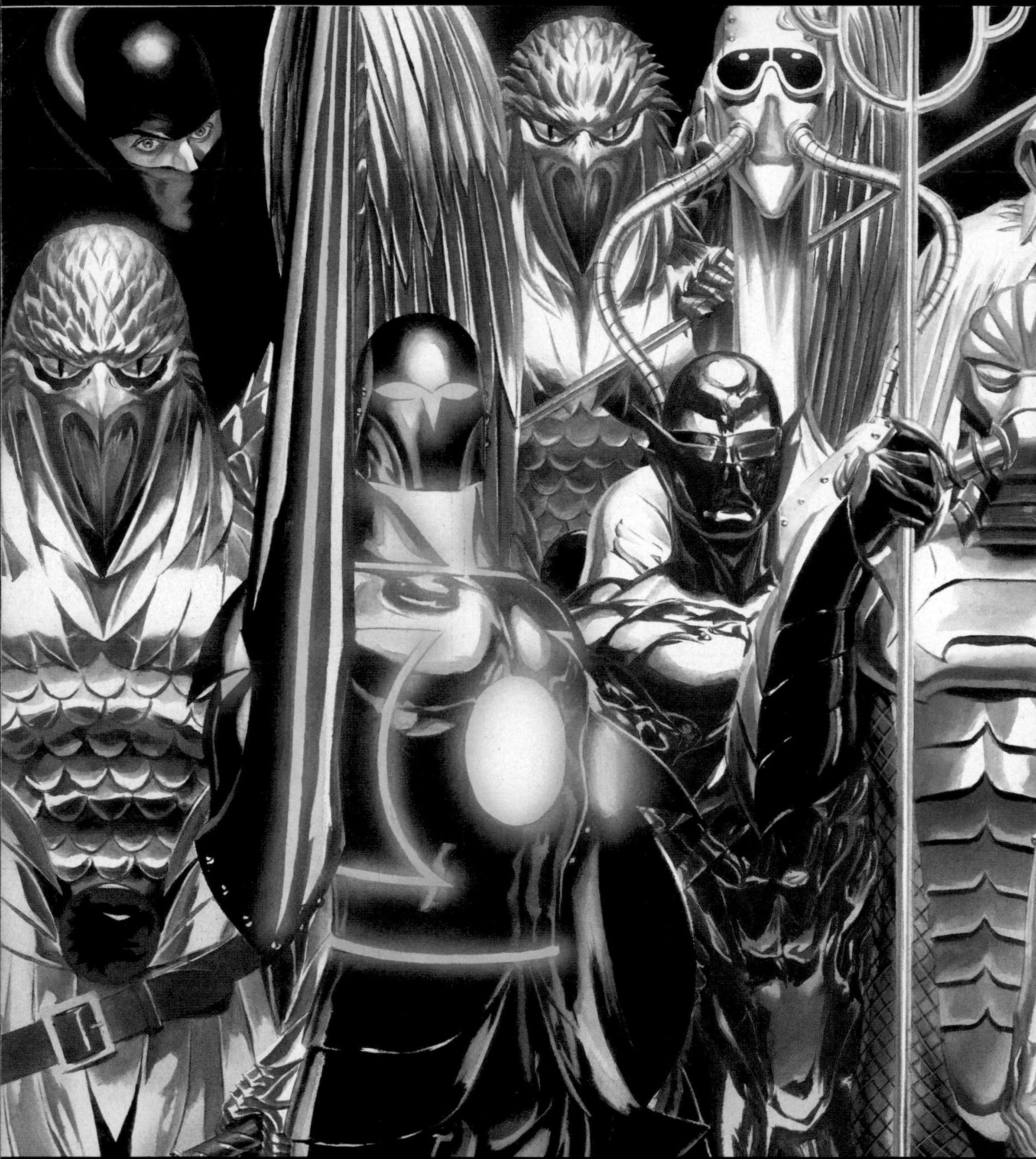

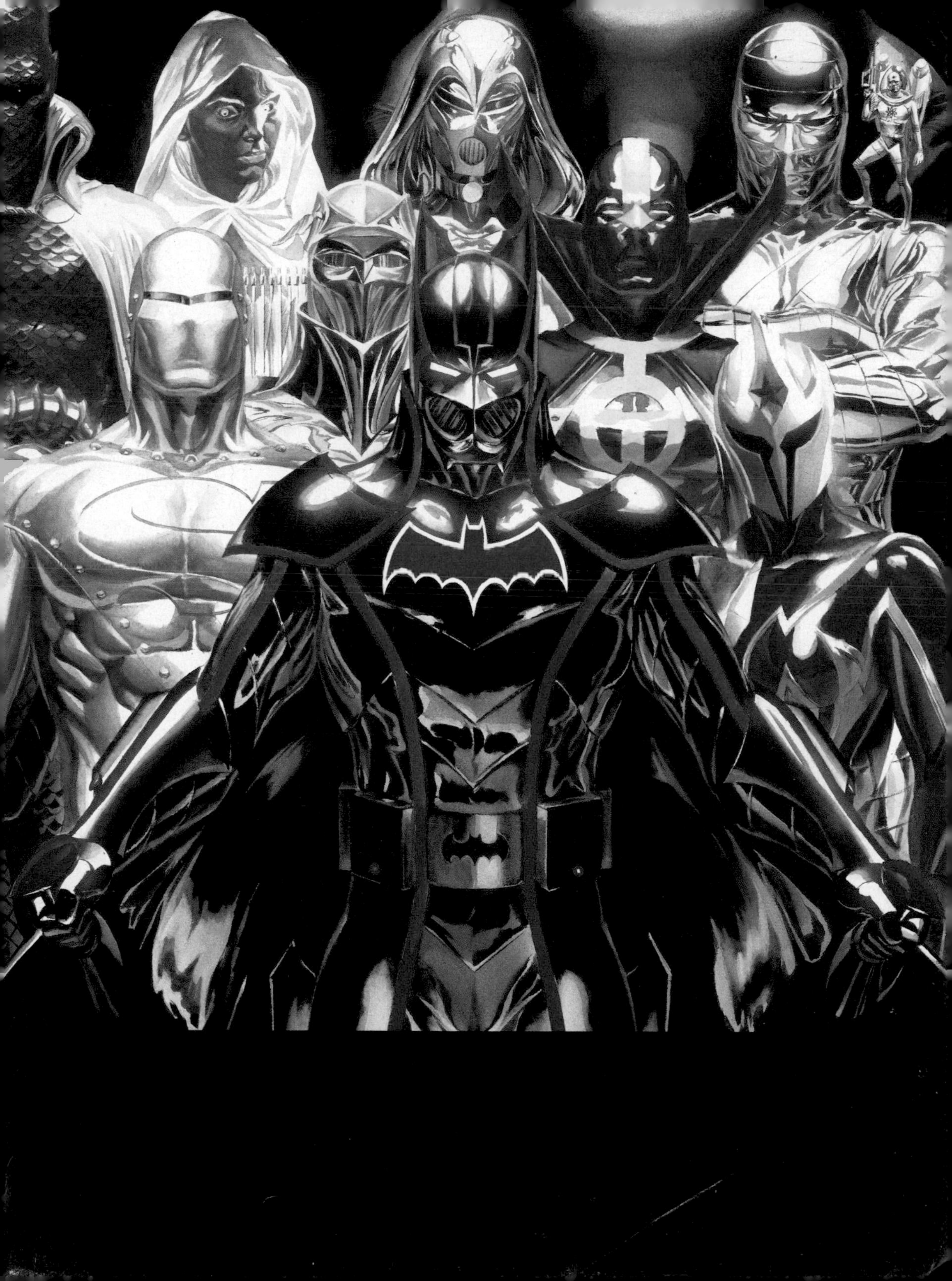

"Groundbreaking."
—USA TODAY

"It's film noir in cartoon panels."
—VANITY FAIR

"Frank Miller absolutely revolutionized the Dark Knight
and his influence can be felt throughout comics, even
20 years later...true masterpiece of storytelling."
—IGN

FROM THE CREATOR OF *300* and *SIN CITY*

FRANK MILLER
with KLAUS JANSON

**BATMAN:
THE DARK KNIGHT
STRIKES AGAIN**

**BATMAN. YEAR ONE
DELUXE EDITION**

with DAVID MAZZUCCHELLI

**ALL-STAR BATMAN
& ROBIN, THE BOY
WONDER VOL. 1**

with JIM LEE

BATMAN: THE DARK KNIGHT RETURNS

FRANK MILLER
with KLAUS JANSON and LYNN VARLEY

DC COMICS™

FROM THE WRITER OF *JUSTICE LEAGUE* & *GREEN LANTERN*

GEOFF JOHNS
with GARY FRANK

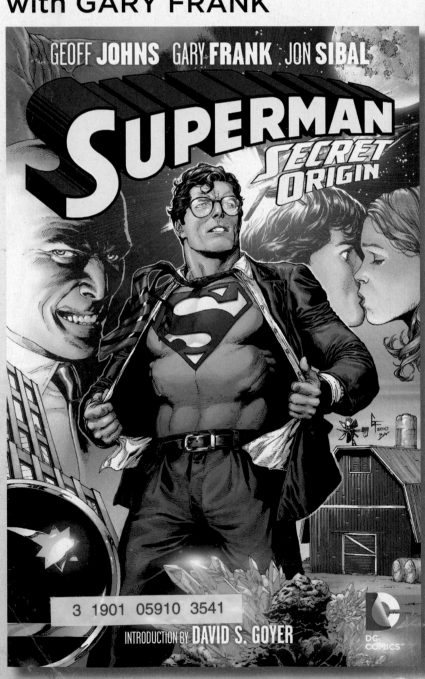

GEOFF **JOHNS** GARY **FRANK** JON **SIBAL**

SUPERMAN SECRET ORIGIN

3 1901 05910 3541

INTRODUCTION BY DAVID S. GOYER

DC COMICS™